TEACH YOURSELF BOOKS

GUIDE TO MODERN WORLD LITERATURE
Volume 1

'A quite remarkable feat . . . this is an astounding and outstanding book. He doesn't just copy out accepted opinions. Drama is there as well. I'm very much afraid he'll prove indispensable.'

CYRIL CONNOLLY, *Sunday Times*

'I have greatly enjoyed it, and I admire it immensely. I can think of no comparably prodigious effort of literary evaluation . . . altogether a noble achievement.'

ANTONY QUINTON, *Sunday Telegraph*

'The word "indispensable" is the only one that will do, and if only because there is surely no other book which deals so thoroughly with so many different national literatures.'

PHILIP TOYNBEE, *Observer*

'The energy of writing hardly flags, author after author is characterised in terms which a student may easily grasp, but which also satisfy readers wanting something more than teachers usually say . . . this book will become a critical classic.'

ROBERT NYE, *Spectator*

'I have read it from cover to cover, and feel an infinitely better informed man.'

ANTHONY POWELL, *Daily Telegraph*

'Mr. Seymour-Smith's commentary exemplifies at almost every point an active engagement with the works he is discussing . . . (his) book embodies both the myths of literature and a sense of what it is like to encounter the thing itself. That is the merit—indeed, the distinction—of his excellent book.'

MARTIN DODSWORTH, *Encounter*

'Essential if reading (or writing) is your essence of life; a book for exploration and discovery, an excited book, and one which stimulates argument and controversy, as well as agreement.'

GEOFFREY GRIGSON, *Country Life*

Martin Seymour-Smith, son of the distinguished librarian and bibliographer Frank Seymour-Smith, was born in London in 1928. Educated at Highgate School and St Edmund Hall, Oxford, he taught abroad and in Britain from 1954 to 1960, when he became a full-time writer. He is married, and lives on the Sussex coast. He has written, compiled or edited over twenty-five books, among them his distinguished collections of poetry, *Tea With Miss Stockport* (1963) and *Reminiscences of Norma* (1971); the subject of much controversy, these have led to his being hailed by C. H. Sisson and others as the best English poet to emerge since the war. His innovatory old-spelling edition of *Shakespeare's Sonnets* (1963) was acclaimed by such scholars as John Dover Wilson, Robert Graves and William Empson. *Poets Through Their Letters* (1969), also highly praised, elicited from Anthony Burgess a comparison of the author to Dr Johnson. The writer's other publications include an annotated edition of Ben Jonson's *Every Man in his Humour* (1966), the anthology *Longer Elizabethan Poems* and *Sex and Society*. His wittily irreverent *The Bluffer's Guide to Literature* (1966, rev. 1972) was a best-seller. An illustrated edition of *Who's Who in Twentieth Century Literature* is at the press.

In 1971–2 he was Visiting Professor of English at Wisconsin University. At present fiction and poetry reviewer for the *Financial Times*, he is currently engaged on several projects, including *Fifty Great European Novels*, and a critical biography of Percy Wyndham Lewis.

Seymour-Smith's growing reputation is based on his erudition, his humour and his stimulatingly different approach to literary criticism. As the critics' evaluations quoted on the first page of this book suggest, both students and the general reader will find this attitude as refreshing as it is illuminating.

BY THE SAME AUTHOR

Poetry:
Poems (with Rex Taylor, Terence Hards), 1952
All Devils Fading, 1954
Tea With Miss Stockport, 1963
Reminiscences of Norma, 1971

Criticism:
Robert Graves (1956), 1971
Poets Through Their Letters, I: Wyatt to Coleridge, 1969
Fallen Women, 1969
Sex and Society, 1975

Satire:
The Bluffer's Guide to Literature (1966), 1972

With James Reeves:
A New Canon of English Poetry, 1967
Selected Poems of Andrew Marvell, 1969
Inside Poetry, 1970
Selected Poems of Walt Whitman, 1975

Editions:
Shakespeare's Sonnets (1963), 1966
Ben Jonson's *Every Man in his Humour*, 1966
Longer Elizabethan Poems, 1972

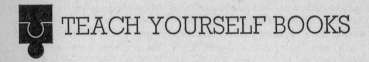
TEACH YOURSELF BOOKS

GUIDE TO MODERN
WORLD LITERATURE
Volume 1

Martin Seymour-Smith

'*Real literature can be created only by madmen, hermits, heretics, dreamers, rebels, and sceptics, not by diligent and trustworthy functionaries.*'

Evgeny Zamyatin

TEACH YOURSELF BOOKS
HODDER & STOUGHTON
ST PAUL'S HOUSE   WARWICK LANE   LONDON EC4P 4AH

First published in one volume by Wolfe Publishing Ltd 1973
Teach Yourself Books, Hodder & Stoughton, corrected and revised edition in
four volumes 1975

Copyright © 1973, 1975 editions
Martin Seymour-Smith

ISBN 0 340 19505 3

Printed and bound in Great Britain
for Teach Yourself Books, Hodder & Stoughton,
by Hazell Watson & Viney Ltd, Aylesbury, Bucks

To the Memory of My Father
and
To My Mother

When Scaliger, whole years of labour past,
Beheld his Lexicon complete at last,
And weary of his task, with wond'ring eyes,
Saw from words pil'd on words a fabric rise,
He curs'd the industry, inertly strong,
In creeping toil that could persist so long,
And if, enrag'd he cried, heav'n meant to shed
Its keenest vengeance on the guilty head,
The drudgery of words the damn'd would know,
Doom'd to write lexicons in endless woe.

(From Dr. Johnson's Latin poem 'Know Yourself', written after revising and enlarging his lexicon, or dictionary; translated into English by Arthur Murphy, in his *Life*, 1772.)

Contents

Preface to the Second Edition

This second edition, in four paperback volumes, contains revisions, corrections and some additions. The introduction, the abbreviated references, and the bibliography, are printed in their entirety in each volume. When the abbreviation q.v. refers to an author, concept or literary movement that is discussed in another volume it is followed by the number of that volume; otherwise it appears alone. Each of the volumes has been given a new and separate index.

For criticism of and corrections to this edition I am indebted to the following: Ronald Bottrall (most especially), Geoffrey Grigson, Miron Grindea, Peter Jay, Dr. S. Jacobson, Professor A. H. Johns, Anthony Rudolf, Jorge Silva, Istvan Siklos (especially) C. H. Sisson (again), I. D. Waldie, Graeme Wilson (especially).

As in the case of the first edition, some of these names appear in the text of the book: in no instance were any of the persons involved aware of any changes or additions that I may have made in my discussions of their own work. None, of course, sought to influence my views in any way. All errors remain my sole responsibility.

I must also gratefully thank the printers of this reset edition for their skill and forbearance.

Since the publication of the first edition I have received many helpful letters from all parts of the world. I invite more, not the least because they help to improve a work of reference that by its very nature cannot be perfect—but which, so far as my own imperfections allow, can be improved with each successive edition. Would those who wish to write to me please do so in care of the present publishers, Teach Yourself Books.

Bexhill-on-Sea,   25 November 1974
Sussex.

Introduction

I

The scope of this book extends to writers, of all nationalities, who survived 31 December 1899. In certain instances (e.g. Hopkins, Mallarmé) I have had, for obvious reasons, to discuss writers who died before that; but I have strictly limited these. I have given an account of the major literary movements of the past century and a half; the names of these will be found in the respective indexes. The system of putting 'q.v.' after names of literary movements, authors, and titles of books, is intended to be a practical aid to the reader: if he turns to the indicated index he will find the main entry he requires in **bold** type. If no number follows 'q.v.' he will find the entry in the volume he is reading. This should make cross-reference quick and simple. Such philosophers and concepts and so on (e.g. Bergson, *Künstlerschuld*) as are not dealt with at length in the body of the text are discussed or explained in this introduction, which appears at the beginning of each volume.

Complete accuracy in a comprehensive work such as this is, alas, impossible: errors of dating are repeated from reference-book to reference-book; it is frequently impossible to check the dates of first publication of books without seeing the original editions. . . . I have made every effort to give correct information (e.g. my dates of birth for Tennessee Williams and E. Lasker-Schüler differ from most authorities, but are right). I shall be glad to correct any errors, with acknowledgements, in future editions—as I have done in this second revised edition.

The dates given for dramatic works are of publication, not first production.

Dates after individual books are of earliest publication, wherever or in whatever form this took place.

The list of abbreviations consists mainly of books in which translations into English of works by writers (other than English-language) discussed in the text are conveniently available. It cannot pretend to completeness, since more and more such collections are being published each year; all libraries and bookshops in large cities stock them. Not all books listed are currently in print.

Unsigned translations are by me.

The emphasis, since in the interests of space I have had to place emphases, is on the more universal areas of interest and language-knowledge (English, German, French, Spanish, Russian, Italian); and on the earlier rather than the later part of the period, which may less surely be assessed. But I have discussed some authors I believe to be neglected or misunderstood or underrated (e.g. George Moore, Céline, Ford) at length; and one great literature that is neglected, at least in Great Britain, the Japanese, has received a fuller treatment.

II

All Western literature has developed, with some national exceptions and variations, to a consistent pattern. In the succeeding brief sketch I have kept definitions as broad as possible: our understanding of literature does not benefit from attempts to narrow down the meanings of terms too precisely: the terms themselves lose their value.

By the mid-century *realism*, particularly in the novel, was well established. Realism in its broadest sense is an essential aim of any work of literature: it simply means verisimilitude to actuality—and points so the aspects of life the author selects as meaningful. But this leaves entirely open the question of how actuality is regarded—as an outward or an inward phenomenon, or both, or whatever. Nineteenth-century realism, the method out of which modern literature developed, does, even though it remains one of the broader literary concepts, have a less vague connotation.

First, realism is essentially a part of romanticism—however much it may sometimes look like a reaction against it, and however certainly the romantic movement may have seemed, in the positivist Fifties, to have collapsed. We are still living in a romantic period—nor, indeed, will there ever be any return to the limitations and artificialities of classicism.

Realism has no significant relationship to the literary classicism of antiquity or to the neo-classicism of the eighteenth century. It originates in the age-old tendency towards accuracy of representation (usually manifesting itself as an anti- or non-classical depiction of plebeian life—Cervantes, Jonson, Shakespeare, Smollett—or as regionalism), and in philosophical empiricism and all proto-pragmatic and proto-utilitarian inclinations. Nineteenth-century realism, at various times and in various writers, exhibited the following characteristics: objectivity (in the sense of concentration on facts rather than on interpretations of them); lucidity (rather than style or rhetoric); 'ordinary', quotidian experience; a search for an immedi-ate, verifiable, truth, even if this be no more than relativistic; secularism; emphasis on the psychological motivations of the char-acters, often at the expense of 'plot'. In general the good realist authors (for example, George Eliot, Howells, Henry James) had good, or even idealistic, intentions towards their audience; but they refused to uplift their hearts, thus raising false hopes. A few realists (to some extent Flaubert; certainly Maupassant) had more aggressive intentions towards the bourgeois. But the milieu chosen was emphatically middle-class.

In many countries (but most notably in France) realism turned into *naturalism*. This term is frequently used, particularly by journalists and reviewers of plays (but also by critics who should know better) as a synonym for realism. This is seriously misleading. Naturalism is a more precise term than realism: a narrowing-down of it. (Zola's programme—described in the account of him—is entirely naturalist; his practice is not.) Naturalist fiction is guided, or thinks it is guided, by the principles of scientific determinism. This arose largely from 'Darwinism', a movement or climate of thought that has less connec-tion with Charles Darwin, from whom it derives its name, than might seem apparent. Darwin had in fact given a new and viable interpreta-tion of the theory of transformism; according to 'Darwinism' he invented and 'proved' it. Actually it went back, as a theory, to at least 550 B.C. The naturalists extracted from Darwinism the notion of man-as-animal, of his life as a bloody struggle (they could have found this more definitely and confidently stated in Hobbes' *Leviathan*, as distinct from hypothetically in Darwin; but Darwin seemed *scientifically* respectable)—'the strongest, the swiftest and the cunningest live to fight another day', said T. H. Huxley. This persistent fallacy has been given the name of 'Social Darwinism'. The lives of the poor, to the depiction of which the naturalists turned, gave ample justification for such a view. However, in practice the best naturalists (e.g. Zola, Dreiser) have transcended their deterministic programmes. Zola is as romantic as he is naturalistic, and Dreiser is massively puzzled as well as sentimental: both are naturalists, it is true; but both gain their ultimate effects from their power of psychological penetration.

The so-called *neo-romanticism*, and then *decadence*, that manifested itself in nearly all the Western literatures between about 1885 and 1905 was not as remote from either realism or naturalism as may have seemed apparent at the time.

All great literary movements eventually deteriorate: into preciosity, over-aestheticism, over-self-consciousness, trivial scholarship, cultivation of debility and whatever society may at the time determine as perverse behaviour. . . . The decadent movement (it is more of a tendency) at the end of the nineteenth century is sometimes called *fin de siècle*, a term I have occasionally employed. It is as much a development, or etiolation, of *Parnassianism* and *Symbolism* (both these terms are discussed in the section on French literature) as a reaction against positivism and naturalism. Symbolism had contained the religious or 'Platonic' impulses inherent in human beings, never completely submergeable, during the realist-naturalist period. The decadent writers—they range from the only partly decadent, like Verlaine, to the wholly decadent, like Dowson—were nearly all 'religious' (if only in the sense that they embraced 'Satanism' or aspects of it and died incense-sniffing Catholics); but they viewed civilization as in decay rather than growth: they worshipped entropy, degeneration, disorder; they transformed the romantic cult of the individual into the romantic-decadent cult of the self (narcissism)— hence their interest in or cultivation of homosexuality. They made a cult of the erotic and hurled themselves into hopeless loves. They worshipped the urban and the ugliness it offered—but in a deliber-ately perverse spirit. They romanticized the then dominant principle of the Second Law of Thermodynamics, seeing it as operative in the evolutionary sphere.

The foregoing are the chief characteristics of decadence in general; no single writer manifests all of them—except, possibly, some entirely trivial one. In its least extreme form this neo-romantic spirit began to pervade the works of realists and naturalists—for example, Zola's novels are increasingly full of deliberate symbolization.

In the course of literary history movements (or tendencies) provoke reactions to themselves; but these reactions absorb the essences, the genuine discoveries, of the movements that have engendered them. To give an over-simple illustration: romanticism at its best contains the essence of classicism. The best neo-romantic writers had learned the important lessons of realism. And it was essentially from neo-romanticism that modernism arose.

Expressionism, which I have fully described in the section on German literature, was a specifically German movement. However, literary modernism can most usefully be described as expressionism: every modern movement after Symbolism (which was in any case nineteenth-century in origin) may conveniently be described as a form of expressionism.

Modernism, which often arouses great hostility, has a number of characteristics (the writer who combines every one of them in his work is likely to be a charlatan). Realism remains committed—more or less subtly—to a *mimetic* theory: literature is an imitation, a photograph, of life. Modernism (in the sense used in this book) is fundamentally non- or anti-mimetic. In its extremest form, modernism may resolutely omit what is 'essential' in societal, communal or simply representational terms. On the other hand, it will stress precisely what is 'unessential' in such terms. This amounts to an emphasis on inner life, and therefore on the life of the individual. Causality, carefully observed in the nineteenth century, may be deliberately deleted. This does not mean, of course, that it is rejected. It means that it is not an essential part of what the modernist writer is trying to say.

An even more important aspect of modernist writing—and one which puzzles many of its readers, for whom 'time' remains, consciously, a means of manipulating reality into acceptable forms—is its jettisoning of conventional chronology. I have explained this at some length in my treatment of the French *nouveau roman* (q.v. 2).

It is here that the French philosopher, Henri Bergson, is relevant. Bergson did not 'discover' either unconventional time or *stream-of-consciousness*; but his philosophy reflected much contemporary thinking. Bergson is part of the neo-romantic reaction against positivism; he also complements the phenomenology of the German philosopher Husserl (discussed with the French *nouveau roman*) inasmuch as he concentrates upon the concrete rather than the abstract (Husserl was not himself at all interested in this problem; but the effect of his work has been to draw attention to perceptual actualities). It is appropriate that Bergson, although not an imaginative writer, should have received the Nobel Prize for Literature (1928): his influence on literature has been wide and deep. He demanded a return to the 'immediate data of consciousness', and he believed that this could be grasped by means of what he called 'intuition'. Like a number of modern novelists he saw character not as 'personality' but as a process of ceaseless becoming.

The actual term *stream-of-consciousness* originated with Henry James' brother William James; stream-of-consciousness fiction tends to lay emphasis on pre-verbal types of experience; by implication, therefore, this type of fiction regards internal experience as more 'important' than external. (However, stream-of-consciousness can be used simply as an extension of realist technique: the fact that mental minutiae are recorded is not in itself guarantee of a phenomenological approach.) Bergson's attitude was similar: for him consciousness was *duration* (*la durée*); intellect conceptualizes this flow into something static; intuition *thinks in duration*. Sartre has summarized Bergson's position well: 'on going into the past an event does not cease to be; it merely ceases to act and remains "in its place" at its date for eternity. In this way being has been restored to the past, and it is very well done; we even affirm that duration is a multiplicity of interpenetration and that the past is continually organized with the present'.

Bergson is important above all for his anti-intellectuality and his continual suggestion of new ways of seeing ourselves in the world. 'There is one reality, at least', he wrote, 'which we all seize from within, by intuition and not by simple analysis. It is our own personality in its flowing through time—our self which endures'. The relevance of this to the work of Proust (q.v. 2) is immediately clear.

III

I have referred throughout to a number of concepts, and used certain terms, which require initial definition.

I have categorized some writers as *naïve* and others as *sentimentive*. In 1795 Goethe's friend and contemporary, the German poet, dramatist and critic Friedrich Schiller published his essay *On Naïve and Sentimentive Poetry* (*Über naive und sentimentalische Dichtung*)—I have followed the sensible practice of translating 'sentimentalische' as 'sentimentive'; 'naïve' is misleading, too, but 'simple' does not help; 'sentimentive' is less hopelessly misleading, if only because less familiar, than 'sentimental'. This great essay has not had, in the English-speaking world, the recognition that it deserves. However, the questions of Schiller's exact intentions and of its significance in its time are not relevant here. What I have done is to borrow Schiller's terms and to simplify them for the purposes of this book. For, even in my modified and restricted usage, they convey indispensable information that is not contained in the more familiar romantic-classical opposition.

For Schiller the naïve poet is one who is in perfect harmony with nature—with, indeed, the universe; his personality cannot be found in his poetry. He may even seem 'repulsive', 'callous', 'invisible'. The sentimentive poet, on the other hand, has lost his contact with and even his faith in nature, for which he yearns. Naïve poetry (Schiller says) is characteristic of the ancients: an immediate, inspired, detailed representation of the sensuous surface of life. In sentimentive poetry the author is everywhere present; he is self-conscious. The object does 'not possess him utterly'.

On Naïve and Sentimentive Poetry was originally prompted by the example of Goethe, whom Schiller saw, as he saw Shakespeare, as a serene and naïve poet born out of his time. It was Goethe, too, who made the most profound comment on the essay: '. . . he plagued himself with the design of perfectly separating sentimentive from naïve poetry. . . . As if . . . sentimentive poetry could exist at all without the naïve ground in which . . . it has its root'.

Schiller was contrasting the objective (naïve) poetry written in the early (progressive) stages of a culture, and the subjective (self-conscious, sentimentive) poetry written in its decline. Goethe, again, summed the matter up: 'All eras in a state of decline and dissolution are subjective . . . all progressive eras have an objective tendency'. Thus, in the poetry of Shakespeare there is a centrifugal tendency (called 'healthy' by Goethe), an inwards-outwards movement; in most of the poetry of Schiller's contemporaries, and more of that of our century, there is a centripetal tendency, an outwards-inwards movement.

Now Schiller wished to justify his own kind of (sentimentive) poetry in the light of what he felt to be Goethe's naïve poetry. As I have remarked, his precise concerns and (in particular) his programme need not—in this context—be ours.

Here I mean by the naïve writer the writer whose inspiration is above all drawn from his unsophisticated, uncomplicated, *direct* view of the universe. His view is uncluttered by intellectualization. The naïve writers of the nineteenth and twentieth centuries have been poor thinkers—this is a point of which I have made a good deal. Hardy, Dreiser and Sherwood Anderson (for example) were all writers of great power—but poor thinkers. (True, Anderson was something of a sage: but sages are not thinkers.) The naïve writer does not proceed by thought. The phenomenon can still only be explained by recourse to Schiller's distinction. And even where a writer—Pablo Neruda, pioneer explorer of the unconscious, comes immediately to mind—neither wants or tries to 'think', Schiller's essay immediately enriches our understanding.

I mean by the sentimentive writer—but always bearing in mind Goethe's stipulation that no work that has not roots in the naïve has any creative status—the writer who is sophisticated, trained in thinking, self-conscious. Thomas Mann is perhaps the prime example in the twentieth century.

Of course there is no such thing as a purely naïve writer—any more than there can be a purely sentimentive writer. But this applies to the romantic–classical opposition as well. Schiller's distinction is essential; and very important for our time. It reveals not only how the naïve writer can wreck and corrupt his work and himself by betraying his impulses, but also how sentimentive writing is becoming increasingly sterile as it draws cunningly away from the naïve; it reveals, too, the terrible predicament of the sophisticated creative writer in this second half of our century. It is towards the truly mysterious—and yet authentic—that the creative writer must now aim. This is why much of the newest poetry and fiction is coming from Latin America: an exotic and largely unexplored region of the world that well matches our own even more exotic, even less explored regions. Recourse to the purely surreal can lead to nothing better than the raw material of the dream—which, as it comes into consciousness, is censored, screened. What is needed—we have had it in Rilke, Vallejo and some others—is the *real dream*: the meaning of the dream in terms of *its own original, unknown, mysterious, day-haunting images*—not in those of (say) a psycho-analytical interpretation. This truth contains, absorbs and accepts death.

The problem is one of control as well as of inspiration: what kind of control must the writer exercise over his immediate impulses to return to his naïve realm? Here the animal cunning of sentimentive writers such as Vallejo or Rilke can be useful. One thinks in this connection of the cunning art of the 'primitive' man who hunts, for food, animals he loves: this is nearer to the required sentimentive than is the cleverness of the regular academic critic, for all the ancient wisdom that is locked up—one might say fossilized—inside the notions with which he plays.

*

Another concept that I have used freely is what I have christened *Künstlerschuld*: 'artist-guilt'. Increasingly in this century poets and writers (Rilke, Mann and Broch are examples) have been beset by the fear that literature fulfils no useful, but only a selfish function. The writers who feel this particular kind of anguish have been or are almost invariably dedicated to literature to the exclusion of everything else (Broch is an exception). The question is, of course, as old as Plato (this was how Aristotle and others understood Plato); but for some writers of the past hundred or so years it has become crucial. Broch tried not to be a writer. At one point Rilke wanted to be a country doctor. Laura Riding has repudiated poetry. Mann portrayed the writer as a sick Faustus. . . .

This is of course a relevant theme in an age of 'committed literature' and *socialist realism* (this is discussed fully in the section devoted to Russian literature; it must, of course, be distinguished from mere *social realism*, which means no more than it implies). The naïve writer has no doubts: Neruda, the most substantial naïve twentieth-century poet, had no difficulty in reconciling his poetry with his 'communism'.

But the more sentimentive the writer the more wracked he is by doubts. ...

*

I have very often spoken of *midcult* and *middlebrow*. This is a dangerous but essential concept in an age that is desperate to reject the wildness of the imagination by absorbing it (hence literary prizes, government-sponsored culture-feasts, and so on). One of the chief features of the truly middlebrow literature is that, however 'tragic' or 'modern' it may seem, it consists of material manipulated to satisfy the *conscious* desires of a pseudo-cultured (some would simply say cultured) audience: an audience that still thinks of the world-as it-is as essentially the best; an audience of individuals who, in varying degrees, reject their endogenous suffering ('decent', externally prompted grief is allowed: in midcult novels relatives die young, girls get raped or crippled, babies are murdered by 'beasts' and/or so on, and it is 'very sad') : that suffering they experience as a result of their failure to attain authenticity. Middlebrow literature is, in Sartre's existentialist sense, *slimy, viscous*: it helps us to remain *filthy swine* (*salauds*). Some middle-brow literature is apparently *avant garde*; at its worst it may not even be intended for reading, but simply for display (hence the phrase 'coffee-table book'). The great midcult successes are seldom, probably never, planned. They arise from the innate vulgarity and ignorance or (usually) pretentiousness of their progenitors.

Of course few works are entirely middlebrow; equally, some works are merely tainted with middlebrowism in one or another aspect. Some of the characteristics of the kind of midcult literature with which I have been concerned here (where this has not been taken seriously by critics regarded as serious I have happily ignored it), though they never co-exist all together, are: 'uncanniness', 'weirdness', 'occultness'; 'profundity' in the sense that dictionaries of 'great ideas that have changed the world' are profound; fashionableness—whether in the matter of being sexy or using 'dirty' language or whatever; slickness of technique; pseudo-complexity, conferring upon the reader the sense that he is reading a 'difficult' (and therefore 'worthwhile', 'deep') book; potential for discussion at lounge-, drawing-room-, or pub-level (or in the foyers of theatres) ; liability to excite certain reviewers.

*

The useful term *objective correlative* was first used by the American painter Washington Allston in 1850; T. S. Eliot revived it in 1919. It has been much criticized as putting either too much or too little emphasis on the objectivity of works of literature. . . . I am not concerned with this: here I mean by it simply: *objective equation for personal emotion*. If the writer, in expressing a personal emotion about having killed his wife, composes a work about a toad eating dry, red eggs, then that situation is the *objective correlative* for his emotion at killing his wife. I imply absolutely nothing more by my use of the term: it is purely descriptive.

*

For a truly viable (non-commercial) theatre to exist there has to be a truly viable audience. This certainly exists—or existed until a few years ago—in Belgium. The theatre of today is largely in the hands of the directors (hence the term, used pejoratively by me, *director's theatre*), who do not work in true conjunction with the authors of plays but rather as more or less commercial *entrepreneurs*, 'realists' who manipulate such dramatic texts as they decide to exploit to meet the needs of their (alas, mostly middlebrow) audiences. The genuine dramatist has to survive this and to assert himself. All he has on his side is the spirit of the genuine theatre—but this, fortunately, survives along with (and often in the purveyors of) the commercial theatre. There are two tests of a genuine dramatist: his work must be playable on the stage, in some form, at any time during or after his lifetime; and it must stand the test of reading as well as viewing. Perhaps there are a score of twentieth-century dramatists who will fulfil these requirements. I have discussed these and a number of other interesting ones. But it must be remembered that this is a guide to literature and not to the entertainment industry or the history of intelligently motivated socio-anthropological phenomena.

IV

Finally, many people have helped me in many ways with the writing of this book. None is of course in any way whatever responsible for any of the opinions expressed in it, or for any errors. The following have given me aid, of kinds too various to mention, that I found invaluable: of my colleagues on the English Faculty at the University of Wisconsin-Parkside, where I am currently spending a happy and instructive year as Visiting Professor: James and Angelica Dean, Andrew Maclean, James Mehoke; my family, which has worked harder than I have—

and suffered much: my wife, my daughters Miranda Britt and
Charlotte Seymour-Smith, my son-in-law Colin Britt (in particular),
who made things memorably cheerful at a time when they were
difficult; Ivar Ivask, for generously overlooking some of the material
—and correcting me on a number of points; Toby Zucker, for help
with the German section; S. K. Pearce, my bank manager, without
whose practical understanding and help I could not have proceeded;
and B. H. Bal, George Barker, Robert Bly, Edward Charlesworth,
Sally Chilver, Tony Gottlieb, Robert Graves, Fujio Hashima, Wing-
Commander Vernon 'Coils' Pocock, James Reeves, C. H. Sisson,
Hilary Spurling, Anthony Thwaite, David Wright. I should also like
to thank the printers, who have performed a difficult task (and not the
first one composed by me) with exemplary intelligence and fortitude.
My greatest debt is expressed in my dedication; the greatest sorrow of
my life in its first part. Libraries have as always been helpful and
courteous beyond the line of duty: The London Library; the East
Sussex County Library, both at Bexhill-on-Sea and at Lewes (this is in
process of being destroyed by faceless bureaucrats as I prepare this
revision for the press); and the Library at the University of Wisconsin-
Parkside.

The University of Wisconsin-Parkside,   18 April 1972
Kenosha, Wisconsin, U.S.A.

Abbreviations

AD: *Absurd Drama*, P. Meyer, 1965
ad.: adapted
add.: with additional matter
AL: *Albanian Literature*, S. E. Mann, 1955
AMEP: *Anthology of Modern Estonian Poetry*, W. K. Matthews, 1955
AMHP: *Anthology of Modern Hebrew Poetry*, A. Birman, 1968
AMYP: *Anthology of Modern Yugoslav Poetry*, J. Lavrin, 1963
ANZP: *Anthologyy of New Zealand Poetry*, V. O'Sullivan, 1970
AP: *Africa in Prose*, O. R. Dathorne and W. Feuser, 1969
ARL: *Anthology of Russian Literature in the Soviet Period*, B. G. Guerney, 1960
ASP: Apollinaire: *Selected Poems*, O. Bernard, 1965
AU: *Agenda*, Vol. 8, No. 2, Ungaretti Special Issue, Spring 1970
AW: *Australian Writing Today*, C. Higham, 1968
AWT: *African Writing Today*, E. Mphahlele, 1967
BAP: Bella Akmadulina: *Fever and Other Poems*, G. Dutton and I. Mezhakov-Koriakin, 1970
BAV: *Book of Australian Verse*, J. Wright, 1956
BEJD: Josef Brodsky: *Elegy for John Donne and Other Poems*, N. Bethell, 1967
BISS: *Penguin Book of Italian Short Stories*, G. Waldman, 1969
BP: Bert Brecht: *Plays*, 2 vols, J. Willett and E. Bentley, 1960–2
BRV: *Book of Russian Verse*, C. M. Bowra, 1943
BRV2: *Second Book of Russian Verse*, C. M. Bowra, 1948
BSP: André Breton: *Selected Poems*, K. White, 1969
CCD: *Chief Contemporary Dramatists*, 3 vols, T. H. Dickinson, 1915–30
CFP: *Contemporary French Poetry*, A. Aspel and D. Justice, 1965
CGP: *Contemporary German Poetry*, J. Bithell, 1909
CGPD: *Contemporary German Poetry*, B. Deutsch and A. Yarinolinsky, 1923
CIP: *Contemporary Italian Poetry*, C. L. Golino, 1962
CIV: *Contemporary Italian Verse*, G. Singh, 1968
CLP: *Century of Latvian Poetry*, W. K. Matthews, 1957
CP: Anton Chekhov, *Plays*, 1959

CRP: *Anthology of Contemporary Rumanian Poetry*, R. MacGregor-Hastie, 1969

CTP: Albert Camus: *Caligula and Three Other Plays*, S. Gilbert, 1958

CV: *Caribbean Verse*, O. R. Dathorne, 1967

CWT: *Canadian Writing Today*, M. Richler, 1970

DFP: Friedrich Dürrenmatt: *Four Plays*, G. Nellhaus et al, 1964

ed.: edited by

ESW: Paul Éluard: *Selected Writings*, L. Alexander, 1951

FBS: Marcel Raymond: *From Baudelaire to Surrealism*, 1950

FCP: *Five Centuries of Polish Poetry*, J. Peterkiewicz, Burns Singer and J. Stallworthy, 1970

FGP: *Four Greek Poets*, E. Keeley and P. Sherrard, 1966

FMR: *From the Modern Repertoire*, 3 vols, E. Bentley, 1949–56

FTP: Max Frisch: *Three Plays*, M. Bullock, 1962

FTS: Frank Wedekind: *Five Tragedies of Sex*, B. Fawcett and S. Spender, 1952

FWT: *French Writing Today*, S. W. Taylor, 1968

GED: *Anthology of German Expressionist Drama*, W. H. Sokel, 1963

GMS: *Plays of Gregorio Martínez Sierra*, H. Granville-Barker and J. G. Underhill, 1923

GSP: Michel de Ghelderode: *Seven Plays*, G. Hauger and G. Hopkins, 1960

GSS: *German Short Stories*, R. Newnham, 1964

GWT: *German Writing Today*, C. Middleton, 1967

HE: *Heart of Europe*, T. Mann and H. Kesten, 1943

HW: René Char: *Hypnos Waking*, J. Matthews, 1956

HWL: Joseph Reményi, *Hungarian Writers as Literature*, 1964

IMPL: *Introduction to Modern Polish Literature*, A. Gillon and L. Krzyzanowski, 1964

IMSL: *Introduction to Modern Spanish Literature*, K. Schwartz, 1968

IN: P. J. Jouve: *An Idiom of Night*, K. Bosley, 1968

IP4: Eugene Ionesco: *4 Plays*, D. Watson, 1958

IQ: *Italian Quartet*, R. Fulton, 1966

ISS: *Italian Short Stories*, R. Trevelyan, 1965

ISS2: *Italian Short Stories 2*, D. Vittorini, 1972

IWT: *Italian Writing Today*, R. Trevelyan, 1967

JDP: Max Jacob: *Drawings and Poems*, S. J. Collier, 1951

JLME: Y. Okazakix: *Japanese Literature in the Meija Era*, V. H. Vigliemo, 1955

LAP: *Anthology of Latin-American Poetry*, D. Fitts, 1942

LTT: Federico García Lorca: *Three Tragedies*, J. Graham-Luján and R. L. O'Connell, 1961

LWLF: *An Anthology of Byelorussian Poetry from 1928 until the Present Day*, 1971

LWT: *Latin-American Writing Today*, J. M. Cohen, 1967

MAP: *Modern African Prose*, R. Rive, 1964

MBL: *Introduction to Modern Bulgarian Literature*, N. Kirilov and F. Kirk, 1969

MBSP: V. Mayakovsky: *The Bedbug and Selected Poetry*, P. Blake, 1961

MEP: *Modern European Poetry*, W. Barnstone, 1966

MFC: *Four Modern French Comedies*, A. Bermel, 1960

MGL: *Introduction to Modern Greek Literature*, M. P. Gianos, 1969

MGP: *Modern German Poetry*, M. Hamburger and C. Middleton, 1962

MHP: *Mayakovsky and his Poetry*, H. Marshall, 1965

MJL: *Modern Japanese Literature*, D. Keene, 1956

MJS: *Modern Japanese Stories*, I. Morris, 1961

MPA: *Modern Poetry from Africa*, G. Moore and U. Beier, 1963

MRD: *Masterpieces of Russian Drama*, 1933

MRP: *Modern Russian Poetry*, V. Markov and M. Sparks, 1966

MSP: Oscar Venceslas de Lubicz Milosz: *14 Poems*, K. Rexroth, 1952

MST: *Modern Spanish Theatre*, M. Benedikt and G. E. Wellwarth, 1968

MSW: Henri Michaux: *Selected Writings*, R. Ellmann, 1968

MT: *Modern Theatre*, 6 vols, E. Bentley, 1955–60

NVSP: *Selected Poems of Neruda and Vallejo*, R. Bly, 1970

NWC: *New Writing in Czechoslovakia*, G. Theiner, 1969

NWP: *New Writing from the Philippines*, L. Caspar, 1966

NWSD: *The New Wave Spanish Drama*, G. E. Wellwarth, 1970

NWY: *New Writing in Yugoslavia*, B. Johnson, 1970

OBCV: *The Oxford Book of Canadian Verse*, A. J. M. Smith, 1960

PBAV: *Penguin Book of Australian Verse*, H. Heseltine, 1972

PBFV3, PBFV4: *Penguin Book of French Verse 3, 4*, A. Hartley, 1957, 1959

PBGV: *Penguin Book of Greek Verse*, C. Trypanis, 1971

PC: Anton Chekhov: *Plays*, E. Fen, 1959

PGV: *Penguin Book of German Verse*, L. Forster, 1957

PI: *Poem Itself*, S. Burnshaw, 1960

PIV: *Penguin Book of Italian Verse*, G. Kay, 1965

PJV: *Penguin Book of Japanese Verse*, G. Bownas and A. Thwaite, 1964

PKM: Kai Munk: *Five Plays*, R. P. Keigwin, 1953

PLAV: *Penguin Book of Latin-American Verse*, E. Caracciolo-Trejo, 1971

PLJ: *Poetry of Living Japan*, D. J. Enright and T. Ninomiya, 1957

PP: Alfred French: *The Poets of Prague*, 1969

PPC: *Selected Poems of Paul Celau*, Michael Hamburger, 1972

PPPP: *Post-War Polish Poetry*, C. Milosz, 1965

PRP: Robert Pinget: *Plays*, 2 vols, S. Beckett, B. Bray, 1965–7

PRV: *Penguin Book of Russian Verse*, D. Obolensky, 1965
ps.: pseudonym of
PSAV: *Penguin Book of South-African Verse*, J. Cope and U. Krige, 1968
PSV: *Penguin Book of Spanish Verse*, J. M. Cohen, 1956
pt.: part
PTP: Luigi Pirandello: *Three Plays*, A. Livingstone, 1923
PWT: *Polish Writing Today*, C. Wieniewska, 1967
rev.: revised
RP: *Russian Poetry 1917–55*, J. Lindsay, 1956
RSP: Pierre Reverdy: *Poems*, A. Greet, 1968
SAWT: *South-African Writing Today*, N. Gordimer and L. Abraham, 1967
SCO: *Swan, Cygnets and Owl*, M. E. Johnson, 1956
sel.: selected by
SL: *Soviet Literature, an Anthology*, G. Reavey and M. Slonim, 1933
SP: Bert Brecht: *Seven Plays*, E. Bentley, 1961
SSP: *Six Soviet Plays*, E. Lyons, 1934
SSW: Jules Supervielle: *Selected Writings*, 1967
TC: Anton Chekhov: *The Tales*, 13 vols, C. Garnett, 1916–22
TCG: *Penguin Book of Twentieth Century German Verse*, P. Bridgwater, 1963
TCGV: *Twentieth Century German Verse*, H. Salinger, 1952
TCSP: *20th Century Scandinavian Poetry*, M. S. Allwood, 1950
TGBP: *Two Great Belgian Plays about Love*, 1966
TMCP: *Three Modern Czech Poets*, E. Osers and G. Theiner, 1971
TMP: *Twenty-five Modern Plays*, S. F. Tucker, 1931
TNM: *Two Novels of Mexico*, L. B. Simpson, 1964
TT: *Tellers of Tales*, W. S. Maugham, 1939
tr.: translated by
UP: *Ukrainian Poets*, W. Kirkconnell and C. H. Andrusyshen, 1963
VA: Andrey Voznesensky: *Antiworlds*, P. Blake and M. Hayward, 1967
VCW: Paul Valéry: *Collected Works*, J. Matthews, 1962
VSW: Paul Valéry: *Selected Writings*, 1950
VTT: Paul Éluard: *Thorns of Thunder*, G. Reavey, S. Beckett, 1936
WNC: *Writers in the New Cuba*, J. M. Cohen, 1967
ZS: Nikolay Zambolotsky: *Scrolls*, D. Weissbert, 1970

American Literature

I

Henry James' statement, made in a letter of 1872, that 'it's a complex fate, being an American, and one of the responsibilities it entails is fighting against a superstitious valuation of Europe' is hackneyed; but it sums up, with splendid aptness, the heart of the American dilemma at the time he wrote it. (In 'Europe', of course, he included England: the parent country whose political, but not literary, shackles had been wholly thrown off.) The Americans as a whole were slow to recognize their native geniuses: no country likes to discover its true nature too quickly. Emerson was widely acknowledged and highly influential, but, although a major writer, he was not a major creative writer. The American public took Longfellow, an inferior poet, to its heart, but was not happy with Melville; and Whitman—the first wholly American poet—was to the end of his life read only by a minority which misunderstood the nature of his achievement, leading to the establishment of a legend that took more than fifty years to dispel. Many Americans of the nineteenth century tended to regard their own literature patronizingly, as an inferior cousin of English literature: they reckoned that English earth, and not that of America itself, the new country, was the proper place for its roots.

This situation has now changed drastically. If there is a cultural capital of the English-speaking world, then it is New York—that it might be London is now no more than a joke. Since America is by far the bigger and more varied country, and since English literature has temporarily exhausted itself, it is not surprising that this state of affairs should have come about. What is more interesting is how American self-discovery developed into a major world literature. This may be seen most clearly in the way American writers discovered and achieved realism.

*

America had her indisputably great nineteenth-century writers: Melville, who failed to achieve real success and was forced to spend all but six of his last twenty-five years as a customs inspector; Whitman, who had even less popular success; Hawthorne, who did achieve fame with *The Scarlet Letter*, but who was not fully understood. But these had done their best work by the end of the Civil War: Hawthorne died (1864), Melville 'retired' to his custom-house, Whitman began his long decline into mage-hood, and added nothing of consequence to *Leaves of Grass*. Few in the quarter-century after the Civil War would have thought of these writers as particularly important. The fashion was first for the so-called 'Brahmin' (the name was good-naturedly applied, by analogy with the highest caste of Hindus) poets and thinkers (Longfellow, J. R. Lowell, Holmes, Prescott and others), centred in Boston—once revered, then too severely misprized, now more temperately revalued as creatively limited but tolerably liberal gentlemen—and later for such popular pseudo-realist fiction as that written by 'the Beau Brummell of the Press', RICHARD HARDING DAVIS (1864–1916), a clever newspaper reporter, the more skilful romantic novelist F. MARION CRAWFORD (1854–1909), every one of whose forty-five novels has dated, the solid 'conscientious middle-class romantic' historical novelist WINSTON CHURCHILL (1871–1947), and the more gifted O. HENRY (ps. WILLIAM SIDNEY PORTER, 1862–1910), a writer of short stories of humour and technical adroitness (his speciality was the surprise ending) but no psychological depth. The more important writers were not at first much heeded. But there is a major exception: MARK TWAIN (ps. SAMUEL LANGHORNE CLEMENS, 1835–1910), a nineteenth-century figure the importance of whose legacy to the twentieth is beyond question. The 'Brahmin' James Russell Lowell as well as the so-called 'literary comedians' ('Artemus Ward', 'Josh Billings', 'Bill Arp' and so on) of the Fifties and Sixties had tried to create a truly indigenous prose style, and had failed. In *Huckleberry Finn* (1844), sequel to *Tom Sawyer* (1876), Twain portrayed a complex but free American boy, in genuinely American prose; he also wrote a great novel of innocence and experience. But, like Whitman, Twain was a naïve (q.v.) writer, the one great naïve American novelist of the latter half of the nineteenth century. He had also lived close to nature and to the experience of action. He could always write directly and un-inhibitedly of experience; but only once, in *Huckleberry Finn*, did he produce a masterpiece. The realists were, however, for the most part sentimentive (q.v.) writers. They admired Twain—Howells (q.v.) was his friend and collaborator—but could not emulate him; nor, to do them justice, could he help them much in their aims: to portray truthfully, and to anatomize psychologically, American urban society.

Howells, James and the other realists had honourable precursors:

writers whose realism was more than nominal, superficially regional —in the sense of patronizingly recording quirks and customs—and fashionable. Such was JOHN WILLIAM DE FOREST (1826–1906), who influenced Howells. De Forest, born in Connecticut, fought as a captain on the Union side; he wrote a number of readable novels, the most important of which is *Miss Ravenel's Conversion from Secession to Loyalty* (1867). This is didactic and its plot is sentimental, but its realism consists not of photographic set pieces but of a serious examination of the origins of the 'Southern' prejudices of Lillie, daughter of an abolitionist New Orleans doctor who has voluntarily come north at the outbreak of the war. Particularly well done is the portrait of one of her suitors, John Carter, a Virginian officer in the Union army, dashing, dissipated, heroic, morally ambiguous. It was in his battle scenes, however, that De Forest was most in advance of his time. His more happily titled *Honest John Vane* (1875), about a corrupt congressman, is also realistic in its study of political background. De Forest had impulses towards realism, awakened by his war experiences, which might, as a critic has suggested, have borne even richer fruit if he had lived later.

The clergyman EDWARD EGGLESTON (1837–1902), founder of a 'Church of Christian Endeavour' in New York, was one of the best of the many regionalists then writing. Encouraged by J. R. Lowell, and an important influence on Hamlin Garland (q.v.), Eggleston described Indiana backwoods life in *The Hoosier School-Master* (1871), based perhaps on the experiences of his brother. Overall this is a sentimental and didactic novel, but it is important for the author's use of Indiana dialect and the realism of some isolated passages. Eggleston wrote a number of other novels, none as good as this, but nearly all distinguished by some realistic facet. EDGAR WATSON HOWE (1853–1937), who was born in Indiana, was another forerunner—one who lived to see the aftermath. Howe was essentially a small-town sage, in the American tradition; a sort of provincial H. L. Mencken (q.v.). He edited newspapers and magazines, produced cynical and homely aphorisms, and wrote memoirs. But when a young man he wrote one powerful, crude novel of the midwest: *The Story of a Country Town* (1883). Howe was not a good novelist, and the plot of this book is so melodramatically pessimistic as to be absurd. It is also monotonous. But Howe's savage misanthropy caused him to look for unpalatable facts, and since he was intelligent as well as completely sincere (as Mark Twain told him) Howe selected some facts that had not previously been presented in fiction. Howe's picture of midwestern life and human scullduddery and scullduggery (for example, the stern patrician farmer-preacher turns out to be a randy hypocrite) is not vivid—but is more truthful than anything that had preceded it in its category, and with its intended scope. It helped to set a tone for such later writers as Sherwood Anderson (q.v.).

WILLIAM DEAN HOWELLS (1837–1920), son of a newspaperman and printer, was born in Ohio. During the middle years of his long life Howells was considered by most critics to be the doyen of American writers. He was important not only as a pioneer realist, but also as a judicious and generous—but not indulgent—critic of the American writers of half a century, and as the introducer of much vital foreign literature. As a young man Howells, who knew how to get on, was taken up and blessed by Brahmin culture. He wrote a campaign life of Lincoln (1860) and was rewarded with the consulate at Venice, where he spent the years of the Civil War. Highly thought of by his elders, Howells joined the *Atlantic* in 1866 and soon became its editor (1871), and printed both their work and that of promising newcomers such as Henry James (q.v.). During the Seventies he began to form his ideas about fiction and to write novels. The best of these came between 1881 and 1892. Howells' reputation declined during his final years, and he was in due course equated with Victorianism, prudery (it was unfairly asserted that he had 'censored' Mark Twain) and facile optimism. Now Howells was a 'gentleman', and he did not think it right to be profane, obscene or gloomy; nor did he have the genius of Mark Twain. But he was not a pre-Freudian relic: his criticism is still valuable, and the best of his fiction has subtlety and depth. It comes from a mind that, even while it believed in a 'respectable' facade, was well aware of the violent impulses that rage beneath the surface of consciousness: he knew and admitted (to Twain) that the whole 'black heart's-truth' about himself could not be told. That was not something that more than one nineteenth-century liberal gentleman in ten thousand would admit; not many gentlemen will admit it now. Howells' achievement is a monument to what can be done in literature without genius. To understand him it is necessary, as one of his recent critics has well said, to have a taste for 'both James and Twain'. . . . Certainly it is grossly unjust to dismiss Howells and yet absolve James. For it was Howells above all who helped to make the decently written novel an acceptable form in America: who helped American readers to understand that fiction, too, could have a 'moral' message—that the absolutely serious writer need not confine himself, as had Howells' mentors, to the oracular essay or to verse. And his own best novels courageously, if never dynamically, examined American mores. *Dr Breen's Practice* (1881) traces the private and public fortunes of a woman doctor; it sympathizes with her ambitions, but in making her a puritan fit for satire Howells reveals, perhaps with deliberate slyness, lurking anti-feminist prejudice. His two best novels are *A Modern Instance* (1882) and *The Rise of Silas Lapham* (1885), both of which were more unusually subtle and penetrating for their time than is realized today. *A Modern Instance*, which handles divorce and got Howells blamed both for over-boldness and 'moral timidity', is a study in the spiritual squalidity of a relationship in which hatred has replaced attraction (not, I think, love). This, written under the direct influence of Zola (q.v. 2), is Howells' boldest book. In *The Rise of Silas Lapham* Howells satirized the hollow snobbishness of Brahmin families (reflecting his committedness to his own kind) and at the same time showed how a vulgar, self-made man could attain moral authority. Lapham is a brash paint-manufacturer with high social ambitions for his family. He is humbled and forced out of Boston society because, although his way to wealth has been ruthless, he refuses to commit a dishonest act; thus he grows in stature, but, as Howells remarks, 'It is certain that our manners and customs go for more in life than our qualities'. Some critics have hailed the panoramic *A Hazard of New Fortunes* (1890) as Howells' best work—and so it might be if it had the power of the psychological novels. After *An Imperative Duty* (1891) Howells' fiction became more self-consciously didactic and illustrative of the Tolstoyan socialism he had now adopted. But until the very last novel, *The Leatherwood God* (1916), published when he was seventy-nine, he maintained his high standards of craftsmanship and style. It is, strangely enough, this last book—a moving study of a historical character, an Ohio smallholder of the mid-nineteenth century, who persuaded a number of women to regard him as God—that is the least didactic of them all.

It is probably correct to regard Howells as one of the native sources of what we may call the naturalist strain in American fiction—if only because others followed where he led. But his own realism was never really naturalistic, even in *A Modern Instance*. Howe's rudimentary *The Story of a Country Town* was nearer. The fact is that there is always something 'ungentlemanly' about true naturalist fiction—even when, as it seldom is, it is written by gentlemen such as Frank Norris (q.v.). Howells was also, and more obviously, an exemplar for—and frequently an encourager of—the other American realists who eschewed naturalism. Many of these, both major and minor, were temporary or permanent expatriates. If you stayed in the new America, it seems, you thought you understood it in assured, scientific, Darwinian—evolutionary—terms: you were a sort of determinist. Otherwise your impulse was to escape from a reality that you could neither deny nor affirm.

Escapism at its most obvious is seen in the case of the eccentric

LAFCADIO HEARN (1850–1904). Lafcadio Hearn was born on the Aegean island of Santa Maura (once called Leucadia, hence his name) of Irish-Greek parentage, with a goodly admixture of gipsy, English and Arabic—but no American—blood. However, he spent twenty-one years (1869–90) in America as a journalist before sailing for Japan, where he married into a Japanese Samurai family, raised children, turned Buddhist, and became a lecturer in English literature at the Imperial University at Tokyo. (His successor was Natsume Soseki, q.v.4). As a journalist Hearn presented himself as a believer in the evolution of human society into complex higher forms; but really he wanted to get away from the ruthless drive that this 'evolution' implied. When competitiveness became increasingly evident in the life of Meiji Japan, Hearn made plans to return to the States, but died before he could put them into effect. His real inclinations are revealed in the exotic character of his novels, *Chita* (1889), about a girl who survives a tidal wave on an island in the Gulf of Mexico, and even more in *Youma* (1890), on the theme of a slave-girl's devotion—till death— to the girl whose 'mammy' she is, and whom she has promised never to desert. Hearn never showed any inclination, despite the optimism of his journalism, to harness his creative imagination to the purpose of analyzing modern society. He knew that had he done so he would have taken a view too gloomy for the comfort of his social conscience.

His case is one of simple escapism. That of HENRY ADAMS (1838– 1918), great-grandson of the second President of the U.S.A. and grandson of the sixth, is more complicated. The two novels he wrote, *Democracy* (1880) and *Esther* (1884)—the first anonymous, the second pseudonymous—are not important as literature; but Adams as a thinker is. He was the first great American pessimist. Where his illustrious family had been public servants, he took refuge in letters. Had he, however, sought to express himself creatively rather than philosophically he would perhaps have discovered an objective correlative for the personal problems of his marriage (1872) which ended in 1885 with the suicide of his wife. But this period of his life (with the seven years following it), is missed out of his remarkable autobiography, *The Education of Henry Adams* (privately issued 1907; published 1918). Adams was a distinguished historian, and in writing his huge *History of the United States during the Administrations of Jefferson and Madison* (1889–91) he had seen something like evolution at work; his argument here was that men cannot change the course of history. He wrote, it must be remembered, as a member of a family who had actually made history. . . . So he had a superior, or a stronger—less journalistic—sense of evolution than Hearn. But, like Hearn, he sought to escape: in restless travel to Mexico, Japan, Europe. In *Mont-Saint-Michel and Chartres* (privately issued 1904; published 1913) the religiously sceptic Adams postulated a unified medieval universe, the centre of which was the Virgin. This was perhaps more fictional, if unwittingly, than either of his novels: thirteenth-century stability is to a large extent a myth in the mind of nineteenth- and early twentieth-century Catholic apologists. He showed the world of 1150–1250 as in equilibrium, 'pre-evolutionary', centripetal. In the *Education* he shows the modern 'multiverse' as accelerating towards disaster, centrifugal, spinning towards what in a letter he called 'an ultimate, colossal, cosmic collapse . . . science is to wreck us . . . our power over energy has now reached a point where it must sensibly affect the old adjustment. . . .' He used the Second Law of Thermodynamics to show the individual, the victim, as so to say being whirled (by the symbol of the Dynamo, opposed to the Virgin of the earlier book), run down and dissipated into a nothingness: into entropy, disorder. Here and in the posthumous *The Degradation of the Democratic Dogma* (1919)—which was edited by his brother, the historian Brooks Adams (1848–1927), who shared his gloomy view of history—Adams rationalized his theory into an exact prophecy, with dates. This prophecy was wrong—the date of final dissolution was doubtless made early in order to fall into Adams' own lifespan—but few intelligent men reading Adams fifty years after his death are likely to find his apprehensions entirely unjustified. He published his two most important books after the first heyday of American naturalism was over; he had no influence on it. But his thinking in these books—and even more so in his *Letters* (1930; 1947), where he is at his most fascinating and vigorous—is more representative than merely influential. Of course he has nothing in him of the material or cultural optimism that was then one of the characteristics of America, nothing of the pure joy in becoming and feeling pure American, un-English, that distinguishes, say, William Carlos Williams (q.v.). But his work is a response to the same sort of mental crisis that Hofmannsthal describes in his *Chandos* letter (q.v. 2). Not being a poet, Adams does not see the problem in terms of language. Basically he fears for the integrity of his human, and therefore the human, personality in the face of scientific advance. The proto-fascist and futurist Marinetti (q.v. 3) hailed the new technology. Adams shuddered before it, his sardonic mind casting fearfully back for a static and stable paradise, for 'some great generalization which would finish one's clamour to be educated'. 'Modern politics is, at bottom, a struggle not of men, but of forces', he wrote. In the new 'multiverse' 'order [is] an accidental relation obnoxious to nature'. Adams, however, was a historian, not a creative writer: all he wanted was to get out, have nothing to do with it: 'All the historian won was a vehement wish to escape'.

Each man sees his own death differently: he colours his apprehensions of it according to his personal and historical circumstances. Adams, a historian, a scion of mighty history-makers who had more excuse than most for treating the world as his particular oyster, faced by a crazily accelerating and already over-confident science (the 'score or two of individuals' who controlled 'mechanical power' he described as 'as dumb as their dynamos, absorbed in the economy of power'), coloured his idea of death with zestful meaninglessness. It is instructive to compare his non-creative reaction to the creative one of the first German expressionists (q.v. 2), with its distorting rapid wobble between ecstatic hope and horror. Adams' importance is that he shared such men's awareness of the time.

AMBROSE BIERCE (1842–?1914), born in Ohio, was as sardonic as Adams—and more creative. But although his best short stories are distinguished, he never wholly fulfilled his genius, preferring for the most part to substitute for the wisdom he could have attained a mordant but too folksy and self-indulgent cynicism. Bierce was a man of principle (he refused the back pay he had earned as a soldier in the Civil War), and a soul genuinely tortured by what Henry Adams called 'the persistently fiendish treatment of man by man'; but in his case journalism, and the pleasure of being literary dictator of the Pacific States (for a quarter of a century until he resigned in 1909), distracted him from literature; it was easier to indulge himself in his vitriolic epigrams—often cheap and gratuitous, and in any case never on the level of his best stories—than to write creatively. The epigrams are in *The Devil's Dictionary* (1911), originally called *The Cynic's Word Book* (1906); the stories are in *Can Such Things Be?* (1893) and, notably, in *In the Midst of Life* (1898), which was originally called *Tales of Soldiers and Civilians* (1891). The famous Civil War tales, including 'An Occurrence at Owl Creek Bridge' and 'The Horseman in the Sky', in which a young Union soldier has to shoot his father, make a valid use of Poe—and remain original, economic, appropriately macabre: they are secure minor classics. But Bierce did not want to use his imagination to grapple with the problem of contemporary America— his cynical journalism was in a sense as much of an 'escape' as Japan was for Hearn. He made his final escape when he disappeared into Mexico, in 1911, to join Pancho Villa. He was never heard of again.

*

The achievement of HENRY JAMES (1843–1916), born in New York and educated mostly abroad, is so great as hardly to abide all questions of

American realism. Son of a formidable, eccentric Swedenborgian father, and younger brother of William James—an important and seminal thinker—Henry offers in one sense a contrast to Howells: his achievement is a monument to how literary genius can surmount crippling personal difficulties. For James was fated to be only an observer. His friend Henry Adams complained that he knew of women only from the outside—'he never had a wife'. But, as Alfred Kazin rejoins, 'because he knew so little, he could speculate endlessly'. His mind was a brilliant and sensitive instrument of speculation. He is certainly one of those whose work transcends its psychological and historical occasions; the only question is to what extent.

James expressed one important theme of his fiction when he passionately expostulated at the unfairness of fate's treatment of Howells' daughter, Winifred, who died young after a long, disabling, mysterious and unrelieved illness: 'To be young and gentle, and do no harm, and pay for it as if it were a crime'. James as an adolescent had felt himself crushed by his father and his clever older brother; he had not gone to the war as his younger brothers had, and never felt himself able to fulfil a masculine role. His biographer Leon Edel has now revealed, for those who had not detected it from the work, that James' sexual impulses (at least as a middle-aged man) were homosexual, and that he had a bad conscience about it. Whether or not he was ever an active homosexual is an as yet unanswered question. Probably not. Hugh Walpole (q.v.), whom he fell for ('Beloved Little Hugh') and overrated as a writer, is supposed to have offered himself to the master and to have been repudiated with 'Si la vieillesse pouvait!'. These facts throw new light on such works as 'The Turn of the Screw' (printed in *The Two Magics*, 1898), *The Other House* (1896) and *What Maisie Knew* (1897), all written at the height of James' crisis of homosexuality—which coincided with his humiliation in the theatre and with the trials of Oscar Wilde. It was in 'The Turn of the Screw' above all that James (unconsciously) analyzed his condition, defensively referring to it as a 'jeu d'esprit', hoping to throw himself and his readers off the scent. James' personal sexual predicament actually affects our interpretation of all his work, from his first novel *Roderick Hudson* right up until his last unfinished one, the posthumous *The Ivory Tower*. For the young novelist not only wanted to get away from America—although not from his Americanness, a different thing— but also from the 'masculine' obligations of love for a woman and the heavy commitments of marriage. The 'horrid even if . . . obscure hurt', probably a strained back, he claimed to have suffered while helping to put out a fire at about the time of the outbreak of the Civil War, served him in a number of ways: it linked him with his father, who when a child had lost a leg while fighting a fire; it excused him from joining the army; it enabled him to be passive, feminine; the nature of the 'injury' was supposed to be sexual, but no one could of course ask about it directly—thus giving 'sex' the *frisson* it nearly always has in James' fiction. The hurt was 'obscure'—but mere mention of it none the less drew a kind of attention to it. It reminds us of those 'things' little Miles, in 'The Turn of the Screw', said to those he 'liked', and which were 'Too bad' 'to write home about'. . . .

Europe attracted James from the beginning. He felt that America was too crude for his own artistic purposes. His first novel, *Roderick Hudson* (1876), explores his dilemma: Europe is beautiful, sinister, wicked—like Christina Light, who tortures the genius hero into 'horrible' dissipations which all, of course, as always in James, take place off-stage, and which eventually lead to his death. In *The American* (1877), not one of his most convincing novels, he rationalizes his doubts about his inadequacies. Wealthy American Christopher Newman (the name is significant) goes to Paris (where, said James elsewhere at this time, modern French books resembled 'little vases . . . into which unclean things had been dropped') and falls in love with an aristocratic girl whose family are most reluctant to approve the match. Christopher finds an ally, however, in her younger brother Count Valentin. He discovers that the mother of the girl he loves is a murderess, but eventually decides not to use the information to gain his objective: he will not use such knowledge for material ends. Thus James launched himself into fully fledged writerhood.

By 1881, at the age of thirty-eight, with *The Portrait of a Lady*, he had become an undisputed master, for all his shortcomings one of the most important of all English-language novelists. It was in the Eighties that James wrote the novels of his so-called 'middle period': the most notable are *The Bostonians* (1886), *The Princess Casamassima* (1886) and *The Tragic Muse* (1890). The novels of the last period—*The Ambassadors* (1903), *The Golden Bowl* (1904)—are more difficult: the sentences are long, the motivations that are examined are ambiguous: the whole approach seems anfractuous, not to say tortuous. And yet many regard *The Wings of the Dove* (1902), with good reason, as James' masterpiece. This is the story of an innocence betrayed and of the terrifying and irrevocable corruption of spirit that this betrayal brings in its wake. Kate Croy persuades her lover, a poor journalist, to attach himself falsely to a rich, dying girl, Milly. He does so, and gets her money. But he cannot take it, and asks Kate to have him without it. Now herself 'infected' by the innocence of Milly, she will not do so because she rightly suspects him of loving the dead girl's memory. In this hideously accurate portrayal of how a man acts in bad faith, of unmelodramatic evil, James the detached observer triumphed—as he did in so many of his short stories (ed. L. Edel, 12 vols., 1962–5).

Right through his fiction, from *Roderick Hudson* onwards, James had maintained a technique for suggesting, without ever detailing, evil. He had not, of course, experienced evil—only his 'evil' homosexual impulses. He was highly professional, as well as emotionally rather innocent, in the way he dealt with this problem. It is actually one of his strengths that the horrors he hints at are not really, by normal sophisticated standards, particularly horrible at all. The point is that this highly sentimentive (q.v.) writer was not, in calling 'debauchery' 'unclean', simply being reactionary or hypocritical. It was his lack of knowledge that lamed him; but he turned it into a crutch. We do not look, in James, for any kind of enlightenment about or illumination of actual sexual matters: his fiction deals with the innocent or inexperienced preliminaries to them. They lie horribly in wait at the ends of twisting and turning corridors.

In *The Portrait of a Lady* the good and generous Isabel Archer is not experienced enough to realize that the widower Gilbert Osmond—a shallow pseudo-aesthete whose worst failing, however, is his capacity to manipulate others' emotions for his material advantage—wants her fortune. She marries him, and discovers too late that she can do nothing for him—as she had hoped to do for whatever man she might love. Eventually she admits to her former American suitor that she loves him, but nevertheless chooses to return to her husband: to give up her freedom in return for that of his bastard daughter, Pansy, whose interests she will continue to protect. The reader can and does easily fill in the missing sexuality here: Osmond is as self-indulgently lustful for Isabel's virginity as for her money; her own disillusion is as much sexual as psychological. If any reader wonders how she could be taken in by so evidently insincere a man, then he need not wonder for long: the reason is sexual. James had the feminine sensitivity and intuition to understand these things: he earned it by the integrity of his self-analysis—for, in one aspect, all novels are either rationalizations or self-analyses. In *The Portrait of a Lady* James is Ralph Touchett, the tubercular (crippled) observer who loves Isabel, and renounces her from the start (because of his condition) but who stolidly looks after her interests. The real tragedy of the book lies in his death: James' touching account of his own death to sexual life. But he also presents himself as Isabel, who initially turns down both a straightforward New Englander and a decent English aristocrat, then falls into the snare of a cosmopolitan—finally choosing, now a natural and detached moralist, to endure him (as James chose to remain in Europe—but he was happier in England than Isabel was with Osmond, for he found there 'an arrangement of things hanging together with a romantic rightness that had the force of a revelation'). James wrote criticism of great subtlety, travel books and a number of interesting but bad plays and adaptations from his novels (*Complete Plays*, ed. L. Edel, 1949). When the First World War broke out James was agonized: 'that to have to take it all now for what the treacherous years were all the while really making for and *meaning* is too tragic for any words'. He became a British citizen, did what war-work his failing health would allow, received the Order of Merit, and died in 1916. James understood that 1914 meant the disintegration of the old order of things, but was too old to contemplate it. He was one of the greatest of the writers of that vanished world. But he has relevance to the literature of today because his fiction is ultimately a commentary, often exquisite, on what it is to be a creator. Most of the important considerations—the relationship between virtue and creativity among them—are there. James saw with some ruefulness what he could never be; but he never hid from his creative responsibilities. There will always be controversy about the stature of his last three major books—*The Wings of the Dove*, *The Ambassadors*, *The Golden Bowl*. Are they a 'trilogy' that embraces a new form, akin to the drama of Racine? Or was the profound self-adjustment (after his failure to capture a big audience or even to avoid ignominy as a dramatist) of which these books are undoubtedly the fruit, achieved at a high cost to the universality of his art? *The Wings of the Dove* is surely exempt; of the other two novels one is less sure. But all the work of James has much more to yield. Supposing he did, in his last period, create a new kind of fiction; he was still not an innovator in the sense of clearing ground for anyone else; but he cannot be ignored because his whole life was in one way an anticipation of the practice of the writers who came after him: he created his own world, understood that he was God in it—and took his responsibilities with the utmost seriousness. He has been denigrated both by Marxist critics and members of the indigenous 'Black Mountain' school (q.v.); there also existed in the Forties and Fifties an over-fanciful image of James that had little relationship to the man or the writer. Close study, new understanding, increase our respect for him.

His friend EDITH WHARTON (1862–1937), although pessimistic in her view of life, was another who rejected the determinism of naturalism. She came of a distinguished family and, like James, was introduced to Europe in childhood. Her marriage was unhappy, since Edward Wharton became mentally ill; this helped to drive her into literature. She settled in France in 1907 and five years later divorced her husband. Mrs. Wharton insisted that the duty of a novelist was to discover what the characters, 'being what they are, would make of the situation'—but in reality her people are less free than James'. In her world, usually of high society, vulgarity overwhelms fineness; the choice to go against the conventional leads to disaster; opulence corrupts; where James' women are convincing angels, Mrs. Wharton's are defeated harpies. Edith Wharton wrote well of a society she knew, but as a whole her fiction lacks tension. The author knew too well from the beginning, one feels, that vulgarity would triumph: her characters do not assert themselves strongly enough to be tragic in their defeats. The short stories (*Best Short Stories of Edith Wharton*, 1958), ironic and satiric, are slight but in this respect more satisfactory. However, there are amongst the novels some notable exceptions; and Mrs. Wharton invariably maintains a high standard. Her observation is impeccable. One compares her to James and inevitably finds her wanting; and yet she is incomparably better than the Nobel-winning Galsworthy was, even at his best. In her best works she partially overcomes her shortcomings, and has something entirely of her own to offer. An account of *Ethan Frome* (1911), which is one of the only two novels (*Summer*, 1917, is the other) Edith Wharton set outside polite society, makes it sound naturalist; but it is no more than bleak. The story is told wonderingly, by a stranger. Ethan Frome barely wrings a living from the barren earth of his Massachusetts farm; his hated wife Zeena (Zenobia) is a whining hypochondriac. Her cousin Mattie comes to live with them, and Ethan and she fall in love. Zeena forces her out; when Ethan is taking her to the station he yields to the impulse to end it all by crashing the sledge in which they are travelling. But the couple are crippled. Zeena is transformed into their devoted nurse, leaving Mattie to become the whining invalid and Ethan to his despair and certain economic failure. This is not absolutely convincing, but the portrait of Zeena—the nagging, loathed wife—the growth of affection between Ethan and Mattie, and the ironic ending are all beautifully done. Her two other major books are both society novels: *The Custom of the Country* (1913) and *The Age of Innocence* (1920). The character of Undine Spragg, the ruthless social climber of the first, has been objected to on the grounds that Mrs. Wharton's disgust with her type is too great to permit of psychological accuracy. This is not altogether fair. Undine Spragg is a shallow monster driven by ignoble motives; but when critics object that the drama of her marriage to a Frenchman more decent than herself is 'weakened' by this, they are in effect trying to tell novelists what kind of characters to use in order to get their plots right. People like Undine Spragg do exist, and *The Custom of the Country* is better than is generally allowed. *The Age of Innocence* is an acid, ironic but touching study of a love whose happiness is destroyed by adherence to a code, and by the kind of people 'who dreaded scandal more than disease, who placed decency above courage'. *Hudson River Bracketed* (1929) is not wholly successful, but is peculiarly subtle and poignant in its portrait of the creative side of its hero, a novelist who discovers that the 'people' he understands best are the ones he has invented. . . . There is something very attractive about Edith Wharton even at her worst—when she is too gloomy or when she is copying Henry James in some of her supernatural tales—for she is always intelligent and humane. Probably her best work has been underestimated and her originality not fully recognized.

*

'New England transcendentalism' is even less susceptible of exact definition than most such phenomena. But, although it was never a school, it is important, for all subsequent American movements may be seen to stem from it. Essentially it is a first religious step after the repudiation of the Christian doctrine; it can fairly be called a form of rationalistic religion. Its chief figure was of course Emerson, and his lecture 'The Transcendentalist' came in 1841, when transcendental-ism was at its peak. One can most profitably study transcendentalism as it manifested itself in individuals—in Henry David Thoreau, in Emerson himself, in the poet Jones Very—but, while there was never a doctrine, some ideas were held in common. Every transcendentalist is a Platonist, and the inclination towards Oriental religions (exempli-fied in the later Emerson), 'creedless creeds', is typical. The spirit of transcendentalism was eclectic, individualist, reformist. On the specifically American subject of slavery the transcendentalists were abolitionist, although initially they were more sympathetic than active—but for the honourable reason that they were sceptical of all group action.

In the fiction of Henry James the implications of transcendentalism were realized. Its consistent background was a non-dogmatic—indeed, a being-sought-for—moral system, something as ghostly but as effectual as that of any Platonic realm of perfections. Thus Mrs. Wharton, despite her gloom and her apparent belief that men's circumstances are stronger than themselves, is no naturalist: she follows James when she says: 'Every great novel must first of all be based on a profound sense of moral values . . .'. And one does feel her sense of values more strongly than her gloom, which in any case does not arise from an intellectual determinism. That same moral sense lurks behind Howells' fiction, too.

The source of naturalism—which only in America produced a crop of major or potentially major novelists—is, as Charles Child Walcutt has pointed out in an essay on Dreiser (q.v.), the 'Divided Stream of . . . transcendentalism'. The transcendentalists, not always uncon-usedly, regarded spirit and matter as two aspects of the same thing. But, as Walcutt observes:

> The monist stream did not stay One . . . time and experience divided it into poles of optimism and pessimism, freedom and determinism, will and fate, social reformism and mechanistic despair . . . the Nature which was assumed to be a version of a man's spirit and therefore of his will appeared under scientific analysis as a force which first controlled man's will and presently made it seem that his freedom was an illusion, that there was no such thing as will but only chemicals performing reactions which could (theoretically at least) be predicted.

First, Walcutt continues, Americans believed that the human spirit could be liberated by mastering nature; but their 'devotion to science and fact' led them to the point where the natural law seemed to deny both freedom and spirit . . . .

The atmosphere that produced the powerful movement of American naturalism was well summed up by Henry Adams in 1894 when he wrote '. . . if anything is radically wrong it must grow worse. . . . If we are diseased, so is all the world. . . . Europe is rather more in the dark than we are. . . .'

But there is more in a major novelist than a philosophy or, more usually, a pseudo-philosophy. As Nietzsche (q.v. 2) once said, talking about realists: 'What does one see, and paint, or write? In the last analysis, what one *wishes* to see, and what one *can* see'. And so, grateful as we are to determinism and gloom for sometimes inspiring such as Dreiser, we do not go to him for his thinking (God forbid). As always, the truly gifted went altogether beyond dogmatism, to produce something certain and knowable. But let us first look at the minor novelists who anticipated or participated in naturalism.

HAMLIN GARLAND (1860–1940) is more interesting as a pioneer than as a novelist. Harold Frederic (1856–98), a similar pioneer, produced, in *Seth's Brother's Wife* (1887) and *The Damnation of Theron Ware* (1896), novels psychologically far in advance of anything of Garland's; but the latter does have his importance. An autodidact, Garland was born in Wisconsin. As a young man he sweated on the land: he knew the farmers he wrote about, and the conditions under which they worked. He was influenced by Howells, and even more by the economist Henry George (1839–97). George, a lucid and fervent writer, was

highly influential. Imbued with the Pelagianism that still characterizes most Americans, he devised an economic scheme by which he
believed social justice might be ensured: a 'single tax' on land. By
means of this, he believed, the community would recover what it had
lost in rents. George's effect on economic thought probably amounted
to little more than the stimulation of more lucid theories of rent (as an
economist, it is said, he was 'a little more than a child'), but his passion
for justice and the style of his thinking, were and to some extent still
are influential (to the dismay of some economists). George's theories
lie behind Garland's early short stories, collected in *Prairie Folks* (1893)
and *Wayside Courtships* (1897): these villainize landlords and mortgage-
holders. In the mid-Nineties Garland put forward a theory of
literature that he called 'veritism'. This may be described as a meliorist
extension of realism. It was naturalist only in that in proposing a
literature that would change social conditions it assumed that those
conditions determined men's lives. Garland's best work is a short
novel called *A Little Norsk* (1892), about a Dakota farm-girl's hard lot;
next best is the longer *Rose of Dutcher's Coolly* (1895), the story of
another farm-girl—but this one studies at the University of Wisconsin
and succeeds in becoming a writer in Chicago. Garland projected
himself into his heroine, but then got interested in her for her own sake.
The result is a convincing realist novel. Garland's most serious work
was not popular, and before the turn of the century he began to write
romances of the far West; after this he turned into a dull memoirist
and, ultimately, weak-minded devotee of psychical phenomena.

ROBERT HERRICK (1868–1938) was not a naturalist, but like Garland
he anticipated and influenced the mood by his critical and reformist
attitude. A graduate of Harvard, he was a professor of English at the
University of Chicago. An older professor, writing of him in 1909,
could allude to him as 'something of a pessimist, but not unwhole-
some'. Herrick partly made up for his lack of power and psychological
penetration by his honesty. He was perhaps temperamentally a
determinist, but frustrated by guilt about the consequences of such
an attitude. The scientist of his first novella, 'The Man Who Wins'
(1897), believes in the freedom of the will—but his very circumstances
seem to deny it. Herrick did not resolve his problem, but turned to the
(sometimes acute) analysis of the corruptions and strains in industrial
society. In his best novels he succeeded in his aim of dealing with social
problems 'less in an argumentative . . . manner than as crises in human
lives'. *The Web of Life* (1900), his most psychologically ambitious
book, indicates the direction he might have liked to follow. Herrick
was obsessed with the figure of the doctor, the healer (an inferior 1911
novel is called *The Healer*), and this early book is about one who saves

the life of an alcoholic by an operation in which, however, he injures the brain. He falls in love with the man's wife; she collapses under the strain and kills herself. This was melodramatic and, except in parts, unconvincing; Herrick was wise to turn to the more social theme of *The Common Lot* (1904), his best novel, which traces the moral degradation of a young Chicago architect in his dealings with crooked builders, which finally lead to a fire and a number of deaths. His moral 'regeneration' by his wife is tacked on as a gesture. Herrick later became more ponderous, his characters less interesting. His greatest success, the sentimental novella *The Master of the Inn* (1908), is now dated and unreadable.

The prolific UPTON SINCLAIR (1878–1969) was from any kind of 'Jamesian' point of view never more than a simplistic romancer, but he cannot quite be ignored—he is, as one critic has said, 'an event in nature'. *The Jungle* (1906) displays real power and concern, and is possibly the most sheerly vivid exposée in American literature of humanly intolerable economic conditions. It tells of the exploitation of an immigrant Lithuanian family in the meat-packing industry. The message is socialist, but what was heeded was the revelation of the filthy conditions in which meat was packed in Chicago—Sinclair had himself investigated the situation. The Federal Pure Food and Drug Act was hastened through, with the assistance of Theodore Roosevelt; but the lot of the workers was not improved for many years. Sinclair was humourless, a crank and an idealist—but of a personal nobility enough to make most humorous and sensible realists feel at least a pang of shame. He wrote well over one hundred books. He remained a socialist all his life, but was one of the first to rumble the nature of the Russian regime. After *The Jungle* his best known novels are the 'Lanny Budd' series, beginning with *World's End* (1940): these feature Lanny Budd, the bastard son of a munitions king who is, in his grandiosely well-intentioned way, a kind of Yankee Jules Romains (q.v. 2) in that writer's unfortunate self-appointed capacity of world's chief trouble-shooter. Lanny knows everyone, including the top men, and they take note of him. Sinclair, who sunk his money into or took part in several Utopian projects, including Helicon Hall (burnt down), and a single-tax colony, was at heart a big, dear romantic booby. But he was not middlebrow: he did not tell his audience anything at all they wanted to hear. And although, like Henry George (q.v.), he believed in the innate goodness of man, he was a true naturalist at least in the sense that he was able to bring to the notice of a reluctant public the evils they lived amongst.

STEPHEN CRANE (1871–1900) was almost forgotten until some quarter of a century after his death from tuberculosis. Then the novelist, pleasantly ironic short-story writer and critic THOMAS BEER (1889–1940)—famous for his later study of the Nineties, which he christened *The Mauve Decade* (1926)—wrote his *Stephen Crane* (1923), which was one of the initial steps in the rehabilitation of a major writer. (Beer himself combined the economy of Lytton Strachey with the sardonic style of Henry Adams, q.v., and was a notable biographer; unfortunately he later came to over-sound the sardonic note, and some of *The Mauve Decade* reads like self-parody.) Since Beer's book and the issue of his *Collected Works* in twelve volumes in 1926 Crane has, and without doubt properly, attained the status of a classic. The fourteenth son of a Methodist preacher and a religiously zealous, well-educated mother, Crane was a thorough rebel by the time he came of age. Part of the secret of his achievement lies in the absoluteness of his rejection of the values of his age—which went with an intelligent curiosity, a sense of humour, and a natural compassion in acute competition with a bitter and sardonic nihilism. Even when Crane seems to throw the whole of himself into what he is describing, a part of him is usually detached and amused.

Crane starved, worked as a freelance journalist, and then, in 1893, published his first book, under the name of 'Johnston Smith', at his own expense. *Maggie: A Girl of the Streets* was reprinted, in a slightly abridged form, in 1896. At the time of its first publication only Garland and Howells noticed it. *Maggie*, whatever its faults, is a pretty remarkable effort for a twenty-two-year-old: what it lacks in maturity it more than makes up for in attack, candour and confidence. Critics have suggested several sources of this stark tale of a pretty girl forced by the brutal squalor of her home, and then by seduction and desertion, into prostitution and suicide: '*Madame Bovary* recast in Bowery style', the novels of Zola, or a sermon of De Witt Talmage which visualizes the suicide of a prostitute called Maggie. . . . It is not certain how much Crane had then read. But the book's tone is Crane's and no one else's. It is, as a critic said, 'violent and absurd like a primitive film'—but not, as the same critic incautiously adds, 'dated'. The 'primitive film' effect is an impressionism that anticipates the innovatory pointillism of *The Red Badge of Courage*. The scenes in which Maggie's parents quarrel are perhaps absurd; they are also vivid and powerful—one feels how the hopelessly pretty, weak girl was deafened by them. (An old woman asks Maggie, amid shrieks, 'Is yer fader beatin' yer mudder, or yer mudder beatin' yer fader?') Regardless of whether naturalism is a 'true' philosophy or not, Crane gave an unforgettable account of one poor creature whose life was quickly snuffed out by her environment. And he strengthened his novel by bringing to it the moral indignation of his preacher father, but not the moral judgement. Its abundant irony is apparent only to the sensitive or humane reader. It remains as truthful a picture of Bowery life as could at that time have been achieved. It has the authority of imagination and a painterly exactitude that reminds one of the fine New York slum paintings of George Bellows and the 'Ashcan' group of painters whom he joined.

Encouraged by Howells and Garland although ignored by almost everyone else, Crane continued to write. In his laconic, debunking poetry, published in *The Black Riders* (1895), *War is Kind* (1899) and collected in 1930 and again, in a variorum edition, by J. Katz (1966), Crane created a tough, rhythmical free verse: it was well fitted to accommodate what John Berryman (q.v.) has called his 'sincerity . . . bluntness . . . enigmatic character . . . barbarity'. It is subtler than the directness of its manner makes it seem, and in it Crane has absolutely no truck with respectability—or anything that seems to him to be respectable. This poetry, influenced as much by the verbal compression of Emily Dickinson as by the cynicism of Bierce (q.v.), has not perhaps had its full due in spite of the full recognition now accorded to Crane. However, he did not wholly succeed in finding his own poetic voice, which might well have combined his parabolic with his symbolist, 'Baudelairian' manner, when this had been purged of its immature neo-romantic tendencies. Crane's poetry is important, though, because in it he is investigating the meaning of his deepest and most mysterious impulses.

Crane subscribed to Garland's 'veritism', but had had no personal experience of war, the subject of *The Red Badge of Courage* (1895). This is an extraordinary demonstration of the complex nature of fiction: it may be 'realism', it may even be 'naturalism' in so far as it presents men helpless in the grip of events—but the 'reality' it embraces is evidently wider than that of mere reportage. As one of Crane's leading critics, R. W. Stallman, has pointed out, it 'is a symbolic construct'. And because it succeeds so triumphantly on the realistic level, it is also about many other things: the fearful plunge of men into maturity and responsibility, into sexuality, into the raw, chaotic unknown. Henry Fleming is not named until half-way through the book. A farm-boy, he swaggers to himself, is frightened, is reassured, is caught up in battle and runs, gains his 'red badge' by an accident, returns and becomes a demon of aggressive energy. But it is all for nothing: his regiment takes up its former position. If he has become a 'man' (as he tries to believe) then what, asks the ironic structure of the book, is a man? In a short sequel, 'The Veteran', Henry really does become a 'man' when he goes into a burning barn to rescue two horses; but after that conversion he is a dead man.

Another interesting thing about Henry Fleming and some of Crane's other characters is that they have nothing dishonestly to offer outside his own pages. As Berryman points out, they are not 'types', but they are not 'round' characters either: they move significantly only in their context, of Crane's impressionistic imagination. This not only anticipates but also disposes of all the philosophical claptrap surrounding the *nouveau roman* (q.v.2). He does not tell us meaninglessly that the *sun shone red*. He puts it honestly into the text that is his own picture, his invention of a battle: 'The red sun was pasted in the sky like a wafer'.

Crane's novel 'The Third Violet' (1897), on bohemian life, is more conventional than *George's Mother* (1896), a competent tale of a working-class mother whose son is the opposite of what she fondly and pathetically imagines he is. Besides novels, poetry, unfinished plays and fiction, and a mass of journalism, Crane left behind him a number of short stories as classic as *The Red Badge of Courage*. The most famous of these are 'The Open Boat', based on Crane's experiences when, sent as correspondent to cover an expedition, he was shipwrecked off Cuba, and 'The Blue Hotel', a wickedly knowing tale about a Swede who creates the death-trap, the hostility of tough Nebraskans, that he most fears.

Crane drove himself ever more frenetically towards an early death. He took jobs covering the Spanish-American and the Graeco-Turkish wars, got into debt, desperately and vainly tried to write himself out of it. His last years were shared in England in a dilapidated manor house at Brede, Kent, with Cora Taylor, divorcee, prostitute and madame. There he made close friends of H. G. Wells, Ford Madox Ford and Joseph Conrad (qq.v.), and enjoyed as much friendship and understanding as any young writer has had. But he wore himself out entertaining on a regal scale, projecting—and writing. It was characteristic that he should have taken no heed of a serious warning (a lung haemorrhage) six months before he died. His self-destructiveness remains enigmatic, but one senses an enormous secret despair behind the sardonic and even gay phthisic energy. We can suspect that as his Henry Fleming turned after the battle to 'tranquil skies' with 'a lover's thirst', so he turned to death. Certainly Hemingway was right in saying that modern American literature begins with *Huckleberry Finn*; but rivers do not come from one spring, and it is as true to say that it flows from Crane's fiction. This may become increasingly apparent. It is sometimes objected that Crane's fiction and 'perverse' poetry ultimately function only 'as a fresh symbol of the universe's indifference to human needs' (Alfred Kazin). Crane did feel that. But there is something else locked away in that blandly autonomous prose, a creative intelligence like a great bird of prey, anticipating American writing not yet seen.

Chicago, to become the centre of the new literature, was an appropriate birthplace for FRANK NORRIS (1870–1902), who shared the given names of 'Benjamin Franklin', but little else, with Wedekind (q.v. 2). Norris did not have Crane's genius or sense of style, but he left some powerful fiction, and usefully demonstrates the limitations of such terms as naturalism when they are allowed to apply to anything beyond conscious method: we cannot heed Nietzsche's warning too much: 'What does one see, and paint, or write? . . . what one *wishes* to see, and what one *can* see'. Norris was a romantic who studied art in Paris at seventeen, and while there became hooked on medieval chivalry (or what passed for it) rather than realist or naturalist literature. Later, however, at Harvard, he chose the naturalist method as he had observed it in the novels of Zola (q.v. 2) in order to have a literary principle, and thus to get his fiction written. He carried out journalistic assignments, including one in Cuba, married, and became well known as a novelist before his death. Norris wrote his best novel, *Vandover and the Brute* (1914) while at Harvard during 1894 and 1895; the manuscript was believed lost for a time, in the San Francisco earthquake; it was not published until twelve years after his early death of peritonitis. *McTeague*, written at about the same time, was published in 1899, after the issue of the later and inferior *Moran of the Lady Letty* (1898). Norris' reputation rests on *Vandover*, *McTeague*, and the first novel of a planned but uncompleted trilogy on the production and distribution of wheat: *The Octopus* (1901); *The Pit* (1903), the second, is inferior. His first published work, a long phoney-medieval poem in three cantos called *Yvernelle: A Tale of Feudal France* (1892), is of no literary value but is useful as an indication of the romanticism that he never wholly shed.

Norris' importance has been acknowledged, but his achievement has been underrated because he has been judged as a naturalist and therefore by the standards of realism. Norris was, however, like Crane, a symbolist, and his three best books are all symbolic novels; but unlike Crane, he had no inkling of the fact, and when he announced, 'By God! I told them the truth', he equated the telling of truth with the simple act of holding a mirror up to the unpleasanter facts of nature. He had been very worried by the consequences of his (apparently ordinary) sexual excesses, and suffered from some measure of the gentility then endemic in America. The simple fact of sex existing at all haunts his fiction as a terrifying background grossness. *McTeague* is about a huge and physically gross dentist who is driven to bestiality, and the murder of his whining, miserly wife Trina, because of the circumstances created when his jealous friend betrays him to the authorities for practising illegally. *McTeague* is indebted to Zola, and even to actual incidents in his novels, and it is plainly intended as a naturalist novel, with simple symbols (such as the huge, gilded tooth that Trina gives McTeague for his sign: 'tremendous, overpowering . . . shining dimly out . . . with some mysterious light . . .', or his canary). McTeague is usually described by critics as 'stupid and brutal', and as thoroughly deserving of his fate; and possibly Norris himself consciously thought this. Actually, however, he is initially a sympathetic character, not in the least brutal except when aroused—as when a friend bites his ear. His lapse in 'grossly' kissing Trina while she is anaesthetized is not too serious, since he goes no further—and in any case the episode too obviously arises from Norris' own anxiety about sexual desire originating in a menacing beasthood (which he was simultaneously trying to resolve in *Vandover*). In *McTeague* each incident and object, and not just that gilded tooth, has symbolic force. The whole does not quite hang together, but the clumsy and deliberate style (like that 'of a great wet dog', John Berryman suggests) is more appropriate than is at first apparent. McTeague's degeneration—after his friend has denounced him—is convincing; but is it 'realistic'? Not more than the detail of his carrying his little singing canary about with him under impossible circumstances, or more than the habit he gets into of biting his wife's fingers (which have to be amputated) to punish her.

The Octopus is a more truly realistic novel. The 'octopus' of the title is the railroad, which threatens California wheat-ranchers. The description of the battle between the farmers and the railway men is justly famous, and the whole novel—although like all of Norris' fiction it has grave faults, one of the chief of which is unconvincing and stilted dialogue—deserves its reputation. *Vandover*, however, remains his masterpiece. It deals with the descent into madness, despair and penury of a decent and well-bred man. It quite transcends its origins: Norris' fear of syphilis, which masked his even profounder terror that sexual indulgence might drive him into a mysterious insanity; and a programmatically naturalist desire to show a man at the mercy of his 'bad' heredity. This is not a moral tale, as is sometimes alleged, because Vandover's fate is ironically contrasted with the good fortune of his vulgar friend Geary, a dishonest man who sows as many wild oats as Vandover, but merely prospers. Vandover's illness is not venereal, as has been suggested, but mental: once a promising painter, he sinks into a fatal decline, ending up by prowling naked and barking like a dog, earning his living by cleaning up filth. His decent friend Haight, however, does get syphilis—apparently from a mere kiss and the accidental slippage of a court plaster. Out of a neurotic anxiety and a fairly crude programme Norris produced a satisfying comment on the nature of both sexuality and creativity. It has been objected that he was inconsistent, putting the blame for Vandover's madness variously on himself, an indifferent universe, and society. . . . But Norris' creative bewilderment is honest; the pert critical objection is sterile. The book has a power and cohesiveness that cause us to take it on trust. Norris did more than enough to ensure survival.

If THEODORE DREISER (1871–1945), the Indiana-born son of a crippled and intermittently employed mill superintendent, had sought fame as a thinker he would have been lucky to get as far as the middle pages of a local newspaper. His fiction, the best of which is not far below the best of the century, is related to his ideas (if we care so to dignify them); but it is fatal to an understanding of the fiction to try to interpret it in terms of the ideas. Most people with such sets of notions as Dreiser possessed remain comparatively inarticulate cranks, or, at best, write books whose appeal is strictly limited to the semi-educated. But Dreiser's fiction is what his ideas were really about. And although his determinism is philosophically shabby and his 'science' a vulgarized jargon and travesty, H. L. Mencken (q.v.) was entirely justified in his remark that 'Dreiser can feel, and, feeling, he can move. The others are very skilful with words'. And when a critic as highly intelligent as Lionel Trilling, an academic rationalist and intellectual incensed by such reactions as Mencken's, tried to demonstrate that Dreiser was not good and wrote poorly (clumsily and not like a professor) because he thought poorly (not like a rationalist professor), instead of damaging Dreiser's status (who, admiring him, does not know that his style and thinking are not models for emulation?) he most painfully and needlessly exposed his own shortcomings. Dreiser is an exception that tests almost every known rule.

Dreiser was an emotional, not an intellectual man. We have to treat his ideas as simplistic rationalizations of his feelings; in his fiction they become transformed. Since his parents were poor, Dreiser was all his life profoundly moved by poverty. Few if any serious modern writers actually believe in capitalism as a system, although many do believe that liberalized forms of it may be the least of a number of evils; Dreiser, however, loathed it, and at the end of his life he joined the communist party, convinced that a Marxist revolution would provide the only just solution. On the other hand Dreiser, himself a compulsive womanizer, was obsessed by capitalist tycoons and crooks, and by the compulsive sexuality they frequently display. The character of Frank Cowperwood, the central character in the trilogy comprising *The Financier* (1912), *The Titan* (1914) and the posthumous *The Stoic* (1947), is partially based on the swindler and transport magnate Charles Yerkes. (Dreiser himself, after a year at Indiana University and some years working on newspapers, attained huge success before he became a famous writer: although his first novel failed in 1900, he went on to become editor of the women's magazine *The Delineator* at the then unprecedented salary of $25,000.) Brought up as a strict Catholic, he came to hate religion and to profess to see the workings of the mind as 'chemisms', mere predetermined chemical reactions. But he remained as interested in religion as in socialism and communism; his last novel—most of *The Stoic* was written many years before his death—*The Bulwark* (1946), some of which was written at the end of his life, has for its hero Solon Barnes, who is sympathetically portrayed as a Quaker and a seeker after religious truth. As for 'chemisms': he could never fully make up his mind about free will (what novelist really can if he tries?), and one of the strengths of his fiction is its ambiguity on this point (for all the unnecessary pseudo-philosophical asides). As Dreiser drifted into communism, he also drifted into a sympathy with the transcendentalism of Thoreau, and with Hinduism.

In terms of thought all this is of small interest. But when Dreiser came to write his fiction he stopped thinking, his imagination started to work, and he dramatized the conflict within himself. Those asides that disfigure even the finest of his novels are irrelevant to them. Critics say that Dreiser in *An American Tragedy* 'makes society responsible' for the tragedy of Clyde Griffiths' execution. That is not so. Dreiser does not know. He shows us Clyde's pitiful moral weakness, the terrible unwitting callousness with which he plans Roberta's death. Beside this he shows us the hypocritical and equally callous indifference of society, concerned with procedures and not at all with understanding or even guilt. Dreiser's book is important in that it gives us the actual grain of, the sense of being of, a specific human being going towards extinction; it warns that 'life' is frightening because it is 'like that'; but it offers—whatever Dreiser himself may say when he abandons his proper business of rendering Clyde and his story—no easy junketing of responsibility onto society. Clyde is forced to leave Kansas and the Green-Davidson by chance (the running down of a child, for which he is not responsible); thus he meets his uncle, his good fortune—and his end. Here Dreiser offers no facile comment as to whether there is free will. There is nothing essential to the novel that demonstrates choice as an illusion—

except in that universal and bitter sense which the retrospective view confers.

Sister Carrie (1900) was accepted for Doubleday by Frank Norris (q.v.), but Doubleday himself—influenced by his wife, who was horrified because in it 'sin' is not 'punished' (it is the duty of society to keep this dark, lest the underprivileged should try it)—'privished' it: he kept to his contract, printed and bound one thousand copies— but did not push it at all hard. So Dreiser had to wait until 1911 and the publication of *Jennie Gerhardt* for recognition. After the first two of the 'Trilogy of Desire' (on Cowperwood) came *The Genius* (1915). *An American Tragedy*, which was occasioned by the Chester Gillette-Grace Brown case, was published in 1925. Apart from these novels and the final posthumous two, Dreiser wrote many short stories, travel and political books, essays and (atrocious) verse.

The view (later modified) of the influential biographical critic Van Wyck Brooks (1886–1963) that American literature was impoverished by puritan dualism (isolated idealism starved by practical material-ism) was over-simplified, especially since it wrote off Mark Twain and Henry James as failures; nor was it a new idea; but it had truth in it. Dreiser helped American literature out of the 'genteel tradition'; again, although critics do not enjoy admitting it, he offered some-thing that Henry James could not offer. Where Dreiser is massive is in the illusions he gives of lives as they are lived, of people as they seem: Clyde weakly appealing in his good looks and ambitiousness (right from when the 'captain' at the Green-Davidson engages him as bellboy), Carrie Meeber and Jennie Gerhardt innocent—although in different ways—of the nature of the lusts they arouse in men. . . . Dreiser—notwithstanding the philosophies in which he was interested, ranging from Herbert Spencer to Elmer Gates' Laboratory of Psychology and Psychurgy—can convey the texture of life itself as few other novelists can. It is the kind of 'realism' for which there will always be a place.

Dreiser's best novels are *Sister Carrie* and *An American Tragedy*, followed by *Jennie Gerhardt*—here the heroine, whom some critics still describe as 'sinful', is morally superior to the other characters, whereas Carrie was morally neutral—and *The Financier*. Then, a long way back, come the last two of the Cowperwood trilogy. Here there are too many authorial asides—we hear too often the voice of Elmer Gates of the Laboratory of Psychurgy—and Dreiser's con-fusion over Cowperwood loses dramatic power. *The Genius* (1915), whose chief character Eugene Witla is a self-portrait—with some added details drawn from a painter and an art-editor Dreiser knew— was banned and then drastically rewritten. It is the odd one out of

Dreiser's books. Here Dreiser tried to resolve his sexual difficulties, but pseudo-intellectual scruples interfered; there are far too many irrelevant intrusions. However, some sections of the novel—such as that describing Witla's decision, after a breakdown, to give up painting and become a manual worker—are extremely good. *The Bulwark* is interesting, but lacks creative steam.

A word about the so famously bad style and the gauche dialogue. Too much is made of this. Dreiser was not a sophisticated writer; a sophisticated or elegant style would not have suited him. His style is admirable—for its purposes. That it is rebarbative, 'as lacerating to the sensibility as the continuous grinding of pneumatic drills' (Walter Allen) is neither here nor there: so is the life and death of Clyde Griffiths, so is the fact that only a little ruthlessness on his part would have brought him success, so is the transformation of the matter of his guilt or innocence into a political issue, so is the massive and never withdrawn pity. To lament that Dreiser's style was not 'better' is to miss the whole point of what Dreiser was. It is not of course sensible to praise Dreiser at the expense of a very different writer, Henry James. It is less sensible to condemn him, as Lionel Trilling tried to do, because he was not James (or, more precisely, James-as-seen-by-Trilling). Trilling sneers at the concept of Dreiser's 'great brooding pity' and attacks him for the 'failure of his mind and heart'. It is an interesting and curiously contorted bitterness—in a fine critic—that can miss Dreiser's achievement in *An American Tragedy*. What has gone wrong here? It is something more fundamental than Dreiser's doubtless hideously non-professorial notions of culture. . . . In a comment on *An American Tragedy* Irving Howe shrewdly quotes George Santayana (q.v.) on one kind of religious perception, that 'power of which we profess to know nothing further', and through which we feel 'the force, the friendliness, the hostility, the unfathomableness of the world'. As Howe says, this power 'flows, in . . . feverish vibration, through *An American Tragedy*'.

JACK LONDON (1876–1916), bastard son of a wandering Irish astrologer whom he never saw, is wrongly regarded in Russia as a great writer. He is, however, a remarkable one, with a gift for storytelling unsurpassed in his time. Before he found fame and a huge public in the early years of the century Jack London (he adopted his mother's husband's surname) had roughed it: had drunk heavily, whored, been to jail, poached oysters, slaved in a canning factory, prospected for gold, been a tramp, gone sealing. . . . He is another writer whose achievement need not be discussed in terms of his crude attempts to systematize his reading; but he has neither the compassion nor the weight of Dreiser. London achieved enormous success, wrote fifty books in sixteen years, married twice—and finally killed himself (half-unpremeditatedly) with an overdose of morphine when ill health (ureamia), financial worry and legal troubles exerted too great a pressure upon him.

The main influences on London, apart from the fact of his bastardy, which he suppressed and which drove him to seek fame, fortune and respectability, were the writings of Kipling (q.v.) and Stevenson, then in the ascendant in America, and the ideas of Marx, Darwin (through his popularizer Haeckel) and Nietzsche. There is usually something worth while in all London's fiction, if only narrative and descriptive vigour. But as he grew older he tended to dissipate his gifts in his increasingly frenetic quest for security. His best books are: *The Call of the Wild* (1903), which dealt with his own problem (compare Norris) of wildness by giving an account of a dog that returns to its ancestors, the wolves; *The Game* (1905), a boxing tale (perhaps only for those who like and have a knowledge of its subject); *The Iron Heel* (1907), which prophesied a 300-year period of fascism, followed by socialism; *Martin Eden* (1909), an autobiographical novel in which London made the more personal prophecy of his suicide seven years later; and *The Star Rover* (1915), interconnected short stories about a convict who learns to transfer himself to another body. London was acutely aware of the conflict between instinct and reason, retrogression to primitivism and progress to utopia; in his inferior fiction he too crudely advances either socialism or his misunderstanding of Nietzsche. It was in *The Call of the Wild* that he discovered his most satisfactory objective correlative (q.v.). He wrote beautifully about animals, with whom he had a sympathy that extended beyond his obsessions with brutality and strength. London is not only still readable, but still worth reading (a different matter).

SHERWOOD ANDERSON (1876–1941), born in Camden, Ohio, does not always get his due, even in America. To some extent this is understandable. At his death Lionel Trilling (once again) struck; he has reprinted his vicious and patronizing obituary piece, with added material, in his widely-circulated collection of essays *The Liberal Imagination* (1950). This helped to put Anderson out of fashion. Furthermore, the best writing of his last twenty years (written off too confidently by Trilling as a time of absolute and 'poignant' failure), the autobiographical material, was unavailable. Paul Rosenfeld's *Sherwood Anderson's Memoirs* (1942), however good its editor's intentions, was bibliographically a disgrace, consisting largely of rewritten material. Not until 1970 did *Sherwood Anderson's Memoirs: A Critical Edition*, impeccably edited by Ray Lewis White, appear. The best writing in this has the kind of impact of the stories of

Anderson's undoubted and acknowledged masterpiece, *Winesburg, Ohio* (1919).

Anderson's moment of truth at the age of thirty-six is a legend. He was sitting in his paint factory in Elyria, Ohio, dictating to his secretary in the winter of 1912, when he suddenly walked out. He turned up in a Cleveland hospital four days later, with 'nervous collapse'. This myth that Anderson himself established about his escape from soulless commercialism to creative freedom contained an element of truth. For he did eventually reject the non-values of his existence as an advertising copywriter and salesman of paint and, previously, other merchandise. But he had been struggling for some years with writing before he made the famous break; and he did not give up writing advertising copy until 1923—as he tells us in the memoirs he wrote in the Thirties, when his fame had passed. Superficially the businessman Anderson was not very different from his neighbours: public churchgoer and private out-of-town brothel-patronizer, country club member, and so on. There are similar men in almost every small town in America, and some of them even walk out. But Anderson differed from them because, in the privacy of an attic, out of the way of his university-educated wife who was always informing him of his inability to become the kind of man she envisaged as a writer, he indulged himself in what at first seemed like fantasies but later turned out to be the imaginative realities of a born writer. Although the actual moment of walking out came to symbolize for him his dramatic escape from the crass materialism of America, the process really took a number of years. The incident of walking out was the result of a real breakdown, occasioned by domestic tension and financial anxiety; these elements were played down, and led first to Anderson's being lionized as a great antiphilistine and enemy of Babbittry (q.v.), but later to his being attacked and subsequently neglected as a crude apostle of instinct. And yet in 1956 William Faulkner (q.v.) affirmed that Anderson was 'the father of my generation of American writers and the tradition of American writing which our successors will carry on', and he asked for 'a proper evaluation'.

Six of Anderson's seven novels amount to little more than a distraction from his real achievement, which lies in his short stories and in the sections of autobiography collected together by Ray Lewis White. Parts of the first, *Windy McPherson's Son* (1916), are good, and in all of them, even the disastrous *Dark Laughter* (1925), there are fine passages. The best, and worth revival, is *Poor White* (1920), a successful projection of the author into Hugh McVey, a 'poor white' telegraph operator who becomes successful when he invents a corn-cutter. He awakens from his mathematical dreams only when Bidwell, Ohio, has been turned into a strife-torn industrial hell. *Poor White* has the faults of too glaring symbolism, but the grotesque and then distorted character of Hugh, and much of the detail of Bidwell's transformation into a factory town, are described with the power and subtlety of *Winesburg, Ohio*.

But Anderson was superior in shorter forms; the pressure put upon him to write long fiction was not good for his work. He was a lyrical and truly naïve (q.v.) writer; his outbursts against criticism, some of it sensible criticism, did not help readers to understand him or critics to follow him. Hemingway (q.v.), an inferior writer, pillaged him and then tried to parody him in his *Torrents of Spring*. After a difficult period in the Twenties, Anderson met his fourth wife, with whom he was happy, and retired from the literary scene to edit two Virginia newspapers, one democratic and the other republican. It was in this period that he did much of the autobiographical writing that provides a full answer to Trilling's charge that 'what exasperates us is his stubborn, satisfied continuance in his earliest attitudes'. After his first great success Anderson was too eager to publish whatever he wrote, and in his efforts to fulfil his genius in a novel he momentarily lapsed into the midcult image of himself that had been created by the widest section of his public: that of prophet and mystic. But he was too fond of life itself to stand the strain of this falsity for long. He refused to become or to pose as a mage—the fate of so many naïve writers, from Hauptmann through Jammes to Giono (qq.v. 2)—and instead, never stubbornly or satisfiedly, strove for self-knowledge. In the best of his autobiographical writings his effortful honesty comes naked off the page: it *is* embarrassing in so sophisticated, so intellectual and so reticent an age. But literature would entirely dry up without its stream fed so copiously by Anderson. The *Memoirs* contain writing that is genuinely inspiring (again, an embarrassing concept today): it fills the reader with the desire to search for and try to attain a similar simplicity and similar honesty. There is very little like it in twentieth-century literature. It is beautiful in the important sense that it illuminates and adds meaning to that increasingly difficult word.

For so seminal and original a book *Winesburg, Ohio* has some strangely obvious sources. The structure is that of the poems of Edgar Lee Masters' *Spoon River Anthology* (q.v.); the self-revelatory characterization is reminiscent of Turgenev's *A Sportsman's Sketches*; the deliberately oral, indigenous style owes much to Mark Twain (q.v.), though it up-dates him; the tone sometimes approaches Howe's in *The Story of a Country Town* (q.v.). Finally, Gertrude Stein, whom

Anderson early recognized as being essentially, 'a writer's writer', liberated him from conventional usage, teaching him what she could not herself achieve: the lyrical expression of intuitions. The episodes in *Winesburg, Ohio*, all centring around the writer-figure of George Willard—a man who brings out something in each of the characters, if only the desire to confess—reveal men as both cursed and blessed by their gift of language: even as they are trapped, they live, they exist, they believe. This arises from a profound scepticism, set out in the prologue to the book and too often ignored. Anderson saw the citizens of Winesburg, and the whole of the modern world, as trapped in what Keats so famously called 'an irritable reaching out after facts and certainties'. Rejecting that multiplicity of apparently contradictory truths that is the actual sum of human knowledge— refusing to be in those 'uncertainties, mysteries, doubts' (Keats) that are proper to the human condition—we (Anderson said) grasp at and appropriate single truths; this distorts us and turns us into grotesques. Anderson's notion throws more light on the nature of society than many searchers after or possessors of systems may care to admit. There are some other short stories by Anderson that reach the level of *Winesburg, Ohio* from *The Triumph of the Egg* (1921), *Horses and Men* (1923) and *Death in the Woods* (1933). These may be found in *Short Stories* (ed. M. Geismar, 1962). Hart Crane (q.v.) said of this unique writer that his strong sense of nature 'colours his work with the most surprising grasp of what "innocence" and "holiness" ought to mean'. Despite what we know about the financial and domestic pressures, the quiet and beautiful work of Anderson's last decade does, after all, take us back to that winter afternoon in Elyria. ... He at least did not spoil his myth.

The connection between Anderson and GEORGE SANTAYANA (ps. JORGE RUIZ DE SANTAYANA BORRÁS, 1863–1952), who was born in Spain and retained his Spanish nationality, may seem tenuous. Santayana was an intellectual, and was more important as a philosopher than as a creative writer. Yet he and Anderson are curiously bound together by the sceptical and electic philosophy that Santayana ambitiously formulated in *Scepticism and Animal Faith* (1923) and its successors. If Anderson typifies the naïve (q.v.) approach to a certain apprehension of reality, then Santayana typifies the sentimentive (q.v.). Santayana left Spain at the age of nine and was educated in Massachusetts. From 1889 until 1912 he was a professor at Harvard. Then, on receipt of a legacy, he resigned. After many productive years he settled (1939) in a Roman nursing home—the fascists left him alone in the war because of his Spanish nationality. Santayana has written the best prose of any philosopher of the century. His poetry, although technically graceful by the standards of its time, entirely fails to reconcile the disparate sides of his nature; had it succeeded he would have been a great poet. As it was he called himself, rightly, 'almost a poet'. His philosophy is essentially an attempted reconciliation of idealism and realism. It is rightly described by orthodox philosophers as not being thorough-going or 'of [philosophical] consequence': it is more important than any of their sets of rigorous games, in that it may be immediately related to how men actually feel and live. It is significant that Santayana's initial approach resembles that of a philosopher who stands behind much modern literature, Husserl (q.v. 2): the application of strict logic results in everything being doubtable. But 'animal faith' compels us to believe in a matter from which what Santayana called 'intuitive essences' have arisen. It is a subtle philosophy, and a profoundly intelligent and ironic modification of scepticism (it is by suffering, Santayana says, that we gain the clue to matter, which we must affirm in a suitably sardonic manner); it contains anticipations and understandings of modernism in literature. Santayana wrote one distinguished and interesting novel, *The Last Puritan* (1935), in which he contrasts Oliver Alden, the last puritan of the title, with other, hedonistic characters. For a reason that no one could explain, this became a best seller.

In 1931 Santayana had written a book called *The Genteel Tradition at Bay*. This attacked, although with much more cogency, the same tradition that had been Van Wyck Brooks' (q.v.) target. But Santayana was specifically criticizing the movement of the 'new humanism', which was led by IRVING BABBITT (1865–1933), who taught French at Harvard for most of his life, and PAUL ELMER MORE (1864–1937), a more interesting figure who interrupted his teaching career to become a distinguished journalist (he edited *The Nation* 1904–14). T. S. Eliot (q.v.) was loosely associated with this movement, although critical of it. The new humanism was thin-blooded, anti-romantic, classical conservative, anti-modernist, intellectual, with some elements of authoritarianism. Essentially it was a foredoomed attempt, by men in general non-creative, to revive what they thought of as transcendentalism. It drew on Christianity, but substituted for its central tenets a universal ethical code. Babbit advocated an 'inner principle of restraint'. This movement flourished in the Twenties but petered out, after being much attacked and defended, in the Thirties. It is one of the least distinguished of the theories that have come from the better minds of our century. Santayana revealed the new humanism, which claimed to be opposed to decadence, as itself decadent and attenuated. He was

particularly withering on the question of the new humanists' super-
naturalism, upon which they were vulnerable. *The Last Puritan* was
conceived both as a criticism of and a satire on this continuation of
the genteel tradition; it was also for Santayana a happy return to
the Nineties, when he was still young enough (he said) to sympathize
with youth but old enough to understand it. However, in the
character of Oliver Alden, and the tragedies of his love and end,
Santayana got beyond satire.

*

Four important women fiction writers emerged in this period. KATE
CHOPIN (1851–1904), born in St. Louis, did not begin to write
seriously until after the death of her Creole husband in 1882. She
won a notoriety (unwelcome to her) with her novel *The Awakening*
(1899). Interest in her has grown so much that her *Collected Works*
have recently been issued in a scholarly edition, in two volumes
(1970), edited by Per Seyersted. Among the many 'local-colourists'
then working she is immediately distinguished by her superior
objectivity and psychological conscientiousness. Her best stories are
in *Bayou Folk* (1894), often poignant and sometimes ironic studies of
the Creoles of Louisiana. In 'Désirée's Baby', her most famous tale,
a wealthy aristocrat turns his wife and son out of the house because
he suspects them of having Negro blood; then he discovers that he
has; meanwhile Désirée kills herself and her child. Kate Chopin's
stories are slight, but are among the earliest of their kind to show real
sensibility and freedom from prejudice.

Her major work, however, is her novel *The Awakening*. This tells
the torrid story of Edna Pontellier, who fails in love but succeeds in
lust—and kills herself. This could fairly be described as a kind of
Creole *Madame Bovary* (Kate Chopin had read Flaubert), although
its purpose is different. It is a tragedy that the hostile reviews of this
fine book should have broken her spirit.

Another gift that deliberately confined itself to a single locality
(Maine), but that displayed itself in tales rather than novels, is that
of SARAH ORNE JEWETT (1849–1909). It would be impertinent to
describe her as a local-colourist: her wide culture and worldly
humour are always in evidence. Her novels are negligible, and the
series of sketches with which she made her reputation, *Deephaven*
(1877), are slight in comparison with those of her acknowledged
masterpiece, *The Country of the Pointed Firs* (1896). By then she had
assimilated the influence of James as well as of Flaubert, Tolstoy and
other Europeans; but she wisely confined herself to the limits of her

experience. *The Country of the Pointed Firs* consists of loosely connected tales about the people in the beautifully evoked seaport town of Dunnet. This deserves its status as a classic because in its unobtrusive way it says so much about old age (most of the characters are elderly) and the manner in which a place may embody both decay and hope, as well as about Maine. Willa Cather (q.v.) was deeply influenced by it.

ELLEN GLASGOW (1874–1945), born of an aristocratic family in Richmond, Virginia, came to revolt against the tradition into which she was born and in which she began—although not with absolute obedience—writing: the sentimental tradition of the old domain of the South as a lost cause, and of the Civil War as an affair between honour and commerce. Ellen Glasgow's fiction set out to investigate this legend. She had a highly developed sense of humour, and, like Sarah Orne Jewett, she chose to write about the locality, Virginia, that she knew best. The teacher and critic H. S. Canby claimed, with justice, that Ellen Glasgow in her nineteen novels 'was a major historian of our times, who, almost singlehandedly, rescued Southern fiction from the glamorous sentimentality of the Lost Cause'. The work in which she accomplished this was mostly done in the Twenties; in old age she became over-conservative, though not unintelligently so, in the sense that she found she could not accept such manifestations of the modern age as bad manners or William Faulkner (q.v.). Her main theme was the consequences of the Southern myth on Southerners themselves. She is also notable for her resistance to the notion that all Southerners are alike. She always, in her own words, 'preferred the spirit of fortitude to the sense of futility'. To some extent Ellen Glasgow anticipated the concerns of the 'Fugitives' group (q.v.), but her approach was more mordant and even, judged just as an approach and not as a breeding ground for poems, preferable. There was not so much to recommend about life in the South before 1860 as Margaret Mitchell's best-selling romance, *Gone With the Wind*, suggests. But later Southerners, and much more intelligent and sensitive ones than Margaret Mitchell, have cherished such an image.

Like most of the novelists of her generation, Ellen Glasgow was of a pessimistic turn of mind, although it was doubtless personal experience that led her to the limiting view that life consists of specifically sexual disappointment followed by stoical acceptance. In her treatment of her thus sexually defeated people there is sometimes an element that goes beyond irony and becomes gloating and almost cheap. From the quality of this irony and of her not always successful epigrammatic writing, one may discern, in fact, that she is not of the first rank. But she is consistently adult, and her best books rise above her intentions. In *Barren Ground* (1925) the 'poor white' Dorinda Oakley, crossed in love, turns her father's barren ground into a farm with as much determination as Ellen Glasgow had put into her fiction writing just before the turn of the century; ultimately, having contracted one marriage of convenience, she marries the man, now a drunk, who turned her down, caring for him until he dies. Dorinda is a memorable creation. *The Romantic Comedians* (1926) is a surprisingly sympathetic treatment of a hypocritical and lustful old judge, Gamaliel Bland Honeywell. The book begins as he buries his wife. A respectable man who disapproves of sexual looseness, he marries a young cousin of his dead wife; she immediately makes him a cuckold, and runs off with her lover. The old man becomes ill and depressed, but we leave him cheered up by spring and the charms of his young nurse. Neither we nor the author dislike him half as much as we should. The Judge, shallow and self-deceiving, is rightly described by Walter Allen as a 'considerable comic creation'; but, as Allen goes on to point out, his fantasies of romantic love are—surprisingly and unusually—given a genuinely lyrical quality, so that he becomes a character actually touching in his defeat. *Vein of Iron* (1935) is not as a whole quite as psychologically acute, but contains fine passages, and effectively sums up Ellen Glasgow's attitudes to the South and to life. Her title expresses her recommended philosophy. Ada Fincastle displays this 'vein of iron' throughout all her and her loved ones' vicissitudes; it enables her to endure her father's lack of reality, the pregnancy she cannot (out of love) disclose, ostracism by the community, her husband's bitterness, poverty during the Depression. Ellen Glasgow makes an excellent 'introduction to the South' and to the more complex novels of Faulkner: she makes explicit much of the knowledge of the South that, as Walter Allen has said, Faulkner assumes in us.

But the most considerable woman novelist of the period was undoubtedly WILLA CATHER (1873–1947). She was born in Virginia but moved to Nebraska, whose people are the subject of most of her novels and stories, at the age of nine. She never forgot the pioneering spirit of the immigrants, who in her childhood often lived in sod houses or caves. Nor, it must be added, could her later fiction adjust itself to what America became. She was a late developer. She was educated at the University of Nebraska and had a tough journalistic apprenticeship on *McClure's Magazine* (1906–12). She had been writing verse and short stories since before the turn of the century, but did not publish her first novel, *Alexander's Bridge* (1912) until she was nearly forty. This was a failure because of a too intrusive symbolism; but the subtly flawed, nostalgic character of its engineer hero already indicated that Willa Cather's scope was larger than that of any previous American woman novelist. In the more successful *O Pioneers!* (1913) she went back to her greatest love and inspiration: the late nineteenth-century settlers in the Nebraska prairie. Like Ellen Glasgow, Willa Cather excelled in the portraiture of strong-minded women; here Alexandra has to assume responsibility for the farm after her Swedish father dies. Her moral superiority to those around her is convincingly conveyed. The episode of 'The White Mulberry Tree'—the story of the doomed romance of Alexandra's younger brother Emil with Marie, whose husband murders them both—fits in and perfectly complements the main narrative.

In *The Song of the Lark* (1915) Willa Cather tried unsuccessfully to deal more or less directly with the subject of herself: her opera-singer Thea Kronberg is clearly based on herself although supposed to be modelled on an actual singer's career. The author told herself that she was most interested in the way in which her heroine 'escaped' through a fortuitous falling together of commonplace events; actually she was interested in, but ultimately afraid to deal with, the nature of her sexuality. On the one hand she shows Thea as regretful of the ascetism that she feels is a penalty of art; on the other, it is clear that her irritation with men does not originate in her creativity but in lesbianism.

My Ántonia (1918) is probably Willa Cather's finest novel. It is an unhappy New York lawyer's middle-aged recollections of his Nebraska childhood, and of his dear companion, the Czech Ántonia. This is one of the most moving and powerful of pastoral evocations; the lawyer Jim Burden's present unhappiness is the result of his urban existence, with its betrayal of the values of his childhood. *A Lost Lady* (1923) is as moving but not as convincing: here Willa Cather is beginning to manipulate her characters in order to prove her point about urban corruption. Ántonia remains a saved character; in *A Lost Lady* Mrs. Forrester yields to the corrupting embraces of Ivy Peters, a vulgar, slick lawyer: her worth is destroyed. This is a good novel, but one may see in it the germs of Willa Cather's sentimentalization of the pioneer age: the idealized portraits of the pioneers themselves, the too easy dismissal of those born to a commercial and urban way of life. In her great success *Death Comes for the Archbishop* (1927) she goes back to the middle of the nineteenth century and the organization of the diocese of New Mexico by two close friends, Bishop Jean Latour and his vicar Father Joseph Vaillant. This is more satisfactory because Willa Cather is writing about the era she loves: there is no temptation to load the dice against the present. In this book Willa Cather's style reached its apogee, achieving epic qualities. There is deep understanding of both the missionary Roman Catholics' and the Indians' point of view. Willa Cather was a major writer, but not one big enough to take creative account of the changes in her century. This is not to say that her hatred of urbanization was wrong; only that it was too intense. She failed to understand that *some* men are victims of their circumstances. She did in the end turn spinsterish and difficult. But she gallantly resisted the intrusion of journalistic vulgarity (it must be remembered that she had been a journalist) into the novel, and her best books offer a unique evocation of the midwest of her youth.

*

Finally, an unclassifiable odd man out: will anyone ever revive even the best-known novels of JAMES BRANCH CABELL (1879–1958)? Cabell, born in Virginia, was an expert in genealogy—and was what might be described as a latter-day escapist. Hatred of modern life caused him to invent his own country, Poictesme, his epic of which is much and tiresomely concerned with the imaginary genealogy of its leading family. His books are 'naughty', and now seem desperately dated; indeed, his reputation collapsed in the Twenties because it had been founded, unfortunately, upon an unsuccessful prosecution of his novel *Jurgen* (1919). This, irritating though it is in its highly self-conscious artiness and sly phallicism, may be a book that will deserve to be looked at again. In this sceptical tale of a middle-aged Poictesme pawnbroker who has a series of fantastic adventures Cabell examined his romanticism and found it wanting. An age only a little later than our own may more easily be able to penetrate the tortuous style and discover the wisdom that it obscures. Cabell was the victim of a cult and shaped his style according to it; unfortunately his bitterness when he went out of fashion did not result in any recapture of the genius underlying *Jurgen*.

II

Although American poetry did not show its true strength until after the First World War, the poets from whose example its most modern manifestations spring were active before that war—and nearly all of them had to wait a long time for public recognition. The first fully and authentically American poet was Walt Whitman. But Whitman was not fully understood until as late as 1955, when Richard Chase's book *Walt Whitman Reconsidered* was published. Interest in him continued to grow after his death in 1892 and he was the rallying cry of many splinter movements; but he was treated as a mystic, a mage, a socialist, a homosexual, a 'transexualist', anything rather than as a discoverer of an American voice who was also a complicated hider behind various masks. Whitman had his faults, and his intellectual equipment was hardly superior to Dreiser's; but he and Emily Dickinson, unknown in her lifetime, were the only major American poets of the nineteenth century.

The poets most highly considered in the first decade of this century have vanished from sight; nor is there much of value or even of interest to salvage from their work. RICHARD HENRY STODDARD (1825–1903), called in the year of his death 'the most distinguished of living American poets', was no more than an imitator of English Victorian poets who celebrated Abraham Lincoln in the English Victorian manner. THOMAS BAILEY ALDRICH (1836–1907) was not quite un-distinguished as a novelist, but as a poet was a scented and weak imitator of Tennyson. Of somewhat more account was the Ohio poet PAUL LAURENCE DUNBAR (1872–1906), who was at least the first Negro to use Negro dialect (he was preceded by a number of white men); but he did not know the South, and the most that can be said of his best work is that it has some grace and style.

The 'Harvard generation' of the Nineties promised much, but performed little. WILLIAM VAUGHN MOODY (1869–1910) was intelligent and even tried to achieve a modicum of sexual realism; but in spite of his skill no poem he wrote deserves to survive, and his verse drama —*The Fire-Bringer* (1904) was the best known—is stilted. It is some-times claimed that Moody influenced Wallace Stevens (q.v.), and this may be true; but only of the Wallace Stevens of juvenilia, which he destroyed. That Moody was a formative influence is unlikely. Moody's best work was done in the prose drama, and is mentioned in the section devoted to theatre.

More poetically gifted was Moody's Harvard friend [JOSEPH] TRUMBULL STICKNEY (1874–1904), whom Santayana (q.v.) recollected as one of the two most brilliant men he had ever known. Stickney's life was cosmopolitan. He was born in Switzerland, and spent his childhood in Europe. After he graduated from Harvard in 1895 he again left immediately for Europe. He was the first American to receive the *Doctorat des Lettres* from the Sorbonne. Stickney finally returned to Harvard, to the post of Instructor in Greek. After only one unhappy year of teaching he died of a brain tumour. Stickney, like his friend Moody, wrote plays: his *Dramatic Verses* (1902) made no

impact whatever, but when Moody and two others collected his
Poems (1905), interest was briefly aroused. The English poet James
Reeves (q.v.), with Seán Haldane, made a selection, *Homage to
Trumbull Stickney* (1968), which contains a valuable biographical and
critical introduction. Messrs. Reeves and Haldane quote lines such
as 'Your face possesses my despair', 'He stubborned like the massive
slaughter-beast', 'That power was once our torture and our Lord'
and 'I have it all through my heart, I tell you, crying' to illustrate
their contention that he is 'more a rejected than a neglected
American poet of genius'. Another view puts him on a level with
Moody and suggests that both 'occasionally capture the modern
manner, only to lose it again in a plethora of words' (Marcus
Cunliffe). It seems to me that, moving though some of Stickney's
poems are, his language would need to be considerably less archaic
for him to be as exceptional as Reeves and Haldane claim. Cunliffe's
'the modern manner' is perhaps misleading; what Stickney needed
was a language capable of expressing—primarily, indeed, of discovering—a set of highly complex prepossessions. Now Stickney certainly
had a 'modern' sensibility but in almost all his poems he tends to
lapse into a diction and tone which are alien to this sensibility.
Feeling in his poetry tends to be robbed of sharpness and impact
by muddy, self-indulgent diction, and sometimes by an ear that is
more metrical than rhythmical. He lacks a formed style. But
certainly he is, as Donald Hall has said, one of America's 'great
unfulfilled talents'.

While most of these poets and others—such as the Canadian-born
BLISS CARMAN (1861–1929), whose 'carefree' verse now seems so
laboured, the verse playwright PERCY MACKAYE (1875–1956), or
JOSEPHINE PRESTON PEABODY (1874–1922), who was influenced by
Moody—were enjoying some esteem, EDWIN ARLINGTON ROBINSON
(1869–1935) was ignored. He did not achieve real recognition until
he was fifty. For the duration of the Twenties he was America's most
popular poet (Frost's ascendancy came later), but before he died of
cancer in 1935 his stock had begun to go down, and between the Second
World War and the beginning of the Sixties he was almost forgotten
by critics (although his massive *Collected Poems* has sold consistently
at about twelve copies a week since it appeared in 1937). In the last
decade there has been a revival of interest: his excellent letters are
now being collected, and eleven books have been devoted to him
since 1963. Even at the height of his fame, which did not go to his
head, Robinson was never at the centre of any coterie or cult, and
no one knew much of his private life—except that he was unmarried,
rumoured (I believe incorrectly) to be homosexual and had an

alcohol problem. Neither Eliot nor the usually percipient, just and generous Ezra Pound (qq.v.) seem to have troubled to read him. The fact is that he was the only fully-fledged American poet to come out of the 'gilded age' (the title of Mark Twain's and Charles Dudley Warren's melodramatic novel denouncing its instability and acquisitiveness) that followed the Civil War; in this age Robinson was formed. Nor is Robinson as far behind the vastly more ambitious Frost as the difference between their reputations suggests. Robinson did not write the handful of nearly perfect poems that Frost did as a young man; but he had a wider range and wrote more penetratingly about people. In many respects he remained a child of the nineteenth century, his roots in Crabbe, Hardy, Browning; but if one compares the diction of his early poems to that of Stickney's (q.v.), the best of the poets who failed to attain a twentieth-century manner, it will be obvious that Robinson did at least find a language appropriate to what he had to say. That does not of itself guarantee the value of the poems themselves; but in this case they are good poems precisely because their author has discovered a new language to say new things. In Stickney the sentimentality and easy assumptions of the age linger on—alas—in the diction and style; Robinson's manner cuts through all this like a knife. What he can do in his best poetry, besides expressing some personal emotions, is to give an authentic account of what it is like trying to be a nineteenth-century man in a twentieth-century society. That is something.

He was born at Head Tide, Maine, but moved to Gardiner, in the same state, six months after his birth; this environment marked him for the rest of his life, and the Tilbury Town of his poems is Gardiner. Robinson became aware of his lonely poetic vocation there (he was an exceptionally lonely man), and there too he learned to identify himself with failure. His mother and father kept him at such a distance as to imply to him their rejection of him; his two brothers were always expected to outshine him. Ultimately, however, he was the success of the family: his father failed financially and went to pieces under the strain and the eldest brother turned from a promising doctor into a drug addict. Robinson himself attended Harvard until the money ran out, then turned—still in his twenties—into a lonely and alcoholic drop-out. He published two books privately, and for the third, *Captain Craig* (1902), the publishers Houghton Miflin had to be guaranteed against loss. President Theodore Roosevelt was given this book to read in 1905, enthused, and obtained a sinecure for Robinson in the New York Customs House, which he retained until the change in the presidency in 1909. During that time of comparative independence Robinson drank heavily and wrote little. It was the poems of *The Man Against the Sky* (1916) which finally gained him public acceptance; but it was not until the eve of his fiftieth birthday that critics and poets alike joined together in tribute to him. From 1911 until the end of his life Robinson spent his summers at the MacDowell Colony, founded by the widow of the gifted (and, outside America, still neglected) American composer Edward A. MacDowell, as a refuge for creative artists of all kinds. He published two plays, which are interesting but not viable theatrically, and wrote fiction, all of which he destroyed. Eventually he confined himself entirely to the long verse narrative: *Tristram* (1927), a national success, completed an Arthurian trilogy; he was at work on *King Jasper* to within a few weeks of his death. It is always said that Robinson fails in these very long poems. And so he does. What is not said often enough is that he comes nearer to success in this form than any other poet writing at the time.

One of Robinson's subtlest and most characteristic poems is 'Flammonde', in which he exploits commonplace and cliché in a strategy that is quite certainly 'modern' in its implications. Yvor Winters dismissed it as 'repulsively sentimental'; but William J. Free, in an important essay, has shown how Robinson in this instance did succeed in finding a suitable, if ambiguous, language to express his uneasy situation. As Free says, 'he was trying to restore life to a worn-out language without abandoning that language'. Flammonde is just such an enigmatic and alienated character as Robinson felt himself to be, but Robinson ironically presents him as seen through the eyes of the townspeople: he has wisdom, but this is remarkable because he is not respectable; he has 'something royal in his walk' and has been 'accredited' 'by kings', but has been banished from that kind of life. Robinson turns Flammonde's *noblesse oblige* into a caricature by making him befriend an ex-'scarlet woman'—one of the worst clichés of the period. In his brain the kink is 'satanic'. Flammonde is the poet seen from the angle of the crowd, vulgarly mysterious, cheaply sinister, and yet necessary:

> We cannot know how much we learn
> From those who never will return,
> Until a flash of unforeseen
> Remembrance falls on what has been.
> We've each a darkening hill to climb;
> And this is why, from time to time
> In Tilbury Town, we look beyond
> Horizons for the man Flammonde.

'Flammonde' demonstrates Robinson's inability to define his poetic function directly, and incidentally explains why he invariably expressed himself through a strategy of characterizations. Thus he found his Flammonde in an Englishman called Alfred H. Louis, a well-connected failure; when in the more famous and longer *Captain Craig* he tried to be more explicit, to dissolve some of the mystery, about the objective correlative he had discovered in this person he was not as successful—although this, too, is an interesting poem.

Robinson wrote a number of other excellent short poems. The celebrated 'Miniver Cheevy' sums up his own situation even more tersely. It has been pointed out that the fourth 'thought' of

> Miniver scorned the gold he sought
> But sore annoyed was he without it;
> Miniver thought and thought and thought
> And thought about it

'comes as an authentic kick in the womb of a stanza that proves the existence of a live poet'; it has the touch of a master. Equally good are 'Eros Turannos', 'Isaac and Archibald', 'Saint-Nitouche' and some others. The narrative poems, naturalistic in the sense that they show people at the mercy of their passions, are unrivalled in their field—Masefield's (q.v.) aim at so much less—in that they are all, even the lushest (*Tristram*), readable and interesting; one may come across a good passage at any time. A properly selected Robinson—still lacking—would have to include some of these, as well as the best of the shorter poems and such medium length narratives as 'Isaac and Archibald'. Robinson may have been a late romantic and even a transcendentalist, who allowed a false optimism to mar much of his poetry; but his was the only nineteenth-century sensibility to express itself effectively in twentieth-century terms. His influence has been considerable although, except in the case of Robert Lowell's *The Mills of the Kavanaughs* (q.v.), unobtrusive. His stock is certainly rising.

Now for three lesser, but undoubtedly important poets, all from the state of Illinois: EDGAR LEE MASTERS (1868–1950), CARL SANDBURG (1878–1967) and VACHEL LINDSAY (1879–1931). All of these were quintessentially American as distinct from English-style poets. In this sense, but only in this, each was superior to Robinson. Masters was the son of a lawyer who himself became a lawyer; born in Kansas, moved to Illinois at one, he wrote much both before and after *The Spoon River Anthology* (1915), but never produced anything remotely near to it in quality. A newspaper editor gave him Mackail's *Select Epigrams from the Greek Anthology* in 1911, and this acted as the catalyst required to manufacture the acid of his own genius, compounded of an innate bitterness, a passion for truth, and a rare sympathy for human beings. Spoon River was an amalgamation of Petersburg and Lewistown. In a flat, laconic free verse Masters makes the inhabitants of the Spoon River hill cemetery state their own epitaphs. He resembles Robinson, but is more direct and less officially optimistic:

> Did you ever hear of the Circuit Judge
> Helping anyone except the 'Q' railroad,
> Or the bankers . . . ?

This was a poetry in the prose tradition initiated by Howe, Garland (q.v.) and others; but the compression he learned from the Greek Anthology enabled Masters to improve on it. However *The Spoon River Anthology* is better considered as prose than as poetry, as which it is undistinguished.

Vachel Lindsay, born in Springfield, Illinois, obtained a good education, and then studied art for five years; but he failed at it, and decided to become a tramp. His drawings look like meagre and talentless imitations of Blake. Lindsay had always wanted to be a missionary, and in 1905 he alternated winter lecturing with summer tramping and declaiming; he would exchange leaflets of his poems for a bed and food. By 1913 he had become well known. Harriet Monroe began to publish his poetry, and *General William Booth Enters into Heaven and Other Poems* (1913) and *The Congo and Other Poems* (1914) were successful. For some fifteen years he enjoyed fame as declaimer of his own work all over America and in Great Britain as well. Public interest in him lessened soon after his marriage in 1925; in 1931, in despair and ill-health, he took poison.

Lindsay was a midwestern populist and revivalist whose views never altered or expanded with his experience of the greater world. His father was a Campbellite minister (member of the Church of the Disciples of Christ, which had broken away from Presbyterianism to a simplicity based solely on the Bible). Lindsay combined this evangelical creed with worship of Lincoln and other local heroes, religious ideas of Swedenborg, and the economics of Henry George (q.v.). He was vulgar and parochial, but at his best he knew it and exploited these very failings. His sources are revivalist hymns and sermons, Whitman's manner and tone, temperance tracts, Negro jazz, all the sayings and doings of Lincoln and other lesser known, local heroes, and Salvation Army brass band music. He learnt much about the performance of poetry from the readings of S. H. Clark, a professor at the University of Chicago. His best poems succeed because they are impassioned and wholly unsophisticated. To put it at its most simple: he meant every word of them, and for a few years he found exactly the right combination of sources. He introduced a genuinely new rhythm into American poetry; he was also America's first genuine folk poet—at his best he is superior to Sandburg. Later he went to pieces and produced too much weak and self-parodic verse. The novelist Richard Hughes (q.v.) heard him at Oxford, and has recorded for the British Broadcasting Corporation some remarkable and highly illuminating renderings of his poetry.

It was Harriet Monroe's *Poetry* that gave Sandburg fame. Born at Galesburg of Swedish immigrant parents, from thirteen he was an itinerant labourer all over the West; he served in the Spanish-American war, worked his way through college in his home town, and became a journalist and socialist. His master was Whitman, but although more genuinely 'of the people' than Whitman he is a minor poet by comparison because he is never more than a reporter. He used very free forms, and his poetry resembles Masters' in that it is by no means certainly properly judged as poetry, but rather as a rhythmical prose. At his worst he is whimsical, sentimental and falsely tough; at his rare best colloquial, tender and precise. He could be defined as an ideal 'unanimist' (q.v. 2): he responded to and thoroughly understood the corporate longings of the new industrial folk, and he fervently believed in their happy future. His weakness is that he has no creative means of confronting evil. The famous stanza about John Brown

They laid hands on him
And the fool killers had a laugh
And the necktie party was a go, by God.
They laid hands on him and he was a goner.
    They hammered him to pieces and he stood up.
They buried him and he walked out of the grave, by God,
    Asking again: Where did that blood come from?

owes all its strength to the presentation of John Brown's vitality as a folk hero; Sandburg could not cope with, and was a child in trying to deal with, the forces of evil. But his best poems reflect midwestern speech and in rigorous selection they will continue to survive. He wrote a monumental biography of Lincoln (1926–39) and made two important collections of local American folk ballads, *The American Songbag* (1927) and *The New American Songbag* (1950).

At his death ROBERT FROST (1874–1963) was America's most famous poet and unofficial laureate. No other American has reached his eminence in letters. And yet he waited as long as—and even more bitterly than—Robinson for recognition. He was born in San Francisco of a New England father and a Scots mother; when he was eleven his father died, and the family moved to Salem, New Hampshire, where his mother taught in a school. Frost worked in mills and as a newspaper reporter, taught, married, spent two years at Harvard and tried to be a poultry farmer—all unsuccessfully. At the age of thirty-six he sold his farm in Derry and went to England, where he settled down to write. In England he met Wilfred Gibson, Ezra Pound, Lascelles Abercrombie and, most importantly, Edward Thomas (qq.v.), whom he encouraged to write poetry. While he was in England his first two books of poetry were accepted: *A Boy's Will* (1913) and *North of Boston* (1914). The second was published in America by Holt in the same year, and when he returned to the States early in 1915 he found he was the author of a best seller. For many years after this he spent periods as poet-in-residence in various academic institutions. The rest of the time he spent on farms he bought in Vermont and, finally, in Florida. He had much sorrow with his children: one died of puerperal fever, and his son Carol shot himself. At the end of his life, although an outspoken and fierce conservative, and a lifelong enemy of all things academic, he had twice been greeted by the Senate (on his seventy- and eighty-fifth birthdays), taken part as unofficial laureate in the inauguration of John F. Kennedy, and received nearly fifty honorary degrees (including ones from Oxford and Cambridge).

To say that Frost has been overrated is not to say that he is unimportant. He was a naïve (q.v.) poet, and when he took thought never more than a skilled folksy epigrammatist, who in order to cling on to his so hardly won fame had to write too much and not always in his natural vein. His pose as sage seldom led to wisdom, and hardly does the true poet in him credit. The poems of *A Boy's Will* are less certain than those of *North of Boston*, his best book, and the confidence of this extends into some of the poetry of its two successors, *Mountain Interval* (1916) and *New Hampshire* (1923). After this Frost was increasingly intent on subscribing to an image of himself largely formed by people who had little knowledge of or love for the arts in general. His poems can be optimistic and cheerful when he does not really feel like that—he conceals his blackness—and he can be arch and self-consciously Yankee.

But when this has been said Frost is still a unique and original poet both in short lyrics and in certain comparatively short narrative poems. The famous 'Mending Wall' is a good enough example of his strength; it alone is enough to give pause when we are told that the claim that Frost is a major poet is 'ridiculous'. This is a genuinely tragic poem: it spells out how things are between people. Lawrence Thompson, Frost's biographer, suggests that 'the conclusion resolves the conflict in favour of the poet's view. . . .' It seems to me that this judgement does not do it justice: it is more than an expression of a mere point of view, for while the wall is a real wall, it also stands for that barrier of reserve which neighbours erect between each other— to avoid being friends, or to protect themselves. We are told that 'Something there is that doesn't love a wall': *frosts* break it up. Hunters have the same effect. At 'spring mending-time' he gets in touch with his neighbours, and together they make the repairs, piling the boulders up. It's only a game, the narrator tells us: a wall isn't necessary at this point, since his neighbour is 'all pine' and he is apple orchard. He tackles his neighbour with this—'Spring is the mischief in me', he explains, thus surely negating Thompson's assertion that the notion of having no wall is his seriously held point of view—but the neighbour only says 'Good fences make good neighbours'. However, mischievously he continues to taunt his neighbour, who goes on rebuilding the wall 'like an old-stone savage armed'; and the narrator concludes

> He moves in darkness as it seems to me,
> Not of woods only and the shades of trees.
> He will not go behind his father's saying,
> And he likes having thought of it so well
> He says again, 'Good fences make good neighbours'.

This is 'about' the barriers between people and the worth of love; maybe the conservative neighbour is right. Frost could and did moralize in his lesser poems; in this good one he is content to leave things as they are, tragically in balance. Yes, spring has made him challenge (with 'mischief') the notion of a wall; but there is no pat conclusion, no suggestion that it is his neighbour's state of mind that is responsible for the state of affairs. . . . The poem works so well because its full meaning arises so naturally out of the situation it describes; there is no straining for a meaning in the account.

Again, it would surely be risky to dismiss the narrative 'The Death of the Hired Man', also from *North of Boston*, as only a minor poem. It is true that Frost's people are cardboard, and that they do not act upon each other or change each other; it is also true that his technical arrangements are static—the oft-made claim that he used

American speech-rhythms cannot be carried far. But this account of the return of a hired man, and the differing views of a husband and wife about charity and their duty, attains such simplicity—

> 'Home is the place where, when you have to go there,
>   They have to take you in.'
> 'I should have called it
>   Something you somehow haven't to deserve.'

—that it cannot be ignored. It offers, for the time being, something other than the urban sophistication of Eliot (q.v.). So do a half dozen other similar narratives, most of them included in *North of Boston*. Frost is not usually a 'nature poet', for he does not observe natural objects minutely; he rather observes man in natural surroundings, and tries to find consolations for nature's indifference. He can be falsely sweet, as when he asks us to come with him while he cleans out the pasture spring (he does not mean it); but he achieves true sweetness when he reveals his desire for a valid and unsentimental universal love, as at the end of 'The Tuft of Flowers', from his first book:

> 'Men work together,' I told him from the heart,
>   'Whether they work together or apart.'

Frost's influence on American poets of account may, surprisingly, be somewhat less than even that of Robinson. Robinson remains enigmatic, unexplored; there does not at present seem to be very much to go to Frost for. The same can under no circumstances be said of the prince of American regionalist poets, WILLIAM CARLOS WILLIAMS (1883–1963), who was born in Rutherford, New Jersey, practised there as a doctor all his life, and died there. He studied dentistry at the University of Pennsylvania, where he met Pound, and later went to Europe to study medicine. By 1912 he was married and settled into his lifelong practice at Rutherford, partly the Paterson of his long poem of that name.

'Williams . . . is . . . the most innocently tedious, insufferably monotonous, and purely mental of modern poets . . . polythene verse. . . . [His] form conceals that he is saying very little, and has very little to say. . . .' (An English critic.)

'Williams' poems contain a generosity of spirit, a humane warmth, ability to translate daily life and ordinary objects into an unsentimental order of personal and universal significance, which are unique in modern poetry and rare at any time. . . . His ear for rhythm is practically perfect. . . .' (An American critic.)

The first judgement may be turned somewhat to Williams' advantage if we grant that, for all his multifarious pronouncements, Williams was a naïve (q.v.) poet—a good deal more naïve than Frost, himself disingenuous in his intellectual pose. His overriding passion (it was never a thought) from early on was that poetry should reflect experience exactly and that therefore rhyme and metre were falsifications: non-American, Anglophile devices. He attacked Eliot and Pound for not staying in America, and imagism (q.v.) for being mere free verse. His 'objectivism' (q.v.) postulated the poem itself as object, presenting its meaning by its form. 'No ideas but in things', he insisted, seeking until the end to describe the universal only in the stubborn particular. He went his own singular way, inconsistent, obstinate, publishing his poetry with obscure small presses—and ended up as a grand old man of American letters, inspirer not only of Olsen, Ginsberg, Creeley (qq.v.), but, less logically, also of the formalists Roethke and Lowell (qq.v.). He wrote autobiography, impressionistic criticism (*In the American Grain*, 1925), plays, short stories and fiction.

All Williams' work flows out of his insistence upon the local and the particular. He saw the world 'contracted to a recognizable image'. His poems are his namings of the objects in his world as it unfolds itself to him. His own words, written when he was at his most energetic, and when he was hardly heeded, are incomparably the best expression of his intentions:

> There is a constant barrier between the reader and his consciousness of immediate contact with the world. . . . I love my fellow creature. Jesus, how I love him . . . but he doesn't exist! Neither does she. I do, in a bastardly sort of way. . . . In the composition, the artist does exactly what every eye must do with life, fix the particular with the universality of his own personality. . . . The only realism in art is of the imagination. It is only thus that the work escapes plagiarism after nature and becomes a creation. . . . [Shakespeare] holds no mirror up to nature but with his imagination rivals nature's composition with his own. . . .

That last remark gives us the clue both to Williams and the appeal he had for so many Americans. Here is a man who insists on the evidence of his own perceptions. As Marianne Moore (q.v.) shrewdly said of him: he has 'a kind of intellectual hauteur which one usually associates with the French'. Indeed, we have only to remember the philosophy behind the French *nouveau roman* (q.v. 2) to recognize this: but this is a doggone, non-intellectual, Yankee approach. Williams exists on the strength of his perceptions or he does not exist. After some early imitations of Keats, he began writing in the vein that he maintained until his death. It is seen at its best in 'This Is Just To Say'—surely an irresistible little lyric?

This Is Just To Say

I have eaten
the plums
that were in
the icebox

and which
you were probably
saving
for breakfast

Forgive me
they were delicious
so sweet
and so cold

Williams' long poem *Paterson* (1946–58), his attempt at an epic, in five books, is distinctly American in its attempt to recover innocence and a sense of community. It is characteristically impressionistic: in large part it consists of seemingly casual collage of undoctored raw material: heard conversation, private letters, news clippings, official reports, bald anecdotes, and so on. It contains some vigorous and compelling passages, but suffers from two contradictory defects. Williams wants to appear non-literary, ordinary, and so to this end he includes far too much unedited material in the poem; this makes it tedious. However, at the same time the essentially naïve poet artfully and disingenuously tries to superimpose a symbolic pattern on the poem: for example, an analogy is worked out between the poet's and the physicist's function, even to the extent of comparing the splitting of the atom to the splitting of the (metrical) foot. . . . The first two books hold together better than the rest, but even these contain dull passages; the rest fails to convince or to cohere, although some enthusiastic critics have stated otherwise. Williams' technique here more closely parallels that of painters than poets: 'he strives', writes a critic, 'for a poem that will, in its own process, answer the question it continually poses'. This is no more than the old, anti-mimetic insistence on creation, the necessity he felt to 'rival nature's composition with his own. . . .' It does not work, but comes near enough to doing so for us to wish that Williams had not tried to be so artful : he was not good at it.

However, Williams' anti-mimetic preoccupation is enough to demonstrate that he is no spurious modern, as the English critic quoted above has suggested. It is true that in an intellectual or metaphysical sense Williams has nothing whatever to say. But is he that kind of writer? Is he not, rather, simply a recorder of his perceptions? That these are often simplistic is beside the point. They are almost inevitably unspoiled. However, can Williams, on the strength of his best things—such fragments as 'El Hombre',

> It's a strange courage
> you give me ancient star :
>
> Shine alone in the sunrise
> toward which you lend no part!

—be called a major poet? As a pioneer he is obviously of importance. But is his poetry intrinsically major? The poem of his old age, of some 350 lines, called 'Asphodel, That Greeny Flower' is probably his crowning achievement. It is hard not to respond to it. But are we not perhaps responding to the integrity and sweet cussedness of personality, to a devoted life, rather than to a poetic achievement? The answer to the question is not to be easily found. In my own judgement there is as much of the simple-minded as of the simple about Williams, so that he is finally a physician and minor poet rather than a major poet and a physician. He always wanted desperately to be 'average', and I think that his simplicities, too, were near the average. . . . (Evidently Wordsworth's, say, weren't.) One appreciates the way he lived and felt and talked; but even 'Asphodel, That Greeny Flower' offers no insight, only a chance to applaud that performance. In order to attain to it he eschewed all alien devices, so that his poems lack tension. And a whole poetry that lacks tension is inexorably minor.

And now, since it is relevant to most of the American poetry that follows, a word about Williams and poetic technique. Williams many times announced that he had discovered a new, American poetic technique, which he referred to as the 'variable foot'. Williams was no prosodist, and his attempted definitions of this variable foot are worthless. But it does mean something in terms of his own practice:

Of asphodel, that greeny flower,
    like a buttercup
        upon its branching stem—
save that it's green and wooden—
I come, my sweet,
    to sing to you.
We lived long together
    a life filled
        if you will. . . .

Each of those 'lines' is a 'variable foot'; at one time Williams would
have called it a 'triadic foot', comprising a single 'line'. And the
reader will quickly appreciate that while Williams himself achieved
a personal rhythm by writing in this way, his imitators have not.
This way of writing verse should be discussed, and there are new
elements in it (even though one can treat Williams' verse in terms
of the various traditional approaches to prosody); but it has not
been usefully discussed yet—least of all by Williams, who waded
thigh deep into the old bog of confusion between accent and quantity
that has bedevilled English prosodic studies since Elizabethan times.
Williams' confused theory comes nearest to the 'temporal' prosody
advanced by the American poet Sidney Lanier, who died in 1881.
What is original in his practice—'not that,' he wrote, 'I know
anything about what I have myself written'—is the accommodation
he gives to quantity without straining its function in the vernacular:
without, as the Elizabethan Stanyhurst, and Bridges (q.v.), and
even Tennyson, did, trying to destroy accent. If his pronouncements on Thomas Campion are embarrassing, his poems do achieve
a kind of musicality, and a new musicality at that, which most
others of this century lack.

It is appropriate at this point to deal with a movement in which
Williams played a major part. Objectivism never hit any headlines,
even though Pound (q.v.) was officially associated with it, and
besides Williams only one other 'objectivist' has since become at all
well known: LOUIS ZUKOFSKY (1904). But this small group is important both as a refinement of imagism (q.v.), and as a forerunner of a
now flourishing branch of American poetry exemplified in the work
of Robert Duncan, Robert Creeley, Gary Snyder (qq.v.) and many
others. It began when a wealthy young man (the description is
Williams'), GEORGE OPPEN (1908), decided to lose his money on
publishing poetry. At first his press was called TO, and in 1932 it
published An "Objectivists" Anthology, edited by Zukofsky. Then it
became the Objectivist Press, with an advisory board consisting of

Williams, Zukofsky and Pound; other poets involved included CARL
RAKOSI (ps. CALLMAN RAWLEY, 1903), born in Berlin, and CHARLES
REZNIKOFF (1894), a lawyer born in New York. Acknowledging
Williams as their master, these poets (this does not include Pound,
whose relationship was avuncular and postal) published his *Collected Poems 1921–1931* (1934), with an introduction by Wallace
Stevens (q.v.). But their own work has its importance in twentieth
century American poets' search for simplicity. All possess an integrity
and a lack of interest in personal fame—as distinct from poetic
achievement—that could be a lesson to their modern successors.
There is much in the claim that while the American poetic tradition
appeared to be, during the Thirties, in the hands of such as Tate
and Ransom (qq.v.), it was really in the hands of these relatively
obscure poets. That this tradition, stemming directly from Whitman
and running through Sandburg and Williams to Creeley and others,
has not yet produced a truly major poet since its originator does not
constitute a negation of the claim.

The objectivists were agreed that imagism, having helped to get
rid of mere verbiage, had 'dribbled off into so much free verse. . . .
There is no such thing as free verse! Verse is measure of some sort . . .
we argued, the poem . . . is an object . . . that in itself formally
presents its case and its meaning by the very form it assumes . . . it
must be the purpose of the poet to make of his words a new form: to
invent, that is, an object consonant with his day . . .' (Williams).
These words bear heeding, because they sum up the credo of every
kind of disciple of Williams.

Zukofsky is a quiet, unassertive man who has been possibly the
most persistent and courageous experimentalist in the English-
speaking world in this century. Once again, it is his procedures that
are important—as indeed one might expect in a work that 'in itself
formally presents its case and its meaning by the very form it
assumes. . . .' To the reader nourished on conventional pap Zukofsky's poetry and criticism seem thin and insubstantial; nor indeed
does he display anything of the emotional robustness of a Williams.
But this should not distract attention from the significance of what
he has been doing in the last forty years. It is characteristic of
Zukofsky that his chief work, the long poem—unfinished—*A*, should
be continuous, a day book. For Zukofsky it is absurd to be a good
poet at one point of one's life, then a bad one, and so on. So *A* is
his continuous poetic reaction, as often concerned with sounds as
with music. He reminds us of Gertrude Stein (q.v.) at least inasmuch
as meaning in his verse is very often no more than an overtone to
sound. (All the objectivists shared Gertrude Stein's important notion

of words as words, things-in-themselves.) Zukofsky is continually playful, and yet he is always thinking—if in a somewhat primitivistic (and why not?) sense of the word—very closely indeed about words as meaning and words as sound. The context of his work is almost always his domestic life; his wife and son Paul (now a well-known violinist) are both musicians. The theme of *A*, in fact, is marriage: marriage as a bastion against the ruins of 'civilization'. For poets at least it is always readable, always an evocation of a sweetly lived life. Some clues to the passages that look like nonsense, but which are in fact various sorts of experiments with sound, may be gathered from Zukofsky and his wife Celia's *Catallus* (1969), in which they have transliterated the entire works of Catullus from Latin into an American that 'tries . . . to breathe the "literal" meaning with him'. Thus the famous

> Odi et amo. quare id faciam, fortasse requiris.
>   nescio, sed fieri sentio et excrucior

becomes

> O th' hate I move love. Quarry it fact I am, for that's so re
>   queries.
> Nescience, say th' fiery scent I owe whets crookeder.

Now: can the texture of the sound of Latin be woven into that of American? Apart from one or two remarkable *tours de force*, it seems not. The vast majority, however well disposed, would consider the above transliteration, for example, a grotesque failure: not only in terms of the literal Latin meaning but also in those of the American language. But it is the failure of an intelligent man; and the experiment is not a useless or a foolish one. However, the question that wholehearted partisans of this version of Catullus (few of whom, curiously, seem to possess the Zukofsky's knowledge of Latin) need to answer is: what can be the function of such a language as is here invented? What is interesting is that an answer can be made. Just as sense can be made of Williams' 'theory' of prosody so even 'O th' hate I move love' for 'Odi et amo' can be defended. We must consider it—and Zukofsky. The poems have been collected in *All: The Collected Shorter Poems 1923–1958* (1966), *All: The Collected Shorter Poems 1956–1964* (1967), *"A" 1–12* (1967), *"A" 13–21* (1969). Criticism is in *Prepositions* (1967), and fiction (a useful method of approach to this important poet) in *Ferdinand* (1968). *Bottom: on Shakespeare* (1963) is criticism combining poetic and musical interests.

Carl Rakosi, a social worker and psychotherapist, is the least well known or committed of the objectivists, but his poetry is as clean as it is slight; *Selected Poems* appeared in 1941, *Amulet* in 1967. Oppen is more substantial. *Materials* (1962) collects thirty years of his work, and he has published three collections since then. He has been described, in terms characteristic of recent criticism, as being 'one of the best and one of the worst of poets'. He has been important to some of the Black Mountain poets (q.v.) because his project has been to express his existence and the use he has made of it:

> Yet I am one of those who from nothing but man's way of thought and one of his dialects and what has happened to me
> Have made poetry

Oppen, unlike Zukofsky and Olson (q.v.), has not received even belated critical recognition, despite his Pulitzer Prize of 1969. And yet his understanding of the problems of diction has been as acute as Williams', and since his first book appeared in 1934 he has provided an object-lesson: a poetry that 'presents its case . . . by the very form it assumes'. Like Zukofsky, he aims for a full articulation of his engagement with life; he is fascinated, too, with objects-as-them-selves (cf., again, the *nouveau roman*), objects not anthropomorphized. But his method is complex; cutting across his purely objectivist preoccupations are intellectual and abstract concerns that might contort the face (often the Black Mountain equivalent of raising the eyebrow) of a true disciple of Williams. Sometimes he has been guilty of smuggling thought into his poetry, in such lines as those describing women in the streets 'weakened by too much need/Of too little'; and yet careful study of his poetry shows that he, more than any other poet in his tradition, has seen the possibilities of using content to create its own form. He is not trivial, and his methods are more original than some of his admirers think.

Charles Reznikoff, a considerably older man, has written distinguished prose in his novel *By the Waters of Manhattan* (1930), and in *Family Chronicle* (1963); as a poet he is more of an imagist:

> This smoky morning—
> do not despise the green jewel shining among the twigs
> because it is a traffic light.

His poetry, much of which is collected in *By the Waters of Manhattan: Selected Verse* (1962), is as enjoyable (in the full sense of the word) as any imagist's could possibly be; though evidently sometimes impelled to widen his scope, he has chosen to limit himself to the minimal, with in this case excellent results. Reznikoff has not been, like Oppen, a pioneer; but because he has decided to narrow his scope, his picture-making impulses have not been frustrated, and many of his poems have the freshness of such paintings as 'Early Sunday Morning' by Edward Hopper, with whom he has indeed been compared.

EZRA POUND's (1885–1972) part in the new American poetry has been more cosmopolitan. No writer of the twentieth century has had more personal influence on modern literature or has known and encouraged more individual poets. His importance in connection with imagism (q.v.), vorticism, W. B. Yeats (q.v.), T. S. Eliot (q.v.), William Carlos Williams (q.v.) and other men and movements has been or will be noted. His immense historical importance has never been in question; the matter of his individual achievement is more controversial.

Pound was born in Idaho. He began to attend the University of Pennsylvania, Philadelphia, at the age of fifteen, owing to his good Latin. Here he met William Carlos Williams, then a student in dentistry. After two years he transferred to Hamilton College in New York State. By 1906 when he received his M.A. he had for some time been experimenting with various forms of verse. He had also already begun to develop the eccentric behaviour—a mixture, it seems, of exhibitionism, excitability, devotedness to his ideals and something that looks like hypomania—that was to characterize his life, and eventually lead him to incarceration in a mental hospital for thirteen years. After a short time spent in an academic job, for which he was totally unsuitable, Pound left for Europe. He published his first book of poems, *A Lume Spento* (1908; reprinted as *A Lume Spento and Other Early Poems*, 1965—with a note by Pound addressed to William Carlos Williams referring to it as 'A collection of stale cream puffs . . . why a reprint? No lessons to be learned save the depth of ignorance . . .'). Soon afterwards he arrived in England and, with typical effrontery, 'took over' T. E. Hulme's (q.v.) and Henry Simpson's 'Poets' Club' of 1909 and turned it into the imagist group. In 1914 T. S. Eliot (q.v.) called on him in London; his poetry immediately aroused Pound's enthusiasm. Before this he had met Yeats (q.v.), and the Irish poet was to acknowledge his influence.

Pound was active on the English literary scene until after the end of the First World War. He helped, encouraged and publicized the work of James Joyce (q.v.), Wyndham Lewis (q.v.) and many others, a few of whom are still almost unknown today. Pound has never bothered much about reputation, and has frequently treated his own simply as a means of helping other writers' work to become recognized. In this sense he has been the most generous poet of the century. He began writing his (still unfinished) Cantos in 1915, but had been planning them for some time before that. The first collection, *A Draft of XXX Cantos*, was published in Paris in 1930 (Pound's *Cantos* are now available as follows: *The Cantos of Ezra Pound*, 1957; *Thrones: 96–109 de los Cantares*, 1959; *Drafts and Fragments of Cantos CX–CXVII*, 1970). He lived in France and then in Italy until his arrest at the end of the Second World War.

In 1918 Pound met Major C. H. Douglas, who had devised an economic scheme called Social Credit, which, he claimed, could avert economic depressions. Pound very soon became taken up with these ideas; he was convinced that in monetary reform lay the key to the creation of a society in which perfect beauty and perfect justice would co-exist. Previously his views on art and society had been less unusual: the writer was to be valued by the degree of his clarity and precision (compare the programme of imagism); of society and social systems Pound was contemptuous: only the individual deserved respect.

Douglas' ideas have never been taken seriously by economists— not necessarily an indictment of them, but perhaps of their originator's sense of tact—but they have had some influence on minority politics in Canada and elsewhere. Douglas himself was not a fascist, and he did not see his theories as being implemented either in Mussolini's Italy or in Hitler's Germany. Pound, unhappily, despite his later confused denial that he had ever been 'for Fascism', was deluded into thinking that Italy's fascist government was leading the country in the cultural direction he found desirable. His anti-semitism, never personal, now began to flare up dangerously; it became increasingly distasteful as the Nazi attitude towards the Jews became clearer. Pound gradually came to see all wars and social misery as a conspiracy of 'top' Jews, based in usury. Markedly greater than his anguish at the unhappiness caused to ordinary people by wars and poverty, however, was his own frustrated rage at not getting his ideas accepted. An element of grandiosity entered his calculations—or projects, as they had better be called—even as his anti-semitic language became more abrasively insulting (and puerile); he thought seriously of gaining the ear of American government officials, and at the same time developed a violent dislike of President Roosevelt. He did have some doubts about fascism, and on occasions he even tried to be fair, in his own terms, about the Jews; but more attracted him in fascism than did not, and he was clearly ideologically committed to it by the late Thirties.

His thoughts and utterances were a fantastic ragbag of theories both wild and sane, and indignations just and unjust. He seems to have had not the faintest idea what the war of 1939 was really about: he told the popular novelist and Nobel prizewinner Pearl Buck that it was 'mainly for moneylending and three or four metal monopolies'. When America entered the war Pound seems to have made an effort to leave Italy, but finally to have been prevented from doing so. It is likely that he found it hard to make decisions.

It is clear that Pound's mind began to cloud, seriously, from the beginning of the Thirties—although a tendency to retreat into a position from which reality was inaccessible had been apparent since early youth. In 1933 he gained an audience with Mussolini, the only one he was ever to have, and came away with the delusion— amazing in anyone of his intelligence—that the dictator really cared for poetry and beauty, and was working passionately for a just society. Pound even thought, from a polite remark, that Mussolini had read and understood the *Cantos*.

It is evident that throughout the war years Pound was in a state of considerable distress. He had been taking small sums of money— which he needed—for broadcasts from Rome radio since before the American declaration of war. He continued to do so after it. The broadcasts were rambling, ill-delivered, dense and perhaps technically treasonable. They had no adverse effect on anyone on the Allied side: since they were almost always on the subject of economics or literature, very few could have understood them. His wife could not follow them for the same reason that some of his readers cannot follow his poems: because of the abrupt jumps from one subject to another. These radio talks were clearly the work of a man at the verge of, or perhaps at times immersed in, insanity.

At the end of the war Pound was eventually arrested and sent to the Disciplinary Training Camp at Pisa. Here he suffered exceedingly, at one point collapsing into a state of 'violent and hysterical terror'. But he recovered sufficiently to write the continuation of his *Cantos*, called *The Pisan Cantos*, and published as such (1948). Brought back to America to face treason charges in 1945, he was correctly judged to be unfit to plead, and was confined to St. Elizabeth's Hospital in Washington. His state at this time was worse than it had ever been: symptoms included scattered wits, inability to concentrate, and an insistence that his new versions of Confucius were the only rational foundation upon which to build a new world. He maintained throughout that he had not committed treason; it was plain that the matter had worried his conscience at all times.

Released (after too long) in 1958, Pound went back to Italy, where he died. He suffered from periodic depressions, and was never wholly coherent. He said on several occasions that he had 'botched' his life work, and made 'errors'; but he continued to publish fragments of poetry. The *Cantos* remained unfinished.

Pound has of course aroused great controversy. This reached its height when he had not long been in St. Elizabeth's, and was awarded the Bollingen Prize for *The Pisan Cantos*. Since many of his disciples then appeared to share his political views, it was natural that his detractors, however unfairly, should identify his poetry with those views—with, in fact, a virulent brand of anti-semitic fascism. One of these erstwhile disciples, Pound's best biographer (*The Life of Ezra Pound*, 1970), Noel Stock, has put all this into a proper perspective. 'I will not dwell on the rubbish which we, his correspondents, fed to him [in St. Elizabeth's], or the rubbish which he in turn fed to us . . . a good number of us . . . helped to confirm him in the belief that he alone possessed a coherent view of the truth. . . .'

The fact is that Pound's political views, such as he has expressed them, would not do credit to a sixth-former. They were partly inherited from the American populism of the Nineties of Pound's childhood, a movement that originated in poverty and was quickly dissipated by a return to prosperity. Like all populism, Pound's is characterized by a practicality (he had been a good handyman all his life), a love of folk poetry, a genuine love of and feeling for the very poor and a cluster of negative attitudes: anti-capitalistic, anti-legal, anti-semitic and (tragically and confusedly in this case) anti-intellectual. Certainly the brilliance of some of Pound's insights has been vitiated by his evident insensitivity to human suffering (e.g. the suffering going on around him in Italy during the war) and his increasing tendency towards incoherence. Fortunately this is only half the story.

Pound's first book to attract wide attention, *Personae* (1909) was attacked both for being incomprehensibly 'modern' and for being absurdly archaic. Much of the modernism was actually Browning put into a distinctly new rhythm. Here Pound writes of a down-at-heel old scholar (these lines, from 'Famam Librosque Cano', come originally from *A Lume Spento*):

> Such an one picking a ragged
> Backless copy from the stall,
> Too cheap for cataloguing,
> Loquitur,

> 'Ah—eh! the strange rare name . . .
> Ah—eh. He must be rare if even *I* have not . . .'
> And lost mid-page
> Such age
> As his pardons the habit,
> He analyzes form and thought to see
> How I 'scaped immortality.

But where Pound was already most original was in his method. He adapted from the Provençal, mixed archaism with modern slang, resurrected (to adapt his own words from his *Credo*) forgotten modes because he found 'some leaven' in them, and because he saw in them an element that was lacking in the poetry of his own time 'which might unite' it 'again to its sustenance, life'.

In the succeeding years Pound produced more books of short poems, and a brilliant adaptation (complete with presumably deliberate howlers, such as a rendering of the Latin 'vates' as 'votes') of the poems of Sextus Propertius called *Homage to Sextus Propertius* (1934; written 1917–18). *Hugh Selwyn Mauberley* (1920), a group of poems originally prompted by the correct conviction that the free verse movement had 'gone too far', was written just afterwards. For those critics who see the *Cantos* as a failure not substantially relieved by excellent or beautiful passages, these two works represent the height of Pound's achievement. Free verse has probably never been handled more firmly or effectively in English than in *Homage to Sextus Propertius*, which, like *Hugh Selwyn Mauberley*, has a coherence that Pound never found again. 'Mr Nixon' is as acid and yet serenely good-mannered a satire against literary opportunism, commercialism and lack of integrity as the twentieth century has seen; and the famous 'Envoi' (1919) that Pound offers as his own poetic credo is as beautiful as anything he has ever written:

> Go, dumb-born book,
> Tell her that sang me once that song of Lawes:
> Hadst thou but song
> As thou hast subjects known,
> Then were there cause in thee that should condone
> Even my faults that heavy upon me lie,
> And build her glories their longevity.

> Tell her that sheds
> Such treasure in the air,

Recking naught else but that her graces give
Life to the moment,
I would bid them live
As roses might, in magic amber laid,
Red overwrought with orange and all made
One substance and one colour
Braving time.

Tell her that goes
With song upon her lips
But sings not out the song, nor knows
The maker of it, some other mouth,
May be as fair as hers,
Might, in new ages, gain her worshippers,
When our two dusts with Waller's shall be laid,
Siftings on siftings in oblivion
Till change hath broken down
All things save beauty alone.

And yet even in this poem, as good as anything ever written by Pound, we may see his limitations. 'Beauty' is still sensed as itself something of a generalization. There is nothing in Pound's poetry about human behaviour as such: no psychological hint as to what beauty itself might consist of, either behaviouristically or in understandable, human terms. The beauty in Pound's verse is nearly always elusive in its nature.

Pound had previously defined the image as 'an intellectual and emotional complex in an instant of time. . . . It is the presentation of such an image which gives that sudden sense of liberation; that sense of freedom from time and space limits; that sense of sudden growth, which we experience in . . . the greatest works of art'. His own participation in the imagist movement had really only been a dramatization of his own developing programme; and yet, like Reznikoff (q.v.), but on an infinitely grander scale, he was to remain an 'imagist' all his life.

Pound first learned about Japanese poetry from F. S. Flint (q.v.), but he soon took over as the pioneer in the study of it. In fact, although he did not understand the Japanese language, he understood some of the more important qualities of Japanese poetry long before they were fully explained to Western readers. It is in this understanding, and the use he made of it, that his greatest achievement lies. His famous poem 'In a Station of the Metro',

> The apparition of these faces in a crowd;
> Petals on a wet, black bough

perfectly illustrates his discovery: a straightforward non-meta-
phorical statement is followed by a striking image, in the manner of
the Japanese *haiku* (q.v.). In this 'super-pository' method one idea
'is set on top of another'. The beauty and the meaning of the poem
are to be discovered in the imaginative leap necessary from the
statement to the metaphor for it. In a slightly longer poem, 'Coitus',
Pound employs essentially the same method to describe a well-
known experience:

> The gilded phaloi of the crocuses
>   are thrusting at the spring air.
> Here is there naught of dead gods
> But a procession of festival,
> A procession, O Giulio Romano,
> Fit for your spirit to dwell in.
> Dione, your nights are upon us.
>
> The dew is upon the leaf.
> The night about us is restless.

Pound's inspiration here was Japanese—specifically the Japanese
haiku. Now this is essentially a miniature art—one that the modern
Japanese poets have themselves found largely inadequate. Pound's
genius perceived its possibilities for English verse, but nevertheless
could not turn miniaturism into epic—which is, however, exactly
what he tried to do in the *Cantos*. In the epic he hoped that his own
unifying sensibility would successfully gather together all the frag-
mentarily presented poetries and cultures. Instead, the poem became
a game for adepts, as Noel Stock has demonstrated (*Reading the
Cantos*, 1967). As Stock says, they 'do not constitute a poem, but a
disjointed series of short poems, passages, lines and fragments, often
of exceptional beauty or interest, but uninformed, poetically or
otherwise, by larger purpose'. They are, he insists, poetry—not
poems. Although there are books, notably one by Donald Davie
(*Ezra Pound: Poet as Sculptor*, 1964), which claim that the *Cantos* do
possess a unifying purpose, these are not convincing, they have not on
the whole convinced readers, and it seems unlikely that the view they
put forward will prevail. It is very difficult indeed to credit the epic
poet Pound with a 'unifying sensibility'—as difficult as it is to credit
the man with one; and there is, after all, his own recent view of the

poem, which cannot altogether be attributed to senile depression: 'I picked out this and that thing that interested me, and then jumbled them into a bag. But that's not the way to make a *work of art*.' As Santayana (q.v.) put it to Pound in a letter in 1940: ' . . . Your tendency to jump is so irresistible that the bond between the particulars jumped to is not always apparent'; and he himself, in Canto CXVI, has confessed: 'I cannot make it cohere'. It is both ironic and significant that Pound's greatest triumphs and failures should consist of 'leaps'. In the *Cantos* the leaps too often become impenetrable ellipses.

In Pound mental instability has certainly vitiated poetic achievement. His imagery of beauty and its permanence, and of light, is often strangely beautiful; but even his achievement here may ultimately be seen to have been vitiated by a lack of emotional solidity, an absence of wisdom, reflecting an inability to learn through experience. Probably his reputation has been unduly inflated, and he has certainly attracted a large number of inferior cranks.

But Pound stood notably, if never very diplomatically or tactfully, for poetic values against commercial ones; he was generous and perceptive; and he searched, as well as his wrecked mind would allow him, for the truth. Posterity may dub him a minor poet: minor because even in his best poetry he lacks conviction; but he will be called a vital critic (sometimes in his poetry), and the failure of his mind will always be regarded as tragic.

The novelist and poet H. D. (ps. HILDA DOOLITTLE, 1886–1961), born in Bethlehem, Pennsylvania, went to Europe in 1911, was for a time married to the English writer Richard Aldington (q.v.) and was associated with the imagists in England; but she remained essentially an American poet in her attitudes and her use of the short line. Like Williams, she was much influenced by the hard precision of Greek poetry. Read by almost every poet of the century and recognized by them as an exquisite minor poet, H. D. has been extraordinarily neglected by critics. Her translation of Euripides' *Ion* (1937) is probably the best translation from Greek drama of the century—only MacNeice's *Agamemnon* can rival it—if faithfulness to the text be taken into consideration. H. D.'s gift, slight but tempered, survived: alone of those imagists who did not merely travel through the movement, she continued to write well. Her earlier poems subscribed exactly to the imagist programme; but she differed from the other imagists, such as her husband Richard Aldington, in that the manner was natural to her. She did not come to imagism; imagism came to her. Her style rigidly excludes sentimentalities, and concentrates on producing objects (poems) that do not pretend to evoke, but instead present themselves as themselves. Her poems have a dateless quality, which calls attention not only to their strength but also to her general weakness: commonplace emotion may be subsumed in 'classical' style, as such lines as

> your insight
> has driven deeper
> than the lordliest tome
> of Attic thought
> or Cyrenian logic

hint. Except at their very best, there is in her poems always an element of pastiche that raises suspicion. This suspicion is partly confirmed by the trilogy she wrote during the Second World War: *The Walls Do Not Fall* (1944), *Tribute to the Angels* (1945) and *Flowering of the Rod* (1946), which dealt with themes of war. In style and taste this is an impressive work; but the symbolism and thought behind it are tawdry. When H.D.'s poetry is not at its best the manner conceals this; when she is at her best the manner itself is, becomes, the poem. She wrote a number of novels, including an interesting *roman à clef*, *Bid Me To Live* (1960), about London in 1917. This contains a valuable portrait of D. H. Lawrence (q.v.).

MARIANNE MOORE (1887–1972), who was born at St. Louis, Missouri, has been praised and loved by poets of every persuasion. It was H. D. and the English novelist Bryher who, unknown to the author, published her first book, *Poems* (1921), which collected twenty-four poems that had appeared in periodicals. She was editor of the magazine *The Dial* from 1925 until its demise in 1929. Hers is a reputation that has never suffered vicissitudes.

Marianne Moore's *Complete Poems* were issued in 1968, but one also needs her *Collected Poems* (1961): her alterations are revealing. She is unique in that she alone has made a 'modern' (by means of procedures) poetry out of an experience that deliberately excludes that rawness which we associate with the modern. She cut, in her eighty-first year, the twenty-odd lines of her famous poem 'Poetry' to just these four:

> I, too, dislike it.
>> Reading it, however, with a perfect
>> contempt for it, one discovers in
>> it, after all, a place for the genuine.

The end of the original version, which includes the celebrated lines about 'imaginary gardens with real toads in them' (it is the real toads she eschews), runs:

> ... if you demand on the one hand
>   the raw material of poetry in
>   all its rawness and
>   that which is on the other hand
>   genuine, you are interested in poetry.

Miss Moore really does dislike it; but she is interested in it, and in a thorough-going, respectable manner that is not shared by many other poets.

All this is not a mask. Miss Moore's external personality is what she presents it as: she is a Presbyterian (like her father) who approves of Bible classes. Hart Crane (q.v.) called her 'the Rt. Rev. Miss Mountjoy', and protested 'What strange people these ——[the omission is by the editor of Crane's letters] are. Always in a flutter for fear bowels will be mentioned. . . .' This aspect of Marianne Moore must, I think, be faced up to. And Crane's verdict is the right one: 'She is so prosaic that the extremity of her detachment touches, or seems to touch, a kind of inspiration'. This is the shrewdest remark ever made about her poetry, which is indeed about rejecting almost everything in modern experience—but rejecting it without loss of grace or authenticity. Out of a sensibility applied to a world she rejects she has created a genuinely poetic style, a body of work that confers vitality and meaning upon a propriety that we might otherwise reject as either incredible (in a poet) or absurdly provincial.

Her most sustained and exact and, in its way, confessional poem is 'The Pangolin'. This has been taken as a description of an animal so precise and loving that its object becomes a paradigm of a certain kind of human virtue. But it is both more and less than this. For here she describes her own life-style. And in the gentleness of the poem there is an implied rejection of an ungentle world:

> to explain grace requires
>   a curious hand. If that which is at all
>   were not forever,
>   why would those who graced the spires
>   with animals . . .
>   have slaved to confuse
>   grace with a kindly manner, time in
>   which to pay a debt
>   the cure for sins . . . ?

In Marianne Moore's poetry the disliked 'poetry', the peerless, imaginative thing that she sees she must reject, is relentlessly eschewed by a technique that makes enjambement a rule and not an exception, and takes as often as not an almost cynical, mechanically syllabic pattern as its norm—and yet the poetry returns, as a gift, in the form of subtle rhythms and light rhymes, as delicately as a butterfly alighting.

WALLACE STEVENS (1879–1955), born in Pennsylvania, was admired by Williams, but is on the whole eschewed by the 'native American' school; academic critics and poets, however, have taken him up. Stevens is not only modern in appearance—recondite, wanton in his imagery, holding back explicitness—but in substance as well. Thus two of his best-known lines are: 'The poem is the cry of its occasion/Part of the res itself and not about it'. He wasted much of his gift in meandering, ineffectual poetry ('The Man with the Blue Guitar') that is little more than an appropriate screen for the projections of ingenious critics; he needs rigorous selection; but at his second-best he is delightful, and at his rare best, superb. His first book, *Harmonium*, appeared in 1923 when he was nearly forty-four, and, unusually, he wrote the bulk of his poetry after he was fifty. He was at Harvard, then read law, and then joined the Hartford Accident and Indemnity Company in 1916; in 1934 he became its vice-president, a position which he held until his death. He was, then, a full-time business man for the whole of his life. This is often remarked upon. Perhaps the only relevant comment is that he is the only poet of the century, of comparable stature, thus to combine business with poetry; and that this is a formidable undertaking simply because the values of insurance and those of poetry do not appear to mix too easily.

Stevens' manner is polished, aesthetic, literary, exotic—at its worst whimsical and contrived—alogical and rhetorical. In terms of feeling his poetry is thin and deliberately reticent: that kind of experience is not its subject. Stevens is above all a civilized poet; his project is usually taken to be philosophical, but it can also be described as a search for a style, an answer to the question, 'How can an insurance man also be a poet?' 'What! Wally a poet', one of his illiterate colleagues exclaimed when told of it. The usual critical approach is to grant that there is what Professor Frank Kermode calls a 'poetry of abstraction', and to judge Stevens as a master of it. However, Stevens is at his best when he is being non-abstract—even if about the pains and difficulties of trying to maintain abstractness. The whimsical, recondite surface of the inferior poems is not always as masterly as it appears. As Stevens told his future wife when he was a very young man: 'Perhaps I do like to be sentimental now and then in a roundabout way. . . . I certainly do dislike expressing it right and left'. Thus 'The Man with the Blue Guitar' conceals not feeling but sentimentality beneath its artful veneer of vaguely symbolist preciosity; the complex aesthetic philosophy it contains may provide grist for such interesting neo-scholiasts as Professor Frank Kermode (a fine if contentious expositor of Stevens), but poetically this is neither here nor there. Too often Stevens was practising: a business man who, instead of questioning the moral sources of his affluence, played scales on an old chocolate bassoon (as he might have put it). Kermode says 'There is a poetry of the abstract; if you do not like it, even when it is firmly rooted in the particulars of the world, you will not like Stevens'. It is not quite as simple as that. One may dislike or not accept as valid the existence of 'a poetry of the abstract', but one may still like a little of Stevens. The trouble with 'The Man with the Blue Guitar' is that it is wholly cerebral: there is nothing to anchor it to any sort of emotional particular. 'Owl Clover', a longish poem rightly omitted from the *Collected Poems* (1954) but restored in its original version in *Opus Posthumous* (1957), shows him to least advantage: not because it maintains a poet's right to pursue his function despite politics, but because its view of Marxism, for all the sonorities, is as vulgar and insensitive as one might expect from an insurance man (no more than an 'it', in E. E. Cummings', q.v., words, 'that stinks excuse me'). But William York Tindall has reminded us that Stevens was a 'Taft Republican who thought Eisenhower a dangerous radical', and in a poet of his sensibilities what is 'fine and private . . . heroic . . the romance of lost causes finds its happiest concentration here'. However, Stevens skated on thin ice; we have good reason to suspect his aestheticism— if we are among those who do not believe the possession of genius is an excuse for lack of sensibility. 'Owl Clover' is crass reactionary propaganda from a man who never visited Europe in his life, and knew nothing of it at first hand—as bad as crass communist propaganda or tractor doggerel, and perhaps worse because wrapped up in an aestheticism that looks so advanced. (Stevens once wrote in a letter: 'The Italians have as much right to take Ethiopia from the coons as the coons had to take it from the boa-constrictors'; he then nervously qualified this by saying his own sympathy was with the coons and the boa-constrictors—but finally stated that Mussolini was 'right, practically'.)

Still, that is enough said. If he kept off politics, especially the kind that threatened his good living and his picture collecting (he believed, and wrongly, that people who could afford to buy pictures were better judges of them than those who could only talk about them), he was, after all, subversive: his early poetry, with its new words and gaiety, deliberately sought to annoy. 'The Emperor of Ice Cream' (equally, 'The Emperor of "I Scream" ') analyzes its material into its Freudian components in spite of himself.

Stevens' first inspiration may well have been Moody (q.v.); at all events, those poems (his juvenilia), he said, 'gave him the creeps'. The sources for his mature manner were mostly French, and perhaps his greatest debt was to Léon-Paul Fargue (q.v. 2), whom he sometimes resembles quite closely. His American forebears were inferior poets: DONALD EVANS (1884–1921), a now forgotten Greenwich Village decadent who killed himself, and ALFRED KREYMBORG (1883–1969), a lesser imagist and a friend of Stevens', from whom he may have gathered some more general hints. Lacking (or eschewing) a central core of experience that compelled poems from him, Stevens' chief theme is the supremacy of the creative imagination. Like Robbe-Grillet (q.v.), Stevens sees order, form, as coming only from the creators of imaginary worlds. For all his sophistication he is, as Marius Bewley has observed, a romantic, who believes in the transmuting powers of the imagination. This faith is most succinctly defined in the sequence called 'Notes Towards a Supreme Fiction', which some would put amongst his best poems. However, 'Sunday Morning' and the subtly autobiographical 'Le Monocle de Mon Oncle', both early poems, have the feeling this often verbally beautiful, but over-cerebral sequence lacks. In both Stevens' manner functions as vitality, but is subdued by personal concerns rather than philosophizings. Nothing touches the note of such lines as 'but until now I never knew/That fluttering things have so distinct a shade' or 'We live in an old chaos of the sun' until the serene final poems, when the threat of death edged safe business and prime living out of the foreground:

> Ariel was glad he had written his poems.
> They were of a remembered time
> Or of something seen that he liked.

It has been claimed that Stevens is the most important poet of the first half of the century with the 'possible' exceptions of Eliot, Pound and Frost: 'There are no other serious competitors'. This, it seems, is to put philosophy above poetry. Williams' poetry is surely much more 'important'; and Ransom's (q.v.) achievement in individual poems is as great or greater. But to exegetic critics, it is true, Stevens offers most of all; ironically, it is his best work, mostly in *Harmonium*, that most strongly resists such attentions.

E. E. CUMMINGS (1894–1962), born in Cambridge, Massachusetts, is still regarded by some as a 'modern' poet. But he was a quirky traditionalist in all respects save two: he showed that typography—visual variations—could be useful; and his ear for the vernacular was sometimes, though not always, good. There are two Cummings: a versifier who disguises his sentimentalities and sometimes irregular but always conventional metrics by typographical tricks; and a magnificently aggressive comic and satirical poet who—alas—never quite grew up. Cummings had wanted to be a painter, and he did in fact execute strangely atrocious paintings all his life (his sense of colour can only be described as nauseous). Instead of maturing he surrendered to—as his photographs and self-portrait show—self-love and arrogance: his language lost its edge, and he descended increasingly into the cliché from which his love poetry had never been wholly free. No amount of critical interpretation can disguise the tawdry third-rateness of the language in the following poem (drawn from Cummings' later work):

> now all the fingers of this tree(darling)have
> hands,and all the hands have people;and
> more each particular person is(my love)
> alive than every world can understand
>
> and now you are and i am now and we're
> a mystery which will never happen again,
> a miracle which has never happened before—
> and shining this our now must come to then
>
> our then shall be some darkness during which
> fingers are without hands;and i have no
> you:and all trees are(any more than each
> leafless)its silent in forevering snow
>
> —but never fear(my own,my beautiful
> my blossoming)for also then's until

This is the work of a man who has gone soft at the centre and likes himself too much to be able to see it. And yet he had once been very good indeed; more, I think, than the 'slight and charming' which has been allowed to him by his detractors. He had been able to criticize false patriotism and outworn literary language to admirable effect in such poems as 'come, gaze with me upon this dome'. Cummings has always been enormous fun, and if one sounds a dissenting note it is only because during his lifetime he had too much attention as a serious lyrical poet. He certainly deserves respect for his part in dismantling the genteel tradition. But diligent search fails to produce a single completely effective love poem: every one is marred by tentativeness or portentousness if not by that unquestioning sentimentality that is so odd in so fierce a satirist. The early poems are full of promise, but it was a promise that did not fully materialize. Cummings' originally childlike whimsicality and tweeness ('the little/lame balloon man'; 'hist whist/little ghostthings'—and so on) need not have been offensive; but he came to indulge it and, eventually, to confuse it with lyricism. The early love poems contain hints of a manner that Cummings might have developed, but most of them only conceal, by their eccentricity, which is of course often typographical, Cummings' failure to find a language. An exception is the fifth of the 'Songs' in *Tulips & Chimneys*: 'Doll's boy's asleep', in which a nursery rhyme insouciance is transformed into a note of genuine menace. But Cummings chose not to investigate his sexual emotions—he chose to avoid the crux of sexuality—and his best energies went into a satire that can be piercingly accurate, or merely hilarious—or funny but curiously diminishing, uncompassionate and perhaps insensitive. There are many poems like the one ending 'i try if you are a gentleman not to sense something un poco putrido/when we contemplate her uneyes safely ensconced in thick glass', and they are certainly funny; but there is an absence, elsewhere in Cummings' work, of a compensating pity: perhaps he imagined that the lyrics filled this role. The fact is that for most of the time Cummings' fun is not quite good enough: not quite first class. The vernacular he reproduces has not always been listened to carefully enough—the poet has been too keen to impress. If he does not diminish he patronizes. It has, however, been salutary to have someone like Cummings to ridicule and generally slam our philistine society of politicians and business men—and the pseudo-culture that nurses and sustains it. And then there are the splendid tough-guy poems, and the descriptions of low life. Cummings is seldom as empathic as Williams in his descriptions ('It really must/be Nice, never to', XIII from *Is 5*, is one of the fine exceptions), since he is concentrating on a kind of audience that Williams has rejected, but his immense gaiety and humour ('what's become of maeterlinck/ now that april's here?) give him a unique importance. The oft-repeated judgement that he is 'the Catullus of the modern movement' is quite wrong; he is cheerfully and most enjoyably obscene (as in his car poem: 'she being Brand/-new; and you/know consequently a/little stiff I was/careful of her . . . just as we turned the corner of Divinity/avenue i touched the accelerator and give/her the juice, good . . .), as Catullus is, but the Latin poet could never have indulged in Cummings' sentimentalities. We are grateful to Cummings; but the reservations have to be made. It is astonishing how many readers and critics take Cummings' late nineteenth-century, neo-romantic love poetry to be modern because of its careful but logical surface pyrotechnics. What has not yet been fully grasped is that Cummings' experiments are extensions of traditionalism, not reachings-forward into the unknown.

Cummings went to France in the First World War as a volunteer ambulance driver; as a result of his violation of the French censorship laws in a letter home, he was arrested and spent some time in a French prison camp. *The Enormous Room* (1922) was the result, a classic of its kind—in which, incidentally, Cummings shows his capacity to master the vernacular. *Eimi* (1933), an account of a visit to Russia, is less good, but contains some memorable passages; in it, too, we see Cummings' romanticism at its strongest and least self-indulgent. *Complete Poems* (1968) supersedes previous collections.

A rather more important, but less striking and less heeded writer is CONRAD AIKEN (1889-1973), born in Savannah, Georgia. Aiken is a distinguished novelist, critic and short-story writer as well as a poet. It is often said of him that he did not realize his enormous gifts. But this is to ignore too much: *Senlin* (1918), the *Preludes for Memnon* (1931)—his best poems, still undervalued—the novel *Great Circle* (1933), a number of short stories, the autobiographical *Ushant* (1953). The four main influences on Aiken have been: his physician father's killing of his mother and subsequent suicide (in 1900), music, Freud, and nineteenth-century romantic poetry (from Poe to Swinburne). He combines a luxuriant style with a psychological subtlety that has not been fully appreciated. Famous for such finely simple poetry as 'Discordants' (from *Turns and Movies*, 1916),

> Music I heard with you was more than music,
> And bread I broke with you was more than bread;
> Now that I am without you, all is desolate;
> All that was once so beautiful is dead.

Aiken can sustain such feeling in more complex poetry, as in the tragic Rilkean twenty-ninth prelude which begins:

> What shall we do—what shall we think—what shall we say—?
> Why, as the crocus does, on a March morning,
> With just such shape and brightness; such fragility;
> Such white and gold, and out of just such earth.
> Or as the cloud does on the northeast wind—
> Fluent and formless; or as the tree that withers.

It takes much to maintain such pantheistic lyricism against the harsh sense of being human.

Aiken's weakness is his romantic imitativeness; but at his best he has—as in the lines above—been able to find his own voice. He has been neglected because he has chosen to express himself, for the most part, in long poems or sequences, and these have simply not been explored. They should be. More than any other poet, he has wanted to allow the subconscious mind to speak for itself; but— paradoxically—he has organized the surface of his poetry most elaborately to that effect. This is to say that he has modified his flow only by such devices as have suggested themselves at the moment of composition; but the devices themselves are often complicated.

His short stories often deal poignantly with psychotic situations; more than any others, they are the stories of a poet. *Ushant* treats of the men he has known: it was he who showed Eliot's poems to Pound; he who helped to orient Malcolm Lowry (q.v.) imaginatively, truthfully and yet with a tact that he may have learned during his long stay, between wars, in England. Of his novels, *Great Circle* (1933), a treatment of the catastrophe of his childhood, seems certain to be revived and admired. An 'essential Aiken', which would be a very fat volume, would contain some of this century's best writing.

By contrast, ROBINSON JEFFERS (1887–1962) seems unlikely to survive, perhaps because his extreme pessimism is uncompensated for by any linguistic energy. He was born in Pittsburgh, Pennsylvania; from 1924 he lived in a stone house and tower—in Carmel, California—which he built himself. His philosophy is not new, but is not in itself uninteresting: man's intellectual capacities are a terrible delusion and they disgrace him and lead him into trouble. Stone, the sea: these endure. Animals: these have dignity and no aspiration. But nothing whatever happens in Jeffers' language, which is clichéridden and more often than not suggests that he was by no means convinced of his own beliefs, which were perhaps formulated as a response to his father's theological certainties. He had some narrative gift, of an old-fashioned kind; but his poems and plays hardly bear re-reading. His *Collected Poems* was published in 1948.

LOUISE BOGAN (1897–1970), whose *Collected Poems* (1954) shared the Bollingen Prize with Léonie Adams (q.v.), was best known for her poetry reviews in *The New Yorker*. She was skilful and precise and did enough to win gallant accolades such as 'the most distinguished woman poet of our time' (Allen Tate); but she lacked attack, and nothing she wrote is memorable.

LÉONIE ADAMS (1899), born in Brooklyn, is a different matter. Not too well known in her own country, she remains unpublished and unknown in Great Britain. Yet she is a most distinguished and original poet. She has been called romantic, but wrongly: rather, she has preserved the metaphysical tradition in a romantic diction. Of a gull alighting without a feather being stirred she says,

> So in an air less rare than longing might
> The dreams of flying lift a marble bird.

Both these poets are vastly superior to EDNA ST. VINCENT MILLAY (1892–1950), who survives in Edward Wilson's poignant memoir of her as a person but hardly at all as a poet. Once very widely read, her proper place (as has been pointed out) is beside Rupert Brooke. A few of her lines have descriptive precision, but she left no single satisfactory poem. Her capacities are well illustrated by her lines: 'God! we could keep this planet warm/By friction, if the sun should fail'.

III

The late nineteenth century in America was a time of highly effective, bewitching actors (Robert Mantell, William Gillette, Richard Mansfield, John Drew, Jr.), but of mediocre drama. Ibsen made a late impact, and the plays through which the Americans were introduced to realism now seem melodramatic as well as sentimental. The energetic actor-manager and dramatist Steele MacKaye (1842–94) developed stage machinery and lighting, and trained actors. He was, if mostly in what he aspired to, an important influence on the future American stage. But not as a playwright: his own plays were pioneer in subject (*Hazel Kirke*, 1880, is the most famous) but weak in structure and dialogue. Much of the work of the real pioneer in playwriting, BRONSON HOWARD (1842–1908) does not now seem an improvement; but, although his primary purpose was always to entertain, he was one of the first to treat his material thoughtfully—and he did develop. He was also the first American to make his living by writing for the stage. The loose ends of *Young Mrs. Winthrop* (1899), first produced in 1882, are sentimentally tied up in the last act; but its situation is realistic. One who did not hinder—though he hardly helped—the emergence of a realistic theatre was DAVID BELASCO (1859–1931), who also wrote plays—Puccini's opera is based on his *Girl of the Golden West* (1905). AUGUSTUS THOMAS

(1857–1934) was in the main simply a successful playwright, but he did have the serious purpose of showing the United States as it was, and he did help—with, for example, *As a Man Thinks* (1911), on faith healing—to clear the way for the 'problem play'. Neither CLYDE FITCH (1865–1909) nor JAMES A. HERNE (1839–1901) wrote what we should call a good play. But both contributed in a small way to a specifically American theatre. The former's best plays were his study of a pathologically jealous woman, *The Girl with the Green Eyes*, and his last, *The City* (1909), which is one of the early stage attacks on political corruption. James A. Herne's *Margaret Fleming* (1890), about adultery, is superior. It seems maudlin and artificial to us now, but its theme deeply shocked the audiences—for the adultery is forgiven. It was praised by Howells and Garland (qq.v). It is unfortunate that all these men worked to create the star system as well as an American theatre, since the star system is in many ways one of the banes of the modern American (and British) theatre; but they had little alternative if they wanted to eat. However, by 1896, with the formation of the first Theatrical Syndicate, the days of the actor-managers were effectually at an end. Philistinism and commerce moved into the theatre: it was hardly to be wondered at that business men, seeing a potential source of profit, should move in. In the first two decades of the century philistinism was countered by the formation of groups who, in one way or another, managed to make themselves independent. Winthrop Ames (1871–1937) inherited a fortune from his father, who was a railway magnate, and made three gallant efforts to found true repertory in New York; later he built two theatres. More important was the equally non-commercial Theatre Guild (1919), which began as the Washington Square Players in 1914. And most important of all was the Provincetown Players. This was founded in 1915 by the novelist and playwright SUSAN GLASPELL (1882–1948), whose plays were competent although not inspired, and her husband George Cram Cook. Their experimentalism was important for giving Eugene O'Neill (q.v.), America's only great dramatist, the chances he needed to develop without commercial restrictions. As vital an influence on American theatre was George Pierce Baker (1866–1935), a Harvard professor who in 1905 set up the '47 Workshop', a course in playwrighting that was taken by, among others, Winthrop Ames, O'Neill, Philip Barry, John Dos Passos, S. N. Behrman, Sidney Howard, Thomas Wolfe (qq.v.). Baker went to Yale in 1925, where he continued until his death. Wolfe's Professor Hatcher, in *Of Time and the River*, is a portrait of him.

The verse plays of William Vaughn Moody (q.v.) have already

been mentioned; he was an intelligent man and an able craftsman, but he did not possess enough originality to achieve a real breakthrough. The best of all his works are *The Great Divide* (1909), a revision of an earlier play, about a girl who marries a man who has bought her against her will, and *The Faith Healer* (1909), about a genuine faith healer whose gift is destroyed by the scepticism of those around him. It was in this latter play that Moody came nearest to a truly modern style; but he was too inhibited to try for the rhythms of ordinary speech, and this failure seriously vitiates his achievement. EDWARD SHELDON (1886–1946) had similar difficulties with language, but had had the benefit of attending George Pierce Baker's classes. He was in fact its first distinguished graduate playwright, and his *Salvation Nell* (1908) was actually produced by the group. *The Nigger* (1909) and *The Boss* (1911) were both profoundly shocking in their day, the first because a white girl finally decided to marry the governor of a Southern state who discovers that he has Negro blood. Sheldon was blind and paralysed for the last fifteen years of his life, but continued until the end to act as consultant to actors, actresses and all connected with the theatre. His worst play, *Romance* (1913), a piece of skilfully executed midcult trash, was easily his most popular. It was Sheldon's skill as an entertainer—and, perhaps, the weakness induced by his progressive disease—that prevented his work achieving real seriousness.

Steele MacKaye's (q.v.) son Percy MacKaye (q.v.) wrote an effective verse drama called *The Scarecrow* (1908), from Hawthorne's tale 'Feathertop'; but although this was the best thing he ever did, it solved no problems for the theatre.

Towering above these, and over all his successors, is the figure of EUGENE O'NEILL (1888–1953), the New York born son of the well-known romantic actor James O'Neill, who was most celebrated in the part of the Count of Monte Cristo. O'Neill's mother was a drug addict and his brother an alcoholic. O'Neill himself suffered from ill-health for most of his life, and was, besides, a tortured soul—so much so that one of his biographers called his book *The Curse of the Misbegotten* (after O'Neill's title *A Moon for the Misbegotten*), and hardly descended into melodrama. O'Neill wrote successful plays in two styles, the realistic and the expressionist (q.v.); he also might be said to have pursued two careers in the theatre, since he was silent for the twelve years between 1934 and 1946. In 1936 he was awarded the Nobel Prize.

The theatre was in O'Neill's blood; but before he came to it he tried Princeton (a year), poetry, mining, marriage (secret and dissolved), the sea (he voyaged to South America, South Africa, several times to England), newspaper reporting, sickness, tuberculosis; and then, after writing some short plays, he joined Baker's course. In 1915 he went to Provincetown, and the Provincetown Players' performance of his one-act *Bound East for Cardiff*—on a makeshift stage in a fishermen's shack at the end of a pier, while fog seeped through the wooden walls—initiated the true birth of the American theatre. It was also the début of a playwright whom no other of his century would outdo. Baker, and the men and women of the Provincetown Players—Robert Edmond Jones, the stage designer, is important among them—had heard of what was going on in Europe: of Antoine (q.v. 2) in France, Reinhardt (q.v. 2) in Germany, Strindberg (q.v. 2) in Sweden, Stanislavski (q.v. 4) in Russia. . . . The American theatre had come of age, and its chief playwright had the required genius and nerve.

O'Neill had passion, gloom and an absolutely uncompromising realism; at the end, anguished, ill and personally unhappy though he was, he achieved a mood of something like reconciliation. The key to his achievement was stated by himself in a letter he wrote about his play *Mourning Becomes Electra*:

> It needed great language . . . I haven't got that. And, by way of self-consolation, I don't think, from the evidence of all that is being written today, that great language is possible for anyone living in the discordant, broken, faithless rhythm of our time. The best one can do is to be pathetically eloquent by one's moving, dramatic inarticulations.

O'Neill was right. No nineteenth- or twentieth-century dramatist has come near to what he called 'great language' (perhaps he was thinking of Shakespeare, as we all do), but he alone authentically yearned after it. Brecht achieved great language—but in his lyrical poetry. Only O'Neill achieved a dramatic framework whose interstices surround poetic silences, and whose 'inarticulations' are truly 'pathetic'. He has been attacked for not producing 'heroes of stature'; but that is one of the reasons why he is truly modern.

Beyond the Horizon (1920), his first full-length play, is a naturalistic study of two brothers, each of whom makes the wrong choice in life, and is defeated through mistakes induced by sexual drive. *The Emperor Jones* (1921) is a piece of expressionism conceived before O'Neill knew anything of the European expressionists: a Caribbean Negro dictator flees from his victims to the sound of a relentlessly beating drum. *The Hairy Ape* (1922), another expressionistic play, deals with a brutish stoker (a sort of McTeague, q.v.), Yank, who yearns for a more human fulfilment; he ends by trying to retreat into what he thinks he is, by embracing a gorilla—which kills him.

Desire Under the Elms (1925), largely prompted by O'Neill's interest in Freudian psychology, is a return to realism, and is one of his most powerful plays.

The Great God Brown (1926) is probably too experimental for the stage, although it reads well. In it O'Neill used masks to try to define the difference between the bourgeois and the creative temperaments—but his chief character Dion Anthony (Dionysus-St. Anthony) is too symbolic, even though his anguished vacillation between pagan creativeness and Christian morality is at times most intensely and movingly conveyed. In *Marco Millions* (1928) O'Neill turned unsuccessfully to satire: this lampoon of materialism is both too obvious and tedious. There is no tension. *Dynamo* (1929) is O'Neill's worst and most theory-ridden play. Aware that he was troubled by the loss of the Catholic faith of his childhood he tried an experiment in which he did not really believe, melodramatically showing a young man's failure to substitute faith in a dynamo for the Calvinistic faith of his childhood. *Days without End* (1934) has two actors playing the same (divided) man: a sceptic and a believer. Nothing demonstrates more clearly O'Neill's failure to rediscover Catholicism, although at the time it was widely believed that he had returned to it.

Between these two disastrous attempts, O'Neill had written the finest of all the plays of his earlier period: the trilogy, *Mourning Becomes Electra*, based on Aeschylus' Orestean trilogy. O'Neill took a New England family in the aftermath of the Civil War and fairly carefully paralleled the Greek story: the returning General Ezra Mannon is killed by his wife Christine, whose lover Adam Brant is then killed by their son Orin, egged on by their daughter, Lavinia. Christine kills herself, Orin goes mad and commits suicide, whereupon Lavinia shuts herself up for ever with an unrelievable guilty conscience in the family mansion. This was presented in relentlessly Freudian terms, which led many critics to describe it as a case-study rather than a tragedy. O'Neill has also been attacked for his prosaic language at moments of enormous stress. But may we not, in retrospect—having had the opportunity to study the 'great language' of the wretched Christopher Fry or even that of Tennessee Williams (qq.v.)—be grateful for this alleged 'flatness'? O'Neill knew he could not attain the great language he yearned for. And so, unlike so many lesser playwrights, he did not attempt it. One suspects that his critics would too easily forgive a heady, contrived rhetoric of the kind so often produced by Tennessee Williams—a pseudo-poetry;

dramatic occasions demand 'high' language. I think O'Neill was right, and that the plays are better without such language.

By 1934 O'Neill had made two more marriages, the latter of which was not unsuccessful. He went into a state of semi-permanent depression from about the mid-Thirties until the end of the war. He destroyed much that he wrote in this period, but by 1946 he felt able to release *The Iceman Cometh* (1946), which he had written in 1939. O'Neill's experiments were necessary to him, but he always returned to the realistic mode. *The Iceman Cometh*, set in a disreputable dive for down-and-outs and outcasts, is entirely realistic; no gimmicks are required. The Iceman of the title is death, which is the only release from the illusions that torment mankind. The salesman Hickey tells all the drinkers in Harry Hope's bar that their only chance of happiness is to renounce hope. Previously happy in their absurd and drunken way, they now disbelieve Hickey and go out to prove him wrong. But each returns: broken. Then Hickey turns out to have killed his wife. When he gives himself up to the police, all but one of them return to their old contentment. Like Dreiser (q.v.), though in an utterly different and more poetic manner, O'Neill here richly conveys the actual grain of life. It does not much matter if you agree with his philosophy or not. Its torpor is counteracted by the lyricism of the outcasts' hope—and of their despair.

O'Neill wrote a number of other plays, none of which was performed in his lifetime. *A Moon for the Misbegotten* (1952) was withdrawn while on trial. *More Stately Mansions* (1964), a study of the breakdown of a poetic soul into madness, has only been tried out in a cut, Swedish version. *A Touch of the Poet* (1957), the sole survivor from a projected eleven-play cycle called *A Tale of Possessors Self-Dispossessed*, contains an unforgettable portrait of a man who seems to attain stature through self-deceit and selfishness. In the one-act *Hughie* (1959) and *Long Day's Journey into Night* (1956) O'Neill rose to the heights of his achievement. In *Hughie* he perfectly captures a vernacular more difficult than that of his early sea dramas: the speech of seedy, boastful New York drifters of the Twenties. *Long Day's Journey into Night*, a semi-autobiographical family-drama, is his simplest play. Here O'Neill demonstrates his genius beyond doubt: there is no plot and no drama, the play is very long—and yet it holds the attention. Alan S. Downer has written wisely of it: 'It cannot be overemphasized that this is a play of reconciliation; the audience that has experienced *Long Day's Journey* cannot go out of the theatre without a greater capacity for tolerance and understanding....'

Not one of O'Neill's contemporaries and successors can be compared to him: his plays are torn from him; theirs are, at best, made.

American theatre, like the British, lacked vitality in the Thirties, and this lack was made even more manifest by the example of O'Neill, who could be criticized for all sorts of faults, but never for lack of vitality or attack.

The verse drama does not seem to be a viable form in our century (the German habit of writing in verse is hardly relevant here), despite valiant attempts; it has been as successful in America as almost anywhere.

ARCHIBALD MACLEISH (1892) wrote *Nobo-daddy* (1926), the labour play *Panic* (1935), and *J.B.* (1958), his most successful play, in which a contemporary Job acts out his story in a circus tent. He also wrote several effective verse plays for radio, including *Air Raid* (1938). MacLeish began as a poet, and his *The Hamlet of A. MacLeish* (1928), one of those long poems inspired by the success of *The Waste Land* (q.v.), was taken with seriousness. He shifted from the extreme subjectivity of this poem to advocacy of full political 'engagement'. He was Librarian of Congress 1939–44 and was influential in the Roosevelt administration. He ranks, David Ray has written, 'with Robinson Jeffers and Carl Sandburg in the penetration of public taste'. But not, one has to add, with Brecht. MacLeish has written sincere and unpretentious verse, and has been an admirable public man—one of the most admirable of the time, a genuinely well-intentioned link between poets and an establishment that cannot take them into account. The poetry of his plays, however, contributes nothing whatever to them. *J.B.* was apparently personally inspiring to a number of those who watched it; this is admirable. But the nature of the inspiration is nearer to that of a good sermon or exhortation than to, say, Sherwood Anderson's (q.v.) various autobiographical writings. These are true literature because they never exhort: the author lives entirely in his imagination. MacLeish appears to have no such imaginative, internal centre.

The same applies to MAXWELL ANDERSON (1888–1959), who wrote plays in verse (and, in 1925, one book of poetry) and yet who was not a poet. He tried for the 'great language' that O'Neill knew could not be got: he felt that there could be no 'great drama' without 'great poetry', and he did not claim that his own verse was well written. He may have been right about 'great drama'; the trouble was that he thought anyone could write poetry—if 'badly'—not realizing that it takes a poet. The career of Anderson, a worthy, gifted and sincere writer, and a fine craftsman of the theatre, affords an illustration of the harsh fact that art and commerce do not and cannot really mix. Art may or may not be successful in terms of the market; once a writer orients himself towards the market, however, he destroys his credibility. Anderson was a serious man who nevertheless conceived it as his duty to entertain middlebrow audiences. His and LAURENCE STALLINGS' (1894) *What Price Glory* (1924), on the American soldiery of the First World War, was a great hit. It was outspoken for its time, but its realism is in fact tawdry and its comedy as second-hand as it is second-rate. Anderson improved on this, but always conceived of a play not only as a dramatically viable entity but also as suitable fare for commercial audiences, whom he believed he could convert to his own humane point of view. And so he did; but this, like a response to Billy Graham, was temporary, because Anderson did not write from his imagination. Verse operates in his drama as an effective rhetoric. *Elizabeth the Queen* (1930), on Elizabeth and Essex, was the first modern blank verse play to pay at the box-office. *Both Your Houses* (1933) attacked political corruption. Probably Anderson's most famous play was *Winterset* (1935), his second attempt to deal with the tragic material of the Sacco-Vanzetti case. It was a success at the time, but a total failure in literary terms: as Edmund Wilson wrote, 'in the text I could not discover anything that seemed to me in the least authentic as emotion, idea or characterization'. He rated Anderson more highly as a prose playwright. Anderson's best is in fact the relaxed musical comedy *Knickerbocker Holiday* (1938), which had a score by Kurt Weill. Anderson came off in his lifetime, and deserved to; it seems unlikely that any of his plays will survive.

SIDNEY HOWARD (1891–1939), a Californian who died prematurely in an accident with a tractor on his farm, was as skilful as Anderson, but more orthodox. He was a member of Baker's '47 Workshop'. His first play, in verse, flopped; he took the hint and did not return to this medium. Howard went on to do fine, conscientious work of all kinds—translations (Vildrac's *S.S. Tenacity*, q.v. 2), adaptations (*The Late Christopher Bean*, 1932), documentaries (*Yellow Jack*, with Paul de Kruif, 1934) as well as original plays. *They Knew What They Wanted* (1924), which was granted a second lease of life in 1957 as the musical *The Most Happy Fella*, was a lively comedy about a Californian grapegrower and his mail-order bride, and immediately established Howard. In the same year Howard collaborated with Edward Sheldon (q.v.) on *Bewitched. The Silver Cord* (1926) was an unsentimental and psychologically accurate portrayal of a possessive mother. *Paths of Glory* (1935), adapted from a novel by Humphrey Cobb, was an excellent anti-war play. Howard listened carefully to common speech, and reported it accurately. He is an example of the man who does the best he can—rather than compromise himself— with a limited imagination.

ROBERT SHERWOOD (1896–1955), a forthright radical who was gassed in the First World War and put much of his energy into anti-totalitarian activities, was perhaps as skilful, but more trivial. *The Petrified Forest* (1935), although its theme is ostensibly the disintegration of the artist in modern society, suffers from technical slickness and sentimentality. The 'continental' comedy *Reunion in Vienna* (1931) is not as intellectually ambitious, and is Sherwood's best play. A psychiatrist thinks that a love-affair his wife is conducting with Prince Maximilian Rudolph, whose mistress she has been, will cure her of an obsession; his complacency is shattered. Apart from this and *Tovarich* (1936), which he adapted, Sherwood is probably better regarded as an admirable journalist than as an imaginative writer. He wrote some of Roosevelt's speeches.

ELMER RICE (ps. ELMER REIZENSTEIN, 1892–1967), a worthy man of the theatre, may be described as an experimentalist of abundant gifts but no genius. Rice, like Sherwood, is a radical, and has on several occasions taken a stand against censorship and witch-hunting by the authorities. His first play, *On Trial* (1914), a thriller, used the movie technique of flashback. *The Adding Machine* (1923), depicts Mr. Zero, executed for the murder of his boss, dissatisfied in the Elysian Fields and returning to the earth to become a perfect slave of the machine age. This is wholly expressionistic in technique, and a fine satire, which Rice has not bettered. Unfortunately Rice has no capacity for psychological penetration or characterization—even of the workmanlike sort practised by Howard (q.v.)—and this has tended to impoverish his drama. His best plays after *The Adding Machine* are the realistic *Street Scene* (1929), *Dream Girl* (1945) and *Cue for Passion* (1958).

PHILIP BARRY (1896–1949), another of Baker's pupils, collaborated with Rice in *Cock Robin* (1928). Barry was another prolific, intelligent and workmanlike playwright. Many of his plays are comedies with a serious note; the others tend to be his best. *You and I* (1923) is a poignant study of a father who discovers his own frustrations when he tries to turn his son into an artist. *Hotel Universe* (1930) was perhaps unfortunate: this drama of an old man who helps people to find themselves was rather too well made and contrived, but some of the individual portraits—including a man who has lost his faith and a girl whose love is unrequited—are excellent. He realized his potential most fully in *Here Come the Clowns* (1938), an odd and disturbing play about the effects of a magician's hypnotic powers on a vaudeville troupe. Barry was also responsible for the smooth and entertaining *The Philadelphia Story* (1939).

S. N. BEHRMAN (1893), yet another of Baker's pupils, tried to combine comedy with social drama, and dealt, in *No Time for Comedy* (1939) with his own predicament. Once again, too much skill at entertainment vitiates seriousness. He adapted, with Joshua Logan, Pagnol's *Fanny* (q.v.) as a musical comedy in 1945.

GEORGE S. KAUFMAN (1889–1961) and MARC CONNELLY (1890) began in collaboration, with several plays, the most successful of which was *Beggar on Horseback* (1924), an expressionist satire on the oppression of the artist (here, a composer) by bourgeois society. Kaufman went on to write several smooth farces, some with MOSS HART (1904–61), including the famous, and deftly written, portrait of Alexander Woollcott, *The Man Who Came to Dinner* (1939). Connelly's Negro play, *The Green Pastures*, has a little more weight; but this well-meant picture of the Negro conception of the Old Testament is at heart both folksy and patronizing rather than dignified and poetic.

The Thirties saw the rise of a more aggressive social theatre, whose white hope was CLIFFORD ODETS (1906–63). Odets was a protégé of the important Group Theatre, founded by Harold Clurman, Lee Strasberg and Cheryl Crawford in 1931. The actor and director Elia Kazan was early associated with this venture, which devoted itself to Stanislavsky's (q.v.) principles of group acting. (Kazan later, 1947, founded the influential Actors' Studio, which taught the Method, a technique in which the actor is exhorted to 'become' the part he is playing. The Method is less different from other methods of training actors than some have thought, since every actor should in one way or another 'become' the stage-person he is representing—provided he does not forget the audience.) Odets began with *Waiting for Lefty* (1935), an effective and bitter piece, without characterization, about a taxicab strike. *Awake and Sing* (1935), ecstatic, well made, at times funny, established him as the leading playwright of his generation. *Golden Boy* (1937) is so well done that its central character, a musician who turns under economic pressure to professional boxing, is made almost credible. By the time of *The Big Knife* (1948) Odets, while he retained all his skill, had become affected by the pressures involved in producing big, successful plays: this indictment of Hollywood seems to come right out of Hollywood itself.

SIDNEY KINGSLEY (1906) was another competent social dramatist, responsible for the originals of the movies *Dead End* and *Detective Story*. His first play, *Men in White* (1933) about a young doctor's indecisions, is among his best. *They Shall Not Die* (1934) by JOHN WESLEY (1902) and *Stevedore* (1934) by PAUL PETERS (1908) were more strident: written with the leftist fervour of Odets, they lacked his passionateness and concern for character.

JOHN HOWARD LAWSON (1895) preceded all these left-wing or Marxist playwrights. Lawson began with expressionist plays, such as *Roger Bloomer* (1923) and *Processional* (1925), all of which harped on class distinction. In 1936 he wrote a Marxist textbook of proletarian theatre. Once again, although he is a very skilful writer, he is best considered as a journalist and a propagandist for social change. Really only Odets, of the social and Marxist dramatists, achieved anything beyond the journalistic—and he did not altogether fulfil his promise.

LILLIAN HELLMAN (1905), who was born in New Orleans, is as radical as any of these, but is less ideological and more interested in characterization. Her one attempt at a proletarian piece, *Days to Come* (1936), about a strike, failed. She is one of the most able and effective of modern dramatists in the old 'well-made' technique. Her first play, *The Children's Hour* (1934), about a schoolgirl who maliciously accuses her two headmistresses of being lesbian, is skilful but ambiguous in that it leaves the audience in doubt as to whether the greater vileness in the play is the child's false accusation or lesbianism itself; Lillian Hellman might well now rewrite the play so that the two headmistresses actually are discreetly lesbian—and show them as still victimized. *The Little Foxes* (1939) is an excellent study of greed and unpleasantness: a Southern family seizes its opportunities as industrialism rises there. Her next two plays, *Watch on the Rhine* (1941), and *The Searching Wind* (1944) were finely made propaganda against fascism and opportunistic appeasement respectively. Then came her best play: *Another Part of the Forest* (1946), a comic study, rightly described as Jonsonian, of hateful people cheating each other. *Toys in the Attic* (1960) embodies Lillian Hellman's most memorable portrait of an evil person, and her most hopeful (if defeated) one. Charges of misanthropy against Miss Hellman are frivolous, and come from those whose optimism is flabby. But the 'well-madeness' of her plays does tend to vitiate them, even though one recognizes that she cannot proceed except in this way. *Another Part of the Forest* is a picaresque comedy, and is freer from the limitations of 'sardoodledom' (q.v. 2) than any other of her plays. (*The Little Foxes*, written earlier, is its sequel in time.)

WILLIAM SAROYAN (1908), born of Armenian parents in California, has exuberance, energy and tenderness; he might have been a major writer, and as it is he is now an undervalued one; unfortunately he has seldom been able to control his sentimentality, or force himself into moods in the least discriminatory. For this naïve (q.v.), all that matters is the glory of the dream. 'He puts everything in', one critic has said, 'in case he misses anything important'. He never went beyond his fictional début, *The Daring Young Man on the Flying Trapeze* (1934), short stories written with a strikingly innocent eye and a direct, appealing lyricism. Saroyan went on to produce much more fiction of the same sort, but the good bits become harder to find. He made his début as a playwright with *My Heart's in the Highlands* (1939) and *The Time of Your Life* (1939), the curious opposite of O'Neill's *The Iceman Cometh* (q.v.) since the somewhat similar central character dispenses happiness, not despair. For a time it looked to many people as though Saroyan might become an important figure in the theatre, but he lacked craftsmanship and discipline, and all his promise petered out into showy, patchy, sentimental drama such as *The Beautiful People* (1941) or improvisations such as his more recent *Sam the Highest Jumper of them All* (1960). One play stands out among all the others: *Hello Out There* (1942), a genuinely tragic one-act piece about the lynching of a tramp. Saroyan can be silly ('I am so innately great by comparison others who believe they are great . . . seem to me to be only pathetic, although occasionally charming'), and he has produced masses of rubbish; but his best is worth looking for.

THORNTON WILDER (1897), born at Madison, Wisconsin, novelist and playwright, has certainly been an odd man out throughout his career; his work, unquestionably skilful, intelligent and technically resourceful, has been the subject of much controversy: is he at heart a middlebrow charlatan exploiting the discoveries and procedures of his betters, or is he an original writer with something of his own to say? The truth is that Wilder seems pretentious because (as he himself has come near to admitting) he can never answer the huge questions he asks. He is by no means a middlebrow in intention, and he has specifically stated that one of the problems of the modern dramatist is to create a theatre that will be genuinely disturbing to the bourgeoisie. But in actually dealing with this problem he has succeeded in pleasing rather than worrying them. He lacks an inner core of imaginative resilience, or passion, and consequently too quickly falls back on mere cleverness, laced with folksiness and sentimentality. In other words, his unconventionality resides in his daring technique rather than in his somewhat unoriginal content. The impact of his plays (and novels, with one exception) is perfectly middlebrow in that it provokes 'discussion' rather than meditation or wonder. *Our Town* (1938) gives the intimate history of a New Hampshire town by means of a bare stage (a shrewd reaction against the theatre's obsession at this time with décor) and a choric stage manager, who describes the characters and talks casually to the audience. It is a dazzling performance, but all it ultimately offers is the rather mundane thought that there is 'something way down deep that's eternal about a human being': a Yankee inarticulateness underlies the high articulateness of the bright presentation. In *The Skin of Our Teeth* the Antrobus family represent humanity and the escape, by the proverbial skin, from most of the terrors that are known to have beset the race. This is again brilliant; but an arch folksiness precludes real warmth.

Wilder's first popular success was the novel *The Bridge of San Luis Rey* (1927), which traces the fortunes of a number of people killed when a South American bridge collapses. But this was meretricious compared with his first novel, *The Cabala* (1926), or with the most solid of all his works, *Heaven's My Destination* (1935), about a book salesman called George Brush, a foolish saint, who reminds one of Duhamel's Salavin (q.v. 2). In this comic story Wilder found his own voice, and although his plays have their moving moments, they never measure up to this (he did not come back to fiction until 1967, with *The Eighth Day*; this has all the old brilliance of technique, but is otherwise sadly disappointing), which is a major work.

*

Since the Second World War the theatre almost everywhere has got increasingly into the hands of the directors; in certain cases the public are even more interested in the producers of plays than their authors. Americans have reacted to this by going 'off Broadway', and now this is where most of the dramatic energy lies. Great Britain is beginning to follow suit. The development is a healthy one, because it means that playwrights, writing for tiny audiences, are able to get away from commercial demands to fulfil artistic ones. This kind of theatre sees as much rubbish as the commercial theatre; but the good writers have more chance. However, the playwrights who dominated the immediate post-war scene—Tennessee Williams, Arthur Miller and, to a lesser extent, William Inge—had to fight for recognition in the commercial theatre.

TENNESSEE WILLIAMS (PS. THOMAS LANIER WILLIAMS, 1911) was born in Mississippi. His father was a salesman who was probably (accord-ing to a gossipy book Williams' mother wrote) a mean drunk; at all events, in his childhood he knew more anger and alienation than love. After much struggle to establish himself, Williams found an agent who believed in him, and in 1945, with *The Glass Menagerie*, he became accepted. His persistent theme is the agonized, even shriek-ing alienation of violent and crippled eccentrics: homosexuals, madmen, sex-driven women. The air his characters naturally breathe is that of romantic hysteria; without it they would wilt and die immediately. He combines lush vulgarity with lyrical despair to produce plays of undeniable power. But their language is not enduring, and they fade in the mind. He is adept at presenting nerve-shot situations, but has never written a successful play of reconciliation. His characters are happiest at not being happy, and when his plots contrive to satisfy them they protest by being totally unconvincing: a tribute to the power of his depiction of despair. Williams shows sensitive people as being ravished by the brutal and materialistic demands of society. But this is not genuine social comment: his sensitives are too often hopeless and irremediably crippled neurotics, and 'society' is represented by persons whose greed or lust or dishonesty is pathological. He loves the grotesque, and in effect he pays tribute to it by lyrically depicting hells on earth.

His first success, *The Glass Menagerie*, is his tenderest and best play: this account of a slightly crippled girl's coming briefly out of the world of dreams she lives in—symbolized by a menagerie of glass animals—is moving within a non-pathological realm. The rest of Williams' plays are set in a pathological world that does not often allow the spectator to visualize his own world—equally tragic—that is not entirely peopled by freaks. *A Streetcar Named Desire* (1947) almost succeeds, but Blanche, its heroine, destroyed and driven into madness by the hideous Stanley, is herself too impossible to gain full sympathy. *The Rose Tattoo* (1951), about Gulf-coast Sicilians, declines into sentimentality and a false vitality. *Camino Real* (1953), a fantasy, is another failure: it has theatre-life, as a clever rhetoric, but a cool reading exposes its pretensions—and reveals the meagreness of linguistic resource which is Williams' basic weakness. The more realistic *Cat on a Hot Tin Roof* (1955), dealing with the frustrations and anguishes of a Southern family, contains some marvellously evocative individual portraits—Big Daddy, his alcoholic son Brick who cannot face up to the homosexual component in himself, his wife Maggie—but does not altogether succeed in setting them against each other. This is a play in which Williams, not dishonestly, tries to suggest the possibility of future happiness (for Maggie and the too detached Brick); but it remains unconvincing. In the Gothic *Suddenly Last Summer* (1958) the homosexual 'poet' Edward, the unseen hero, is eaten by the boys he has used (a typically vague allusion to Orpheus being devoured by furies). His mother, in order to inherit his fortune, is glad to submit her daughter-in-law to a lobotomy. The language here is particularly thin, and the intentions confused; but there are moments of power. More recently Williams has written *Sweet Bird of Youth* (1959), the factitious *The Night of the Iguana* (1961) and *The Eccentricities of a Nightingale* (1965). Williams, gifted as a realist, has chosen—and on balance the choice is probably a correct one—to work in more or less expressionist modes. This leads him into some difficulties with language; but he does gain poetic, and sometimes heartrending, effects from his juxtapositions of characters and settings. He is a writer as flawed as any of his heroes; but more of a genius, too, than any of them. In 1969 he joined the Roman Catholic Church, perhaps as a substitute for the writing of plays, which had served (he has said) as 'therapy' to reduce tension. He is the author of a not outstanding novel, *The Roman Spring of Mrs. Stone* (1950), many short stories (*One Arm*, 1948; *Hard Candy*, 1954) and some fuzzy, mystical verse that is collected in *In the Winter of Cities* (1956 rev. 1964). He has not really, as a writer, faced up to the problem that obsesses him: sexual anguish.

ARTHUR MILLER (1915), who was born in New York City, has by contrast more of the journalist and social reformer than of the poet in him, but is as important as Williams. Miller began to write plays while at the University of Michigan, won prizes, and after graduation (1938) worked for the Federal Theatre Project. (This, which lasted from the autumn of 1935 to the summer of 1939, was the first American state-sponsored theatre project, a typically New Deal enterprise which invented such devices as the Living Newspaper, and encouraged Negro theatre; it was suppressed by reactionary elements in Congress.) *Situation Normal* (1944) was a rather flat and starry-eyed piece of reportage about military life; *Focus* (1955) is an ironic novel about anti-semitism: the protagonist is an anti-semitic Gentile who gets demoted when a new pair of spectacles makes him appear Jewish; but he is slow to learn the lesson, and when he finally does his transformed character is unconvincing.

In 1947, with the strong drama of *All My Sons* (1947), Miller established himself as, with Tennessee Williams, America's leading young dramatist. This is a straightforward, traditional play, which shows the strong influence of Ibsen (whose *Enemy of the People* Miller adapted in 1951). Joe Keller has in the war allowed some faulty engine parts to be sent to the air force, which has meant the deaths of some pilots; his partner has been wrongly blamed and imprisoned, while he was exonerated. Now, after the war, his son discovers his guilt—and that his own elder brother, having realized their father's guilt, has allowed himself to be killed as a kind of expiation. Joe, after trying to wriggle out of his responsibility in every way, kills himself when he realizes that those dead pilots were all his sons. . . . This is a good, well constructed play, but nothing out of the ordinary.

Far superior is *Death of a Salesman* (1949), which was directed by Elia Kazan (q.v.) and had the excellent Lee J. Cobb in the leading role. Willy Loman, who is presented with great compassion, is perhaps still the most vivid example on the modern stage of the 'other directed' man of modern industrial societies that David Riesman postulated in his (and collaborators') *The Lonely Crowd*: the social character who is controlled by the expectations of other people, the 'marketing character' of Erich Fromm (who has influenced Riesman), who becomes anxious when he lapses from the standards of selling himself to other people. Like all his kind, Willy preaches the bourgeois virtues to his family; but in reality he accepts dishonesty. But Miller shows him as possessing a humanity that, deep down, recognizes this. His suicide is genuinely tragic.

The Crucible (1953), about the notorious Salem witch trials, was performed at a time when witch-hunting for communists was prevalent in the United States. This is a play about commitment, and the French movie script was written by Sartre (q.v.): condemned to die for witchcraft, John Proctor confesses to it to save his life—but then refuses to live, and thus triumphs.

In 1956 Miller married the film-actress Marilyn Monroe, and became the object of a good deal of publicity which did not help his creative life. He wrote a film for her, *The Misfits* (1961), which is presented in its published form as a kind of novel; this is interesting, but its attempt to show how innocence (Miller had seen Marilyn Monroe as innocent) is destroyed was vitiated by the nature of the medium itself. The ending is sentimental—and Miller does not really suffer from sentimentality. He and Marilyn Monroe were divorced in 1960.

After the Fall (1964) is overtly autobiographical: Maggie is clearly a representation of Marilyn Monroe (who had recently died) and Quentin is the 'intellectual' Miller. It is as good as any of Miller's previous plays, and is most notable for its maturity—a maturity beyond that of any commercial audience—and its refusal to find easy or glib solutions. In *Incident at Vichy* (1964), a semi-documentary, about the Nazis' treatment of various Frenchmen, he seemed to be marking time.

It is in Miller that 'social realism', in the most intelligent, Ibsenian sense, has found its best and most compassionate playwright. The future of this kind of play, which requires audiences more educated than most at present are, could well be in his hands.

WILLIAM INGE (1913–1973), who was born in Kansas, is more conventional in technique than either Williams or Miller; his plays are not as ambitious, but he has successfully portrayed midwest people, intelligently revealing them as they are beneath the public surface. *Come Back, Little Sheba* (1950) is one of the best of modern plays on the subject of alcoholism. *Picnic* (1953) and *Bus Stop* (1955) became famous in movie versions; in the latter the old technical device of bringing strangers fortuitously together is given new life by fine characterization and convincing dialogue. *The Dark at the Top of the Stairs* (1958) is that darkness into which both the child of a family and its parents dare not—whatever they pretend—climb up to. *A Loss of Roses* (1960) was a disappointment: the relationship between a mother and her son clearly springs from a psychiatric textbook rather than from a human situation. Inge is perhaps not more than a useful playwright (in the sense that Telemann and Hindemith are useful composers)—but this is something considerable in its own right.

The off-Broadway movement has not yet brought many playwrights to prominence; but prominence may not be what the real theatre needs. However, three dramatists who have graduated from this milieu to some commercial success should be mentioned. The best known, EDWARD ALBEE (1928), is not necessarily superior, although his *Who's Afraid of Virginia Woolf?* (1963) is more substantial than anything so far written by JACK GELBER (1932) or JACK RICHARDSON (1934). Albee is unusual in that he seems to have nothing in him of American optimism, and actually began—with *The Zoo Story* (1959)—with an example of the Theatre of the Absurd (q.v. 2). Even so, this brilliant dialogue does end both violently and sentimentally: a gesture, it seems, to the American insistence on one or the other (in the absence of actual Utopian choruses). Its theme— a young homosexual inveigles an ordinary bourgeois into killing him—foreshadowed that of its successors, except for *The Death of Bessie Smith* (1959) and *The American Dream* (1960). The adventure into realism of the former has a shocking subject: the real reasons for the refusal of a hospital for whites to admit the injured blues singer, whom they could have saved. But it is no more than a dreary and uninteresting protest piece. *The American Dream* abandons realism, and is better. This is a send-up of America in terms of its clichés, beautifully heard and reproduced, that resembles Karl Kraus (q.v. 2) even more than Ionesco (q.v. 2), upon whose techniques it greatly depends.

Who's Afraid of Virginia Woolf? (1963) is superbly inventive theatre, but is ultimately sterile inasmuch as it amounts to an alyrical assault not merely on marriage but on all heterosexuality. Or that is how I read it. But its dialogue is masterly in its capture—or deadly parody—of a certain kind of upper middle-class Americanese; and throughout there is a yearning for understanding. *Tiny Alice* (1965) is a kind of disguised well-made play. A story of the richest woman in the world who seduces, marries and destroys a Catholic lay-brother, it works well on the stage, but reads badly except to critics set on interpreting its incredibly complicated symbolism. Once again, the real theme is the horror any man lays in store for himself by having truck with the evil trickster Woman. But for some the mood and language raise the play above this. In *A Delicate Balance* (1966) Albee returns to more realistic family horrors, but the message is similar. Albee does not of course load the dice against women, or make his men paragons—he is too intelligent; it is simply that one gets a strong sense, from his plays, that for him femininity is the ultimate destroyer and spoiler of happiness. But the greatly inferior William Burroughs (q.v.) is completely (and stupidly) explicit on this point, whereas it would certainly be doing Albee an injustice to suggest that this is his rational view. Albee has made excellent adaptations of Carson McCullers' *The Ballad of the Sad Café* (q.v., 1963) and *Malcolm* (1965), James Purdy's (q.v.) novel.

Jack Gelber's *The Connection* (1960) vacillates too uncertainly between realism and expressionism—Gelber is not sure whether he wants to protest against the drug laws or to depict a group of junkies waiting for their fix—but is nevertheless a vivid and accurate presentation of people who simply don't want anything to do with society. Its form is interesting: a jazz quartet improvises on the stage, two film cameramen become involved in the action; the aimless dialogue is authentic. *The Apple* (1961), an improvisation, departs more radically from the conventional theatre, but is less successful. *On Ice* (1965), a novel about a hipster called Manny, is surprisingly low in energy and humour.

Jack Richardson's *The Prodigal* (1960), an acerb and witty treatment of the Orestes theme, came from off Broadway; so did his *Gallows Humour* (1961). *The Prison Life of Harris Philmore* (1961) is a novel.

Another American dramatist who has attracted attention by serious work is PADDY CHAYEFSKY (1923). He began as a television playwright, and became famous when *Marty* (1953) was filmed, with Ernest Borgnine. *The Bachelor Party* (1954), a touching but not quite unsentimental play, was also filmed. Chayefsky was attacked for his 'tape recorder' realism, and has unwisely tried in his stage plays for symbolic effects which do not really suit him. For *The Tenth Man*, his best play, he combined an authentic Bronx setting with the Jewish legend of the Dybbuk.

IV

GERTRUDE STEIN (1874–1946), born of a wealthy family near Pittsburgh, was not altogether modern—she has even been put forward as one who belonged essentially to the 'sunset phase' of the nineteenth century—but she understood the importance of modernity. Her writings were not, as Sherwood Anderson (q.v.) saw, necessarily very important in themselves; but they provided incomparable signposts for others more imaginatively gifted. Gertrude Stein studied at Radcliffe under, among others, Santayana and Moody (qq.v.); the most important influence on her there, however, was William James. She planned to become a psychologist, and so began medicine, including brain anatomy, at Johns Hopkins. In 1903 she went abroad, learnt about art from her brother Leo, who—though he kept in the background—was always a better art critic than she, and set about establishing herself as an expatriate queen and patron of artists. She bought the work of Picasso, Braque, Matisse and others, and amassed a famous collection. She lived with her secretary and companion Alice B. Toklas in Paris for the rest of her life (except for a period during the war, when they lived in Vichy), only returning to America once—for a lecture tour in 1934. Her early books appeared so difficult that she had to publish or guarantee them herself. But when she had acquired fame as a personality, through both her *salon* and her assumption of the headship of the *avant garde* of the Twenties, she was able to write a popular book: *The Autobiography of Alice B. Toklas* (1933), which purported to be her life as told by her friend. She repeated this with *Everybody's Autobiography* (1937). Gertrude Stein encouraged Anderson, Hemingway, Wilder, Fitzgerald (qq.v.) and others gifted, talented—and mediocre. No poet gained anything from her example. But she was certainly regarded as the most influential English-speaking writer in Paris in the early Twenties—Pound ('Gertrude Stein liked him', said Miss Stein in *Toklas*, 'but did not find him amusing. She said he was a village explainer, excellent if you were a village, but if you were not, not') and Ford Madox Ford (qq.v.) were also there. In her last years she and Miss Toklas entertained many American soldiers; she had known the Americans of two wars, and wrote of them in the popular *Wars I Have Seen* (1944) and in *Brewsie and Willie* (1946). This latter was her last; it reconstructs the language of the G.I. Joes of 1944–5 with brilliance and affection as well as sentimentality.

Apart from her popular works, which are not only witty and readable but also sometimes egocentric and surprisingly arch, *Three Lives* (1909), and some posthumously printed earlier writings, Gertrude Stein's books are hard to read: child-like but repetitious, monotonous and not always justifiably inscrutable. It was after *Three Lives* (her best work) that she began to evolve the style for which she is known. By that time she had come to understand what Pablo Picasso and his friends were trying to do in painting: to elevate the picture itself over its 'subject'. Thus, for her, words became objects-in-themselves. Meaning became an overtone. Picasso and the others concentrated on *the painting*; she concentrated on *the writing*. (This offered, perhaps, a convenient enough way of evading the issue of self-appraisal.) Her teacher William James had 'discovered' the 'stream of consciousness'; as a psychologist he was interested in the flux itself—whereas she was more interested in the moment of 'the complete actual present': in the capturing of instants. One of the intentions of her repetitions is to convey an illusion like that of a motion picture; each sentence is a 'frame', and differs only slightly from its predecessor. Once the novelty has worn off, this tends, of course, to be as boring as exposing each frame of a movie not for a fraction of a second but for several minutes. But perhaps it had to be done. Gertrude Stein had the effrontery and self-confidence to do it.

She was also against the 'objective' or transcendent self: the self of which James claimed psychology could give no account. In that hopeful, Utopian manner common to many Americans she believed in the present—and thought the future was a rosy one. Perhaps such optimism requires to ignore sequence, structure and what I have called, in relation to Dreiser, the grain of life. The substantial, or transcendent, or objective self—what Wyndham Lewis (q.v.) thought of as 'the eye of the artist'—did not interest her any more than 'realism': she was peculiarly modern in this concentration on the qualities of objects, and in her opposition to 'stories'. She tried to get rid of narrative and put into its place a technique of extracting the essential quality of a thing or person. For example, this piece called 'A Cloth' from *Tender Buttons* (1914): 'Enough cloth is plenty and more, more is almost enough for that and besides if there is no more spreading is there plenty of room for it. Any occasion shows the best way'. Witty, intelligent—but trivial, and, when in bulk, tiresome. . . . This was the trap into which she fell. Not perhaps wishing her imagination to be free to investigate her personality, she allowed herself to create abstractions that were inexorably separated from life or anything like it. *Ida, a Novel* (1941), for example, is really 'about' all that is least important in its protagonist's life—or at any rate it tells us nothing that is significant. The mimetic or representational was for Gertrude Stein a vulgarity and a sentimentality. Her writing tried to be 'abstract' in the sense that painting is abstract. It is curious that of her modern non-representational or would-be non-representational successors (Olsen, Creeley, qq.v. etc., etc.) only the American poet Robert Duncan has shown any real interest in her; but he is an 'intellectual', as she was; the others cannot really be described as such.

Gertrude Stein was in her own way, from her 'home town' of Paris, an American pioneer. She saw how American procedures—indecorous and adventurous—differed from English, which are neat and traditional because 'Nothing is perplexing if there is an island. The special sign of this is in dusting'. In other words, she saw the right direction for American literature. But she became increasingly megalomanic and remote, and it is not strange that she early turned from novelist to critic (demonstrator of how things ought to be done). *Things As They Are* (1950), a straightforward (though not 'obscene') treatment of a lesbian theme, written in 1903, gives us some clue as to why she chose the course she did. It is fortunate that she wrote *Three Lives* (1909) before she made this choice, for it is a masterpiece—as well as being the most accessible of all her writings. There are hints of the future manner, but it has not degenerated into a method and become tiresome. The book consists of three stories of women, all of whom are defeated by life. Outstanding is 'Melanctha', about the daughter of a Mulatto mother and a Negro father who hates her: this, as has many times been pointed out, is almost the first American fiction to treat a Negro as a human being. The vigour and scope of this book make it clear that Gertrude Stein abandoned imaginative for critical fiction for reasons other than experiential capacity.

*

No fiction could have been further from Gertrude Stein's than that of SINCLAIR LEWIS (1885–1951); if she was super-literary, he was never more than super-journalistic. He is one of the worst writers to win a Nobel Prize (he was the first American to do so, 1930), and the worst American writer to achieve fame on a more than merely popular level. Yet although he was in no way as serious or as good as Gertrude Stein, he was in a certain sense as historically important as her. The son of a doctor of Sauk City, Minnesota, he went to Yale, became a journalist, and fell under the influence of the journalist H. L. MENCKEN (1880–1956), an important debunker and satirist who despite his crudities was a magnificent destroyer of hypocrisy, cant and pretentiousness. Lewis wrote a number of realistic and partially satirical novels, but did not achieve recognition until *Main Street* (1920). This attacks Sauk City (here called Gopher Prairie) and every similar town in America on very much the same lines as Mencken and the critic George Jean Nathan (1882–1958) were currently doing in their magazine *The Smart Set*—but rather more ambiguously. For Lewis makes his symbol of freedom, Carol Kennicott, return to the dull doctor husband she has walked out on; not only that, but we can now see very easily that Carol Kennicott herself is an extremely sentimental and middlebrow creature—she is merely a bit smarter than the others. Lewis followed this with *Babbitt* (1922), a portrait of an average American business man which its readers took as satirical at the time but which may now be seen as loving as well as critical. Still, this added a new word to the language. *Arrowsmith* (1925) is about a scientist, and *Elmer Gantry* (1927), by far his best novel, is an almost Dickensian extravaganza about the attractions of phoney religion and a fake preacher who takes advantage of them. *Dodsworth* (1929) is a sentimental novel on the obligatory theme of the American being educated in Europe. The books of Lewis' last twenty years are more overtly in favour of what he began by satirizing; but the tendency was always there.

Lewis appealed to so vast a readership because he was 'safe'. As he confessed, he had written of Babbitt with love and not with hate. He could oppose nothing to the materialism of the small towns he portrayed. He was intellectually feeble. His powers of characterization were nil. What, then, were his virtues? First, he had a masterly journalistic grasp of his material: he really knew about the society of which he wrote. And if he did not really hate it, he none the less depicted it with vitality. He owed something to Wells, but most of all to Dickens. For essentially he was a caricaturist of great energy and zest. His readers were easily able to kid themselves that they were not like Babbitt; but the accuracy of his fine detail still fascinates— and in Elmer Gantry he has created a monster of Dickensian proportions and of some complexity.

*

WILLIAM FAULKNER (1897–1962), born in New Albany, Mississippi, and raised in Oxford in the same State, won the Nobel Prize nineteen years after Lewis, and was the fourth American to do so (if Eliot is regarded as British); he was incomparably the better writer; he is regarded by some, in fact, as the greatest of all American novelists.

Faulkner joined the Royal Canadian Air Force in 1918, after the American Air Force had rejected him because of his smallness (5 feet 5 inches); he did not see any active service, but was able to enter the University of Mississippi, for which he could not qualify academically, as a veteran. He stayed there for just over a year, and then took a variety of jobs. He worked on a newspaper and in 1924 published a book of poor, imitative verse called *The Marble Faun*. His first novel, *Soldiers Pay* (1926), published with the help of his friend Sherwood Anderson (q.v.), *fin de siècle* in style, is about a dying soldier's return. *Mosquitoes* (1927) is a mannered satirical book; no one would notice it now if it had not been Faulkner's second novel. In 1929 he published his first important novel, *Sartoris*. For this he drew on his family history (his great grandfather's colourful life was ended by a bullet fired by a rival only eight years before Faulkner's birth), and created the domain for which he became famous: Yoknapatawpha County, county seat Jefferson. This place has a relation to Lafayette County, and Jefferson has a relation to Oxford (and other towns, such as Faulkner's birthplace, New Albany). It is also Faulkner's 'world': a world as untidy as the real one, and as vivid as any created by a novelist in this century. Within this world, with certain inconsistencies that make it more rather than less convincing, Faulkner traced the decline of certain families (the Compson, Sartoris, Benbow and McCaslin families) and the rise of the Snopes. The scheme is a vast map of Faulkner's imagination: it blurs somewhat at the edges, and there are undefined areas; but much is illuminated and illuminating. Faulkner is an example of a writer who managed, for a period—of about twelve or fourteen years—to keep his powerful imagination under control. His genealogies and complex accounts of the 'history' of his region were essential parts of this process. He had to bring his internal world into line with the external world. In the end, and understandably, he gave way under the strain of maintaining his gloomy but not life-denying vision: his speech of acceptance of the Nobel Prize is dutiful, a series of clichés almost worthy of a politician, unworthy of the creative writer. The view implied in Faulkner's works is not the view expressed by the winner of the Nobel Prize: '. . . man will not merely endure: he will prevail . . . because he has a soul, a spirit capable of compassion and sacrifice and endurance'. The view of the best work is more sombre. It has been well summed up as follows: '. . . the Faulkner novel is designedly a silo of compressed sin, from which life emerges as fermentation'. Faulkner believed in no system; he was at his best when he tried to discover the patterns of his internal world—this is of course, in part, a result of the impact the external world made on him. The values of Christianity will do for him; but there is no evidence that he believed that God had ever intervened in human affairs. His late novel *A Fable* (1954), an attempt to re-enact Christ's Passion against the background of the First World War, is imaginatively an atrocious failure: laboured, its bitterness misplaced, its use of the Christ-theme palpably erroneous because of Faulkner's clear lack of belief in it.

His first wholly characteristic novel was *The Sound and the Fury* (1929). Here the Compson family are shown degenerating, fallen from their former gentility, leading a doomed life. The story is told through the consciousnesses of three members of this family: Benjy the idiot, the sensitive Quentin and the twisted, mean Jason. Quentin kills himself through shame at his incestuous desire for his sister Candace; Jason's is a tale of pettiness and greed. A final section centres on the Negro servant, Dilsey, whose goodness and whole-someness contrast with the horror of the Compsons' decline.

Faulkner made the interior monologue his chief technical device. He enters too bodily into his characters—white, black, successful, defeated—ever to speak confidently of men prevailing. . . . His world is infinitely more complicated than the platitudinous one in which such utterances can be made.

Faulkner's best work was written between *The Sound and the Fury* and *Intruder in the Dust* (1948), the story of how a Negro is saved from lynching by a white boy who has grown into understanding and humanity. After this—which is itself seriously vitiated by the intro-duction of a character who will insist on interpolating his unconvinc-ing theories about race relations into the narrative—although none of his books is without some virtue, Faulkner tended to make optimistic intellectual inferences from his earlier works and elevate those into a kind of moral system. The three finest novels of all came early in Faulkner's career: *The Sound and the Fury*, *As I Lay Dying* (1930) and *Light in August* (1932). *As I Lay Dying* deals with the last journey of Addie Bundren: in her coffin as her family—her husband, her three legitimate sons, her bastard and a pregnant daughter—carry her to Jefferson. When there her husband finds himself new teeth and a new wife. This is a great novel because it reads perfectly as a realistic novel, and yet its symbolic possibilities are infinite. *Light in August* sets the bastard Joe Christmas, who may be half Negro but in any case feels and behaves as if he were, amongst a strict Calvinist community. This book touches, more closely than any of its predecessors, on one of Faulkner's main themes: that the doom and decline of the white man springs from his inability to treat the Negro as a fellow human being. This conviction—that all people should treat others as human beings—is one of the mainsprings of Faulkner's creative impulse. It is not 'political', but merely human. But there are characters as primitive and evil, in Faulkner's books, as some Southern demagogues with whom we are familiar: he penetrates their minds with his understanding, too. His job is not to satirize or to make judgements: he presents people as they are, and he can do so. Although *Light in August* is a grim book, it is a positive one because it is made clear, from the beginning to the end, that Joe Christmas' tragedy is his refusal to take or give love, and that he got into this condition because he was originally denied love.

Absalom, Absalom! (1936) brings back Quentin Compson, who is preparing for suicide in *The Sound and the Fury*, but only as narrator. The story is of Thomas Sutpen, the 'demon' poor white who has ambitions to achieve aristocracy and destroys everyone who gets in his way. Sutpen marries a planter's daughter and they have a son, but he abandons them when he discovers they have Negro blood. He goes to Yoknapatawpha County, obtains land by dishonest means, marries again, and has a son and a daughter. Later his son Henry goes to the University of Mississippi and meets and admires Charles, not knowing who he is. Charles falls in love with his own half-sister, Judith—and it is Henry who kills him when he learns about his Negro blood. Then Henry disappears. Sutpen is obsessed with begetting a male heir, and when he abandons a poor white girl on his land because she bears him a daughter her grandfather kills him with a scythe. Ultimately it is only Sutpen's Negro heirs who live on his land; in the end, finding the aged Henry come back and hidden in his own house, one of them burns it down. Thus Faulkner gives his most complete version of the doom of the South; once again he spells out the message: the fatal flaw is its refusal to accept the Negro on equal terms. This working out of the flaw is presented with passion, for Faulkner truthfully shows it to come of a horrible innocence. A Marxist explanation of the South simply will not do—and it is Faulkner who shows this most clearly. It would be more comforting if it would do. To have to report that this attitude to other human beings arises from an innocence is agonizing; but Faulkner, himself a Southerner, found the courage to tell the truth. There is a sense in which he had earned the clichés of his Nobel Prize acceptance. What else could he say but read *Absalom, Absalom!*? *The Unvanquished* (1938) linked episodes previously published as short stories into a novel about the fortunes of the Sartoris family in the Civil War. There are many more short stories, collected in *These Thirteen* (1931), *Doctor Martino* (1934), *Go Down Moses* (1942), *Knight's Gambit* (1949) and then in *Collected Stories* (1950). *The Wild Palms* (1939) relates the defeat, through love, of a New Orleans doctor who performs an abortion on his mistress.

The Hamlet (1940), *The Town* (1957) and *The Mansion* (1960) are a trilogy on the Snopes family; the first part is the best, but the second two contain the most humorous writing of Faulkner's latter years.

Faulkner is a very difficult, even forbidding writer. He is also, perhaps largely because of the strain and responsibility imposed upon him by his concern with the nature of evil, the most uneven of all the major writers of our time. His metaphors and similes can seem forced and even jejune. He can be pretentiously complex. He can be portentous and confused. But his best work is not more difficult than it has to be. Those long and intricate sentences are not too long and intricate when they are describing the processes of a mind. Few techniques more effective in doing so have been evolved. The subject of the beauty and innocence contained in evil is a difficult and paradoxical one, which can lead to misunderstandings. The sheer energy of Faulkner's stories of perversion, horror and despair gives the lie to those who would accuse him of doing the dirty on life itself, for his own creative ends.

*

F. SCOTT FITZGERALD (1896–1940), born at St. Paul, Minnesota, was the laureate of the Jazz age, of what Gertrude Stein called 'the lost generation'. These were people who were 'so deliberately and determinedly cynical that [they] became naïve'. Fitzgerald belonged to this age, but he knew that it was all wrong. In *The Great Gatsby* (1925), he achieved a balance between empathy and analysis, and produced the most memorable and accurate description of the American Twenties—a devastating criticism that is none the less rich and romantic, for Fitzgerald was an out-and-out romantic, and it was in large measure his offended romanticism that produced his disgust.

He began as very much one of his age. His family was prosperous, and when he went to Princeton in 1913 he was anxious to distinguish himself in every field including football: in 1920 he published his first successful novel, *This Side of Paradise*, which is about Princeton. Here Fitzgerald romantically sets his (immature) notion of true love against the corrupting power of money; the novel's strength, apart from its brilliant descriptive passages, lies in Fitzgerald's convincing grasp of what is unselfish in his initially snobbish and hedonistic hero. Fitzgerald had married a beautiful girl, Zelda, and he now began to live it up in one plush hotel after another, going from party to party, consuming himself rapidly but of course, in his twenties, imperceptibly. Zelda wanted to be a ballet dancer—she was very good, but she had started too late, and was not mentally stable —and she insisted on competing with Fitzgerald, which upset him, tearing him in two directions. Eventually she entered an institution; she was in one—in America—when she was burned to death in an accidental fire in 1947. Fitzgerald, earning a lot of money but increasingly in debt, wrote two volumes of short stories, a novel— *The Beautiful and Damned* (1922)—and a play before his first masterpiece, *The Great Gatsby*. The action takes place in the valley of ashes, beneath the huge eyes of Doctor T. J. Eckleburg (an advertisement). The story is told by Nick Carroway, a device that gives Fitzgerald the precise distance he needs between himself and his material. Poor Jay Gatz from Dakota quickly becomes one of the rich ('They are different from you and me. They possess and enjoy early, and it does something to them, makes them soft where we are hard, and cynical where we are trustful, in a way that, unless you were born rich, it is very difficult to understand') because he wants to win back Daisy Buchanan, Nick's cousin. After an affair with Jay when he was an army lieutenant, she had married the brutal, materialistic proto-fascist, Tom Buchanan—a prophetic portrait. Through Nick Gatsby meets Daisy again, and is able to make her his mistress. Tom takes a garage proprietor's wife for his mistress; her jealous husband locks her up, she runs out into the road—and is killed by Daisy, who does not stop. Gatsby takes the responsibility and Tom tells his own mistress's husband, Wilson, that it was Gatsby who killed her and drove on. Wilson shoots Gatsby in his swimming-pool, and then turns the gun on himself.

The Great Gatsby is another of those seminal books that manage to exist simultaneously and convincingly on both the realistic and the symbolic plane. Fitzgerald depicts the rich society into which Gatsby hoists himself as empty of all but putridity; the object of his simple romantic dreams, Daisy, is no more than a treacherous whore without the discrimination or inclination to diagnose the evil in her cruel and stupid husband. But Gatsby, as is often and rightly pointed out, comes, 'divided between power and dream', to represent America itself, and he (Nick says) 'turned out all right at the end; it is what preyed on Gatsby, what foul dust floated in the wake of his dreams that temporarily closed out my interest in the abortive sorrows and short-winded elations of men'. Fitzgerald is able to see Gatsby as both ex-criminal, vulgar member of the *nouveau riche*, and as a dreamer: as the man who had believed in Daisy's kiss so fervently that he had dedicated his whole being to what he thought it represented. In this way Gatsby embodies the American dream, which will (Fitzgerald implies) founder on its preference of appearance to reality.

Tender is the Night (1934; rev. 1951) is the love story of Dick Diver, psychiatrist, and his rich patient Nicole Warren. This is a more personal, more autobiographical book (for Nicole's mental illness he obviously drew on his experience of Zelda's); it does not have the universality of *The Great Gatsby*. It is none the less a masterpiece. The manner in which sick Nicole attracts Dick, and how she then corrupts him, is truly tragic. He loses his sense of vocation and becomes merely charming. Even though mentally ill and utterly dependent when she is sick, Nicole is somehow superior, the victor: she destroys her husband because in their marriage there is a tacit understanding that he is being paid for staying with her. In the end Dick returns to America, to—it is implied—rot away and waste his substance.

The Thirties were bad years for Fitzgerald. He worked in Hollywood, drank too much, behaved in such a manner as to give inferior men the opportunity to pity him, and almost stopped writing. At thirty-nine, in 1936, he experienced what he himself called a crack-up: Edmund Wilson (q.v.) edited the interesting notebooks, papers and essays describing this nervous breakdown in the volume *The Crack-up* (1945): why, Fitzgerald asked himself, had he gone so far as to have become identified with all he loathed and pitied. He had a daughter by Zelda, and it is clear that he desperately wanted to appear to her as a good and decent father—and that he felt he could not do so. Luckily for his personal happiness he met a journalist, Sheilah Graham, who sweetened his difficult final years, and helped him to get himself into a fit state to attempt his last novel, *The Last Tycoon* (1941). Fitzgerald died, after two heart attacks, before he could finish it. Essentially it is a self-portrait: Monroe Stahr, a film-producer at the end of his rope, tries to struggle on although he no longer believes in life. It is clear that Fitzgerald's alcoholism and involvement with commerce had not weakened his powers, and if this had been finished it might be safe to agree with those critics who find it his best novel. Fitzgerald wrote many short stories, of varying merit; there is a selection of eighteen of the best of them in *The Stories of F. Scott Fitzgerald* (1951).

ERNEST HEMINGWAY (1898–1961) also came from the midwest— he was the son of an Illinois doctor—and, as Fitzgerald had done, but to much greater point, he sat at the feet of Gertrude Stein in Paris. As a young man he made many hunting and fishing expeditions;

his descriptions of these activities were one of the high points of his writing. Hemingway was a reporter in Kansas City, volunteered as an ambulance driver and was wounded in Italy in 1917. He served with the Italian infantry until the Armistice. In Paris he came to know Gertrude Stein, Ford Madox Ford and Ezra Pound (qq.v.), all of whom encouraged him. (His memoirs of his Paris years were published posthumously in *A Moveable Feast*, 1964. This is an example of Hemingway at his worst: self-parodic, arch, untruthful.) His early short stories were collected in *In Our Time* (1925). The tedious *The Torrents of Spring* (1926) parodied Sherwood Anderson's (q.v.) style—a style from which Hemingway had already appropriated what he wanted. *The Sun Also Rises* (1926), called *Fiesta* in Great Britain, his first novel, is his best. This was followed by the short stories *Men Without Women* (1927) and the novel *A Farewell to Arms* (1929); the short story collection *Winner Takes Nothing* (1933) was Hemingway's last book of account.

Hemingway was famous for his style, his four marriages (only the final one, lasting from 1944 until his death, took), and his various sporting exploits. The record is not very clear on his prowess as a sportsman. It seems that he was not always as good as he said or thought he was. When he went to the front in the Spanish Civil War he nearly killed someone with a grenade, and was regarded as a nuisance. But he could fish and he had enthusiasm for bullfighting. During most of the Thirties Hemingway lived in Key West in Florida. After the Second World War, during which he was a correspondent with the Fourth Division of the First Army, he lived on an estate near Havana, Cuba, until the Castro revolution. After this he settled in Idaho. But he was already mentally and physically ill, and in 1961 he shot himself. After 1933 his main publications were: *To Have and Have Not* (1937), *For Whom the Bell Tolls* (1940), on the Spanish Civil War, the badly received *Across the River and into the Trees* (1950), *The Old Man and the Sea* (1952), all novels, and *The Green Hills of Africa* (1935), on big game hunting. *The Fifth Column*, a hollow and cliché-ridden play about a newspaperman in Spain, was included in his collected short stories: *The Fifth Column and the First Forty-nine Stories* (1938). A posthumously issued, excruciating novel, *Islands in the Stream* (1970), is best ignored.

Hemingway, especially the late Hemingway, has been an over-rated writer; but this does not mean that he was not a good one. The earliest influence on him, RING LARDNER (1885–1933), whose style he was imitating at school, deserves a paragraph to himself.

Lardner was better known as a sports columnist than as a short-story writer. He did not fully realize his genius, but he was the first to listen properly to and carefully reproduce the speech of the lower classes, the speech of people who went to prize fights and baseball matches. He refrained from judgement, and his idea of what was comic was also very often (as he knew) tragic; he missed greatness because there was just too much of the casual about his misanthropy. His lunatic short plays anticipate the Theatre of the Absurd, although they did not influence it.

The mature Hemingway of the Twenties owed the authenticity of his dialogue and his toughness to Lardner's example; in the latter the toughness was unassumed, in Hemingway it functioned laconically and truthfully as a guard against sentimentality.

Hemingway's style was self-conscious and carefully worked out, but it arose from a simplicity of feeling that he gradually lost. Apart from Lardner, its sources are in the economy of the newspaper report, the purity of Gertrude Stein, the honesty and lyricism of Anderson, the innocence of Huckleberry Finn, the simplicity of Stephen Crane (qq.v.). The Hemingway of the Twenties is complex; but he has not yet fallen prey to cliché or to noisy exhibitionism about 'action'. He is not as much of a 'man' as he would like to be: the hero of *The Sun Also Rises* has been emasculated by the war. But he lives to a code —the famous Hemingway code of 'grace under pressure'. For Jake Barnes there can be no meaning in life except to live gracefully. He cannot have the girl he loves, Brett; but she returns to him at the end because the novelist Robert Cohn, to whom she has briefly given herself, has nothing to offer—he is the victim of mere words and fine sentiments—and because she fears she will injure the bullfighter she loves if she stays with him. This is Hemingway's most moving novel, fine in characterization, pellucid in style, and contrasting without sentimentality the anguish of futility with the dignity of a few people's graciousness. *A Farewell to Arms* is poignant but the English nurse, Catherine Barkley, is quite unreal. Aside from Brett in *The Sun Also Rises*, whom he observes but upon whose qualities he does not comment, Hemingway could not create women. There was, it seems, a homosexual component in his nature which led him both to want to establish himself as masculine (i.e. not 'feminine'), and to make up soft, yielding, sweet women—too obviously the ideal complement for strong and hairy warriors. Catherine is the beginning of this line of girls, who get younger and more improbable as his heroes age along with him. But apart from this *A Farewell to Arms*—with its implied comments on the futility of war, its descriptions of battles, and its depiction of the state of mind of the hero—runs *The Sun Also Rises* very close.

The best short stories are in the first three collections. In them

Hemingway was getting nineteenth-century culture out of his system, and saluting a primitivistic, non-industrial kind of life in which males (the females are out except for purposes of comfort, and as something a man 'needs') must learn to live and die with courage and grace: people must behave well. The best stories, particularly those about Nick Adams, are laconic and as pure as spring water. Hemingway's fascination with death (he chose it rather than life at the end) was genuine, and he is especially good in describing encounters with death.

But in many ways he never grew up. The kind of badness of his posthumous novel reveals him to have been capable of fantasies of action so puerile that it is hard to believe the author of *Fiesta* could have perpetrated them. His longest novel, *For Whom the Bell Tolls*, has good passages, but is flawed as a novel by its meaningless and sentimental love affair. The symbolism of *The Old Man and the Sea* is portentous, its simplicity false. It is, it is true, a skilful performance, and—the Christian symbolism apart—a sincere one. It conveys Hemingway's message: life is futile, but we must still live it nobly and with courage. However, it is not fresh, but lucubrated; the words have not been drawn up from a deep well, but pondered and put together by 'Papa Hemingway'.

The message itself is not and never was much, of course. Hemingway will be valued, surely, for the discovery of a style that enabled him to make vivid, lyrical and piercingly accurate descriptions of graciousness and male companionship (as in the fishing trip in *The Sun Also Rises*). He is a moving writer, but it is an error to go to him for 'philosophy'.

THOMAS WOLFE (1900–38) was less gifted than Hemingway, and his failure to grow up was more comprehensive. But he cannot be ignored. He was born in Asheville, North Carolina, where his father made grave masonry and his mother ran a small hotel. A giant in height—he was six feet six inches tall—he poured out a gigantic torrent of thinly fictionalized autobiography which his publishers, first Maxwell Perkins of Scribners and then Edward C. Aswell of Harpers, edited into four books (themselves massive novels). He had graduated from the University of North Carolina and then gone to Harvard to try George Pierce Baker's (q.v.) course in playwriting. He took his first novel to Perkins in 1923, and between them they put it into shape—meanwhile Wolfe was an instructor of English at New York University. *Look Homeward Angel*, in which he appears as Eugene Gant, was published in 1929, and was immediately successful; it was followed by *Of Time and the River* (1935). In his next two novels, both posthumously published,

Gant becomes George Webber. Shortly after delivering the Webber manuscript Wolfe caught pneumonia; he died of a brain infection. Aswell edited and published the material Wolfe had left as *The Web and the Rock* (1939) and *You Can't Go Home Again* (1940). Since his death Wolfe's reputation has somewhat declined—no competent critic recommends him wholeheartedly—but he is still read. Clearly, for all his lack of self-discipline and failure to consider any pheno-menon or person except in the light of his own interests, he is a writer of some importance.

He is most important to the young. Go back to him after thirty and you will find yourself selecting; before thirty you take it all in. In the first novel Gant tells the story of his father and mother. Even as edited by Perkins it is badly, inflatedly written; but this does not seem to matter, because Wolfe does create an unforgettably vivid picture of a savagely quarrelling, mutually recriminative family. Probably he could not have done it in any other way. The continua-tion, and the unsuccessful attempt to cover the same ground more objectively in the Webber novels, tell his own story: of the search for success (rather than meaning), for a father (found in his editor Maxwell Perkins) and for a mother (found and finally repudiated in the stage designer Aileen Bernstein, almost twenty years older than himself). And yet through all the inchoateness something does emerge: the ghost of man trying to find, fumbling with, sometimes finding and using, his own self-expression. Wolfe is a romantic rather than a novelist: the author of a vast body of work that seeks to define the myth of the American artist. But he failed—except as a writer of fragments—because he could not altogether discipline Wolfe into the artist, could not sensitively enough separate the ego from the creativity. But for all Wolfe's adolescence, for all the egoism that he drags into his fiction, much of what his prose recreates —his childhood, his tortured romance with Mrs. Bernstein, his relationship with the homosexual Francis Starwick—is as vividly evoked as anywhere in the fiction of our century. It is often as paranoiac, adolescent and unpleasantly egocentric as Wolfe himself was; but it is of legendary proportions, and we do not forget it.

*

Not much of the proletarian literature that flourished during the depression of the early Thirties, and only subsided with the Stalinist purges, the Nazi-Soviet pact, and then (ironically) the alliance with Russia, has survived or deserves to. But there were important writers who sympathized with the proletarians without subscribing rigidly to their Marxist point of view. No writing that subscribes rigidly to any dogma (Christian, Marxist or whatever), where there is a choice, survives for long: this kind of writing is, after all, criticism, or propaganda in which the work of the resolutely non-dogmatic imagination may take only second place.

Chicago-born JOHN DOS PASSOS (1896–1971), whose grandfather was a Portuguese immigrant, had gained fame and flourished before the Depression, but his important work fits most appropriately in with, and even influenced, proletarian literature. He had grave faults; his retreat into conservatism after the Second World War is unconvincing and adds nothing to his literary stature—and he is most important as a technician. But whatever may spoil his work, of whatever period, it is never dogmatism or rigidity.

After graduating from Harvard (1916) Dos Passos saw service in France. His first book was an autobiographical novel about an ambulance driver: *One Man's Initiation—1917* (1920; rev. as *First Encounter*, 1945). His next, *Three Soldiers* (1921), was more characteristic, and although it does not incorporate his later technical innovations it does conveniently illustrate his strengths, weaknesses, and chief preoccupations. During the Twenties Dos Passos wrote plays incorporating 'movie' techniques, and he translated Blaise Cendrars (q.v. 2), whose panoramic methods of composition were to influence him considerably.

Three Soldiers takes three different men and traces the impact of war upon them: the optical worker Fuselli, who wants promotion; the farm-labourer Chrisfield, who only wants to go home; and the educated musician, Andrews. All are destroyed. Fuselli gets not promotion but syphilis. Chrisfield kills a sergeant and deserts. Andrews is unjustly sent to a labour battalion, escapes, is let down by his girl, and is eventually recaptured. He faces a bleak future (death or years of imprisonment), and the sheets of music he has composed blow away.

This is the real, gloomy Dos Passos. *Three Soldiers* was one of the first novels to describe the war as it really did affect people; those who thought it a fine thing, and patriotism meaningful, upbraided Dos Passos; but he manfully defended himself. The novel is vivid, and it manifests the nihilism from which Dos Passos guiltily suffered all his life: he feared anarchy for the obvious reasons, and was not an anarchist; but even more he feared the society for whose portrayal he became so famous: he feared for the survival of the individual. In *Three Soldiers* he shows the destruction of three men by society; this he really, and reasonably, believed to be the fate of individual man in the twentieth century. But naturally enough he wanted to offer some hope, and so he turned to the portrayal of society itself in the hope of reforming it. Whether he had read Romains' *Death of a Nobody* (q.v.) is not clear; but from *Manhattan Transfer* (1925) onwards his thinking had—or tried to have—something in common with unanimism (q.v. 2). He knew French literature well. But he could never make up his mind whether his entities with a life of their own were good or bad. However, one suspects that society itself was for Dos Passos an evil entity; he never, for all his reformist zeal and his active leftism of the Thirties, caught a sense of that authentic corporate life that is explored by the sociologist Durkheim. And, as *Three Soldiers* already makes clear, he could not create character: even his leading figures are types, and they are portrayed without psychological richness.

However, the naturalism of *Manhattan Transfer* and the trilogy *U.S.A.* (1938) escapes drabness for three reasons: his technique is lively as well as skilful; he is responsive to poesy, and had been exposed to imagism and other colourful new developments while at Harvard, so that his writing, too, is often gay and fresh; and although his creative imagination was deficient he was driven by real passions: passion against the injustices caused by the social and economic conditions between wars, and passion against the bigger injustice of life itself. For Dos Passos the naturalist gloom was all-pervading because he had no real imaginative life to set against it. His counterweight was provided by travel; and his travel books, particularly *Orient Express* (1927) are superb—at a time when his novels are, understandably enough, more known about than read, these travel books ought to be reissued.

The technique Dos Passos invented is very fine indeed, and I think it is still useful and valid. It has been utilized, notably, by Döblin and Sartre (qq.v. 2), both much superior as novelists to Dos Passos—but both fertilized considerably by his method. Dos Passos himself derived it mainly from Joyce (q.v.), but he added much of his own, and his approach, although lyrical, was realistic rather than intro-spective. He was not interested in language but social reality; Joyce's books are increasingly an investigation into language itself.

Dos Passos first used this technique in *Manhattan Transfer*, which deals mainly with the teeming life of New York City over a period of some years, and in particular with certain defeated individual lives. Dos Passos takes a number of characters and deals with the rise and fall of their fortunes in parallel (sometimes converging) episodes. These episodes are combined with three other devices: brief 'biogra-phies' of important people (giving obvious opportunities for irony when contrasted with those of poor people); the 'newsreel', a collage of headlines, phrases from popular songs, and so on, that define the general atmosphere; and 'the camera eye', in which the author himself enters the field, mixing prose poetry with impressionistic and stream-of-consciousness passages. These, with some exceptions, are the weakest passages in *Manhattan Transfer* and *U.S.A.*, which consists of *The 42nd Parallel* (1930), *1919* (1932) and *The Big Money* (1936), with a new prologue and epilogue. *U.S.A.* takes twelve characters and treats them with what Marcus Cunliffe well calls 'circumstantial unloving competence'. Each one is supposed to be subordinate to the life of the city; but Dos Passos does not succeed in concealing his despair—a rather sterile despair. His later books— among them the trilogy *District of Columbia* (1952), *Chosen Country* (1951) and the very poor *Most Likely to Succeed* (1954)—collapsed, doubtless from exhaustion, into facile phoney patriotism, flat reportage and a nearly whining self-indulgence. It would certainly be unfair to judge Dos Passos' earlier work by them. He began as a pessimistic individualist and in fact remained one all his life. But in his best works his commitment to collectivism is sincere, arising from that streak of Utopian idealism that runs through most American consciousnesses. Nor does he falsify his sense of doom: both *Manhattan Transfer* and *U.S.A.* are ultimately depressing books. What the novel owes Dos Passos is a still viable method; it was a considerable achievement.

Of Irish-Catholic background, JAMES T. FARRELL (1904), who was born in the South Side section of Chicago that provides the background for his works, set out his literary principles in *A Note on Literary Criticism* (1936), which is Marxist but never in a crude or oversimplified sense: it opposed the official communist literary line. In *The League of Frightened Philistines* (1945) he defends realism sensibly; some of his arguments are reminiscent of those of the French 'populists' (q.v. 2). Farrell owes debts to his Catholic upbringing, to Marx, to Sherwood Anderson, to Proust, and, especially, to Joyce (for his use of stream-of-consciousness) and Dreiser (qq.v.). He resembles Dreiser in being at bottom a true naturalist, with little hope for the poor or the ill-fashioned, but much pity; his prose style is not distinguished. Because Farrell's later prose and many short stories are the products of a comparatively exhausted talent, his *Studs Lonigan* trilogy has been undervalued since the Thirties. Studs is his doomed character; Danny O'Neill makes it, but the pentalogy through which he does so is not much more than competent; in the Bernard Carr trilogy, in which Farrell traces his own literary aspirations, the energy is even more dissipated. But *Studs Lonigan—Young*

Lonigan: A Boyhood in Chicago Streets (1932), *The Young Manhood of
Studs Lonigan* (1934) and *Judgement Day* (1935)—is different. This at
least is worthy of Dreiser. Studs comes from a poisoned place—
Chicago's South Side—and his fundamental decency is shown as
stifled by it. He has the usual adventures; he wants to be a real
human being; but the desire to appear like his gang companions—
tough, unsentimental, ruthless—prevails. When he grows up he
becomes a crook and torturer, and learns to drink unwisely; his girl
rejects him. Finally he marries and tries to make it; but his weak
heart, his lack of real or wholesome experience, the indifference of
society—these conspire to defeat him. He dies at twenty-nine. This
reveals, as it sets out to do, the 'concrete facts' of 'spiritual poverty'.
It has force and passion. It is the most powerful work of naturalism
in a post-naturalist era.

Although he won the Nobel Prize in 1962, JOHN STEINBECK (1902–
68), who was born of German-Irish parentage in Salinas, centre of
the Californian lettuce industry, never produced a single work nearly
as rawly effective and moving as *Studs Lonigan*; but he was a gifted
novelist, who has written many more novels of interest, even if they
are flawed, than Farrell. Steinbeck did not share the natural pessimism of Dos Passos or Farrell, but—although evidently a sturdy
rationalist, and just as indignant an enemy of injustice—substituted
for it something very like the unanimism of Romains (q.v. 2). But
in some of his better books (they all belong to the Thirties), such as
Tortilla Flat (1935), he seems to have grasped a sense of that 'Durk-
heimian' corporateness the lack of which has been noted in Dos
Passos. *Tortilla Flat* consists of tales about the *paisanos* of Tortilla
Flat, on the outskirts of Monterey: people who do not share the
'values' of society and have opted out from it, so that they are idle
and thieving but untainted by commerce and generous to those in
need. There is a strong vein of sentimentality running through
Tortilla Flat, but it does not quite spoil the freshness and liveliness of
the conception.

Steinbeck got his unanimism from the eccentric biologist
Edward Ricketts, whose interest was in groups of marine creatures
functioning as one organism. Writers and others began to get interested in unanimism in this century when the corporateness of
behaviour of human groups became less evident (especially in the
religious sphere). That this interest is fruitful we have seen from the
sociology of Durkheim and the novels of Romains (q.v. 2), to name
only two writers; Steinbeck did add something of his own, in his
insistence on bestowing a loving consideration upon all living things,
even freaks—an attitude he opposed to morality. This produced the

best of his novels, really a novella, *Of Mice and Men* (1937). This, too, is flawed—some of the characters are wooden; the symbolism is lucubrated; Lennie's hallucinations at the end are wildly unconvincing; but the theme of the animal-child, the giant who does not know his own strength, protected by the little, intelligent, physically weak man, is not sentimental even though it is fundamentally homosexual (Lennie is led from 'good' non-sexual friendship to murder by vile uncomprehending women).

Unfortunately Steinbeck did not realize the contradictions in which his unanimistic ideas involved him: why be sorry for the individual if the individual does not matter? Of course Steinbeck cared about the plight of individuals, and about injustice, and with *In Dubious Battle* (1936), the story of a strike of fruit-pickers, he aligned himself with the proletarian school. *The Grapes of Wrath* (1939), about the Joad family which with thousands of others came to California to find work, is epic in proportion and gripping as narrative; the coming of the sharecroppers from the Oklahoma dustbowl to California is seen as a vast instinctive migration. Again, brilliant impressionistic writing is mixed in with some intolerable folksy sentimentality. But the novel's chief fault is that it does not cohere: Steinbeck makes it clear that he believes the behaviour of the profiteers in California is humanly inadequate, but he cannot show why; there is a conflict in him between the philosophical unanimist and the humane socialist. The book's message, that everything that lives 'is holy', is vitiated by its philosophy—and in any case it conveys this message not in imaginative but only in sentimental terms. Steinbeck's later books do nothing to resolve this paradox, and the ambitious *East of Eden* (1952), although it contains a few passages of good writing is, pretentiously symbolic.

ERSKINE CALDWELL (1903), from Georgia, no less gifted, is too easily dismissed by critics today. Like Steinbeck, Caldwell tends to deal in inarticulate or simple characters not only because he wants to depict people depressed by economic and social circumstances but also because he cannot create complex or articulate ones. However, his early work illuminates the lives of Southern poor whites in the Thirties—the backwoodsmen and sharecroppers, whose lives he knew well—in a way that they had never been illuminated before. In *Tobacco Road* (1932), a dramatization of which ran in New York for eight years, and *God's Little Acre* (1933), all these wretched and degraded creatures have is sex. They have been so reduced by circumstances that they are only parodies of human beings—and Caldwell writes of them forcefully. That what he writes is sometimes very funny is (perhaps) beyond his own intention, but has its irony.

Caldwell should not be judged by the self-parodic novels that keep him rich nowadays, but by the two novels already mentioned and by *Journeyman* (1935), *Georgia Boy* (1943), *Trouble in July* (1940), about a lynching, and, an exception, the recent *Miss Mamma Aimee* (1967). A few of his stories are excellent—they were collected in *Complete Stories* (1953)—especially 'Kneel to the Rising Sun' (1935), a tale of racism that has classic stature and ought to be better known than it is.

NELSON ALGREN (1909), once the lover of Simone de Beauvoir (q.v. 2), and written about by her, was born in Detroit and reared in poverty in Chicago, his home for most of his life and the scene of most of his novels. He is connected with the proletarian movement and its predecessor, naturalism, because his immature first novel, *Somebody in Boots* (1935), was deliberately Marxist—and because his fiction seems to resemble Dreiser's or Farrell's in its relentless build-up of detail. Actually his mature work is highly original in its effect. He is, one might say, a naturalist without a philosophy or even interest in a philosophy—he has stuck to his own vision of life. Caldwell's subjects are the dregs of a rural, Algren's those of an urban, society—usually from the slums of Chicago's West Side. He soon lost his political interests, and was honest in doing so—for he is properly the laureate of these doomed dregs: content to perform this minor function, his novels and stories are remarkably successful within their limitations. Algren really isn't trying to say anything at all: just, by implication, to claim human interest for his people, who are tramps, petty criminals with grandiose dreams, hustlers, prostitutes, bar-flies. *Never Come Morning* (1942) is about the Polish immigrants in Chicago, and in particular about Bruno Bicek, whose dream is to be heavyweight champion of the world. He ends by committing murder. In *The Man with the Golden Arm* (1949) Frankie Machine (Majcinek), another Pole, has genius at gambling—and heroin. He could escape; but the poetry of his environment as well as its hellishness, which he recognizes, drags him back: he fails, and kills himself. *A Walk on the Wild Side* (1956) is set on the way to and in New Orleans, and records the self-destruction of an innocent strong man, Dave Linkhorn. *The Neon Wilderness* (1947) contains memorable short stories. Algren is too often ignored; but he is one of the most consistent of American novelists, and while the fact that he does not try to see further than his characters' world limits him, it also gives him purity and power. He has written less than Farrell, but his fiction has not fallen off.

EDWARD DAHLBERG (1900), born in Boston and a friend of Herbert Read, D. H. Lawrence (qq.v.), and many others, is a difficult writer to place. His literary criticism is mystical, his indictment of civilization both Jewish and vituperative, his philosophy learned; but he began as a novelist of the proletariat even if not as a proletarian novelist, as a realist if not as a naturalist. *Bottom Dogs* (1929) is to a certain extent his own story: Lorry Lewis is the bastard of an itinerant woman-barber of Kansas City; he goes to an orphanage and then drifts. This is interesting because although its material is similar to that of Farrell, Dahlberg's method is impressionistic. *From Flushing to Calvary* (1932) less convincingly treats of similar material. Dahlberg, whose *Bottom Dogs* was introduced by D. H. Lawrence, does not seem to have fulfilled its promise, although he has retained a certain small following.

Farrell and Algren were often bracketed together, as 'Chicago realists', with a third: the distinguished Negro writer RICHARD WRIGHT (1908–60). Wright was born in Mississippi and migrated to Chicago on the eve of the Depression. He was a communist from 1932 until 1944. He educated himself during the late Twenties and Thirties, studied sociology, whose compilations of facts, together with his experiences in dozens of jobs, gave him the background for *Native Son* (1940). This, which is often described as 'a Negro *American Tragedy*', tells the story of the Chicago Negro boy Bigger Thomas. Although Wright had already written the four novellas collected in *Uncle Tom's Children* (1938; rev. 1940), this is still the work of a prentice writer. But for all the crudities of its writing, and the structural collapse of Book III owing to confusions between Marxist and creative imperatives, it remains a powerful and seminal book. In essence this novel is as critical of communists as of everyone else; where it isn't, as in the long speech of Bigger's communist lawyer— a Marxist plea that society has made Bigger what he is—the material is extraneous. And it must be admitted that the heart of *Native Son* is a savage and demonic nihilism. Bigger, as underprivileged and conspired against as Studs Lonigan, but black into the bargain, becomes reluctantly involved with the communist friends of the daughter of his white employer. In a moment of panic he accidentally kills her. While in flight he kills his own girl. He is captured, tried and, after rejecting both Christianity and communism, is executed. What is interesting about *Native Son* is that its power comes not from its revelation of society's responsibility for Bigger Thomas but from its nihilism: clearly society is not altogether responsible for him, because he is shown as vicious even amongst his own equally underprivileged contemporaries. The power comes from his violent assertion of himself, his defiance of the whole city of Chicago, his final affirmation of his murderous self.

Wright followed this with *Black Boy* (1945), an autobiography and his best and least confused book. This gives a clue to his nihilistic attitude, for in it he confesses to the extent of his horror of the Negro's collaboration with the white man to keep himself down. Since Wright had been brought up by a strict mother, a Seventh Day Adventist, he had felt doubly alienated in his childhood; when he grew up he was able to sublimate his self-hatred—usual in all creative people—in a generally critical attitude towards his people as a whole. He underestimated Negro culture; tended, in fact, if only by implication, to see the Negro as actually inferior because of his lack of self-assertion. Yet *Black Boy* is a masterpiece, a series of episodes that demonstrate with a terrible dramatic exactitude the predicament not only of the Negro, but of the artist who sees the ills in his society, is punished for it, and yet is of it.

After the Second World War, partly at the behest of Gertrude Stein (q.v.), who had liked a review, Wright settled in Paris. He remained in France until his premature death, at only fifty-two, from a heart attack. Wright was by then a famous man; much of his time was taken up entertaining visitors, travelling and lecturing. The books he wrote in these years did not fulfil the promise of *Native Son* and *Black Boy*. Robert Bone has summed him up admirably: he cannot, he points out, 'convincingly exorcise his demon. His sense of self is too deeply rooted in revolt. To opt for love is to give up his identity as a picaresque saint, metaphysical rebel, lonely outsider'. This explains the failure of his long novel *The Outsider*, which betrays his imagination because it is contrived, stilted, pompous—ultimately, egocentric and insensitive. Because industrialization had freed him from the stultifying traditions of the South, he came to invest too much in it—to ignore the evils inherent in it. But in the posthumous *Eight Today* (1963) there is one novella, dating from the early Forties, in which Wright wholly succeeded. It is called 'The Man Who Lived Underground', and it bears some close resemblances to Ralph Ellison's almost classic *The Invisible Man* (q.v., 1952). Here Wright more or less abandons a painstakingly realistic surface, and concentrates on the sensations and consequences of being driven underground. His hero, Fred Daniels, resembles Bigger Thomas in that he breaks the laws of the white masters and defies them. Furthermore, unlike Bigger, he penetrates to the absurd centre of their inauthentic world, based as it is on exploitation and falsehoods. Here Wright's indignation goes well beyond the Marxist line: it reaches beyond the political. But Fred Daniels wants to integrate himself (as the expression goes): he tries to return, from the sewer where he has been living, to the world. But that white world does not know him, even when he confesses to the crimes he has committed. Eventually he is murdered by policemen, determined not to accept his reality, in his own sewer. On account of this story alone Wright must be given a place in the front ranks of modern American writers of fiction. But the first two books of *Native Son*, and parts of the third, and *Black Boy* also entitle him to this position.

RALPH ELLISON (1914) was born in Oklahoma City, the son of a construction worker and tradesman who died when he was three, leaving his mother to support him, which she did by working as a domestic cleaner. Ellison was and has always been as interested in jazz as in literature. He played the trumpet in his school band, knew Hot Lips Page, is a lifelong friend of Jimmy Rushing. He chose first to study music. Then in 1936 he went to New York, met Richard Wright and LANGSTON HUGHES (1902–67), another Negro writer, mainly a poet with a fine ear for colloquial speech, but also a novelist (*Not Without Laughter*, 1930), playwright and influential and intelligent leader of Negro culture—and began writing. After war service in the Merchant Marine he worked on *Invisible Man* (1952). Ellison's high reputation is unusual since it is based on this novel alone; in the nearly twenty years that have elapsed since its publication he has added to it only a volume of essays, *Shadow and Act* (1964), and fragments from his novel in progress, printed in periodicals.

The style and method of *Invisible Man*, a novel whose prophecies have been realized in its own time, have as many antecedents as those of other highly original novels. The one that is most often pointed to is Kafka (q.v. 2): the hero is not named, and is manipulated in ways mysterious to him. But this resemblance to Kafka, while it does exist, is somewhat misleading. So is the oft-made comparison with surrealism (q.v. 2). For the Negro's consciousness of his predicament—and *Invisible Man* is first and foremost about that—is prophesied, so to speak, by Kafka. And Ellison can hardly be said to be indebted to Kafka for that. As for surrealism: 'reality is surreal', as Ellison himself has said. Joyce is a more certain influence: Ellison has learned much from Joyce's use of modern methods, including stream-of-consciousness and the introduction of comedy. An even greater debt—or is it a resemblance?—is owed to Nathanael West (q.v.). It is often held to be essentially a 'backward-looking-novel'; but this is where the Kafka comparison is misleading. After all, *Invisible Man* is the first Negro novel to transcend its genre. This even led Philip Larkin to (inadvertently) insult Ellison by calling him 'a writer who *happens* to be an American Negro'. That this is wrong is clear from Ellison's proposition that 'we view the whole of American life as a drama acted out upon the body of a Negro giant, who, lying trussed up like Gulliver, forms the stage and the scene upon which and within which the action unfolds'.

Invisible Man uses symbolism, allegory, myth and any other modernist device to hand, but never to the detriment of the mad narrator's account of his alienated and 'invisible' state. He begins as an idealist, studying at a college for Negroes in the South run by an 'Uncle Tom' called Dr. Bledsoe. His rejection by the South is redolent with irony: through the 'accident' of being no more than he precisely is, the narrator brings the school into disrepute. He travels North and, like Fred Daniels in Wright's 'The Man Who Lived Underground', holes up in a Harlem basement: 'invisibility' is for the time being the only endurable condition. His ultimate wisdom—reached after working in a nightmare paint factory, and becoming a noted member of an underground liberal party whose policy, he comes to see, is betrayal and totalitarianism—is disillusionment. The end of the book, describing a Harlem race riot, might have been a piece of impressionistic reporting of events that took place more than ten years after it was written. The narrator ends by asking: 'Who knows but that, on the lower frequencies, I speak for you?'

The most impressive of the fragments from his work in progress that Ellison has published is called 'And Hickman Arrives'. It concerns a small boy acting out, in a coffin, 'the meaning of resurrection', and shows even more daring and power than *Invisible Man*.

*

The truly ideological representatives of the proletarian movement—ROBERT CANTWELL (1908), who wrote *Laugh and Lie Down*, MARY HEATON VORSE, author of *Strike—A Novel of Gastonia* (1930), and so on—did not leave any important fiction behind them. And even the more enduring work of Richard Wright (but not of Ellison, who was six years younger and in any case waited until he was thirty-eight before publishing his novel) is flawed by political conviction rather than otherwise. Steinbeck's view was confused; Farrell's was limited, enabling him to complete only the one satisfactory book, the Lonigan trilogy. However, there are three novelists of the Thirties, all Jews, whose fiction goes beyond politics to, as Walter Allen has rightly claimed, confront 'the human condition in its naked terror'. That is not to say that these men were not affronted by the hideous injustices of the Thirties. They certainly all were. But in their books they went straight to the reasons for them; they did not see the reasons as primarily political or economic. And their general superiority perhaps proves that it is not at any rate the writer's business to see things in economic terms—but rather to examine the human disease that produces the economic symptoms.

DANIEL FUCHS (1909), the least gifted of these writers, but nevertheless a substantial talent, was born in New York City; he long ago turned to the writing of movie scripts as a way of life; his three novels of the Thirties, *Summer in Williamsburg* (1934), *Homage to Blenholt* (1936) and *Low Company* (1937), attracted no attention until they were reissued in 1961 as *Three Novels*, when they were immediately acclaimed. Fuchs' apparently lightweight, Jewish humour, his good-natured irony, anticipated the manner of the 'Jewish novel' with which we have become perhaps too familiar in the last decade. He seems to stand squarely behind Bellow and Malamud (qq.v). And yet he was writing like this—about Jews in New York's Lower East Side during the Depression—long before either of these writers began. Fuchs is a comic novelist; his characters inevitably fail, usually humorously; they are incapable of inspiring any reader with a sense of tragedy. They are knowing, but their knowledge gets them nowhere: they are innocently without innocence, and some of them intuitively realize their futility. There is no tragic resonance in Fuchs' work, but his comedy is the genuine article. Above all he is truthful and never gratuitously unpleasant. He is detached from his characters, but he understands them.

HENRY ROTH (1906) is the author of one masterpiece, *Call it Sleep* (1934). He found himself unable to complete a second novel, and he has never been able to return to writing again—apart from the odd short story. This has been a real loss. Essentially *Call it Sleep* is the story of the anguish of a small boy, David Schearl, the son of European Jewish immigrants to America in 1907. His father is a withdrawn paranoiac who is useless to this sensitive son; so the boy goes to his mother, who is herself alienated from her surroundings by language and custom. The boy haunts the streets, learning about sex, crime and cruelty, all the time in an abject terror of something his irritable Rabbi teacher calls God. At last he finds a way to unify his disparate fears into something meaningful and divine. His teacher has spoken of the coal of fire with which God cleansed the mouth of his prophet, Isaiah. And two young toughs have forced him to drop a piece of metal into the crack between the two electrified streetcar rails. The resultant flash has struck him as something fearful but divine. One day he is forced to fly from his father's sick rage. This phantasmagoric flight through the streets, and its outcome, is one of the most intensely related episodes in American fiction. Had Roth gone on to write more fiction at this pitch he would have been of at least the stature of a Faulkner; Hemingway never wrote better.

The boy thrusts a metal ladle into the electrified crack, and is shocked into an insensibility which purges him of the horrors he has endured. As he recovers he has a reconciling vision. He does not know how to describe this unconsciousness: 'call it sleep'.

NATHANAEL WEST (originally NATHANAEL WEINSTEIN, 1903–40), who lost his own and his wife's life when he failed to stop for an oncoming car in California, was a close friend of many writers, including Farrell, William Carlos Williams and Fitzgerald, but his four novels were not generally appreciated until the early Fifties. He drifted around in the late Twenties in such jobs as sub-managing or managing hotels; and for a time he edited the magazine *Contact* with Williams. He had spent some time in Paris in the mid-Twenties, and he thoroughly absorbed surrealism—but he hardly ever reproduced it. He spent the last six or seven years of his life in Hollywood, a sexually solitary and perhaps tormented man. Then he met Eileen McKenney, the heroine of the silly book *My Sister Eileen* by Ruth McKenney; he married her and they had a few months, it appears, of great happiness before they died in the car accident.

West was not a more powerful or poetic writer than Henry Roth, but he developed a wider range. His first book, *The Dream Life of Balso Snell* (1931), entirely ignored when it appeared, is nothing much in itself, although brilliant in promise. It is a fantasy inspired by surrealism, in which Balso Snell discovers 'while walking in the tall grass that has sprung up around the city of Troy', Homer's 'ancient song'; he decides to enter the wooden horse, and discovers the 'posterior opening of the alimentary canal', by which he enters it, 'O Anus Mirabilis!'

West was not only original in his own right, but he was the original black comedian (and with a surer touch than his successors)—after all, *Miss Lonelyhearts* (1933) preceded Fuchs' first novel by a year. This is not his best book—*The Day of the Locust* (1939) is that—but because in it he discovered the procedures most suitable to his genius, it does sometimes reasonably seem to be. It is certainly a very good, and a very grim, book. The journalist hero is given the job of answering the 'lonely hearts' letters on a popular newspaper. He collapses under the pressure of the job and of the cynicism of his colleague Shrike ('Why don't you give them something new and hopeful? Tell them about art'). He needs to become nothing less than Jesus Christ; and he means it. But he perishes (crucified?), the accidental victim of a cripple whose wife he has seduced and whom he (too sentimentally?) wants to save.

The irony and terror of this was already beyond anything modern America had yet produced. West's next novel, *A Cool Million, or*

The Dismantling of Lemuel Pitkin (1934), was a departure from the realistic surface of *Miss Lonelyhearts*. It has been criticized, and probably underrated, because it adopts a parody of a woman's magazine style. It is sometimes a little jejune, but also very funny— and in the end horrific. There are still few more effective exposures of naïve 'Americanism' and capitalist optimism than this story of the honourable, trusting and parodically innocent Lemuel Pitkin, who loses an eye, his teeth, his scalp and his leg, and after being jailed and used as a tool for both communist and fascist conspiracies, is killed and becomes a martyr in the fascist cause. It disappoints only because it fails to transcend its immediate object—the Horatio Alger legend of the rise to fame and fortune of the honest poor boy —and become a major work of the imagination. The same cannot be said of West's last novel, *The Day of the Locust* (1939). This was composed in a straightforwardly realistic style, and with the great economy West had achieved. Despite its refusal to compromise facts or situation or character with sentiment or, indeed, with emotion of any kind, and despite the despair which pervades it, *The Day of the Locust* is redolent with pity and understanding as well as the terror of the previous books. The events he depicts are outrageous—he knew and lived in Hollywood, which is enough—but he nurses their vitality, celebrating it sadly.

West's decade was that of Jean Harlow, who initiated a line of sex-symbols that culminated in Marilyn Monroe. Both girls died young. In the character of Faye Greener West displays a more perfect understanding of the type, and what it represents, than any writer since. What would his wry, intellectually cruel and yet compassionate genius have made of the Arthur Miller-Monroe marriage, in which the intellectual, however briefly, 'caught' the dream girl? His description of the relationship between his intelligent hero, the painter Tod Hackett, and Faye Greener, suggests an answer. Tod knows what Faye is, but she nevertheless captivates him. He feels that if he can possess her honourably, everything may change. . . . He has qualms about approaching her as a client while she is working in a brothel. He travels hundreds of miles in order to see her misperform brief scenes in movies she has made. 'Her invitation wasn't to pleasure', West writes. The truth of such books as this often has to wait years before it is heeded. 'It is hard to laugh at the need for beauty and romance', West wrote in it, 'no matter how tasteless, how horrible, the results of that need are. But it is easy to sigh. Few things are sadder than the truly monstrous.' West's work relentlessly depicts the truly monstrous, but also expresses the exact and human quality of its sadness.

JEROME WEIDMAN (1913), another New York Jewish novelist, is always a trifle unlucky, I feel, to be given no credit at all by critics. Certainly he is slick and sentimental in his later work (which is nevertheless readable and amusing light reading), but few novelists have been as good at portraying repulsively ruthless (Jewish) characters. His first three books are his best: *I Can Get It for You Wholesale* (1937), *What's in It for Me?* (1938) and the short stories collected in *The Horse That Could Whistle 'Dixie'* (1939). Here, as in none of his succeeding work, Weidman displays a cynicism so shocking that, whatever its motives, it is really fascinatingly effective, even if in a thoroughly minor way. Weidman cannot possibly be considered on a level with Daniel Fuchs, let alone West; but he has his tiny niche as caricaturist of Jewish go-getters.

JOHN O'HARA (1905–70), born in Pennsylvania, is another novelist famous for his portraits of heels and for his brutal realism. He had somewhat more merit than Weidman, especially as a craftsman in the short story. After the Thirties O'Hara's work grew increasingly pretentious, vulgar and lurid; little of it needs to be taken into account, although some of the short stories of his final decade are finely observed and compressed. His best novel is his first: *Appointment in Samarra* (1934). This tells of the events leading up to the suicide of Julian English, of Gibbsville, Pennsylvania. While drunk at the country club English throws a highball into the face of a man who could help him in business. It leads to his self-destruction. For although he promises his wife that he will try to make it up the next evening, events conspire to make him drunk again; he goes off to a roadhouse and dances with the mistress of a powerful local bootlegger; then later gets into a fight and finds himself ostracized on all sides. English's motives are not clear, but presumably the throwing of the drink into his potential business friend's face is seen as a decent (anti-materialistic) gesture that he has not the resilience, the decent substance, to sustain. The analysis of Gibbsville and its mores is masterly and utterly fascinating. But one feels even here that O'Hara is an excellent journalist and sociologist rather than novelist. He has little insight into human character, and his accounts of it resemble good newspaper reporting rather than fiction. All his skill and readability cannot save him from his obtuseness about individuals. The best of his later novels was *Ourselves to Know* (1960), about the life of a successful murderer.

Very different from O'Hara, superior but less well known and prolific, is the Wisconsin novelist GLENWAY WESTCOTT (1901), who was encouraged but then disliked by Gertrude Stein ('... Glenway Westcott at no time interested Gertrude Stein. He has a certain syrup but it does not pour'). Westcott, though an expatriate for many years, has remained obsessed by Wisconsin, and might even be described as its reluctant laureate. Westcott found the repressive puritanism of his native region restricting and oppressive; but it fascinated him, as did the history of his tough pioneering forbears. He began as a poet, and his best fiction tries to recapture the bitter poetry of Wisconsin. *The Grandmothers* (1927), his best work, is in its quiet way of classic status. Although very American it is a highly original novel; the only discernible influence, that of Proust (q.v. 2), has been throughly assimilated. Alwyn Tower, a young man living on the French Mediterranean coast, recreates the lives of his relatives: his three grandmothers (for one grandfather had two wives), his parents, and others. This sometimes painfully nostalgic book recreates the American past with the accuracy and love of a Willa Cather. The short stories in *Goodbye Wisconsin* (1928) have similar power. Later novels—*Pilgrim Hawk* (1940), set in Paris, and *Apartment in Athens* (1945)—have been distinguished but not of similar high quality.

High claims have occasionally been made for JOHN P. MARQUAND (1893–1960), but they can hardly be sustained. At its very best, his writing is that of a bland, shrewd and gentlemanly journalist. He began as a journalist, popular romancer and detective-story writer, but then graduated to a higher-middlebrow comedian of manners. He at once satirizes and indulges New England society, but never so as to offend. On the other hand, he is observant and he writes smoothly and amusingly. Some of his well known, rather smug (but pleasantly readable) books are *The Late George Apley* (1937), *Wickford Point* (1939), *H. M. Pulham, Esq.* (1941). His two best books are *So Little Time* (1943) and *Sincerely, Willis Wayde* (1955). The first expresses his own regrets at his creative mediocrity in the form of a story about a New York play editor who would like to have done something serious; the second is a knowledgeable study of a business man's rise to power.

Rather more extravagant claims have been made for the Chicago-born JAMES GOULD COZZENS (1903), even by serious critics—one of whom has compared him to C. P. Snow (q.v.), and perhaps not without unwitting point. For Cozzens is an arch-middlebrow, although by no means an inoffensive one. The book that rocketed him to fame, *By Love Possessed* (1957), is perhaps the most repulsive of all the pretentious midcult novels of the twentieth century. Its successor, *Morning Noon and Night* (1969), is almost deliriously bad in the pretentiousness of its language. However, no critic takes these books seriously; attempts to put Cozzens forward as a serious writer have mainly centred on *Men and Brethren* (1936), *The Just and the*

Unjust (1942) and, in particular, *Guard of Honour* (1948). What can be said for him? The last book is a fairly meticulous account of three days at a United States Air Force training field in Florida in 1943; but it lacks characterization, and the attitude behind it is that of a business man who has made his pile and simply wants to leave everything to the experienced chaps who know best. In other words, Cozzens has nothing whatever to say. He is a man with a commonplace temperament who has, with happy results for himself, strayed into the field of literature. Cozzens, as *By Love Possessed* shows, has gathered no wisdom, and never had warmth—all one can discern is an extraordinarily virulent hatred of sex. Cozzens hides his coldness and civil servant's smugness behind what his admirers take to be a stoical irony. The combination in him, of sly authoritarianism, unwisdom and iciness, is unique. One must grant him, especially in *Guard of Honour*, a certain technical skill. But his 'objectivity', much vaunted by admirers, is simply insensitivity—a human stupidity of remarkable dimensions. A world that grants Cozzens a place in literature is on a long, steep slide into indifference.

*

HENRY MILLER (1891) is probably best regarded as an educationist. His reputation has been distorted because some of his books were for years banned in Great Britain and the United States. He has been thought of variously as a writer of dirty books (his notorious *Tropic of Cancer*, whined the semi-literary entertainer, Leon Uris—knocking, as Leslie Fiedler has implied, at the gates of gentile heaven—in a court case, 'goes beyond every bound of morality I've ever known in my life—everything I've been taught'), mage, mystic, daddy of the beats. . . . Miller was born in New York City and worked in a variety of jobs, eventually becoming employment manager for Western Union. He was nearly forty when he went to Paris and took up a literary and bohemian life. He has told the story of his early life in a series of autobiographical books, including *Black Spring* (1936) and *The Rosy Crucifixion* trilogy, consisting of *Sexus* (1949), *Plexus* (1953) and *Nexus* (1960). His writing about his family and his earlier life is his best, and is run a close second only by the account of his travels in Greece, *The Colossus of Marousi* (1941) and by his account of Conrad Moricand, an astrologer he had known in Paris and unwisely invited to Big Sur, in the section of *Big Sur and the Oranges of Hieronymus Bosch* (1957) called *A Devil in Paradise*, which appeared as a separate volume in 1956. For the past thirty years Miller has lived in Big Sur, California.

Miller resists classification inasmuch as he cannot be called critic, poet, novelist, essayist—or even all of these things together. Actually he does not have an imagination, and his attempts to write 'poetically' (in imitation of Rimbaud, q.v., whom he does not understand and about whom he has written very poorly) are disastrous. But this gives no cause for puzzlement once it is realized that Miller is a simple-minded and literal heir of American nineteenth-century romanticism. Since he lives in the twentieth century, his romanticism has developed a defensive, nihilist edge: he is famous for his denunciations of America (*The Air Conditioned Nightmare*, 1945). But it is wrong to call this side of him satirical: it is merely vituperative.

Miller is a true naïve (q.v.), as his embarrassing compilation called *The Books in My Life* (1952) demonstrates: here Rider Haggard rubs shoulders with Mary Baker Eddy and Shakespeare in one of the most haphazard lists ever made. The sage of Big Sur, the Whitman-esque celebrator of the body and the enemy of literature, became for the most part a highly 'literary' writer. It is a sad end to the career of the man who tried harder than any other twentieth-century American writer to realize the specifically American dream of absolute freedom. However, Miller has his intrinsic importance as an autobiographer, and his historical importance as a kind of educator of the beat generation. Leslie Fiedler is quite correct in saying that the years of Depression, unemployment and appeasement produced no 'brand of apocalyptic hysteria . . . so eccentric or so heartless as Miller's', and that, deliberately hilarious at his best and undeliberately so at his worst, he is the 'first important . . . anti-tragic writer in America'. But in freeing himself entirely from morality and responsibility—this involved 'being a swine' in the sense of sleeping with his benefactors' wives or stealing the car-fare home from the bag of a woman while laying her—he played a significant role. He has carried 'innocence' as far as it can be carried in this century; those who want to study the results need look no further. He thinks living is more important than writing, and we can judge him as liver as well as writer from his prose. In *Sexus* he tells us: 'I was approaching my thirty-third year, the age of Christ crucified. A wholly new life lay before me, had I the courage to risk all'. This, one might say, is bad life but good writing: good writing because it is true, as true as Miller's lifelong devotions to pseudo-religions and phoney prophets.

Miller is certainly not important for his contributions to the sexual life of the twentieth century. Sex unsettles him so much that a good deal of his writing about it is fairly describable as a way of filling in time (and not much time at that) between orgasms. In his writings about sex Miller proceeds frantically from one encounter to another, a gentle person desperately trying to brutalize his sexual role, not knowing what he is looking for beyond his need to degrade woman, make her comic, not to be tender towards her. He can be compassionate about anyone unless it is a woman in a sexual role; but he tries to push all his women into sexual roles. . . . He is the less likely to represent a woman as already degraded (simply by the fact of her being physically capable of fulfilling his mindless pleasure) the more she genuinely puzzles him or reminds him of his mother. Thus his second wife, Mona, lesbian, taxi-dancer, whore and pathological liar, fascinates him more than any other woman in his writings: his sexual use of her does not exhaust her meaning. Somewhere behind all this, it seems, there is a Whitmanesque homosexual impulse that not even the so much vaunted innocence of total freedom can erase.

Miller is the authentic non-intelligent, natural, 'anti-tragic', free man. One can rightly call him 'eccentric and heartless'. But in him, one might also say, mankind has come some way—from employment manager to lucid autobiographer and clown. His despair, if he has any, has no quality; and his writings about sex are disappointingly pornographic. But can one say more of the silence of employment managers?

Another odd man out of American letters, although in almost every respect at the other end of the scale, is VLADIMIR NABOKOV (1899). Miller is odd because he is *so* representative, Nabokov is so odd because he is, of course, not. One might treat him as Russian, since he was born of a noble Russian family in St. Petersburg (now Leningrad), and he wrote in Russian until 1940. But Nabokov was educated at Cambridge, has been an exile all his adult life, is an American citizen, and has written his more important books in an expert and confident English, and has written them about America. Nabokov taught Russian literature at Stanford and Cornell in the United States before his literary success enabled him to retire. He is a distinguished entomologist.

Nabokov's Russian books, most of which have now appeared in English, deal coldly with the anguishes of exile, which none the less come through strongly. They are brilliant, but only one or two of the short stories show feeling towards the characters. The best is *Laughter in the Dark* (*Camera Obscura*, 1933; tr. 1936), about a man's fatal infatuation for a cinema usherette, the worst—foreshadowing the ignominious depths plumbed by *Ada* (1969)—is *King Queen Knave* (1928; tr. 1968). Nabokov's best books came in his second, American phase, when he decided to accept exile and to become—so far as he could—American. Then he began to analyze, with the genuinely innocent eye of the foreigner, his surroundings. *Pnin* (1957) tells of a Russian professor of entomology at a college in New York State. *Lolita* (1955), banned for a time, is Nabokov's best book. Humbert Humbert becomes obsessed with a twelve-year-old 'nymphet', and in order to gain possession of her marries her mother. After a flight across the United States, as vivid a description of it as has ever been made by a non-American, Lolita · is seduced by a playwright, whom Humbert kills.

Nabokov might have been a major writer, but self-congratulatory cleverness has killed the intensity in him. His stylistic tricks—punning, anagrams—have energy but very soon become monotonous; they do not add anything fundamental. His style is so hard that it is sometimes brittle, and that brittleness indicates that his aristocratic sensibility—early battered beyond repair by exile—is accompanied by an innate romanticism. Nabokov's course as a writer has been to challenge, combat, even at times to deny this romanticism, acknowledging it only as a sort of baroque nostalgia for St. Petersburg. However, in *Lolita* Nabokov was able, by means of a detachment he had cultivated with care and skill, convincingly to describe the enslaving effect of a certain kind of sexual passion—perhaps one of the things he 'means' by Humbert's passion is romantic love—and the opportunities for evil that it opens up. It is not the novel it might have been because it fails to examine the nature of Humbert's sexual pathology; Nabokov's lack of interest in this is a positive defect. The clue to Nabokov's deficiencies lies in *Ada*, where his delight in himself is anything but aristocratic. The only interest in this appalling book partakes of the nature of the solution to a crossword puzzle; but Nabokov has sufficient imagination and literary breeding to learn from the shame he must now feel at perpetrating it.

*

MARY MCCARTHY (1912), born in Seattle, was orphaned when both her parents died in the influenza epidemic of 1918; she has recorded her experiences at the hands of various relatives in one of her best books, *Memories of a Catholic Girlhood* (1957). For a time she was the wife of EDMUND WILSON (1895–1972), one of the best of American literary journalists and, with Geoffrey Grigson (q.v.) and one or two others, the last representative of a dying race of literate and informed periodical critics. Wilson, notable for his generosity and his shrewd judgements as a reviewer, also wrote some good fiction, including *I Thought of Daisy* (1929) and *Memoirs of Hecate County* (1946). Like her ex-husband, Mary McCarthy has always remained a journalist; in recent years she has written persuasive criticism, in magazines, of the American involvement in Viet Nam, which she has visited. She is a readable, successful and intelligent novelist, often described as 'scathing'. Her subject is usually the unwisdom of those who in our time regard themselves as wise: the cultured and the intellectual. She has little love for her own kind, and this may be the reason why she appeals to a middlebrow readership (she has stooped to its level only twice, in her two books about Venice and Florence); it is likely that she has been somewhat undervalued, although her characters tend to be manipulated for the benefit of her admirable wit, and she has little warmth. Her best novels are *The Oasis* (1949), about a modern would-be Utopia; *A Charmed Life* (1955), in which the artistic are castigated; *The Groves of Academe* (1952) and *The Group* (1963), a novel about the fates of eight girls who graduated from Vassar at the same time as Miss McCarthy. This is not psychologically profound, and like all Mary McCarthy's work it lacks a sense of poetry; but it is a brilliant and compassionate piece of social history, which deserves to survive.

The output of JEAN STAFFORD (1915), who was born in California and grew up in Colorado, has been slender but genuinely distinguished. From 1940 until 1948 she was married to the poet Robert Lowell (q.v.), and later, after a second marriage, she had a short (1959–63) marriage to the late A. J. Liebling, journalist and sports writer. Her perceptive and sharp first novel, *Boston Adventure* (1944), subjects Boston society to the scrutiny of Sonia Marburg, the daughter of an immigrant chambermaid; Sonia works as secretary to the wealthy spinster Miss Peabody. *The Mountain Lion* (1947) is one of those rare novels that can penetrate the world of children without shattering or sentimentalizing it. *Children Are Bored on Sundays* (1953) and *Bad Characters* (1965) are collections of short stories.

The South is a violent place, and a conservative one. It is not an easy place for its sensitive or liberal inhabitants, who, like Faulkner, form part of its tradition and yet oppose it—thus opposing a part of themselves. Perhaps the painfulness of living in the South is one of the reasons why the New Criticism—essentially an attempt to evolve an objective criticism—came from there. Following the period of reconstruction after the Civil War the South, given the best will in the world, had nearly insoluble problems. Where, above all, was it to deploy the mass of freed slaves? The problem is not, of course, solved; the South-eastern United States throws up Faulkners, and it also throws up Wallaces. Literature often flourishes under difficult conditions; the Southern renaissance has added greatly to the literature of modern America, even if its contribution has been markedly pessimistic. This has been a defeated area, not one of hope; but it is also a perfect microcosm of crazy modern man as he ruins his world. Faulkner towers above everyone else in this renaissance of letters, both in scope and depth; if in his life he had to hit the bottle, and if he ended in self-parody, in his best works he still sums up the South: its aspirations, its despairs, above all its doomed sense of itself. But there were others besides Faulkner. Some writers, although Southerners, contributed little to Southern literature as such: Thomas Wolfe (q.v.) is one; Erskine Caldwell is another. The first of these is an individualist (or an egocentric); the second is excellent on poor whites, but does not even try to see them in their context. They certainly do not build on the foundations laid by Kate Chopin and Ellen Glasgow (qq.v.).

In 1962 KATHERINE ANNE PORTER (1890), born at Indian Creek in Texas, published a long novel, which had become a legend, having been announced as imminent over a period of twenty years. This was *Ship of Fools*. An 'appallingly obvious and dull' (Leslie Fielder) 'moral allegory' about a voyage, it is a surprising middle-brow negation of her previous and most distinguished work, which consists of short stories and novellas. In these earlier works— *Flowering Judas* (1930), stories, *Pale Horse, Pale Rider* (1939), three novellas and *The Leaning Tower* (1944), stories—she studies the effects of the changes in the South on the personalities of individuals; many of the stories deal with a girl called Miranda—into whose figure Katherine Anne Porter doubtless projects some of her own history— at various stages of her life.

Although Katherine Anne Porter has travelled all over Europe, and has lived in many parts of America (New Orleans, Chicago, Denver, Mexico City, New York, and elsewhere), the central concern of her writing is her Southern heritage. Her life has been dedicated to the subsidization of her creative writing, a vocation she once said she would not herself have chosen; in her earlier days she had to perform many unwelcome journalistic chores. She has destroyed 'trunkfuls' of material. She spoke of herself (1933) as 'a woman who goes with her mind permanently absent from the place where she is'. Her aim was 'to tell a straight story and to give true testimony'. One might describe her best writings as imaginatively in quest of the meaning of herself and of her peculiar heritage. She reveals her awareness by means of 'epiphanies' (q.v.), moments of sudden illumination: the child Miranda, curiously alienated from the tradition of which she is a part, even a kind of freak, understands her situation through seeing a circus performance. Almost always these moments of revelation indicate a tragic situation, meticulously and exquisitely set forth. The nearest to such illuminations is to be found in some of Emily Dickinson's poems. Few writers have been able to suggest such vast accumulations of fact, such complex histories, in so short a compass. *Noon Wine* (1937), included in *Pale Horse, Pale Rider*, is characteristic. It works perfectly on the realistic level, but sets up extraordinary resonances both parabolic and symbolic. Mr. Thompson, married to an invalid, unhappily and inefficiently runs a Texas dairy farm. Then the work of an enigmatic new hired man, Mr. Helton, puts things right. After nearly a decade Homer T. Hatch turns up: he claims that Mr. Helton is an escaped lunatic, and tries to capture him for profit. Thompson kills him, but is acquitted of murder; however, Hatch posthumously succeeds in ruining his life, for he cannot bear his guilt, and kills himself. What really happened? The question forms itself as naturally as it does when we seek explanations in the non-fictional world.

Since Miss Porter is so excitingly and uniquely gifted a writer, the failure of *Ship of Fools* was little short of a tragedy. There are of course fine touches in it; but these touches are those of a writer of short stories or novellas. Miss Porter is not a novelist, and it is a pity that she allowed her understandable ambition to write a long novel to develop into a pressure to produce a 'great' one; inevitably, *Ship of Fools* was turned into a big, *kitsch* movie. But this massive failure in no way detracts from the original achievement of the earlier fiction.

Since most of the members of the Southern Agrarian movement were poets, it is dealt with in the following section. One of the leading spirits was Allen Tate (q.v.), who for over a quarter of a century was married to the Southern novelist CAROLINE GORDON (1895). Caroline Gordon was born in Kentucky; her people on both sides had been tobacco-planters 'since the weed was first cultivated by white men'. Her novels are exceptionally skilful, but their austerity has prevented them from having a wide effect. *Penhally* (1931), her first novel, set the tone for its successors. An account of a Kentucky family over several generations, it demonstrated the author's grasp of the details of Southern history. *None Shall Look Back* (1937), a study of the Confederate general, Nathan Bedford Forrest, is her most severe novel. It gives her picture of the old South: gracious, heroic, feudal but benevolent to its slaves (who are represented as ungrateful!), and yet is, as Walter Allen has said, somehow 'abstract . . . static': has life ever actually been lived like this? But this is nevertheless an important novel, even if an obviously limited one: it gives, at an entirely serious level of intelligence (however its sensitivity is to be judged), the picture of the old South that so many people still hold— and have great nostalgia for. Unfortunately *None Shall Look Back* appeared in the shadow of Margaret Mitchell's *Gone With the Wind* (1936), a piece of midcult trash about the South that made history as a best seller and then as a movie. The best of Caroline Gordon's later novels is *The Malefactor* (1956), which puts to good use her extensive knowledge of literary people, including Tate himself.

Another close associate of the Agrarians, although somewhat younger than the rest of the group, was the Kentuckian ROBERT PENN WARREN (1905), who is a critic, poet and academic as well as a novelist. It was Warren, who cannot be described as other than a liberal, who first saw that Faulkner was being misjudged, in the Thirties, for 'having the wrong politics'; who saw that Faulkner's work went well beyond any kind of politics. A considerable writer in every genre that he has attempted, Warren has some affinities with Faulkner, in particular with his tendency to treat of violence and evil. But Warren's approach is more cerebral, and sometimes tends to lose in power. He has a colloquial liveliness that is rare in a 'new critic' of his generation; certainly, reading some of his criticism, one would not imagine him to be the kind of novelist he in fact is. As a poet Warren is consistently interesting and evidently of high quality; but he has not often succeeded in discovering a voice that is distinctively his own. His and Cleanth Brooks' *Understanding Poetry* (1938), a text book of the New Criticism, revolutionized the teaching of poetry in American universities, and its effects are still felt; it is possible that Warren's critical self-consciousness has weakened or dispersed his poetic impulse. His best poetry is to be found in *Promises* (1957).

He is a self-conscious novelist, too; and again, whatever weaknesses his fiction has may be traced to this (he and Brooks wrote an *Understanding Fiction*, 1943, as well . . .). For example, might not his surprising rhetoric be an attempt to escape from his over-intellectualism? His fiction has rightly been seen as developing straight out of Faulkner; one senses that he would sacrifice much of his critical intellect in order to attain to Faulkner's power. Certainly one sometimes gets the notion that Warren hates being a thinker, and wants to escape from it. And yet this is to judge by the highest standards. Warren is a serious writer, of undeniable quality; it is this that makes his failure to reconcile his strong creative impulses with his intellectual processes a serious and disappointing one. In his most famous novel, *All the King's Men* (1946), a study of a Southern politician suggested by the career of Huey Long (for some—inexplicable—reason Warren denied this), there is an imbalance that results from Warren's attempt to escape his critical self-consciousness. This is a pity, because few more gifted novelists have tackled a more fascinating theme: that of the problem of how or when doing good by corrupt means is wrong or ultimately destructive. Willie Stark does good ruthlessly, and one of Warren's intended messages is perfectly clear: that nothing, even reform and justice and a square deal, is worse than totalitarianism. But Warren chooses as narrator a newspaperman called Jack Burden, a history graduate. Burden begins by accepting Stark at face value, and idealistically supports him. He even causes the suicide of a respected judge by digging something discreditable from his past—only to discover that this judge was his father. Eventually, when Stark is assassinated by an idealistic doctor—but not for political reasons—Burden is supposed 'to understand'. However, he is an unconvincing figure, and the novel as a whole leaves one with a strong impression that Willie Stark is, after all, a hero—that had he not become personally (sexually) corrupted by power, he might have survived to do even more good. Burden is supposed to understand by the end that Willie has been corrupted by power; but Burden is an intellectual, a representative of Warren, and he is not convincing. *All the King's Men* therefore fails, for one reason or the other, to demonstrate that power does corrupt.

Warren has written some notable short stories, collected in *The Circus in the Attic* (1948). His 'tale in verse and voices', *Brother to Dragons* (1953), is his most formidable effort to recapture the horror of the Jacobean era; much more successful than the lurid and theatrical novel *World Enough and Time* (1950). *Brother to Dragons* tells the story of the axe-killing of a Negro by the sons of Jefferson's sister; the author introduces himself as 'R. P. W.', an interlocutor of the twentieth century. This is, again, a powerful work, and yet it is a little too calculated, for all its concentration on evil and the deliberateness of its melodrama, to quite come off.

Claims have been made for Warren's later fiction, especially for *Flood* (1964). But it is likely that posterity will endorse Walter Allen's view that Warren's best novel is his first: *Night Rider* (1939). This is, in a way, on the same theme as the more ambitious *All the King's Men*: Percy Munn joins the Night Riders, an illicit organization formed to destroy a tobacco-buyer's ring that threatens the small growers of Kentucky, out of idealism; but the nature of its activity, which he helps to direct, corrupts him. The scenes of violence here are superbly described, and reinforce the suggestion that the full expression of a tragic vision of life has been prevented by too zealous an adherence to a critical theory.

A lesser novelist, but an interesting one, is T. S. STRIBLING (1881–1965), who was born in Tennessee. He is interesting because his obvious starting-point, his inspiration, was Sinclair Lewis (q.v.): his first significant novel, *Birthright* (1922), appeared just two years after *Main Street* (q.v.). This applies Lewis' methods to a different kind of problem: not one of mere smugness but one of savage injustice. An educated mulatto returns to a Tennessee town to try, as is his just and human due, to make his way. He fails horribly. The novel has more point than Lewis', although it is worse written by any standards, and much less clever; and Stribling, who had practised law in the South and knew his rogues as well as the others, displays as much knowledge as Lewis—which makes this and some of its successors rather neglected novels (two years after his death not a single book by him was listed as in print). *Teeftallow* (1926) is an even more Lewisian study, this time of a confidence-trickster, a small-time Southern politician, Railroad Jones, who climbs to wealth and influence by exploitation of the vileness of the people of his Tennessee mountain town. The couple who love each other and fail to conform are destroyed. Again, this is a novel whose corrosive bitterness is not forced. But better was to come from Stribling: a trilogy consisting of *The Forge* (1931), *The Store* (1932) and *Unfinished Cathedral* (1934). This traces the history of a family, the Vaidens, in Florence, Alabama. It is not a major work of the imagination, nor is it well-written; but it is none the less a truthful novel. Jimmy Vaiden rises from poor white to a position of dominance in the region; but he loses his slaves after the Civil War, and gets into debt to the local storekeeper. His son Miltiades, Klansman and ex-colonel, unscrupulously and dishonestly acquires the store. Finally we see him in his power, president of the local bank, feared and 'loved'. He is building a cathedral as his monument. Stribling is crude and his satire is laboured. But he was a pioneer. We meet the Vaidens again, after all, in the Snopes. Faulkner purchased the Vaiden trilogy as it appeared, and kept it until his death. He owed much to it.

EUDORA WELTY (1909) was born in Mississippi, yet in one important sense she chose to be Southern, for her father was from Ohio and her mother from West Virginia—which does not count, culturally, as a Southern state. Although she has written good novels, Eudora Welty is plainly at her best as a writer of short stories and novellas. She is an original, even an idiosyncratic writer, who was admired and encouraged by, among others, Ford Madox Ford, Katherine Anne Porter and Robert Penn Warren (qq.v.). A writer who has influenced her is Henry Green (q.v.), about whom she has written interestingly.

Eudora Welty is at her strongest in the short forms of fiction probably because she is best of all at compressed portraits of eccentrics. These are often called caricatures, but this is not the right word: Miss Welty seizes an individual at a self-revelatory moment, and the resultant portrait often appears as a caricature. In fact it is more often a truthful account of the person. She has the capacity to create characters that puzzle as much as those from everyday life. Is the postmistress of China Grove, Mississippi, in 'Why I Live at the P.O.'—in the collection *A Curtain of Green* (1941)—schizophrenic or merely alienated? That the story generates arguments on the point is tribute to Miss Welty's powers of characterization. It is true that the characters in the stories are frequently neurotics, eccentrics or in a few cases psychotics; but they are nevertheless seen as they are, and if they provide comedy, they provide quite as much pathos. Of course, dealing with such material invariably produces risks, and when Miss Welty tries consciously for symbolic effects she fails. But when she concentrates on the small-town Mississippi life that she has observed so carefully and understands so well, she frequently makes more universal statements. Besides *A Curtain of Green*, her story collections include *The Wide Net* (1943), *The Golden Apples* (1949) and *The Bride of the Innisfallen* (1955). *The Shoe Bird* (1964) is for children. *Delta Wedding* (1946) and *The Ponder Heart* (1954) are novels. It has been suggested that Eudora Welty is not essentially Southern. The answer is to imagine her fiction without the South. The strangeness of her characters is a Southern strangeness.

Two important Southern women novelists are CARSON MCCULLERS (1917–67) and FLANNERY O'CONNOR (1925–64). Carson McCullers was born Lula Carson Smith in Georgia. She studied in New York, and married Reeves McCullers when she was just twenty. She published *The Heart is a Lonely Hunter* in 1940, at just about the time when she and her husband had agreed to divorce. For the next five years she lived mostly in New York, publishing *Reflections in a Golden Eye* (1941) and a number of short stories. She remarried Reeves McCullers, who had been wounded in the war, in 1945; this broke up in 1951, for Reeves had turned into a drug- and alcohol-addict— he killed himself in Paris soon after Carson McCullers left him. She herself suffered intermittently from heart disease, paralytic strokes, and pneumonia; when she died from a stroke she was also suffering from breast cancer. Her health had been deteriorating since her marriage in 1937. She managed, however, to produce several more books: *The Member of the Wedding* (1946), which she dramatized (1950), *The Ballad of the Sad Café* (1951), an omnibus volume containing her first three novels as well as collecting most of the stories, the play *The Square Root of Wonderful* (1958) and the final novel, *Clock Without Hands* (1961). Edward Albee (q.v.) successfully dramatized her short story *The Ballad of the Sad Café* in 1963.

Although her last years were such a struggle against illness and incapacity, Carson McCullers published in 1964 a charming book of children's poetry: *Sweet as a Pickle and Clean as a Pig*.

Like the other Southern woman writers of fiction (Katherine Anne Porter, Eudora Welty, Flannery O'Connor, qq.v.) Carson McCullers deals in eccentrics and grotesques. This is an effect that the South has upon the minor writer. (It may well be that in trying to meet the challenge with major fiction such a writer as Warren has fallen short of the achievement of this quartet; certainly Wolfe failed so abjectly, so far as the South is concerned, that his fiction has scarcely any relevance to it.)

Carson McCullers is essentially a minor writer, and she has strengthened her best work by keeping strictly to her limitations. She has been misunderstood when critics have judged her analyses of crippled individuals as dissections of poisoned cultures. Miss McCullers was enough of a medical freak to be able to feel sympathy for more drastically maimed persons. But there is no sense, in her books, of horror at physical or mental deformity. She is in one important sense an affirmative writer, for she shows the world of her crippled characters to be beautiful and loving rather than horrible; true, her sense of the whole world is not an altogether beautiful one —but she does show, as few other modern writers have done, that what seems or is taken to be ugly is not necessarily so.

Her best work is in *The Heart is a Lonely Hunter*, the short story, almost a novella, 'The Ballad of the Sad Café', and *The Member of the Wedding. Reflections in a Golden Eye*, set in a pre-war army camp in the South, was a rather disastrous experiment in the macabre and is a thoroughly bad and, by its author's standards, pretentious piece of Gothic. *The Heart is a Lonely Hunter*, set in a small Georgian mill town, is concerned with an intelligent deaf-mute called John Singer and his effect on four people. He lives with the feeble-minded Spiros Antonapoulos, whom he loves. (There is no hint of homosexuality.) When Antonapoulos becomes ill and anti-social and has to be taken to a mental hospital, Singer enters into the lives of four other people, none of whom have an inkling of the grief he is feeling. Most beautifully drawn of these is the twelve-year-old girl Mick, who wants to be a composer. Finally Antonapoulos dies, and Singer kills himself; his disciples are puzzled—for they have never understood or cared about him personally, But each of them, too, is defeated. This book is flawed by over-writing, by a too conscious use of allegory that sometimes ruins the action on a realistic level, and by some too consciously taken—and contradictory—decisions about what Singer represents (Christ? Satan?). But it remains an important and beautiful book; the enigmatic, ambiguous nature of Singer, which is really the point of the novel, is maintained despite such details as his age at death (thirty-three) and his 'look of peace'.

'The Ballad of the Sad Café' is the most perfect of Carson McCullers' fiction. In this grotesque tale of Miss Amelia Evans, grasping merchant and generous healer, her imagination found its real shape; simultaneously she discovered her true voice. In all her other books, even *The Member of the Wedding*, her language is uncertain: she is given to ineffective comparisons and has a penchant for lofty pseudo-poeticisms. *The Member of the Wedding* is Carson McCullers' most realistic book, and her best full-length work. It tells the story of the entry of Frankie Addams into adolescence, and introduces the most straightforwardly sympathetic of all the author's characters, the four-times married, black cook, Berenice Sadie Brown. This is a lyrical, comic and hardly ever sentimental novel, moving and refreshing. *Clock Without Hands* never comes up to this level; its chief weaknesses are linguistic slackness and, again, unfulfilled symbolic pretensions. However, it is at least evident that had its author not been so seriously incapacitated (mainly by paralytic strokes) she could have gone on to write the major novel of which *The Heart is a Lonely Hunter* had shown her capable.

Flannery O'Connor, another Georgian, was also the victim of painful and crippling ill health: she inherited disseminated lupus from her father, and became progressively crippled by the complications the necessary treatment set up, and she must have known that she would die prematurely. Flannery O'Connor was born a Roman Catholic and remained one all her life. She began by trying to become a cartoonist, but soon changed over to fiction. Despite her illness and the discomfort it caused her Flannery O'Connor was a gay and wisecracking woman, who accepted as many invitations as she could to lecture and to appear in public. She found time to write two novels, *Wise Blood* (1952) and *The Violent Bear it Away* (1960), and two collections of short stories, *A Good Man is Hard to Find* (1955) and the posthumous *Everything that Rises Must Converge* (1965).

Flannery O'Connor is a difficult writer, who mixes Southern Gothic (but in a more controlled form than Carson McCullers), grotesque humour and an extremely complex symbolism. Once again, her characters are grotesque. But her Catholicism (her religious 'position' seems to have approximated to, or at least to have been sympathetic towards, that of Teilhard de Chardin) gives her a completely different perspective from any other Southern writer. Her first remarkable novel is about nothing less than an anti-Christ, one Haze Motes who loses his (Protestant) faith while in the army and thereafter tries to establish a Church Without Christ, 'the church that the blood of Jesus don't foul with redemption', in the Tennessee mountains where he lives. Haze believes his blood is wise because it is natural; but his blood is actually wise, since he is, despite himself, the voice of the living God: even if he preaches an anti-Church, his preachings are more authentic than those of the secular contemporary Church: he is holy. Haze, in a book whose symbolism becomes more and more complex and theological, finally blinds himself with lime. Although herself of the Catholic faith, Flannery O'Connor sees Southern Protestant primitivism as an authentic Christianity—as hideously authentic as the truth (to her) of God's love and Christ's redemption. (It is only fair to add that her theme has also been interpreted as 'the spiritual distortions that are the consequence of Protestant primitivism'.) The symbolism of *Wise Blood*, which is very theological, tends to show Haze's life as comic— and distorted—but as a comic and distorted parallel to Christ's. Its fault is that, because of the bizarre and comic elements, no sense of anguish is allowed to come across. The things the author writes about (wearing barbed wire next to the skin, blinding oneself with quicklime) are so painful, so Grand Guignol, that they defeat their own ends: this gospel is ultimately eccentric rather than authentic. However, the manner in which Flannery O'Connor has set up an anti-Christianity is subtle and intelligent, even if, finally, a kind of sermon lies at the very back of it all.

The Violent Bear it Away (1960) has more imagination and less ingenuity, and is the better book. Francis Marion Tarwater's great-uncle, a mad prophet and illicit whisky-distiller, dies; but he has instructed his great-nephew to become a prophet, and to begin his ministry by baptizing his cousin Bishop Rayber. Tarwater, who does not wish to be a prophet, carries out this order—but also drowns him, as directed by Satan, previously only a voice in his head. He does all he can to avoid his calling. But ultimately, drugged and sodomized by Satan, he is driven into madness and authentic prophecy. Tarwater is certainly representative of the true Church, which must become itself—lose reason—to save the world. Clearly Flannery O'Connor, like so many other contemporary Catholics, was desperately unhappy about the present Church, which she saw as betraying itself.

It is possible that posterity will see the best of Flannery O'Connor's short stories—such stories as 'The Artificial Nigger', 'The Lame Shall Enter First' and 'Parker's Back'—as her most enduring work. On the whole these are easier to read in the sense that, while they possess as formidable a symbology, it is not as relentlessly calculated a one. But this view has been challenged, on the grounds that she put everything that was really important to her into the novels. The answer to that might be that she put in everything that she thought most important to her into the novels. . . . Certainly she is the most unusual of the Southern woman writers. As Stanley Edgar Hyman has pointed out, she goes back not to Faulkner but to Mark Twain, as her brilliant use of dialect shows; further, the writer by whom she was most influenced (this again was Hyman's discovery) was Nathanael West. She also resembles certain French Catholic writers such as Bernanos and, even more, Bloy (qq.v. 2): for example, racial integration is for her a sentimentality: what is important is beyond life. And yet, for all her important differences from her fellow Southern writers, it is impossible to consider her as anything but a Southern novelist: 'I have found that any fiction that comes out of the South,' she said, 'is going to be considered grotesque by the Northern critic, unless it is grotesque, in which case it is going to be considered realistic'.

JAMES AGEE (1909–55) was almost the only one of all the serious writers who went to Hollywood to script movies that were above average: *The African Queen* is a real improvement on its original. Agee was a good film critic, one of the best; but he destroyed himself in the interests of the cinema industry—even if he was trying to improve it. He wrote some poetry of quality, though not of genius, and only took to fiction towards the end of his life. *A Death in the Family* (1955), which is an unfinished, partly autobiographical, novel, is one of the few positive novels to come out of the South. It tells of the shattering effect on a happy Tennessee family of the father's death in a car accident. It is important for its picture of decency in Tennessee—not a thing much celebrated in fiction.

The Virginian WILLIAM STYRON (1925) is a most gifted writer who has become progressively the victim of an ambition to write the great Southern novel. *Lie Down in Darkness* (1951) was acclaimed. Since then, with the exception of the novella *The Long March* (1953), he has succumbed to the temptation to try to contain the whole Southern story between the two covers of one book. He has only completely failed, however, with *The Confessions of Nat Turner* (1969), the story of the slave insurrection of 1831 and its leader, in which he simply took on more than he could handle. This novel is of course interesting, but Styron, consciously a liberal and consciously a subtle and sophisticated novelist, left his invention and his imagination too little room. *Lie Down in Darkness*, for all its debts to Joyce and Faulkner and its lofty rhetoric, is, like its successor *Set This House on Fire*, an impressive book, with passages of first-class quality.

The latter has the courage to try to take a leaf out of Dostoevski's book; at least it does not make itself look foolish. One can certainly say that Styron's novels do not cohere, and that the Nat Turner book was a mistake, an attempt to take on too much; but one must concede that his first two books are both readable and continuously intelligent. His potential is still great.

The admirers of Nebraska-born WRIGHT MORRIS (1910) invariably complain that he is neglected. To the extent that he does not enjoy huge sales and that not one of his novels has been a total critical success, this is true. But he is very much an intellectuals' writer: he makes no concessions. (And yet there are many snobs and fools among his admirers.) Wright Morris is an off-beat, original writer, whose sardonic approach to life—which he regards as absurd without making any fuss about it whatever—has not attracted the 'general reader'. His books have not been kept in print. Morris' outlook is neither comforting nor discomforting; he is, rather, acutely sophisticated. He is, apart from his fans (many of whom cannot read him), awaiting discovery. His first novel, *My Uncle Dudley* (1942), is about a long trip and a successful confidence man. Morris is a professional photographer, and two of his books are illustrated with his own photographs. *The Inhabitants* (1946) set out to show 'what it is to be an American', and failed; but the photographs are interesting. *The Home Place* (1948) is a novel about a writer who returns to Nebraska with his wife and children to live; *The World in the Attic* (1949), without the nostalgic photographs, is its sequel. These combine an aching love for the past, felt to be pointless, with a horror of the present that spends itself as nervous comedy. His first substantial, and his most moving, novel was *The Works of Love* (1952), about a midwest egg-farmer who is successful in business but comically unsuccessful with women. This is a subtle variation on the 'holy fool' theme, as exploited in Wilder's *Heaven's My Destination* (q.v.). Wright Morris is a most peculiar and unusual writer in that he expects nothing good whatever from life—but this is none the less a bitter book in effect, since no one to whom the egg-farmer offers his love even recognizes it for what it is. *The Huge Season* (1954) is about money and its corrupting effects. *Love Among the Cannibals* (1957), his most sheerly comic novel, deals with two bad song-writers and the girls they pick up on their way to Acapulco. *What a Way to Go* (1962) is a relentless study of the marriage of a middle-aged small-college professor to a very young girl. Morris is often an over-subtle and too self-conscious writer; he has not always succeeded in being simply the 'photographer' he wanted to be in the sense he meant when he said 'The windmill, the single plough, the grain elevator, the receding horizon, are both signs and symbols at the same time. They speak for themselves. They would rather talk than be talked about. The man who loves these things ... is a photographer.' He also suffers from an archness and an involuteness, a lack of straightforwardness. But he is serious and sensitive, and his peculiar methods force his readers to see things from new angles.

SAUL BELLOW (1915) spent his first nine years in his birthplace, Canada. His parents were Latvian Jews who had emigrated two years previously. The family moved to Chicago in 1924, and Bellow went to Chicago and then to Northwestern University, graduating (1937) in anthropology and sociology.

Bellow was America's first major writer to shift the central concern of his fiction from the social and political to the existential. Although one of the most intellectual of all American novelists, he has discouraged critical examination of his work; his admiration for Dreiser and Hardy, not intellectual writers, is significant. For all his wit and brilliance, Bellow's subject is ultimately what a critic has called 'the porous quotidian texture which is squeezed between the accidents of birth and the fatal sicknesses which end in death'. He is a realist (emphatically not a 'new novelist') armed with a formidable, vigorous poetry—his style. Bellow is above all an individualist, a man concerned to demonstrate that, although society has become so gigantic, individual human beings have not become smaller. He has tended to show Kafkaesque, put-upon man in his absurdity but also in his glory. It is mistaken to miss this essential simplicity in Bellow. One must remember that he has said, of Dreiser, 'I often think criticism of Dreiser as a stylist at times betrays a resistance to the feelings he causes readers to suffer. If they can say he can't write, they need not experience these feelings'. This unfashionable statement tells us much about the novelist who made it; fashionable interpretation of him does not always take it into account.

Although Bellow has developed, by widening his scope and his style accordingly, he sees all his protagonists as 'victims' of life in search of a cure in the Godless twentieth century. In his first novel, *Dangling Man* (1944) he introduces the first version of his hero, Joseph (not Joseph K.; but he has no surname), who is 'dangling' because he has given up his job and is waiting to be called up. The form is a journal. Joseph is passive, resigned, but hypersensitive about life; finally he begs for defeat by asking to be called up as soon as possible. *Dangling Man* shows modern man burdened, bored, by his very liberty—and yet alienated from those around him by his concern. *The Victim* (1947) goes more deeply into the question of Jewishness. Asa Leventhal, a journalist, worries about his position;

he is picked up by a mad, drunken, anti-semite who accuses him of having once done him a wrong. Leventhal becomes aware, through being persecuted by this creature, that he needs something to hate, that he too carries within him an anti-human virus. There is a marvellous scene, characteristic of Bellow at his most powerful and moving, in which the two men come into physical contact—to blows; Leventhal is suddenly aware of his complicity, with his antagonist and torturer, in life itself. The two men are 'brothers'. This novel ends on a serene note, and one of the characters makes a remark that might serve for an epigraph to all Bellow's fiction: 'Choose dignity. Nobody knows enough to turn it down'. This is, of course, an anthropologist speaking.

In the picaresque, technically unambitious, loose *The Adventures of Augie March* (1953) Bellow presents what has been called his first 'above ground' hero, Augie, who refuses to accept defeat although he recognizes that 'everyone got bitterness in his chosen thing'. Augie is different from Joseph or Leventhal: although still a victim, he affirms rather than questions everything. He becomes a gangster, a kind of gigolo, a husband: he accepts it all.

But this (*Henderson the Rain King, Herzog* and *Mr. Sammler's Planet* are its successors) is the first of Bellow's 'big' books, of which only *Herzog* really comes off. There is a sense of strain here. The novel does not cohere: it is a series of episodes, some superb, where its predecessors clearly were not. The novella *Seize the Day* (1956), which as originally published appeared with a play and another shorter story, accomplishes more in a tenth of the length. This is about a failure—as a breadwinner, as a husband, as a son—the most clearly defined of all Bellow's victims. He knows he is unworthy and a fool, and yet he must hand his money over to a crooked psychiatrist, Tamkin, to be 'multiplied on the stock exchange'. He can fulfil himself only as the dupe of a confidence man; must sit and watch as his money is lost. In the end, defeated, stripped of money, turned away by his rich, valetudinarian old father whom he merely embarrasses, Tommy Wilhelm burst into tears in a chapel at the funeral of a complete stranger ('It must be somebody real close to carry on so', someone says). The music plays: 'He heard it and sank deeper than sorrow, through torn sobs and cries towards the consummation of his heart's ultimate need'. This is, curiously or otherwise (as one looks at it), one of the most moving endings in the whole of twentieth-century literature.

Henderson the Rain King (1959) is a comparative failure. This story of a (non-Jewish) millionaire who goes to Africa in quest of wisdom incorporates Bellow's anthropological interests, and despite its exuberance is ultimately bogged down in intellectuality. *Herzog* (1961) is, however, a successful long study of a middle-aged Jewish intellectual, a kind of Tommy Wilhelm but without the final masochistic need to submit to fate. Herzog is, of course, another victim; he is betrayed by his friends and wives and even his doctor, and he is forever writing letters of carefully reasoned complaint. These letters are really to God, the architect of his misery, in whom he continues to believe, 'Though never admitting it'. The greatest challenge to Herzog has been the one who makes him suffer most acutely, his second wife, who is unfaithful to him with the repulsive Valentine Gersbach. Without her choice treachery and her insane charges that he is insane, he feels nothing: she makes him remarkable. The vigour of this novel is the shrill vigour of nervous exhaustion; and yet Bellow succeeds in portraying an intellectual (a brilliant one) more convincingly than any other novelist of his time. *Mr. Sammler's Planet* (1970) is another exercise in the picaresque. Since Bellow's is a major talent, it has exquisite passages. But it hardly coheres around its central character as *Herzog* does. It is largely a vehicle for Bellow's (counter-revolutionary) philosophy. This philosophy, 'old-fashioned' in terms of today's youngest university rebels but in no way reactionary, seems wise and mellow to many of Bellow's readers; but this does not make his novel more than a series of episodes, a product of thought rather than imagination.

Bellow has written a play, *The Last Analysis* (1965), which was produced in 1964, and a volume of short stories, *Mosby's Memoirs* (1969).

BERNARD MALAMUD (1914), born in New York, is like Bellow the son of parents who had emigrated from Russia not long before his birth. It is Malamud who made the famous remark, 'All men are Jews', by which he meant that all men are at heart sensitive, alienated—'chosen'. His first novel, *The Natural* (1952), was a comic masterpiece, a treatment of baseball in terms of the American hero. This contained the germ of Malamud's method—a marriage of realism and fable that had been called 'magic realism' (q.v. 2, 3)—as well as exploiting his pride in being a Brooklyn baseball afficcionado. His next novel, *The Assistant* (1957), a work of rare beauty and affirmation, is on his theme of 'All men are Jews'. It remains his best novel, and is on a level with anything of Bellow's. Bellow undoubtedly has the greater intellect and perhaps the greater potential; but he has not bettered this. *The Assistant* is about nothing less than goodness. Frankie Alpine is a Gentile hoodlum who robs a poor Jewish shopkeeper. Out of a pity he tries to resist—one is

reminded of Flannery O'Connor's heroes resisting their vocation—
he goes to work for him, and gradually becomes involved in his
defeated and unsuccessful life. He falls in love with the grocer's
daughter, Helen, and accepts her criticisms of him. In the end he
actually becomes the grocer (who dies), running the store and
grumblingly performing the same acts of charity. He has himself
circumcised and becomes a Jew.

A New Life (1961) is a campus novel, tracing the progress of
Seymour Levi from rock bottom to a realization that life is holy.
This, although richly comic, is not altogether free from sentimentality. *The Fixer* (1967) is Malamud's most ambitious novel. It is not
as good as *The Assistant* because its effects have been strained for too
hard: it is an attempt to rival Bellow with a 'big' novel, and an
attempt to write the great 'All men are Jews' novel. Considering
this—the sense of strain is apparent—it is remarkably successful. It
is loosely based on the case of Mendel Beiliss, an innocent Jewish
workman who was tried in Tzarist Russia for the 'ritual' murder of
a boy—and acquitted in spite of the conspiracy against him. *The
Fixer* (handyman) describes the ordeal of Yakov Bok; the result of
his trial, however, is left open. *Pictures of Fidelman* (1969) is a picaresque novel set in Italy. This is Malamud's weakest work, in which
he experiments unsuccessfully with surrealism, and where his invention often seems less comic than farcical. Much better are his short
stories, collected in *The Magic Barrel* (1958) and *Idiots First* (1963).
The Jewish stories in the first collection remind one of the Yiddish-
American author, Isaac Bashevis Singer (q.v.); the later stories try
to get away from Brooklyn, as if in preparation for *The Fixer* and
Pictures of Fidelman.

We get another and very different version of American Jewish
fiction in the work of NORMAN MAILER (1923), who was also raised in
Brooklyn. The accent here has been increasingly on performance;
the fiction has deteriorated as the journalism has improved. The
radical sociologist has turned into the white Negro hipster. Mailer is
the most vivid figure on the American literary scene; he is decidedly
not a playboy, although he is, of course, an exhibitionist—and he
has come dangerously near to fragmenting himself. However, he is
contemptuous of any kind of official literary criticism, and with
some justification; and he has to be saluted for his courage in trying
by every means in his power to capture and bring up out of himself
what is unconscious and mysterious. His seeing of himself as a
performer, his unabashed self-appraisal in *Advertisements for Myself*
(1959), where he tells of his vanities and aspirations, may irritate
some. But they should look into their own minds. He is often silly;

but it would not be possible for him to fulfil his existential project in any other way.

His first novel, *The Naked and the Dead* (1948), the best of the American Second World War books, was in the realist tradition; but it foreshadowed the rest of his work. It concerns two different kinds of proto-fascist, a general and a sergeant, and an ineffective liberal lieutenant—in retrospect one can see that this figure is Mailer himself, unhappy in the role of a traditional radical writing a war book in conventional terms. This is a good book, containing in particular shrewd analyses of the motivations of the authoritarian types. But it has little characterization and, curiously enough, little compassion.

In *Barbary Shore* (1951) and *The Deer Park* (1955) we see Mailer making more effort to put himself meaningfully into his fictions. He goes into first-person singular narration and drops pretence of strict realism; the prose is messy, but some of the portraits, such as that of Eitel the radical film director, are unforgettable. However, these are based on real people. They are not invented: they are very good journalism. As one reads on in Mailer's fiction, coming to *An American Dream* (1965) and the disastrous *Why Are We in Vietnam?* (1967), one begins to suspect that he does not have an inventive imagination at all. Certainly he has evolved a 'position', one that is derived in large part from the psychoanalyst Wilhelm Reich, and resembles D. H. Lawrence's. Reich preached the necessity of full, creative orgasm, and towards the end of his life could detect the 'orgone energy' in the universe (it gave off a blueish light). Mailer is not quite so set on the orgasm, or at least not on its blueish light; but the central theme of his later work is the necessity of living life according to instinct. The 'White Negro' or hipster is distinguished from the passive Beat by his active, energetic quest for pleasure. Rojack in *An American Dream* is simply an embodiment of this new kind of overman—and if his story is not biblical in its import, then one has to take it as being very silly and, worse, dangerous in its implications. We have to applaud Mailer for his courage (as he wants us to do); but we are also entitled to ask how much, in fact, he cares about anything but the quality of each of his particular performances. The generalization 'love', which comes easily to the lips of his disciples, is unconvincing in the absence of an answer. Commitment to Reich is one form that current American Utopianism takes. (Another, following Norman O. Brown, is against Reich's 'full genitality', and insists on a return to bisexual 'polymorphous perversity' and play without orgasm.) Bellow has been said to be committed to Reich; but at his best he is a writer rather than a philosopher, and even when he is a philosopher he builds himself a very respectable structure. Mailer is a public man, and he functions as such—like a boxer always forced to put on a performance. The question is whether in this way, without solitude, with public pressures upon him, he can properly function as a writer. The answer may well be that, unless he gets beyond his competitiveness, he is doomed to sink into confusion and fashionably hip reportage— as his report on the 1970 American moonshot, *A Fire on the Moon* (1970), suggests. The energy that drives him is phenomenal; but it can end by driving a husk.

HERBERT GOLD (1924), from Cleveland, is an inventive and often comic novelist who has ambitions to be a Bellow but remains trapped in the meandering picaresque. Even his best novels fragment into comedy or farce just as something interesting is happening in the mind of the central character. His novels include *Birth of a Hero* (1951), *The Prospect Before Us* (1954), *The Optimist* (1959), his best character study, on a man who wants to succeed *and* be loved by all, and *Therefore Be Bold* (1960), a sensitive first-person account of a Jewish adolescence in Ohio in the late Thirties. *Love and Like* (1960) collects short stories.

*

WILLIAM BURROUGHS (1914), born in St. Louis, for much of his life an expatriate, is part of an American sociological phenomenon. The Beat (exhaustion, but also beatification) movement began spontaneously in San Francisco in the Fifties, and was at first entirely sociological. People who were dissatisfied with bourgeois society reacted against it not by rebellion but simply by dropping out. The original Beats had no leaders; their aims were passive. They were influenced by, but did not understand, Zen Buddhism, and they sought private illumination by means of drugs and/or drink. Their spiritual fathers included Whitman and Henry Miller (q.v.); and the good-natured, unconscious business man who put them on the map, and invented several reputations—including that of Burroughs —was the poet Allen Ginsberg (q.v.). Burroughs' best book was his first, published in 1953 under the pseudonym of William Lee: *Junkie*. This is an account of his life as a drug addict. He had held a number of jobs in New York (private detective, factory-worker, barman); then in 1944 he became addicted to heroin and moved to New Orleans and Mexico, where he shot his wife in an accident. *Junkie* was a relatively straightforward book. In 1957 he flew from Tangier to London for the apomorphine treatment, and apart from two relapses immediately afterwards has not touched the drug since. Nowadays Burroughs, having delivered himself of his works—*The Naked Lunch* (1959), *The Soft Machine* (1961), *Nova Express* (1964), and others—is mainly a prophet-interviewer. What is perhaps most impressive about him is his monumental stupidity and naïvety. He discovered Reich late, and refreshes himself in one of those boxes— to gather orgone energy—that earned their inventor a prison sentence he did not survive. He is (or was) a 'scientologist'. He postulates, with apparent seriousness, an all-male community in which reproduction would be confined to test tubes. He admired China's Red Guards not because he could understand anything about them, but because (like Hitler?) 'they feel they have something important to do'.

His creative work is unoriginal but none the less looks different. His techniques consist of: the use of various aleatory devices to produce associations that arise from illogic, especially the illogic of dreams; these are superimposed on pulp type plots, bad SF or gangster books. His 'cut-out' and 'fold-in' techniques, consisting of certain semi-aleatory ways of manipulating existing material, are merely variations of old surrealist games. *The Naked Lunch* counterpoints a realist account of a junkie's life with the subjective horrors he experiences; it is supposed to have been given what little coherence it has by the shrewd Ginsberg, whose own incoherence is voluntary. The real subject, which is what a junkie experiences in withdrawal, is nausea. The organization of *The Naked Lunch* is naïve in the extreme. The themes are *addiction, control* (leading to more control), *power* and *means of cure*. His other works do not radically depart from this scheme. Burroughs submits his original material (which is probably bathetic and ill written) to his various techniques, spicing it up with clippings from his 'favourite' cut-in sources, such as the novels of William Golding (q.v.). But his chief obsessions emerge: the erections of hanged men, anal rape. . . .

What is pitiful is that Burroughs, an essentially simple-minded man, and one perhaps less unintelligent on than off narcotics, has been treated by some critics (including, amazingly, Mary McCarthy, q.v.) as an innovator. He is historically important; but his importance is as, in Leslie Fiedler's words, a 'pioneer mutant', pledged to become a child.

JACK KEROUAC (ps. JEAN-LOUIS KEROUAC, 1922–69), who 'died of drink and angry sicknesses' (Ted Berrigan), had a grotesquely inflated reputation; but as a latter-day Thomas Wolfe (q.v.), though a vastly inferior writer, he has historical importance. Kerouac was always a wanderer, and was thrice married and twice divorced, both times in less than a year. Originally he was a drunken drifter who managed to commit to paper a bad Wolfeian novel called *The Town and the City* (1950). It contains in embryo his stale message: ignorance, incoherence and illiteracy are beatific, crime is lovely, do as you want, get stoned, learn to be naïve, attain sweetness and light. But it took the astute Ginsberg to launch him as a legend. *On the Road* (1957), typewritten on a continuous roll of art paper in three weeks flat, has distinction as being the most non-structured book of its decade. In writing it Kerouac simply followed his own nose. It is in no sense fiction, but a record of the wanderings of three bums; Sal Paradise (Kerouac), Carlo Marx (Ginsberg), and Dean Moriarty (a friend of theirs called Neil Cassady). *The Dharma Bums* (1958) is similar, but puts emphasis on Kerouac's search for realization through some kind of Zen Buddhism. If anyone doubts Kerouac's pretentiousness, and the self-delusion in which he existed, he should read *Satori in Paris* (1966), in which he humourlessly describes a journey to Paris in search of his French ancestry, drinking bouts, and a final Buddhist illumination—as convincing as the 'satori' claimed by an English Buddhist, the judge Christmas Humphreys. Kerouac wrote many books, and in all of them he splashed, a critic rightly said, 'everything energetically with his own boisterous, messy ego'.

*

TRUMAN CAPOTE (1924), who was born in New Orleans, is close to Tennessee Williams (q.v.) in atmosphere; all his books up to *In Cold Blood* (1966) sugar and prettify the same kind of Gothic-invert world. Leslie Fiedler calls Capote a representative of the 'Effete Dandies or . . . Decadents' school, which he sees as deriving from Faulkner. Certainly Capote is flip and his 'amusement' at evil is tiresome and even irresponsible—he can give a sense of a perverse boy liking to annoy his reader by being sick and crippled; but that is only one side of the picture. Capote is a consummate artist, a writer very serious about his craft, who, no matter whether his reader likes it or not, does create a world of his own. Things are seen by Capote not with an innocent but with the goblin eye of a self-retarded soul. In his first book, *Other Voices, Other Rooms* (1948), the boy Joel Knox sinks into a decadent homosexual relationship with the transvestite Randolph in just the same way as his paralyzed father's rotting house sinks gradually into the swamp on which it is built. As John A. Aldridge has said, Capote here achieves a purity, of 'the sort that can be attained only in the isolation of a mind which life has never violated, in which the image of art has developed to a flowerlike perfection because it has developed alone'. Capote is no surrealist; but his world is more dream than real. He does not like to call himself a Southern writer, but there is no doubt that his dream is a Southern one. Its inner coherence is admirable; but its relationship with anybody else's world is problematical. If Joel Knox's pilgrimage is for the father or the Holy Grail then these are fathers and grails few others would know anything about. *The Grass Harp* (1951) is about an eleven-year-old orphan who, with one of his elderly aunts and three others, is driven, by the nastiness of the world, to live in a tree-house. This little community is presented as innocent and even improved in its efficacy to deal with reality; there are allusions to Noah's ark and to Huck's raft. There is much sharply perceptive, fresh writing; but the pretty vision is corrupted by Capote's lack of interest in people as people. With *Breakfast at Tiffany's* (1958) Capote tipped his talent in the direction of the middlebrow: this traced the adventures of a playgirl, Holly Golightly, against the background of modern Manhattan. The book may well have achieved its popularity because Holly is utterly superficial, flip, all phoney; the book has a kind of false vitality, but is quite without warmth. And yet the writing is on an altogether higher level than the cult of the child which the book is advocating. *In Cold Blood* (1966) is a piece of gripping and highly intelligent journalism reconstructing a peculiarly brutal murder; Capote investigated the case in depth. This marked a complete break with the first three, narcissistic novels; but *In Cold Blood*, in spite of its author's claim to have invented a new form, 'the documentary novel', is no more than very good journalism. *Tree of Night* (1949) collects short stories.

Mark Twain was the first American to see the Noble Savage as a child (Huck), and writers have not stopped imitating him, or sharing in his vision, ever since. Truman Capote is a good example. Another is J. D. SALINGER (1919), whose *The Catcher in the Rye* (1951) achieved heights of popularity denied to any other 'quality' novel since the war. Salinger had studied at various establishments before the war without getting a degree; he ended up at Columbia in a short-story class taught by Whit Burnett, founder and editor of *Story*—not to be confused with the writer of superior gangster fiction W. R. BURNETT (1899), author of *Little Caesar* (1929)—a magazine which published his first story in 1940. He entered the army in 1942, and took part in five campaigns. It has been suggested that his military experiences brought his nausea with modern existence to the surface.

Salinger became so popular, a star *New Yorker* writer, because in *The Catcher in the Rye* he discovered the exact tone and flavour of post-war middle-class, adolescent alienation. The use of the vernacular owes much to Ring Lardner (q.v.); but it is Salinger's own (and greatest) achievement. The book is about Holden Caulfield, who flunks school and must go home to tell his parents about it. He spends a weekend in New York failing to connect, being nauseated by everybody, finding everything phoney. Only two nuns he meets at breakfast strike him as genuine. After an experience of feeling 'damn happy', which anticipates the *kitsch* Zen of the later stories, Holden goes home, falls psychiatrically ill, and is psychoanalyzed. The monologue that is *The Catcher in the Rye* is (presumably) part of a healthful therapy. But to what purpose? The book ends: 'Don't ever tell anybody anything. If you do, you start missing everybody'. *The Catcher in the Rye* is limited by its failure to go beyond Holden: it catches a style, and one must concede that it does so marvellously; but it has no wisdom, can imply no alternative either to the phoney world or the, ultimately, tiresome Holden. Here lies another reason for its popularity (although Salinger should not be blamed for this): the young do not want alternatives, or to acknowledge the necessity of compromise with the adult world they reject; so they seized on Holden Caulfield. As Walter Allen has said, Salinger's is the *New Yorker* version of the Beats and hipsters. For his older readers, whose notion of the ultimate in intelligence is to be found in the pages of the *New Yorker*, he had a comforting message: junior has been sick like you once were, but next week he will be coming home and he will go back to school. . . . I do not think this was the intention, but Salinger would have been a really important writer only if he could have written of the defeat (or victory?) of an adult Holden Caulfield; and if he could then have peopled his world not with cliché-shams (that is what the 'phonies' of *The Catcher in the Rye* are) but with real people—shams, yes; but shams with the varyingly concealed humanity that they do have. But the successors to *The Catcher in the Rye*, all short fictions, skilful though they are, do not suggest this possibility; and it is significant that except for a single story published by the *New Yorker* in 1965 Salinger has, in the Sixties, dried up. *Nine Stories* (1953), *Franny and Zooey* (1961) and *Raise High the Roof Beam, Carpenters*; and *Seymour: An Introduction* (1963) form a chronicle of the eccentric Glass family, including Buddy Glass, who is a representation of Salinger himself. Even by the side of *The Catcher in the Rye*, these tend to be cute and to fall back not on any kind of mellowness or comprehension of the real nature of the world, but on pseudo-religiosity.

JOHN UPDIKE (1932) worked for the *New Yorker* after leaving Harvard, and is now the brightest, funniest, most intelligent and entertaining from that stable. His first novel, *The Poorhouse Fair* (1959), is about a revolt of the old people in an institution against their liberal director. *Bech* (1970), his most recent, tells the story of a successful middle-aged Jewish writer who can do everything except write well. It is clearly Updike's effort to justify his own middlebrow success, which has led Leslie Fiedler to say of him that he provides 'the illusion of vision and fantasy without surrendering the kind of reassurance provided by slick writing at its most professionally *all right*'. It fails to explain Bech at all; but Updike does manage to convey a sympathy for this husk, who is presented not as a bad writer but a victim of the middlebrow public. . . .

JAMES BALDWIN (1924) was born in Harlem. He never knew his real father, to whom his mother was not married; but his stepfather, a preacher, rejected him and told him he was ugly—all against a background of bigotry and religious fanaticism. At fourteen Baldwin, in competition with his stepfather and wanting to draw bigger audiences than he did, became a preacher, a Holy Roller in the Fireside Pentecostal Church in Harlem. Except for the few years in which he wrote his two first (and best) novels, Baldwin has been a preacher ever since. His first novel, *Go Tell it on the Mountain* (1953), describes the conversion of a fourteen-year-old; this is a vision of ecstasy brought about by the guilts and stresses of initiation into puberty, by the hatred of his father, and by the desire to escape altogether to a new world. *Giovanni's Room* (1956) is set in Paris and deals with a conflict between homosexual and heterosexual love. *Another Country* (1962) mixes fine fiction with homosexual preaching. As Leslie Fiedler has been most articulate in pointing out, in America Jew, Negro and homosexual have become to some extent identified—because, of course, all are discriminated against. In Baldwin's third novel ('precisely because he is a homosexual as well as a Negro', claims Fiedler) one of the messages—the most important message, to Baldwin—is that hate between white and black is exacerbated by male-female relationships but healed by homosexual ones. Now the predicament of Negroes and homosexuals (how long before we write this word with an initial capital?) is similar (although the real enemies of homosexuality are themselves homosexuals, but repressed); the future of an overpopulated world may well have to be homosexual; but, unless one takes negritude to be a disorder, the nature of the Negro and the homosexual *may* not be similar. At all events, Baldwin has to manipulate his people and his situations to elevate homosexuality into a panacea for the racial human illness. This approach does not really help to resolve the tension between the two ideas which Baldwin has recognized that any writer—but most

particularly a Negro writer—'must hold . . . forever in his mind':
'. . . the acceptance, totally without rancour, of life as it is . . . [and
the idea] that one must never . . . accept . . . injustices as commonplace . . .'. Eric Jones, the bisexual actor who dominates the second
part of *Another Country*, is an unreal figure. *Tell Me How Long the
Train's Been Gone* (1968) deals with Baldwin in his role of publicist in
the person of Leo Proudhammer; it seems to have been thrown
hurriedly together, and shows a marked deterioration. However, as
his creative work has declined, so his strength as an essay writer has
increased. His function has changed: from imaginative writer to
inspired Negro publicist.

There are at least a score of American novelists under fifty who
have some fair claims to importance. Some, like Philip Roth, have
gained commercial success; others, like John Hawkes, have not. The
greatest *succés d'éstime* has been JOHN BARTH (1930), though so far
critical enthusiasm tends to be expressed around publication time.
The immensely ambitious *Giles Goat-Boy* (1967) is one of those novels
that is either a masterpiece, albeit a flawed one—or something very
much smaller. Barth is an academic and has been one ever since he
graduated from Johns Hopkins. His novels, however, are as anti-
academic as they are academic. He is amusing, inventive of situations,
a trained philosopher, a polymath. His work is by a large number of
people (including Nabokov, Kafka, Borges, Beckett, qq.v., Bunyan,
Lewis Carroll) out of James Joyce (q.v.). He relies on puns, slang of
all sorts and pastiche (and parody). His own ability to write prose
has so far been concealed by these intellectual pyrotechnics (his use
of slang is photographic). Barth is an author of 'in-books'; that so
astute a critic as Leslie Fiedler can admire them is evidence that they
contain in-jokes about academe that are good jokes; but a number of
reviewers have knowingly saluted the achievement without, however,
understanding it in the least.

Giles Goat-Boy is the ultimate in the *Bildungsroman* (q.v. 2); like
Barth's preceding three novels—*The Floating Opera* (1956, rev. 1967),
The End of the Road (1958, rev. 1968) and *The Sot-Weed Factor* (1960,
rev. 1967), only more specifically and ironically, it deals in 'education'.
Here the universe is a university, into which are launched a false
Messiah—and a counter-claimant, Giles Goat-Boy, a 'horned human
student'. This is dazzlingly clever, and I suppose some of those who
combine crossword-puzzle mentalities with philosophical inclinations
might have got through its 700-odd pages. The fact is that *Giles
Goat-Boy* is a prototype for a certain kind of book: the new, scholastic,
inturned Joycean epic. The justification comes out of Borges: the
novelist is to re-invent the universe, but adding the coherence 'God'

lacks. The self-caressing, 'fiendish' ingenuity comes from Nabokov, the Nabokov of such books as *Pale Fire* (1962) and, alas, *Ada*, with its whiff of exalted *kitsch*. Barth is serious, a comedian, a man with marvellous ideas—but his own language offers no clue to the presence of a creative imagination.

The enormous success of the 'masturbation novel', *Portnoy's Complaint* (1969) by PHILIP ROTH (1933), who was born in New Jersey, makes it difficult to assess him. It is an amusing comic book, an eminently worthwhile variation on the American Jewish novel; but it is not in the top flight. Roth belongs, as a critic puts it, in the tradition of American writers 'which examines the individual's posture of optimistic wilfulness and finds it wanting'. Thus, the compassionate sensibility of the hero of *Letting Go* (1962), Gabe Wallach, is crippled by his sentimentality and his weakness. But this book was ill organized, and its author's flipness drowned his delicacy of insight. *When She Was Good* (1967) is his best book. Lucy Nelson revenges herself for her inadequate childhood by turning herself into a castrator, a possessor of men-objects; and yet the vitality that throbs in her, tragic substitute for humanity, is vividly conveyed. *Portnoy's Complaint* is intelligent black Jewish comedy; but sheer professionalism, a facility for skating over the difficult explanations, spoils it. Alexander Portnoy cannot learn that his feelings of imprisonment arise from his failure to relate to others; but masturbation is not an adequate symbol for this.

American critics are mostly hostile to JAMES PURDY (1923), who was born in Ohio. One can see why: his homosexual Gothic is unmitigated and his control of it is doubtful, and, in any case, inelegant. But he has unquestionable power. He experienced fierce rejection until Edith Sitwell (q.v.), doubtless in a receptive mood, since she possessed small judgement in her last monomanic years, found him an English publisher. In America he was eventually, and predictably, taken up by CARL VAN VECHTEN (1880–1964), a dilettante old critic who was born out of his time and whose pussy predilections Purdy fulfilled with suitable modern garishness. In Van Vechten's decadent, well written novels —*Peter Whiffle* (1922), *The Tattooed Countess* (1924) and the excellent *Nigger Heaven* (1926)—we may find foreshadowed not only Purdy's anguished quest for love in violence but also a source (or anticipation) of much American fiction concerned with homosexuality. Purdy gets less attention than many inferior writers because, although he has humour, he does not pretend that his view of life is other than despairing. He is unacceptable to the *New Yorker* public because his misogyny is not comfortingly conveyed: not smuggled in, so to speak, between cocktails. *63: Dream*

Palace (1956), the novella that made Purdy's name when it was published with other stories in *Colour of Darkness* (1957), portrays a man, lost and misused in a small town, who kills the brother he loves. He is seen as a victim of urban technology; but the author's Calvinist ancestry is more obvious than any desire to criticize modern society. . . . *Malcolm* (1959) projects homosexual anxiety onto a fifteen-year-old boy who wanders through a world of depravity in search of his lost father, only to be destroyed by ugly and evil forces. This, written in terms of bitter comedy, is a horrifying story, but it illuminates the urban indifference to evil with a real poetry. *The Nephew* (1960), a more integrated novel, and the high point in Purdy's writing, describes a spinster's search for the personality of the nephew, missing in Korea, whom she brought up; she does not find what she seeks—predictably, this nephew was among other things homosexual. The author cleverly and with surprising gentleness reveals the mainsprings of her own personality as she puzzles over her discoveries. If *Cabot Brown Begins* (1965), whose central character makes contact with others by means of rape ('at the rate of about $1\frac{1}{2}$ per diem') is Grand Guignol then *Eustace Chisholm and the Works* (1968), set in the Chicago of the Depression, is fashionable Gothic. The eponymous hero writes 'the Works' in charcoal on old pages of the *Chicago Tribune*. Another character is only able to express his true homosexual bent when sleepwalking; he is disembowelled by a mad Captain, also—it need hardly be added—homosexual. It is sad to see so eloquent a writer reduced to this; but criticism of Purdy, mostly hostile, is oddly silent about why he is granted attention at all—which is because of the quality of his style. This is very carefully based on the speech of Ohio, and is an achievement in itself. Purdy cannot (surely) indulge in more extensions of the Gothic; if he is to survive as a writer he must, it seems, allow this style to lead him into his subject.

JOHN HAWKES (1925), born in Connecticut, has a number of faults, the main one being a tendency to very heavy rhetoric; all his work, too, is uneven. But he is that very rare article: a genuine experimental writer. This is something for which a price usually has to be paid. Hawkes, like Barth, is concerned with the creation of fictional worlds, not with the transcription of events. But his approach is quite different; and less intellectual. Whatever the faults of his prose, it is always evident that an imagination of great power is struggling to express itself—with Barth one does not feel that the great energy arises from more than ingenuity. Hawkes' books are something like dreams, and so is their logic. He has been called a fabulist and a surrealist, but neither term really helps. The fact is that, for all the suddenly emerging rhetorical crudities and fallings-back on brutality when his own procedures break down, Hawkes is one of the most original writers of his time. It is true that his peculiar methods resemble those of DJUNA BARNES (1892); but he seems to me, although not to all critics, superior. Still, the comparison (originally Fiedler's, who called one of Hawkes' novels '*Brighton Rock* rewritten by Djuna Barnes') is useful.

Djuna Barnes, born in New York, for long a member of the between-the-wars Paris expatriates, is a minor Gothic decadent—who was somewhat irresponsibly commended by T. S. Eliot (q.v.), with the predictable effect that she became a cult-object. Eliot wrote that her *Nightwood* (1936) had a quality 'very nearly related to that of Elizabethan tragedy'. This was, quite simply, wrong: the quality of this surrealist study in psychopathology (mostly sexual) is actually related to the French decadence of the Nineties. Djuna Barnes has also written *The Book of Repulsive Women* (1915), *A Book* (1923; rev. as *A Night Among the Horses*, 1929), the stream-of-consciousness novel *Ryder* (1928), and *The Antiphon* (1958), a tedious play in blank verse written perhaps under the influence of Eliot's linking of her with the Elizabethans. Her *Selected Works* were published in 1962. Djuna Barnes undoubtedly possesses originality; she adds to it an element of pretentiousness; and when all else fails her she retreats into irresponsible surrealism; attempts to demonstrate how her images cohere have not been convincing.

Hawkes' work resembles Djuna Barnes' in the integrity of its peculiar atmosphere. *Nightwood* is too long and too full of forced Gothic to be a major book; but it does have its own extraordinary atmosphere. Hawkes' *The Cannibal* (1949), his first novel, has a similar integrity but is less spoilt. It is no more about the horrors of devastated Germany than Robbe-Grillet's *The House of Assignation* (q.v. 2) is 'about' Hong Kong. Hawkes' post-war Germany is, however, as valid as any other: such fiction implies the question, Whose Germany can be viable? *The Lime Twig* (1961) is possibly based on Greene's *Brighton Rock* (q.v.) in the way Golding's *Lord of the Flies* (q.v.) is based on Ballantyne's *Coral Island*. It takes place in what Hawkes calls the London blitz. But this is only his surrender to a certain image he has (uncorrected by any historical investigation) of this event. *The Beetle Leg* (1951), perhaps his most successful novel, is about a worker buried alive while building a dam. It is certainly not realistic, but it is not symbolic either. One might better say that Hawkes' world here illuminates the reader's. . . . Of course he can be merely quaint; one of the stories collected in *Lunar Landscapes* (1970) begins: 'Early in the morning in a town famous for the growing of some grape, I arose from my bed in the inn and stepped outside alone to the automobile'. But that was perhaps to get a start. Hawkes, who has also written the novel *Second Skin* (1964) and some plays, is one of the leading writers of his generation, and one from whom we may perhaps expect the most.

EVAN S. CONNELL (1924) is one of the most accomplished of American novelists. He is always professional, but this never obtrudes into his work; he does not make concessions to gain entertainment value. He is not a loud novelist, but the way he distances himself from his material should not lead any reader to suppose that he lacks feeling. His less good novels (for example, *Diary of a Rapist*, 1966) do, it is true, strain after effect at the expense of feeling; but *Mr. Bridge* (1969) amply demonstrates that this is not lacking. At his worst Connell writes too tastefully well; but his mastery of technique stands him in good stead in *Mr. Bridge*, in which he portrays a modern Babbitt more skilfully and unambiguously than Sinclair Lewis (q.v.) —but not with the same raw power. Here he composes in vignettes, some not more than a page long; the cumulative effect is remarkable, and conveys the picture of a whole man. Connell is not a major writer; but within the limits he sets himself he is an excellent minor one. His other novels include *Mrs. Bridge* (1959); *The Anatomy Lesson* (1957) and *At the Crossroads* (1965) collect short stories. *Notes From a Bottle Found on the Beach at Carmel* (1963), a long poem in the manner of Pound's *Cantos*, is not poetry but is interesting, intelligent and readable.

HUBERT SELBY (1928) achieved notoriety through *Last Exit to Brooklyn* (1964), which the British government tried and failed to ban. It is a book of short stories, essentially in the realist tradition, about homosexuals and transvestites in Brooklyn. Few have written so vividly about the miseries of the extreme forms of homosexuality. It is ironic that Selby should have been selected for prosecution, because his attitude towards his material is somewhat puritanical. Doubtless it was his truthfulness and starkness that offended: he is one of the few writers of his generation to prove the continuing viability of realism. *The Room* (1972), describing the sexual fantasies of an imprisoned psychotic, is at once a terrifying and a deeply compassionate novel.

V

The general tendency in American poetry in the last thirty years might be said to be towards Williams and away from Frost or Ransom (qq.v.), with the figure of Pound in the middle. Thus, such a poet as Marianne Moore is right of centre, whereas Roethke (q.v.) is to the left of it. But this is no more than a useful generalization. The recent poetry of John Berryman (q.v.), although it is disliked or ignored by the Beats and their associates, is not really classifiable.

Two 'schools' do exist side by side, however, and for the most part they sullenly ignore each other. On the one hand there are such poets as Creeley (q.v.), Edward Dorn, Gary Snyder (q.v.)—the sort collected by Donald Allen and Creeley in their *New Writing in the U.S.A.* (1967); on the other there is an academic group, more traditional: this includes Lowell, Wilbur, Snodgrass (qq.v.); James Wright, Robert Bly (qq.v.) and some others occupy a middle position—or, perhaps it is fairer to say, an independent one.

The last serious conservative, traditionalist movement in American poetry was promulgated by the Southern group of poets who called themselves the Fugitives. *The Fugitive*, a bi-monthly little magazine, appeared between 1922 and 1925. The contributors were mostly associated with Vanderbilt University; their leader was JOHN CROWE RANSOM (1888–1974), the son of a Tennessee Methodist minister. After studying at Vanderbilt and Oxford, England (as a Rhodes scholar), Ransom went back to Vanderbilt as an instructor in English. He stayed there for a quarter of a century and played a leading part in the Southern renaissance—that 'renaissance' which was preceded by nothing.

Southern Agrarianism was conservative, but the individuals who propounded it were not illiberal. The Agrarian programme is set forth in the 1930 symposium *I'll Take My Stand*, to which Ransom, Warren, Tate (qq.v.) and other Southerners contributed. One could make out a case for this programme being crypto-fascist, especially since its philosophy flowed from Plato; or a case for its being over-scholarly and, in politics, naïve—which in some aspects it is. Its importance, however, is not as a political programme—whatever its proponents may have thought at the time—but as the matrix for some important creative writing. The programme itself is essentially nostalgic, but being intellectual and scholarly it is carefully non-populist. The Agrarians advocated a non-industrialized, Agrarian South, and thus one not exploited by the North; they wanted culture to take the place of politics in an aristocracy. Their version of the Civil War is, of course, a complicated one; but we may be forgiven for interpreting it as a fight between culture (the South) and politics (the North). Agrarianism was not, however, obscurantist: regarded as something to be re-created. It would have to grow up as the men of the South learned to mould their lives to the natural geography of their region.

What all this actually represented was the last really intelligent, gifted traditionalist movement in American (or British) poetry. A poetry for the most part content to work within the limits of what has gone before it, needs to be attached to a set of real beliefs. (The trouble with the routine Georgians, q.v., in England, or, indeed, with any routine middlebrow versifiers, is that they have only a set of pseudo-beliefs, and slackly sentimental ones at that.) For a short time Agrarianism provided such a set of beliefs. Not all people will condemn a movement that referred to science and technology as new barbarisms 'controlled and directed by the modern power state'. And when it was clear that Agrarianism was no longer viable the same group, the Fugitives, turned to the development of the 'new criticism'. This term had been used as early as 1910 by the critic Joel E. Spingarn to describe his own methods; but what Ransom meant by it—in his book *The New Criticism* (1941)—was different. Taking into account all the critics who have been described as new critics one can fairly say no more than that the new criticism, as generally understood (Ransom's text of 1941 has had a considerable effect on that understanding), introduced higher and more responsible standards into criticism, and put it onto a more, but not of course a wholly, scientific basis. Eventually the movement petered out into the sometimes apparently half-hysterical pseudo-science of such critics as W. K. Wimsatt ('The Structure of Romantic Nature Imagery'). But in its heyday, for all its excesses, and in particular its tendency to artificially isolate works of literature from their contexts (this had begun as an admirable redirection of attentions that had wandered from texts), the new criticism represented a renaissance of sense and sensibility after a period marked mainly by sentimentality and soft thinking.

Ransom's own criticism is ingenious and important but somewhat frigid. Its frigidity, at any rate, confirms the truth of Dryden's remark that 'the corruption of a poet is the generation of a critic'; although 'corruption' is perhaps in this case too strong a word. If we do not (as he does not) count the crude, commonplace and often clumsy *Poems About God* (1919), then Ransom's fecund period—there are only four poems dating from the Thirties—lasted for only four years, from the beginning of 1922 until the end of 1925. In this time, in a series of remarkable poems, he held the balance between an archaic, mannered and ornate conservatism and his own personal, emotional concerns. Invariably these poems are cast in the form of elaborate fictions, sometimes learnedly historical and sometimes ironically idyllic. Everything is carefully removed from direct utterance; but a dark passion imbues every poem.

For Ransom, man was once whole, and able to perceive the world as it really is; now he is split into reason and sensibility, body and soul. Science, for Ransom, is materialism; it gratifies rational impulses. His kind of poetry, 'metaphysical', 'miraculist', is made up of *structure* (the logical sense, the syntax, the metre), and *texture* (tone, imagery, sound, subject). The texture needs to be supported to a certain extent by the structure, but the two may nevertheless be almost independent of each other: in any case the resultant poem is independent of either a rational or a 'platonic' (this is the kind of poetry Ransom dislikes) impulse. Essentially, it will be noted, the poem is a strategy; and as a critic Ransom has undoubtedly enjoyed isolating it—to that extent—from its author, for one of the oblique themes of his poetry is how a passionate man may viably live at a distance from himself.

Ransom's criticism is important and has deserved its wide influence. It is important, incidentally, because based on the experience of being a poet—and not because it is good theory. But it is essential to recognize that the criticism is a transformation of the poetic function into a series of the very abstractions the poet hates: for it is less criticism of specific poetry, illumination of texts, than a theory. In other words, we have to sit patiently on the banks of a pond of theory to trick the secret fish of poetic intuition into biting. The poet Ransom, the anti-abstractionist, is one of those who think of a theory as what someone has called 'a structure of interrelated empirical propositions'; the critic Ransom, who all but renounced poetry (many poets do in one way or another) because it began to bring him too uncomfortably close to himself, is a theorist, a prescriber of rules upon which poetry should be written and read. And by now, forty years after he could not continue with poetry, Ransom (in the definitive *Selected Poems*, 1969) ruins his earlier poems, 'pairing' the original texts of eight poems with 1968 versions, and adding commentaries in most cases longer than the poems themselves.

> Conrad, Conrad, aren't you old
> To sit so late in a mouldy garden

becomes the intolerable, arch

> Evening comes early, and soon discovers
> Exchange between two conjugate lovers.

> 'Conrad! dear man, surprise! aren't you bold
> To be sitting so late in your sodden garden?'

The critic has sat in judgement on the poetry.

In one sense the critic Ransom is a strategist leading us away from one of the main features of the poetry: that the poet got more into his poems than their rigorous composer had planned. In his smaller poems, such as 'Janet Waking'. Ransom does get the effects he plans: here he shocks the reader out of sentimentality into a realization of what the death of Janet's hen, her first experience of death, really means to her. In the justly famous *Captain Carpenter* he goes beyond himself, achieving a major poetry. The personal price paid is great. As he said in his poem about what the poets ate and drank:

> God have mercy on the sinner
> Who must write with no dinner. . . .

Poetry comes out of experience, and there are points at which it becomes intolerable to question experience too deeply.

ALLEN TATE (1899), born in Kentucky, is a critic, historical biographer (of Stonewall Jackson and Jefferson Davis) and the author of a novel, *The Fathers* (1938, rev. 1960), as well as a poet. He was a pupil of Ransom, and was the first undergraduate to be invited to join the Fugitives. Tate's poems were from the beginning brilliantly phrased; he was always an adept at sustaining one manner or another: a brilliant student. All his work is elegant and accomplished, and yet there is a curious neutrality about it: not a lack of distinction, but the lack of a voice distinctive enough to suggest any personal unifying view. His poem 'Ode to the Confederate Dead' (1936) does sum up an ethos—roughly, the ethos of a typical Southern Agrarian—but even this, for so sheerly accomplished a poem, lacks personality. Almost always Tate's poetry seems to be trying to discover a literary language to define *a* position; but one has to persuade oneself that it is his position. Thus, although he has seldom been criticized (by the Williams-Olson-Black Mountain School he has been ignored, like Ransom, simply as an antique) or attacked, Tate has also seldom been warmly praised. There is not often either warmth or passion—or the notion of such feelings being suppressed—in his poetry. He attracts praise, but it is seldom enthusiastic. Conrad Aiken, who had some personal regard for Tate, was forced—in defending him against a severe appraisal—to resort to the word 'useful', hardly a compliment. Is he no more than a model of what a good twentieth-century metaphysical should be? Such a judgement would be unfair to the best of his relatively sparse poetic output. Usually Tate has simply taken too much thought ('So many fine things have a way of coming out all the better without the strain to sum up the whole universe in one impressive pellet' Hart

Crane, q.v., once wrote to him); and for all his insistence on tension ('Tension in Poetry' is the title of his best known critical essay), the intellectual ingenuity of his poems tends to rob them of that very quality. But in such a poem as 'The Swimmers', where the poet remembers the lynching of a black man and a swim he shared with some other boys, he achieves a personal note of indignation and sadness—as in one of his sonnets, where he tells of how he got a Negro beaten unjustly. In the long meditative 'Seasons of the Soul' Tate is at his weakest: the poet is at all times clothing his thinking in suitable linguistic terms—the language is not arising of its own volition. This language has, somehow, a second-hand flavour: 'The living wound of love', 'the mother of silences', 'Irritable spring': very good modern metaphysical poetry, but it fails to convince.

Tate's single novel, *The Fathers* (1938), is a greater achievement than anything in his poetry—not because it is anything very different, but because if you are as clever as Tate is then you can get away with more in fiction than you can in poetry. *The Fathers* is about the old South, the time the months during which the Civil War broke out. It is narrated by an old man, but its central character is really Major Buchan, the narrator's father, a feudal gentleman and an anti-secessionist who has no defences against the commercial, materialistic North. His son-in-law, George Posey, represents man uprooted from tradition. This is beautifully done, and the character of Major Buchan is most movingly conveyed. And even if one is left wondering if Tate's old South is not somewhat idealized, one accepts it as his legitimate view of the way in which the good life has disintegrated.

MERRILL MOORE (1903–57), born in Tennessee, was another member of the Fugitives. For most of his life he practised psychiatry in Boston (he was able to give valuable help to Edwin Arlington Robinson, q.v.); his immense poetic output consisted entirely of sonnets. He did not, eventually, take literature seriously; but if his comic verse were better known it would perhaps rival that of OGDEN NASH (1902–71), who though himself inexorably middlebrow and writing comfortingly for middlebrows, did smuggle a few truths into his deliberately banal and mostly irritating verse.

LAURA RIDING (PS. LAURA REICHENTHAL, 1901) was born in New York. Her father was an Austrian tailor, a naturalized American, and a lifelong socialist. She went to Cornell University, and there married a history instructor, Louis Gottschalk. Her first poems were signed Laura Riding Gottschalk. From her divorce in 1925 she was known as Laura Riding; since she married Schuyler B. Jackson (died 1968), in 1941 her few published works have been signed 'Laura (Riding) Jackson'. From 1926 until 1941, in England,

Mallorca, Rennes (France) and finally America, she was associated with Robert Graves (q.v.), with whom she published a number of books and pamphlets. The Fugitives awarded her a poetry prize and made her an honorary member of their group; she was highly enthusiastic, and devised schemes to publicize their work. Soon after she published her *Collected Poems* (1938) she came to the conclusion 'that poetry had no provision in it for ultimate practical attainment of that rightness of word that *is* truth, but led on ever only to a temporizing less-than-truth (the lack eked out with illusions of truth produced by physical word effects)'. She worked with her husband on a project 'that would help to dissipate the confusion existing in the knowledge of word-meanings', and she has now completed it alone. In the magazine *Chelsea* (12 and 14, 1962, 1964) she has detailed her reasons for rejecting poetry, and told 'the story of human beings in the universe' (*The Telling*, in *Chelsea*, 1967). In 1970 her *Selected Poems* appeared in Great Britain, with a Preface explaining why she considers even her own poetry an inadequate approach to her function of truth-telling. She knows, she says, of 'no one besides myself and my husband . . . who has put feet beyond the margin on the further ground—the margin being the knowledge that truth begins where poetry ends. . . .' *The Telling* appeared in England in 1972.

The notion of poetry—and, indeed, all writing—as humanly inadequate is not new. Rilke, Broch and Thomas Mann (qq.v. 2) all had similar forebodings, and so have many others. In a century in which everything is questioned it is unlikely that art would not have been, too. But Laura Riding has been more specific about it than anyone else. She calls the vanity of 'artistically perfect word-use' 'a parasitic partner in the poetic enterprise'. How American this is! And how interesting that where she, in her own word, '*stopped*', such writers as Charles Olson (q.v.) simply tried to make a new sort of poetry. But, her personal peculiarities apart (they involve her in continual complaints that everyone has ill-treated her and stolen their styles and ideas from her, and have been said to constitute a 'Jehovah complex'), she has drawn attention to a crisis of poetry in our time—and she has done so whether, with her, we abandon poetry, or whether we go on trying to make it.

Laura Riding's own poetry, which has interested only a minority, but a distinguished one—the Fugitives, Graves, Auden, Cameron, Larkin, Bottrall (qq.v.)—is difficult but at its best, as in her first collection, *The Close Chaplet* (1926), astonishing: almost a definition of sense of the poetic. Here is the kind of absolute dedication to poetry of a Rilke: all experience is continuously subjected to the heroically objective scrutiny of a truthful heart. Her quality is as well illustrated in 'The Mask' as in any other short poem:

> Cover up,
> Oh, quickly cover up
> All the new spotted places,
> All the unbeautifuls,
> The insufficiently beloved.
>
> With what? with what?
> With the uncovering of the lovelies,
> With the patches that transformed
> The more previous corruptions.
>
> Is there no pure then?
> The eternal taint wears beauty like a mask.
> But a mask eternal.

In a way the rejection of the poetry that came in 1940 is already there, in the poems: 'if poetry', she often seems to imply, 'won't get me further in my quest for the perfect and the pure, then poetry will have to go'. Her assertions of her knowledge of the direction of truth do not make for her best poetry; the best lies in her descriptions of the sufferings of a woman of genius, with aspirations towards goodness: 'Nor is it written that you may not grieve./There is no rule of joy . . .' is a notable example. This is a poetry that either makes no appeal or deeply fascinates; the full, important and fascinating story of it, and of its aftermath, has yet to be told.

*

HART CRANE (1899–1932), born in Ohio, failed to escape the demons that drove him to drink and homosexual encounters; he died when he jumped from a ship after a bad night gambling with some sailors, who had beaten him up. He was travelling with a woman with whom he had had a satisfactory heterosexual relationship in the previous months; but she came too late into his life to help him to achieve stability. He published *White Buildings* (1926), short poems, and the American epic, *The Bridge* (1930), in his lifetime. *Collected Poems* (1933) incorporates a last group of shorter poems. His *Letters* (1952) are full of acute and generous critical insights into his own and his contemporaries' poetry. Crane, who was patchily self-educated and who was, in an academic sense, unfamiliar with the history of his own country, was quintessentially American and poetically enormously gifted; he is the subject of an increasing number of contradictory monographs, certain of which reach the fantastic in their projections of their authors' involved symbolisms onto Crane's often historically confused conceptions.

Crane was not, it should be emphasized, naïve (q.v.) in the modified Schillerian sense in which I have used it in this book. He was just badly educated, and too frenetic to do anything about it. His parents were unhappily married, and both seem to have been thoroughly unpleasant people. He was a classic victim; and when he emerged from adolescence he was dangerously mother-attached, bisexual with an almost ritual emphasis on the homosexual side, and a problem drinker (whether he suffered from the specific disease of alcoholism, which was even less well understood then than now, is not clear). But Crane's letters make it perfectly clear that his intelligence, when allowed to function unimpeded, was powerful. He has been compared, inevitably, with Dylan Thomas (q.v.); but —as a comparison of the letters demonstrates—Crane was by far the more intelligent of the two (and infinitely the better and more important poet).

The more academic the approach to Crane—that is to say, the more his poetry is approached as an entity separate from his drunken and hell-driven self—the more emphasis is put on *The Bridge* as a more or less successful American epic. But Crane, unlike some other poets, is not well served by an exclusively academic approach. His poetry embodies the drives of his own frenetic personality.

No really aware critic considers *The Bridge* a success. He conceived this epic in a state of desperation in order to get money from a business man patron, Otto Kahn (whose $2,000 he soon spent in drink and debauchery, as well he might—perhaps Wallace Stevens, by then fairly well-heeled, should have advanced the cash). Crane told Kahn that the poem was supposed to represent the American past by showing the present in its 'vital substance'; but it is only good when Crane is doing something else; it can only be judged as a ragbag of fragments, some sentimental and forced, others beautiful. Nothing in *The Bridge* coheres. The concept of it belongs to the semi-literate side of Crane: his *conscious* Americanism is exceedingly laboured. He was not, at twenty-five, equipped to write any kind of epic.

Crane had a number of mediocre and, worse, pretentious friends and acquaintances; he had very little more than his superb intuition to distinguish between the fake and the real. Yet he was not himself pretentious: rather, he overwrote, putting out hot gusts of rhetoric to the sound of jazz and the glug-glug of his throat as he poured alcohol down it. He would interrupt his bouts of drink-writing to indulge in equally heroic bouts of homosex.

Yet after all this has been said, Crane is one of this century's major poets. In some dozen or so poems—they include the 'Voyages' sequence and several other poems from *White Buildings*, and the late 'The Broken Tower'—he found a language as suitable to his time as to himself. It cost him immense pain; the real reason for his death, apart from the local remorse that occasioned it, was that he believed his powers were failing. Crane has much to tell us: of the nature of romantic love; of gentleness, for he was gentle, of sexuality; of the anguish of homosexuality; of poetry and of being a poet. No twentieth-century poet has written more moving poetry. 'The Broken Tower', the poem he believed had failed, is perhaps more moving than any other. This combines the themes of his bisexuality and his capacity as a poet in a complex image of bell-ringing at dawn (which he had helped to do in a Mexican town). Its strength and poetic confidence make a tragic contrast with his state of mind a few weeks after he had written it. These are its last six stanzas:

> And so it was I entered the broken world
> To trace the visionary company of love, its voice
> An instant in the wind (I know not whither hurled)
> But not for long to hold each desperate choice.
>
> My word I poured. But was it cognate, scored
> Of that tribunal monarch of the air
> Whose thigh embronzes earth, strikes crystal Word
> In wounds pledged once to hope—cleft to despair?
>
> The steep encroachments of my blood left me
> No answer (could blood hold such a lofty tower
> As flings the question true?)—or is it she
> Whose sweet mortality stirs latent power?—
>
> And through whose pulse I hear, counting the strokes
> My veins recall and add, revived and sure
> The angelus of wars my chest evokes:
> What I hold healed, original now, and pure . . .
>
> And builds, within, a tower that is not stone
> (Not stone can jacket heaven)—but slip
> Of pebbles—visible wings of silence sown
> In azure circles, widening as they dip

> The matrix of the heart, lift down the eye
> That shrines the quiet lake and swells a tower . . .
> The commodious, tall decorum of that sky
> Unseals her earth, and lifts love in its shower.

Like Rilke's, Crane's poetry in its very different way nakedly poses the dangerous question of just what poetry itself is.

*

YVOR WINTERS (1900–68), born in Chicago, was much better known as critic than poet. He taught at Stanford University from 1928 onwards. He began as an experimental imagist poet, recording life as a series of ecstatic perceptions in an ineffective free verse. Then he became, or tried to become, the moral and classical spokesman of his generation. Since Winters could really think, it is probably fair to call him an exponent of the new criticism (which was never a school); but his criticism does not otherwise resemble that of other well-known critics such as Warren or Ransom (qq.v.). He was ill-tempered, racked with envy and frustration, and pompous; at its frequent worst his criticism is grotesque (as when he claims that Bridges', q.v., verse drama is the best in English since Shakespeare). But at his best, as when he attacks Hopkins and Yeats and Crane (qq.v.), he demands an answer, and is thus provocative. His own poetry, however, tells us why he became the enemy of romantic self-discovery and expressionism. First, there are the early 'modernist' poems. These are commonplace and affected. Then come the 're-strained' models for his contemporaries (almost the only one he wholly applauded was Elizabeth Daryush, Bridges' daughter). These are restrained because there has been no feeling to restrain. This enemy of romanticism does not understand what he hates. Many of the poems, such as 'On the Death of Senator Thomas J. Walsh', are disguised tributes to himself:

> An old man more is gathered to the great,
> Singly, for conscience' sake he bent his brow. . . .

Why did he become so famous as well as unpopular? Because, I think, the deliquescent hatred, product of envy and poetic inner emptiness, that inform his criticism does give it an energy, and when that energy is harnessed to logical argument the results are interesting and stimulating. Here egocentricity shrieks contortedly in the name of 'reason' and 'classicism'. And his passionate exhortations to young poets towards restraint did occasionally have useful results, particularly in the cases of J. V. CUNNINGHAM (1911) and the English poet Thom Gunn (q.v.).

Cunningham was born in Maryland and studied at Stanford. He has interestingly transformed Winters' aim; and his motive is not an impoverished emotional life or an inability to create an energetic language. Therefore his project, at least, is of great interest—particularly to those who are concerned with what I have termed *Künstlerschuld* (q.v.). Poetry, and his own poetic impulse, Cunningham wants humbly to reduce to the level of other 'ordinary' activities: Poetry 'is a concern of the ordinary human self. . . . Its virtues are the civic virtues. If it lacks much, what it does have is ascertainable and can be judged'. This was very much the view of W. H. Auden (q.v.) (dealt with as an English poet), who believed that poetry changes nothing and regarded it as an entertainment (and yet continually acted as a public man who believed in the civilizing virtues of art). Thus Cunningham writes a good deal of 'light' verse—much of it highly accomplished and amusing. His more serious poetry, in such volumes as *The Judge is Fury* (1947), *To What Strangers, What Welcome* (1964), is difficult but of great integrity. He is a neglected poet—but probably not one who would appeal to upholders of the civic virtues of the average American town, which is perhaps ironic. *Selected Poems* appeared in 1971.

DELMORE SCHWARTZ (1913–67), born in Brooklyn, was an extremely brilliant man who perished under the burden of his gifts. In him were uneasily combined two traditions: the Brooklyn Jewish (he planned a baseball novel before he was thirty, but it was Malamud, q.v., who wrote *The Natural*) and the intelligent academic. When he died he was a mental and physical wreck, whose gift had long ago choked on itself. Schwartz's Marxist inclinations (he was at various times concerned with editing *Partisan Review* and *The New Republic*) often clashed with those of his imagination; this may have been one of the reasons why he failed, in poetry, to discover his own voice for more than a few lines at a time. A trained philosopher with an intellect too clear for his own good, he wanted simply to observe, pessimistically; but his acute Jewish conscience would not allow him to do this. Hence the title of his first book, *In Dreams Begin Responsibilities* (1938). He is forever philosophizing against the horrors his imagination involuntarily reveals. Towards the end he became too consciously 'symbolic': the bright heart of his work had entered into a tunnel of gloom. In his poetry the language that his self-consciousness, his guilt, struggles to produce is expected—but never comes. But the Jewish stories of *The World is a Wedding* (1948), the acute criticism—and the so nearly successful poetry, much of which is collected in *Summer Knowledge* (1959)—gave him an important place in modern American literature, as a writer of high quality destroyed, to an alarming and poignant degree, by his predicament and his honesty.

The poetry of MURIEL RUKEYSER (1913), born in New York, is more specifically directed towards socialism than Schwartz's; what isn't tends to the too exuberantly feminine. It is not that the sense of it is embarrassing; but the poet writes too much in the 'open' tradition of Sandburg and does not bother to discover her own voice. She was influenced by HORACE GREGORY (1898), from Wisconsin, a distinguished translator who has not found his own voice, either—because of too easy philosophical and Marxist predilections. Both these poets have floundered intelligently about, but have been too much at the service of simplistic ideas. Better, because resolutely minor, was KENNETH FEARING (1902–61), born in Chicago, who in his fiction—notably *The Big Clock* (1946)—achieved a level of intelligence seldom seen in the thriller: he influenced the Englishman Julian Symons, who achieved a similar distinction. His poetry (*New and Selected Poems*, 1956), in free verse, is funny and sometimes compassionate: a readable and sarcastic rebuke to the pretentious excesses of others more ambitious.

Minnesota-born RICHARD EBERHART (1904) has experimented with too many forms; he has diffused his considerable gift into a too rambling poetry, which ranges from the metaphysical through the allegorical to the descriptive-romantic. He protests against the anonymity of the 'system' that pseudo-orders life, but cannot seem to set against it anything personal enough to convince us of more than his own, rather than his poems', excellence. He has published his *Collected Poems* (1960), *Selected Poems* (1965), and two volumes since then. No clearly serious poet is, perhaps, so uneven. His 'philosophy' shifts between a pessimism that he will not sufficiently explore and a mild religiousness that is unconvincing. One of his best known poems begins

> You would think the fury of aerial bombardment
> Would arouse God to relent. . . .

It is slack, careless, undistinguished writing: too generalized even to call forth a personal rhythm. And yet when the poet becomes personal, his poetry leaps into life: that same poem ends with these four lines:

Of Van Wettering I speak, and Averill,
Names on a list, whose names I do not recall
But they are gone to early death, who late in school
Distinguished the belt feed lever from the belt holding pawl.

The long quarry into the vague mud of his poetry yields similar jewels, and is worthwhile.

STANLEY KUNITZ (1905), born in Massachusetts, whose *Selected Poems 1928–58* appeared in 1958, is one of the most skilled poets of his generation. His achievement stands, like Eberhart's, but more solidly, behind the poetry of Lowell and others; but this is not yet fully acknowledged. His first book, *Intellectual Things* (1930), appeared when Lowell was twelve years old. His is one of the earliest poetries to concern itself exclusively with the naked, solipsist self, unconsoled, in a hostile world. There is in the earlier poems too much dependence on Yeats, and a corresponding rhetoric; but personal suffering and a refining of style has modified this to a spareness of diction in the later work. He has recently made excellent translations from Russian poets.

*

American poetry since the war has divided itself into two diverging streams. Some of the more or less traditionalist poets—such as Lowell, Jarrell, Roethke, Elizabeth Bishop, Snodgrass, Hecht (qq.v.)—have been influenced by, or at least enjoy, the poetry of William Carlos Williams (q.v.), who is the real twentieth-century father of the anti-traditionalists: Olson, Creeley, Duncan, Snyder. But these latter will have no truck with the Fugitives ('antiques'), Frost, or Lowell himself. The one figure to which nearly all acknowledge allegiance is Pound (q.v.). It is the Black Mountain poets and their disciples, however, who have most decisively broken away; and their immediate prophet is Charles Olson (q.v.). To be fully aware of what they have broken away from it is necessary to look, first, at the continuers of the tradition: those who, whether in fact *avant garde* (as Lowell is) or not, have not been self-consciously, programmatically so. Mostly they are poets of self-revelation, who have written 'confessionally' in the belief that by exploiting their verbal gifts in the interests of self-analysis they may create a world comprehending enough to allow the realization of all individual values. The danger, as one soon sees, is that under the strain of confession they become self-publicists, cultural film-stars: that their imagination may be robbed of authority, so that they themselves subscribe to sentimental photographs of themselves as midcult poet-heroes. Thus society pulls them into the very life-impoverishing system they set out to destroy: gives them a glossy place, reports on their pain, panders to their ideals.

Thus, ROBERT LOWELL (1917), scion of a great family, is now a public figure whose poetry has lately (whether temporarily or not remains to be seen) degenerated into a sterile, exhibitionist journalism: the confessionalist puts himself on show, inserting into an account of his selected private and public activities the odd striking line. This is *Notebook 1967–8* (1969, rev. 1969, rev. 1970). No mistake should be made about this: it is rank bad, a coffee-table book, and if its author does not go back on it he ends his serious career as poet.

Lowell's early poems, the best of which are to be found in *Poems 1938–49* (1950) and *The Mills of the Kavanaughs* (1951), were metrically tight and invariably rhymed. Lowell had learned about prosody from Bridges (q.v.)—that master technician who had nothing of poetic importance to say—as Auden did, and these early poems show him as the leading technician of his time. These youthful, livid, melodramatic poems look rather like a magnified, violent revision of Allen Tate (Tate and Ransom were Lowell's first masters):

> Wallowing in this bloody sty
> I cast for fish that pleased my eye
> (Truly Jehovah's bow suspends
> No pots of gold to weight its ends);
> Only the blood-mouthed rainbow trout
> Rose to my bait. . . .

The tone has been well described as one of 'baroque exaltation'. During the war Lowell ('a fire-breathing Catholic C.O.') was a conscientious objector and went to prison; the themes of the early poems are generally speaking Jansenist (he left the Catholic Church in the Fifties), and harp on the punishment that man must resign himself to for his failure to fulfil his obligation to God. Their mood, if nothing else, is not unlike that of the earlier novels of Mauriac (q.v.). From the beginning Lowell carried within him a consciousness of a certain regality; he studied, so to speak, to assume the regal duties of appraising Boston and, in due course, his family. He had evaded his background at first; but during the Fifties, experiencing divorce (from the novelist Jean Stafford), remarriage and madness, he went back to it: the result was *Life Studies* (1959). The fuller American edition of this contains a prose autobiography and auto-

biographical poems—the method of which, Lowell has acknowledged, he borrowed from his pupil W. D. Snodgrass. This collection
included the famous 'Skunk Hour', with the lines:

> One dark night
> My Tudor Ford climbed the hill's skull;
> I watched for love cars. Lights turned down,
> they lay together, hull to hull,
> where the graveyard shelves on the town. . . .
> My mind's not right.

These are the poems, beautifully accomplished in their relaxed
rhetoric, for which Lowell is most celebrated. His *Imitations* (1961),
often deliberate distortions or alterations of European poets, are also
admired—and arouse interest as part of the education of an allegedly
major poet. But some have preferred the crabbed, tightly restrained
energy of the earlier Lowell, seeing in *Life Studies* the beginnings of
the process that leads through *For the Union Dead* (1964) and *Near
the Ocean* (1967)—some original poems and more translations—to
the self-vulgarizing disaster of the *Notebooks*, which read, says Donald
Hall cruelly but justly, 'like prayers to Stockholm'. The poems of
Life Studies, and some of those that come after them, are masterly in
technique; but the autobiographical ones often seem less good than
the prose. Comparison establishes that the poem is often a fiercely
worked up version of the prose: often nothing has come up from the
well of the unconscious—rather, the poet has manufactured a poem
out of his raw material, tricking it up and making it rhetorical. The
best poems, the ones to Ford, Schwartz and Santayana (qq.v.),
'Skunk Hour' and others, are minor rather than major: the distinction is nearly all in the way style manipulates tone and feeling. The
poetry is impressive, fashionable, superbly appropriate for treatment
in approved critical modes. One can see why Lowell got into a state
of mind in which he felt obliged to imitate his friend John Berryman
(q.v.)—to the extent of even copying the form of the *Dream Songs*.
Notebooks often looks like what it is: a rival to *Dream Songs*. The
career of Lowell, and the embarrassing impasse into which it has
led him, exemplifies the difficulties of poetry in our time. The poet
is transformed into politician; he has to justify himself, get glass
eyes; his imagination is threatened. That Lowell in 1970 came
quietly to England for a period gave hope that he meant to retreat
into himself and keep away from publicity; only thus can his poetry
survive. But the hope remains unrealized.

Another poet who suffered from bouts of madness throughout his difficult life was THEODORE ROETHKE (1908–63), the Michigan-born son of the Prussian owner of a huge and well-known nursery business, the details of which figure greatly in his poetry. Roethke's subject is the state of his being as it comes into contact with reality. He is not 'confessional', is not, like Lowell, interested in making his subject his own awareness of his behaviour. He presents his biography in lyrical, semi-mystical terms that were notably influenced, at various times, by Blake, Yeats, Eliot, Auden, Dylan Thomas and Léonie Adams (qq.v.). His first poems, published in *Open House* (1941), were in strict forms; but those of *The Lost Son* (1948) are in a freer verse. They consist of interior monologues, in which Roethke incorporates microscopic descriptions of plants that are not in fact scientific or even very carefully observed—rather they remind one of Graham Sutherland's close-up paintings, which try to define the nature of their subjects by pictorial metaphor. *Praise to the End* (1951), which contains much pastiche of Yeats (q.v.) and mimicry of Dylan Thomas (q.v.), is at once less original and more visionary.

Roethke's poems were collected in *The Waking* (1953), again in *Words for the Wind* (1958), and finally and posthumously in *Collected Poems* (1968). He was an insecure poet, and his most serious fault is his parodies—or mimicries—of other poets. It makes most of what he has to say unconvincing. Such tender poetry as 'The Meadow Mouse' is spoiled because, in it, all that is not imitated from John Clare is petty moralizing. Eliot is drawn upon not only for manner but for a whole symbolic method that Roethke himself was not close to.

What is left and may survive is a small body of minor love poetry, such poems as 'The Apparition', 'Her Reticence' and 'The Happy Three'—all of these from his posthumous collection *The Far Field* (1964).

Roethke often looks very good indeed. His poetry nearly always has a most attractive surface. His technique seldom lets him down. But close investigation usually shows the poetry to be second-rate and second-hand, the ecstatic voice something the poet jollied himself into. The long para-surrealist poems about greenhouses and plants have a certain value, but ultimately they fail to take us beyond the experiences of mental disintegration and regression to childhood which they record. Again, the purely physical love poetry, which is not as plagiaristic as most of the rest of his work, is of little value because when one comes down to it, it does no more than find various ingenious ways of describing physical desire. Roethke's 'mystical vision' consists of nothing at all. But his breathless, lyrical manner (often, in him, trite—as in 'The Geranium', with its banal ending) had a wide and probably beneficial because releasing influence.

A poet admired by Lowell and others of his group is ELIZABETH BISHOP (1911), who published her complete poems in 1970. If this quiet and fastidious poet, who was born in Massachusetts and has spent much of her life in South America, has a model then it is Marianne Moore (q.v.). She is not immune from awfulness ('Invitation to Miss Marianne Moore' begins 'From Brooklyn, over the Brooklyn Bridge, on this 'fine morning,/please come flying' and continues in that vein), but in general she is more discriminating in what she publishes than most. Although she has written competent ballads and done some translations from the Portuguese of some Brazilian poets, she is mainly a poet of description so accurate and skilful that she suggests something beyond her subject. She owes part of the curiosity of her style to Marianne Moore, and her method is rooted in imagism—but a Bishop poem has its own unmistakable stamp. When she tries anything other than this she is liable to sentimentality and tweeness, as in 'Cootchie'. But, with a group of some twenty-five poems, such as 'The Fish' and 'The Weed' she has made a special place for herself in modern American poetry.

There can be no more technically skilful poet living than RICHARD WILBUR (1921), who was born in New York. Wilbur is graceful, learned, civilized—but he cannot allow himself to mean as much to his readers as they would like. He cannot be wild. His discretion, his control, insists on decorum. He observes well, writes beautifully, translates exquisitely; but of course it is all just a little too good to be true. No one really important, alas, *could* be that fastidiously perfect. And yet. . . . One finds oneself lamenting that Wilbur, so intelligent and decent, lacks 'attack'. Even 'Beasts', one of his finest poems, lacks a really cutting edge. Yet *Poems 1943–56* (1957), published in England and collecting the best of three American volumes, contains many pleasurable poems, as do his next three books, the most recent of which is *Walking to Sleep* (1970). Perhaps a British critic, writing of this latest volume, has put his finger on the trouble when he suggests that Wilbur's poetry may not cost him enough. Much bad verse doubtless costs dear; but all good poetry must do so.

SYLVIA PLATH (1932–63), who was born in Boston and died in London, was the exact opposite of Wilbur: at the end of her life, her marriage to the English poet Ted Hughes (q.v.) broken up, the surface of her life was, quite literally, poetry. She had had a nervous breakdown in America in 1951, when she had tried to commit suicide. She wrote about this time of her life in her novel *The Bell*

Jar, which was first published in 1963 under the pseudonym Victoria Lucas. When she became seriously ill in London in 1963 she had no one to look after her, and she finally gassed herself. She had published *The Colossus* in 1960; but it is generally agreed that it is the poems of the posthumous *Ariel* (1965) that are her most important. More has been and will be issued; but none of this appears to have much intrinsic value.

Most people are dedicated to the surfaces of their lives, and this protects them from the stresses of poetic thinking: from caring intensely about what does not, in material terms, matter. Because for a few months Sylvia Plath made all her existence into poetry (her children were her only distraction), critics have too confidently assumed that her ostensible subject matter, of concentration camps and the plight of Jewishness, is their real subject matter. One, calling her a 'minor poet of great intensity', yet states that 'the last, greatest poems culminate in an act of identification, of total communion with those tortured and massacred'. This is mystical. Another critic (no doctor) assumes that her illness was schizophrenic and pronounces that her poetry 'defines the age as schizophrenic'. But the chances are that her illness was a form of manic-depression—a form in which euphoria and depression may mysteriously co-exist (cf. Campana, Bacovia, qq.v.). That, certainly, is the mood of the last poems.

These are minor poems—although they may in an age of increasing urban stress and consequent madness be historically prophetic—because their subject is never really more than her own illness. So 'minor poet of great intensity' is right. But that is enough. For they tell us much of the nature of her mental and therefore of human illness. But fashionable criticism has been wrong in emphasizing 'the contemporary predicament' in her poems. They should read the French diarist and essayist Simone Weil to find this: she really writes about the contemporary predicament. Sylvia Plath was writing about herself. The comparison is a revealing one.

When A. Alvarez, an able critic and, to a point, good on Sylvia Plath, says that she 'gambled . . . and lost', implying she 'did it' for poetry, he is projecting his own poker-playing preoccupations onto her. For it evades the issue. Her predicament was not to gamble but to remain truthful while she suffered madness; and the best of her poems do remain truthful, if only to her condition of a suicidal depression shot through with euphoria. They tell us about this condition—not about 'the schizophrenic world', a critic's ambitious and rhetorical abstraction.

However, Sylvia Plath did find apt words to describe her condi-

tion as she waited to die. In 'Death & Co.' she imagines death as
two business men calling, one of whom 'exhibits

> The birthmarks that are his trademark—
> The scald scar of water,
> The nude
> Verdigris of the condor.
> I am red meat. His beak
>
> Claps sidewise: I am not his yet
> He tells me how badly I photograph. . . .
>
> The other . . .
> His hair long and plausive.
> Bastard
> Masturbating a glitter,
> He wants to be loved. . . .'

The tone comes straight out of Roethke's greenhouse poems, but it is
sharpened by knowledge of self-inflicted death. These are suicide
poems. They are not at all, and cannot be, about any kind of love.
They are about horror. But however much this diminishes their
stature, they will remain important for the chilling accuracy of their
descriptions of terror.

ANNE SEXTON (1928–1974) is usually described as of the 'confessional'
school, although she would prefer to be classed as 'an imagist who
deals with reality and its hard facts'. She writes, inevitably, in the
shadow of Sylvia Plath, since some of her poems are about mental
breakdown. The title of her first book was *To Bedlam and Part Way
Back* (1960), and this dealt with, among other things, a suicide
attempt. She published her *Selected Poems* in 1964. Two more collections followed: *Live or Die* (1967) and *Love Poems* (1969). Anne
Sexton is an excellent writer of lyrical autobiography. She writes of
her own experiences—illness, motherhood, love—descriptively, not
moralistically or squeamishly. Her poems set up few resonances, are
autobiographically 'regional'. Her love poems, for example, are
splendidly physical, and extremely feminine inasmuch as they make
no attempts to extrapolate 'meanings' from the pleasures they record
As that kind of love poet, writing as a woman, she is probably
unsurpassed.

JOHN BERRYMAN (1914–72), who was born of strict Roman Catholic parents in Oklahoma, and whose father shot himself in front of
the twelve-year-old son's window, could well be described as the

confessional poet *par excellence*. His style is frequently cryptic, mannered, convoluted; but the subject (beginning with his *Sonnets*, which he wrote in the Forties but did not publish until 1967) of his poetry has increasingly been himself: his mental instability, his adultery, his friends, his general agony. Obviously Berryman is in the *Dream Songs*—77 *Dream Songs* (1964), *His Toy, His Dream, His Rest* (1968)— frequently a very bad poet indeed: impenetrably obscure, ruthlessly making use of private references, crabbed, archaic, over-dramatic. . . . This is hardly denied unless by the kind of uncritical reader whom no one wants. The question, in the *Dream Songs* as much as in the *Sonnets*, is whether by taking these risks Berryman has achieved a new, more lucid, better poetry. Well, he has achieved a very fascinating and different kind of poetry, which demands to be studied. Berryman does not pretend that he does not lust for fame:

> He can advance no claim,
> save that he studied thy Word and grew afraid,
> work & fear be the basis for his terrible cry
> not to forget his name.

And yet he said (in an interview on British TV) that he had only six readers who really understood what he was doing. . . . Did he mean this? The number of private references in his poems suggests that in one sense he did—but it is unfortunately not a question he chose to answer, perhaps because he remained Roman Catholic enough to leave such matters to God. Berryman, an alcoholic, killed himself during a spell of depression partly caused by his going off drink.

Berryman began as an almost academic poet, writing in tight stanzas; Dudley Fitts found in them 'an aura of academic contrivance'. He collected together such of his early poems as he wished to preserve in *Short Poems* (1967); but these are quite different from the three later sequences. *Homage to Mistress Bradstreet* (1956) is a poem-sequence based on the twin conceits that the Puritan Anne Bradstreet, America's first poet, is his mistress—and that she is his alter ego. By participating in her life—into which Berryman made research—the poet illuminates his discovery of his own country.

The organization of *Dream Songs* is calculated to allow the writer to explore himself and his world in as free a manner as possible. Each poem consists of eighteen lines divided into three stanzas of six lines each; but lengths and stress of line, and rhyme pattern, vary. Berryman projects himself into several voices: Henry, a white man in black face, who speaks like a nigger minstrel (Berryman says the poem is 'essentially about' him), an unnamed friend who calls him

Mr. Bones, and some other not definitely identified voices. This Henry and his friend are not more than acknowledgements on his part that no poet can himself be the 'I' of any poem; he can only pretend it. This pretence is not necessarily reprehensible; but it will not do for so long and ambitious an epic—a rival to the *Cantos*?— as Berryman planned. The poem has rightly been called artificial, uneven and pretentious. The question is: How much more artificial, uneven and pretentious than its author (or its readers)? Could one get such comic effects as Berryman gets in the following stanza by not being 'quirky'?:

> Henry sits in de plane & was gay.
> Careful Henry nothing said aloud
> but where a Virgin out of cloud
> to her Mountain dropt in light,
> his thought made pockets & the plane buckt.
> 'Parm me, lady.' 'Orright.'

This of course shows a poet being himself (in just the way Wilbur will not be himself) with a vengeance. It has attendant risks, and it can lead to an egocentric and even offensive verse. But someone who cared about the past of poetry, and for the notion of effort in making it, had to take this plunge. It could prove of more historical than intrinsic interest: it is very uneven, and we must wait to see what cumulative effect it has after at least a decade. But its importance is unquestioned.

RANDALL JARRELL (1914–65), who was born in Tennessee, threw himself under a truck at the age of fifty-one. He was a leading member of the gifted generation of Schwartz, Lowell and Berryman (qq.v.), and like them, he taught in universities. In the Second World War he served in the United States Air Force. He was a critic of genius (*Poetry and the Age*, 1953), being particularly funny at the expense of the wholly academic critics; and he wrote a good novel satirizing small college life, *Pictures from an Institution* (1954). Jarrell was a poet of, above all, sensibility: sensibility about man's doomed quest for decency and goodness. He wrote much about childhood because innocence was what interested him. He was a very friendly poet—the friendliest of all of his generation. But he fell into sentimentality, his obvious temptation, less often than Schwartz into windy abstraction, Lowell into regal exhibitionism. Roethke into pastiche, Berryman into private and idiosyncratic muttering. . . . He will no doubt be called a minor poet; he is not as ambitious as Lowell (although history will see him, I think, as effective), and does not try for so much as Berryman; Robert Fitzgerald was possibly justified in his stricture that we 'admire' Jarrell's poetry, but are 'unrelieved; we miss the great exhilarations of art'. Or was he? When one remembers Lowell and his recent struggles to achieve something that *looks* like those great exhilarations, one is thankful for the more modest Jarrell. But then Jarrell was more sceptical and less personally ambitious; he might even, at his best, have avoided the phrase 'the great exhilarations of art'. One is above all grateful for him when thinking of the gush that has gathered around such apocalyptics as Dylan Thomas (q.v.): like Thomas, Jarrell stood for poetry, and was against its impoverishment by the sort of criticism he called 'nearly autonymous'; but unlike Thomas he resisted the fake-Bardic in himself.

His war poetry, *qua* war poetry, is probably the best to come out of the Second World War. It has some of the bitter irony of Owen, and great compassion. Reading it one really does wonder about those 'great exhilarations': doesn't he have here what Fitzgerald meant?

> In bombers named for girls, we burned
> The cities we had learned about in school. . . .
>
> The soldier simply wishes for his name. . . .
>
> Strapped at the centre of the blazing wheel,
> His flesh ice-white against the shattered mask
> He tears at the easy clasp, his sobbing breaths
> Misting the fresh blood lightening to flame,
> Darkening to smoke. . . .

The best of these, with others, were included in *Selected Poems* (1955). The post-war Jarrell, with his love of Grimm and the *Märchen*, could not always keep away from the whimsical. And such poems as 'Nollekens', based on the famous book, are a little too wide-eyed ('All that my poem says he did, he did . . .'). Then, in his last years, Jarrell found a more suitable style. Although it was not Browning's, Browning, with his dramatic monologues, pointed the way. The poems, most of them dramatic monologues spoken by women, are in the posthumous *The Lost World* (1966). At their best these have the exact quality of the nostalgia of his admired Proust. 'Thinking of the Lost World' begins

> This spoonful of chocolate tapioca
> Tastes like—like peanut butter, like the vanilla

> Extract Mama told me not to drink.
> Swallowing the spoonful, I have already travelled
> Through time to my childhood. It puzzles me
> That age is like it. . . .

and later occur the lines:

> All of them are gone
> Except for me; and for me nothing is gone—
> The chicken's body is still going round
> And round in widening circles. . . .
> Mama and Pop and Dandeen are still there
> In the Gay Twenties.

It ends:

> I hold in my own hands, in happiness,
> Nothing: the nothing for which there's no reward.

It has been given to few American poets to write so beautifully and so simply—and to avoid the psychopathic, the abnormal, the terrible, at the same time.

*

HOWARD NEMEROV (1920), born in New York, has not embraced the Beats or the school of Olson; but he is a very knowing, humorous traditionalist—by no means a citizen of Squaresville. His first poems were sophisticated and metaphysical, and often spoiled by their cleverness. But he has evolved to a greater simplicity. And even if there is no special virtue in having simplicity for an aim, there is every virtue in a poet's working to attain the greatest simplicity commensurate with what he has to say. This is what Nemerov, it seems, is trying to do. He is one of the most gifted American poets born in the Twenties—and in many ways the most representative of his time. He has slowly but surely forged his own style, as the carefully edited *New and Selected Poems* (1960), taking only forty-three poems from four volumes and adding fifteen new ones, shows. Nemerov has come to the all-important point of asking why he writes:

> The time came
> He had to ask himself, what did he want?
> What did he want when he began
> That idiot fiddling with sound of things.

Although he appears at present to believe that the answer to this lies in philosophy, it is to be hoped that he will continue to search for his answer in his imagination. The kind of poem he now writes is well illustrated by the fine 'The Iron Characters':

> The iron characters, keepers of the public confidence,
> The sponsors, fund raisers, and members of the board,
> Who naturally assume their seats among the governors,
> Who place their names behind the issue of bonds
> And are consulted in the formation of cabinets,
> The catastrophes of war, depression, and natural disaster:
> They represent us in responsibilities many and great.
> It is no wonder, then, if in a moment of crisis,
> Before the microphones, under the lights, on a great occasion,
> One of them will break down in hysterical weeping
> Or fall in an epileptic seizure, or if one day
> We read in the papers of one's having been found
> Naked and drunk in a basement with three high school boys,
> Of one who jumped from the window of his hospital room.
> For are they not as ourselves in these things also?
> Let the orphan, the pauper, the thief, the derelict drunk
> And all those of no fixed address, shed tears of rejoicing
> For the broken minds of the strong, the torn flesh of the just.

Nemerov has written some highly intellectual, comic fiction: four novels and a number of (uncollected) short stories; and two volumes of non-fiction, the second, *Journal of the Fictive Life* (1965), an interesting account of his inability to finish a novel. It seems likely that this pessimistic but humorous writer has his best work in front of him.

W. D. SNODGRASS (1926), who was born in Pennsylvania, first wrote on very personal subjects; since he tried to widen his range, and deliberately made his language, once straightforward, more complex, he has been notably less good. But this might happen to any poet who has run low on inspiration. His poetry is collected in two books: *Heart's Needle* (1958) and *After Experience. . . .* (1969). Essentially, when one has ruthlessly cut out the over-mawkish, the complacent and sentimental, Snodgrass is another good autobiographical poet like Anne Sexton.

New York-born ANTHONY HECHT (1923) has sometimes been associated—misleadingly—with the 'confessional' school. Actually he is a factitious poet, wholly traditional, who would not dream of letting slip a confession that had been undoctored with wit or irony.

Behind all this care, though, lurks an Old Testament Jewish voice, sometimes very angry; Hecht mutes it but its prophetic bray is still there. *The Hard Hours* (1967) selects from the earlier *A Summoning of Stones* (1954).

w. s. MERWIN (1927), also born in New York, is a most skilful constructor of poetic surface. He began by writing poems, of excellent technique, that looked as though they were meant to satisfy all the requirements of the new critics. They analyzed beautifully, one might say; but they lacked a distinctive voice, and they were not moving or convincing. The experience they reflected was that of thinking about being an acceptable poet. Since then Merwin has gone through a Williams (q.v.) phase, and is now writing in the style of the French poetry that stems from Reverdy (q.v.). He is a good craftsman, and is evidently sincere—he least of all needs to switch from traditional to unrhymed and free modes—but his new poetry looks too much like translation. And he is of course a notable translator from Spanish and from French: he translated Jean Follain (q.v.) in 1969, in a volume called *Transparence of the World*, and the French poet's influence is evident. Merwin's first verse was collected in *A Mask for Janus* (1952); recent books include *The Moving Target* (1967) and *The Lice* (1967).

*

There are probably more than a thousand published Beat poets. We need consider only one: ALLEN GINSBERG (1926). Ginsberg is a socio-anthropological phenomenon, a shrewd business man, and now, ironically, a part of the way of American life. He was educated at Columbia University, after which he went on the hoof. Then in 1955 he published the long poem *Howl*, and he was made: the Beat Generation was accepted. And Ginsberg cannot rebel again; so he boasts 'I . . . achieved the introduction of the word *fuck* into texts inevitably studied by schoolboys'. This is again ironic (if, of course, we accept that he alone did it): for this amiable pseudo-Zen droll is by no means a propagandist for heterosexuality. His poetry, he says, is 'Angelical Ravings'; but he is too comfortable to do more now than worry about his influence. His poetry is actually simply the manifestation of the eclectic, syncretic, 'redskin' American tradition. The first poems, although incoherent, had a pressure of indignation behind them. Their literary badness was deliberate. The poet 'simply followed his Angel in the course of compositions'. There *was* just a tiny bit of Blake in all this: the poet meant it. It expressed the drop-out's attitude to organized society. Ginsberg did have something that

Lowell did not. But all this became corrupt, a way of life; and life has not changed. Ginsberg's latest verse is publicly performed, chopped-up prose, incoherent and self-indulgent. It is preferable to the antics of politicians; preferable even to what passes for literature in the 'literary world'; but if it is indeed the new poetry, then a poetry in which thought, care and effort play a part is dead. And that is false to Gods Ginsberg himself appeals to: Blake, Smart, Shelley. Ginsberg's is a way of life. And so far we have not had a poetry that went along with any accepted way of life—certainly not ones that are sponsored by national institutions like Ginsberg. Whatever Ginsberg does, he is trapped: society has tamed him.

The Black Mountain school of poets, of whom I shall here discuss Olson and Creeley, did not arise from the Beat movement, although Creeley welcomed Ginsberg, who had previously been endorsed by Williams (who endorsed, in fact, pretty well anyone, including Lowell). Black Mountain College began in the Thirties and finally collapsed in the late Fifties. The emphasis was at first on the visual arts, on the art-object as thing-in-itself, and the tradition was that of American pragmatism. So far as literature is concerned, with the exception of Olson's doctrines (to be outlined below) the preoccupations were those of the objectivists (q.v.).

CHARLES OLSON (1910–70), who was born in Worcester, Massachusetts, was fifty before he became well known; and when he did it was in an atmosphere partly created by the Beat generation. At the end of Williams' life all American poets admired and respected him —as they did and do Pound. But Olson, who drew on Williams and Pound, only knew the admiration of disciples. He represents an apostle of Americanness: another step in the voyage of American self-discovery. He published many small volumes; but his main work is to be found in *Selected Writings* (1967), *The Maximus Poems* (1953; 1956; 1968); collected poetry is in the posthumous *Archeologist of Morning* (1970).

Olson's doctrines are to be found in the now famous essay 'Projective Verse'. They too spring directly from the American pragmatic tradition: verse is to be of '*essential* use', must reflect the breathing of the poet. Energy must be immediately transferred from writer (speaker) to reader (listener). This is 'kinetic': 'COMPOSITION BY FIELD'. The old method ('closed verse . . . which print bred') interposes the ego of the writer between himself and his audience; Olson claimed, contentiously, that this was what Keats meant by 'the Egotistical Sublime' (rather as if Keats had been born in Massachusetts in 1910: neither Olson nor his disciples are very strong on the past, except in their own terms of '*essential* use'). The

new poetry Olson demanded in his essay, which was published in
1950, was to put rhyme and metre in the background, and let 'the
syllable . . . lead the harmony on'.

All this, written in sometimes old-fashioned professorial slang
('And the joker? that it is in the 1st half of the proposition that, in
composing, one lets-it-rip. . . . Consider the best minds you know in
this here business . . .' and so on), was interesting as a theory: it was
just one more, rather dogmatic and slapdash, way of looking at the
problem of prosody, about which no one has ever been able to agree
beyond the most elementary points. It was also a plea, of course, for
more poetry readings—but would, in the course of these, the ego of
the poet still not obtrude? Olson's own poetry does not seem less
egocentric, or 'egostistically sublime', than anyone else's; in fact it is
a very noisy poetry. And his theory wholly ignores the fact of a form
(selected or invented by the poet: not necessarily failing to 'extend
the content', one of Olson's prerequisites, which, given his instructions to poets to let their own breathing determine their lines, are
excessively rigid) and a content acting as two poles to generate a
poetic tension. It also ignores the ritual element in poem-making,
which leads to the creation of arbitrary forms. All men live within
a recognisable bodily pattern: two ears, two eyes, a nose, and so on.
And yet all bodies are different. . . . One way of approaching the
problem is, of course, Olson's. What is distressing is his insistence
that only his own way is valid . . . His own poetry noisily insists, too:
is as philosophical and bullying as his criticism. It is so American
that it can have no more than historical interest to British readers; it
looks unlikely to survive long.

ROBERT CREELEY (1926), also born in Massachusetts, began as an
avowed disciple of Olson's although his lines have always been short
where Olson's were long. It is ironic that when he writes at his best,
as in 'Kore',

> As I was walking
>   I came upon
> chance walking
>   the same road upon.
> As I sat down
>   by chance to move
> later
>   if and as I might,
>
> light the wood was,
>   light and green,

and what I saw
　　before I had not seen.

It was a lady
　　accompanied
by goat men
　　leading her.

Her hair held earth.
　　Her eyes were dark.
A double flute
　　made her move.

'Oh love,
　　where are you
leading
　　me now?'

there is nothing peculiar about his rhythms. This is a fair lyric in a distinctive manner: its occasion is emotional rather than theoretical. Much more recently Creeley has written:

Could write of fucking—
rather its instant or the slow
longing at times of its approach—

how the young man desires,
how, older, it is never known,
but, familiar, comes to be so.

How your breasts, love,
fall in a rhythm also familiar,
neither tired nor so young they

push forward. I hate the metaphors.
I want you. I am still alone,
but want you with me.

Now this, unless Creeley adds something special to it in his performance of it, seems to me (as poetry) commonplace. Where the ballad-like clumsiness and archaism of the early poem added something essential to it, the form of this indicates the writer's tiredness. It is very like bad conversation. It—like Olson's theory and indeed any other theory if a poet has nothing to say—leads to the production of work that lacks tension.

Creeley's tightly held dogmas are, of course, a way of life. His novel *The Island* (1963), although autobiographical, and dealing with a hard time in his life, resolutely concentrates upon its author's perceptions (except when it slips); he thus misses much he might achieve. He cannot, or refuses to, say *of what use making poetry is*. Now that is a difficult, a primitive, even a philistine, position to be in if you are a poet. 'Things continue, but my sense is that I have, at best, simply taken place with that fact. . . . Words will not say more than they do. . . .' It is not enough to arouse interest outside the hall where the poem is being performed. Creeley's poetry is collected in *Poems 1950–65* (1965), in *The Finger* (1970) and in many small volumes.

GARY SNYDER (1930), who has studied Zen Buddhism in Japan and has been regarded as a Beat, is a good deal less intransigent about learning from the tradition. His poetry actually works by means of images (in Olson's or Creeley's theory interpositions of the ego), and it has developed in a manner reminiscent of poets working in the tradition. Yet Snyder has learned something from Ginsberg and from Olson and Creeley, for he eschews any kind of literary style. His sense of the world as he records it in his poetry is relaxed, pleasurable and without exhibitionism. Much of his best work is contained in *A Range of Poems* (1966), *The Back Country* (1967) and *Regarding Wave* (1970).

*

ROBERT BLY (1926), who was born in Minnesota, founded the magazine *The Sixties* in 1958, and pioneered—with JAMES WRIGHT (1927) —many important translations (of Vallejo, Trakl, Jimenez, and others). Bly is not a disciple of Olson in any sense, but he has bitterly attacked the whole concept of the new criticism—and the poetry of Robert Lowell. His ideal poet is probably Trakl (q.v.); which means that he eschews rhetoric, and is a poet who dislikes 'talk' in poems: as he has said of Trakl, the images speak for themselves. His own procedures resemble those of Trakl. But in his first book, *Silence in the Snowy Fields* (1962) he has introduced a bareness, an austerity. He wants to allow the things of Minnesota to speak for themselves. Later, in *The Light Around the Body* (1967), he finds he cannot: they are too spoiled by the world. He continues to develop, and has lately taken to writing moving prose—poems which give his work a new dimension.

James Wright has been much influenced by Bly. He began as a disciple of Frost and Robinson (qq.v.), and had been a pupil of Ransom and Roethke (qq.v.). But he was affected by Bly's war against rhetoric, and the poems of his third book, *The Branch Will Not Break* (1963)—the first two were *The Green Wall* (1957) and *Saint Judas* (1959)—are in free verse, and are almost Japanese in their spontaneity and freshness. His most recent poems, in similar style, are collected in *Shall We Gather at the River?* (1968). *Collected Poems* appeared in 1972.

Although LOUIS SIMPSON (1923), who was born in Jamaica, was associated with friends of Bly as an anthologist, he cannot be regarded as one of the 'Sixties' school. His best poetry is in his *Selected Poems* (1965). Simpson, who believes that poetry 'arises from the inner life of the poet and is expressed in original images and rhythms', is a lyrical poet of great power who, perhaps unusually, is also an accomplished ironist. He has absorbed enough of the native American schools, without sacrificing his notion of the uses of knowledge, to suggest that he may be a pioneer of style.

Australian Literature

Twenty-five years ago it was widely held, even by academic critics of repute, that there was no Australian literature worth mentioning outside Australia itself. Today that is an untenable view. Patrick White (q.v.) won the 1973 Nobel Prize and the work of at least three Australian poets (Slessor, Judith Wright, Hope, qq.v.) is well known throughout the world; that of some others deserves to be. Australian woman prose writers have been especially notable.

Australian literature developed along familiar colonial patterns. There was poetry before (creative) prose, and this was inhibitedly based on that of England. Thus an anonymous poet of the late eighteenth century wrote: 'And none will doubt but that our emigration/Has proved most useful to the British nation'. The work of the three leading poets of the colonial period—Harpur, Kendall and Gordon, none of them good except in flashes—must be judged mainly in terms of the late romantic or decadent literature into which their Australian experience happened to fit. More truly native writing, whether superior or otherwise, is to be found in such fugitive writing as J. F. Mortlock's *Experiences of a Convict*, which was not published (ed. A. G. Mitchell and G. A. Wilkes) until 1965.

The foundation of the *Bulletin* in Sydney in 1880 established the nationalist movement, which lasted until after the Second World War, and which still exercises a certain influence—though not at a high level. That this movement has been shown to embody a tradition which is largely mythical is not surprising; most movements are susceptible to similar retrospective reassessments. Not all the Australian writers of the early part of the modern period can be fitted into it. But it is useful to define the 'myth', if only to see it fall apart as we consider individual writers—and, indeed, as we consider some aspects of Australia itself. For the glowing, American kind of optimism could never have existed in Australia: the earliest settlers were convicts, the interior was vast and hostile and apparently unconquerable. There were criminal heroes in plenty, but no 'great men' who struggled for and gained independence—which did not have to be fought for. Sin and the melancholy loneliness of the individual in vast and mysterious places lie at the heart of the true Australian consciousness. This new world was never wholly brave. And, last but not least, the early development of the economy depended upon corporate rather than individual effort—which has had its oblique effect.

The nationalist movement tried to ignore this darker side. It was chauvinistic, democratic (in the early, broad, populist American sense of setting the ordinary man up against the privileged), and in that sense 'left-wing', Utopian, and anti-literary (in that it opposed aristocratic 'polish' as genteel). The main literary figures were HENRY LAWSON (1867–1922), TOM COLLINS (ps. JOSEPH FURPHY, 1843–1912) and ANDREW BARTON ('BANJO') PATERSON (1864–1941). After the heyday of these men, themselves in some ways exceptions, most major Australian writers are to be found outside nationalist tradition.

Lawson, the laureate of 'mateship' (the sense of corporateness that keeps Australians going in the face of hardship) and the outback, had a hard time on his father's farm in his youth—but spent most of his life in Sydney. His bush ballads were popular in his lifetime, but it is his short stories that will survive. Lawson is a sardonic realist, writing of the bush and its inhabitants with naturalistic resignation but also with humour and energy. Early reading of Dickens encouraged his capacity for taking pleasure in eccentric or roguish characters, whom he describes with brilliant zest. His best prose is admirably simple and sharp. It is seldom vague and its observation is keen and exact. Despite lapses into sentimentality, repetitiveness and unevenness, Lawson's genius for selecting what details are significant is not in question. After the turn of the century the quality of his work fell off, and he sought refuge in drink, unhappily divided in mind between outback and city.

The writing of Tom Collins, now usually referred to by his real name because he became well known only some thirty years after his death, is more sustained. Furphy was born in Victoria, and had a harder life than Lawson. After he married a farm he had taken failed, and he became a bullock-driver for some seven years before going to work in a factory. By 1897 he had finished 'a full-sized novel'; this is lost. But it was published in an abridged, revised form as *Such is Life* (1903); some of the material rejected for it appeared in shorter works. *Such is Life* was the first Australian novel to break with the English tradition. It made no attempt at a plot, and satirized effete British gentlemen (understandably but possibly unfairly). Furphy described the book, famously, as in 'temper, democratic; bias, offensively Australian'. He was a semi-naturalist, fascinated by the notion of ineluctable destiny stemming from choices made in a moment (thus, because at one point he does not fill his pipe, the narrator, Tom Collins, gets involved in a series of mishaps). *Such is Life* is crude, but crude in an authentically Australian manner; it is also comic and impolite in a way that (in book form) would have shattered a true Britisher of the time. The title is in itself a criticism of the carefully plotted Victorian novel; and I have called Furphy a *semi*-naturalist because, while he acknowledges destiny as a force, his experience had taught him a measure of scepticism about all aspects of life.

Banjo Paterson, author of *Waltzing Matilda*, is a literary balladeer who reflected native Australian rather than colonial experience; his poems read best aloud. At his least inventive he tends, under careful analysis, to collapse into components of patronization (he was, unlike the people he wrote about, an educated man), chauvinism and populism. But there is an authentic note: 'Clancy's gone to Queensland droving, and we don't know where he are'; and the magical 'There was movement at the station, for the word had passed around/ That the colt from Old Regret had got away . . .'. (PBHV). This vein of popular poetry was continued, but to less good effect, in the work of CLARENCE JAMES DENNIS (1876–1938), in *Songs of a Sentimental Bloke*.

The Victorian BERNARD O'DOWD (1866–1953) will survive only as a figure of historical interest. He corresponded with, and to a certain extent imitated, Walt Whitman, whose subtleties and complexities he lacked. His manifesto is *Poetry Militant* (1909), which is contained in his *Collected Poems* of 1941: this postulates a poet who understands history and can therefore contribute to the building of the future. O'Dowd was a clever versifier of a conventional kind, but his work is overloaded with rhetoric—and suspiciously free of personal concerns —to be of any but historical interest today. (BAV; PBHV). A much better poet is FURNLEY MAURICE (ps. FRANK WILMOT, 1881–1942). He can be both archaic, but with a Housmanesque edge, and—at times —extraordinarily direct. (PBAV)

SHAW NEILSON (1872–1942), born at Penola in South Australia, was a poorly educated manual worker who suffered for most of his life from bad eyesight. He used to compose his poetry in his head and then wait for a suitable amanuensis; many poems, he himself said, were lost in this process. Neilson is a minor poet, at his very best resembling Blake (whom he never read); he was the first unselfconsciously Australian poet, in whose simplicities lie a few jewels of insight and genuine ecstasy. He modelled himself on Thomas Hood, and often his insufferably 'poetical' language ('Plague me no more') spoils his effects. But occasionally his poetry comes through breathtakingly, as in 'The Orange Tree'. His *Collected Poems* appeared in 1934; *Unpublished Poems* in 1947. (BAV; PBAV)

Neilson's was a delightful and touching achievement, and greater than that of the sophisticated and learned CHRISTOPHER JOHN BRENNAN (1870–1932), who went to Sydney University (where he was later a professor), travelled in Europe, and was deeply conscious of the European poetic tradition. To put it briefly, the gifted Brennan went adrift on that notorious sandbank for the poets of his generation: sex. He felt he had to deal with his own failure to find sexual fulfilment in marriage, but he did so—as James McAuley (q.v.) has pointed out—pretentiously. An evader of the true nature of his experience—a central feature of which was that the hopefulness contained in his innocent, overforcefully applied wedding-night lustiness was shattered by his virginal wife's shuddering revulsion—he posed as a 'confessional' poet. He had waited, Victorian-like, for some years for the ecstasy of sexual fulfilment—and when it came he found it not only a let-down but also a focal point for every kind of guilt. He drew on French symbolism (q.v.), German romanticism and Pre-Raphaelite womanology in order to construct an edifice that would look like sexual wisdom. But he was the first Australian poet to be intelligently aware of a poetry outside the Anglo-Australian tradition, and is important for this reason. His ultimate ambition, in conscious terms, was to create a complete symbolist myth; in unconscious terms to erect a Platonic paradise that would compensate him for his sexual disappointment. And his poetry is interesting and skilful. He came under the influence of most of the important poets of his time—Verhaeren and George (notably) as well as the early French symbolists (qq.v. 2)—and he never indulged in pastiche. As a minor poet Neilson does sometimes come off; but Brennan had to come off as major or not at all. And he fails because his impressive structure of intellect, scholarship and literary awareness cannot subsume his personal experience. He was eventually sacked from his post at Sydney University when his wife divorced him and he began to drink too heavily. The definitive edition of his poetry is *Verse* (1960). (BAV; PBAV)

HUGH MCCRAE (1876–1958) has been important to almost every Australian poet. This seems curious to the outsider, because his poetry is not only limited but tiresome. The commonplaceness of McCrae's vitality is hardly compensated for by its abundance; his 'paganism' (satyrs, fauns and so on) is irritatingly simplistic and is inadequate as a poetic response to his times. He was the hero of the *Vision* group that gathered round Norman Lindsay (q.v.) in the Twenties—Australia's first clearly defined literary group. They, like other Australians, chose McCrae as a hero because he seemed so energetically anti-bourgeois. He was the obvious alternative to the new middle-class smugness. The poet R. D. Fitzgerald (q.v.) edited and selected his lively *Letters* (1970). Of his poetry one can now say little; like Lindsay's work and *persona*, it became one of the weekend treasures of the very class whose values it set out to challenge. (BAV; PBAV)

MARY GILMORE (1865–1962) declined into what James McAuley calls 'a repulsive example of a formidable will, cannily sucking homage indiscriminately out of the environment' some years before this attitude was properly rewarded by the D.B.E. (1937). But earlier in the century she had successfully avoided, in her unpretentious short lyrics, most of the vices of inflated diction and the poeticism that disfigured the poetry even of Neilson. She was a pioneer feminist, and a devotee of Aboriginal culture. (BAV; PBAV)

The next stage in Australian poetry came after the First World War, with the publication of the magazine *Vision* (1923). Its inspirer, NORMAN LINDSAY (1879–1969), has to be considered both as an influence (in Australian terms, immense) and as a novelist (minor). He was primarily an illustrator. Like his friend McCrae, Lindsay had boundless energy as mannered draughtsman and crude philosopher of 'vitalism' or 'biologism'.

His 'philosophy' is expressed in *Creative Effort* (1920), an inconsistent mish-mash of pseudo-Nietzschean vitalism, Godless immortality and heavy-handed amorous innuendo. The obvious message of this book, as of *Vision*, is pseudo-Rabelaisian 'vitality, vigour', of any sort—and not necessarily Australian. And this was what the writers in a more settled Australia wanted; they could thus evade their melancholy destiny (a thing we all wish to do) and yet seem to oppose bourgeois complacency. The members of this group did their best work after leaving it; but it did nearly all of them harm. For it was essentially a backwards-looking movement, which avowedly preferred 'being alive' to being modern—and this was inadequate to the inner needs of the best Australian poets. *Vision*, of which only four numbers appeared, vanished from Australia and reappeared in London (briefly) as *The London Aphrodite* (1928), edited by Norman's son JACK LINDSAY (1900), who remained in England and poured out an immense amount of lively Marxist historical fiction, translation, biography and interesting reminiscence.

The best of Norman Lindsay's books is his children's novel *The Magic Pudding* (1918), because here the sheer thoughtlessness of his exuberance cannot offend. As he himself said, its basic themes are 'eating and fighting'. It is said by some to be a children's classic. But his adult fiction, although stylistically offensive, is not negligible. It is probably a testimony to the accuracy of *Redheap* (1930), about life in the Australian Nineties, that it was for over twenty years banned by the Australian government. Perhaps his best novel is *Saturdee* (1933), which helps to explode the myth of boys as angels.

The most gifted member of the *Vision* group was KENNETH SLESSOR (1901-71). But his early poetry consists of little more than energetic and linguistically promising literary inventiveness—sophistications of the subject-matter of McCrae. He is descriptively brilliant, playful (often archly so) and has no content beyond a generally bristling sexuality and materialism. Slessor became a more interesting poet; but it is only in a few individual poems, mostly noted by critics, that he has wholly succeeded. 'Gulliver' appropriately shows what sort of experience his uneasy later poems can explore with success (although even here the exasperated tone of the monologue is somewhat forced):

> I'll kick your walls to bits, I'll die scratching a tunnel,
> If you'll give me a wall, if you'll give me simple stone,
> If you'll do me the honour of a dungeon—
> Anything but this tyranny of sinews.
> Lashed with a hundred ropes of nerve and bone
> I lie, poor helpless Gulliver,
> In a twopenny dock for the want of a penny,
> Tied up with stuff too cheap, and strings too many.
> One chain is usually sufficient for a cur.
>
> Hair over hair, I pick my cables loose,
> But still the ridiculous manacles confine me.
> I snap them, swollen with sobbing. What's the use?
> One hair I break, ten thousand hairs entwine me.
> Love, hunger, drunkenness, neuralgia, debt,
> Cold weather, hot weather, sleep and age—
> If I could only unloose their spongy fingers,
> I'd have a chance yet, slip through the cage.
> But who ever heard of a cage of hairs?
> You can't scrape tunnels in a net.
>
> If you'd give me a chain, if you'd give me honest iron,
> If you'd graciously give me a turnkey,
> I could break my teeth on a chain, I could bite through metal,
> But what can you do with hairs?
> For God's sake, call the hangman.

Clearly McCrae's vitalism is too simplistic for him, and yet he resents a universe in which this should be so: the giant trapped by 'hairs' therefore wants to die. To McCrae himself he said (most Australian poets have written poems to McCrae): 'We live by . . . your masks and images/ . . . But you take passage on the ruffian seas/ And you are vanished in the dark already'. One continually feels, reading the poetry of Slessor, that one is just about to encounter a linguistic revelation; but it seldom really comes. 'Five Visions of Captain Cook' is an interesting and genuinely Australian poem, with some good passages; but as a whole it is not *réussi*: the thought and the language fall together only sporadically. However, 'Five Bells', a meditation on the death of a friend by drowning, is an impressive poem of despair: here at last Slessor is able to see the unhappy nihilism that his vitalism and sensuality papers over, and to respond with words that haunt the mind. Slessor frequently revised his poems in the course of his life; the definitive edition is *Poems* (1957). He wrote no more than three or four poems after 1940. (BAV; PBAV)

The poet REX INGAMELLS' (1913–55) Jindyworobak school of the late Thirties, with its emphasis on the importance of the Aboriginal culture, produced no important poetry even though it hit the (literary) headlines. The *Jindyworobak Review* ran from 1938 until 1948. However, its attempt to bring Aboriginal culture, with its highly poetic central concept of 'dream time' (*altijira*), into the mainstream of Australian poetry may yet have its effect; that this was premature and that Ingamells (who died in a car accident) was a poor poet should not distract us from appreciation of his admirable project.

The only poetically gifted member of this abortive movement was WILLIAM HART-SMITH (1911), whose extreme concentration and economy are remarkable in that they so seldom pull him down into the trivial or whimsical. Born in England, he left there at twelve, and lived in New Zealand for a while (being at one time represented as a New Zealand poet), but he is now permanently in Australia. He has been influenced by Sufic ideas and the teachings of Gurdieff, but these seldom obtrude. There is no collected edition. A representative volume is *The Talking Clothes* (1966). (PBAV)

R. D. FITZGERALD (1902) contributed to *Vision* but was not associated with Lindsay's group as closely as Slessor. Some see Fitzgerald as Australia's major poet of the century: the writer who succeeded where Brennan (q.v.) failed. Certainly he has been as aware as Brennan of European poetry, and his goal has been ambitiously philosophical. An intellectual poet, he also suffers from a brash optimism ('I regret I shall not be around/to stand on Mars') that may either attract or repel; but he is in any case honest. He is to be

seen at his best in such poems as 'The Wind at your Door' (AWT),
a sensitive and skilful meditation on an ancestor, a doctor, 'caught
in the system', which broadens out into a lyrical and humane
exploration of the original sin that lies at the back of the Australian
experience (a nation of convicts and, as bad, their no less criminal
oppressors). 'I find I lack/the hateful paint to daub him wholly
black' Fitzgerald says of this ancestor: 'Perhaps my life replies to his
too much/through veiling generations dropped between'. The
language of the poem is simple almost to clumsiness; but retrospectively one sees that it suits the awkward and agonized honesty—and
makes the poet's vain wish to be a descendant of the flogged man
who (under the medical supervision of Fitzgerald's forbear) guiltily
haunts the poem. Fitzgerald has probably received most praise for
his collection of 1938, *Moonlight Acre*; but these philosophical poems
are less spontaneous than *Between Two Tides* (1952), an epic of
eighteenth-century Tonga, and the lyrics of *This Night's Orbit* (1953).
But like Slessor, Hope and the younger McAuley (qq.v.) Fitzgerald
has never really been able to achieve an authentic Australian voice
more than sporadically; it has been left to Patrick White (q.v.) to
do this, in prose; and to Kenneth Mackenzie (q.v.) to come very near
to, and sometimes attain, it in poetry. (BAV; PBAV; AWT)

A. D. HOPE (1907) did not publish his first collection, *The Wandering
Islands* (1955), until he was nearly fifty. Since then he has exercised
an increasing influence on Australian poetry. He is a ferocious
conservative; but his apparent conservatism and rejection of modernism (including that of Eliot) may appear on closer examination to be
an expression of Swiftian disgust at all developments in human
history since about 1750. Hope is a sexual romantic, highly energetic
(again in a familiar Australian way), operating in severely classical
modes of his own choosing. The sex-fun, however, is basically
McCraen. A similarly gifted poet, JAMES MCAULEY (1917), a witty and
astringent critic, has displayed a similarly intelligent but unhappier
conservatism. Like the New Zealand poet James K. Baxter (q.v.),
he has become a Catholic; but his poetry tends hotly to limit his own
faith rather than to affirm it. Australians bitterly attack their own
'way of life', but, watching the developments in the outside world
(of which they are acutely aware: they are not 'cut off') are unwilling
to let in pop-culture.

A. D. Hope has been a 'literary nuisance' on the Australian scene,
sometimes silly but always amusing; he is at his best when caught between the nervous tension of his deliberately Augustan formalism and
his sexual wildness. And yet even here one wonders if the Australian
predicament itself is not responsible for a refusal to allow rhythms to

develop in their own idiosyncratic way: the traditional forms seem to trap Hope, at his most personal, in poeticisms that the term 'irony' cannot quite accommodate:

> She does not tire of the pattern of a rose,
> Her oldest tricks still catch us by surprise.
> She cannot recall how long ago she chose
> The streamlined hulls of fish, the snail's long eyes.

His has been the most skilful and versatile means of defeating both hatred of Australian philistinism (a very brash phenomenon) and his failure to discover his own voice. But the over-celebrated 'Ode on the Death of Pius the Twelfth' reveals not only his accomplishment but his pomposity and degree of artificiality. Neo-Augustinism is not an adequate response to any modern predicament, let alone an Australian one, and though Hope's performances in this vein are superior to those of Winters (q.v.), they do not ring at all true. He has published *Collected Poems* (1966) and *New Poems* (1969).

McAuley, who has criticized Brennan's personal inadequacies in no mean terms, has brought the influence of Rilke (q.v. 2) into Australian poetry—something Brennan could not have done. It was after his first book, *Under Aldebaran* (1946), and after the Ern Malley hoax—in which he and another poet, Harold Stewart, faked a Dylan Thomas-like poet and successfully put him across on Australian letters—that McAuley became a Roman Catholic and defined his anti-sceptical position: the danger, as he reasonably saw it, was that everyone was being encouraged to be *uncommitted*, 'without fixed principles or certainties'. Considering the self-limiting nature of his own faith, one is bound to consider that McAuley may merely have been urging himself to take arms against the sea of his own troubled scepticism. His own later poetry, as in 'A Letter to John Dryden', is less celebratory of the joys of understanding the true God than shot through with hatred of scepticism. It seems a highly provincial kind of position for so gifted a critic and poet. So far the lyrics of McAuley's first book have been his best work: he has made the mistake of taking up a critical position in his poetry—afraid, perhaps, of what he might find if he did otherwise. His *Collected Poems 1936–1970* appeared in 1971. (BAV; PBAV)

The third force in Australian poetry (as she might be called) is JUDITH WRIGHT (1915), who published her first book, *The Moving Image*, in 1946. She has written intelligently on her contemporaries, and in poetry has been less ambitious and perhaps more healthily stark in her use of language. But she is better on her non-sexual experience than on her position as wife and mother: here, while she is translucently sincere, a puritanically bourgeois attitude becomes too apparent; a typically Australian, frozenly ineffectual resistance to what is happening in the world causes her to cast a rosily sentimental glow over 'family life'. One's own experience is one thing; lack of understanding through a dogged refusal to understand is another—and there is a residue of the latter in her over-fragrant attitude. She has rightly emphasized that poetry must finally depend upon emotion; but she has tended to diminish the role of that hard thought which must so often precede the statement of emotion. Her early despair at loneliness relieved only by sexual contact, which produced her best and most limpid poems, has given way to a less self-explorative assertion of 'old-fashioned' values. (AW; BAV; PBAV)

Two other women poets have been less influential, but both are in the final analysis superior to Judith Wright. ROSEMARY DOBSON (1920) probably has no more to say, but she has found a decidedly less self-consciously 'feminine' way of saying it. Her usually tight forms effectively and unarchaically contain and control her strongly felt sense of erotic and religious dismay, but the influence of Lovell (q.v.) has hardly helped her to achieve a less metrically strict, more rhythmically free form; yet when she achieves it she will be found to have much more to say than, for example, Anne Sexton (q.v.). A *Selected Poems* appeared in 1963. (BAV; AWT; PBHV). GWEN HARWOOD (1920) is an oddity, and an extremely good one. She owes much to Morgenstern (q.v.) in her comic poems, but has an entirely original and powerful lyrical capacity. She is as strange as Stevie Smith (q.v.), but less hit-or-miss, more intelligent and more controlled. Her rewarding work may be found in *Poems I* (1963) and *Poems II* (1968). (AWT; PBAV). Both she and Rosemary Dobson should be more widely read in Great Britain and America.

DOUGLAS STEWART (1913) was born in New Zealand, where he learned to write nature poetry. He belongs to the still flourishing Antipodean tradition of conservative formalism; by not forcing himself into an intellectual stocktaking he has managed to continue writing poetry and vigorous, if conventional, verse drama. 'The Sunflowers' demonstrates his strength and his limitations:

'Bring me a long sharp knife for we are in danger;
I see a tall man standing in the foggy corn
And his high, shadowy companions'—'But that is no stranger,
That is your company of sunflowers; and at night they turn
Their dark heads crowned with gold to the earth and the dew

So that indeed at daybreak, shrouded and silent,
Filled with a quietness such as we never knew,
They look like invaders down from another planet,
And now at the touch of light from the sun they love—'
'Give me the knife. They move.'

This is in certain respects poor: no one can say that the clichés of observation and language are exploited, either ironically or otherwise—and yet it was worth doing. (BAV; AW; PBAV)

EVAN JONES (1932), the best of the younger critics, has achieved a colloquial directness not often seen in Australian poetry. VINCENT BUCKLEY (1925), another helpful critic, has written some poetry of recollected experience that is moving in the honesty of its attempt to capture exactly the mood and feeling of the past moment.

*

Australian dramatists have been few. Douglas Stewart's (q.v.) verse plays have vigour, but their language—read over—is prosy. The one authentic Australian play that has so far been written is by the actor RAY LAWLER (1913): *The Summer of the Seventeenth Doll* (1955). This deserved its success. It is an examination of the legend of the tough Australian outdoor man and his innate superiority; the notion it gave non-Australians of Australia was both truthful and moving. It was not flawless—sentimental box-office concessions were made— but its final departures from psychological accuracy do not challenge the basic conceptions of the play. *The Piccadilly Bushman* (1959) was not as successful, and later plays by Lawler have settings other than Australia. There have been good plays by Patrick White and Hal Porter (qq.v.), but so far no Australian of Lawler's calibre has emerged.

*

The first Australian novelist of importance was HENRY HANDEL RICHARDSON (ps. ETHEL FLORENCE LINDESAY RICHARDSON, 1870– 1946). She was in Europe studying music until 1903, and her first essays into literature were translations from the Scandinavian; Jacobsen's *Niels Lyhne* (q.v. 2), so important to Rilke (q.v. 2) and others, she acknowledged as a formative influence—her translation of it appeared in 1896. *Maurice Guest* (1908), autobiographical in many diverse ways, none of them quite direct, is naturalistic, Freudian and 'amoral'. Although Henry Handel Richardson re- visited Australia only briefly—she lived in England, where her

husband was a professor of German literature, and she died at
Hastings in Sussex—she is still to be considered an Australian
novelist, for the main subject of her most important novel, *The
Fortunes of Richard Mahony* trilogy (1929), is wholly Australian. It
is a brilliantly intelligent work, a late flowering of naturalism; its
theme, of an English Victorian doctor's emigration to Australia and
the crushing of himself and his decent qualities by fate, in the form
of his own characteristics and circumstances, is never forced. The
societies of Australia and England (to which Mahony at one point
returns) are acutely described, and Mahony's defeat and moral
collapse are observed with feline attention to detail. Pity is withheld;
but not understanding.

Naturalism has flourished longer in Australian writing than elsewhere (except perhaps in Canada): the fatalistic habit of mind has
not yet been dispelled. Even the best poets tend to insist on retreating
into conservatism (or, like Slessor, give up after a final nihilistic
fling); the novelists can cling on to naturalism, which after all—
with its insistence on exact mimesis and cruel destiny—is a kind of
faith. A novelist who has had his due neither in his native Australia
nor outside it is LEONARD MANN (1895), a bleak and clumsy writer
whose best fiction approaches the power of Dreiser's (q.v.). Mann
tries to irradiate the darkness he sees over the world with socialistic
hope, but gloom dims his effort; the glow in his novels is one not of
hope but of courage in adversity. *Flesh in Armour* (1932) is one of the
best of the First World War books, and has been unduly neglected.
The ex-schoolmaster Frank Jeffreys is the typical Mann victim: he
tries to make himself into a soldier with the A.E.F., but cannot
manage it; he shoots himself in the hour of the Allied victory. Mann
presents this early anti-hero, the man who *could* not kill, as in one
sense superior to his companions—but doomed. After *Human Drift*
(1935) came *A Murder in Sydney* (1937), a gloomy metropolitan study
of crime and redemption (through the agency of a Dostoevskian
maimed lover), which is set in the years of the Depression. *The Go-
Getter* (1942) is Mann's tensest and finest book: Chris Gibbons is
redeemed from cheapness by his tough challenge to fate. His heartless project to seduce a girl turns into love. *Andrea Caslin* (1959) and
Venus Half-Caste (1963) maintain the high standards of this powerful
and unheeded novelist. The key to Mann's fiction may be found in
his minor but not undistinguished poetry. (BAV)

FREDERIC MANNING (1882–1935) produced one classic; it appeared
anonymously in Paris in 1929 under the title *The Middle Parts of
Fortune*, but is better known under its English title of *Her Privates We*
(1930)—the author called himself 'Private 19022'. This is a contrast

to Mann's pacifistic *Flesh in Armour*, than which it is a more artistically successful—but not more powerful—work: Manning treats the war as a test of character. Where Mann is deliberately anti-heroic Manning is heroic—but not by choice. It is simply that his Bourne *can* what Mann's Jeffreys *cannot*. But there is as much irony in *Her Privates We*: Bourne is, in effect, murdered (by being forced to go on a suicidal sortie) by an officer who fears and envies his qualities. Manning, who wrote other graceful minor prose, suffered from asthma even while serving in Flanders; he died in Italy.

VANCE PALMER (1885–1959), a competent author, was a better writer of short stories than novels: he could deal well with the apparently trivial, but whatever struck him as important seemed to inhibit him. But his novels contain much excellent work. His best books are *Separate Lives* (1931), *Sea and Spinifex* (1934) and *Let the Birds Fly* (1955), all collections of stories, and the novel *The Passage* (1930), in which he fails with the love relationships but succeeds with the description of the stresses and strains experienced within a family. His big trilogy about a socialist politician, *Golconda* (1948), *Seedtime* (1957) and *The Big Fellow* (1959), is honest but more mediocre.

KATHERINE SUSANNAH PRICHARD (1884–1969), although she played some part in the formation of a specifically Australian novel, never produced a masterpiece. Her first efforts were feeble, and almost all her books are flawed by too great a reliance upon a crude Marxism. She was a simple-minded socialist; it did not do her writing much good. She is at her best in *Haxby's Circus* (1930), a humorous and vivid account of circus life which contains no manipulation of character in the interests of theory, and no preaching. *Coonardoo* (1929), reckoned by most to be her best book, is a moving story (based on what used to be called 'real life') of a black Australian's romance with a white man. It is flawed by the poor handling of its melodramatic plot and its inept attempt to emulate D. H. Lawrence's (q.v.) manner of dealing with 'elemental' sex ('deep inexplicable currents of his being flowed towards her'); but the author makes Coonardoo herself understandable. Later books, particularly the gold-field trilogy—*The Roaring Nineties* (1946), *Golden Miles* (1948) and *Winged Seeds* (1950)—are worthy: always worth reading for their author's mastery of the facts of her material and her sincere treatment of it.

For Katherine Prichard the naturalistic gloom of imagination was replaced by Marxist socialism; KYLIE TENNANT (1912) is a more thoroughgoing naturalist who has written several vivid novels of city life. *Tiburon* (1935) is about unemployed relief-workers in the country during the Depression; *Foveaux* (1939) is a vivid picture of Sydney slum-life in the years 1912-35.

Of the expatriates since Henry Handel Richardson, CHRISTINA STEAD (1902) has been the most distinguished. She went to London in 1928, and settled in America permanently in 1937. She was mainly a 'critic's author' until the reprint in America, in 1965, of *The Man Who Loved Children* (1940). Her first book was a collection of stories, *The Salzburg Tales* (1934); this was followed by *Seven Poor Men of Sydney* (1934), about young revolutionaries in Sydney in the Twenties, remarkable for its realistic picture of the Sydney docks. *The Man Who Loved Children* is her masterpiece: a study of the savage warfare between a wild but intelligent woman and her neurotic, proto-fascistic husband, and of their seven children's varying means of evading permanent damage. This is set in America, and it is hard to see anything Australian about it: Christina Stead is a cosmopolitan novelist, nominally left-wing (but without party) and she has studied French fiction—particularly that of Louis Guilloux (q.v. 2), whose influence she has acknowledged. But *The Man Who Loved Children* is entirely original; sovereign among its many qualities, perhaps, is the detachment of its portrayal of Sam Politt, the husband who drives his wife to suicide and 'never thought she meant it'. Other books by Christina Stead include *For Love Alone* (1944), the earlier part of which is set in Australia, *Letty Fox, Her Luck* (1946), *A Little Tea, A Little Chat* (1948), *Cotter's England* (1966) and the four superb novellas in *A Puzzleheaded Girl* (1967). One can at least see the fascination that Guilloux had for Christina Stead: like him, she horrifiedly and fascinatedly dwells on the tiny details of obsessions. *For Love Alone* dwells thus on the behaviour of an Australian girl who falls in love with a student and follows him to London. *Cotter's England*, set in England, looks at the lives of a couple somewhat reminiscent of Sam and Henrietta in *The Man Who Loved Children*. Nell, an unsuccessful left-wing journalist, 'collects' women and fills her house with them; her husband George is more important in the world, less neurotic and cares less about other people. Christina Stead is one of the most gifted novelists of her generation, a master of significant detail.

MARTIN BOYD (1893-1972) improved on his expatriate fiction after he returned to Australia in 1948. In England he had been a monk for a time. Boyd is not a sensational novelist, and although generally readable his books have their *longueurs*; but he is an intelligent and gifted analyst of the Australian past, who deserves more attention than he has had. *The Montforts* (1928), written under the pseudonym of Martin Mills, traces the history of his mother's family over five generations; *Lucinda Brayford* (1946), however, which deals with the same subject-matter, is superior. It traces the fortunes of the Vanes from William Vane's emigration to Australia after being sent down from Cambridge for cheating at cards until the death of his great-grandson in England in the Second World War. This is an intelligent and sensitive 'family saga' novel, and avoids the sentimentalities and dishonesties into which Galsworthy (q.v.) fell. The 'Langton' tetralogy—*The Cardboard Crown* (1952), *A Difficult Young Man* (1955), *Outbreak of Love* (1957) and *When Blackbirds Sing* (1962)—is more substantial and is his best work.

SEAFORTH MACKENZIE (ps. KENNETH MACKENZIE, 1913-55), whose novels but not poetry collections were published under the name of Seaforth (because his publisher had a Kenneth Mackenzie on their list), could well have been treated as poet, for he was equally—perhaps more—distinguished in this field. He has been compared with Dylan Thomas (q.v.): he was Australia's latter-day *poète maudit*: alcoholic (meths drinker sometimes), an isolate, always poor, usually desperate, died young (by drowning). But in his shrugging, complex, sardonic despair he resembles Malcolm Lowry (q.v.) rather than Thomas. He is certainly an odd man out of Australian letters—and an important one. Not one of his four novels is an absolute success, but each achieves something. *The Young Desire It* (1937) and *Chosen People* (1938) are sometimes marred by pastiche of Lawrence's (q.v.) vitalism, or by youthful awkwardnesses. But both introduce something new into Australian fiction. The most successful feature of the first is its sympathetic portrait of an unhappy homosexual schoolmaster. (Clearly Mackenzie had had some adolescent trouble with homosexuality, though he seems to have emerged as a fully fledged heterosexual at adulthood.) There is also some excellent observation of the narcissism natural to certain types of adolescent. One critic, Evan Jones (q.v.), has most unfairly confused his dislike of the manifestation with Mackenzie's portrayal of it. *Chosen People* is a vile story told with hideous conviction and power: a beautiful woman gives up her young paramour—already sucked dry by her—and grooms her equally beautiful daughter for marriage to him. *Dead Men Rising* (1951) is disappointing; but Mackenzie's last novel, *The Refuge* (1954), shows a return to the form of *Chosen People*, and is his best-written book. This is the story of a love affair ending in murder; it reads straightforwardly on a realist level, but has unmistakable symbolic overtones. Lloyd Fitzherbert falls in love with a young woman, a double agent who has renounced both her employers; he renounces her offer of herself to him. Later, however, they marry secretly; the girl takes his beloved son (whose mother died in giving birth to him) as lover; Fitzherbert kills her, with, it seems, her consent. This has mythological and incestuous overtones; it is also about isolation and the tragedies this can lead to: in a diary Mackenzie wrote: 'Perfect moonlight—absolute, utter silence of windless night, cold'. This is the spiritual atmosphere of *The Refuge*.

Mackenzie's poetry, a properly definitive collection of which is only just now in preparation (by Evan Jones and Geoffrey Little), is at its best as good as any Australian's of the century, and perhaps suggestive of greater gifts. From his personal hell Mackenzie seems to have been unique in breaking free of that stultifying kind of traditionalism which even the most brilliant of Australian male poets seem to oblige themselves, in one way or another, with varying reluctance, to cling to (the exception is Hart-Smith, q.v., but he is not fully Australian). Mackenzie at his best has a voice more unmistakably his own than any of his contemporaries; you can never confuse it, as you can even McAuley's and Hope's, with that of a dead age.

> Blackness rises. Am I now to die
> and feel the steps no more and not see day
> break out its answering smile of hail all's well
> from east full round to east and hear the bird
> whistle all creatures that on earth do dwell?

Mackenzie did not always write well, and his poetic achievement will not be truly measurable until we have his complete work; but we have enough to be sure that he almost (although not quite) alone of contemporary Australians was prepared to risk himself in the quest for an adequate response to his time.

HAL PORTER (1917) has, after Patrick White (q.v.), the most versatile and vigorous talent of all Australian contemporary writers. His best prose is in his magnificent autobiography, *The Watcher on the Cast-Iron Balcony* (1963 pt. AWT), which has extraordinary control and detachment as well as a Proustian sense of the past. This is one of the most quintessentially Australian books to be published since 1945—because Porter's experience has been Australian and because his book remains true to it. Its exuberant manner owes something to Dylan Thomas' Welsh idylls. A sequel volume, *The Paper Chase*, followed in 1966. Much influenced by Katherine Mansfield (q.v.), Porter writes well, in short stories, of innocence betrayed by maturity: *A Bachelor's Children* (1962) and *The Cats of Venice* (1965). In his novel *The Tilted Cross* (1961), set in mid-nineteenth-century Tasmania, Porter seemed to be going out of his depth in trying to follow Patrick White. So far his best fiction has been in short stories.

PATRICK WHITE (1912), born of Australian parents in London, educated at Cambridge, only returned to Australia permanently after serving in the Second World War. He began with a book of poems, *The Ploughman* (1935), which has considerable value as an index to his later works. His first important book was *The Aunt's Story* (1948). This dealt with what is really his central theme, the Nietzschean (q.v. 2) one of the lonely atheist's agonized capacity for insight into the nature of existence. Comparisons with Dostoevski and other such writers are not, in White's case, foolish, although he continually experiences difficulty in sorting out rhetoric from what is a kind of truly mantic utterance. *The Aunt's Story* is concerned with Theodora, who in her desire to lose personal identity—she rejects love as a threat to this process—becomes mad, but possibly feels at peace. In *The Tree of Man* (1955) White tried to resolve this problem of solitude by anchoring his characters—husband and wife who build up a large farm from a smallholding—in everyday life; but one can see his obstinate and guilt-ridden obsession with the necessity of loneliness even in this most realistically conceived of his novels. *Voss* (1957) goes entirely the other way: its hero's project is, by making an expedition into the Australian interior, to become God: to turn himself into what is not. Although this profound and beautiful book has sources in the journeys of actual explorers, the most instructive general background to it is undoubtedly the thought of Nietzsche. Voss has to transcend his sense of beauty (one is reminded of Hopkins, q.v., punishing himself for having taken too much pleasure from the landscape) in order to achieve his project: he must not yield to the sensuous. Perhaps he loves his dog: he kills it. In *Riders in the Chariot* (1961) White achieves on a major level, with alienated freaks, what Carson McCullers (q.v.) could only hint at. This takes place in Sarsaparilla, the Sydney suburb that White has made as real as Faulkner (q.v.) made Yoknapatawpha County. All the freaks are in quest of a loss of identity that is not a suicide or an escape. *The Solid Mandala* (1966) is about twins, one apparently simple, the other clever, who are brought to Sarsaparilla by their English parents when young. First we see life from Waldo's point of view: he is 'superior', but he fails and ends his life hating his twin Arthur because he knows that Arthur is his only contact with life. Then we see the same events from Arthur's point of view: Arthur is a 'holy fool', a wise man who from childhood has wanted to climb to 'the red gold disc of the sun'—but he is judged by all but a neighbour, Mrs. Poulter, as a madman. The apparently sordid *dénouement* is seen through her eyes. This is a difficult but immensely powerful novel, another milestone in a strange and poetic journey. *The Vivesector* (1970) is about a painter, and, astonishingly, maintains the classic level of the earlier novels—as, indeed, does *The Eye of the Storm* (1973), which was misunderstood by reviewers. White has written short stories (*The Burnt Ones*, 1964) and four plays of varying dramatic effectiveness but extreme significance in the context of his fiction. He won the Nobel Prize in 1973. (AWT)

The novelist and poet RANDOLPH STOW (1935) is a follower of White. He leans too heavily on him; but it is hard to see how a still young man who genuinely shares White's predisposition to the symbolic could fail to do so. His first two novels were powerful but melodramatic; only in the third, *To the Islands* (1958), about a sixty-eight-year-old Antipodean Lear, did he really begin to find himself. Heriot, a missionary, loses his faith and goes off on a voyage of exploration, accompanied by an old aborigine, to the islands of the dead. *Tourmaline* (1963) is about a ghost-town stricken by drought; a water-diviner who comes there persuades the inhabitants of his magic qualities, but proves to be a fake. This intended fable of man's capacity for self-deceit does not come off: Stow is dealing in fact with his own religious feelings, but tries to rationalize these into generalized comment. In *The Merry-go-Round in the Sea* (1965) he abandons conscious symbolism for a vein of tender realism, and does much better. He only falters at the end, when he tries to contrast the old world of childhood with the new one of adult reality. In his poetry Stow expresses a vision much akin to that of Sydney Nolan (who has illustrated one of his collections); he speaks of his 'sad-coloured country/bitterly admired'. What James McAuley (q.v.), in a lecture on Australian poetry, has called 'the personal element' has so far been missing or ineptly expressed; but of his seriousness there is no doubt.

British Literature

I

Although no country had more good novelists than Great Britain at the beginning of this century, the European naturalist movement had little direct effect on British fiction. It did, however, influence the work of GEORGE GISSING (1857–1903), who in his turn has exercised a strong, although largely subterranean, influence on later writers (particularly on Orwell, q.v.). Gissing, an unhappy and unhealthy man, led a life of almost unrelieved misery. At college he stole to help a prostitute he had befriended; after serving a prison sentence he went to America for a year; he failed to support himself there, returned—and married the same woman. She was a nagging psychopath, and Gissing's life was made hell for ten years. Then she died, and he went out and picked up and married a similarly impossible woman. When she became insane Gissing found a Frenchwoman with whom he was happier. He never achieved financial stability, and only kept his head above water by constant overwork— which subsequently weakened his constitution and led to his early death. His close friend H. G. Wells (q.v.), who was with him at his death, wrote of him with great acumen: he called him 'an extraordinary blend of a damaged joy-living human being hampered by inherited gentility and a classical education'.

There is something a little repulsive about Gissing: a genteel defensiveness and a not always wholly repressed whining self-pity. Yet at his best, as in *Born in Exile* (1892), Gissing is not merely a good but a major novelist—greater in achievement than, for example, his older, more sophisticated and more gifted contemporary George Meredith (q.v.). Some of Gissing's twenty-two novels are poor and thin, and the writing is cliché-ridden and weary. But at least in *Born in Exile*, the bitter tale of a free-thinker who destroys himself by pretending (against his principles) to be a Christian in order to gain love and position, Gissing wrote a major novel—and one of Dostoevskian overtones.

His original model had been the Dickens who recorded the seamy side of life; he wrote of this with sourness and no humour—but managed to add something. Personally doomed by his own foolish propensity to 'redeem' and 'genteelize' lower-class women, he was a naturalist in spite of himself: his characters are often driven— sometimes one must read between the lines—by their anguished sexual preoccupations, as he was. There is much worth reading in him beside *Born in Exile*, his masterpiece: *Demos* (1886), in which he expresses his distrust of the people *en masse*, *A Life's Morning* (1888), *New Grub Street* (1891), *The Private Papers of Henry Ryecroft* (1903), and more. He still requires his due.

GEORGE MEREDITH (1828–1909), although nearly thirty years older than Gissing, is a modernist *manqué*. He deserves credit for his intentions; and if he must ultimately be said to have failed then his was a very notable failure. The spirit of naturalism also influenced Meredith, although in a different and even less direct way: he retained a somewhat obstinate conviction that everything may be explained mechanically—this is at the heart of both his (uninteresting and unconvincing) optimism and his (interesting) sense of the comic, which in some respects anticipates that of Wyndham Lewis (q.v.). He had a hard time establishing a reputation—even at the height of his Victorian fame there were influential cliques who had no use for him—and he had not long been dead before he became widely unread. And yet he was a tireless experimenter; he will never quite lie down. No one's novels sound more interesting in detailed summary. He would have liked to have been an ironic comedian in the manner of the Brazilian Machado de Assis (q.v. 3), whose work he did not know; but his subtle and intelligent novels usually become victim to his meretriciousness, his false philosophical optimism and the puzzling manner in which he transforms his huge imaginative energy into something merely whimsical or even plain crazy. And yet, as Henry James carefully said, he did 'the best things best'. He has his magnificent moments, and these are prophetic of what is to come in the novel.

Meredith was badly hamstrung by the Victorian necessity for sexual reticence: his realistic view of women and of sexual matters in general cut sharply across the Victorian fantasy, which enshrined women only to patronize them and neutralize their (in anthropological terms) magical qualities. His imaginative sympathy really was with women—as victims of this male distortion—and it involved him in the kind of extreme difficulties with which we, in turn, must sympathize. Meredith's sympathy with women and his understanding of sexual problems led to some inspired passages (such as the scene, in *The Egoist*, where Clare watches Vernon Whitford asleep under the cherry tree; or, earlier, the masturbation scenes in *The*

Ordeal of Richard Feverel) but never, alas, to a completely successful novel. The only book in which the notorious Meredithian difficulties are wholly absent is the comparatively early and simple *Rhoda Fleming* (1865). However, despite the existence during his lifetime of a band of loyal (but not all comprehending) 'Meredithians', he has not had his due even for what he attempted. He is, after all, as V. S. Pritchett has said in an excellent study of him, 'a storehouse of ways and means' and 'rather hard and intelligently merciless—which is refreshing in the nineteenth century'. And the best of his poetry, despite his unfortunate penchant for trying to sound—and sometimes sounding—Shakespearean, is at the least interesting.

GEORGE MOORE (1852–1933) deserves to be considered both as a nineteenth- and a twentieth-century writer. He is the most seriously neglected major novelist of the past century: too many critics have confused his best work with his frequently sloppy and foolish persona (even if he was ultimately, in Sherard Vines' oddly apt words, 'a dear good soul'). He was a pioneer, as the 'English naturalist'—a category he may be said to have invented for himself, in order to get a real start as a novelist—as autobiographer and as post-realist novelist; he is one of the best writers of short stories in the English language (yet, in a recent survey of this form by a reputable critic, he gets exactly one sentence). Moore is a remarkable illustration of the fact that great writing frequently springs from personal humiliation: the sources of his energy certainly include his boastful foolishness and his sexual voyeurism. He turned both these humiliating characteristics to creative account.

The key to Moore's imaginative attitude is summed up in a remark from his *Reminiscences of the Impressionist Painters* (1906): 'Life is a rose that withers in the iron fist of dogma. . . .' Creatively he was a consistent sceptic; his diagnosis of the disease that threatens twentieth-century humanity is subtler and profounder than his non-creative (critical) pronouncements, frequently inane, would lead one to believe. Ford Madox Ford (q.v.) called him 'infinitely the most skilful man of letters of his day—the most skilful in the world'. One of Moore's skills consisted in filtering his considerable Irish silliness out of his writings, and yet preserving the energy from which it sprang.

His first important book was the autobiographical *Confessions of a Young Man* (1886 rev. 1926): he needed to satirize what he had been as a very young man in Paris. This book conveys an accurate sense of the genuine (as distinct from the theatrical) element in his immature paganism of those early days—by isolating it and thus keeping it at a proper comic distance. As early, then, as 1886 Moore had abandoned any serious attempt to present himself in conventionally realist terms. This is so incongruous as coming from the later self-styled champion of Zolaesque naturalism that it has been overlooked. By the time he came to write the autobiographical trilogy *Hail and Farewell* (1911-14) he had perfected the process. By then he knew, as he put it in a letter (1913) to Robert Ross, that a 'man only seems natural when he is speaking aside or to himself; he seems quite mechanical when he is uttering little phrases to people standing. . . .'

But his first undoubted masterpiece was a work avowedly natural-ist, and certainly realist: *Esther Waters* (1894). This is a tender study of a servant betrayed and left pregnant, and of her fight for her son. Grudgingly acknowledged as a classic, it has nevertheless been con-sistently underrated. Virginia Woolf (q.v.) claimed that Moore 'had not the strength to project Esther from himself'; but she merely put a finger on a weakness of her own. All Zola's naturalism did for Moore was to give him a method to get started. *Esther Waters* is naturalist in intention, but its effect is, eventually, anti-naturalist: the 'message' is that compassion is all, not that character or environ-ment is destiny. However, naturalism taught Moore not to be reticent about sexual matters, and it purged him of the gentility that even today bedevils English literature and most of the criticism of it.

Moore went on to produce at least three more major novels. The first was *The Lake* (1905); later came *The Brook Kerith* (1916), the story of Paul's betrayal of a Christ who, rescued from the cross, has come to reject his earlier fanaticism; *Héloise and Abelard* (1921) is hardly read now, and is not in print—but it is another masterpiece. These later novels (the new manner began with *The Lake*, but was not developed until *The Brook Kerith*) demand to be read aloud if the reader is fully to appreciate how so lyrical and uninterrupted (but varied) a 'seamless' flow can contain so much complex material. There is, after all, a part of ourselves that perceives our experience as an unstitched and seamless whole (cf. Bergson, q.v.); Moore seized on this aspect of perception and made himself its master.

And yet his greatest achievement of all is in the realm of the short story: from the relatively early *Celibates* (1895), through *The Untilled Field* (1903) and *A Story Teller's Holiday* (1918) to the perfection of *Celibate Lives* (1927), which is the final revision of *In Single Strictness* (1922). 'Albert Nobbs', originally from *A Story Teller's Holiday* but included in *Celibate Lives*, is the greatest comic short story of the century in any language. *The Untilled Field* (as Graham Hough has observed) precedes Joyce's *Dubliners* (q.v.) just as *Confessions of a Young Man* precedes his *Portrait of the Artist as a Young Man*.

There were once excuses for not looking at Moore: in his famous quarrel with Yeats (q.v.) he made himself look foolish; his disciples (they included Charles Morgan, q.v.) were the most mediocre any great writer has ever gathered around him. These excuses are no longer viable: Moore is a very important—and modern—writer in-deed, both extrinsically and intrinsically: far from ever having left him behind, there is a whole readership that has yet to catch up with him.

w. h. hudson (1841–1922) was of American parents who emi-grated to Argentina; he returned to England in 1870 and became an English citizen in 1900. Although he gained wide recognition with *Green Mansions* (1915), he is now a rather neglected writer. Conrad said of him to Ford: 'He writes as the grass grows. The Good God makes it be there. . . .' He was a brilliant and unusual observer of countless small natural things; his observations fly, like richly coloured birds, across the bleakness of his recollections of Spanish-American savagery and of his own poverty and neglect. *Green Man-sions*, the story of a bird woman, is still insufficiently acknowledged as a classic; that it was derived from an earlier and inferior novel (Lady Morgan's *The Missionary*) makes little difference, since it transforms and improves it.

r. b. cunninghame graham (1852–1936), once the toast of many distinguished authors (including Ford), is now buried in oblivion. This is not quite deserved. Three-quarters Scottish and the rest Spanish, he was a fierce and flamboyant personality, who lived an adventurous life: as a young man he pioneered in South America and America; later, in England, he got himself jailed for champion-ing the then unpopular cause of justice for working men. He should be revived in selection. Edward Garnett's selection, *Thirty Tales and Sketches* (1929) and *Rodeo* (1936), edited by A. F. Tschiffely, reveals an original minor writer, one of the few British masters of *costumbrismo* (q.v. 3), a portraitist of wild places, whose lawless bohemianism has—despite its over-dependence on rhetoric—a fine and genuine quality. Cunninghame Graham is a Kipling-in-reverse: he suffers from the same violent anarchic passions, but channels them into socialism instead of imperialism. He shamelessly indulged himself in both his Scottish-dour and Spanish *hidalgo* aspects, but had a clear sense of the places he wrote about, and his uncompromisingly shame- (as distinct from guilt-) directed approach is sincere—more sincere, less puerile, than that of, say, Roy Campbell (q.v.).

joseph conrad (originally teodor jozef konrad kornzeniowski, 1851–1924), a Pole, was the son of a literary man who was sent into political exile; he went to sea, and soon began serving in English ships—he passed for master in 1880, and took up British citizenship in 1886. He began writing while still at sea. His first novel, *Almayer's*

Folly, was published in 1895, and gained critical success; but he did not get public recognition and the relative financial independence that flows from it until *Chance* (1913). He wrote English much better than he spoke it; and each of his novels cost him an inordinate amount of nervous energy. The influence and help of Ford Madox Ford (q.v.) has been deliberately underestimated by critics; it was, however, vital in his development. Conrad and Ford wrote three novels in collaboration. *The Inheritors* (1901), *Romance* (1903)—and *The Nature of a Crime* (1924), which was written in 1906–7 and first published by Ford in his *English Review*.

The best of Conrad's fiction has been the subject of an exorbitant amount of critical exegesis, both in Great Britain and the United States. Recognition of his supremacy as a novelist was a cornerstone of the ultra-dogmatic school of the critic F. R. Leavis (q.v.) at Downing College, Cambridge, which was influential between 1930 and 1960 (Leavis has written well on him). There have been remarkably few dissentients from the basic assumption of his greatness; his position as a great novelist remains secure and undisturbed. The case for the prosecution (if there is one) has never really been presented. And at the very least this does pay tribute to Conrad's massive seriousness, his great struggle with himself, his wide range—and his extraordinary mastery of written English. Henry James (q.v.), it seems, could turn his sexual deficiency into a triumph of art; Conrad, likewise, turned both a clumsy incapacity for full human relationships (perhaps this culminates in the partial portrait of his wife Jessie as Winnie Verloc in *The Secret Agent*), and a difficulty with the English language, into a triumph. Here is another sceptic, anxiously probing at heroic and moral truisms, masterfully avoiding what he hardly understood, though personally yearned for: friendship, love, communion. It so happened that Conrad's genius coincided in certain respects with that of the English language, which (as is natural in a Pole) he approached for its Latin rather than its Anglo-Saxon qualities. But he worked desperately hard to achieve the coincidence.

Conrad's masterpieces are *Typhoon* (1902), *Heart of Darkness* (1902), *Nostromo* (1904), *The Secret Agent* (1907) and *Under Western Eyes* (1911). *Heart of Darkness*, which contains the quintessence of his art, is set in the Congo—where Conrad himself, in difficult circumstances, discovered his true vocation. This is Conrad's exploration of his narrator, Marlow's recollections (on the Thames in London) of a nightmare journey into the interior. It demonstrates the firmness of his control through style and tone, of his material; agonizedly, it shows human sympathy existing where an 'official' view would allow of none.

Conrad's chief subjects include revolution—its causes, its excesses and its betrayal; and the evils of acquisitiveness. His concern is always imaginative rather than political. There lies at the heart of Conrad's best fiction a horrified awareness of evil, a scepticism about the validity of human attitudes, and a terrified recognition of human solitude. In *The Nigger of the 'Narcissus'* (1897) he shows how sympathy itself can threaten survival; in *Lord Jim* (1900), again narrated by Marlow, he demonstrates how imagination and idealism can corrupt and lead to cowardice—and also how impossible non-intuitive moral judgement (the prerogative of establishments and the systems they perpetuate) is to achieve (in *Heart of Darkness* we find two moral opposites in profound kinship. . . .). In *The Secret Agent* Conrad found a sardonic objective correlative (q.v.)—Ford provided the material—for his uneasiness over his marriage (which was, at bottom, an unhappy one) and over the role of the writer (his treatment of the *Künstlerschuld*, q.v., theme), whom he projects into the morally insensitive dealer in pornography, Verloc, who gets more involved in the game of spying and terrorism than he had intended (he thought he could play with evil); but the characters transcend their origins in the author's mind. It is probably true to say, as a critic has, that Conrad does not 'explore human relationships'; but he does use this incapacity to show how they can fail to exist; at other times he can imply them very cleverly. The lack of one between the comically sinister Verloc and his wife is one of the most chilling things in the whole of his work. There is often a ponderousness about Conrad's style that not everyone finds to their taste (he is sometimes a bit too much the Polish 'master of English prose'); but of his stature, his subtlety, his seriousness, there can be no serious doubt.

RUDYARD KIPLING (1865–1936) is a strange case indeed. He is certainly not less than a major writer of fiction (though only a minor poet) and yet, more than any writer of his stature, he seems to suffer, not simply from ignorance or lack of education, but from an advanced philistinism and, at times, an insensitive proto-fascism. His attitudes, taken simply as attitudes, form an offensive constellation: racist, blindly imperialist, British 'public school' in the worst sense, feudal. . . . But actually, of course, his thought is confused. The real man does not hold these views at all: unlike his actually philistine counter-part, the stupid British Tory (not the intelligent one, of whom Ford's Tietjens, q.v., was the last), Kipling has an imagination. A good deal of Victorian imperialistic sentiment (which was not of course as 'offensive' then as it is now) undoubtedly released repressed sexual energies: Elgar's symphonies, for example, are as much 'about' a series of sexual climaxes and sexual guilts as they are 'about' anything else. It is hardly necessary to point out, at this date, that one of the functions of the British Empire was phallic. But Elgar was a robust and relatively uncomplicated Roman Catholic. The evidence suggests that Kipling—and here lies the secret of his creative strength —was a sadomasochistic bisexual. His rationalizations of his (in his own Victorian terms) hideous impulses took two forms: one was his political doctrines; but the other was often a true objective correlative, a creative resolution of his severe emotional and sexual problems. And in many of Kipling's stories and one or two of his novels we find instinctive wisdom, love, kindness—and, sometimes, terror. As a writer he was, after all, at his best, very good—his Nobel Prize of 1907 is not incongruous, as is, say, Galsworthy's—and that is perhaps what is important in a writer. He is one of the best of the immensely popular writers of the twentieth century.

Kipling was born in Bombay; after some unhappy years in England with a relative and then four years at school in Westward Ho in Devon, he returned to India. W. E. Henley, who among other better things was a chauvinist, enthused about his early *Barrack-Room Ballads*, and printed them in the *National Observer*. Kipling collected his first stories in *Plain Tales from the Hills* (1888) and *Soldiers Three* (1888). *Barrack-Room Ballads* were collected in book form in 1890 and 1892. In the latter year Kipling married the sister of an American journalist, Wolcot Balestier; he seems to have been in love with both brother and sister, and he lived in Vermont until 1896, when a quarrel with Wolcot caused him to leave. After this he settled in Sussex, eventually purchasing a large house, Batemans, from which august headquarters he continued to issue prose and verse until the end of his life.

Kipling's tales are at their best when their sheer realism becomes independent of the code of 'honour' that he consciously built up— and which was largely responsible for his immense popularity. Kipling, when he was not trying to think, possessed an uncanny insight into the mind of the common soldiers and officers about whom he wrote so vividly. Kipling's code consists of 'fair play' (approximating rather to the 'fairness ethic' that Erich Fromm has wryly distinguished as a capitalist contribution to society), British public school solidarity and loyalty (this was partly fantasy on Kipling's part, as he showed in *Stalky and Co.*, 1899, where he transformed his own timid role at a rather enlightened non-public school into that of a rebellious hero playing the game against the game), self-reliance and paternalism. He applies this, in the course of his fiction, to many situations, in particular to animals (*The Jungle Books*, 1894, 1895) and to simple masculine situations—military, engineering and so on. As C. S.

Lewis pointed out, Kipling longed to be in on all masculine mysteries, to be 'one of the boys'. Max Beerbohm (q.v.) put his finger on Kipling's motivations when he wrote: 'Mr. Kipling is so far masculine that he has never displayed a knowledge of women as they are; but the unreality of his male creatures, with his worship of them, makes his name ring quaintly like a pseudonym. . . . Strange that these heroes . . . were not . . . created out of the inner consciousness of a lady novelist. . . .' This is malicious but just. Eliot (q.v.) tried to defend Kipling from the charge of fascism by calling him a Tory. But Kipling was not a Tory: he was a Tory-anarchist—a passionate, confused man—whose confusions, however, passionately appealed to the thousands of Englishmen like him. Ford's Edward Ashburnham, from *The Good Soldier* (q.v.), would have read and admired Kipling; but he would not have seen that Kipling projected his own 'cheap cynicism about the female sex', his own propensity and 'relish' for 'The ugly word, the ugly action, the ugly atmosphere' (Beerbohm) into his characters. He has, too, a pathic slyness and cunning that give his tales, with their pristine and lyrical feelings, not only technical mastery but also great power. His best novel is *Kim* (1901): here the writer took over entirely, and the British and Indian characters are seen with equal imaginative sympathy.

In verse Kipling is what Orwell (q.v.) called 'a good bad' poet. 'Danny Deever' has an authentic *frisson*, but the conflict in Kipling's mind between his false code ('a sneakin' shootin' hound': "e shot a comrade sleeping') and his sexual and sadistic fascination with hanging is too nastily apparent, and the poem doesn't have the strength to resolve it. His poems, whether ballads or nostalgic lyrics, seldom get beyond the bounds of self-indulgence.

Kipling's best work arose out of confusion and even viciousness; it also has a strange beauty, something not altogether definable—a gentleness and child-likeness—that functions as a soother and a neutralizer of the violence of the 'Freudian' elements. He was ungenerous in his views; but it would be ungenerous of us to take these at face value, and to refuse to judge him from his best books. His collected works were published in thirty-one volumes (1913–38), and are still available.

If ARTHUR CONAN DOYLE (1859–1930) will eventually be forgotten as a historical novelist, he will be immortal for his creation of Sherlock Holmes. His historical romances are excellent, and some remain in print; but they are romances. His photograph of his fantasy-self as Sherlock Holmes, however, is an offbeat literary achievement: a Victorian portrait of an eccentric, with innumerable implications, and embellished with a splendid and absorbing ingenuity. Conan Doyle's Holmes is the dream-paradigm of the brilliant decadent, cunningly written from a non-decadent point of view; it transcends most of the decadent literature of its time.

H. G. WELLS (1866–1946), despite his huge and continuing popularity with all sections of the public, is with critics a persistently underrated and misunderstood writer. He himself disclaimed interest in his literary reputation and stated, in a mock-obituary of 1936, that he was 'much more the scientific man than the artist, though he dealt in literary forms'. But he was a major novelist, praised fulsomely by Henry James (q.v.), and told (1920), by Ford, one of the most perceptive men of this time, that he was a 'genius' who wasted too much of his time on 'social speculation'. The reasons why Wells the propagandist, the inconsistent and irascible generalizer, was led to betray the creative writer in himself, and the ways in which he unconsciously rapped himself over the knuckles for this betrayal, are exceptionally interesting.

The most destructive criticism of Wells the 'thinker', the Utopian, is Max Beerbohm's (q.v.) deadly parody 'Perkins and Mankind', in which he has Wells writing an account of an old man happily going to the 'Municipal Lethal Chamber' on 'General Cessation Day', 'walking with a firm step in the midst of his progeny. . . . He will not be thinking of himself. . . . He will be filled with joy at the thought that he is about to die for the good of the race . . . for the beautiful young breed of men and women who, in simple, antiseptic garments, are disporting themselves so gladly on this day of days. . . .'

But Wells the Utopian, the public figure with 'brains but no tact' (his uncle said this of Wells when he was fourteen), is only the least important part of a story that is more complicated than is generally acknowledged. The popular idea of Wells—publicist, novelist, pioneer of science fiction—seems to be that he betrayed the glowing optimism of a lifetime only in his gloomy last work, *Mind at the End of its Tether* (1945). Nothing could be further from the truth. The root of the false view lies in the notion that Wells was an optimist. He was nothing of the sort. He was, it is true, a cheeky satyr, full of good humour and tactlessness, who thoroughly enjoyed gatecrashing a high society that he despised; but his continuous sexual curiosity (he was exceptionally good to his many cast-off mistresses) and his ebullience hid a gloomy dreamer: a man of profound imaginative capabilities, who read Blake as well as science text-books. Allying itself to this pessimistic streak was Wells' feeling of social inferiority, which never really left him, and which he exploited to superb comic effect in his early straight novels. It was the submerged poetic, subversive elements in Wells, working through the scientifically trained exterior, that led him to make his most startling prophecies and anticipations. For besides the better known scientific prophecies, some of which we cannot yet assess, Wells made many astute sociological guesses; all of these are negative, satirical, gloomy.

The cannibals of Rampole Island (in the neglected dystopia *Mr. Blettsworthy on Rampole Island*, 1928) who call their enemies 'cannibals' are as good an example of doublethink as anything in Orwell's *1984* (q.v.); their failure to refer to unpleasant manifestations of state authority by their proper names (criminals are 'reproached', not punished) is worthy of Swift. Compare this morbid side of Wells— the far future envisaged in *The Time Machine* (1895), the death of Griffin in *The Invisible Man* (1897)—with the antiseptic, imagination-free, laboured naïvety of a *Modern Utopia* (1905) or the lecture on the World Encyclopaedia project (1936). . . . In all the fiction in which Wells tried to creat a Utopia he never quite knew what to do with it: he did not believe in Utopias.

Wells' range is very wide. As a writer of science fiction he has not been equalled for versatility, ingenuity or credibility; the atmosphere of those early tales is unforgettable, unrepeatable, poetic. He is a great comic novelist: *Kipps* (1905), *Tono Bungay* (1909), *The History of Mr. Polly* (1909). His later and more complex fiction has been unjustly neglected. *Mr. Blettsworthy on Rampole Island*, although flawed, is one of the most memorable of modern dystopias; *The Bulpington of Blup* (1933), in part a portrait of Ford (q.v.), is a notable psychological study. Wells' work as would-be shaper of human destiny and popularizer of science did partly undermine his creativity: he never, after *Mr. Polly*, reached the point at which his imagination could function positively. But his earlier work deserves the praise James conferred on it ('You are a very swagger performer indeed' who 'makes even dear old Dickens turn . . . in his grave'); the best of his later work demands responsible reconsideration.

By contrast the talent of JOHN GALSWORTHY (1867–1933) is drab. He cannot hope to achieve more than his recent enshrinement as author of the original script (so to speak) of the (for ever?) current soap opera of *The Forsyte Saga*. His best work, which is very modest in achievement, is in the drama and the earlier part of the *Saga*. He won the Nobel Prize in 1932. Easy as it is to sneer at him, D. H. Lawrence's (q.v.) attack on him as a 'sneaking old cynic' cannot really be countered: we find ourselves apologizing rather than pointing to positive virtues.

Galsworthy wrote nothing of account before *The Island Pharisees* (1904) and the first of the *Forsyte Saga: The Man of Property* (1906). The latter remains the best of his novels, and even Lawrence conceded that its satire on the upper crust of society 'really had a certain noble touch'. But even this and its successors *The Country House* (1908) and *Fraternity* (1909) can hardly be described as important books. One has only to think of Ford's *The Good Soldier* (q.v.) to realize just how ordinary they are. The characters are flat and lifeless; the redeeming factor is the author's genuine social indignation, which expresses itself in the form of satire. By 1922, introducing the first Forsyte trilogy (*The Man of Property; In Chancery*, 1920; *To Let*, 1921), he was able to say: 'Human Nature, under its changing pretensions . . . is and ever will be very much of a Forsyte, and might, after all, be a much worse animal'. He remained a courteous, considerate, conscientious man; but as a serious writer he was finished. The Forsytes who had been the villains of the early novel now became the heroes; nor in the later volumes (the trilogy is called *A Modern Comedy*, 1929) did Galsworthy display the least understanding of the post-war generation. And in all these later novels Galsworthy indulges himself in the middlebrow habit of manipulating his characters according to his emotions, which became progressively more sentimental and conservatively 'worthy'. He was not at any time a major writer. His dramas, notably *The Silver Box* (1903), *Strife* (1909) and *Justice* (1910), are well made, restrained, and display a genuine passion for social justice. They represent Galsworthy at his most skilful and agreeable. But his undeservedly high reputation justifies the harshness of D. H. Lawrence's verdict: 'Vulgarity pays, and cheap cynicism smothered in sentimentality pays better than anything else'.

ARNOLD BENNETT (1867–1931) is both more gifted, and more puzzling. To many readers of modern poetry he is no more than a footnote to Ezra Pound's unkind poem 'Mr. Nixon':

> . . . 'Consider
> Carefully the reviewer.
>
> I was as poor as you are;
> When I began I got, of course,
> Advance on royalties, fifty at first,' said Mr. Nixon,
> 'Follow me, and take a column,
> Even if you have to work free. . . .
> I never mentioned a man but with the view
> of selling my own works. . . .
>
> And give up verse, my boy,
> There's nothing in it.' . . .

This goes well enough with 'I write for as much money as I can get' and the admonition by Bennett to those 'parasites' (poets) to try to understand that nothing matters so much as cash and the preservation of 'decency'. Galsworthy, possibly to his credit, would never even have considered such philistine sentiments; the irony is that Bennett was, incomparably, the better novelist. Even in the late Twenties, when rising critics such as Edwin Muir (q.v.) found it necessary to dismiss Bennett, they would admit that in *The Old Wives' Tale* (1908) he had 'beautifully and profoundly expressed the passing away of human delight in possessions'.

The truth is that Bennett's 'philistinism', while tactless and reprehensible in itself, was part of an ironic self-defence. He could not quite understand how his ambition had driven him into being a *writer*: there must have been something wrong there: he had been a cocky, self-confident law-clerk and prentice-journalist down from Hanley (one of the Five Towns) to escape from a puritanical atmosphere and his father's domination: a man with an eye on the brass should have been able to do better than *that*. The puritan in him felt guilty, too, about the self-indulgence (he was a famed sybarite) that success in letters had allowed him. As a popular recommender of books to a middlebrow audience (in his capacity as critic of *The New Age* and *The Evening Standard*) he did much to push his fellow authors, displayed as consistently high standards as any such columnist ever has, and was remarkably unspiteful and unpretentious. 'Mr. Nixon' is a fair comment on the value of certain of Bennett's pronouncements, many of which were as absurd as George Moore's (q.v.); it is not a fair comment on the man himself—who was generous, sensitive and vulnerable—or on his best work.

Bennett is a strange case. Throughout his life he issued a stream of pot-boiling novels, instructive handbooks on *Self-Help* lines and popular 'philosophies of life'; yet this did not corrupt his creativity. As late as 1923, when he was fifty-six, he produced a novel whose flaws of style and presentation cannot prevent its being a masterpiece —in creation of atmosphere, in psychological acuteness and, above all, in warmth of feeling: *Riceyman Steps*. His really important books are: *The Old Wives' Tale*; the *Clayhanger* trilogy (*Clayhanger*, 1910; *Hilda Lessways*, 1911; *These Twain*, 1915); *The Card* (1911); *Riceyman Steps*; *Lord Raingo* (1924). His last novel, *Imperial Palace* (1930), is as sceptical about great hotels as it is awe-inspired; and is a lively and amusing performance. He knew nothing whatever about poetry, and was silly when he talked about it (hence Pound's justified satire); but although he regarded literature as a business, his imagination

never became corrupt; the quality of *Riceyman Steps* is as high as that
of anything he ever wrote.

Bennett's first models were the 'French' George Moore (q.v.) and
the later French nineteenth-century novel. He was always more at
home in French than in English literature. Although influenced by
naturalism, Bennett was a realist without (in his novels) any philosophy; however, the grim puritanism and drab ugliness of the Five
Towns affected him deeply, and are reflected in the best books. *The
Old Wives' Tale* is his greatest achievement: its people, as Frank
Swinnerton (q.v.) has said, 'are within his heart as well as his head';
he is at his best here because he is 'both humorous and humane'.
This is a great unsophisticated classic. *The Card* (called *Denry the
Audacious* in America), a kind of delightedly objective self-study, did
something that had not previously been done in English fiction, even
by Wells—the thread was taken up again by William Cooper (q.v.)
forty years later; but *The Card* has not been bettered. For all his
lapses, his spasmodic puritanism, his unevenness, Bennett succeeded
in achieving the 'all-embracing compassion' that he believed to be
the 'essential characteristic of the really good novelist'.

STEPHEN HUDSON (ps. SIDNEY SCHIFF, 1868–1944) presents a complete contrast: a member of the so-called Bloomsbury Group (centred
in Cambridge and the Bloomsbury district of London, and including
Leonard and Virginia Woolf, q.v., the art-critics Clive Bell and
Roger Fry, the painter Duncan Grant, the writers Lytton Strachey,
E. M. Forster, the economist John Maynard Keynes, and many
others; chief common or overlapping interests were Fabianism,
beautiful young men—such as Rupert Brooke, q.v.—and humanism),
he was self-consciously literary. He completed Scott Moncrieff's
famous translation of Proust—notoriously badly. But his fiction
deserves to be remembered. His best book is *A True Story* (1930, rev.
1949), which is a revision and condensation of three earlier novels
and part of a fourth: *Richard Kurt* (1919), *Elinor Colhouse* (1921),
Prince Hempseed (1922) and *Myrtle* (1925). This, the story of Richard
Kurt, is an original and economically written study of motivation—
and of, as Walter Allen has pointed out, 'the Oedipus Complex
working its doom throughout a man's life'. Hudson was aware of
the discoveries of psychoanalysis, and his unobtrusive use of them
was both intelligent and pioneering. The beginning of *A True Story*
is the best part: the account of Kurt's adolescence and of his life in
America. I agree with Walter Allen (who has been largely responsible
for drawing attention to Hudson's distinction) that the succeeding
parts, in which Kurt's relationships with two women are explored,
are less satisfactory: Hudson was weak when dealing with women,

and he cannot disguise this. But when he deals with Kurt's own motivations he remains impressive. His technique consists of selecting certain incidents in his hero's life, and concentrating upon them with great psychological intensity. *Tony* (1924), a portrait of Kurt through his brother's eyes, is more interesting than the modest and over-sophisticated Hudson himself would allow.

The Powys brothers—JOHN COWPER POWYS (1872–1963), T. F. POWYS (1875–1953) and LLEWELLYN POWYS (1884–1939)—sons of a Church of England parson, were a remarkable trio of eccentric writers; the first two have become the subjects of cults. John Cowper's virtues, and in particular his sexual philosophy, have been urged by the critic G. Wilson Knight; and T. F. Powys is or was compulsory diet for budding Leavisites (q.v.). The least unconventional of the three was Llewellyn, who spent most of his life struggling with tuberculosis, to which he finally succumbed. He wrote well of this struggle (*Skin for Skin*, 1925) and of his travels (*Ebony and Ivory*, 1924); he was also a competent biographer. But he was hardly a creative writer, and his two novels are negligible.

John Cowper is a writer on a huge—even cosmic—scale; Theodore Francis is a miniaturist. But both brothers see the universe—as do Bernanos and Jouhandeau (qq.v. 2)—as a battleground for the forces of good and evil. Both writers have been overrated by their admirers; both had genius; both too rapidly become bores by harping on their particular obsessions. Of the two, T. F. Powys is more likely to survive: he used shorter forms.

John Cowper Powys' best book, by far and away, is his *Autobiography* (1934); this should be read in conjunction with the American edition, *The Art of Happiness* (1935), which differs considerably. Powys' self-insight and honesty are here displayed at their best. His massive novels tend to be both boring and pretentious; there is an element of charlatanism in them. The imagination of the author is less in evidence than the grandiose schemes suggest: there is usually more of his philosophical world-view than of invention: he tells us about his characters' conflicts, but cannot convince us of their existence. The 'imaginative power' with which he is so often credited consists in large measure of a vulgarly 'cosmic', pseudo-mystical approach to life, which ignores individuality and concentrates on mere largeness of conception. *A Glastonbury Romance* (1933), a modern treatment of the Grail legend, is unreadable except by those who want to escape from themselves into a vague pantheism. *Wolf Solent* (1929) is better, but suffers from the same grandiosity. And yet there was a grand obstinacy here, and an occasional achievement of colloquial style (when Powys tried to be archaic he was excruciating;

but his vernacular is often excellent). At the heart of all this high intention and self-inflation is a minor writer of distinction, best savoured in short passages. Like his brother Theodore Francis, John Cowper Powys was a miniaturist; but he would not accept this limitation.

T. F. Powys is superior. Certainly his sadistic morbidity becomes absurd when taken in quantity. The perverseness and cruelty of his rustic characters are too easily caricatured. It is not that he had an exaggerated picture of the beastliness inherent in human beings; it is rather that he usually (he wrote eight novels and more than twenty collections of short stories) fails to place this beastliness (often sexual) in a convincing context. It becomes *grand guignol*, too much of a joke. In *Mr. Tasker's Gods* (1925), a notorious example, a rapist feeds his father to his pigs, who are his Gods. Despite the power and the conviction, it does not come off. Powys is not, in H. Coombes' words, a 'great and extraordinary writer' who has 'the terrifying honesty of genius'. But he is an extraordinary writer and he sometimes has genius; but even he is neither great nor quite terrifying. One can see (this has often been pointed out), in Dylan Thomas' (q.v.) early short stories in *The Map of Love* (1939), how this kind of semi-surrealist perversity can spill over into a sick and ill-accomplished nastiness. From the difference between Thomas and Powys one may discern that whereas Thomas (in this aspect at least) was a dirty little boy playing with evil, Powys was genuinely and more maturely obsessed; he might, indeed, have been a great writer if he could have got things into better balance. But he fails (unlike another similarly obsessed writer, Céline, q.v.) to reveal his charity. One needs at least one 'normal' rustic as a foil for the others. His best novel, *Mr. Weston's Good Wine* (1927), an allegory in which God appears in Dorset, has a lightness of touch and a gentleness that neutralize his usual concentration on the bestial side of man; but one must resist, as grotesque, the comparisons with Shakespeare that have been made. However, for this, the novel *Black Bryony* (1923), and for a handful of the short stories, Powys has his place as an original minor writer.

C. E. MONTAGUE (1867–1928), one of the last of the great journalists, wrote four competent but now dated novels, of which the best is *Rough Justice* (1926), and one masterpiece of non-fiction: *Disenchantment* (1922), a description of the Western Front, and one of the earliest and finest denunciations of the cruelty and stupidity of militarism. *Fiery Particles* (1923) contains some good short stories.

NORMAN DOUGLAS (1868–1952) is possibly more memorable as a personality than as a writer. But at least *South Wind* (1917), *Old Calabria* (1915) and his two books of autobiography—*Looking Back*

(1933) and *Late Harvest* (1946)—will survive. *South Wind* is a unique light satirical novel, a study of a group of expatriated English on Capri (an island which he made, so to speak, his own). Nothing is as harmless and tolerant as Douglas' 'hedonism', although his own sex-life, which included the purchase of children from their Italian parents, is not altogether attractive.

MAX BEERBOHM (1872–1956) is just about as substantial as a minor writer can become—and a warning to those who regard minor writers as mere *repetiteurs* of their elders and betters. Beerbohm was, in fact, minor entirely by choice: he preferred to wound with arrows shot from the periphery. He is distinguished as an essayist, as a parodist and a short-story writer ('Enoch Soames' is a masterpiece). He was also a notable caricaturist. He understood more than his deliberately lightweight style suggests—as the parodies in *A Christmas Garland* clearly demonstrate.

G. K. CHESTERON (1874–1936) could never be uninteresting, as man or writer. It has been said that he is a 'master who left no masterpiece'; and this seems just—or does some masterpiece-like quality inform at least the conception of Father Brown? . . . The vitality of Chesterton's best writing is not a consequence of his Roman Catholicism, the intellectual content of which may now be seen as an accidental. Chesterton spent his creative life indulging his nihilism, but rendering it powerless with brilliant final twists. Terror is the father of his ingenuity. His ostensible message—bluff, matter-of-fact, 'jolly', beery, genial—is 'Everything's all right *really*: see how harmless I render these fascinating horrors'. But a little examination reveals a profound unease: a spirit wrestling with the notion of absurdity as far as it dared without madness. The wonderfully ingenious *The Man Who Was Thursday* (1908), the best of his novels, reveals all evil as non-existent: six of the anarchists are really detectives, and the seventh is God. But the figure of Sunday (God behind the mask of Nature) is ambiguous and ill-defined: a confession of 'faith' but a failure of the imagination.

HILAIRE BELLOC (1870–1953) never achieved the creative level of his friend Chesterton, but he did certain small things well. He is most distinguished of all as a writer of comic verse: here he was relaxed; his essential decency and gaiety found their best and purest form in parodying smug, false Victorian didacticism.

SAKI (ps. HECTOR HUGH MONRO, 1870–1916), who was killed in the First World War, was born in Burma; but at the age of two he was sent home to Devon in the care of two sadistic maiden aunts. This experience formed him as a writer. He first became known as a journalist, but before his death he had established a reputation for his grotesque short stories about Reginald and Clovis, those clever young assailants of the pretentious, the fake-adult and the orthodox. His short stories were collected in 1930; he wrote one novel, *The Unbearable Bassington* (1912). Saki could be as cruel and sick as those maiden aunts: they prompted in him (and in his sister) a desire for revenge that lasted all his life. His standard procedure is original: the gruesome or sinister is wrapped up in a farcical package. The novel is an exception: here Saki seriously tries to account for his hero's sadism; there is evidence that he took this book more seriously than his short stories. It was on an unusual theme for its time, and psychologically it is penetratingly accurate; it suggests that, had he not been killed (by a sniper), he might have developed into a major novelist. He has been compared with Beerbohm, Wilde and Firbank (q.v.); a more telling comparison, allowing for nationality, might be with Wedekind (q.v. 2): Saki has the same gay grimness, the same hatred of gentility and of its life-denying emptiness.

OLIVER ONIONS (1873–1961) is now a somewhat neglected writer who wrote one minor masterpiece: *In Accordance with the Evidence* (1912), the first of a trilogy, about a clerk who murders a rival and gets away with it by tricking him into writing a suicide note. This is a powerfully unpleasant novel, with an uncanny and oppressive air of reality about it. Its two successors (*The Debit Account*, 1913; *The Story of Louie*, 1913) are not quite as good. The whole trilogy was issued as a single volume in 1925. There are a few effective stories in the *Collected Ghost Stories* (1935). The best of his later fiction is *The Story of Ragged Robyn* (1945).

FORD MADOX FORD (originally FORD MADOX HUEFFER, 1873–1939), if only for five novels (he wrote, counting collaborations, thirty-two, plus countless other books of criticism, travel, history and belles lettres), is one of the dozen greatest novelists of the century. The most generous of men—only Pound (q.v.), himself conspicuously loyal to Ford, has been as generous and helpful to other writers—Ford was a boastful and often grotesquely silly liar and, like Coleridge, made a mess of his life; yet, like Coleridge, he was a better human being than most of those who denigrated him. Stella Bowen, who lived with him for many years and bore him a daughter, said: 'Ford's weakness of character, unfairness, disregard of truth and vanity *must* be accepted. . . . On the other hand, his tenderness, understanding, wisdom (about anything that didn't apply to himself!) and the tremendous attraction of his gorgeous mind, must make him always regretted. . . .' England, to its eternal discredit, more or less rejected him; in recent years Graham Greene (q.v.) has crusaded for him almost alone; all the substantial studies of him, as well as the standard biography by

Arthur Mizener (1971), are American. When he is praised by English critics it is almost always grudgingly, or in the shadow of his friend Conrad (of whom his study remains one of the best), than whom, however, he was not in his own way less good. No man was more persecuted by women—Ford suffered unreasonably from his wife, but more from the woman he left her for, Violet Hunt—and he was lucky to find some happiness with Stella Bowen and then even more, in the last nine years of his life, with Janice Biala. Robert Lowell, who met him, sums it all up in the last line of one of the most moving of his poems: 'You were a good man, Ford, and you died in want.'

Ford's five great novels are *The Good Soldier* (1915) and the Tietjens tetralogy, consisting of *Some Do Not . . .* (1924), *No More Parades* (1925), *A Man Could Stand Up* (1926) and *Last Post* (1928). His good, if flawed, novels include the *Fifth Queen* trilogy (1906–8), on Henry VIII's Katherine Howard, and *When the Wicked Man* (1931). Throughout his life he wrote charming poetry; the series of poems he wrote in the Thirties to Janice Biala, *Buckshee*, are rather more than charming, and deserve revival: they convey a sense of the absolute—and holy—sweetness at the heart of Ford the bumbling, romantic, self-deceiving, vain man. That wise sweetness glows at the heart of all his best work.

Pound, Joyce, Wyndham Lewis, Eliot (qq.v.) and Ford are sometimes, because of their pioneering spirit and innovations, known as the 'men of 1914'. Pound, Joyce and Eliot have had their due (and more); Lewis and Ford have not. And yet in terms of intrinsic importance Lewis' and Ford's achievements are greater: their best prose is of higher quality than Pound's or Eliot's poetry.

Ford, thrust by his parents into the Roman Catholic Church when a youth, remained a nominal Catholic all his life; when it suited him, as his biographer Arthur Mizener has said, he could be very Catholic indeed. But he was never a believing Catholic. Considering the impartiality of his treatment of Roman Catholics in his novels, particularly in *The Good Soldier*, Ford cannot other than disingenuously be claimed as a real member of the fold. (Nor, to be fair, has the claim been made: few groups, to their shame, have wanted Ford among them.) By 1914 he had painted a picture of himself—it was not truer to life than anyone else's picture of himself—as an honourable, radical, romantic Tory. This Toryism was of the old-fashioned sort (as George Orwell said in 1946, and it still applies, there are now no Tories: only 'liberals, fascists and the accomplices of fascists'). He was always thoroughly humanitarian in his political opinions, which seldom showed any of the silliness of which he was so capable.

His sense of history and of current political situations was excellent. There is an important sense in which Christopher Tietjens, although a character in a book and not a real man, really is the 'last Tory'. Much has been written about Ford's personal involvement in the characters of *The Good Soldier*; but while it is of course true that there are elements of both his wife and Violet Hunt in the two chief woman characters, and of himself in Dowell, the narrator, and in Edward Ashburnham, he here entirely transcended his own difficulties. No better novel in the realist mode has appeared in this century in any language. The story is simple enough: of the American narrator's unconsummated marriage to a shallow but lustful and deceitful woman, and of their apparently placid but actually fatal relationship with an English couple: a 'good soldier', an honourable and brave man who is corrupted into a liar and a betrayer by his compulsive womanizing, and his Irish Catholic wife. There is disagreement about the narrator: is he a sexual and moral idiot, or a sensitive man? The first view, which depends on a Lawrentian (or Reichian) view of men as undeveloped unless fulfilled sexually, of course reads more irony into the novel as a whole. It is, I believe, untenable: nothing in the text suggests that Dowell would be 'better' as a sexual he-man. There is enough irony in the fact that these four people are 'well behaved': Edward Ashburnham is stupid, but he is a conscientious magistrate and a benevolent and humane landlord. And there is irony in Dowell's well-bred failure to get sexual possession of his wife (and evidence that he wants her); but he is by no means an idiot. *The Good Soldier* is the complex and ironic presentation of an Edwardian tragedy. The novelist is always in perfect control. There is no more formally perfect novel in the language.

Ford became dissatisfied with *Last Post*, the final novel of the tetralogy *Parade's End*; but as Arthur Mizener says, 'it cannot be made to disappear': it was undoubtedly a mistake to reprint the series, as was done in recent years, without it. Fundamentally *Parade's End* is the story of how the Edwardian Tory Christopher Tietjens transforms himself into a modern man: the story of endurance (of war, of a fearsome bitch, of misunderstandings) and finally of survival and love. Christopher's brother Mark, by contrast, chooses to die rather than live in a new age. No books, fiction or non-fiction, reflect more exactly or more profoundly the radical changes that British society underwent between 1910 and 1925. Walter Allen has suggested that the 'Tory Christian' character of Christopher Tietjens is laid on a little too thickly: that it is difficult not to see him as a sentimental creation. This is not a frivolous charge—nothing Allen says is less than sensible and carefully considered—but I think it misses one of the central ironies of the book as a whole: whatever Ford's conscious intentions, Tietjens does not come across simply as the wholly 'good man', who will not break his code. There is an element of caricature in him—of self-criticism. Ford's picture of him hovers, throughout the book, between these two views—as a piece of music may hover between a major and a minor key. He is too good to be true. . . . But is he? This adds to, rather than detracts from, the excellence of *Parade's End*.

Much else might be said of Ford: as a critic, as a writer of travel books, as an editor (the most impractical, but the best of the century), as ,a man. Arthur Mizener's fat biography is sound, sensible and sensitive, and should do much to gain Ford his rightful place—even if it tends slightly to underestimate him. There has been no English novelist like Ford; it is time he had some of the praise that has been so willingly lavished on his contemporaries.

w. somerset maugham (1874–1965) wrote many skilful but now mostly dated (though still playable) plays and farces; his fiction cannot be so easily dismissed. With the exception of Franz Werfel (q.v. 2), he is the most serious popular writer of this century; if he wrote nothing as good as Werfel's earliest poetry, he wrote nothing as nauseous as *The Song of Bernadette* (q.v. 2). His fiction, even at its slightest, was always intelligent and craftsmanlike, and although he appealed to a middlebrow public he was neither pretentious nor did he manipulate his characters in accordance to set formulas. Maugham is neither brilliant nor profound; he is a sardonic, or sometimes merely wondering, observer of human nature. Even at his tritest he serves up an interesting assemblage of odd facts about human nature. In his best work he is not as limited as some critics have made him out to be. His first novel, *Liza of Lambeth* (1897), written out of his experiences as a medical student, is a warmly indignant book, influenced by Zola but not much resembling him. He wrote a number of other goodish but not spectacular realistic novels, conquered the London stage (*Lady Frederick*, 1912, ran for over a year) and then, in the second year of the First World War, produced his finest although not his best written novel: *Of Human Bondage* (1915). This is a fine realistic novel, and it is not a minor one. It is largely autobiographical, although in it, because of the time at which it was written, Maugham was unable to face his problem of bisexuality. The waitress to whom Philip Carey becomes enslaved may well have been (in Maugham's own life) a vicious and beautiful young man; but the transformation is in any case entirely successful. The 'bondage' in which Philip feels himself to be is not only that of the waitress with whom he is infatuated, but also the whole constellation of beliefs that he has inherited; finally he succeeds in casting them off. But the world of the book is nevertheless an exceedingly bleak and hostile one. This is a novel to which one returns gratefully: for the account of Philip's schooldays, of his years as an art student in Paris (this is particularly vivid and well-realized), above all of his fatal infatuation. What prevents Maugham from being a major writer, the mundane (although beautifully styled) quality of his point of view, is, paradoxically, one of his strengths: he is never pretentious. At his worst, as in *Theatre* (1937), he is simply trivial—but even here he manages to be entertaining. The rest of Maugham's best work is to be found in various short stories and in one more novel, *Cakes and Ale* (1930), a malicious and subtly observed tale about writers; it contains an unfair but uproariously funny caricature of Hugh Walpole (q.v.) as Alroy Kear.

E. M. FORSTER (1879–1970) is Great Britain's chief representative of humanism. He published five novels in his lifetime—*Where Angels Fear to Tread* (1905), *The Longest Journey* (1907), *A Room with a View* (1908), *Howards End* (1910) and *A Passage to India* (1924)—a number of short stories (collected in 1948), criticism, essays and biographies; *Maurice* (1971), a weak novel dealing with his own problem of homosexuality, is posthumous. His finest achievement is, without doubt, *A Passage to India*; after it he wrote no more creative work of significance. Forster's stature as a major novelist undoubtedly depends on this novel: his earlier books are seriously flawed and over-contrived, and in them his blandly old-fashioned technique is usually a hindrance. In *A Passage to India* Forster's creative impulse was strong enough to generate an organic plot, hinging on an ambiguity (what happened in the Marabar Caves between Adela Quest and Aziz? Aziz is tried for attempted rape; but we never know). He conveys a unique sense of the tragedy of the gap that lies between Indians and Englishmen, even if they do not desire it. Further, while this novel works perfectly on a realistic and psychological level, it also functions on a symbolic level—with the Marabar Caves themselves, and the strange figure of Mrs. Moore, as the two central symbols.

In an excellent (because intelligent and provocative) book of criticism, *Aspects of the Novel* (1927), Forster very interestingly examined and then rejected Henry James' (q.v.) notion that the writer of fiction must above all avoid giving his own point of view; and in his own fiction he is very much the omniscient narrator. And yet, apart from Jane Austen and Samuel Butler, his master is Proust (q.v. 2). . . . His technique was deliberately old-fashioned, then; but his practice in the last and best of his novels was twentieth-century.

The wisdom of Mrs. Moore, although it consists of no more than human good will, is thoroughly 'modern' in its function, and it is still as valid as it was in 1924.

The formative influences on Forster were his life at Cambridge at the turn of the century, his extensive travels—and Cavafy (q.v. 3), whom he knew. He might well have achieved more had he been able—which he was not—to come to terms publicly (as a novelist) with his homosexuality. The posthumous *Maurice* is sensitive, but it shows how far off he was from facing up to the aspect of himself which so disturbed him.

COMPTON MACKENZIE (1883–1972) wrote two excellent novels, *Sinister Street* (1913–14) and the less well known *Guy and Pauline* (1915), many distinguished others—and a number of light novels that are among the funniest of their time (*Buttercups and Daisies*, in America *For Sale*, 1931, is perhaps the funniest of all). As late as 1956 he turned out a first-class story of a homosexual politician who becomes the victim of blackmail: *Thin Ice*. He has written many books of essays, travel and autobiography. Like Maugham, Mackenzie expresses no higher aim than to 'entertain'; in his comic novels that is just what he does, and without offence; the earlier novels—and to some extent *The Four Winds of Love* (1937–45)—possess a lyricism, a keenness of observation and a psychological insight that go beyond entertainment. Most of his other fiction is spoiled by over-indulgence in sentimental romanticism or deliberate Gaelic eccentricity; but *Sinister Street* at least is genuinely realist throughout.

R. H. MOTTRAM (1883–1971) wrote competent and worthy traditional fiction throughout his long life; but his *The Spanish Farm Trilogy* (1924–6) is important. It is a valuable document of the First World War—the first part, *The Spanish Farm*, was one of the first books in any language to take a detached view—and a notable work of fiction. Mottram was a friend and an admirer of Galsworthy, who encouraged him; but *The Spanish Farm Trilogy* is superior to anything of Galsworthy's: as a critic has pointed out, it escapes Galsworthy's 'social evangelism' (which is not genuine—as D. H. Lawrence saw) and his 'worse sentimentality'. *The Spanish Farm Trilogy* is a quiet book, full of compassionate and restrained observations of the horrors and the courage that characterized the First World War.

FRANK SWINNERTON (1884), who has written invaluable (though not always critically discriminating) friendly-malicious memoirs of his friendships with Bennett, Wells (qq.v.) and many others in *The Georgian Literary Scene* (1935 rev. 1950) and its successors, has been another practitioner of competent fiction throughout a long life. He began with some good (and now neglected) novels in the mode of

Gissing (q.v.): he had come up the hard way, and he had known bad health. His study of Gissing (1912) is still one of the best. He has written only one really distinguished novel, *Nocturne* (1917), a charming and memorable love story; as Wells said, 'he can count on this much of his work living'. The best of his later novels is *A Woman in Sunshine* (1944).

HUGH WALPOLE (1884–1941), gifted, promising, immensely successful, never achieved more than competence. The best of his many readable novels is his third, *Mr. Perrin and Mr. Traill* (1911), a psychologically acute study of two schoolmasters. Walpole was intelligent—so much so that Henry James admired him, and not for wholly extra-literary reasons—and he had feeling; when he did not try to do too much he could be highly effective. But he preferred keeping his name in front of the public to cultivating his craft; consequently he produced some atrocious work, such as the pseudo-historical *Rogue Herries* (1930) and its sequels. One of the reasons for this may well have been that he was a (notorious) homosexual with sadistic inclinations (the flogging scene in *Jeremy at Crale*, 1927, clearly shows this)—but he could hardly work out this theme in public. When he tried to do so, as in *Portrait of a Man With Red Hair* (1925), he was near his best. There is a sympathetic biography of him, omitting details of his homosexuality, by Rupert Hart-Davis (1952).

P. G. WODEHOUSE (1881–1975) began by writing conventional school stories; but before the First World War he had turned to the books for which he is famous. These are farcical fantasies, unconnected with any kind of reality, featuring (most notably) the drone Bertie Wooster and his man Jeeves. The Jeeves books, his best, are set in an upper-class world, nominally Edwardian (later Georgian), but essentially timeless. Wodehouse wrote the same book scores of times (he was still working when he died) but his skilful use of upper-class slang and his highly professional skill at handling plot give many of them what Orwell (q.v.), who wrote well on him, called a dated and nostalgic charm. Unfortunately there is a cult of Wodehouse which takes him to be a great writer: a master of style, creator of a convincing and 'truly imagined' world. This is not so. Wodehouse's style is limited (if delightful), he can become boring, and his world is one of escape. True, he is one of the great escapist writers of the century; but no escapist writer, no novelist who cannot convey a sense of the real, can be major. It is foolish to try to make an occasionally gorgeous entertainer into a serious writer.

II

Victorianism and its last burst of (partial) vigour, Pre-Raphaelitism, survived into this century as Georgianism. This was an actual movement, named after Edward Marsh's anthology *Georgian Poetry 1911–12* (1912), which was the first of five similar collections. The movement itself is unimportant, because Marsh was (by literary standards) a conservative dilettante. It was his love for Rupert Brooke (q.v.), and for Brooke's youthful enthusiasm for some of his contemporaries, that first set him off. (Brooke is Georgian, but, for reasons of contrast, is dealt with as a war poet.) Not all those represented in *Georgian Poetry* were in fact Georgians: D. H. Lawrence and James Stephens, for example, certainly were not. The word 'Georgian' has come to have a pejorative meaning, and understandably so. One's sympathy must be historical or sociological. As a literary movement it has no redeeming features. It was really a commercial venture (only Marsh's pleasant sentimentality conceals this); and it cannot really be said to have succeeded in its aim of creating a large reading public for poetry (the volumes were to sell very well, as of course verse does in wartime) because what it actually created was a large reading public for verse (with a bit of poetry accidentally thrown in). Georgianism, even as war-clouds gathered, insensitively aimed to perpetuate Victorian values at a time when Victorian standards, procedures and practice were no longer adequate. What may fairly be described as Georgian poetry continues to be written today, both in Great Britain and America: it is escapist in the worst sense (rural fantasies set in a countryside both unthreatened by technology and commerce, and inhabited by servile dream-peasants), flatly traditionalist and uninventive in form, sentimental in attitude, crudely mechanistic in its assumptions about human nature. Much verse that looks modern, either because it is in free verse or because it is spiced up with fashionably up-to-date mannerisms, is also fundamentally Georgian. Here I shall discuss only those Georgian poets who transcended the insulting category. But what of the background out of which both Georgianism and imagism developed?

Of the Victorians ROBERT BRIDGES (1844–1930), the Poet Laureate (1913), THOMAS HARDY (1840–1928) and ALGERNON CHARLES SWINBURNE (1837–1909) survived into this century. Little need be said of Swinburne, who was a spent force long before the turn of the century. It is impossible to say what kind of poet—with his enormous metrical

facility, his vigour and his learning—Swinburne might have been
had he possessed emotional maturity. Unfortunately he never grew
up sexually, and this seriously affected his intellect. It was natural
enough for the poets of this century to react against the rhetoric of
even his earlier, better poetry; the imitation of Swinburne's lush and
imprecise manner (at its most reprehensible in Gilbert Murray's
translations of Greek drama, as Eliot, q.v., observed) would have
been fatal to a viable new poetry.

Bridges was a conservative innovator (in matters of technique),
but wrote not one single good poem. He lacks the energy necessary
to a poet. Attempts have been made to rehabilitate him as a poet
(notably by Yvor Winters, q.v.), but they are unconvincing. He is
at his least conventional in the conversational 'Poor Poll' (in its least
attractive aspect an envious and ineffective parody of Eliot's poly-
lingual *montage* in *The Waste Land*, q.v.), but this is not incisive
enough, and is too labouredly and exasperatedly eccentric (in place
of the modernism Bridges knew he could not achieve) in manner to
be of much appeal today. All his poetry, especially the long philosophical *The Testament of Beauty* (1929), is marred by artificiality,
lack of feeling (once called restraint but now recognized as frigidity)
and unintelligent conservatism. He shrank too much from life—nor
could he examine his reasons for doing so. The age still allowed such
lack of robustness to be 'good form'. The last long poem, which
purports to prove that the natural order is 'good', does not do so in
spite of its length. His friend Gerard Manley Hopkins (q.v.) praised
Bridges' poetry in general but criticized it in particular. The critic
Sir Walter Raleigh, his contemporary, summed up Bridges best:
'Just a shade too little of a blackguard. . . .' Bridges' experiments
with classical, quantitative metres have some importance, and
doubtless he deserves credit for dimly recognizing the genius of
Hopkins—and for eventually giving his poems to the world.

Hardy's novels were all written in the nineteenth century; I shall
not discuss them here, since they are essentially of their century. He
continued to write poetry, however, until his death. Although he
was a traditionalist in both conscious attitude and technique, his
poetry has been influential in this century. He is a major poet, and
the sheer bulk of his best work continues to surprise. Nor is the good
easily separable from the bad. Hardy's poetry springs from a tension
between overpowering feelings (for people, for landscape, for justice
and for women—whom he saw as instruments of men, whose function in this respect he equated with careless or malign fate) and a
courageous and toughly held conviction that life is purposeless or
even subject to the dictates of a wanton or malevolent God:

> Let me enjoy the earth no less
> Because the all-enacting Might
> That fashioned forth its loveliness
> Had other aims than my delight.

Hardy represents the tragic and imaginatively articulate side of Victorian unbelief; but he was not an intellectual. He had simplicity. But what continually buoys him up above his faults (they would have been faults, at least, in other writers)—clumsiness of diction, reliance on the poetical rather than the poetic expression ('all-enacting Might'), the simplistic polemicism of his naturalism (for this can be seen as a version of naturalism, even though Hardy believed in fate rather than character or environment as destiny) when it is functioning unimaginatively—is, quite simply, beauty of spirit. To state that a man means what he says is to make no claim at all for him creatively; but to say that he means it when he says such things as Hardy said is to make a very large claim. And Hardy is, indeed, the last indisputable great naïve writer in the English language. He is also the most accomplished portrayer of women in English literature since Shakespeare. Like all naïve writers, he was content to be a part of his times—but he imaginatively transformed the drab rationalism of the late nineteenth century, with its various humanistic consolations: at the heart of his work, as at the heart of Shakespeare's, is a vision of absurdity quite as complete as Camus' (q.v. 2)—but more robustly tragic. That is why Hardy is 'modern'. He is intrinsically of more importance than any British or Irish poet of the twentieth century, if only because his poetry is validly accessible to a greater audience without playing down to that audience; and his range is wider. And, as Ford (q.v.) wrote in 1925, it was 'first Browning and then ... Hardy' who 'showed the way for' the imagists (q.v.); '... his power to excite—is that ... he simply takes his lines by the throat and squeezes them until they become as it were mutinously obedient. ...' Hardy has not attracted the same volume of academic criticism as Eliot and Yeats, but he has been as much read and assimilated. He is an infinitely greater writer.

A. E. HOUSMAN (1859–1936) published his first collection of poems, *A Shropshire Lad*, in 1896; within a few years he was one of the best selling of all twentieth-century poets. He issued *Last Poems* in 1922, and *More Poems* appeared in the year of his death. The best collected edition is *Complete Poems* (1960). While at Oxford Housman fell in love with a fellow-student, Moses Jackson. The exact nature and extent of their relationship is not known, but it affected Housman so much that, a gifted classical scholar, he failed his finals. To make up for this he turned himself into one of the most formidable classical scholars of his day, ending up at Cambridge, 'the other place'. As a poet he worked within the limits of a narrow epigrammatic tradition. Much of his poetry is trite and speciously pessimistic; and it is hardly 'classical', as its admirers used to claim. One of Housman's models is Heine, another is the Greek Anthology; a third, less happily, is Kipling (and his imperialistic ideas). However, despite his frequently poetical triteness, he is at his best an exquisite and moving poet. His poetry arose from the conflict between strong homosexual feeling and a genuinely acute horror of this, reinforced by convention. He remained emotionally immature, as possibly many homosexuals do; but within his limits he did something no one else has done. His 1933 address *The Name and Nature of Poetry*, published separately and then in *Selected Prose* (1961), is wrong-headed in places (as when it equates 'nonsense' with 'ravishing poetry') but contains an understanding of poetry greater than that of the critics (themselves incapable of any poetry) who deplore it. His best poetry is not pessimistic—as he glacially intended—but heartrendingly gloomy and yet tender. His brother LAURENCE HOUSMAN (1865–1959) was an efficient minor essayist, novelist and illustrator; he is most famous for his dramatic biography of Queen Victoria, collected in *Victoria Regina* (1934); this is skilful but sentimental.

No account of modern British poetry is complete without mention of Gerard Manley Hopkins (1844–89). Hopkins, although he was an innovator, was a Victorian poet and a Jesuit priest and he needs to be considered in those contexts if he is to be properly understood. But (with the exception of a few poems that appeared in an anthology published after his death) his poetry did not become available until 1918. Within a decade he had become a major influence.

Hopkins was caught between his duties as a priest (one of the factors in his decision to enter the Society of Jesus two years after his conversion must have been his discovery of his homosexual leanings) and his intense and sensuous joy in the details of nature. His observation of these details was so sharp that he was impelled to invent an ecstatic language to match it. He also expressed his negative moods in violent and vivid language. Hopkins succeeded in his aim of rejuvenating poetic language; he showed the way for the poets of the twentieth century who were trying to break away from the stale Victorian conventions. His 'sprung rhythm' is, essentially, a more flexible, musical way of looking at poetic technique than the metrical one. It is an accentual system, taking into account rising and falling movement; the poet is in effect freer and has more equipment at his command. Attempts to imitate Hopkins' own extreme use of his technique are invariably grotesque: it is too much his own. But the example he set had enormous influence on both the development of 'free' (or irregular) verse and the amount of licence poets allowed themselves. It was Hopkins, too, who first turned to the seventeenth century and the 'metaphysical' tradition of deliberate exploitation of the ambiguities inherent in language.

A rather better and more interesting poet than Bridges was THOMAS STURGE MOORE (1870–1944), a classicist of some skill who 'made' poems rather than dealt with any strong pressure to do so, but whose work is executed with taste and precision—and in an awareness of the exhausted state of fashionable Victorian diction. His poems were collected in four volumes (1931–3); the 1934 *Selected Poems* is still a useful introduction. His correspondence with Yeats (q.v.) is interesting (1953).

Thirteen years older, and considerably less well adjusted to the world, JOHN DAVIDSON (1857–1909), a Scot, was a more gifted and incisive poet who became a victim of what Hugh MacDiarmid (q.v.) admiringly calls 'giantism': the disease of attempting to create a grandiose system, a 'philosophy of life'. When he killed himself a journalist said of him that he had been murdered by Nietzsche (q.v.), of whom he was one of the earliest English explicators. He was a prolific writer: the author of fiction, criticism, translations, epic poems and plays. . . . His philosophy was that 'Man is but the Universe grown conscious'. It is a pity he did not leave it at that. Davidson was right in seeing the need to destroy the pseudo-values of his environment and (this he learned from Nietzsche) the 'Christianity' that it had erected as a defence against the terrors of authenticity. But he expressed this more effectively as a lyrical poet than as an epic poet and dramatist—although there are good things buried in the five *Testaments* (*The Testament of a Vivisector*, 1901; *The Testament of a Man Forbid*, 1901; *The Testament of an Empire-Builder*, 1902; *The Testament of a Prime Minister*, 1904; *The Testament of John Davidson*, 1908). His best poetry, which was popular for a time but then went out of fashion, was published in the Nineties. *John Davidson: A Selection of his Poems* (1961) is an excellent introduction. Among the best of his ballads are 'Thirty Bob a Week', 'A Ballad of a Nun', 'A Ballad of Hell'. Davidson began as a Pre-Raphaelite and decadent, but soon developed out of this manner, discovering his true voice in the ballad-form, in which he has a strength most of the Pre-Raphaelites lack. At his best he was a fine urban poet. And few of his contemporaries could equal 'The Runnable Stag' as a lyric.

W. E. HENLEY (1849–1903) was an invalid (a tuberculous disease

brought about the eventual amputation of a foot), and he consequently worshipped not only health, and the feelings of strength
that stem from its possession, but also imperialism. His politics were,
in fact, offensively jingoist; and one has to say that the spirit of the
too famous 'Invictus', rousing at first, is specious. But Henley had
another and preferable manner: light, impressionistic, sensitive,
delicate. He is at his best in the 'Hospital Sketches', graceful and
vivid impressions, in a nearly free verse, of his ordeal in hospital.

The unhappy career of FRANCIS THOMPSON (1859-1907) is a monument to the failure of more or less traditional methods to express the
complex and baroque. One has only to compare Thompson's poetry,
particularly the famous 'The Hound of Heaven', with that of Hopkins (q.v.) to see its shortcomings. Thompson was a passionate
Roman Catholic (his parents were converts) who tried, first, to
become a priest, but was refused as unsuitable, and, secondly, to
enter his father's profession of physician—he failed here, too. He
took to opium and the streets, and for a while lived off the earnings
of prostitutes. By the time he was discovered and rescued by a
magazine editor, Wilfred Meynell, his health was ruined. Thompson,
though gifted, was weak, lazy and without inner resource. 'The
Hound of Heaven', influenced by the seventeenth-century poet
Richard Crashaw, has some academic virtues (speed, shape, high
style), but does not achieve real poetic success: Thompson tries for
tough, metaphysical paradox but lapses into semi-hysterical self-
indulgence. Hopkins, who dealt with his tendencies towards hysteria
and self-indulgence by embracing a strict monkhood, never found
the way to God so easily. However, there is something touching
about Thompson's work, which is not quite at its best in 'The
Hound of Heaven': he manages, at times, to convey both his observation of nature and his profound suffering. His weakness is that he
lacks originality of style, and falls back on earlier manners: he is not
strong enough to transmute Crashaw's baroque ecstasy, and depends
too much on a vague, 'Shelleyan' style.

ERNEST DOWSON (1867-1900) was similarly weak, but a few of his
poems are more effective than anything of Thompson's, because he
had less grandiose aspirations. He, too, embraced that brand of
Roman Catholicism peculiar to the decadents of the late nineteenth
century. As a member of the Rhymers' Club he knew Lionel Johnson, Oscar Wilde and W. B. Yeats (qq.v.), its co-founders. The
famous 'Non Sum Qualis Eram Bonae Sub Regno Cynarae' ('I have
been faithful to thee, Cynara! in my fashion') is only limited, so to
speak, by its innate decadence: it perfectly sums up the attenuatedly
romantic attitudes of the Nineties poets; it is well done, and, as

Eliot observed, it escapes the traditional metres of the time 'by a slight shift'. Better and even more original, however, is 'Spleen'.

OSCAR WILDE (1856–1900) is of course primarily a playwright; but all his plays belong to the nineteenth century, and form no part of modern literature. As a poet he was simply another decadent— although parts of *The Ballad of Reading Gaol* have a certain crude power.

The most gifted of this group of poets was LIONEL JOHNSON (1867– 1902), a brilliant classical scholar who, although English, identified himself with his Irish contemporaries: Yeats was his close friend. Johnson had much more to offer, in the way of learning, intelligence, skill and inner poetic resource, than Thompson or Dowson. His critical book on Thomas Hardy (1894) remains one of the best. He became a Roman Catholic in 1891; when he fell off a bar stool (he drank heavily) eleven years later he cracked his skull and killed himself. Johnson looked intelligently to the Caroline poets of the seventeenth century for inspiration; through this he was able to achieve a more austere poetry than that of others in his group. He had assimilated Greek and Latin poetry, and unlike most of his contemporaries he designed his poems; even his over-ornamentation (which we can now see as a fault) has elegance. Johnson was not a major poet: his mystical outlook is too vague: his hard-headedness comes out in style but not enough in irony (this was needed to slash sarcastically across the too inebriating God-yearnings). But he was a distinguished minor poet.

Nothing need be said of the turgid poetaster STEPHEN PHILLIPS (1868–1915), whose vastly inflated verse plays, which lack any vestige of merit, captured, for a few years, an audience that could not stomach Kipling or Masefield (qq.v.). His cousin LAURENCE BINYON (1869–1943) is in a different class altogether. Binyon was a scholar and art historian; his translation of Dante's *Inferno* (1933) is still the best: it solves more problems than any other version, including even that of new ones. His poetry was traditional and restrained; his poetic drama (*Brief Candles*, 1938, is the best) is well executed. He did many graceful translations from the Japanese. Then, in old age, he produced his best sequence of poems: *The Burning of the Leaves* (1944), first published in Cyril Connolly's (q.v.) magazine *Horizon* in 1942 under the title of 'Ruins'. All Binyon's poetry had up till then been marred by excessive restraint: here is an example of a fastidious, discerning and deep-feeling poet whose energy was certainly the victim of gentility as well as native diffidence. This was partly overcome in the collection *The North Star* (1941), and then more so—but not wholly—in the final sequence.

Binyon's achievement in these poems should not be exaggerated: ultimately he evades the issue (of the Second World War and what it stood for); and the influence of Eliot—on one who had hitherto been a traditionalist—is sometimes unfortunate. But they do show an unusual sensitivity—and flashes of linguistic power. Binyon's earlier poetry, which is also worth investigation, was collected in two volumes in 1931.

JOHN MASEFIELD (1878–1967), who became Poet Laureate on the death of Bridges, is now undervalued. It is true that he never quite realized his poetic gifts; but he achieved something vivid and vigorous in the difficult realm of narrative verse (*The Everlasting Mercy*, 1911, and *Reynard the Fox*, 1919, are his best) and he was a competent novelist in the vein of Robert Louis Stevenson (*Lost Endeavour*, 1910; *Sard Harker*, 1924). None of his later verse, or his verse plays, is of account. The forthrightness of the earlier narrative poetry, which shocked some people at the time, is not absolute, and seems tame enough now; but it did introduce a new anti-genteel element (Masefield went to sea and knocked about a good deal before settling down to a literary career); the story of the poacher Saul Kane's conversion in *The Everlasting Mercy* is by no means wholly specious, though when it came to it Masefield could never face up to the full implications of the non-respectability that he implied. One of the most intelligent general comments on Masefield's poetry was made by the critic John Middleton Murry: 'He is seeking always to be that which he is not, to lash himself into the illusion of a certainty which he knows he can never possess. . . .' The illusion was that he could ever be wholly free of that stifling gentility which he seemed, to his first admirers, to be so effectively challenging. But all his prose remained vigorous; and *William Shakespeare* (1911 rev. 1955), although unscholarly, is stimulating where many more sophisticated or learned performances are not.

CHARLOTTE MEW (1869–1928), an eccentric figure, wrote a few memorable poems in an idiom that she forged for herself out of an extremely unhappy life that ended in insanity and suicide. Her talent was recognized by Monro, Hardy, Masefield and de la Mare (qq.v.). Charlotte Mew had something of the gnarled wisdom of W. H. Davies (q.v.); she wrote not of a fanciful world, as she might be expected to have done, but of the unhappy real world that she observed, bird-like, from her sad, shabby-genteel experience: of prostitutes and sailors, in a dramatic verse that is from time to time remarkably effective and moving. Her poetry was collected in 1953.

A younger woman poet of similarly eccentric and lonely demeanour ANNA WICKHAM (1884–1947), may conveniently be classed with

Charlotte Mew. She hanged herself when the Chancellor of the Exchequer increased the tax on cigarettes, of which (like Charlotte Mew) she was an inveterate consumer: she lived the latter part of her life in poverty and neglect. She had begun with marriage and hope. Anna Wickham's poetry, which has never been collected, lacks Emily Dickinson's linguistic power, but has something of her epigrammatic quality, and is distinctly individual and, at its best, wisely sardonic. She published three books: *The Contemplative Quarry* (1915), *The Man with a Hammer* (1916) and *The Little Old House* (1921). The contents of the first two books were gathered together in America under the title of the first (1921).

By comparison with these two, ALICE MEYNELL (1847–1922), although a sensitive mind, is ungifted: the language of her poetry never comes near to doing justice to the delicacy of its impulses.

*

J. C. SQUIRE (1884–1958) was a typically Georgian figure: he was critically obtuse, being all for 'straightforwardness' (but at times robustly sensible in spite of this beery pseudo-simplicity), over-prejudiced against poetry he could not understand; and he usually stifled his genuine poetic impulses with a blanket of bluff English-ness. In his parodies (*Collected Parodies*, 1921), however, he was often brilliantly funny, for he had the parodist's knack of intuitively catch-ing his victim's manner and then caricaturing it. He was a highly influential editor, and champion of Georgianism, and was knighted in 1933. He ended his days as a forgotten, agreeable drunk, occasion-ally giving lectures to schools for small fees (he would frequently turn up on the wrong day, or on the right day of the wrong week). He was a kind and generous man, and a better poet than many who now enjoy temporary reputations and have not heard of him. His *Collected Poems* appeared in the year following his death.

EDWARD THOMAS (1878–1917), who was killed in France, is some-times classified as a Georgian, but he did not appear in Marsh's anthology; nor is he really one of the 'war poets' (Rosenberg, Sorley, Graves, Sassoon, Owen, qq.v.). Though claimed by the Georgians, he does not deserve the epithet except in a few isolated instances. He spent most of his life as a hack critic and editor, under conditions of great poverty (asked for his address, he retorted: 'Ask any publisher in London'); he wrote one novel, *The Happy-Go-Lucky Morgans* (1913). His work in prose is discerning but not distinguished, although his nature essays contain descriptions that anticipate his poetry. He did not begin to write in verse, in his adult life, until persuaded to do so by Robert Frost (q.v.), who was visiting England (1912–14). His first collection, *Poems* (1917), appeared under the pseudonym 'Edward Eastaway'; he was dead before he acquired fame. His *Collected Poems* (1920 rev. 1949) represents, there is no doubt of it, a major achievement. Norman Douglas (q.v.) said of his years as a hack writer (three books a year) that 'the lyrical love of his mind was submerged, imprisoned, encysted in an impenetrable capsule'. But in the last four years of his life this capsule exploded. His range is wider than the frequent label, 'nature poet', implies. He is not a merely descriptive poet: although his observation of the English countryside is exact, he is almost all the time probing the core of sexual melancholy, of solitude, of nostalgia. He used only the technical equipment available to him, but was plainer, less rhetorical, freer, than any true Georgian—and as a whole Georgian editors did not much respond to him. They could not find enough metre or full rhyme; the poems are too conversational; there is an originality that would have disturbed a Georgian.

Thomas often falls into what looks like cliché ('The glory of the beauty of the morning') but then successfully invests the tired phrases with life (he can do it because he means it) as he illustrates them with the beautifully observed particular ('The cuckoo crying over the untouched dew;/The blackbird that has found it, and the dove/That tempts me on to something sweeter than love. . . .'). He knew that he could not penetrate to the heart of what he felt as beauty ('I cannot bite the day to the core'), but in his poetry he strove for a language that would do so. Miraculously he avoided, but without ever evading, the ugly and the urban; his is the last body of work that seeks to define a rural concept of beauty that was finally invalidated by the First World War, by the growth of technology—and by that complex process whereby the anti-human has crystallized, or is still crystallizing, into the political. Given the hideous context of today, the kind of solitude Thomas' poetry explores—as a man he had wandered through it for his nearly twenty years as a hack writer—no longer exists. But it still functions as a metaphor for solitude and for solitudes relieved and/or threatened by love. One of his most remarkable poems is 'The Other', in which he follows a phantom of himself, and tries to come to terms with it; this beautifully illustrates his quality of toughness, by which he refuses to depend on any body or thing to arrive at his answers.

HAROLD MONRO (1879–1932) hardly realized his considerable poetic gifts. Ezra Pound (q.v.) summed it up in a letter to him (of about 1922): 'only HELL—you never had a programme—you've always dragged in Aberbubble and Siphon. . . . One always suspects you of having (and knows you have had) sympathy with a lot of lopp . . .' Monro did weakly succumb to Georgianism, and as generous proprietor of the Poetry Bookshop he did sympathize with far too much 'second-rate lopp'. None of his own verse is as bad, as flaccid and uninventive, as really bad Georgian; but some of it is undeniably Georgian. Monro compromised with his own standards, as the unevenness of his book *Some Contemporary Poets* (1920) clearly shows. And yet Eliot's tribute to him is justified: 'His poetry . . . is more nearly the real right thing than any of the poetry of a somewhat older generation than mine except . . . Yeats's . . . like every other good poet, he has . . . done something that no one else has done at all'. Monro's achievement rests on about a dozen poems, nearly all of them written towards the end of his life. In at least two of these poems ('Friendship', 'The One, Faithful . . .') Monro went further towards a resolution of his bisexual problems than most English-language poets of the twentieth century in similar predicaments have been able to do:

> But, probing, I discovered, with what pain,
> Wine more essential in the end than you,
> And boon-companionship left me again
> Less than I had been, with no more to do
> Than drop pale hands towards their hips and keep
> Friendship for speculation or for sleep.

Even if Monro did dissipate his poetic energy by giving aid to inferior talents, this arose from a generosity that is apparent in the best poems, the most famous of which is 'Bitter Sanctuary', a poem surprisingly far, in manner, from the sonnet-sequence 'Weekend', or the much anthologized 'Milk for the Cat'. What he did in this poem is indeed 'something that no one else has done at all'. There is a valuable (and painful) portrait of the man Monro, as Arnault, in Conrad Aiken's (q.v.) *Ushant*.

W. H. DAVIES (1871–1940) was self-educated; he had been a tramp and pimp in America and England, and wrote lucidly and well of this in *Autobiography of a Super-Tramp* (1908), a minor classic that has remained in print. Before that he had hawked an ill-printed collection of his poems—*The Soul's Destroyer* (1905)—from house to house. It was through the encouragement of Shaw (q.v.) that he became established as a writer. His *Complete Poems* (in texts not impeccable) appeared in 1963. Most of Davies' later poetry and prose is bad: artfully simple, deliberately appealing, slyly mock-innocent (Davies was nothing like as 'simple' as he liked to make out), banal, insipid. But, when he was not trying, he wrote some highly original lyrics—charmingly whimsical, blackly melancholic, mysteriously impudent (as in the famous 'The Inquest'), or, very occasionally, of a genuinely Blakeian simplicity. Davies has been neglected because the bulk of his output is poor and because there is nothing in him for academics; but the reader who does not take the trouble to pick out the jewels from the rubble of imitation stones is missing an exquisite and highly individual minor poet.

WALTER DE LA MARE (1873–1956), undoubtedly in certain respects a Georgian, is a very difficult case; he has not had the serious critical attention he deserves, although there is a general awareness of his worth. The best study of him (1929) is by Forrest Reid; later criticism has been poor. He is distinguished not only as a poet but also as a children's poet (indisputably the greatest of his time), novelist, anthologist and short-story writer. At his weakest De la Mare is lush, excessively romantic and imprecise (as in 'Arabia'); at his best he is unique: quite certainly a poet of major proportions. He has often been described as an 'evader of reality', even by his admirers; this seems obtuse. What is usually called unreality was, for De la Mare, a reality. It is of no use to try to judge the achievement of his finest work by the values propounded in his more self-consciously poetical verse, where he is often thoughtlessly romantic. But although he did so often make what H. Coombes has well called 'a routine use of the properties [of] verbal magic and romantic symbol', De la Mare was a master of the world of childhood. Such lines as

> 'Grill me some bones,' said the cobbler,
>   'Some bones, my pretty Sue;
> I'm tired of my lonesome with heels and soles,
> Springsides and uppers too;
> A mouse in the wainscot is nibbling;
> A wind in the keyhole drones;
> And a sheet webbed over my candle, Susie.
>   Grill me some bones!'

from the (ostensibly) child's poem 'At the Keyhole' make his mastery perfectly clear. He is rhythmically inventive; and he can enter into the world of children—sinister and cruel as well as innocent—with uncanny ease. 'The Song of the Mad Prince' is unthinkable outside the context of childhood, but it is not simply a children's poem: it is unusual in that it is for both child and adult. This poem, in which De la Mare takes on the mask of the 'mad'

Hamlet, is one of the subtlest, dramatic and most beautiful that he ever wrote; it shows him at strength: rooted in literature, but not in the literature of escape:

> Who said, 'Peacock Pie'?
>   The old King to the sparrow:
> Who said, 'Crops are ripe'?
>   Rust to the harrow:
> Who said, 'Where sleeps she now?
>   Where rests she now her head,
> Bathed in eve's loveliness'?
>   That's what I said.
>
> Who said, 'Ay, mum's the word'?
>   Sexton to willow:
> Who said, 'Green dusk for dreams,
>   Moss for a pillow'?
> Who said, 'All Time's delight
>   Hath she for narrow bed,
> Life's troubled bubble broken'?
>   That's what I said.

There is rather more of this calibre in De la Mare than has usually been allowed, as his *Complete Poems* (1969) made apparent. A reading of the whole of this strengthens the impression that De la Mare is a major poet. What he alone does, he does so well. It has been something to have, in this century, so exquisite a ponderer on the various mysteries that life offers (even such simple ones as described in the haunting 'The Railway Junction'); after all, the crasser scientists and the least creative critics have between them attempted to remove all element of mystery from life.

De la Mare's fiction is uneven, but at its best it, like the poetry, does what no one else has done. The novel *Memoirs of a Midget* (1921) is a sinister *tour de force* that would long ago have been seen as genuinely expressionistic if it were not for its unashamedly archaic manner. It is a strange and degenerate book; attempts to neutralize its undoubted power and originality by attributing 'unsound' opinions to De la Mare have failed. As to the short stories: as Graham Greene has written, here 'we have a prose unequalled in its richness since . . . Robert Louis Stevenson'. It is, of course, a certain kind of richness ('Stevenson', says Greene, 'comes particularly to mind because he played with so wide a vocabulary—the colloquial and the literary phrase'), and it has its obvious limitations; but as the investigator of what is odd or spectral or puzzlingly 'lost' in experience De la Mare has no peer. His total achievement is undoubtedly an important one.

WILFRED WILSON GIBSON (1878–1962), a Yorkshireman, began as a Victorian, but later developed into a determinedly realist poet. During the Thirties he sank into oblivion, although most people are aware of his name through certain narrative poems by which he was well represented in school anthologies. He was one of those (De la Mare was another) who inherited Rupert Brooke's estate. Most of Gibson's best poetry—there is not much of it—is to be found in *Collected Poems 1905–1925* (1926): shrewd, Hardyesque character studies, dramatizing ordinary lives. Unfortunately, although Gibson deserves credit for helping to purge poetry of pseudo-romantic trappings, he is on the whole a somewhat dull and linguistically uninspired poet. He fought in the First World War as a private; his war poems are lucid and realistic, but they lack power—as does most of his work. Yet, mainly in the character studies (not in the schoolbook narratives, which lack sufficient edge), he did achieve a tiny distinction: a reward for fifty years of 'worthy' writing. His last collection, *Cold Knuckles* (1947), shows no falling off. He wrote a number of moderately efficient verse dramas.

LASCELLES ABERCROMBIE (1881–1938) stands out from amongst the Georgians for his intelligence and excellent criticism. He showed a greater awareness of the seventeenth century than any of his Georgian contemporaries; his *Colloquial Language in Literature* (1931) shows that he wanted to transcend the Georgian limitations. But he was, as one might fairly put it, 'no poet'. His imagery is sometimes interesting and original, but its source seems to be Abercrombie's interest in the metaphysical poets rather than in his poetic impulse. His language as a whole, notwithstanding his images, continually lapses, just as his theme is becoming interesting, into Victorian bathos. He is at his best in his plays (the best are included in *Collected Poems*, 1930), where his psychology is powerful and his plots subtle; but once again it is his language that lets him down. Had he employed prose in them he might have been a major dramatist. His *A Plea for the Liberty of Interpreting* (1930) has some marginal importance in the history of Shakespearean bibliography.

RALPH HODGSON (?1871–1962), who may have been even older than he gave out, was a tough eccentric who from 1940 lived in Ohio (U.S.A.), where he owned a farm. Before that he had worked on newspapers in America and as a graphic artist—and had bred and judged bull-terriers; he was a dedicated spectator of boxing. He is most famous for his poems condemning cruelty to animals. Such a poem as 'The Birdcatcher' not only categorizes the malevolent hunter himself but also, by extension, a certain kind of frigid intellectual. Hodgson, a man of steadfast integrity and strong personality, possessed true distinction; the following famous short poem, 'Reason', displays his epigrammatic and lyrical power:

> Reason has moons, but moons not hers
>   Lie mirrored on her sea,
> Confusing her astronomers,
>   But O! delighting me.

Hodgson (like Andrew Young, q.v.) is an excellent example of the man who can write really good and relevant poetry strictly within the tradition (De la Mare, who has seemed so much part of it, has unwittingly strained and distorted it to a point where, paradoxically, he is considerably more 'modern' than, say, Cummings, q.v.). His *Collected Poems* appeared in 1961, and is an essential book for real connoisseurs. In both 'Song of Honour', an ecstatic meditative poem reminiscent of Smart, and 'The Bull', which comes as near to Clare's unsentimental sympathy with animals as any poet has, Hodgson achieved convincing poetry.

JAMES ELROY FLECKER (1884–1915), whom tuberculosis early killed off, was regarded as one of the central figures of the Georgian movement. And he was, it is true, low in vitality, firmly anti-realistic and a somewhat pallid pursuer of 'beauty'. However, his poetry is stylistically more distinguished than that of a mere Georgian: he was intelligently aware of foreign literature—particularly that of France—and he learned from the Parnassian (q.v. 2) poets, whom he tried to emulate in English. His poetry does have a fastidiousness, a deliberate and studied lack of diffuseness, that is alien to the vague Georgian ideal—and for this he should be remembered. Flecker spent most of his adult life in the East, in diplomatic posts. He wrote a good deal, including some readable fiction and the verse dramas *Don Juan* (1925) and the more famous, lush, dated but not ineffective *Hassan* (1922).

W. J. TURNER (1889–1946) was born in Australia; but he came to England as a very young man and remained there until his death. He was a well known music critic, a novelist—and a notable playwright in *The Man Who Ate the Popomack* (1922). Turner seldom succeeded in reconciling his wild romanticism (so wild that it sometimes ran over into irresponsibility and irascibility) with his satirical impulses; but he was an interesting although uneven poet, who sought for subtler and profounder themes than he was able to cope with. His passion for music led him to treat his poetry as a sort of music; this spoiled much of it. But at his best he is memorable and deceptively simple:

> The sun has come, I know,
>   For yesterday I stood
>   Beside it in the wood—
> But O how pale, how softly did it glow.
>   I stooped to warm my hands
>   Before its rain-washed gold;
>   But it was pebble-cold,
> Startled to find itself in these dark lands.

There is a *Selected Poems* (1939); his last collection, *Fossils of a Future Time?* (1946), is as interesting as anything he did. Yeats (q.v.) was an admirer of his poetry.

*

Some poets of the Georgian generation remain entirely immune. For all that the poetry of the Scottish parson (he changed from non-conformist to Church of England, and was vicar of a parish in Sussex for many years until his retirement) ANDREW YOUNG (1885–1971) is firmly traditional in form, it is never tainted with the poetical, and it always has acuteness of observation and fine sharpness of style. Furthermore, Young remained a minority taste until after the Second World War—his first collections were pamphlets issued somewhat late in life; his first collection from a regular publisher, *The White Blackbird* (1935) was issued when he was fifty. His poetry has no Georgian affinities, and he, a fastidious user of words, could never have tolerated the slack and styleless meandering that generally characterizes Georgian verse. Young is a tough, precise, even dour poet who says almost all that he has to say through a rapt contemplation of nature. Watching birds through binoculars, he feels his shoulders prick as though he himself were sprouting wings. He has much—if only incidentally—to say about the phenomenon of anthropomorphization. Above all, because of his remarkable sensibility, he is a describer of the natural world of Great Britain that no discerning reader could do without. His *Collected Poems* appeared in 1950. This includes all his lyrics; a later, narrative poem, *Into Hades* (1952), which begins with the poet's funeral, is lively and interesting but less successful. *Nicodemus* (1937), included in the *Collected Poems*, is a straightforward and effective verse play, quite as good as most essays in this, in the twentieth century, impossible genre.

HUMBERT WOLFE (1885–1940), a Jewish civil servant born in Milan and brought up in Bradford (Yorkshire), was an extremely popular poet: so much so that he stands in danger of being forgotten. This would be a pity, for when not trying to be lushly lyrical (a vein he was very clever at emulating, but in which in fact he never got beyond sentimentality) Wolfe was an accomplished minor satirist and ironist, with a devastating sense of humour. No one has quite this touch ('The Grey Squirrel'):

> Like a small grey
> coffee-pot,
> sits the squirrel.
> He is not
>
> all he should be,
> kills by dozens
> trees, and eats
> his red-brown cousins.
>
> The keeper, on the
> other hand
> , who shot him, is
> a Christian, and
>
> loves his enemies,
> which shows
> the squirrel was not
> one of those.

This is an admittedly fragile and slight exposure of Christian pretensions; and Wolfe usually spoiled such an effect as he gains here by his own pretentiousness. But in the early *Kensington Gardens* (1924) and in *Requiem* (1927) there are several poems as good. He cannot be dismissed as easily as most coffee-table poets.

CHARLES WILLIAMS (1886–1945), poet, dramatist and novelist, had his admirers—including such critics as C. S. Lewis. But his work normally raises grave doubts. His 'cosmic thrillers' are frankly middlebrow, written to raise money. In them the 'belief in the supernatural' is insincere and vulgar: he so patently *disbelieves* in their action. They are nearer to the crudely written occult romances of Dennis Wheatley than to literature. He was a confused, unsatisfactory critic: an obscurantist without even the resources of a C. S. Lewis. His early poetry is a semi-Chestertonian attempt to revive a Victorian style. His most highly praised poetry is in *Taliesin through Logres* (1938) and *The Region of the Summer Stars* (1944), a sequence on the Arthurian legend. No critic, however, has made out a satisfactory case for it: C. S. Lewis could only call it 'gorgeous', with 'profound wisdom'. In fact it is muddy work; what looks like originality is simply disguised archaism; the 'grand style' proceeds to nothing. Behind all Williams' work—particularly the novels—there seems to be something thoroughly unpleasant: the orthodox Christian apologetics conceal a human rather than a merely Christian heresy: one senses Williams hanging masturbatorily over his nasty, midcult images of evil.

FRANCES CORNFORD (1886–1960), wife of the classical scholar Francis Cornford, is most famous for the clever, nasty triolet 'To a Fat Lady Seen from the Train' ('O why do you walk through the fields in gloves,/Missing so much and so much?/O fat white woman whom nobody loves. . . .'); but she wrote some tiny but charming and distinctive poems. She seldom, unless in her diction, fell victim to Georgian sloppiness. Her *Collected Poems* appeared in 1954.

ARTHUR WALEY (1889–1966) has exercised a considerable influence on the development of English poetry through his brilliant and poetic translations from the Chinese. These, admired by Pound (and superior to Pound's essays in the genre) and Yeats, represent a remarkable achievement, and are perhaps as substantial a contribution to modern poetry. The translations—*170 Chinese Poems* (1919), *The Book of Songs* (1937), *Chinese Poems* (1946)—are done into a sensitive, rhythmically impeccable free verse; the sense is not really Chinese (how could it be?), but it introduced into English poetry as many new attitudes as new procedures. Waley's translations helped English poets to regain something of the spontaneity and lyricism that are so difficult to attain in twentieth-century poetry without resort to cliché. Again, in his less direct way, Waley has influenced the use of imagery in English poetry almost as much as Pound: the Chinese poems he translated employed concentrated images in place of mere description. His influence has been subterranean but (almost) all-pervasive.

*

The burst of creative activity that took place in Ireland at the turn of the century is sometimes called the Irish literary renaissance. It was not, however, a movement, but rather the result of the sudden diversion of national energy from politics to literature after the Parnell scandal (1892). The main activity was in the drama (this is discussed in the appropriate section), but there was also a Gaelic revival (and some translations out of the language of Ireland's only wholly native culture) and a resurgence of poetry. PADRAIC COLUM (1881–1972), dramatist (he helped to found the Irish National Theatre), autobiographer and folklorist, wrote attractive poetry for almost the whole of his long life. (He came to America at the beginning of the First World War and remained there until his death.) Colum's poetry has a quality with which, as L. A. G. Strong said, 'literary criticism has little to do': 'simplicity', which 'cannot be analyzed'. Colum's plays, discussed elsewhere, are important; but so is his poetry, which ought to be better known. Some of it has passed back into the folk tradition from which it came. . . . It is remarkable that Colum never spoiled the purity of his gift in his near sixty years of exile in America (and Hawaii); his fairly frequent visits to Ireland seem to have protected him from sentimentality and feyness. His *Collected Poems* (1953) is an essential part of any comprehensive library of twentieth-century poetry in English. Although his poetry always has a lilt, it is not a monotonous one—he has an exquisite and original ear, as the deservedly famous 'She Moved Through the Fair' demonstrates. His subtlety, elegance and fine craftsmanship are all evident in 'Wild Ass':

> The wild ass lounges, legs stuck out
> In vagrom unconcern:
> The tombs of Archaemenian kings
> Are for those hooves to spurn.
>
> And all of rugged Tartary
> Lies with him on the ground.
> The Tartary that knows no awe
> That has nor ban nor bound.
>
> The wild horse from the herd is plucked
> To bear a saddle's weight;
> The boar is one keeps covert, and
> The wolf runs with a mate.
>
> But he's the solitary of space,
> Curbless and unbeguiled;
> The only being that bears a heart
> Not recreant to the wild.

Colum, 'whose goodness and poetic innocence speak at once to all that is good and innocent in his audience' (L. A. G. Strong), is one of the very few English-language poets to draw his strength from tradition throughout his career. *Poet's Circuits* (1960), a collection of poems published in his eightieth year, is as pure and strong as ever.

Æ (ps. GEORGE WILLIAM RUSSELL, 1867–1935)—he wrote an early article under the pseudonym 'Aeon'; the printer dropped the last two letters, and he stuck to the result—was a prolific and active member of the Irish revival: in fact, he and his close friend Yeats dominated it. He was an interesting man, helplessly divided between active social idealism (half his time was given up to founding co-operatives and trying to persuade the farmers to abandon their wasteful and inefficient methods) and a mysticism that he acquired from the reading of oriental literature. His activities are often described as political. This is unfair: Russell was no purveyor of clichés or seeker after power, but was honest, meant what he said, and was a competent economist and, far from being an 'expert' (in the meaningless manner of politicians), was actually an authority on agricultural matters such as soil conditioning; he retained his sympathy for the poor. Furthermore, Russell so disliked Irish politics after the First World War that he spent his last years in England, where he died of cancer. One may learn much about the personality of Russell from his *Letters* (1961), which have been well edited and annotated by Alan Denson. So far as his poetry is concerned (there is a *Collected Poems* of 1926; *Selected Poems*, 1935, contains much of his best poetry) Æ (he kept this name for his 'mystical' and poetic identity) is essentially an Irish Platonist: this world is unreal, and our only clues to that real world, of which it is the shadow, are dreams and visions of beauty. Yeats said, brilliantly, that his poems had 'a mind of scented flame consuming them from within'. At their best they faithfully describe their author's trance-like mood—for Æ was not a vague dreamer: he had experienced what he tried to convey. But whereas Yeats, who shared his combination of interests, was able to evolve his own style, Æ had to fall back on a diction and manner not quite his own: he could only talk of 'the breath of Beauty', where Yeats could eventually supply actual particulars of beauty. . . . But as a minor Celtic twilight poet Æ is distinguished: delicate, sincere, with a subdued glow. 'Exiles' is characteristic:

> The gods have taken alien shapes upon them,
> Wild peasants driving swine
> In a strange country. Through the swarthy faces
> The starry faces shine.

Under grey tattered skies they reel and strain there:
Yet cannot all disguise
The majesty of fallen Gods, the beauty,
The fire beneath their eyes.

They huddle at night within low, clay-built cabins;
And, to themselves unknown,
They carry with them diadem and sceptre
And move from throne to throne.

One of Æ's most valuable books, which deserves revival, is about his own poetry and how it came to be written: *Song and its Fountains* (1932). His religious thought, which contains some cogent criticisms of Christianity, is interesting and original; as thought—although not as a vehicle for poetry—it is superior to Yeats' elaborate system. There have been few kinder literary men in this century.

It was Russell who rescued JAMES STEPHENS (1882–1950) from life in an office, and introduced him to the literary world. A few years afterwards, with the generosity and shrewdness characteristic of him, he spoke of him as 'a poet without a formula', 'perplexed' but moving 'down to earth'. Russell was referring to the division in Stephens between comic, faun-like, impudent elf—and poet-as-angel; this conflict was resolved in his best poetry. In his prose Stephens succeeded admirably both as realist and as fantasist. Joyce (q.v.) regarded him very highly. His first success was the novel *The Crock of Gold* (1912), one of the best of modern fairy stories. The stories in *Etched in Moonlight* (1928) show him in more realist vein: he is in debt to Moore (q.v.) for his material, but introduces a lyrical quality that is his own. As a poet he is most attractive: more sophisticated than Colum, he is nevertheless simple and innocent without guile. His Irish charm (of the best variety) is revealed in the celebrated 'The Centaurs'; occasionally he strikes a deeper, almost Blakean note, as in 'The Shell' and 'What Thomas An Buile Said in a Pub': here God is going to strike the unsatisfactory earth, but Thomas (he claims) tells him

'Stay,
You must not strike it, God; I'm in the way:
And I will never move from where I stand.'
He said, 'Dear child, I feared that you were dead,'
And stayed his hand.

'Little Things', too, strikes exactly the right sweet and simple note. Some of the poems in *Strict Joy* (1931) and *Kings and the Moon* (1938)

are as good as anything in the *Collected Poems* (1926); Lloyd Franken-berg's *A James Stephens Reader* (1962) is an excellent job—but a more substantial selection from the poetry is still urgently needed.

The poetry of WILLIAM BUTLER YEATS (1865–1939) has attracted much criticism and exegesis, a high proportion of which consists of wilful projection (of the critics' own predilections) or frigid abstractions. Considering his intrinsic and extrinsic importance he has, in fact, attracted surprisingly little really good, lucid criticism—although a few of the straightforwardly explanatory guides and handbooks collect facts that are indispensable to an understanding of his poetry. Yeats is clearly a major poet; but the high reverence in which he is held frequently conceals an inability to come to terms with him. The 'philosophical' system which he developed is, in fact, one about which it is impossible not to have reservations.

He was the son of J. B. Yeats, a lawyer turned painter, whose family originally came from England—but had been in Ireland since the seventeenth century; his mother's family, also English, had been in Ireland for a considerably shorter period. Yeats began as a vaguely Pre-Raphaelite poet; but from the beginning his manner was different from that of his friends Dowson and Johnson (qq.v.) because he had Sligo folk-lore to fall back on: this acted as an effective antidote to his Pre-Raphaelite vagueness and dreaminess. Of the poems of this first period, much of it spent in London, the Irish ones are the strongest: they are the most down to earth, precise, natural, unforced. That Yeats was likely to develop into a poet of genius was already apparent in 1889, when he wrote 'Down by the Salley Gardens', 'an attempt to reconstruct an old song from three lines imperfectly remembered by an old peasant woman' in Sligo. Clearly the author of this beautiful song understood how real poetry sounded. During the Nineties Yeats wrote plays, and was active with Lady Gregory (q.v.) and Douglas Hyde in founding the Abbey Theatre (1900).

As he matured Yeats sought to purge his language of excessive romanticism (the extent to which he succeeded may be seen in the *Variorum Edition* of his poems, 1957; the fullest, definitive *Collected Poems* appeared in 1956). He clung on to the poetically formal (he never really abandoned it) as his expression of the high, aristocratic calling of the poet, and as an appropriate response to the mysterious-ness and magic of the natural—as distinct from the 'ordinary', sordid, commercialized—world. But he laced his formal language with colloquialese, to achieve an effect unique in English poetry. The style he wanted to create eschewed abstraction and cliché, and yet it was based in Irish tradition. Yeats, although he fell early under the influence of Blake, Shelley and neo-Platonic ideas in general, could not remain immune to Irish aspirations. The conflict between the ethereal, the immaterial, and the concreteness of Irish national-ism produced, in fact, some of his best poetry. During the Nineties he was associated with the Socialist League; but in the first ten years of this century, under the influence of visits to Lady Gregory's country house, Coole Park, and of his convictions of the poet's high calling, he began to evolve his feudal idea. This, which involved a total rejection of middle-class materialism, an enlightened aristo-cracy and a partly idealized peasantry (which knew how to keep its place), was both unrealistic and politically naïve; but it did not prevent Yeats writing meaningful poems in the important collec-tions *The Green Helmet* (1910) and *Responsibilities* (1914). It was in this period that Yeats was in love with the actress and patriot Maud Gonne, who refused to marry him and caused him much sexual frustration and despair. In 1917 he married.

By this time his poetry had entered into a third phase: in response to Pound (whom he knew well) and imagism (qq.v.) he began to evolve a laconic, even epigrammatic manner; at the same time, more independently, he had become increasingly concerned with mysticism (oriental and neo-Platonic) and with the 'occult'. His wife claimed mediumistic powers, and she faked (with the best of intentions: to help him) 'automatic writing', which he used as raw material for his poetry. Yeats believed that this writing was dictated by spirits, and it helped him to evolve the symbolic system he out-lined in *A Vision* (1925 rev. 1937). The poetry of *The Wild Swans at Coole* (1919), for all its conversational quality, is technically finer than anything preceding it. It is rhythmically more subtle, and it plays an important part in freeing English verse from metrical (i.e. iambic) monotony.

From here on Yeats proceeded into his penultimate phase. This is the period of his richest poetry, in which he combines a number of themes: the conflicts between the spirit and the flesh, 'madness' and cool reason, permanence and change. In 1934 he underwent the Steinach 'monkey gland' operations—for sexual 'rejuvenation'—and this ushered in the poetry of his final phase: wild, lustfully romantic once again—and yet conscious of 'sin' and 'the foul rag-and-bone shop of the heart'. Yeats won the Nobel Prize in 1923. Since his death he has been almost universally regarded as the greatest English-language poet of this century. However, the viewing of him from a position of over-reverence has not helped towards an understanding of him—any more than it has helped in the case of Shakespeare. . . . A good deal of nonsense has been written about

Yeats by academic critics who know nothing of poetry's roots in real life. It has become exceedingly difficult to tell the truth about him—to criticize him at all—without heaping abuse upon one's head. Thus, when Conor Cruse O'Brien (the most gifted Irish critic of his generation), who admires him, asked the question, 'How can those of us who loathe [Yeats'] politics continue . . . to love the poetry . . .?', he brought coals of fire upon his head. However, he convincingly proved that Yeats' politics, *qua* politics, were naïve, disagreeable and opportunistic (his record as a Senator in the Twenties, when he supported Protestant landed interests, is not good by any standards); and critics do have the right to ask the question. The relationship between poetry and virtue is hardly an irrelevant one; and Yeats' politics, naïve or not, are humanly reprehensible. Auden (q.v.) has asked a similar question of the 'occult' beliefs: 'How on earth . . . could a man of Yeats' gifts take such nonsense seriously?' And he goes on to point out, further, that since Yeats was a 'snob' (it is a fair word, and it fits in with his politics), it is all the more remarkable that he believed in 'mediums, spells, the Mysterious Orient'.

The problem is this: Yeats' politics are stupid or humanly disgraceful, or both; his 'philosophical' system, as outlined in *A Vision*, is a synthesis of vulgar rubbish, intellectually ill-digested lore from neo-Platonism and what Auden calls the 'Mysterious East', and Ancient Greece and elsewhere—and of the insensitive, authoritarian politics, too; and yet the poetry is admired—and is almost always interpreted in the terms of *A Vision*. . . .

The short answer is that it does not matter in the least what Yeats' ideas actually mean—*but what, in his poetry, he meant by them.* By no means all the elements in his system are specious in themselves; one may argue, without granting intellectual or philosophical respectability to the system itself (it simply doesn't have it), that Yeats responded intuitively to what was important in it, and that his responses are contained in his poems rather than in his obscure and difficult expository prose. Or one might agree with L. C. Knights: 'Measured by potentiality, by aspiration, and by the achievement of a few poems, it is as a heroic failure that one is forced to consider Yeats' poetic career as a whole'. For, as Knights goes on to say, Yeats thought that 'Unity of Being' is impossible without 'Unity of Culture'; and yet he realized that 'Unity of Culture', in the face of a mechanized society drifting towards cultureless technocracy, is itself increasingly impossible.

The fundamental symbolism of the poems in the two books regarded by the majority of critics as Yeats' greatest—*The Tower*

(1928) and *The Winding Stair* (1929)—and of the later poems, is fairly simple: our life is a walk up a spiral staircase in a tower; we keep covering the same ground, but at a different height; because we travel in a 'gyre' (Yeats' word for a spiral), we both go round in a circle and yet make progress; the point, of final understanding, the tip of the spiral, where we are 'above' every place we have been before, is also the point of death; thus the summit of the tower is ruined. History, too, is for Yeats composed of gyres (cycles), as he makes most clear in 'The Second Coming', which he wrote in 1920 and published in 1921:

> Turning and turning in the widening gyre
> The falcon cannot hear the falconer;
> Things fall apart; the centre cannot hold;
> Mere anarchy is loosed upon the world,
> The blood-dimmed tide is loosed, and everywhere
> The ceremony of innocence is drowned;
> The best lack all conviction, while the worst
> Are full of passionate intensity.
>
> Surely some revelation is at hand;
> Surely the Second Coming is at hand.
> The Second Coming! Hardly are those words out
> When a vast image out of *Spiritus Mundi*
> Troubles my sight: somewhere on sands of the desert
> A shape with lion body and the head of a man,
> A gaze blank and pitiless as the sun,
> Is moving its slow thighs, while all about it
> Reel shadows of the indignant desert birds.
> The darkness drops again; but now I know
> That twenty centuries of stony sleep
> Were vexed to nightmare by a rocking cradle,
> And what rough beast, its hour come round at last,
> Slouches towards Bethlehem to be born?

This is an example of Yeats at his most powerful; it embodies both his rejection of Christianity as a system, and his religious sense; furthermore, it does not really depend for its full poetic effect on a knowledge of the system of thought behind it: the opening image of the first two lines is self-evident: the falcon breaks free, goes out of control.

It is often asserted that the two famous Byzantium poems, 'Sailing to Byzantium' and 'Byzantium' (they appear, respectively, in the

1928 and 1929 volumes), written some years later, exercise their power before any knowledge of their symbolic patterns has been gained by the reader; this is true, but perhaps to a more limited extent than has been realized or admitted. These and other poems of the late Twenties and early Thirties contain magnificent lines, but they also contain elements as pretentious as the 'system' upon which they are too carefully and calculatedly based; either the spontaneity of the original impulse has been eliminated (Yeats first wrote them out in prose), or there never was a true impulse; after they have been fully examined they shrink into something less profound than their grand surface suggests. Perhaps the poems in *The Wild Swans at Coole*, however, have had less consideration than they deserve: are not these more central to humanity, less concerned with the poet himself, than the more spectacular ones of the late Twenties and early Thirties?

In any case, Yeats is not on the level of Rilke, Vallejo, Valéry, Blok. . . . He failed because his sophistication failed. Being sensitive to and monumentally aware of the demands of this century, he tried to transform himself from a naïve to a sentimentive poet (qq.v.); his effort appeared to be much more successful than that of (say) Gerhardt Hauptmann (q.v. 2); but ultimately it was not successful. He possessed consummate technical skill and epigrammatic mastery —but his intellect was not strong, and he sought refuge in the over-factitious. The metaphysical complexity of the Byzantium poems, for example, is ultimately a factitious rather than a poetic element in them. The much vaunted 'intellectual power' of these poems has been exaggerated; whatever qualities they may have, real intellectual power is hardly one of them. Passion is. But, despite the public air, it is an egotistic passion. The incredible richness of most of these poems has been bought at a price; the comparative simplicity of the poems in *The Wild Swans at Coole* suggests this. And yet they, too, can attain simplicity:

> When such as I cast out remorse
> So great a sweetness flows into the breast
> We must laugh and we must sing,
> We are blest by everything,
> Everything we look upon is blest.

*

T. S. Eliot (q.v.), although not officially one of the imagist poets, stated (1953) that the London imagist group of 1910 is 'usually and conveniently taken, as the starting-point of modern poetry' in the English language. Ezra Pound (q.v.) was the moving spirit behind this group; but others in it were important. Imagism was never clearly enough delineated to allow of precise definitions; however, one can fairly say of it that it represented 'British-American expressionism'. It was, however, less violent and aggressive, generally less self-confident and extensive in its aims, and more limited in its results, than German expressionism (q.v.). Its poets were on the whole less gifted. The intrinsic importance of every self-consciously 'imagist' poem is minor—or even trivial. But to claim that 'apart from Pound, and also Lawrence, . . .' the imagists 'have no importance' (John Holloway) is plainly wrong: Eliot's statement that modern Anglo-American poetry has its starting-point in imagism is authoritative. The actual poetry of the imagist anthologies was trivial, theoretical. But it was not unimportant.

Apart from the effervescent and ever-active Pound, the chief figure in the imagist group was the philosopher T. E. HULME (1883–1917), a victim of the First World War. Hulme did not have time to mature, but he is none the less an important and prophetic thinker. The work he left was collected by his friend Herbert Read (q.v.) in *Speculations* (1924; 1960) and *Notes on Language and Style* (1929); *Further Speculations* was edited in 1955 by Sam Hynes. Five of his poems were printed by Pound at the end of his own *Ripostes* (1912) as 'The Complete Poetical Works'; further poems were added by Alun Jones in his useful *The Life and Opinions of T. E. Hulme* (1960). Hulme's poems, delicate, elegant, beautifully phrased, are the best produced by the imagist movement; we have tended to take them for granted. His thinking was confused: he preferred, as Read wrote, 'to see things in the emotional light of a metaphor rather than to reach reality through scientific analysis', and this led him to some foolishly extreme conclusions, such as that *all* romantic poetry was sloppy, or that 'fancy' is to be preferred to 'imagination' (his argument on this point is peculiarly confused and inane). However, it is unfair to call him a 'premature fascist'. He was perceptive about the faults of democracy and made noises about authoritarian or monarchist regimes—but he was never exposed to the reality of fascism, and actually put to the test; there is much in the fragments he left behind that could be taken as 'proto-anti-fascist'. . . . He studied for a time under Bergson (q.v. 2), and from him he gained his predilection for the concrete and for the notion of qualitative, 'real time'. Bergsonism hardly chimes in with authoritarianism. . . .

However, this is not the place to examine the inconsistencies of Hulme's thought; the main point is that he was prophetically aware of the fact that the twentieth century would see a drastic break away from types of thinking that had been traditional since the late fifteenth century. He misdiagnosed the nature of this revolution, confusing it with his own brash neoclassicism, and he was guilty of over-simplifications (as when he claimed that blank verse, being new, had alone been responsible for the Elizabethan efflorescence); he wrongly thought of all romantics as Pelasgian optimists. But his programme for poetry—and for intellectual life and art in general— was, although confused, symptomatic: neoclassical, abstract (non-representational), 'royalist', 'hard' (as against 'romantic', 'softness' or sloppiness), intellectual (not emotional), precise (not vague), 'religious' (in the broad, public sense), pessimistic (man is seen as a limited and sinful creature; only his art raises him above the status of an animal). We can see many of these lines of thought converging in the positions taken up by Eliot and Wyndham Lewis—and by the anarchist Herbert Read. Yet Hulme's own poetry, instructive in intention, is by no means, of course, non-romantic:

Three birds flew over the red wall into the pit of the setting sun.
O daring, doomed birds that pass from my sight.

The actual starting-point of imagism may be traced back to Hulme's formation of a 'Poets' Club' at Cambridge in 1908; he wrote and published one of his most famous poems, 'Autumn', in that year. Soon afterwards he got into a fight in a pub and was expelled from the university, whereupon he appeared in London. Here he met F. S. FLINT (1885–1960) and Pound. In 1909 a group of poets, including Hulme, Pound and Flint, began meeting in a Soho restaurant. Out of these meetings, the subject of which centred on poetic technique and French and Japanese poetry, was eventually evolved the following credo (published by Flint in 1913): '1. Direct treatment of the "thing" whether subjective or objective. 2. To use absolutely no word that does not contribute to the presentation. 3. As regarding rhythm: to compose in the sequence of the musical phrase, not in sequence of a metronome'. And Pound added a note in the course of which he referred to an image as 'that which presents an intellectual and emotional complex in an instant of time'.

By 1913 Pound, as was his wont, had taken over: the group he now called 'Les Imagistes' (active in 1912–14 and rightly regarded as the true imagists), which did not include Hulme but acknowledged his influence, was organized and publicized by him. The chief members, besides Pound and Flint, were the American H.D. (q.v.) and the Englishman who became her husband for a time: RICHARD ALDING-

TON (1892–1962). The first anthology of imagism, *Des Imagistes*, appeared in 1914. The British poets included, besides Aldington and Flint, were Ford and Joyce (qq.v.). Soon after this the American poetastress Amy Lowell gained control of the imagist group—and imagism quickly turned into what Pound called 'Amygism'. (This is a part of literary history—several good poets, including Lawrence, q.v., and some of the original imagists, were represented in Amy Lowell's anthologies—but it is not important.)

Many of the attitudes subsumed under the term imagism are peculiar to Pound, or were initiated by him, and have been discussed in the section devoted to him. The imagist poems themselves were, as has been mentioned, small or trivial affairs; but the state of mind which produced them was modernist. The actual imagist poem concentrates so hard on being visually exact and vivid that it hardly has time, in its brief life, to demonstrate the anti-logical direction of its origins. But both Hulme (through Bergson) and Pound rejected ordinary logic as an acceptable surface for poetry: Hulme spoke (1908) of a new impressionism, and of an introspective (rather than heroic) poetry that would deal 'with expression and communication of momentary phases in the poet's mind'; Pound resorted to the Chinese ideogram, or to his understanding of it— which was entirely alogical. It was the imagists—again, chiefly Hulme and Pound—who put forward 'free verse' as the most appropriate vehicle for poetry. This, then, was what was most modernist, most expressionist, about imagism: its assumption that poetry communicated metaphorically rather than logically.

Milton and, in the nineteenth century, Arnold had written 'free verse': verse in irregular lines. Whitman had not obeyed metrical laws—although his verse is by no means 'free'—and neither had a number of other nineteenth-century poets after him. But imagist free verse is not really 'free' at all; rather, as Pound wrote, it is 'a rhythm . . . which corresponds exactly to the motion or shade of emotion to be expressed'. This left the poets themselves free of rules; it did not mean that poetry was now to become a kind of chopped up prose.

Whenever English poetry has radically changed its direction (in, for example, the sixteenth and twentieth centuries) it has turned to foreign poetries. Surrey and Wyatt and their minor contemporaries turned to Italy for the sonnet and blank verse; Pound and his contemporaries turned to the poetry of China and Japan, and of the French symbolists. Directly and indirectly, then, English-language poetry of this century has taken sustenance from elsewhere.

Flint, an important figure in the history of imagism, but possessed of an 'almost imbecile modesty' (Aldington), was a civil servant (Chief of the Overseas Section, Statistics Division); he translated Verhaeren (*Love Poems*, 1916; *Plays*, 1920) and others, and published three volumes of original poetry—the last of these appeared as long ago as 1920. Flint, whom Ford called 'one of the most beautiful spirits of the country' (did he suggest some aspects of Tietjens, also in the Statistics Division?), had an exquisite gift; unfortunately it was too slight—or perhaps fragile is the apter word—to fully convey the acuteness of his sensitivity. He rather too frequently fell back on visual preciosity: 'Under the lily shadow/ and the gold/ and the blue and mauve/that the whin and the lilac/pour down on the water,/the fishes quiver. . . .' (Flint) is not of the quality of the briefer 'Green arsenic smeared on an egg-white cloth. . . .' (Pound). Nor do Flint's longer poems ('Hats', 'Otherworld') quite come off. 'Hats', an attack on the complacent bourgeoisie very much in the manner of Richard Aldington, lacks originality and linguistic edge. However, a few of his shorter poems have the vivid sharpness of good etchings: this one is actually called 'Eau Forte':

> On black bare trees a stale cream moon
> Hangs dead, and sours the unborn buds.
>
> Two gaunt old hacks, knees bent, heads low,
> Tug, tired and spent, an old horse tram.
>
> Damp smoke, rank mist fill the dark square;
> And round the bend six bullocks come.
>
> A hobbling, dirt-grimed drover guides
> Their clattering feet—
>   their clattering feet!
>   to the slaughterhouse.

Richard Aldington, poet, novelist, translator, critic and biographer, never realized his potentialities. A man of learning, sensibility and even some genius, he turned into an exhausted hack. His last works, critical and biographical, are worth reading; but they are enervated and frequently exasperated in tone (especially the biography of T. E. Lawrence). Aldington, who fought in the First World War, suffered from a tendency to incoherence and bitter, convulsive rage; it is most apparent in his novel *Death of a Hero* (1929)—about war and its prelude and aftermath—which has passages of power but which is written in too headlong a style. When Aldington had his emotions under control he was interesting; too often he is either debilitated or hysterical; he seldom does justice to his intelligence. His *Complete Poems* appeared in 1948. One of his best and most self-revealing books is the autobiographical *Life for Life's Sake* (1941).

As a poet, Aldington was seldom self-confident enough even to search for his own voice. From elegant imagist he moved (perhaps under Pound's influence) to pastiche of the styles of previous centuries (in his 1923 collection, *Exile*). The phantasmagoric *A Fool i' the Forest* (1925), one of the long poems of disillusion written as a response to Eliot's *The Waste Land* (Aiken's *Senlin* is another), is his most original work, and the one that most nearly pinpoints the nature of his disabling pain—an alarming combination of cynicism, sense of failure, blurred emotionalism, hysteria, frustration and satirical indignation. As a whole Aldington's poetry fails to throw off sufficiently the mere posture of romanticism; surprisingly, a good deal is taken for granted, and this operates as a sort of background of cliché. Aldington knew ancient Greek poetry well, but did not learn enough from it. His violently anti-bourgeois attitude is unsubtle and over-romanticized.

The poetry of Eliot, which to a large extent developed out of imagism and the poetic mood in which that movement originated, was one of the factors that led to the clear emergence of a 'modern' style in the Thirties. Another, less immediately obvious, factor was the poetry of some of the men who fought in the trenches in the First World War; their work originated in an ambience more or less Georgian—the exigencies of the war jerked them out of this complacency.

The Sitwells offered a third, minor but lively challenge to Georgianism. The comment that this trio belong 'more to the history of publicity than to the history of poetry' (Leavis) is manifestly unfair in the case of SACHEVERELL SITWELL (1897), and both EDITH SITWELL (1887–1964) and OSBERT SITWELL (1892–1969) did many things that transcended mere publicity. Undoubtedly the Sitwells, especially Edith, were frequently tiresome and exhibitionistic; the 'progressive' anthology *Wheels* (1916), edited by Edith, contained mostly mediocre work; there was a strident egocentric note about most of Edith's public statements and critical pronouncements; her fiction (*I Live Under a Black Sun*, 1937, on Swift), criticism and biography are spoiled by a jarring, sometimes hysterical note that is in fact, not confidence or certainty, but spinsterish self-love. None the less, although she became a bore, Edith's earlier poetry has seldom, since her death, had its due.

Osbert Sitwell was an amusing, accomplished and clever satirist

(*England Reclaimed*, 1927, 1949; *Wrack at Tidesend*, 1952; *On the Continent*, 1958); but, as Conrad Aiken (q.v.) said in 1928, he 'never disturbs us, he never reveals'. As an essayist and critic he is pompous but often shrewd and informative. His best book, and this really is 'revealing', is his five-part autobiography: *Left Hand, Right Hand* (1944), *The Scarlet Tree* (1946), *Great Morning* (1947), *Laughter in the Next Room* (1948) and *Noble Essences* (1950). The autobiography is good because it does not take up a defensive position (I belonged by birth, education, nature, outlook, and period to the pre-war era'), but simply records. Not the least excellent passages deal with the eccentric Sitwell father, Sir George, who, among other things, invented a toothbrush that played 'Annie Laurie' as it brushed the teeth and a 'small revolver for shooting wasps'. Osbert Sitwell also wrote one perceptive novel about the provincial England of 1914, before the holocaust of the First World War: *Before the Bombardment* (1926).

Sacheverell Sitwell is a more limited writer. His many travel books are self-consciously aesthetic, and evade seriousness; his writings on baroque art and architecture are learned but curiously neutral in their effect. His poetry, notably *Canons of Giant Art* (1933), is eccentric, accomplished, artificial; it has unmistakable quality, but the most diligent investigation fails to yield an answer to the question, 'What quality?' What Sacheverell Sitwell has is a manner; but this, elegant and assured, conceals a total lack of poetic conviction—the sad emptiness of a man born into the wrong time.

Edith was at once the most eccentric and most poetically gifted of her family. She was never more than a minor poet; but her verbal virtuosity and dexterity have hardly been equalled, within traditional limits, in this century. She chose not to draw upon her personal experience, but instead to construct an aristocratic-surrealist world that owed much to her interest in painting. The value of this lies in its style and its arch pseudo-innocence; resolutely avoiding the serious, the grotesqueness of Edith Sitwell's play-world reflects the grimness of the sexual experience (itself a narcissistic indulgence, or even celebration, of lack of sexual contact) she eschewed. 'Colonel Fantock', one of the more revealing of her poems, is haunted by the shadow of incest and degeneration. The most successful of her poems is undoubtedly *Gold Coast Customs* (1930), a rhythmical *tour de force*.

With the advent of the Second World War Edith Sitwell adopted a new, earnest, apocalyptic manner, which culminated in her (surely too triumphal) entry into the Roman Catholic Church in 1954. This new style, cruelly referred to by James Reeves (q.v.) as 'death-bed repentance', was disastrous. Edith Sitwell attempted to fuse the richness of Yeats, a grand high style, and the seventeenth-century complexity of such poets as Crashaw and Vaughan. The result is pretentious, vacuous, rhetorical, as at the beginning of 'Dirge for the New Sunrise', which has the solemn epigraph 'Fifteen minutes past eight o'clock, on the morning of Monday, the 6th of August, 1945':

> Bound to my heart as Ixion to the wheel,
> Nailed to my heart as the thief upon the cross,
> I hang between our Christ and the gap where the
> world was lost. . . .

Rhapsodies of praise flowed from certain knighted cultural *entrepreneurs*, but not from critics. These later effusions of Edith Sitwell—Dr. Leavis, having been read one of them in a suitably lugubrious manner by an enthusiastic pupil, is supposed to have asked 'What do I do now? Ejaculate?'—are now for the most part unread. Edith Sitwell's *Collected Poems* appeared in 1957; this is supplemented by *The Outcasts* (1962).

*

RUPERT BROOKE (1887–1915), a dazzlingly good-looking young man who held Henry James (he 'took for *his* own the whole of the poetic consciousness he was born to, and moved about in it as a stripped young swimmer. . . . Rupert expressed us *all*. . . .') as well as Edward Marsh spellbound, was in many ways the epitome of Georgianism. But he is best treated as a war-, or rather a 'pre-war-', poet, because here he provides the clearest example of the limitations of Georgianism. He wrote some pleasant (and graceful) light verse, but was not a good poet and could never have been one. His rebelliousness is schoolboy—his father was a master at Rugby School, which he attended and apparently enjoyed; nothing he wrote is ever in bad taste, nothing is profound. The excitement he caused in his male contemporaries was largely sentimental and homosexual in origin, although he himself was heterosexual. Because of his energy, his skill and his accomplishment, he seemed more original to his contemporaries than he actually was. Had he not died of blood-poisoning (at Skyros) while on his way to Gallipoli he would not have continued to write verse—his proficiency at it was but one of his accomplishments: there is no pressure behind his work—but would have become a publisher, or, most likely, a moderately reformist politician and then a peer. His famous sonnet 'The Soldier' sums up a mood that was almost universal among young people in the autumn of 1914; one can hardly blame Brooke himself for it. But it is bad poetry: under the guise of specious patriotism the poet celebrates a

racial and therefore personal superiority ('a richer dust') that he has
in no sense earned: God ('the eternal mind') is coolly equated with all
things English. Now Brooke could hardly have known what the First
World War was going to be like; but this sonnet is none the less non-
poetry, a piece of inadequate traditionalism that sets out to supply
what its public desires. It is still better known and more widely read
than any single poem by any of the genuine poets of the First World
War. Brooke's fundamental unoriginality is shown in one of his better
poems, 'Dust': this, we realize, is all he can do with the new and
exciting influence of Donne: all that comes through is a self-
consciously bluff, 'young' tone.

The first poet—and an incomparably more important one than
Brooke—to realize the true nature of war in this century was CHARLES
HAMILTON SORLEY (1895–1915), killed before he had time to develop
his remarkable poetic gifts. His *Letters* (1919) are, for their time,
extraordinary: they anticipate attitudes not taken up until after his
death. In one of them he condemns Brooke for his 'fine words' and
sentimentality. 'There is no such thing as a just war', he wrote:
'England—I am sick of the sound of the word. In training to fight
for England, I am training to fight for that deliberate hypocrisy, that
terrible middle-class sloth of outlook . . . after the war all brave men
will renounce their country and confess that they are strangers and
pilgrims on the earth'. Before writing this he had diagnosed the
hypocrisy underlying the British public school system (he experienced
it at Marlborough); there is enough here to make it clear that the
loss to English literature and life occasioned by his death is incalcul-
able. His poetry is, for the most part, no more than immensely
promising. But its eloquence, studiedly unrhetorical, already points
to an astonishing integrity of purpose.

ISAAC ROSENBERG (1890–1918), a Bristol Jew who began as an art-
student, is not often given his due. The usual verdict is 'greater in
promise than achievement'. His *Collected Works* (1949) suggests that
this is an unfair verdict. He is patronized for his 'imperfect education', but this did not in fact 'obscure his genius' any more than the
more 'perfect' education of other aspiring poets illumined theirs. . . .
On the whole critics have failed to understand that his poems, far
from being 'unfinished', are rhythmically original—and they have
failed to recognize the intense Jewishness that underlies everything
he wrote. Sorley (who was not twenty-one when he died) apart,
Rosenberg was the most naturally gifted of all those who fell in the
First World War: although of course war drew poetry from him (he
suffered greatly at the front, as his health was poor: he was not in
fact medically fit for service), it was not a decisive factor—as it was

in the case of Owen. There is a complexity (sometimes wrongly referred to as 'verbal awkwardness') in Rosenberg's poetry that is absent from that of any of his contemporaries. Siegfried Sassoon saw it as a fusion of British and Hebrew culture, 'a strenuous effort for impassioned expression . . . he saw things in terms of sculpture . . . a poet of movement. . . . Words which express movement . . . are essential to his natural utterance'. The most substantial and sensitive critical account of him so far is in C. H. Sisson's (q.v.) *English Poetry 1900–1950* (1971).

'Expression' illustrates the intensity of Rosenberg's poetic awareness—and his courage in not limiting the complex sense of what he is trying to say:

> Call—call—and bruise the air:
> Shatter dumb space!
> Yea! We will fling this passion
>   everywhere;
> Leaving no place
>
> For the superb and grave
> Magnificent throng,
> The pregnant queens of quietness
>   that brave
> And edge our song
>
> Of wonder at the light
> (Our life-leased home),
> Of greeting to our housemates.
>   And in might
> Our song shall roam
>
> Life's heat, a blossoming fire
> Blown bright by thought,
> While gleams and fades the infinite
>   desire,
> Phantasmed naught.
>
> Can this be caught and caged?
> Wings can be clipt
> Of eagles, the sun's gaudy measure
>   gauged,
> But no sense dipt
>
> In the mystery of sense.
> The troubled throng

Of words break out like smothered
fire through dense
And smouldering wrong.

The 'wit' (in the metaphysical sense) of this poem works: here—in a poem written in 1914 or 1915, before Rosenberg enlisted—is 'modern' writing apparently arising from nowhere. Actually Rosenberg sensed the 'seventeenth-century' aspirations in the poetry of the intelligent Lascelles Abercrombie (q.v.)—one is tempted to say that he admired it because of what it tried to do rather than for what it did—and put these to work. . . . Rosenberg's view of the war that destroyed him was extraordinarily objective and comprehensive (more so than Owen's): he realized that the hideous destructiveness of 'shrieking iron and flame/Hurled through still heavens' nevertheless called forth, from men, what D. W. Harding (one of Rosenberg's editors) calls 'a simplified greatness which they could never have reached before'. Rosenberg is quite as 'modern' as Eliot; but he has more experience—and much more to say. The neglect in which he has been held is puzzling; probably the main reason for it lies in the difficulties his poems present. He is unique in English-language poetry inasmuch as, like Vallejo (q.v. 3), he passionately seeks to turn his poems into actual *things*, spells; too often this differentness has been dismissed as 'immaturity'. For the ex-painter Rosenberg, however—he did not finally decide to devote himself solely to poetry until 1915, when he was staying with a married sister in Capetown, South Africa—words had a magical value: they existed for him, as they do for some contemporary writers in Spanish, as the actual mysterious doubles of the things or qualities they denote (cf. Asturias, q.v. 3). He sees, in 'On Receiving News of the War' (1914), the ill tidings as 'Snow', 'a strange white word'. In 'Dead Man's Dump' a 'choked soul stretched weak hands/To reach the living word'; the dead lie in 'great sunk silences'. Rosenberg's poetry only requires close attention to be more widely recognized as the greatest to come from any soldier poet in this century. No contemporary English-language poet has had greater potentiality.

WILFRED OWEN (1893–1918), who was killed only a week before the Armistice, was unknown to the public in his lifetime; he saw only four of his poems in print. Owen was the son of a Shropshire railway clerk. The account of him by his brother HAROLD OWEN (1897–1972) in his memoirs, *Journey From Obscurity* (1963–5)—itself a masterpiece of reluctant, doggedly honest self-revelation—suggests that he was in many ways a prissy and self-absorbed youth. His earliest poems are

Keatsian exercises—without anything very special about them. His parents could not afford to keep him at London University, where he matriculated in 1910; instead he was forced to take up a post as assistant to a vicar; he was supposed to decide whether to take orders. This exposure to the Church itself led him to a mental crisis: naturally enough, he lost the simple Christian faith of his childhood. Between 1913 and 1915, when he enlisted, he was a private tutor near Bordeaux. In September 1914 he wrote from France to his brother Harold (Owen's *Collected Letters* appeared in 1967) about a visit he had made, in the company of a doctor, to a hospital where some of the earliest casualties of the war were being cared for. Considering that Owen was the man who, less than four years later, was prepared to sacrifice the poetry ('Above all I am not concerned with Poetry' he wrote in the famous preface he drafted to a future volume) for the pity ('The Poetry is in the pity'), this is an odd letter: ostensibly written to 'educate' Harold 'to the actualities of war', it gives a clinical account, with illustrations, of the wounded. 'I was not much upset', Owen told his brother. But nearly all the poems of pity by which he is now remembered were written in the last eighteen months of his life.

Now that we have Owen's letters and his brother's remarkable reminiscences we are able to see more clearly that his rather frozen and forbidding manner as a young man arose largely from sexual confusions. Joseph Cohen has shown in his *Owen Agonistes* (1967) that Owen was in fact a passive homosexual and what he aptly calls an 'injustice collector'. It seems that he fully discovered this fact about himself when he was in hospital in Craiglockhart after his first spell of active service (1916–17). While there he met Siegfried Sassoon—who was also a homosexual; one letter to Sassoon settles the matter beyond dispute. (There is, furthermore, a fairly well-founded suggestion that he was buggered by C. K. Scott-Moncrieff, the translator of Proust.) All that we know about Owen tends to support this view: there is sometimes a certain morbidity in him which, despite the indignation and the anger which undoubtedly seared him, is not even, perhaps, primarily compassionate. This is particularly apparent in 'The Show', whose subject is not only the 'pity of war' but also an undiagnosed sickness in Owen's mind:

> My soul looked down from a vague height with Death,
> As unremembering how I rose or why,
> And saw a sad land, weak with sweats of dearth,
> Gray, cratered like the moon with hollow woe,
> And fitted with great pocks and scabs of plagues.

Across its beard, that horror of harsh wire,
There moved thin caterpillars, slowly uncoiled.
It seemed they pushed themselves to be as plugs
Of ditches, where they writhed and shrivelled, killed.

By them had slimy paths been trailed and scraped
Round myriad warts that might be little hills.
From gloom's last dregs these long-strung creatures crept,
And vanished out of dawn down hidden holes.

(And smell came up from those foul openings
As out of mouths, or deep wounds deepening.)

On dithering feet upgathered, more and more,
Brown strings towards strings of gray, with bristling spines,
All migrants from green fields, intent on mire.
Those that were gray, of more abundant spawns,
Ramped on the rest and ate them and were eaten.
I saw their bitten backs curve, loop, and straighten,
I watched those agonies curl, lift, and flatten.

Whereat, in terror what that sight might mean,
I reeled and shivered earthward like a feather.
And Death fell with me, like a deepening moan.
And He, picking a manner of worm, which half had hid
Its bruises in the earth, but crawled no further,
Showed me its feet, the feet of many men,
And the fresh-severed head of it, my head.

This is one of Owen's most powerful and self-revealing poems: often he himself remains curiously uninvolved in the 'pity' he describes—it is a legitimate criticism of the body of his later anti-war poems—but here he is a part of the horrible murder-process he is describing. Almost all of the anti-war poems are of course effective and deeply moving. However, we have, I think, to look again at Vallejo's (q.v.) poetry to see clearly that in Owen there is something morbid— something that actually *enjoys* the suffering that is being described, something nearly self-indulgent. (This is to judge by the high standards that the poems demand.) Further, the poems do not altogether avoid a note of personal resentment: 'Miners' ('. . . they will not dream of us poor lads/Lost in the ground') does read like the poem of an injustice collector: it has that note. Sassoon was wrong when he said 'he did not pity himself'; had he said it of Rosenberg he would have been nearer the mark. There is a sullen, homosexually oriented resentment of women that, every so often, surfaces in the poems ('all women, without exception, *annoy* me', he wrote in 1914).

But this is only to redress a balance: Owen has long been slightly overrated, Rosenberg miserably underrated. Owen at his best is a poet of great power, who discovered, in his complex response to the war, new poetic procedures that were to influence the next generation of poets. His experiments with half-rhyme and what Edmund Blunden called 'para-rhyme'—most effective in the famous 'Strange Meeting', where he meets the man he has killed—were extensive and intelligent. His blend of irony and pity, too, was new in English poetry.

SIEGFRIED SASSOON (1886–1967) was the most satirical of the war poets. He had started (in his anonymous *Poems*, 1906, *Hyacinth*, 1912, and other collections of pre-war poetry) as a fairly conventional post-Pre-Raphaelite; his originality first made itself evident, not in his war poems of *The Old Huntsman* (1917) and *Counter-Attack* (1918), but in *The Daffodil Murderer* (1913), published under the pseudonym of Saul Kain: this was intended as a parody of Masefield's *The Everlasting Mercy* (q.v.), but it ended as a serious poem. Sassoon's attitude to the war was at first orthodox ('war has made us wise/And, fighting for our freedom, we are free'); experience of it soon changed this, and he became perhaps the most savage satirist of war that has ever been known. A captain in the Royal Welch Fusiliers, he was a close friend of Robert Graves (who held the same rank in the same regiment) and, later, in hospital at Craiglockhart, of Wilfred Owen —upon whom he exercised a decisive influence both sexually and poetically. *The Daffodil Murderer* (which Sassoon never made re-available) revealed what can only be described as a strange inner twistedness: a kind of half-crazy, delirious, pathic decadence, mixed in with strong feelings of guilt, lyrical compassion (expressed in the famous 'Everyone Sang') and whatever love for the 'wholesome', aristocratic, distracting 'sport' of fox-hunting represents. . . . Sassoon never succeeded in resolving his problems; but the horrors of war— which turned him into a lifelong pacifist—brought out in him a (valid) satirical ferocity and power: paradoxically, he found a kind of spiritual peace in the hellish sufferings of war. The war poems are crude and even uncontrolled, but in that lies their power: as D. J. Enright has written, they are 'so clearly written out of honest rage and decent indignation'. It took war, however, to push him into this kind of honesty and decency. His only effective poetry between the end of the First World War and his death is satirical; most of it is in the short sequence called *The Road to Ruin* (1933). During and after the Second World War he reverted to facile patriotism—a kind of 'dash . . . of Winston Churchill in an ocean of water' (D. J. Enright). He ended in the Roman Catholic Church (he entered it at 70). His many volumes of fictionalized autobiography, such as *The Complete Memoirs of George Sherston* (1937) and *Siegfried's Journey* (1945) have been much admired; *The Old Century and Seven More Years* (1938) is the least contrived, the most lucid and touching and informative, of these. But for the essence of Sassoon, a good minor satirical poet, one must go back to those angry poems of the war which he so hated and in which he fought with such courage.

Although he saw longer service and was badly wounded, the war did not prompt such powerful work from ROBERT GRAVES (1895), who matured considerably later. His poetry may, allowing for anticipation and regressions, be divided into four main phases: from his schoolboy beginnings in 1906 until his discovery of the poetry of the American poet Laura Riding (q.v.) in 1926; the duration of his literary and personal association with her (1926–39); the period of his war-time sojourn in a South Devon farmhouse and of the first years of his return to Mallorca (1939–56); and what may be called the years in which he has emerged into world fame. The two main events in his poetic life have been the impact upon him of four years' trench warfare in the First World War, and his response to the poetry and personality of Laura Riding. While the effect of Graves' war experiences has been adequately appreciated by his critics, the influence of Laura Riding has been very seriously underestimated—owing, one feels, to failure to understand her poetry.

Graves' faith in the poem he has to write—although not attended by careless arrogance about his capacities to write it—has been as great as that of any English poet, perhaps greater. In this sense the poem, for Graves, is a thing outside himself, a task of truth-telling—and not a thing to be invented or 'composed'. Poem-writing is a matter of absolute truthfulness to the mood of self-revelation. Graves is not the kind of craftsman who invents shapes in stone, to his own desires; but one who seeks, by means of intuition, to discover the exact shape in the middle of the stone, in which he has absolute faith.

If one of the signs of a major as distinct from a minor poet is development, then Graves is certainly a major poet. Yet his technical experiments have always been within the limits of tradition. As a schoolboy he worked on hosts of complicated rhyme-schemes and verse-forms, including the Welsh *englyn*, as well as with assonance and dissonance. For his subject-matter he drew on the worlds of chivalry, romance and nursery rhyme. Much of his technical facility and his capacity to use folk-themes without parodying them he owed to his father, ALFRED PERCEVAL GRAVES (1846–1931), himself a graceful minor Irish poet.

Graves has rejected not only nearly all his war poetry but also much of his immediately post-war poetry, written under the twin (and opposing) influences of war-trauma and pastoral marriage. This is technically accomplished, charming, and with an underlying complexity that is by no means as typically Georgian as its surface. Graves was at this time working—under the influence of W. H. R. Rivers, the anthropologist—on the Freudian theory that poetry was therapeutic, a view he largely abandoned in the later Twenties.

Little of the poetry of Graves' first period has been preserved in his *Collected Poems*; but its main positive features—delight in nonsense, preoccupation with terror, the nature of his love for women—have survived into his later poetry. What was purged was softness and cloying over-sweetness. Yet it was not Laura Riding's procedures that influenced him, but the content of her poems—and the personality that went with this. The poems of his maturity are in no sense at all imitations of hers; but her remarkably complicated view of life (and therefore the work in which she expressed this) are relevant to them: he shared, or rather, attempted devotedly to learn, this view, and the material of the poems is his struggle to accommodate himself lovingly to it and to her. The process proved impossible in the end, as he foresaw in 'Sick Love', written in the late Twenties: 'O Love, be fed with apples while you may', this begins; and it ends,

> Take your delight in momentariness,
> Walk between dark and dark—a shining space
> With the grave's narrowness, though not its peace.

The poems Graves wrote in his second period record, with great directness and in a diction of deliberate hardness and strength, the nerve-strains of impossible love ('To the galleys, thief, and sweat your soul out', one begins) and his attempt to achieve an existence that accorded with the goodness that Graves and (at that time) Laura Riding saw as residing in poetry above every other human activity. These are therefore 'existential' poems, and to be understood they must be read in this way: they are at once an account of the condition of romanticized devotedness, of a search for perfection (always tempered with ironic realism and earthy masculine robustness) and of human failures. Poems such as 'The Legs' describe the distractions that Graves saw as tempting him from the concentration his single-minded quest for poetic wisdom required. His 'historical grammar of poetic myth', *The White Goddess* (1947 rev. 1952), is essentially a generalization from his experiences of these years of devoted struggle to serve a savagely demanding muse, whom in 'On Portents' he had seen as a vast propeller, a 'bladed mind' strongly pulling through the 'ever-reluctant element' of Time. These poems, by which—together with those of the succeeding phase—Graves will probably be chiefly remembered, provide what will almost certainly become the classic latter-day record of romantic love; this is so not least because of their unsentimentality, their tough and unidealistic acceptance of the author's strong masculine recalcitrance. Thus, his mood changes from confidence—

> We tell no lies now, at last cannot be
> The rogues we were—so evilly linked in sense
> With what we scrutinized that lion or tiger
> Could leap from every copse, strike and devour us.

to zestful gloom—

> Yet why does she
> Come never as longed-for beauty
> Slender and cool, with limbs lovely to see . . . ?

As he wrote in 1965, 'My theme was always the practical impossibility, transcended only by miracle, of absolute love continuing between man and woman.' It is the tension between 'practical impossibility' and 'miracle' that gives Graves' poetry its power.

The poems of Graves' third phase, written when he had abandoned his prodigious enterprise of creating—with Laura Riding—an existence in which poetry and what it represents would be a natural way of life—reflect upon the meaning of his experience:

> her image
> Warped in the weather, turned beldamish.
> Then back came winter on me at a bound,
> The pallid sky heaved with a moon-quake.
>
> Dangerous had it been with love-notes
> To serenade Queen Famine. . .

They also discover new love, in some of the most beautiful love lyrics in English:

> Have you not read
> The words in my head,
> And I made part
> Of your own heart?

Finally, they humorously state his position and accept that fame has caught up with him, as in 'From the Embassy', where he refers to himself as 'ambassador of Otherwhere/To the unfederated States of Here and There'.

The poetry of Graves' most recent phase lacks the tension of the earlier work. It owes a good deal to the Sufist ideas by which Graves has been influenced in recent years; it discovers, but not wholly convincingly, the peaceful figure of the Black Goddess who lies behind the crueller one of the White Goddess. Love, to Graves in these new poems, walks 'on a knife edge between two different fates': one fate is to consort with the White Goddess, and is physical; the other, more difficult yet more rewarding, is to find peace in the domains of the Black Goddess. Frequently the poems are so lapidary as to remind the reader of Landor; but they reach a greater power than Landor usually achieved when they envisage the hell of a world made dead by a too great reliance upon physical passion. Of one who is trapped in this hell, who in departing too casually has said, 'I will write', he says in a poem of the same title:

> Long letters written and mailed in her own head—
> There are no mails in a city of the dead.

These late poems provide, in their explorations of the possibilities of a world purged of what he calls 'the blood sports of desire', and of the agonies of alienation from such a world, a fitting sequel to those of his earlier years. He will be, perhaps, the last romantic poet to operate within traditional limits. His mastery of these is not in question.

Graves has also written some important prose. The best of his many historical novels are the two Claudius books: *I, Claudius* (1934) and *Claudius the God* (1934), *Wife to Mr. Milton* (1943)—an account of the first marriage that has been called 'distorted', but never on evidence—and *The Golden Fleece* (1944). His autobiography, *Good-bye to all That* (1929) is rightly regarded as a classic. *The Nazarene Gospel Restored* (1953), which he wrote in collaboration with Joshua Podro, is a remarkable reconstruction of the Gospel story; it was damned out of hand by orthodox theologians, but has gained wide currency —and was highly praised by Reinhold Niebuhr.

For EDMUND BLUNDEN (1896) too, the war (in which he was gassed) was a devastating experience; but for the most part he reacted to it in a very different way: in a pastoral, although gnarled and highly original poetry. Blunden, a self-effacing and modest man, has been a useful although not a trenchant critic—he has been absurdly although touchingly over-generous to his contemporaries; carrying on where Norman Gale and Arthur Symons left off, he became the pioneer of the major eighteenth-century poet John Clare; *Undertones of War* (1928), though somewhat archly written, is one of the better prose books to come out of the First World War.

Nearly all Blunden's best poetry was written between about 1914 and 1929; it may be found in *The Poems of Edmund Blunden 1914–1930* (1930); the most substantial later collection is *Poems of Many Years* (1957), which is supplemented by *A Hong Kong House* (1961). The best of the poems, with a very few notable exceptions such as 'Report on Experience', come into the category perhaps unfortunately called 'nature poetry'. Blunden's poems about nature combine accuracy of observation with an odd (and by no means always 'pleasant', in the sense that this word is understood by devotees of the pastoral and the bucolic) imaginative malice. This is when he is at his best and most disturbing. At other times he is artificial and literary. 'The Midnight Skaters' shows him at his best:

> The hop-poles stand in cones,
>   The icy pond lurks under,
> The pole-tops touch the star-gods' thrones
>   And sound the gulfs of wonder,
> But not the tallest there, 'tis said,
> Could fathom to this pond's black bed.
>
> Then is not Death at watch
>   Within those secret waters?
> What wants he but to catch
>   Earth's heedless sons and daughters,
> With but a crystal parapet.
> Between, he has his engines set.
>
> Then on, blood shouts, on, on,
>   Twirl, wheel and whip above him,
> Dance on this ball-floor thin and wan,
>   Use him as though you love him;
> Court him, elude him, reel and pass,
> And let him hate you through the glass.

Blunden edited a selection of the *Poems* (1954) of his friend, the Gloucestershire man IVOR GURNEY (1890–1937). Gurney, who was a gifted composer of songs as well as a poet, is unaccountably neglected: as a poet he was far superior to, for example, Brooke. Though he survived it, Gurney was really a victim of the war: soon after it was over he became afflicted with mental illness, which resulted in his spending most of the last years of his life in institutions. He published two volumes in his lifetime: *Severn and Somme* (1917) and *War's Embers* (1919); much of his poetry has never been published. It is often painfully inchoate and rambling, reflecting his disturbed mentality; but every so often it flashes into its own unique and passionate life. Gurney's manner, in his best poems, is very far from Georgian.

HERBERT READ (1893–1968), who also fought in the First World War, was unquestionably a great eclectic critic. He was also an influential art critic. Probably his finest creative work is the novel, *The Green Child* (1935). His poetry (*Collected Poems*, 1966) is very seldom as successful as one feels it should have been. He was a man of great sincerity and exquisite sensibility—over-tolerant towards bad art because of his generous assumption that others shared his qualities— but, like Bridges (q.v.), 'just a shade too little of a blackguard'. He was, of course, a stronger poet than Bridges; but he very seldom achieved a manner of his own ('To a Conscript of 1940' is an exception). Ultimately he acknowledged this, quoting Yeats' remark to the effect that 'perfection' is to be found in the 'life' or in the 'work', but not (presumably) in both. However, his acknowledgement of the fundamental problem of *Künstlerschuld* (q.v.) made him into an important creative critic.

*

HUGH MACDIARMID (ps. CHRISTOPHER MURRAY GRIEVE, 1892) is—as he would wish it—unclassifiable. He has been somewhat overrated by Scottish critics, who tend, as David Daiches does—to confuse his extrinsic importance to Scots literature with his intrinsic value as a poet; but he is undoubtedly a figure of stature. Until the Sixties he was unjustly neglected outside his own country; since then there has been a good deal of irrelevant hullabaloo; there is no proper collected poems (the book of that title, 1962, is not nearly what it purports to be; it is only partially supplemented by its successors: a decently edited retrospective collection is badly needed). MacDiarmid's achievement is uneven. His egotism (he can seldom write about anyone else without concentrating upon himself— although he is not ungenerous) and much of his militant communism often seem frustratingly irrelevant to his poetry. His endorsement of the Russian invasion of Czechoslovakia (1968)—'fraternal entry'— as of Hungary twelve years earlier has raised doubts about his decency and, indeed, his historical judgement. But for half a century he has waged war against philistinism and against the tendency of

the vast majority of his fellow Scots to affect an unnatural English-
ness—thus emasculating themselves and undermining their native
genius, of which they are as timidly afraid as a law-clerk ot a cut lily
(to adapt a phrase of Pablo Neruda's, q.v. 3). The strain, accompanied by neglect and hostility, has told: MacDiarmid's external
persona is not wholly attractive: he thinks too much of himself too
solemnly, and his grandiosity is frequently a bore. But it is a natural
enough response to the treatment he has had, and it may easily be
disregarded.

MacDiarmid is the pioneer of, and the most gifted figure in, the
Scottish literary renaissance (which came twenty-five years later
than the Irish); he provided its 'programme . . . focus, and . . .
models' (David Daiches).

MacDiarmid has done more than any other Scottish writer to
develop Lallans, a synthetic language that draws upon Middle Scots,
English and modern local dialects. Lallans has unique vitality in the
right hands; in the hands of inferior poets it is laboured and tedious.
As Daiches has pointed out, Lallans is in fact no more 'synthetic'
than the language of Dunbar or Burns; it has closer links with Anglo-
Saxon than modern English; it preserves English words that English
has lost. . . . Here, in a well-known poem, 'Lourd on my Hert', is
MacDiarmid using it as it should be used:

> Lourd on my hert as winter lies
> The state that Scotland's in the day.
> Spring to the north has aye come slow
> But noo dour winter's like to stay
> > For guid
> > And no for guid.

> O wae's me on the weary days
> When it is scarce grey licht at noon;
> It maun be a' the stupid folk
> Diffusin' their dullness roon and roon
> > Like soot
> > That keeps the sunlicht oot.

> Nae wonder if I think I see
> A lichter shadow than the reist
> I'm fain to cry 'the dawn, the dawn!
> I see it brackin' in the East.'
> > But ah
> > —It's just mair snaw!

MacDiarmid's concern for Scotland is better shown here than in his many cantankerous utterances on the subject. Practically all his best work was done by the mid-Thirties, including the long poem-sequence *A Drunk Man Looks at the Thistle* (1926), a linguistic *tour de force* of immense vitality in which satirical verve exists side by side with self-contemplation. Here Lallans is triumphantly appropriate: it functions as the poet's pure voice. MacDiarmid never reached this level again, although some of his short Scots lyrics are arresting in their freshness and depth of emotion. Much of MacDiarmid's later verse is in English: long poems (such as *In Memoriam James Joyce*, 1955, and 'A Raised Beach') setting forth arguments. Most of this resembles dull prose: MacDiarmid is not impressive as a thinker (there is something distinctly ingenuous about his polymathic enterprises), and he lacks an ear for English rhythms. Intelligent critics speak of 'the cumulative pattern of meaning' (much of this English verse consists of mere catalogues of facts), but this is over-charitable. The claim that MacDiarmid is the best Scottish poet since Burns is a just one; but this is on the strength of his earlier Scots poetry.

Of poets born in the nineteenth century, the most distinguished successor to MacDiarmid was WILLIAM SOUTAR (1898–1943), who was a bedridden invalid for almost a quarter of a century. Soutar's Scots poems (his English are negligible) are narrow in range of subject and feeling, but none the less exquisite in tone, style and execution. His *Collected Poems* appeared posthumously, in 1948; *Poems in Scots and English* (1961) adds more good poems. Soutar's moving and perceptive journal, *Diaries of a Dying Man* (1954), deserves to be better known.

The most eminent Scots poet to use English was EDWIN MUIR (1887–1959), one of the most modest and self-effacing of contemporary writers. Muir, who came from the Orkneys, had a bitter struggle to establish himself: for nearly twenty years he lived a grim and miserable life in Glasgow. His first book, of literary criticism, appeared under the pseudonym of 'E. Moore' in 1918, when he was already past thirty. Muir and his wife Willa Muir made many translations from contemporary German writers; the most important were from Kafka (q.v.). Muir was one of the best critics of his time (the book-reviewing he did towards the end of his life is his least important criticism: the best is in *The Structure of the Novel*, 1928, comparable in importance to Lubbock's *The Craft of Fiction* and Forster's *Aspects of the Novel*). His three novels—*The Marionette* (1927), *The Three Brothers* (1931) and *Poor Tom* (1932)—are of a high standard as well as being important guides to the nature of his complex sensibility. Muir's unambitious and diffident nature gives his poetry a unique quality;

unfortunately these qualities were also responsible for his too frequent lack of linguistic distinctiveness and energy. He could rarely develop a rhythm of his own: his poetry, traditional in form, relies too much on metrical norms; he often evades, one might say, the sound of his own voice. And yet he is a remarkably original poet, who avoided both the Scottish and the English traditions. There is nothing of the Georgians and little of Eliot in his work. He took his inspiration from fable and myth, and from his observation of the natural world of animals. He was not a major poet only because he lacked procedures adequate to fully express the combination of the visionary and the metaphysical that characterizes his attitude. And yet he is a rewarding and often beautiful poet, in whom there is no fatal failure in humour (see 'Suburban Idyll'); one is prepared to accept his faintly stilted, strained diction and his awkwardness—arising from the fact that his poetic impulses usually fail, very oddly, to find their complete verbal counterparts: there is little verbal excitement in Muir—because one has such faith in his integrity, sweetness of disposition and wisdom. He is not a sensuous poet—this means that he lacks the force and conviction of a Yeats or a Graves—and he is sometimes given to a kind of too obviously symbolic, abstract writing that lacks experimental reference ('The Actor on the Tree'; 'like the happy doe/That keeps its perfect laws/Between the tiger's paws/And vindicates its cause'), but his best poems, such as 'The Horses', have their own substance. Muir's first book of poetry appeared in 1925; the definitive *Collected Poems* was published in 1965. His *An Autobiography* (1954; originally *The Story and the Fable*, 1940) is deservedly a classic.

*

Two women poets born in the Nineties stand out above others: RUTH PITTER (1897) and SYLVIA TOWNSEND WARNER (1893). The latter is a distinguished novelist, and her fiction is mentioned elsewhere; but her poetry has been unduly and strangely neglected. Ruth Pitter is less resourceful and usually less interesting linguistically, but she is a graceful craftsman. and her quiet manner can be attractive. She is one of those rare woman poets who, like Marianne Moore (q.v.), can make a poetic virtue out of an apparently genteel and orthodox respectability. Often her themes are Christian; her gentle optimism functions pleasantly, as a kind of innocence. She has just a handful of truly distinguished and original poems which, beneath an unruffled surface, combine pastoral charm with emotional vitality. 'Time's Fool' ends with lucidity and serenity:

I knew that the roots were creeping under the floor,
That the toad was safe in his hole, the poor cat by the fire,
The starling snug in the roof, each slept in his place:
The lily in splendour, the vine in her grace,
The fox in the forest, all had their desire,
As then I had mine, in the place that was happy and poor.

Sylvia Townsend Warner is a musician learned in the church
music of the fourteenth, fifteenth and sixteenth centuries. Her prose
achieves what T. F. Powys (q.v.)—an admirer—tried but so seldom
succeeded in achieving. Her poetry only needs to be better known to
be more widely acclaimed. She has never had her due; perhaps this
is because she knows her limitations too well. 'Nellie Trim' is one of
the most effective of modern literary ballads, and conveys an
authentic poetic *frisson* in a way that many more ambitious poems do
not. She has an epigrammatic style, a fine technique, and the
capacity to employ traditional diction without distorting her meaning.
Her best poetry is to be found in longer works, such as *Opus 7* (1931).
But 'Song from the Bride of Smithfield' illustrates her skill and wit:

A thousand guileless sheep have bled,
A thousand bullocks knelt in fear,
To daub my Henry's cheek with red
And round the curl above his ear.

And wounded calves hung up to drip
Have in slow sweats distilled for him
To dew that polishes his lip.
The inward balm that oils each limb.

In vain I spread my maiden arts,
In vain for Henry's love I pine.
He is too skilled in bleeding hearts
To turn this way and pity mine.

Sylvia Townsend Warner's poetry has not been collected; it may be
found in *The Espalier* (1925), *Time Importuned* (1928) and *Whether a
Dove or a Seagull* (1933), half of the poems in which are by her lifelong
friend the late Valentine Ackland.

*

T. S. ELIOT (1888–1965)—who, although loosely associated with the imagists, requires separate treatment—was born in St. Louis, Missouri, and educated at Harvard. After study in Paris and Germany, and a short period as an assistant in the department of philosophy at Harvard, he settled permanently in England. He gained his living as an editorial director of the distinguished publishing firm of Faber and Faber (originally Faber and Gwyer). He married an Englishwoman (who subsequently became insane) in 1915. In 1927 he became an English citizen; it was in the following year that he issued his famous statement (influenced by *Action Française*, q.v. 2) that he was 'Anglo-Catholic in religion . . . classicist in literature, and royalist in politics.' He won the Nobel Prize in 1948. He made a second marriage in the Fifties.

Eliot's enormous extrinsic importance is undoubted. It is so great that Geoffrey Grigson's (q.v.) comparison of him with Cowley, the minor late seventeenth-century poet who in his lifetime was regarded as a major figure, is hardly appropriate: Grigson is certainly correct to draw attention to Eliot's extremely limited intrinsic achievement—but he was very much more influential, and accomplished, than even Cowley.

Eliot poses a formidable problem: the distance between his remarkable critical sensibility and perceptiveness, and his poetic achievement, is so great as at first to seem impossible; furthermore, he possessed the technical accomplishment—if not the rhythmical energy—of a major poet. Eliot was one of the first to see that, as he put it in his tribute to John Davidson (q.v.), it was necessary for a poet to 'free himself completely from the poetic diction of English verse of his time. . . .' Eliot saw this more clearly than any one else of his generation (he owed much to Pound, who established him; but his mind was always clearer than Pound's); he had the capacity to demonstrate it in a practical form—in 'The Love Song of J. Alfred Prufrock' (written while Eliot was at Harvard and published, with other poems, in *Prufrock and Other Observations*, in 1917). This poem, like most of its successors, is full of technical excellencies: the control of tone and the juxtaposition of the literary and the colloquial are perhaps the main ones. At all times Eliot demonstrates a superior intelligence—in fact, when one thinks of the English-language poets who dominated the scene at the time Eliot was actually writing the poem this intelligence is not short of astonishing.

But it is primarily a critical intelligence. 'Prufrock', like the best of its successors, is a minor poem. Eliot is a minor poet: he cannot write about love; he lacks real sympathy, or empathy; he is frigid. . . . Skill, accomplishment, sensibility—even these are not enough to make a major poet. Emotional substance is needed. 'Prufrock' is the best as well as the earliest of Eliot's important poems: it is the only one that tries to deal, fully, with his own problem: with his lack of feeling. That is to say, it states his predicament and it laments it; ultimately it is thin stuff, for all the delicacy of manipulation and the cleverness and the sensitivity. Eliot's use of Laforgue and other French poets is masterly, as is his pastiche of Gozzano (q.v. 3); his importation of French symbolist techniques into English poetry has been valuable; but even as early as 'Prufrock' his procedures tend to function as a substitute for an original poetic impulse. This he never really has. That is why, in later poems, his techique of *montage* becomes poetically reprehensible: the reason for it is that he cannot make his own poetry, and so—with the exquisite sensibility that can so beautifully discern poetry, he uses other people's. It amounts to a splendid and judicious patchwork; but it is critical, anthological—not, in the final analysis, poetic.

The fact is that Eliot, although extremely sophisticated in literary matters, was sexually and poetically naïve to a quite extraordinary degree. His inability to write about love is illustrated by the disastrous 'A Dedication to my Wife', written to his second wife: however touching this may seem in everyday terms, it amounts to a confession of total poetic failure in an area that is surely important. Again, Eliot's political position—although not 'fascist' as has often been urged—is simply naïve, insensitive and humanly ignorant. The celebrated disdainful contempt for humanity that emerges in Eliot's plays, particularly in the final comedies (*The Cocktail Party*, 1950; *The Confidential Clerk*, 1954; *The Elder Statesman*, 1959), is not the product of suffering or bitterness, but of a near-giggling frigidity and an ultra-conservative insensitivity. The crucifixion, on an ant hill, of his character Celia—in *The Cocktail Party*—is the supreme, atrocious example of this element in his attitude: of his failure to see ideas in terms of their human results. His attitude was not 'fascist', but it was insensitive; thus he could subscribe, at the end of his life, to a lunatic-fringe right-wing newspaper (now happily out of business, its owner bankrupted). Eliot's notion of the England he adopted as his own country was as simplistic as that of one of its military servants in the last century, and it had less justification. The contrast between that fantasy and his literary judgement—when this operated freely and autonomously—is extraordinary.

The Waste Land (1922) coincided with a universal mood of disillusion and despair. Its near-nihilism is more dignified than that of the icy and sneering little commercial verse-comedies of the Fifties —for in the early Twenties Eliot had no sustaining orthodoxy to cling to. The notion that *The Waste Land* is a unity, however, is incorrect: it is a ragbag of satirical and pseudo-lyrical and sensitively dramatic pieces, all on the general theme of present decay and past beauty. The satirical feeling is poetic, but the carpentry is obtrusive—and already the positive element, the beauty of the past, is factitiously presented, and is unconvincing. The sense of present degradation is well conveyed; there are scenes of genuine comedy; but the non-satirical sections (especially at the end) are pretentious. As a satirical poem—or, rather, a series of satirical poems—*The Waste Land* is successful. As a poem it fails: all traces of the experience that prompted it have been carefully removed. The critic John Peter implied, in an essay that was withdrawn (out of courtesy) when Eliot's solicitors threatened to take action, that it is (in part) an elegy for a young man who was killed at Gallipoli. . . . Whether this is so or not, there is little doubt that, at a personal level, it examined the problems of 'the waist land'; the fact of sexual as well as spiritual loss and frustration.

Eliot's poetry after his conversion to the Anglican religion becomes empty. E. M. Forster, writing in 1929, put his finger on the reasons for this conversion: 'if it [religious emotion] exists [in Eliot's books], it cannot be relegated. He has not got it; what he seeks is not revelation, but stability . . . . Most writers . . . ask the reader in, to co-operate or to look. . . . Mr. Eliot does not want us in. He feels we shall increase the barrenness. . . . He is difficult because he has seen something terrible, and (underestimating . . . the general decency of his audience) has declined to say so plainly'. Eliot saw not one but two 'terrible' things: he saw not only the repellently commerical and mechanized nature of modern life—but also the arid nature of his own heart. The *Four Quartets* (1936–42) consist of theological and philosophical abstractions piled up on one another in a skilful and sometimes entrancing manner; but they represent an evasion of experience, a failure to examine an incapacity for experience. For all the many ambitious exegeses that have been made of them, it is safe to predict that they will not survive as major poetry.

Eliot, then, is a vitally important influence; but the enormous edifice of his authority stands on a pin-point of actual poetic achievement. It remains to say that in his public life he was courteous, scrupulous, modest and generous.

III

The drama in Great Britain in the Nineties was in just such an attenuated and totally exhausted state as it was in Europe. Although Ibsen (q.v. 2) had been known to a devoted few since about 1880, London audiences refused to accept him. He did not pay. Oscar Wilde's comedies, particularly *The Importance of Being Ernest* (1895), represented the very best that could be commercially viable. ARTHUR WING PINERO (1855–1934), of Portuguese-Jewish ancestry, represents the best of the popular theatre outside Wilde and Shaw. Like many playwrights Pinero began as an actor (with Irving's company); his many plays show a mastery of the technical side of the theatre. He made his reputation with *The Second Mrs Tanqueray* (1894), a social tragedy which still plays entertainingly. Pinero manipulated his characters; they do not develop; they are two-dimensional. But he lacked the innate vulgarity of his German contemporary Sudermann (q.v. 2), and within his limitations he is an effective, extraordinarily skilful and sometimes witty dramatist.

GEORGE BERNARD SHAW (1856–1950) is a part of history; he made the world of his intellectual or enlightened contemporaries a more lively place; he was a skilful technician; he was an on the whole humane and generous man; he had a most engaging personality. But he was a superficial thinker and a third-rate creative writer. His career as a whole is a monument to the failure of reason alone to solve human problems. His importance in the history of the theatre, as an Ibsenite revolutionary, has been exaggerated. Shaw is an excellent dramatist of ideas; few can go to the theatre and fail— in the theatre itself—to respond to the lively entertainment he usually offers. He is a man of almost infinite theatrical skill. But his drama is not literature, and his characters are not alive—actually they don't even pretend to be so. His portraits of real creative writers (the 'poet' Marchbanks in *Candida*, 1894, is the chief one) show no understanding whatever of the creative process or the creative character: they are, in fact, hopelessly conventional. Shaw was brilliant and he was lucid; but he entirely misunderstood the nature of the imagination. He thought himself to be in the tradition of Molière, and was seriously disturbed because no one would agree with his own estimate of himself as superior to Shakespeare. His attempt to write an imaginative, a 'great', play, which deals with emotion, is *St. Joan* (1924): when it tries to be moving it is execrable—as embarrassingly false as the 'passion' expressed in his letters to the actress Mrs. Patrick Campbell (published in their *Correspondence*, 1952). Shaw's lack of emotion, which was not accompanied by any sort of unkindness, enabled him to be acute on occasions, as well as obtuse (as in his failure to see anything wrong with Mussolini's 'castor oil treatment' of his political opponents, or his sentimental worship of 'great' men). Shaw undoubtedly belongs to the history of the theatre; his place in literature, however, is a very minor one. One may say, indeed, that the place of the 'drama of ideas' itself—when it is no more than that —in literature is a very minor one. Given the audiences of today, it has been little more than midcult journalism. Shaw won the Nobel Prize in 1925.

In attacking the complacency of the Nineties theatrical audience —*The Quintessence of Ibsenism* (1891)—Shaw concentrated on the reforming, didactic element in Ibsen, entirely ignoring the imaginative; his own plays, while full of outrageous (rather than genuinely vital) dialogue were structurally conventional. With his long and elaborate stage directions he helped to create the anti-linguistic, 'director's' theatre that still dominates the English and American stages, and stifles real drama. He did help to initiate a theatre with more life in it; but as is now generally recognized, it was in no sense really new.

The most important and enduring work of HARLEY GRANVILLE-BARKER (1877–1946) is contained in his *Prefaces to Shakespeare* (5 volumes, 1958); but, a man of quite exceptional intelligence, he was also a more than competent playwright. Long a protegé of Shaw's, he was one of the earliest pioneers for the British National Theatre—which has still not actually been built. In 1911 he published his 'paraphrase' of Schnitzler's *Anatol* (q.v.). He also translated plays by Romains (q.v. 2) and the Quintero Brothers (q.v. 3). His best plays, *The Voysey Inheritance* and *Waste* (published, with *The Madras House*, as *Three Plays*, 1909), are reminiscent of Galsworthy; but Granville-Barker is better at the creation of character.

The failure of JAMES BARRIE (1860–1937) to fulfil his high potential has most usually been attributed to his over-attachment to his mother. Certainly this played a part in his life and work: his best play and his greatest success, *Peter Pan* (1904), about the boy who wouldn't grow up, is clearly related to his maternal problems. But Barrie's unresolved Oedipus complex was by no means as crippling to him as has been supposed; he failed to fulfil his gifts because he wilfully and slyly chose to indulge his sentimentality (and the sadism that went with it)—and he refused to remain in Scotland and become a Scottish instead of a popular British writer. . . It was Edwin Muir who first pointed out that he was really tough, not soft at all; but Beerbohm (q.v.) had hinted at it when he said, a propos of the newly produced *Peter Pan*: '[Barrie's preoccupation with children] forces me to suppose that Mr. Barrie has, after all, to some extent, grown up. For children are the last thing with which a child concerns itself'.

Barrie began as a journalist, then succeeded as a novelist in the 'kailyard' tradition, which exploited Scottish humour and peculiarities in a manner that combined whimsicality, sentimentality and acute observation. His best book was *My Lady Nicotine* (1890), about his journalistic experiences; this is delightful. After that he sank into a cunning utilization of his audiences' most immature and crude instincts: a hard, subtle little Scot almost cynically purveying the cult of the child. *Peter Pan*, like the later *Mary Rose* (1924), is a masterpiece of polymorphous perversity, a Freudian joy-ride whose whole existence furiously denies the efficacy of beastly Freud. . . . It is as irresistible and as horrible as a nasty day-dream.

*

More important than Shaw or anyone operating in England or Scotland was the group of playwrights associated with the Abbey Theatre in Dublin. This came into being in 1903. It gathered its inspiration from a desire to treat Ireland and her problems in an honest manner (the recalcitrance of the censor was thus a negative stimulus) and from the austere style of acting just then initiated in Paris by Antoine (q.v. 2). Because of the cosmopolitan policy of Edward Martyn (1859–1924), Moore's cousin, the Abbey Theatre became more than a mere platform for Irish peasant plays: it looked beyond England, to the continent. Yeats (dealt with here in his capacity as a verse dramatist), George Moore, Colum, Joyce and Æ (qq.v.) were among those who were concerned with the venture; the most gifted playwright of the first period was J. M. SYNGE (1871–1909). Synge trained as a musician, but became interested in literature while in Germany. In Paris he met Yeats, who encouraged him and sent him off to the Aran Islands to express 'a life that has never found expression'. Synge was a naïve (q.v.) writer who never had time to ruin his work with 'thought'. Yeats said to Moore of him: 'Synge has always the better of you, for you have brief but ghastly moments during which you admit the existence of other writers; Synge never has'. And he added that he did not think that Synge 'disliked other writers': 'they did not exist'. And Moore himself spoke (1914) of Synge's strangeness and solitariness; he 'was interested in things rather than ideas'. (Moore also suggested that Yeats 'could not keep himself from putting rouge on Synge's face and touching up his eyebrows'.) What Synge, second only to O'Neill (q.v.) in the English-speaking theatre of this century, gave to an enervated drama was the vitality of non-literary, country people and their speech. But he rejected realism: his greatest play, *The Playboy of the Western World* (1907), is poetic in all but its actual prose form. Synge, even though his greatest achievement lies in the theatre, was primarily a poet. An excellent linguist, he made some fine translations (many of them in prose) from the Gaelic, Hebrew, French, Italian and German (his *Translations* were collected in 1961). In the Aran Islands he spoke Irish and listened to the English that the Irish spoke—the English of which Yeats said: it 'takes its vocabulary from the time of Malory and of the translators of the Bible, but its idiom and vivid metaphor from Irish'. His own poem 'In Kerry' reflects this linguistic experience —and Synge's own fear of death:

> We heard the thrushes by the shore and sea,
> And saw the golden stars' nativity.
> Then round we went the lane by Thomas Flynn,
> Across the church where bones lie out and in;
> And there I asked beneath a lonely cloud
> Of strange delight, with one bird singing loud,
> What change you'd wrought in graveyard, rock and sea,
> To wake this new wild paradise for me. . . .
> Yet knew no more than knew those merry sins
> Had built this stack of thigh-bones, jaws and shins.

Synge died of cancer in 1909 just as he was beginning to achieve fame. His plays deal with and draw their energy from the untamed wildness of Ireland; the greatest, *The Playboy of the Western World*, functions at a number of levels. The language is as fresh as Jacobean English (it is interesting and significant that, like O'Neill, Synge knew better than to employ verse): exuberant, extravagant, tender, beautiful. It is splendidly primitive—its first audiences were profoundly shocked because it cut sharply and neatly across their pseudo-sophisticated gentility and false patriotism—with its roots deep in the true Irish tradition. Its theme, that a man can become what people think of him, anticipates the contemporary drama of Europe rather than that of Ireland or Great Britain. A properly edited *Collected Works*, edited by Robin Skelton, began to appear in 1962. Synge, a truly poetic dramatist, has never really been understood or accepted by the Irish urban audience, to whom he is superior. As a critic has said, 'his plays demand that kind of attention from ear and brain and heart, which appears to have been lost to the English-speaking theatre three centuries ago'. He stands almost alone in a century in which most theatre has belonged to managers and directors.

None of the other Irish playwrights of the first decade of this century (with the exception of Yeats) was of Synge's stature; but many vigorous plays were written. Padraic Colum's *The Saxon Shillin'* (1903) was effective both as nationalist propaganda (it protested the enlistment of Irishmen in the British army) and as drama; his *Thomas Muskerry* (1910), set in a small rural community, recalls both Ibsen (in its social awareness) and Synge (in its language). ISABELLA GREGORY (1852–1932), Lady Gregory, manager of the Abbey, was a graceful minor dramatist whose *The Rising of the Moon* (1907) and *The Gaol Gate* (1908) deserve to survive. LENNOX ROBINSON (1886–1958), who also ran the Abbey Theatre for many years, produced a number of workmanlike realist plays; he lacked Synge's or even Colum's power over language, but he was absolutely faithful to Irish experience. *The Lost Leader* (1918) is about Parnell; his best play, *The White-Headed Boy* (1920), is a shrewd comedy of peasant life. Later, in *Church Street* (1934), he successfully attempted a Pirandellian experiment.

LORD DUNSANY (EDWARD DRAY PLUNKETT, 1878–1957), a somewhat isolated figure, should also be mentioned. Dunsany developed a highly individual style as a writer of fiction as well as of one-act plays. He was educated at Eton and Sandhurst, and saw service with the British army in the Boer War, and the First World War—he had, in fact, a sardonic *persona* as a 'correct', cricketing, Englishman; but, as Ernest Boyd shrewdly pointed out, he failed 'in some slight . . . details to conform exactly to type'. It is easy to see why Dunsany is one of Borges' (q.v.) favourite authors: he is a thoroughgoing fantasist, one of the few who succeeds in this form. As the marvellously perceptive Ford (q.v.) put it, 'Says he: "I am sick of this world. . . . I will build up a world that shall be the unreal world of before the fall of Babylon. . . ." And all [his] effects . . . are got by the methods of sheerest realism'. One need add little more. He was a master of the one-act play and the short story (his verse has dated); one who builds his own worlds, and adventures in them—rather than indulging himself in them. Yeats introduced a *Selection* from his earliest work in 1912; there are a number of collections of the plays and stories.

The next major Irish dramatist to emerge after Synge was SEAN O'CASEY (originally JOHN CASEY, 1880–1964), whose best plays are his first three: *Shadow of a Gunman* (1925), *Juno and the Paycock* (1925) and *The Plough and the Stars* (1926). O'Casey came from the slums of Dublin and educated himself. His three great plays are set against the background of the Irish revolution and civil war. O'Casey, too, rejected that kind of realism of which Yeats had said that it 'cannot become impassioned, that is to say vital, without making somebody gushing and sentimental'. He chose highly melodramatic plots, but these were no more obtrusive than Shakespeare's. O'Casey, in these early plays, was able—as Synge had done before him—to create something that was so intensely Irish as to transcend it. These will continue to be played as long as the theatre lasts; they bring out the best in their audiences. By the time O'Casey arrived, the true genius of the Irish theatre had been almost stifled; but at first the Dublin audience accepted him, if only because his tragedy is screened by an inspired, savage farce. His vision is pessimistic, but tempered by comic irony; in *Juno and the Paycock* the violence and the horror are continuously redeemed by ebullience and vitality. O'Casey's indignation and hatred of priestly bigotry later got the better of him: where once his sense of the comic had operated lovingly and affirmatively, as an organizing and controlling factor, his later work tends to be either frozen into too consciously expressionist modes or merely chaotic (as in the case of his six volumes of autobiography, 1939–54). But in *The Plough and the Stars*, which caused so much anger that he left Ireland for England, O'Casey was still at the height of his powers. No play, even *Juno*, so successfully describes and defines the peculiar tragedy of Ireland—a tragedy that continues into our own times. Of course O'Casey's later plays contain much excellent work. Some critics have even seen *The Silver Tassie* (1929), which is certainly one of the fiercest and most moving anti-war plays ever written, as his finest. And his expressionist experiments, influenced by film techniques, are valuable. But it is a pity that O'Casey's hatred of the capitalist system led him to embrace the *dogma* of communism: the imagination—so far as any dogma is concerned—is a sceptical instrument. Too much of the language of the later plays is factitious; too many of the targets are objects set up by the author simply to indulge his rage. O'Casey began as an eloquent, compassionate and comic diagnostician of the Irish tragedy—of both the beauty and the terror in the Irish soul. He ended as a victim of violence and hatred, sustained only by the lyricism of his sense of justice and love of humanity. He failed (as, after all, even Marx did not) to see that individual members of an oppressive class may be as, or even more, 'human' than individual members of an oppressed class. . . . His plays were collected in four volumes (1949–51); *The Bishop's Bonfire* (1955), *The Drums of Father Ned* (1960) and three shorter plays, collected under the title of *Behind the Green Curtains* (1961), followed.

The only Irish dramatist of real stature since O'Casey is DENIS JOHNSTON (1901), who has been living in America since 1960. Johnston was a co-director of the Gate Theatre (which became a rival of the Abbey when the latter became state subsidized and respectable) for a number of years before joining the British Broadcasting Corporation. He lacks the sheer power and wildness of O'Casey, but has more control and perhaps more intelligence. He is one of the few English-language dramatists who has thoroughly absorbed and understood expressionist (q.v.) techniques. His first two plays are his best: *The Old Lady Says 'No'* and *The Moon in the Yellow River* (published together in 1932 under the latter title, and now included in *Collected Plays*, 1960). The first explores both sides of the myth of Ireland. The second, Johnston's simplest play in terms of technique, contrasts the reality of an independent Ireland with the dream: a German engineer comes to Ireland to supervise an electrical power project. The time is the Twenties, when the Irish had newly won their independence. Johnston, while characteristically refraining from actually making judgements (this is one of his strengths), shows that the impact of technology on a rural society is not a happy one—it must be remembered that when the play was first performed the notion of 'progress' was more respectable among intellectuals than it now is. In 1936 Johnston adapted a play of Ernst Toller's (q.v.) as *Blind Man's Buff*. Johnston has continued to produce highly intelligent plays, including *The Dreaming Dust* (1940), about Swift, and *The Scythe and the Sunset*, which is set in Dublin in 1916.

One more Irish playwright deserves mention. BRENDAN BEHAN (1922–64) was a diabetic alcoholic; the dangerous combination killed him early. He had little skill of any kind, but his enormous energy partly compensated for this. Wilful egocentricity and self-adoration drowned his gift, and before he died he had become a pitiful and tiresome self-publicist; but he produced three memorable works: the plays *The Quare Fella* (1954) and *The Hostage* (1958), and his memoirs, *Borstal Boy* (1958). *The Quare Fella* is a fine, moving, indignant exposure of the villainy of capital punishment and of the cruel hypocrites who believe in and operate it. *The Hostage* is a lively, if formless, depiction of the Dublin underworld. *Borstal Boy*, an account of authoritarian and official infamy and stupidity, is sharp, amoral, objective.

*

Unlike James Barrie (q.v.), JAMES BRIDIE (ps. O. H. MAVOR, 1888–
1951) remained in Scotland: for most of his adult life he practised as
a doctor in his native Glasgow. But his star, once thought to be
rising, fell into the sea with a hissing plop: he simply could not be
serious enough. He could write superb scenes, but he never managed
to produce a single satisfactory play. His weakness springs not only
from lack of imaginative self-confidence but also from a feyness that
archly replaced creative recklessness. Like Shaw, whom he resembles,
Bridie lacks emotional substance and tries to make up for it by
ingenuity. And yet he has enormous energy and inventiveness, and
his best work (*The Anatomist*, 1931; *Jonah and the Whale*, 1932; *The
Black Eye*, 1933; *Dr. Angelus*, 1950) reveals what is best and worst in
the middlebrow Scottish audience—and that is one way of being
superior to it. But he disappointed many serious Scots by his failure
to initiate a revival in the theatre that would match the one begun
by MacDiarmid (q.v.) in poetry.

NOËL COWARD (1899–1973) is middlebrow in all but one respect:
he has never been pretentious. His sophisticated comedies of modern
life (the best are *Hay Fever*, 1925, *Private Lives*, 1930, and *Blithe
Spirit*, 1941) are, within their admittedly—but unashamedly—
extremely narrow limits, accurate, truthful, cynical and funny. He
also has a sentimental, semi-jingoist, 'patriotic' vein (*Cavalcade*, 1932;
This Happy Breed, 1942), which is surprisingly inoffensive: one has
never been asked to take him seriously, and one accepts this as part
of him. His movie *Brief Encounter* (scripted and directed by him) is
rightly considered a cinema classic: this tale of a provincial love-
affair is marred only by a sentimental fifty-second sequence at the
end, and even this is defensible within its context. His books of
autobiography—*Present Indicative* (1937), *Future Indefinite* (1954)—
are well written and shrewd. Coward's fault is brittleness; but when
one considers his work as a whole one is impressed by the tolerance
and decency that—I use the word advisedly—shine through. This is
particularly apparent in the short stories, collected in 1962. Coward
is the most successful of all the non-'profound' writers in the theatre
because he has a generous heart as well as being a professional to his
finger-tips.

FREDERIC LONSDALE (1881–1954), though less gifted, was similarly
professional. His greatest success was *The Last of Mrs. Cheney* (1925),
a clever post-Wildean comedy with a melodramatic plot. He wrote
for the moment. 'He delighted the millions', wrote W. Bridges-
Adams, and 'the party over, his mirror reflects an empty mask'.

Some other successful playwrights who emerged in the pre-1956
(that is, pre-*Look Back in Anger*, q.v.) period are TERENCE RATTIGAN

(1911), an excellent technician, PETER USTINOV (1921) and RODNEY ACKLAND (1908). All of these, and some others, have provided intelligent and skilful fare for London's theatregoers. But their technique, and with it the whole notion of the 'well-made play', have been repudiated by the post-Osborne dramatists.

*

As Eugene O'Neill (q.v.) realized, great drama needs 'great language'—which is usually in verse rather than prose. Has any English-language dramatist of the twentieth century been capable of great language? Only Synge, perhaps. ... Certainly the contemporary attempt to revive verse drama has been an almost unrelieved failure. The most poetic verse play of this century, Hardy's *The Dynasts* (1903–8), was not designed or written for the theatre. There has been no audience for real, contemporary poetry in the English theatre (and there is no sign of one developing). Hardy saw this, and in *The Dynasts* he anticipated the technique of both radio and cinema. It is not free from faults, but it is considerably more profound that its sometimes portentous surface suggests. When one compares it to Bridges' attempts at verse drama ('I spake too roughly, Margaret; I was angry:/I knew not what I said. Margaret, I am sorry. ... My God, oh, if I have killed her! Margaret, Margaret!') one realizes its strengths. *The Dynasts* has not yet been subjected to really intelligent, extensive, critical examination. Its stage directions alone represent a high point of English prose—and once it is realized that no verse at that time could have come much nearer than Hardy's to success in dealing with so comprehensive and vast a theme, the magnitude of his achievement may be grasped. Kenneth Muir's verdict that he writes in a 'strange jargon', an understandable enough response, is not, however, a fair one. This 'jargon' expresses a remarkable complexity of thought.

The century's best verse dramatist in the theatre itself is certainly Yeats. But (and surely this is as significant as O'Neill's conscious eschewal of 'great language' and Hardy's refusal to write for the actual theatre) his finest play, *The Words Upon the Window Pane* (1934), written in the last years of his life, is in prose. ... In the verse play Yeats very nearly, in the words of his compatriot Frank O'Connor, 'made good': he, almost alone, came to understand that no verse play in which the verse is merely ornamental to the action (the fault of, e.g., Fry, q.v.) can be poetic. His very early *The Countess Kathleen* (1891) has some good (minor) poetry in it—but this has no relevance to the action. Later Yeats came to realize that his drama could appeal only to a minority; this minority did not constitute the kind of audience that could have prompted a real revival of poetic drama—but it enabled Yeats to do almost as well as anyone could have done. The best of his verse plays are in one act. He had a good sense of theatre (he learned this while trying to run an actual theatre), but was poor in characterization. However, since most of his plays are on mythological themes, this hardly matters. His plays were collected in 1952.

The history of the verse drama since Yeats is uninspiring. Masefield (his best play is *The Tragedy of Nan*, 1909, which is in dialect) and Binyon made serious efforts, but they have dated. Abercrombie, as already noted, failed as a playwright actually because he chose to write in verse instead of prose. . . . Eliot's verse drama, which lay very near to his heart, was a disastrous affair that would not have attracted attention but for his fame in other fields. When *Murder in the Cathedral* (1935) is stripped of its Christian pretensions it is revealed as an empty, pseudo-liturgical affair, devoid of psychological interest; skilfully executed though it is, it can only be of real interest to churchgoers. *The Family Reunion* (1939) has dated. The comedies of the Fifties have already been mentioned. In his plays Eliot betrayed poetry by trying to make it unobtrusive: his fashionable audiences believed they had been watching drawing-room comedies—and so, as it happens, they had.

GORDON BOTTOMLEY (1874–1948) wrote accomplished verse; but not one of his plays, which include glosses on *Macbeth* and *King Lear*, really hits the mark. He was always devoid of dramatic sense, and as he grew older he tried to turn his plays into rhetorical performances. His verse is better than that of most Georgians, and for this reason one searches in it for something more than mere verbal beauty—but, alas, in vain. His gift consisted of little more than a capacity for concealing clichés.

Auden, Spender and MacNeice (qq.v.) all wrote verse plays during the Thirties. Three of Auden's were written in collaboration with Isherwood (q.v.), who supplied the plots. *The Ascent of F6* (1936) and *On the Frontier* (1938) are no more than lively reflections of fashionable preoccupations; *The Dog Beneath the Skin* (1935) anticipates the later interest in Brecht and in the 'musical'. Verse is not an essential element in any of these. MacNeice made a splendid verse translation of *Agamemnon*, but his original verse play, *Out of the Picture* (1937), is weak. His plays for radio are excellent, but ephemeral. The best of the Thirties verse plays, although it is gravely flawed, is Spender's *Trial of a Judge* (1938): this is more mature than anything comparable of its time, and has at least the virtue of trying to make use of poetry to express an agonizing situation—that of a liberal judge trapped between extremes. The language fails; but the attempt is testimony to Spender's political and critical awareness.

After the Second World War there was a revival of Eliotian 'Christian' drama; some of this was moderately successful in the theatre, but none has survived. Andrew Young's *Nicodemus* (q.v.), written earlier, is superior to all these productions. Then CHRISTO-PHER FRY (1907) burst on the scene. Fry began as an imitator of Eliot, but soon switched to comedy with *A Phoenix too Frequent* (1946) and *The Lady's Not for Burning* (1949). Later he did *Venus Observed* (1950). Soon after this he began to go out of fashion, although he has tried to make several comebacks. Fortunately for himself he was able to earn money writing scripts for Hollywood. Fry's verse is perhaps most clearly defined by the adjective 'non-poetic': his language is inorganic, over-confident, slick, pseudo-effervescent, grovelling for the superficial response of an inattentive audience. His sense of 'wonder' and 'delight' is as meretricious as his sense of character. One feels sorry for him as a victim of fashion (the fickle-ness of the middlebrow audience is one of its chief characteristics)— but on the other hand he has perpetrated an offensive pretentious-ness (thus a newspaper critic once spoke of his 'great hymns to living'): a smug prosiness snuggles cosily at the heart-cavity of the false vivacity: '. . . in the heart/Of all right causes is a cause that cannot lose. . . .' His skill works most effectively in translation, where he is controlled by meanings outside the area of his own self-indul-gent fancy.

*

The English theatrical revolution is usually dated from 8 May 1956, when JOHN OSBORNE'S (1929) play *Look Back in Anger* (1956) was staged. This was certainly an important date in the history of the theatre: theatrical impresarios—who are seldom intelligent in a literary sense—became interested in the work of young authors, and the theatre became more lively: the age of the drawing-room comedy was past. A shrewd journalist and theatrical historian, John Russell Taylor, has claimed that, now, 'there is a hard core of exciting new writing in the theatre'. This is partly justified, although the influence of Osborne's play (which has already begun to date badly) is limited to its effect on the mentality of the people who run the theatre—as Taylor himself remarks, there was no 'School of Osborne'. There were more active good playwrights in 1970 than

there were in 1950. . . . However, Taylor's term 'exciting' should not
be taken to imply that there has been a genuine theatrical revival:
there has not. This would have required an audience, and it could
not take place in the commercial theatre—or under the present star
system. The general improvement of the British theatre in the third
quarter of this century is largely due to the belated influence of
Brecht (q.v. 2)—and of other continental playwrights. The theatre
of an essentially conventional playwright such as ROBERT BOLT
(1924), for example, is probably rather more lively for its cautious
assimilation of Brechtian and other innovations; but Bolt writes for
stars, and never strays over the boundary of the generally acceptable. The other beneficial influence on the new British theatre has
been that of the music hall. N. F. SIMPSON (1919), for example, is too
confidently treated as an absurdist by Martin Esslin in his book *The
Theatre of the Absurd*: he is (as Taylor, again, has pointed out) much
nearer to the wartime radio show *Itma* (*It's That Man Again*) and the
Goons than to Ionesco (q.v. 2). *One Way Pendulum* (1960) is theatrically excellent—'it plays itself', as one experienced member of the
original cast put it—but its nonsense is that of the old variety comic
rather than that of a Lear or a Carroll or a Morgenstern (q.v.). . . .
When Simpson has tried to be allegorical or 'significant' the result
has been disastrous.

Osborne's own progress since *Look Back in Anger* has been disappointing. *Look Back in Anger* was a muddled but passionate play
which caught the muddled and passionate mood of young people in
the Fifties, and provided a younger generation with a portrait of
itself in Jimmy Porter. *Epitaph for George Dillon* (1958), written,
before *Look Back in Anger*, in collaboration with ANTHONY CREIGHTON,
is an even better, more psychologically dense play, about a playwright who decides to sell out. (The situation is the same, Allardyce
Nicoll has discovered, as that of a 1910 farce; he might have added
that it is also an English variation of Renard's *The Sponger*, q.v.2). In
The Entertainer (1957) Osborne's confusions vitiate the play; nor does
he successfully convey the spirit of the old Edwardian music hall
which he so admires. *Luther* (1961) is simply pseudo-Brechtian documentary; the words (mostly Luther's) are effective, but the dramatist's selection of his material is oddly uncreative. *Inadmissible Evidence*
(1965), although admired by some, and certainly the best of
Osborne's plays since 1956, is basically a rehash of *Look Back in
Anger*. At his best Osborne is, in Raymond Williams' words, 'uncontrolled, unresolved but directly powerful'. A major playwright
needs more than that. When Osborne takes control he becomes a
writer of (perfectly good) commercial documentary; and he loses

power. The worst of his faults is his inability to rid himself of trivial obsessions.

JOHN ARDEN (1930) is more original than Osborne, but has not achieved comparable commercial success. Arden uses verse in parts of some of his plays, but this is not poetic—or, I think, intended to be so. Arden, though himself what would be described in newspapers as a 'radical', used not to write 'committed' plays. In fact it is this that upset his audiences, who expected him to take sides. Actually he is an individualist, a man more in love with vigour of personality and vitality than with morality. He has more control over language than Osborne, and more complexity. His first substantial play, *Serjeant Musgrave's Dance* (1959), met with a fairly hostile reception because, although 'about' pacifism, it had no comforting message. It showed instead a man of semi-pathological personality spear-heading a confused pacifist movement in a provincial town in the North of England. This is 'about' Arden's own confusions, and it resolves them in human terms: Serjeant Musgrave, the central figure, is as splendidly puzzling as Brecht's Mother Courage (q.v.), with whom he has often been compared. The language is the richest in the modern British theatre. It ran for twenty-eight performances, but was later presented as a television play. *The Workhouse Donkey* (1963) is a comedy: a caricature of local politics in a northern town. *Armstrong's Last Goodnight* (1964), set in sixteenth-century Scotland, fails because Arden has invented an unsuccessful and pointless equivalent for the Scottish speech of the time; but in other respects it is an impressive and subtle play. Since then he has tried to write 'committed' plays, and these have been disastrous.

Few approach the level of seriousness once achieved by John Arden, although there are many skilful dramatists who can put together effective theatre pieces. HAROLD PINTER (1930), a Jewish actor from the East End, continues to write brilliantly original plays. Pinter is an ironic super-realist whose first three plays hold up a mirror to nature—to life as she is really lived—with a quite remarkably artful artlessness. When asked what his work was about he replied: 'The weasel under the cocktail cabinet': in 'real life' there are weasels under cocktail cabinets; but not in fiction. . . . Again, the oddness of Pinter's dialogue is simply that it reproduces everyday speech—which, in dramatic contexts, seems very odd indeed. The 'Kafkaesque' elements in Pinter's plays, the hired killers, the strange instructions given down the shaft of a dumb-waiter, the menacing atmosphere (of the first three plays: *The Room, The Birthday Party, The Dumb Waiter*)—all these are super-realistic: the author merely withholds the 'explanation': why is Stanley to be killed in *The Birthday*

Party? Who gives the instructions in *The Dumb Waiter*? You only need to be supplied with a limited number of answers, and you have solved the riddle. Pinter, then, is a very different kind of 'absurdist'. There are elements of caricature (of reality), and an atmosphere of horror as well as comedy—but the dramatist's position is still basically realist. These plays were published in 1960 under the title of *The Birthday Party*.

The Caretaker (1960) is even more overtly realist: although the play is strange in atmosphere, and one of the characters is (medically) depressed, there is a perfectly acceptable 'explanation': Mick wants to get rid of an old tramp his depressed brother has picked up—but without offending the latter. *Tea Party*, written like a number of Pinter's other plays for television, is a masterful study of a man descending into catatonic schizophrenia—it ends with his complete paralysis. Again, this is absolutely realist once we have the explanation (which in this case we do have). *The Homecoming* (1965), written for the stage, is also realist; it moves yet nearer to the conventional realist formula. The notion that Teddy—who comes home, having achieved success in America, to confront his awful family—is a liar has no more evidence to support it than any other unverifiable statement by anyone else. . . . That is one of Pinter's points. And in the case of this play we can even begin to discuss it in 'Bradleyan' terms: in terms of the characters' psychological motivations. With Arden, Pinter stands head and shoulders above his contemporaries in the theatre.

The third substantial post-war English dramatist, JOHN WHITING (1915–63), died prematurely. He did not, in fact, fulfil his potential —nor did he ever have a real commercial success. *Saint's Day* (*Three Plays*, 1957), winner of the Festival of Britain Play Competition, anticipated a good many future techniques: 'absurdity', deliberate lopsidedness of structure, abandonment of realist intentions. *Marching Song* (*Three Plays*, 1957) is one of the few really outstanding postwar plays: so much so that John Russell Taylor calls it 'formidably intelligent' but 'a little cold and lifeless': it 'could never take an unprepared audience by storm'. For *The Devils* (1961), commissioned by the Royal Shakespeare Company, Whiting drew on Aldous Huxley's study of mass hysteria, *The Devils of Loudon*, but treated the material in the light of his own unusual preoccupation with man's tendency to undermine his material position—in which process Whiting discovers much poetry. *The Devils* should not be judged by realist standards: it needs (like Shakespeare's histories) to be judged in its own, not in historical, terms.

ARNOLD WESKER (1932) is less gifted, but his *Wesker Trilogy* (1960) at least—*Chicken Soup with Barley* (1958), *Roots* (1959), *I'm Talking About Jerusalem* (1960)—deserves to survive. The first of these is set in Wesker's native East End, the last two in Norfolk. These are sprawling, muddled—but passionately alive. They do not succeed in portraying the post-war working-classes, but they do present some convincing characters—notably Beatie in *Roots*. However, the plays, for all their vitality, do not stand up well to close examination: the Norfolk speech is badly done, there are some pointless faults of construction and inconsistencies, and at times Wesker's simplistic idealism is revealed in all its stupidity—not as innocently lovely or Blakean, but as something a little awkward. . . . *Chips with Everything* (1962), a portrait of life in the R.A.F., has its moments—but in general Wesker's attitudes (which are not the result of processes one would normally describe as intellectual) are obtrusive. During the Sixties Wesker worked hard on his impossible and noble Centre 42 project, and his plays of that period (*The Four Seasons*, 1966; *Their Very Own and Golden City*, 1966) have increasingly reflected his over-optimistic view of society—a view that unfortunately has less and less, of a lyrical nature, to sustain it.

JOHN SPURLING (1936) is the most promising of the new playwrights. He combines hard neutrality of outlook with interest in Latin-American possibilities, and is already technically adept. *Macrune's Guevara* (1969) is a relentless and yet moving examination of a legendary character, and is one of the most outstanding and serious plays of its decade.

IV

D. H. LAWRENCE (1885–1930), despite his international reputation, was one of the most English of all English writers. He wrote novels, stories, drama (at the end of the Sixties this was revived, in London, with some deserved success), travel books, criticism and poetry. Much of his best poetry (the fullest edition is *Complete Poems*, 1964) is about birds, beasts or flowers; but in this form he tends to be over-diffuse: very few of his poems are wholly successful. They aim at truth to feeling, but too often language fails. However, judicious selections from his poetry show clearly that it cannot be lightly dismissed: apart from any other consideration, it contains invaluable indications of his attitudes. His criticism (conveniently assembled in Anthony Beal's *Selected Literary Criticism*, 1955) is frequently whining, self-indulgent and unfair; it is, quite as frequently, piercingly brilliant in its insights.

Whether one ultimately likes Lawrence or not, he is undoubtedly a writer of immense importance, indisputable genius, and power. He lived and died poor; although a sick man—he suffered from tuberculosis for much of his life, and it killed him—the concept of compromise with commerce was totally unknown to him. He was the most honest of all writers. Moreover, there are some things he could do perfectly (like the sketch 'Adolf', about his father; and some of the short stories): things that no one else has done. 'There was', his friend Richard Aldington said, 'no taming him'. And so even if he could be vicious (as in his letter to Kathleen Mansfield, q.v., as she was dying), unkind, prejudiced, a would-be sex-mage whose practical grasp of his subject was notably imperfect—still, this century has needed and still needs more like him: untameable, dedicated to their project, undeflectable from it by any pieties— political, academic, polite or dogmatic. . . . The price of all this is likely to be a personality difficult to deal with; but it is a price worth paying.

Lawrence's father was a Nottingham miner married to a woman who was—and felt herself to be—a little above him socially and intellectually. For the whole of his life Lawrence sought (unsuccessfully) to resolve his fierce Oedipal feelings, which were complicated by his extreme (and equally unresolved) difficulties in relating to women. Almost always a petulant, small-minded egoism undermined his marvellous tenderness. He refused to recognize his limitations— which in terms of technique (as his poetry demonstrates) were considerable—and too frequently tried (angrily and aggressively) to express his attitude in its entirety in single works. His marriage to Frieda Lawrence, originally the German wife of an etymologist at Nottingham University, was probably about as stable as any marriage he might have made; but neither Frieda, nor any other woman, could have supplied his demands, which were unquestionably neurotic. In so far as Lawrence is a creative writer, he is liberating; but in so far as Lawrence was a sexual prophet, he was a dangerous man, insensitive to the effects of the tyranny of himself and others. His philosophy, that what is right is what feels right—in the 'solar-plexus', the 'blood'—is certainly much more dangerous and ambiguous than Nietzsche's (q.v. 2) philosophy, which was the result of intellectual processes far more complex, and of a much deeper self-insight. Lawrence acted on his instincts and intuitions, but, at some relatively early stage, his sexual self-exploration became arrested: he became identified with the position in which he found himself. He furiously and truculantly generalized from this position, refusing to try to create better balanced books. Even though he preached instinctive life, his own instinctive life was evidently more crippled than that of many men; the power of his message surely derives from the fierceness of his compensation for this—in the Adlerian sense. He seems to have suffered from some kind of impotence (his friend John Middleton Murry, the critic, Utopian and 'professional sufferer', stated that he did), and the descriptions of love-making in his novels are embarrassing and unconvincing, and are decked out with vulgar and pretentious language. However, his descriptions of male contacts are often authoritative (the wrestling in *Women in Love*, the massage in *Aaron's Rod*): there was a quality in women that sent him into a retreat whose ignominy, like his concomitant homosexual inclinations, he entirely refused to face. Thus, in the middle of *The Rainbow* (1915), in which the characters have been allowed a life of their own, Lawrence hysterically intrudes with something entirely personal to himself. ... 'What is the meaning', asks David Daiches, 'of the incident' in which 'Ursula and Skebrensky have some sort of tremendous crisis ... symbolized by Ursula's compulsive desire to lie on her back ... and by the particular way she accepts Skebrensky's love-making'? The meaning is that Lawrence is substituting himself for his imagination at the point where this fails. ... He, the prophet of sexual liberation, was not sexually liberated. ... He was, in fact, sexually ignorant: his defensive sexual dogmatism destroyed his sexual freedom. It is strange that so few critics have thought it worth while to examine this discrepancy. But it is interesting, in this connection, that Lawrence's wholehearted admirers are never only critics, but also themselves committed to sexual or moral prophecy. Since it is Lawrence whom Dr. F. R. Leavis has set above all other writers of this century it is appropriate at this point briefly to discuss this influential and gifted critic—whose own excellence is so similarly flawed. Leavis is a self-assertive moralist, and he has chosen to select what he likes from Lawrence's work and then to erect this as a kind of monument of twentieth-century genius—while 'wilfully' (Daiches) ignoring Lawrence's limitations. Now Lawrence's faults, which are bad ones, go along with great virtues—the chief of them is the intuitive capacity to present hidden truths about human beings and their relationships in terms of their apprehensions of nature—but the faults need to be mentioned.

Leavis as a critic suffers from similar limitations: he is a critic of great gifts, insight and integrity; but those who are not entirely for him are wholly against him; he seeks not pupils but 'disciples';

those disciples he has attracted who have not broken away have been, like the master, rancid and fanatic in manner: the chip on the shoulder of every 'Leavisite' (as his followers are called) is a splinter of the cross upon which the master himself has been crucified by society's less than absolute acceptance of his creed.

It is no wonder that Lawrence has been raised up, in this atmosphere, as a God. And it is a pity: while Leavis in his book on Lawrence's novels, *D. H. Lawrence: Novelist* (1955), gives a valuable account, he has also been responsible for an uncritical acceptance of Lawrence's dangerous, because so confusingly presented, ideology: that life is a mystery, not to be solved by dogmas, and only to be known by itself: by acceptance of itself, by vitality.

There are of course inspired passages in every one of Lawrence's twelve novels; but each one is flawed in the same way as Daiches points out that *The Rainbow* is flawed: by a sudden, raw, personal, ideological intrusion into the imaginative texture. The best of the novels are *Sons and Lovers* (1913), for which he drew on the experiences of his own childhood—and in which he managed to be fair to his father (who appears as Morel), *The Rainbow*, and *Women in Love* (1920) in part—but this is ruined by his attempt to *judge* Gerald Crich instead of explaining him, and by the untruthful presentation of Birkin (himself) as a sexually self-fulfilled man.

But Lawrence's supreme achievement is in the best of his short stories, which were collected in three volumes in 1955 (the short novels appeared in two volumes in 1957). Here, in this relatively short compass, he did not always feel impelled to intrude. Here his sense of humour (in Lawrence's writing this seldom manifests itself more specifically than as a sense of general relaxation) emerges. In 'The Prussian Officer', one of his greatest stories, he is able to draw upon his homosexual proclivities without strain: writing it, he did not have time to become upset and confused about this problem. It is in the stories that Lawrence reached perfection uninterrupted by the sort of neurotic turbulence that led him, in his final novels, to authoritarianism and (in *Lady Chatterley's Lover*, unexpurgated version 1961) hysterical manipulation of a female character—the noble lady in the arms of the gamekeeper, a wishful portrait of Lawrence.—under the disguise of writing a hymn to the life of the instincts. It has been said that although we must condemn 'the murk and unassimilated excitement' when 'it comes into the novels', we nevertheless pay the price 'for the Lawrentian genius . . . gladly'. We do pay it; but not 'gladly': we are only 'glad' when we discover the genius unpoisoned, as in the best stories.

VIRGINIA WOOLF (1882–1941) was a very different sort of writer.

The daughter of the Victorian man of letters Leslie Stephen, and the wife of Leonard Woolf—a liberal and humane journalist, publisher and (latterly) autobiographer—she suffered for most of her life from a type of manic-depression. Eventually she drowned herself. That Virginia Woolf was a genuinely innovatory novelist, critically aware of the changes in sensibility that were taking place around her, goes without question. The extent of her actual achievement, however, has been challenged. Just how much more conventional was she than she thought? Are her innovations chiefly technical?

Her theories will sound familiar to anyone who knows something of modernism. The novel was not to be a photograph, not even a critical photograph, of life: it was to be a recreation of experience. 'Clock'-time was to cease to dominate it. But Virginia Woolf's work frequently suffers from her own lack of experience. She understood that trivialities were only apparent, but—herself always rich and protected—she tended to underrate the obviously non-trivial: 'it's not catastrophes, murders, deaths, diseases, that age and kill us; it's the way people look and laugh, and run up the steps of omnibuses'. One knows what, in reaction to the realism practised by Bennett and Wells and by a host of poor novelists, she meant; but these things *do* age and kill (too)—and all the more amongst the poor, about whom Virginia Woolf failed to be as sensitive as she would (to her credit) have desired. She would have done better if she had worried less. One might say, without being wholly unfair, that her awareness of the inadequacy of conventional realism was an advantage to Virginia Woolf: she employed it as a strategy to avoid the 'cruder' aspects of life (murder, death, diseases—poverty) with which she guiltily could not deal. She remains, despite her immense potentialities, very 'literary'; she could not quite escape from that into literature, as other greater modernists (Joyce, Céline) have done. Joyce chose the stuff of 'normal' life (to reveal that it was there, rather than anywhere else, that abnormalities were to be found). Virginia Woolf was less at ease about her subject matter. In her two most important novels (*Mrs. Dalloway*, 1925; *To the Lighthouse*, 1927) her technique suggests new and rich possibilities; but clearly the imaginative stuff on which she is concentrating, even in these books, is somewhat lacking in substance: her imagination cannot quite visualize a world, a society: her characters swim in water that has been sterilized and distilled—its salt, its fish, its teeming life destroyed—by purely literary considerations. Thus, those significant moments that it was her so intelligent intention to capture are not always particularly revelatory; her world seems impoverished because it is composed of people like herself. The ghost of her father's

Victorian rationalism is nearly always lurking in the shadows: as a 'philosophy' to console us for our loss of belief; thus the imagination's freedom is curtailed. But *Mrs. Dalloway* succeeds at least in its vivid, impressionistic evocation of London and in its consciously Proustian revelation of life-as-flux. Her finest novel, *To the Lighthouse*, is much influenced by Romains' *Death of a Nobody* (q.v. 2), which her friend Desmond MacCarthy had co-translated: although it is in no sense a product of 'unanimistic' thinking, its theme is the influence of a person after her death, and its concept of time is the Bergsonian one of Romains. And although it is limited by Virginia Woolf's usual lack of substance, by an emphasis on sensibility that is made at the expense of robustness, it is none the less a beautiful book. *The Waves* (1931), which consists of a series of interior monologues keyed in with the progress of the sun over the sea, has its admirers; but it is too self-conscious, the life-substance ebbs away like the waves: Virginia Woolf was not a poet, and when she tried to be she was inclined to be embarrassing. Throughout the Thirties, except for occasional flares, the flame of Virginia Woolf's genius guttered; her last novel, *Between the Acts* (1941), shows all the old intelligence, but lacks power and conviction (although it is worth noting that Walter Allen, q.v., seldom a critic to dismiss lightly when he has had time to consider, regards it as her best novel).

Less need be said of DOROTHY M. RICHARDSON (1872–1957)—for a time one of H. G. Wells' many mistresses—whose sequence of twelve novels *Pilgrimage* (1915–38) is rather lucky to have attracted the amount of attention that it has. She was certainly a pioneer of the stream-of-consciousness (q.v.) method; but in an ultra-realist rather than a phenomenological direction. Dorothy Richardson's protagonist Miriam is not an interesting woman, and the progress of her life is (alas) made more dull and more monotonous by the author's dogged and humourless refusal to leave much of it out. The method is of course interesting; but it is not as interesting as some have made it out to be. After all, it cuts out the physical; it ignores (as Walter Allen has pointed out) the entire implications of what Freud and others of his generation brought out into the open. Dorothy Richardson held feminist views; but her feminism is impoverished by her refusal to acknowledge woman's sexuality (she herself was not short of sexual experience: she was married, and in any case H. G. Wells would have educated her in any shortcomings —if that term may be used advisedly).

The most important of experimental writers of his generation in English literature is JAMES JOYCE (1882–1941), a Dubliner who lived in exile from 1904 until the end of his life—in Zurich, whither he had fled from France—after an operation. Joyce has often been attacked for his insensitivity to contemporary history, but in his case this is hardly just: his subject-matter was not the life of literary people (far from it), but of 'ordinary' people (he wanted above all— he, too, saw the awful, tragic irony of it—to reconcile the function of good-bourgeois-husband-and-father with that of writer): he saw that he could not do this in a priest- and politician-ridden Ireland, and he left it. *Ulysses* (1922) is a celebration of, a monument to, the life of ordinary, 'vulgar' people; had Joyce directed his energies to polemical indignation over Irish—and, later, European—politics he could not have created this monument, which in itself is an antidote to the dehumanized and dehumanizing efforts of politicians. (Joyce's admirer Eliot cannot be acquitted of the same charge: in his work there is neither indignation nor pity.)

Joyce received a good although painful education in Jesuit schools. He soon rejected the ideals of the Irish literary revival as being too nationalistic; he even went to Paris with the intention of studying medicine. The poems of *Chamber Music* (1907)—the pun is, of course, intentional—which went unnoticed, reveal the lyrical springs of his genius. He had already written the stories in *Dubliners* (1914), but could not find a publisher for them. These describe the Ireland from which he had deliberately chosen to exile himself, from which he had painfully torn up his roots. They render it with perfection: the prose loves compassionately the dreary awfulness even while it comments ironically upon it. Joyce had already taken the guts and bone out of Catholicism: he left behind only the bloated skin of its tired dogmatic insistencies. He had learned from Ibsen to be realistic; his awareness that life consisted of moments of continuous 'sin' (the official Roman Catholic word for a constellation of emotions including guilt, shame, anxiety, lovelessness) redeemed by equally continuous moments of joy and blessedness was his own. Until after *Ulysses* he was an optimistic writer.

The protagonist of *A Portrait of the Artist as a Young Man* (1916) is Stephen Dedalus, who reappears in *Ulysses*, which, in tracing the progress of an artist to maturity, represents him as necessarily un-committed and free—and lonely.

In *Ulysses*, a masterful combination of realism (of an undeniably naturalist flavour) and symbolism, we find Stephen confronted with Leopold Bloom, an 'ordinary' man. Gradually, throughout the twenty-four hours of time covered by the novel, these two come together. Bloom is the father whom Stephen seeks; but he must finally refuse his offer of hospitality (a bed for the night). Signifi-cantly it is Bloom, Ulysses, the 'ordinary', 'dirty', 'little' man whose experiences are the richest: the artist is represented as the calculating son of the universal, decent, threatened man. This is Joyce's resolution of the universal problem of what I have called *Künstlerschuld* (q.v.). Even Joyce, one of the most dedicated writers of the century, once thought of being a physician. . . . *Ulysses* is a colossal celebration of life—including its miseries—biologically (in Marion Bloom's final thoughts as she goes off to sleep) emotionally (in Bloom's mind) and intellectually (in Stephen's mind). To describe his technique as an exploitation of 'stream-of-consciousness' is inadequate; his own theory of 'epiphanies' is more revealing. In scriptural terms an epiphany is a 'showing-forth'; for Joyce it was 'a sudden spiritual manifestation, whether in the vulgarity of speech or of gesture or in a memorable phase of the mind itself'. *Ulysses* is a subtle and rich book, but it is not a difficult one. It is, at once, a despairing, amoral, drunken Irish joke, a retelling of an ancient myth in symbolic terms, an immense, rueful parody of Catholic 'order', a quasi-naturalist tragi-comedy. . . .

Joyce's wife (they lived together from 1904, but did not get legally married until 1931), Nora Barnacle, was a non-literary woman ('Why don't you write sensible books that people can understand?') —as 'ordinary' (but how extraordinary she was!) as one would expect from the author of *Ulysses*. She bore him two children, a son and a daughter. The latter, Lucia, became schizophrenic and eventually had to be permanently hospitalized. This broke Joyce: it touched off his enormous guilt. The guilt was not connected with his leaving the Roman Catholic Church, but with the price (paid by others) for his devoting himself to creative writing. Like most of the great writers of this century, he blamed himself for being creative. In *Ulysses*, as I have suggested above, he had been able to some extent to resolve this problem. The progressive dissociation of Lucia's personality revived his guilt. *Finnegans Wake* (1939) is his anguished response to his daughter's gradual retreat from reality. He took her to Jung, who told Joyce that she had schizophrenic tendencies. Desperately he objected: why were her verbal games not just like his own? 'You are both going to the bottom of the river', Jung replied, 'but she is falling and you are diving'. Joyce had his own troubles, too: fame had by no means made him rich; he was almost blind; *Ulysses* ran into trouble in almost every country in which it appeared: he may well have felt that he was being driven deeply into himself. *Finnegans Wake* is the dream of H. C. Earwicker (*Here Comes Everybody*) and of Joyce himself, written in multiple puns. Although it has become a book to which a number of scholars have written keys, *Finnegans Wake* is an inaccessible failure, the work of a man whose masterpiece had already been written. It is fascinating, comic, ingenious; but as a whole it fails. Joyce's associative technique becomes a desperate, empathic parody of Lucia's disastrous compulsion: the guilty father searches the bottom of the river for the daughter he feels he has abandoned and allowed to drown. *Finnegans Wake* is wonderful food; but we cannot really eat it. 'I could not', he wrote of this book, which was seventeen years in the making (scrawled out painfully, between eye operations) 'I felt I could not, use words in their ordinary connections. . . . When morning comes of course everything will be clear again. . . . I'll give them back their English language. . . .' But morning (Lucia's miraculous recovery; his own clear sight) never did come. The project of *Finnegans Wake* arose as an intuitive response to the oddness apparent in the fifteen-year-old Lucia: to the effect that Joyce saw himself having, as a dedicated writer, upon his family's life. But the answer to his doggedly private and bitter attempt to turn words into nothing but counters is to be found in the humanity of *Ulysses*. Joyce's letters have been collected (1957), and his *Critical Writings* (1959). Richard Ellmann's excellent biography appeared in 1959. *Giacomo Joyce*, a short but exceedingly interesting story from about 1914, was published in 1969.

As important (and exciting) a writer as Joyce, though few have recognized it, was PERCY WYNDHAM LEWIS (1882–1956). Although Joyce learned much from Lewis, no two writers could be more different. Lewis was a painter of genius, as well as a writer; he, too—although much later in life—went blind. Wyndham Lewis (who is not to be confused with an often witty humorist, Catholic apologist and biographer called D. B. Wyndham-Lewis, also blind in his old age and now also dead) was literary critic, art critic, polemicist, satirical poet—and, above all, novelist. In general Wyndham Lewis has been, and is, ignored; when granted a place in surveys of literature it is usually as a right-wing obscurantist. But discerning critics (T. S. Eliot was one of them; Pound, Grigson, Walter Allen, qq.v., are others) have recognized his strange genius.

Lewis embarrassed everyone, including—in the end—himself. His faults are soon dealt with—sooner, indeed, than some, because of the lack of attention he has suffered. But these must be enumerated.

He frequently tried to do too much at the same time: some of his polemical writing is inexcusably slapdash—as well as being irrelevant to his real concerns. He became too involved in his function as polemicist, and neglected to develop his imaginative and intuitive gifts—until it was almost too late. For much of his life (until he found himself exiled in Canada, during the Second World War) he used the intellectual side of himself as a protective shield against compulsions that can only be described as romantic. These he nervously rationalized as 'privacy': it is as well to remind his detractors that, while he wilfully over-indulged his paranoid tendencies, he also enjoyed a tenderly happy marriage. But in his capacity as the hard-headed, self-styled 'Enemy', this (personally) timid, kind and gentle man wilfully refused (1931) to see Hitler as anything but a comic 'gutbag', and even appeared to praise him. This was a worse case, as Lewis finally saw, than merely doing it to annoy because he knew it teased the left. He failed to discern the humanity and sense of alarm that were genuine elements in the liberal protest against Hitler. *The Hitler Cult* (1939) was his official apology; but he later examined the causes of this failure (and what it implied) in one of the most self-castigating novels of the century: *Self-Condemned* (1954), published only three years before he died. He lived to suffer for his excesses, and to expose his failures to himself—and in the process to write a work, *The Human Age* (1955–6) that, although it is unfinished, will in due time be seen to be a classic (as T. S. Eliot said, alluding to the treatment of people as puppets—'hallucinated automata': here 'the puppets begin to get the better of the puppet-master'). So Lewis' grave faults did not destroy or even diminish him as a creative writer. He is ultimately a giant of letters not in spite of them but—like all such giants—because of them. Most of Lewis' novels are in print, and there are two excellent selections from his work: E. W. F. Tomlin's *Wyndham Lewis: An Anthology of his Prose* (1969) and Raymond Rosenthal's paperback *A Soldier of Humour and other Writings* (1966), which contains much otherwise inaccessible early work.

What Lewis the critic, satirist and sociologist was interested in was what he called, in *The Art of Being Ruled* (1926), 'the life of the intelligence'; the pride of 'its servants', he wrote, 'if they have it, is because of something inside themselves which has been won at no one else's expense, and that no one can give them or remove from them'. Lewis the satirist was at his best an apostle of the life of the intelligence unique in his time. Savagely humorous (usually over the heads of his targets), he used *thought* where most *literati* slackly used fashion or facile emotion. He cast himself into isolation partly by exercising his human right to objectivity. His thinking about time, flux, and the role of the intellect may most conveniently be found in *Time and Western Man* (1927), a book which anticipates and transcends many of the more important ideas of the four decades that followed its publication; here he is at his least rigid in his application. The basis of his notions about art arose from his practice as a painter: '. . . I am for the Great Without', he wrote, 'for the method of *external* approach'. And he tended to describe his people in wholly external terms. So far as satire was concerned, this was effective: in the massive *The Apes of God* (1930), a fearful account of the silliness of *literati*, the dehumanizing process is justified. But that was Lewis functioning as the Enemy—and in him there lurked an enemy of the Enemy. . . . Even in his most ferocious satire, Lewis was always straining after something else, something imaginative and creative; but this was not really compatible with his dehumanizing descriptive technique. His satire became phantasmagoric horror: the romantic element cannot express itself, but is held rigidly down by the cold technique (in such paintings as 'The Surrender of Barcelona' the romantic richness is more apparent, because Lewis was able to use actual colour). Lewis' powerful imaginative yearnings hid beneath the cool or comic surface, a metaphor for the graphic, a result of the ruthless and behaviouristic exploitation of the 'eye'—like red-hot lava waiting to erupt. It has been asked why the strangely original early writings—'Bestre', 'The Cornac and his Wife'—'had no later fulfilment'. But they did: partially in *Self-Condemned*, fully and linguistically in the last great unfinished tetralogy. Lewis was in 1914 a pioneer of the short-lived vorticist movement: in other words an English cubist. Vorticism (of which Pound, q.v., was the chief champion) in painting and literature was essentially an anti-mimetic movement: the artist was urged to *invent* in his own right (cf. cubism, q.v. 2). As Walter Allen has remarked, 'Lewis's prose at its best is as exciting as any written in English this century'. And in Lewis' earlier prose we may see the germs of an astonishing experimentalism. Consider the beginning of 'Cantleman's Spring Mate' (1917):

> 'Cantleman walked in the strenuous fields, steam
> rising from them as though from an exertion,
> dissecting the daisies specking the small wood,
> the primroses on the banks, the marshy lakes,
> and all God's creatures. The heat of a heavy
> premature Summer was cooking the little narrow
> belt of earth-air, causing everything innocently
> to burst its skin, bask abjectly and profoundly. . . .'

Or this from the 'advertisement' to 'The Enemy of the Stars' (it is not possible here to reproduce the startling typography):

DRESS. ENORMOUS YOUNGSTERS, BURSTING
EVERYWHERE THROUGH HEAVY TIGHT
CLOTHES, LABOURED BY DULL
EXPLOSIVE MUSCLES, full of
fiery dust and sinewy energetic
air, not sap. BLACK CLOTH
CUT SOMEWHERE, NOWADAYS, ON
THE UPPER BALTIC.

VERY WELL ACTED BY YOU AND ME.

Lewis tinkered with this amazingly original style, in which disparate elements seem to clash, diverge and come together, until *The Childermass* (1928), in which he tried to discover to where it might lead in a full-scale work. Then, in illness and possibly in despair, he abandoned it and fought his battles in a different way. (This negative phase of his creative life is perhaps best described as one of heroic behaviourism.) But towards the end of his life he resumed the task, with renewed lucidity and courage: *Monstre Gai* and *Malign Fiesta*, which, with the revised *Childermass*, form *The Human Age*, explore the meaning of existence. The mass of humanity, in a limbo outside heaven, awaits examination by the Bailiff. This visionary work, 'magnificent and dreadful' (Walter Allen), which will undoubtedly be seen as one of the major achievements of the present century, was written by Lewis when he had become (by a savage stroke of irony) blind (the pressure of an inoperable tumour on his optic nerve) and was dying.

Other notable works by Lewis, one of the major art critics of his time, include *The Demon of Progress in the Arts* (1954) and the novels *Tarr* (1918) and *The Revenge for Love* (1937).

L. H. MYERS (1881–1944), like T. F. Powys, has long been championed by F. R. Leavis and his school (q.v.); without the critical attention thus accorded to him he would perhaps have been forgotten—which would certainly be critically unjust. Myers, especially in the trilogy *The Root and the Flower* (1927–35)—*The Pool of Vishnu* (1940), a sequel, is not on the same level—is a distinguished philosophical novelist; in fact, he is so distinguished that he clearly shows the limitations of this genre. Myers, son of F. W. H. Myers the psychical researcher, was rich, fastidious and mystical. As a young man he had a mystical experience: a sense of the goodness of man as seen from the eye of God. This—together with his guilty hatred of his own class—remained his guiding light until his suicide. He began as a verse dramatist, and did not publish his first novel, *The Orisers*

(1922), until he was forty-one. Myers failed to resolve the problem of his sense of alienation from his environment until he set his fiction in the past (in an Elizabethan India). Even here he does not entirely succeed in a creative capacity, for, subtle and intelligent as he is, his real purpose is didactic: briefly, it is to demonstrate that personality and all that man does to form it and exercise it is an obstacle to his self-realization. In *The Root and the Flower* a young prince, Jali, is shown as being presented with various temptations, the main one being that of becoming a personality instead of a fulfilled person. Myers' thinking is interesting and important—but it precedes his invention and conception of character. Finally he rejected art and fiction altogether, became a somewhat desperate communist, and tried to pinpoint the evils of society in an auto-biographical study; he destroyed this before destroying himself, thus incidentally answering the question that had plagued him for the whole of his life: why do men choose to live? Like Martin Buber, the author of *I and Thou*, to whom he owes much, Myers fiercely resisted the tendency of the modern, commercial world to treat people as objects—and, as G. H. Bantock has remarked, 'he has . . . a sense of evil'. Judged by the highest standards, he failed; but no novelist of greater imaginative power has yet tackled his subject-matter. He is an important figure.

A. E. COPPARD (1878–1957), a short-story writer who never essayed a novel, is nowadays almost as neglected as Myers. His *Collected Tales* appeared in 1948; it was followed by *Lucy In Her Pink Jacket* (1954). Coppard came up the hard way: apprentice to an East End tailor, office boy, professional athlete, clerk. He was well over thirty before he began writing poetry and stories seriously. His poetry is not successful; but his best short stories are among the most poetic of his time. Although self-educated, he was an exceedingly cunning and studied writer, who worked very hard (sometimes too hard) to gain his apparently spontaneous effects. A grand anarchy lay at the heart of his work; his most deeply felt stories (such as 'Dusky Ruth') involve characters whose real concerns are entirely anti- or non-social. He also has charm, comedy and beauty. Coppard, who came from Kent, is one of the most English of writers; perhaps only his failure to keep to his roots prevented him from being major.

CARADOC EVANS (1879–1945), although one of the most ferocious satirists of Wales (he was a Welsh-speaking Welshman writing in English), was as Welsh as Coppard was English. His first collection of short stories, *My People* (1915), was remarkably original, even though the author went back to the style of the Bible for his sharp, gleefully realistic and honest accounts of the dark idiosyncrasies of his people. After two more volumes of stories he brought out a satirical play, *Taffy* (1923), which caused a stir when it was produced in London: a critic said it 'hit, hurt and heartened'. His first novel, *Nothing to Pay* (1930), embodied an even more deliberate and angry caricature of the Welsh than he had yet attempted—and it did not increase his popularity in his own country. Evans was above all the denouncer—often in its own brand of powerful rhetoric—of the Welsh nonconformist institution known as Chapel. It is in Evans' novels and collections of stories that we may find a more morally engaged, less self-indulgent version of the more popular *Under Milk Wood* (q.v.).

RONALD FIRBANK (1886–1926), a cultivated taste is ever there was one, presents a complete contrast. He was a pathetic and yet genuinely agonized trivialist, a chic fugitive from life who hid, in aestheticism, what his giggling response to terror could not neutralize; his substanceless fiction attracts fellow-homosexuals—and writers whose roots are in, or half in, the Nineties. His technique and mood have influenced writers as diverse as Osbert Sitwell, Anthony Powell, Carl Van Vechten, Aldous Huxley, William Gerhardie, Evelyn Waugh, Ivy Compton–Burnett (qq.v.). He wrote twelve novels and a play; the best known novels are *Valmouth* (1919) and *Concerning the Eccentricities of Cardinal Pirelli* (1926); *The Works* appeared in 1928, later to be supplemented by *Santal* (1931), stories, and *The Artificial Princess* (1934). Firbank cannot be called serious, and he was also silly—but it must be conceded, even by those who are repelled by the pointlessness of his concinnity, that, in Evelyn Waugh's words, he 'negligently stumbled' upon 'technical discoveries': the efficacy of dialogue, conversational nuance, the withdrawal of the kind of cause and effect associated with conventional *mimesis*. . . . *Sorrow in Sunlight* (1924), called *Prancing Nigger* in America, played an important part in the cult of things negro which swept France in the Twenties—and which indirectly influenced the progress of negritude (q.v. 3, 4). Firbank's work, always valetudinarian, hovers between the ingenuous and the cunning; its tittering nihility has no more than a touching, childish quality—but in Waugh it becomes a blackness, in Powell an observational position, in Van Vechten a self-caressing pussiness, in the early Huxley a cleverness. . . . Firbank belonged inexorably to the Nineties, but he managed to anticipate—largely by influencing—that twentieth-century vein which exploited, more or less successfully, decadence.

Another source for these writers, as for Firbank himself, was FREDERICK ROLFE (1860–1913), self-styled baronet and priest, who was both more comic and more poisonous than Firbank. He was a confidence-man, pauper, tutor, blackmailer, paedophile, translator

—and author of seven novels and a number of short stories. Rolfe was a trickster whose failed life stank to himself as to the few friends whom he had and betrayed. But he was a fascinating figure: a bore, but also a pseudo-Borgian freak whose vindictiveness and paranoia have deservedly become legendary—largely through A. J. A. Symons' famous biography, *The Quest for Corvo* (1930). Rolfe's one decent novel, *Hadrian the Seventh* (1904; 1950), is by no means the 'masterpiece' Symons called it; but it is a psychopathological *tour de force*, an autobiographical fantasy about a man who, rejected as a priest (as Rolfe was), is elected Pope and proceeds to revenge himself upon—or to reform?—the Church. . . . Even this novel, told in an over-mannered and hysterical prose, depends upon our knowledge of Rolfe himself to gain its full effect: it is the self-recorded case-history of a remarkable patient.

IVY COMPTON-BURNETT (1892–1969), whose novels are constructed entirely out of dialogue, is a unique phenomenon in English fiction: a very respectable and aristocratic lady (one thinks of Marianne Moore, q.v.) whose one 'moral failing' (in purely Victorian terms), her lesbianism, gave her uncannily sharp intelligence a window onto the world of real human evil: this bitter and severe intelligence, in the privacy of the author's consciousness, made its ironic decision some time between the publication of a first, wholly conventional tale, *Dolores* (1911) and that of *Pastors and Masters* (1924), the first genuinely 'Compton-Burnett' novel. Ivy Compton-Burnett was an artful prestidigitator: her bland procedure—the recording of dialogue—conceals: the very highly melodramatic nature of her plots; her lack of interest in realism—all her 'characters', after all, share in their creator's delight in style and epigram; her limitations (the late Victorian upper middle-class world), which are as severe—she recognized it—as her opinion of existence; her lack of psychological expertise—of knowledge of actual mental process; the strong, uncreative, mushy element of sentimentality in her. . . . Here is a case of the triumph of a self-prescribed, drastic therapy. Her theme, most broadly defined, is exploitation: she sees her specimens as exploiters or exploited—but the former may prove to be the latter in disguise, or the position may become transformed. One can be sure of only one thing: that the surface of the story will remain conversational, an imperturbable parody of the ravaged and ravaging minds of the protagonists. Her plots almost invariably involve such vicious, violent or sensational crimes as incest, murder, forgery and so on. Ultimately these are not, perhaps, novels at all—but marvellously entertaining Indic fantasies, in which nothing really happens in peoples' minds. As she has said, with a characteristically misleading, sardonic directness: 'real life' is 'of no help at all'. This hardly matters, though: ultimately the quality we gain from these observations is as tragic as their classically educated progenitor intended. There are more than twenty novels, from which one might select *Brothers and Sisters* (1929), *Parents and Children* (1941), *Manservant and Maidservant* (1947), called *Bullivant and the Lambs* in America, and *A Heritage and its History* (1959) as being particularly excellent.

ALDOUS HUXLEY (1894–1963) was more versatile and, during his lifetime, very much more widely read than Ivy Compton-Burnett. In the years following his death his reputation has slumped drastically, doubtless because he had throughout his career—right from clever young man through fashionable mystic to psychedelic vulgarian—a journalistic flair. This may seem odd in so esoteric and highly educated a man; but Huxley bristled with contradictions—his failure to resolve them prevented him from progressing from brilliance to the seriousness of a major writer. The adroit, studiedly cruel young imitator of Firbank jostled in Huxley with the aesthete of guiltily ascetic tendencies; the theoretical hedonist with the deficient monk. Because Huxley began as an entertainer and ended as a mystic it is often supposed that he changed drastically; such is not the case. As D. S. Savage, one of the most astute of modern critics, has pointed out, both the early attitude of 'Pyrrhonic hedonism' and the later mystical one—essentially this amounts to rejection of the ego and its works, including time, for the sake of union with the absolute—'originate in a common dislocation of being'. The early Huxley of those bright comedies of manners, *Chrome Yellow* (1921), *Antic Hay* (1923) and *Those Barren Leaves* (1925), felt himself to be as detached from the crude, raw stuff of life as did the later mystic. The early writer has no mercy on his characters; he caricatures the disgustingness of human physicality in them; the later writer has dropped caricature and learned compassion (although he was never able, in his fiction, to achieve warmth); he still rejects physicality.

The three early novels are coruscating, farcical, worthy successors to the Ben Jonson of the 'humour' plays. *Those Barren Leaves*, more serious, is more questionable because its characters, which ought to be endowed with their own vitality, are rather too obviously vehicles for Huxley's own reflections on futility. *Point Counter Point* (1928), a *roman à clef* that owed a good deal to Gide's *The Coiners* (q.v. 2), is Huxley's best, most felt, novel—although it is significant that even here the most moving episode revolves around a Beethoven quartet. Huxley lacked warmth as a novelist; but he had decency and gentleness, and *Point Counter Point* does succeed to a limited degree in ' exhibiting sympathy towards that humanity which does not aspire but simply suffers and lives. Huxley examines himself in the person of the novelist Philip Quarles and finds himself wanting: 'All his life he had walked in . . . a private void, into which nobody . . . had ever been permitted to enter'. He throws himself (humbly) up against the vitalistic Mark Rampion (D. H. Lawrence, a friend of Huxley's), and in the book gives Rampion the edge ('the intellect', Quarles ends by believing, 'ought to humble itself . . . and admit the claims of the heart, aye and the bowels, the loins. . . .'). But that was to falsify the true state of affairs. Savage calls the novel an inept failure, shoddily written, 'puerile in conception and presentation'. . . . There is something to this judgement, and even to the charge that here more than anywhere Huxley betrays 'the fatal juvenility which . . . vitiates his understanding of life'. But it is none the less too severe. Huxley is only juvenile as a novelist when compared to, say, Lawrence at his very best; at times *Point Counter Point* is far from inept; the sincerity and, perhaps more to the point, the seriousness of Huxley's project is evident on every page, and Rampion is realized with power and some understanding. After this Huxley's powers as a novelist collapsed: *Eyeless in Gaza* (1936), *After Many a Summer* (1939) and all its successors are intelligent; but they are thesis-fiction, written in an entire absence of imaginative pressure. *Brave New World* (1932) is a clever but somewhat cold dystopia. Of Huxley's retreat into mysticism the less said, perhaps, the better: it never seems, even to a reader of good faith who is interested in mysticism and not prejudiced against it, to be more than journalistic; one assumes, or at least hopes, that his personal experience was of a more substantial calibre. His two best later books are historical studies: *Grey Eminence* (1941) and *The Devils of Loudon* (1952). *Texts and Pretexts* (1932) is one of the most lively and provocative anthologies— linked by commentary—of its time. His *Letters* (1971) are interesting.

WILLIAM GERHARDIE (1895)—the final 'e' is his own recent reversion to an older family spelling—is a better novelist, who has never had his due; even a uniform edition initiated in the late Sixties has not really established him. He did in truth 'go off' (like the ladies in Mrs. Oliphant's Victorian novel *Miss Marjoribanks*) very badly during the Thirties, and his latter-day manner (in letters to the press and so on) has been irritating and off-putting; but this is not an excuse for the neglect of his accomplished and unusual early novels. His originality owes much, no doubt, to the fact that Gerhardie—an Englishman—was brought up in Petrograd: he looks at things from a very unusual point of view. That is his strength. *Futility* (1922) and *The Polyglots* (1925) are both true English-Chekhov—and both deal with Englishmen abroad. Here Gerhardie is both sad and comic, with a certain modest deftness of touch that he later mistakenly sacrificed in the interests of a wider scope. *Resurrection* (1934), about a young man who has the mystical experience of becoming divorced from his body, is his attempt at a major novel, and it almost comes off. But Gerhardie is too ambitious and self-consciously experimental, as if he wishes to produce a rival to *Ulysses* or *Point Counter Point*; and it is here, too, that a self-defeating tone of superiority begins to creep in (just the same kind of preening but mistaken self-delight that wrecks Nabokov's *Ada*, q.v.). *Of Mortal Love* (1936), a sentimental love story of the Twenties, shows his talent stretched to its utmost—and fragmenting under the strain.

EVELYN WAUGH (1903–66), another predictable admirer of Firbank, has the same horror of life as Huxley; he has more energy, Dickensian inventiveness, but is much sicker—he early (1930) rationalized his inability to respond to people into an all-embracing orthodoxy: Roman Catholicism. Essentially, however, his world is the nihilistic one of Firbank; but it was enriched by the manure of an intelligent and religious gloom. It is obvious enough that Waugh dwelled darkly and at length upon the mysteries of Christ; but it is equally obvious that, whatever he achieved in his own life, self-centredness deflects his work from true seriousness. Religion in his work seldom functions as more than something to console his sense of hatred (not dislike or distaste) for the world—and everyone in it. His aggressive Catholicism has assured him of many more readers than Huxley—but he is not really a better novelist, even if he looks like one (and it must be conceded that he usually does): his religion is seen, by his readers at least, as his excuse for condemning not merely the modern world but also the people in it. Waugh's early novels differ from Huxley's in that they are fantasies where Huxley's are farces; they are less brilliant, but more crazy. In *Decline and Fall* (1928) and *Vile Bodies* (1930) there is a sense of autonomous life missing in even the earliest Huxley; the atmosphere is entirely antinomian. Only the kind of seriousness that expresses itself in the form of solidity is absent—present, instead, is an indifference of which the author is obviously unaware. It might have been youth; later books showed that it was not. *A Handful of Dust* (1937), the story of a man's falling apart under the strain of his broken marriage, has been admired as Waugh's best novel and a masterpiece; but it is neither. It is rather, as Graham Martin has suggested, a piece of elaborate and skilful fakery: Waugh uses his famous detached manner—much vaunted as 'objectivity'—to cover up his own incapacity for that psychological understanding which amounts to compassion. Whereas in the comic novels (*Scoop*, 1938, and *Put Out*

More Flags, 1942, are to be included in this category) Waugh could
to some extent rationalize his terror into shuddering, quick laughter,
here he inhibits himself by attempting to deal with ostensibly realist
material. All Waugh's later fiction—with the exception of the scari-
fying satire, *The Loved One*, 1948, on the Hollywood cult of death—
is spoiled in this way. The trilogy formed by *Men at Arms* (1952),
Officers and Gentlemen (1954) and *Unconditional Surrender* (1961) is an
imitation of Ford's *Parade's End* (q.v.), and collapses by the side of
it: Guy Crouchback is a wistful technicoloured photograph of
Waugh, whereas Tietjens has an existence independent of Ford. It
is true that in this trilogy, especially in the concluding book, Waugh
tried to assert interest in humanity; but it came too late to make any
difference to his achievement: the relevant passages read like sermons preached by worthy but linguistically ungifted parsons. The
best of the later novels is *The Ordeal of Gilbert Pinfold* (1957), a treatment of his own experience of a series of hallucinations induced by
the paraldehyde he took in order to alleviate his manic-depressive
illness. A gifted writer—but either neutral or nasty in just the places
where niceness counts.

*

JOYCE CARY (1888–1957) did not publish his first novel, *Aissa Saved*,
until 1932, when he was forty-four years old—so that as a writer he
belongs to a generation later than his own. He is an exuberant
novelist, whose poor sense of form is usually more than counter-
balanced by his remarkable gift for identifying with his characters.
What matters to Cary is vitality and integrity: these are more
important than morality—and in the life of an individual they are
more important qualities than success. Cary's earliest novels, written
out of his experiences in the Nigerian Political Service, are as good
as anything he ever did. *Aissa Saved* is an objective account of the
effect of missionaries upon those they convert, *Mister Johnson* the
memorable story of an African who tries, with first pathetic and then
tragic results, to live like an Englishman. The sequence *Herself
Surprised* (1941), *To Be a Pilgrim* (1942) and *The Horse's Mouth* (1944)
is a study in different sorts of innocence and integrity; the novels are
narrated, respectively, by Sara Monday, Mr. Wilcher and Gulley
Jimson. The first and the last of these are criminal; Wilcher is a
senile exhibitionist. But all three represent life to Cary, and, whether
they irritate the reader or not, there is no mistaking the gusto and
the energy which have gone into their making. *A House of Children*
(1941) recreates an Irish childhood with great charm and verve. It
is true that the actual world of Cary's novels is unvaried and limited,

and even that he is unimaginative ('there is ... much less ... than meets the eye' in his writing, wrote Anthony West); but he is inventive, and he does convey the sense of life in which he so desperately believed. Cary is a representative of the same religious tradition as Bunyan, but in his hands it becomes secularized into a kind of humanism, a combination of pragmatism and ecstasy that for many readers is unsatisfactory—but is nevertheless a fact of British life and is not artificial.

ROSE MACAULAY (1889–1958) was a humane, shrewd and witty novelist whose best work will assuredly survive. Her best novels are *Potterism* (1920), an excellent, rather Forsterian satire on the society of its time, and her last, *The Towers of Trezibond* (1956), the self-told story of a man who goes to Turkey to escape from an adulterous love-affair—an extremely unusual and sad comedy.

STELLA BENSON (1892–1933), who died young of tuberculosis, should not be forgotten. Probably her diary, which is now allowed to be published, is her most important work; but *The Poor Man* (1922) and *Tobit Transplanted* (1931) are both original, painfully self-probing, witty novels; the latter tells the story of Tobias and the Angel in a modern, Manchurian setting.

REBECCA WEST (ps. C. I. FAIRFIELD, 1892) is very much a novelist of her period: intelligent, solid, sensibly feminine, determinedly enlightened. She is a brilliant journalist—though in this field her work, of which *The Meaning of Treason* (1949) is the most notable, remains journalism. Her second novel, *The Judge* (1922), was hailed as the 'best psychoanalytical novel'; and so it was, but now it reads just a little too pat. In fact Rebecca West's best novel is the comparatively late *The Fountain Overflows* (1956), which is the first of a sequence in progress. This is a retrospective account of an Edwardian family broken up by the defection of the brilliant but self-destructive father. *Letters to A Grandfather* (1933) is an unusual work about the religious impulse, in which God appears as a tired Negro in faded scarlet evening dress.

More gifted as a novelist than any of these, and now unduly neglected (not a single book of hers is in print) is Rebecca West's older contemporary MAY SINCLAIR (1865–1946). Like Rebecca West, she is very much of the Edwardian period (she was a suffragette, or at least took part in some marches), but her grasp of character is greater; clever, again like Rebecca West, in her best fiction she transcends this entirely. *Mary Olivier: A Life* (1919) and *The Life and Death of Harriett Frean* (1922), both acute psychological studies of women, are probably her finest novels; but *A Cure of Souls* (1924), the portrait of a sybaritic vicar, runs these very close. May Sinclair was also a very good writer of short stories; one of these, 'Where Their Fire is Not Quenched', is a small masterpiece of the supernatural.

ELIZABETH BOWEN (1899–1973), as obviously a disciple of Henry James as L. P. Hartley, has written about a dozen worthy novels, full of delicate and sensitive descriptions of moods and places, but has never equalled *The Death of the Heart* (1938), the story of the destruction of a young girl's sensibility and capacity to love by a group of cold-hearted, affected people. In her other novels, one of the best of which is *The Little Girls* (1964), Elizabeth Bowen is better, so to speak, at description than psychology. And she has made her incapacity to deal with any but a specific type of upper-class person into a more severe limitation than it needs to be by trying, from time to time, to overcome it.

DAVID GARNETT (1892) wrote some unusual novels of fantasy—'a perfect literary nick-nack', Desmond MacCarthy said of the first, *Lady Into Fox* (1922)—but gradually dried up until in the middle Fifties he produced a very ordinary comedy of manners. *Lady Into Fox* is, indeed, a slight work; but it is beautifully done, with exactly the right touch, as are its successors *A Man in the Zoo* (1924) and *The Sailor's Return* (1925). Sylvia Townsend Warner (q.v.) began in something like the same vein with her story of a witch, *Lolly Willowes* (1926); but she went on to produce a much more substantial novel, a remarkable account of fourteenth-century convent life, *The Corner That Held Them* (1948). Garnett wrote *No Love* (1929), a realistic picture of life in the first quarter of the twentieth century, which is marred by preciosity of style, but contains some vivid portraits. He wrote no fiction between 1935 and 1955; when he began again he had lost his touch.

J. B. PRIESTLEY (1894) has been a best-selling novelist since the panoramic *The Good Companions* (1929); he has also had successes as a playwright—sometimes an interestingly experimental one. It has long been fashionable to dismiss him from serious consideration—but this is not fair. Priestley does have certain middlebrow vices: long-windedness, over-heartiness—an insecure, bluff, Yorkshire manner—sentimentality; and he is in the realm of fiction an entirely conventional realist. But he has virtues: and he is a better novelist than his master and close friend Hugh Walpole (q.v.), with whom he collaborated in a letter-novel. Even *The Good Companions*, the tale of a concert party, has virtues: strong characterization, a good sense of place, a sense of the comic. But he has written better than this: good, intelligent thrillers (*Black-Out in Gretley*, 1942, is the best) and *Lost Empires* (1965), a really moving story of the old-time music-hall.

His plays are well made, and the 'time' plays—*Time and the Conways* (1937) and *I Have Been Here Before* (1937)—and *Dangerous Corner* (1932) are as good as anything seen in the commercial theatre in their decade.

L. P. HARTLEY (1895–1972) is an uneven writer—some of his tales of the supernatural are really shoddy—but at his best he earns the comparison with Henry James (q.v.) that is often made. *Simonetta Perkins* (1925) is as much an exercise in the manner of James as Lubbock's *The Region Cloud*. Hartley's strength lies, rather surprisingly, in his stern morality. His attitudes are what would be called 'old-fashioned', and one assumes that he would reject such things as psychoanalysis as tending to excuse 'evil' conduct. And yet his own work is very 'Freudian': it gains its power from the fact that the evil in it is never really defined. *The Go-Between* (1950) is a Jamesean tale of the adult world interpreted by a boy. The *Eustace and Hilda* trilogy—*The Shrimp and the Anemone* (1944), *The Sixth Heaven* (1946), *Eustace and Hilda* (1947)—is the subtle and beautifully told account of a brother and sister doomed, by their characters, to destroy each other; terror and comedy are perfectly blended here. Although Hartley is himself a moralist (his non-fiction work leaves this in no doubt) he is not in fact a moralist as a writer, but rather what Paul Bloomfield has described as 'the transmitter of a civilized ethos'. He has not only an awareness of evil but also an awareness of inevitability; moreover, he makes no judgements in his novels. *Facial Justice* (1960) is a powerfully imagined dystopia.

L. A. G. STRONG (1896–1958) never fulfilled his early promise. A prolific and successful writer of competent and intelligent novels, the really substantial novel just eluded him. He was highly professional —perhaps too much so—but could only create types, rather than developing characters. His best work is to be found in the early novels *Dewar Rides* (1929), *The Garden* (1931) and *Sea Wall* (1933), and in his short stories of Irish rural life. He was a graceful minor poet: *The Body's Imperfection* (1957) collects his poems.

CHARLES MORGAN (1896–1958), regarded by the French as a leading British novelist, has gained the unenviable reputation of the middlebrow novelist *par excellence*: he is pretentious,' deep' without depth, politely mystical—and pompous (one of his favourite phrases was 'the eternal verities'). 'X marks the spot where I read *Sparkenbroke*' (1936) V. S. Pritchett said of his most pretentious book. But Morgan did write one good novel: his first, *The Gunroom* (1919), based on his naval experiences. This was relatively simple, and came out of real suffering. Within six years, with *My Name is Legion*, Morgan had learned how to get himself compared with Dostoevski in

The London Mercury. . . . His elaborate prose style is as bad as his 'philosophy': he became a Golf-Club novelist, and entirely deserves his bad reputation.

The Irish writer LIAM O'FLAHERTY (1896) wrote some excellent short stories and one good novel, *The Informer* (1925), but seems to have dried up in mid-career. The stories in *Spring Sowing* (1924) were lyrical, elemental, highly readable without, however, making any concessions to popularity. They marked him out as one of the leading writers in this form of his generation; but the two collections since *The Short Stories* (1937; 1948) have not been on the early level.

Another writer who lost his fine early form, perhaps because he decided to tackle novels—for which he had a commercial but not really an artistic capacity—is H. E. BATES (1905–1974). Bates' early stories, in such volumes as *Day's End* (1928), *The Woman Who Had Imagination* (1934) and *The Beauty of the Dead* (1940), are unsurpassed in English in their time. 'The Kimono' for example, a magnificent story, could have been written by no one else. But since serving in the R.A.F. during the Second World War Bates' work coarsened considerably, although it remained highly professional. The earlier Bates is a sensuous, powerful writer, expert in portraying women and their moods and the atmosphere of the countryside or the small country town. Latterly he became mannered, and sometimes declined into self-parody.

V. S. PRITCHETT (1900) was never, perhaps, as good as Bates at his best. But he is more versatile and his work has not fallen off. His stories—collected in 1956—are often about eccentric characters or absurd situations. His novels, which contain passages of exquisite comedy, are studies of tormented puritans: *Nothing Like Leather* (1935), *Dead Man Leading* (1937) and *Mr. Beluncle* (1951), the best, a sympathetic and penetrating study of an enthusiast for odd and out-of-the-way nonconformist religions. Pritchett is one of the very few good contemporary literary journalists.

*

We now come to the three novelists, all born in the first decade of the century, who are generally regarded as the most important of their generation: Graham Greene, C. P. Snow and Anthony Powell.

GRAHAM GREENE (1904) is, like Waugh, with whom he is sometimes bracketed because of it, a convert to Roman Catholicism. But he is a very different sort of Catholic. For one thing, while Waugh was obviously of a Tory mentality, Greene is aggressively left-wing; again, where Waugh revered orthodoxy and decorum, Greene is openly against the conservative elements in his Church—and in his obsessive concern with seediness and evil he has even appeared to many of his fellow Roman Catholics to be heretical. However, Greene's Catholicism is an even more essential element in his fiction than Waugh's. Essentially Greene is concerned with what in Catholic terms is the idea of the mercy of God; but we do not need to be Catholics ourselves to respond to his work—for this idea functions in it as human compassion. Thus, in *Brighton Rock* (1938), the first major novel, the young gangster and murderer Pinkie is presented as in some sense 'holy': he is at least dedicated to evil, whereas his pursuers are merely decent—they lack Pinkie's faith in God, which continues to exist in spite of his desperate project to deny it. This is not in fact a realist novel (how would a semi-literate young gangster remark 'Credo in unum Satanum'?), although the seedy realist background is superbly filled in. Greene has never seriously sought to imitate life (as, say, Snow does so industriously). *Brighton Rock* is a thriller-as-metaphor (Paul West calls it a 'structural oxymoron'), a superb novel that misses real distinction only because of a certain patness on the part of the author, a professionalism that most unfortunately functions as an over-simplifying, even a coarsening, agent. This criticism applies in more or less degree to all Greene's novels, and is perhaps the reason why they do not wear as well as one expects them to. And yet I think it is truer to put it in this way than in the way the Leavis-inspired (q.v.) F. N. Lees (1952) put it. He spoke of 'popular fiction ... crude analysis, the obtrusive and deformed emotionalism ... defective presentational technique. ...' That is to say, I believe Greene's view of life has more power and creative validity than this approach allows: one does see it as modified by sensationalism, but at least its power is always there. His view of life, repellent to so many people, is not really 'popular' (i.e. middlebrow): it involves no manipulations of reality, and it cannot be called sentimentality.

His first novel, *The Man Within* (1929), was influenced by both Robert Louis Stevenson and—thematically—Conrad, a novelist whom he closely resembles. Even here Greene's hero is educated by guilt into grace. And for those who are not Catholics, and doubtless for some of those who are, grace in Greene often means simply *being human* rather than being *moral-before-the-event*: defensively rigid, reaching forward aggressively into the texture of life to make judgements. Greene's whisky-priest in *The Power and the Glory* (1940) is a coward, dirty, the father of a bastard—but he is none the less a priest. He represents man, doomed to sin (always depicted in Greene as various kinds of squalor or shabbiness), redeemed by grace. He is the only priest in a Mexico that has prohibited both Catholicism and alcohol, and his enemy is a policeman who is as dedicated as himself. Before the priest is shot the two come together, in a passage whose irony is sometimes missed, to recognize each other's type of goodness.

Greene has tended to parody himself in some of his later novels, in particular in *The Heart of the Matter* (1948), which is technically one of his finest achievements. This dramatization of theological abstractions (how can a sinner in the eyes of God's Church be a saint in the eyes of God?) is almost convincing; but Orwell (q.v.) was right to charge that it led to 'psychological absurdities'. However, although the context into which Greene has put his hero, Scobie, is unsatisfactory, the man himself is nevertheless invested with a kind of life. The best of the later novels are *The Quiet American* (1955), which contains a masterful portrait of a hysterically bad man, and *The Comedians* (1966), about Haiti under the malevolent regime of the late Duvalier, 'Papa Doc'.

Although C. P. SNOW (1905) has by now attracted almost as much attention as Greene, he is not in the same class. He provides, in fact, an excellent example of an approach that is not merely traditional— Greene is not an innovator in the technical sense, but no one can accuse him of refusing to confront the problems of the twentieth century—but also positively inadequate and obscurantist. As Rubin Rabinovitz has demonstrated in his *The Reaction Against Experiment in the English Novel 1950-1960* (1967), Snow as a critic has been resolutely against every kind of modernism. His favourite novelists include—as well as Proust, whom he wishes to emulate—Daphne du Maurier, James Gould Cozzens (q.v.) ('one of the few novelists now practising whom a grown-up person can read with respect'; 'intellectually and morally hard'; 'the soundest of his generation . . . which includes . . . Faulkner. . . .'), Nevil Shute and Nancy Mitford. Of satire he has said that it is 'cheek'; and he has quoted with approval his wife Pamela Hansford Johnson's remark that it is 'the revenge of those who cannot really comprehend the world. . . .' Snow, who has been a scientist, civil servant and government minister, is the author of a *roman fleuve* called *Strangers and Brothers* (1940-70). The narrator is Lewis Eliot—a figure resembling Snow himself in education, background, profession and temperament. The books' reading order is *Strangers and Brothers* (1940), *The Conscience of the Rich* (1958), *Time of Hope* (1949), *The Light and the Dark* (1947), *The Masters* (1951), *Homecoming* (1956), *The New Men* (1954), *The Affair* (1960), *Corridors of Power* (1964), *The Sleep of Reason* (1968) and *Last Things* (1970). They trace the progress of Eliot from a

Midland working-class childhood through legal training and practice as a barrister, wartime service at a Ministry, to eminence in the
political world; Eliot's two marriages and his friendships are re-
viewed. Now this novel-sequence is an achievement. But it is not a
literary achievement. The reason is, simply, that Snow lacks
imagination. His Lewis Eliot is a mostly flattering photograph of
himself: the stiff-lipped man of affairs, compassionate and understanding, but controlled in the interests of the commonweal. It
has as much relationship to life—life in the sense the novelist must
feel it: life out there, not-as-I-want-it, the lived, mysterious thing—
as a well-run office of the civil service. Admirable, perhaps; but
certainly limited. That definition of satire—'cheek'—is surely relevant. Not all literature, of course, is satire; but all except the rare
literature of pure joy (and no one is going to accuse *Strangers and
Brothers* of being that: it is as drab as Monday morning at the
Ministry of Social Security) springs out of what may be described as
the difference between man as he is and man as he might be. . . .
Snow's attitudes, although humane, function throughout his
sequence as a kind of self-satisfaction. The man writing this book is
an excellent public man (if public men can be excellent), but he is
not what we usually think of as a novelist. Walter Allen speaks of
Snow's 'massive fairness' (he is thinking particularly of *The Masters*,
1951, about the struggle for power in a Cambridge college), but is
this not the fairness of an enlightened civil servant? Is not the 'moral
agnosticism' from which it springs a result, not of a mature scepticism, but of an improverished imagination? Is not his 'wonderfully
subtle' (Paul West) sense of character merely the shrewdness of an
interviewer quick to smell out a candidate with problems or habits
that might lead him to put himself before The Firm? Shrewd, yes.
But understanding?

One might say that it was, at least, all very worthy—if it were not
so clearly inadequate, so sociologically unsophisticated (has he read
Romains or Durkheim? Does he think he comprehends them? One
would give much to know the answers)—and if the self-satisfaction of
Lewis Eliot, the man (after all) of affairs, were less apparent. What is
shocking in the sequence is that Eliot, the great inside-man to whom
supreme reality is bureaucratic procedure, is so uncritical of the
world in which he lives. Nothing is *really* wrong—but if only officials
wouldn't indulge in so much humanity: the great reality isn't being
yourself at home but compromising in committee. Snow has little
style, no humour, no recognition of the religious side of man (even
in the sense that the sociologist Durkheim wrote of it) or of its
function. Eliot's world is colourless: no tenderness, no lyricism—no

enthusiasm or passion. However, Snow treats politicians and the lives they lead with absolute solemnity—indeed, with reverence. No 'cheek' or 'revenge' here. And Eliot himself ('in depth . . . myself' admits Snow): is he admirable—or, as Geoffrey Wagner has put it, 'obnoxious'? The answer is not relevant to Snow's achievement. The more important question is, Is he real? The answer must, I think, be that he is not real in terms of his century: he is as blind as his creator to the real nature of twentieth-century man. Snow, the most reactionary of novel reviewers (he is not and presumably has not set out to be a literary critic), has consistently attacked all forms of modernism; he and his wife's violent objections to 'absurdity' and 'cruelty' are as well known as they are one-sided; the nature of his attitude is revealing. As Frederick R. Karl has pointed out, the characters in Snow's novels are not real; the code they live by is illusory: 'Snow is not really concerned with people . . . he gives a sense of the *things* that exist. . . . This way of treating *things* is carried over to people. . . . What pompous fools these administrators and scientists are as Snow describes them, and yet he takes them seriously. . . .' Let us grant Snow's good intentions; let us grant that he is nice enough to attract kind criticism from people who ought to (and no doubt, privately, do) know better. We still cannot escape from judging him with the utmost severity. His enormous yarn, or head-boy's prospectus-in-form-of-tale, is extremely ambitious: it demands an answer of the same magnitude. That answer is that it is reprehensible—I use the mildest term available—to treat human beings as objects in any kind of games—even in office games. Our response must be: 'No, people are *not* like this; and we must not allow them to become so'.

ANTHONY POWELL (1905) provides a complete contrast: his attitude is sardonic 'High Tory' (Snow is nominally a socialist); he has the aristocratic background that Snow makes it obvious that he lacks; he is sophisticated and has a sophisticated style; above all, he has a highly developed sense of humour. Members of Parliament can read Snow with pleasure; one cannot imagine their having much time for Powell.

Powell wrote five novels before the Second World War, of which the last, *What's Become of Waring?* (1939), is perhaps the best. They established him as the best comic novelist of his generation; but recognition of this fact has been slow to come, despite the fame of his novel-sequence (still in progress), *A Dance to the Music of Time*, begun in 1951 with *A Question of Upbringing*. Powell's method in the early novels is decidedly aristocratic and omniscient; but he knows not to try to do more than expose the follies and stupidity of his characters. There is more than a touch of Wyndham Lewis, although the tone is softer, and the laughter elicited considerably less strident.

A Dance to the Music of Time continues the comic work with confidence, brilliance and an admirable coolness; it is also a technical *tour de force*. Powell is one of those novelists who make a virtue of their limitations. While it is true that his attitude is unmistakably upper-class—as a novelist he cannot take the lower classes seriously—it is to his credit that he has not tried to change this: *A Dance to the Music of Time* never purports to be more than an upper-class comedy. However, it must be conceded that the sequence lacks variety, that the reasons for 'strangely formalized dialogue' are not yet fully apparent, and that the area it covers is small. All these are valid objections to its evaluation as a major work.

Powell's narrator, Nicholas Jenkins, is evocatively unobtrusive, a worried ironist whose own personality is for most of the time in the background. His narrative consists of carefully selected recollections; objectivity is attained by a balletic scheme in which 'human beings, facing outwards like the Seasons, move hand in hand in intricate measure'. Whether or not this is a viable or even relevant concept, the spell of the storyteller is present. Powell's type of comedy has been compared to Evelyn Waugh's; but the hypomanic and cruel element in Waugh is absent; where he is frenetically gleeful, shrieking the truth of (his own) religion, Powell is thoughtful, as if in his attitude he were trying to define what social sanity might consist of.

The sequence opens with *A Question of Upbringing* (1951). After a Proustian introductory paragraph, Nicholas Jenkins is back at school, at Eton. Its successors are: *A Buyer's Market* (1952), *The Acceptance World* (1955), *At Lady Molly's* (1957), *Casanova's Chinese Restaurant* (1960), *The Kindly Ones* (1962), *The Valley of Bones* (1964), *The Soldier's Art* (1966), *The Military Philosophers* (1968) and *Books Do Furnish a Room* (1971).

Some objections to the consideration of Powell as a major novelist have been mentioned. Against these is the fact that—despite the restricted area of life treated—few fictional techniques employed in the English language today convey as well as Powell's the sense of life as it actually passes before us: hence the plotlessness, the wild improbabilities and coincidences, the flatness of narrative manner. The passing of time is for once seen—without metaphysics or passion—as it is: without even such feelings about it as Powell himself possesses. But this does not create a sense of boredom. Widmerpool, one of the true monsters of modern fiction, is anything but a bore. There is residual wisdom enough in the sequence for us to want to know, not what Powell will do with Widmerpool, but what life will do with him. . . . We shall not be sure of the status of *The Music of Time* until it is finished: certainly, however, Widmerpool is a major comic-evil creation. Behind Powell's comedy and irony, and perhaps behind the Proustian ambitions, lies a serious concern with what human obligations are, or might become. The American critic Charles Shapiro's judgement, 'England's best comic writer since Charles Dickens', may well prove to be right.

*

RICHARD HUGHES (1900), a pioneer of radio drama as well as a novelist, has written so little that he probably has not had his full due. Each of his three novels is excellent and highly original. The first, *A High Wind in Jamaica* (1929), is the story of some children in the Sixties of the last century; on their way home from a Jamaican plantation they are captured by pirates; eventually they are rescued, and learn to accept an adult version of their experience. But the subject of the novel is the truer nature of this experience: its nature as seen from the viewpoint of a child. This lucid tale of children, brutal and yet strangely gentle, is poetic in the best sense. Hughes' now unjustly forgotten poems (they are collected in *Confessio Juvenis*, 1926) were successful—they are influenced by Skelton and by Hughes' friend Robert Graves, yet are original and eloquent—but lightweight. *In Hazard* (1938), equally unusual and beautifully accomplished, is about a steamer caught in an unexpected hurricane. The narration seems to be artless, but is in fact highly sophisticated and carefully planned—one presumes that Hughes has written so little because he revises at length. The revelation of the true characters of some of the ship's officers and crew is done with consummate skill and subtlety; the descriptive writing is masterly. Hughes' third novel, *The Fox in the Attic* (1962), the beginning of a three- or four-volume work with the rather unhappy title of *The Human Predicament*, is 'a historical novel of my own times'. A young Welshman, just too young to have fought in the First World War, comes down from Oxford and goes to the Germany of the Weimar Republic. Here we meet Hitler, Goering, Röhm and other historical personages; the hero, a curiously innocent and bewildered creature, understands little of what is going on around him. It will be impossible to judge this novel until we have the whole.

EDWARD UPWARD (ps. ALLEN CHALMERS, 1903), close friend at Cambridge of Isherwood (with whom he devised the private, satirical world of 'Mortmere'—as Isherwood recounts in his autobiography *Lions and Shadows*, 1938), was the only British writer of fiction—as Gascoyne (q.v.) was of poetry—successfully to absorb both Kafka and surrealism (qq.v.). This was in the novel *Journey to the Border* (1938), and in a few short stories (now collected, together with the novel, in *Railway Accident*, 1969). This early work is brilliant and exciting, but it has been a little overrated; the stories are better than the novel because the latter peters out into crude communist propaganda. Communist dogma is what frustrates Upward's very different novels *In the Thirties* (1962) and *Rotten Elements* (1969), which are the first two of a projected trilogy. They trace the progress of Alan Sebrill, who, like Upward himself, joins the communists in the Thirties but leaves them in the Forties. Sebrill is an unsympathetic character: a humourless puritan rigidly devoted to his creed. The writing is deliberately muted: it is as if Upward had determined to sacrifice all his imaginative gifts. However, the account of Sebrill's dedication to communism is of historical interest. In effect Upward recounts the process of a man's destruction by his lack of humour and flexibility; but he does it unwittingly.

Upward's early prose was more effective than that of the overrated REX WARNER (1905). Warner is a gifted stylist and a classical scholar of distinction, but in his fiction he has consistently failed to find a satisfactory objective correlative (q.v.). It is obvious that he has feelings and ideals, but his fiction is always spoiled by coldness and over-intellectuality. In the earlier, Marxist books—*The Wild Goose Chase* (1937) and *The Professor* (1938)—Warner created, with undoubted skill although little conviction, a Kafkaesque atmosphere; but this tended, in fact, to obscure his intentions—which were simply allegorical. In *The Aerodrome* (1941), his least unsuccessful novel, the allegory becomes more explicit, although an over-complicated plot interferes with its impact. Since the end of the war Warner has written efficient but less ambitious historical novels.

ARTHUR KOESTLER (1905) has treated the problems of fascism and communism with more success. He is a Hungarian whose better fiction was written in Hungarian and German rather than English. Before becoming an Englishman and settling in England Koestler spent some time in gaols in Spain (under sentence of death) and France; he has written books about this. After temporarily giving up fiction Koestler wrote a series of useful, influential books on sociological and religious subjects. His first two and best novels were written in Hungarian and German respectively: *The Gladiators* (tr. E. Simon, 1939) and *Darkness at Noon* (tr. D. Hardy, 1940). The first is an intelligent and moving account of the slaves' revolt of Spartacus in ancient Rome; that it examines it in twentieth-century terms does not subtract from its power and force of characterization. *Darkness at Noon* is Koestler's finest novel: it is the story of an old-guard communist who falls victim to Stalin's purges. He is a 'just' victim to the extent that in his heart he regards Stalin as a betrayer of communism. This was one of the earliest really lucid revelations—in the West —of the true nature of Stalin's rule. But its political implications are incidental—they gain their strength from Koestler's very matter-of-factness. Rubashov, the protagonist, is presented not only as a victim of a tyrannical system and a mad logic: we see him attaining an ultimate freedom as he contemplates his destruction. That the book is so convincing psychologically is a strong argument against those who hold that it is not really a novel at all. Koestler's later novels are in English. None is dull, and all are acutely intelligent; but they lack the power of the two already discussed. *Thieves in the Night* (1946) is an impassioned but propagandist tale of the struggle of the Zionists in the Palestine of 1937–9; *Arrival and Departure* (1943) tries to demonstrate that ethical imperatives transcend neurosis—a secret agent is shown by psychoanalysis that his motivations are private, but he continues the fight—but the bones of the argument show through the thin psychological skin and flesh much too obtrusively.

GEORGE ORWELL (1903–50), who died young, of tuberculosis, has been much discussed since he published *Animal Farm* (1945), his satire on the Soviet Union; but his fiction apart from this has been consistently underrated. He has been called many things: leftist, conservative, sick satirist. . . . His last great novel, *Nineteen Eighty-Four* (1949), has been systematically denigrated, despite its great power: it is too near the truth. Even David Daiches, usually a reliable critic, calls it 'masochistic' and tiptoes backwards into the safety of the drawing-room (home of 'serious political reflections') as he gasps, 'as a criticism of English socialism it is fantastically irrelevant and even as a picture of the ultimate evil of the totalitarian state it is too obsessed and self-lacerating to arouse serious political reflection'. *Nineteen Eighty-Four* is not a criticism of English socialism, but a warning of the consequences of contemporary 'politics' in general. What Daiches may have failed to realize is that it is just conceivably possible that Orwell's warning has actually postponed or even prevented the horrors that he foretold. This novel represents an entirely valid resolution of Orwell's conflicts. Big Brother and the rest are convincing: the critics have shrunk back in horror. Irving Howe is right when he observes that the book 'trembles with an eschatological fury that is certain to create . . . the most powerful kinds of resistance'. Once that fury is recognized, the timid little Aristotelian and other objections of the awed critics can be seen for what they are—and ignored. For, as Howe points out, of course we should all 'feel more comfortable if the book could be cast out'. It is certainly, to employ C. P. Snow's unforgettable term, 'cheek'; but it will take more than Snow or even Daiches to transform the nature of twentieth-century affairs into something genteel and acceptable at office- or cosy seminar-level. *Nineteen Eighty-Four* is a vision of Swiftian proportions which belongs, horribly, to our time.

Orwell was a fine (if often confused) journalist—all his occasional writing is in *The Collected Essays, Journalism and Letters of George Orwell* (1968). He can be obtuse (what columnist is not from time to time?) but he makes up for this with his many unique insights. He is, in fact, for decency and readability and intelligence combined, the best journalist of the century—and it is by studying his journalism all together that we can best see that his potentialities, in the realm of psychological fiction, were enormous. But his best work is in *Down and Out in Paris and London* (1933) and in his novels (a fact not sufficiently recognized), chiefly of course in *Animal Farm* (a classic), and the final book. It has been said that Orwell was not interested in character; but to condemn him as a novelist because of this is to misunderstand both his purposes and the type of fiction he wrote— as well as to ignore his actual achievement. After all, *Animal Farm* is an animal fable. And a characterization of Winston Smith, the protagonist of *Nineteen Eighty-Four*, would be wholly out of place: the man is fighting for the right to have a personality. Thus he makes effective his ultimate verdict on those who are *not* interested in character. His autobiographical sketch of pre-school life, *Such, Such Were the Joys* (it is in the *Collected Essays*), shows considerable aptitude for presenting character, and suggests that, had he lived, he could have carried out his intention of breaking away entirely from polemics to write about 'human relationships'—this is what he told his wife in the last days of his life. But his earlier novels are better than is often admitted: *Burmese Days* (1934), *A Clergyman's Daughter* (1935), *Keep the Aspidistra Flying* (1936), *Coming up for Air* (1939): all these have lasted for over a quarter of a century or more—and they will survive as invaluable and sensitive portraits of the Thirties where more ambitious books will fall into oblivion. They are the nearest we have in fiction to the novels of Gissing (q.v.): they evince a similar kind of disgust at all the manifestations of modern life, and a similarly obstinate belief in integrity. But I cannot agree with Walter Allen that Orwell resembles Gissing in deficiency of 'human sympathy'. True, some of Gissing's novels are thus deficient; but I do not think one feels this in Orwell. He is not concerned with the compassionate portrayal of character; but he is concerned with the portrayal of the conditions that cause men to lack compassion. Did Swift lack compassion? Allen admires *Burmese Days*, but feels that an impression of misanthropy 'finally chills'. But how was the young Orwell, fresh from Eton and service with the police in Burma, to deal with such conditions? Was there anything at all likeable about the British administration there? I think that what Allen feels is misanthropy is in fact despair of Swiftian proportions: compassionate concern. Orwell achieved more in his fiction than almost any critic is prepared to allow.

CHRISTOPHER ISHERWOOD (1904), once a great hope of English fiction, petered out into a skilful and intelligent entertainer—a novelist of high quality, but not of the first or perhaps even the second rank. His genius all but vanished, possibly under the pressure of personal problems, in a cloud of mysticism: like Huxley, he took up the study of Eastern religion—which he at first combined with writing film scripts in Hollywood. Isherwood, as all his novels and his autobiography (*Lions and Shadows*, 1938) show, writes very well indeed—too well, perhaps, for his own good, since he is able to make trivialities pass for more substantial stuff. Between 1928 and the outbreak of war (and his departure to America, where he has eventually settled—as an American citizen) Isherwood wrote four good minor novels. He was as gifted in prose as his friend Auden was in verse. But, again like Auden—many of whose characteristics he shares—he has never really grown up. Hence his retreat into an unconvincing mysticism. The early novels were comic and brilliant, but depthlessly so: the later ones well describe the miserable lives of immature men, but fail to explain the misery or the immaturity. For all the recommended mysticism (or Quaker austerity), one's strongest impression is of a clever, seedy, hopped-up kid. . . . The first two novels, *All the Conspirators* (1928) and *The Memorial* (1932), are clever and well observed Audenesque indictments of the bourgeois for their sickness of mind and acceptance of falsity; they do not go deep psychologically, but are technically adept. *Goodbye to Berlin* (1939) is Isherwood's best novel (the third, *Mr. Norris Changes Trains*, 1933, is an amusing, in-joke novel partly based on the exploits of a real-life homosexual): a series of sketches that superbly evoke the atmosphere of pre-Hitler Berlin; Isherwood is the neutral observer—and is at his best in this relaxed and undemanding position. *Prater Violet* (1945) was a disastrous attempt at a Hollywood novel; its successors are more readable and amusing, but entirely fail to account for their protagonists' inability to come to terms with themselves or the world.

A less clever, stylistically inferior, vastly more substantial (and, alas, more neglected) novelist is JAMES HANLEY (1901). Hanley is an irritating writer: he has obstinately refused to learn much about technique through over forty years of writing; he is diffuse and humourless; but he has a power and intensity of vision that all but a very few of his contemporaries lack. In certain respects he may be compared with Thomas Wolfe (q.v.); he does not run to length, and is generous and outward-looking where Wolfe was egocentric—but he has the same kind of crude energy, and is moved by the spectacle of life in somewhat the same way. *Boy* (1931), the stark tale of the ordeal and death of a twelve-year-old boy on a sea voyage, was foolishly banned, which discouraged the sensitive Hanley—who, however, continued with the first of his *Furys* tetralogy, about a Liverpool-Irish family (Hanley was born in Dublin): *The Furys* (1934), *The Secret Journey* (1936), *Our Time is Gone* (1940) and *Winter Song* (1950). This suffers from Hanley's usual faults of diffuseness and clumsiness—but it does have the inestimable advantage of reading like an account of a 'real' family. His most sombre work, however, is *Say Nothing* (1962), which deals with the despairing inhabitants of a boarding-house; this has a truly Dosteovskian power. Hanley's adaptation of this novel provided British television's finest play of the Sixties. Hanley's technique has not advanced, but he has developed into one of the subtlest exponents of inarticulate emotion; it is time that he gained the recognition that he deserves.

*

CYRIL CONNOLLY (1903–74) was not primarily a novelist; but *The Unquiet Grave* (1945), the book for which he will be remembered, is certainly an imaginative work. For many years Connolly—editor of the widely read magazine *Horizon* (1940–9)—was, with Pritchett and Grigson (qq.v.), one of the few literary journalists whose critical opinions were worth noting. His best criticism is collected in *Enemies of Promise* (1938 rev. 1949), *The Condemned Playground* (1945), *Ideas and Places* (1953) and *Previous Convictions* (1964). He is often provocative, and is unreliable on poetry—but always civilized (in the best sense) and worth reading. Like Jocelyn Brooke, Isherwood, and Rayner Heppenstall (qq.v.) he writes with a rare lucidity. He is an ironic pessimist of the civilized Irish variety ('It is closing time in the gardens of the West' . . .), puckish, an expert parodist, an authoritative historian of the educated sensibility of his age. Most of what may be said against him has been said by him in *The Unquiet Grave*, which he published under the pseudonym of 'Palinurus'. Since for his last few years Connolly (no longer at his most interested) was the chief literary columnist of the London *Sunday Times*, this book is in danger of being forgotten—or at any rate of being ignored by a generation too young to remember it. It is a work of courageous self-revelation, whose chief achievement is to cut self-love out of the self-portrait it renders. It is said that many intellectuals of Connolly's generation immediately recognized themselves in *The Unquiet Grave*; what is more surprising is that almost any cultivated person born not later than 1932 (or thereabouts) can still recognize something of himself in this wry, rueful and self-mockingly sensitive account of an intellectual's attempt to lead a tolerable existence. Connolly found it hard to be at his best—the novel *The Rock Pool* (1935), about a young man's disintegration when he falls into the hands of an arty group in France, is amusing but resolutely minor—but *The Unquiet Grave* is a classic, and it has not dated. *The Missing Diplomats* (1953), on Burgess and MacLean, both of whom he knew well, is a superb piece of journalism. Connolly, who produced little because he has not wanted to produce mediocre work, was almost the last of a dying breed: the genuine man of letters.

FLANN O'BRIEN (ps. BRIAN O'NOLAN, 1911–66), a civil servant, journalist and Gaelic scholar, who was born and lived all his life in Dublin, is a very different kind of Irishman, but is similarly unclassifiable in the context of the more or less conventional novel. O'Brien's prose combines Joyce (q.v.), who praised his first book, with the great nonsense writers—Lear, Carroll and Morgenstern (q.v.); only his tendency to whimsicality prevents his being a major comic writer. His lightness of touch, however, does not detract from his achievement: it is, indeed, a relief to have one of the most familiar of modern themes (a novel about a man writing a novel about men writing a novel, which is the subject of O'Brien's best book, *At Swim Two Birds*, 1939) treated lightly rather than heavily. *At Swim Two Birds* is funny in a unique manner. It is the quintessence of Irish responsibility, which means that it lacks serious emotional substance but not wisdom. A characteristic notion introduced by O'Brien is that the water we drink is too strong. . . . The other novels, *The Hard Life* (1961), *The Dalkey Archive* (1964), *The Third Policeman* (1967), are excellent comic tales on a smaller scale.

*

HENRY GREEN (ps. HENRY YORKE, 1905–1973), a Midlands industrialist, is a major novelist who pursued the trivial, of which he has an exquisite sense, to the point where his subject-matter disappeared and he stopped writing. But his achievement is a major one. *Living* (1929) is about life in a Midlands foundry just such as Green worked in after he came down from Oxford; it is a joyfully optimistic novel, simply celebrating the fact of life against a background of drabness, personal disappointment and hard work. Although it was for years taken as a proletarian novel, *Living* is concerned essentially with what Green considers the proper subject of modern fiction: 'the everyday mishaps of ordinary life'. Green is often called a symbolist; but the fog (*Party Going*, 1939) and birds (*Living, Party Going, Loving*, 1945) and other entities that haunt his novels are both more or less than symbols: they 'stand for' qualities just as such entities do so—if they do so—in 'real life'. Green, for all his carefully selective technique and lyricism, is a realist more than a symbolist. In *Party Going* a group of idle parasites are waiting to set off for France, but are delayed by fog in a hotel that becomes surrounded by workers waiting to go home. The scales are not weighted: this is a realist treatment. The metaphor for the 1939 situation is all the more effective for not being contrived—as in the novels of Rex Warner (q.v.) or some of the poetry of Auden (q.v.). *Caught* (1943) is about life in the London fire-service just before the German Blitz began in earnest. *Loving*, set in an Irish country house in the early years of the Second World War, is Green's most beautiful and subtle novel. It is the love story of the English butler, Raunce, and the housemaid Edith. Raunce is one of the most complex and solid portraits in modern British fiction. Raunce emerges so clearly because morality (judgement) never intervenes: the result is a product of pure imagination, a character as rich in contradictions as a real man. Green was not able to maintain this standard; in *Loving*, one of the most original novels of its time, he exactly caught the elusive poetry of 'everyday life'; his work was done. Its successors—*Back* (1946), *Concluding* (1948), *Nothing* (1950), *Doting* (1952)—concentrate, Pinter (q.v.)-like, on capturing exact nuances of speech, and become slighter and slighter.

JOCELYN BROOKE (1908–1966), another writer of unusually lucid prose, never achieved anything near the recognition he deserved, although his highly original autobiographical works—*The Goose Cathedral* (1950) and *The Dog at Clambercrown* (1955) are the best—received good notices. His finest book is *Private View: Four Portraits* (1954), four beautifully delineated, shrewd portraits of people whom he had known well. Brooke was at his best in this shadowy area between fiction and reminiscence, but one of his straight novels comes nearer to creating a genuinely Kafkaesque atmosphere than anything except Edward Upward's (q.v.) fiction of the Thirties: this is *The Image of a Drawn Sword* (1950), a beautifully written account of a nightmare that begins when the protagonist is awakened in the middle of the night and drafted into a unknown, mysterious army. . . . This at least of his fiction should survive; as a Proustian autobiographer he seems certain to be remembered.

ROSAMUND LEHMANN (1903) derives, like Elizabeth Bowen (q.v.), from Henry James as much as she derives from anyone. She is a sensitive writer, gifted with compassion and psychological understanding; but it sometimes seems that she seeks, vainly, to escape from her own feminine intensity. She has never found a really distinguished style, and her main subject—the sufferings of women in love—often becomes cloying and over-obtrusive. She has maintained a high standard, but probably has never done better than her first novel, *Dusty Answer* (1927), and *The Weather in the Streets* (1936). Both of these are excellent period pieces. In the much later *The Echoing Grove* (1953) her real intentions (to dissect and perhaps destroy, or reveal in its full unworthiness, the male object of female suffering) seem to be at odds with the story she tells, in which her gentleness and reconciliatory nature operate against her impulses. Her brother JOHN LEHMANN (1907) has written fiction, autobiography, criticism and graceful minor poetry; but he is most famous for his discriminatory help to young writers through his magazines (*Penguin New Writing, The London Magazine*) and his publishing firm.

WILLIAM COOPER (ps. HARRY S. HOFF, 1910) is a disciple of C. P. Snow (q.v.), but a more gifted novelist. The Joe Lunn of his *Scenes from Provincial Life* (1950) is the first of the unlikeable nonconformist heroes of whom Kingsley Amis' Jim Dixon is the most famous. In *Scenes From Married Life* (1961) Joe has settled down into a useful member of the community as a civil servant (he is also, of course, a well known writer) and accepted that what he once disliked and rebelled against is really the best of all possible worlds. . . . In this and his other novels Cooper is only as funny as an establishmentarian can be. There is, however, one exception: *Disquiet and Peace* (1956), a most perceptive and moving study of a woman afflicted with depression, set in Edwardian times. This is a distinguished and delicate novel, and stands in strange contrast to the mixture of crude, cocky brashness and conformity that characterize the other, markedly inferior, books.

PATRICK HAMILTON (1904–62), famous as the author of the excellent stage thriller *Rope* (1929), and of a really remarkable and underestimated play called *The Duke in Darkness* (1943), was a novelist who never received the critical attention he deserved. He was an expert (and envenomed) castigator of the speech habits and stupidity of the pseudo-gentry—the sort that congregate in the saloon-bars of large pubs (exactly the kind of people who refer to the lower classes as 'the great unwashed' and to Harold Wilson as 'Flash Harold').

This infinitely foolish and pathetic section of society is triumphantly well represented in *Mr. Simpson and Mr. Gorse* (1953), but too facetiously in the trilogy *Twenty Thousand Streets Under the Sky* (1935), the important parts of which, however, are entirely successful—and compassionate. Hamilton realized the poetic side of his genius most fully in *The Duke in Darkness*; he never went on to do, in the novel, what *Twenty Thousand Streets Under the Sky*—a touching and psychologically acute story of ordinary, underprivileged people—had promised. He became over-obsessed with evil (rather as L. P. Hartley, q.v., is, in his terror-driven 'punish bad children' mood, when his imagination is not functioning fully), with stupidity and with vulgarity. Still, the three novels about Ernest Ralph Gorse (a cross between the post-war British psychopathic multiple killers Heath and Haigh) are effective and intelligent: *The West Pier* (1951), *Mr. Simpson and Mr. Gorse*, which anatomizes the pseudo-genteel of Reading, and *Unknown Assailant* (1955). It is a pity, however, that Hamilton did not present Gorse in the round instead of simply as a psychopathic villain. It is probably true that some human beings cannot avoid being evil; but even these have motivations—and Hamilton does not try to explain these. His best novel is *Hangover Square* (1941), in which he fully explores the invitations of the latter.

*

MALCOLM LOWRY (1909–57), born in England and educated at Cambridge— but resident abroad (America, Mexico, Canada) for most of his life, although it was at the little village of Ripe in Sussex that he finally put an end to his life—was a heroic alcoholic who succeeded, more than any other who resembled him, in resolving his terrible problems in creative form. His *Selected Poems* (1962) show him to have been a gifted poet; his posthumous fiction—which includes *Hear Us O Lord from Heaven Thy Dwelling Place* (1961) and *Lunar Caustic* (French tr. 1956; 1968)—reveals massive gifts; his early hallucinated sea-story *Ultramarine* (1933), which was influenced by and written with the help of Conrad Aiken (q.v.), is full of promise. But his masterpiece, one of the most powerful novels of its time, is *Under the Volcano* (1947). Lowry dedicated himself to work on this as desperately as he dedicated himself to self-exploration and self-destruction through drinking. Its setting is Mexico—a Mexico that symbolizes Hell—on the Day of the Dead, and its hero is an alcoholic, Geoffrey Firmin, the last day of whose life this is. Firmin is dedicated to his own death, and *Under the Volcano* is the terrific vision that his voluntary sacrifice of his life vouchsafes him. Finally he is murdered and thrown into a ravine; but it is of course drink, or rather what drink stands for, that kills him. Lowry knew his subject well, and only ten years after finishing this novel he killed himself. Firmin, British Consul in a Mexican town between two volcanoes, represents Lowry himself—and, on the level that matters to the reader, the artist. If Vallejo (q.v.) and some other writers have given us a positive answer to the problem of what I have called *Künstlerschuld* (q.v.), then Lowry certainly gives us a terribly negative one. Perhaps it is a limitation. And yet Firmin—himself in deliberate flight, to hell, from all those who love him and seek his salvation (his ex-wife, his anti-fascist brother)—knows of heaven as well as hell. His self-destructive drinking (a Faust figure, he has taken drink to gain the power of insight— and now he must pay) enables him to see heaven—as well as to anaesthetize him from a rotten world that (1939) is destroying itself just as he is. *Under the Volcano* operates successfully on both the realist and the symbolic planes; Firmin is a true modern Faust, a tragic figure of our times. Lowry, after all, endured the agonies of alcoholism (some details appear in Aiken's *Ushant*, where he figures as Hambo) to some purpose: perhaps in his own terror-haunted mind Lowry did equate the Faustian drunk Firmin with an ineluctably guilty artist; but in relentlessly recording his anguish he showed a courage and sense of compassion (this, of course, is apparent in the characters of those who desire to save Firmin) that merit our gratitude.

A writer who has something of Lowry's power, and who is regarded by some as Britain's leading living novelist, is WILLIAM GOLDING (1911). Although he had published a volume of poetry as early as 1934, Golding did not attract attention until he was fortythree, with *Lord of the Flies* (1954), still his most famous novel. This is a savage gloss on the Victorian writer R. M. Ballantyne's *Coral Island*, in which some British boys are wrecked on a desert island, and create a decent Christian society. Golding's boys create as memorably horrible a dystopia as anyone has thought up since Wells' Rampole Island. There is something modish about Golding's vision of these prep-school boys' vileness, and I am not even sure that all 'the disagreeables', in Keats' famous phrase, fully 'evaporate'; but there is no denying his conviction and force. He is, however, a writer who requires to be separated rather firmly from the many fashionable critics that his work has attracted. These critics have represented him as every kind of writer: allegorist, fabulist, realist, mythographer, Christian—and so on. This is, as Walter Allen has pointed out, 'a considerable confidence trick'. Here there really is a negative vision —and one in which, when we think about it, Golding has cheated somewhat: this is fantasy. Yet, because of the modishness I have mentioned, because of a certain element of pretentiousness, *Lord of the Flies* escapes the censure that *Nineteen Eighty-Four* (q.v.) attracted. . . . Of Golding's later novels *The Inheritors* (1955), *The Spire* (1964) and *The Pyramid* (1967) seem to me to be the best. *The Inheritors*, about Neanderthal man, is flawed by the same wilfully negative attitude (I mean that the negativity seems to be contrived, to deliberately omit something from the author's response, in the interests of fashion or rhetoric), but it is a *tour de force* by virtue of its brilliant presentation of the Neanderthal people. Golding gives no reason why *Homo Sapiens* (supplanter of Neanderthal Man) should be vile, murderous and predatory; but his picture of his predecessor does have a kind of gentleness. *Pincher Martin* (1956) and *Free Fall* (1959) fail to cohere, although they contain superb passages; *The Spire*, a medieval novel about the erection of a phallic spire, without proper foundations, to the glory of God, is another study of the evil grounds upon which the apparently good establishes itself. It is too confused to be satisfactory, but the portrait of the Dean, Jocelin, is superbly clear. In *The Pyramid*, his best, least pretenious, novel so far, Golding appears to take up a realist approach; but closer examination reveals that it is as symbolic, if less obtrusively so, as its predecessors. However, the treatment of the background, a provincial town (Stillbourne) in 1930, and its Operatic Society's production of *The King of Hearts*, is well done in a realist mode. Golding has been overrated; his symbolism is strained; but he remains one of the most interesting of contemporary novelists.

Golding's contemporary RAYNER HEPPENSTALL (1911) is yet another neglected British novelist. Heppenstall, like Connolly and Jocelyn Brooke, is an excellently lucid writer; but he has always been uneven—and latterly he has become off-puttingly eccentric in reviews, putting forward such views as that the pornographer Ian Fleming (perpetrator of James Bond) is the finest stylist of our time. . . . This must be ignored, for Heppenstall is almost the only English novelist to have properly absorbed the influence of the modern French novel. He has written well on Léon Bloy and Raymond Roussel (qq.v. 2). Heppenstall's best novel is *The Connecting Door* (1962), which renders the surface of things with great acuteness and feeling. *The Lesser Infortune* (1953) and *The Greater Infortune* (1960) are also interesting novels. *The Fourfold Tradition* (1961) is one of the most illuminating books on the differences between French and English fiction—and on the French 'new novel' (q.v. 2).

WALTER ALLEN (1911), author of deservedly standard books on the novel in English, is in danger of being ignored as a good novelist in his own right. This would be unjust, for he is a master of colloquial understatement and an unusually careful observer of society. His modest, almost casual manner is deceptive. His first mature novel was *Rogue Elephant* (1946), a comic and ironic study of an ugly and unpleasant writer. *Dead Man Over All* (1950), which gained scant appreciation, is one of the best of modern novels about technocracy. Allen does not have Snow's (q.v.) reverence for the public, official over the private, individual, life, and he traces the real lives of his characters with a compassionate psychological adeptness. But his best novel is *All in a Lifetime* (1959), which traces, through a bed-ridden narrator, the changes in British working-class life since the latter years of the reign of Queen Victoria. This is a subtle socio-logical study, in which Allen's knowledge of fictional techniques has stood him in good stead. It is moving, as well as shrewd and skilful: the most successful working-class novel since Green's *Living* (q.v.).

The fiction of PAMELA HANSFORD JOHNSON (1912), wife of Lord Snow, has been progressively impaired by a simplistic, authoritarian, anti-imaginative moralism. She began with real gifts—of comedy and of character realization. By *The Honours Board* (1970) these had been entirely squandered in the interests of her prurient, neo-Victorian obsession with the 'permissive society': thus, in this disastrously poor novel, the villain reads 'dirty books': all is mani-pulated to the simple-minded, self-indulgent pseudo-sociological fantasies of the author. There was always in Pamela Hansford Johnson's fiction a basic, unsophisticated, perhaps semi-hysterical, appeal to middlebrow (i.e. a manipulative, self-indulgent) morality; but this did at least reflect a concern with the results of the loss of official morality. That she was ever a seriously excellent novelist is a fragrant British myth. American critics have always been puzzled by it: as Carlos Baker wrote of the characters in *Night and Silence! Who is Here?*: 'These, one and all, are people whose predicaments can be enjoyed without our feeling the slightest compulsion to believe in their actuality'. But it is a pity that her preoccupations should have eventually led to something as non-creative as *Cork Street, Next to the Hatters* (1965)— a weak, because uncomprehending, satire on aspects of modernism misunderstood by the author—and *The Honours Board*. For it might have resolved itself into something more creatively viable: the humour, psychological accuracy, skill and elegance of the earlier fiction certainly gave some compensation for the basic orthodoxy of attitude underlying it. Her most amusing novel is *The Unspeakable Skipton* (1958), in which she takes a Rolfe (q.v.)-like character, a bad and selfish novelist, and traces his career of exploitation.

LAWRENCE DURRELL (1912) was for many years best known as a

poet and youthful friend of Henry Miller (q.v.). His *Collected Poems* (1960) contain, in fact, his most enduring work. An Irishman born in India, and for much of his life a British government official in the Middle East, Durrell's most consistent characteristic is his anti-puritanism, and his best poetry presents an Anglicized, thoroughly heterosexualized, wafer-thin but absolutely genuine slice of Cafavy (q.v.): it is an achievement. What brought Durrell real fame, how-ever, was the tetralogy known as the Alexandria quartet: *Justine* (1957), *Balthazar* (1958), *Mount Olive* (1958) and *Clea* (1960). This has been an enormous popular success, hailed by modish critics; it amounts, however, to little more than what Leslie Fiedler has called 'warmed-through Proust'. The French see the same kind of pro-fundities in it as they saw in Charles Morgan (q.v.). The clue to its lack of real quality is contained in Durrell's pretentious prefatory note to the second novel in the series: 'Three sides of space and one of time constitute the soup-mix recipe of a continuum. . . .' The vulgarity of 'soup-mix' is characteristic. How could the coffee-table public fail to fall for something that was not only as 'deep' as this pompous statement implies but also sexy and overwritten ('beautiful' or 'poetic' writing)? Durrell based the series on a vulgarization of the relativity principle. As Pursewarden, one of the characters, pronounces: 'We live our lives based on selected fictions. Our view of reality is conditioned by our position in time and space—not by our personalities, as we like to think. . . . Two paces west and the whole picture is changed'. The quartet is full of such gobbets of 'wisdom'. The four books deal with the same material—a series of (mostly sexual) incidents in Alexandria—from different viewpoints. The whole is supposed to be an investigation of modern love (of physical sex as the true reality), or perhaps a representation of life as significant only when it becomes art. But it is muddled, and the self-consciously lush writing is an indication of its essential meretricious-ness. The characters have no solidity; the entire conception is robbed of whatever atmospheric power it might have had by its author's ambitious, polymathic vulgarity: his adolescent obsession with decadence, his preoccupation with occultism, his fatal penchant for potted wisdom. This is the kind of thing that naturists read aloud to one another after sunset and before exhanging sensual essences (or whatever). If Colin Wilson—who perpetrates a rather similar though vastly less well educated mixture of Nietzsche-and-water, sexiness, personal immortality, 'superman crime' and the occult—is the mage of the lounge, then Durrell is the savant of the drawing-room. By 2000 his quartet will be as dead as *Sparkenbroke* is today—and orgasms will still be non-philosophical.

ANGUS WILSON (1913) is an altogether more serious and substantial writer. He has been much misunderstood ('scrupulously prolongs the tradition running from Trollope to Hugh Walpole') for two reasons: he is a brilliant realist, and he has made attempts to revive the solid, Victorian novel. In fact he is not a traditionalist—and even if his attempts to create a twentieth-century equivalent of the nineteenth-century novel are over-ambitious failures, they are nevertheless experimental failures, for Wilson is a sophisticated critic, well aware of the difficulties confronting him in his project. Wilson is a very gifted novelist and one eminently justified in harbouring major ambitions: he is a deadly satirist of the stupid and the pretentious, he has the sort of compassion that goes with a capacity for self-criticism (this is all too clearly what the latter-day Durrell has lost), he can construct his big novels properly. . . . But his very ambitiousness is in a sense his worst enemy: it has led him to attempt the impossible, the construction of massive realist novels, when his real gift is for the fantastic, the grotesque—the richly imaginative. His best novel, *The Old Men at the Zoo* (1961), is in fact satirical fantasy: set in (what was then) the future, 1970. We see England invaded by Europe and the Zoo taken over so that the new rulers can throw their opponents to the beasts. All this is presented as if it were 'ordinary' subject-matter; but the result is merely an increase of ironic tension. Wilson's first novel, *Hemlock and After* (1952), is his most successful purely realist work (outside the short story); it suffers from its failure to build up a complete enough portrait of the hero, Bernard Sands, a novelist who falls victim, in middle life, to the homosexual impulses that he has so far successfully repressed. Wilson has a Dickensian gift for caricature, and this has never been seen to better advantage than in his devastating picture of London's homosexual underworld. This is hardly, alas, an advertisement for what in the United States of America is called the Gay Liberation Front. *Anglo-Saxon Attitudes* (1956), full of excellent things, and an acute character study, is nevertheless too long; it tries to achieve what is today an inappropriate kind of solidity. *The Middle Age of Mrs. Eliot* (1958) is, as has often been pointed out, too near to clinical case-history. *Late Call* (1964) is less novel than satire—on the deadness of modern life as lived (or not lived) in a British New Town.

P. H. NEWBY (1918) is an excellent minor comic novelist, but when he has tried to be more ambitious he has not succeeded in writing more than a few superb but isolated scenes. The context is always highly intelligent, but it is not really imagined; one feels that Newby has taken too much thought, that he lacks a single vision of his own because of his awareness of others'. And yet the potentiality is there to such an extent that one wishes that Newby would abandon his nervous, play-safe pastiche of other writers' life-views (Conrad's, Lawrence's, in particular), and abandon himself to himself. As it is, a certain meanness of spirit (a deliberate avoidance of robustness), an over-prudence, seems to vitiate what could clearly be—and in part is—a major achievement. If only, one feels, Newby could sustain the power and sensitivity of *A Step to Silence* (1952), the first of two books about Oliver Knight (the sequel is *The Retreat*, 1953): the descriptions of Midland landscape, of the teachers' training college which Oliver attends before joining up, of (in particular) Oliver's older friend Hesketh's model geography lesson, given to satisfy the examiners of his efficiency as a teacher. But even this novel fails to hold together: Newby is too reticent with Knight; and he is too eager in the sequel to turn him into a freak, to disown him as a character and transform him into a stock symbol of alienated man. Basically what has happened is that Newby's empathy has failed. In later novels the symbolic intentions are excellent, and there are always sensitively rendered scenes; but there is a lack of psychological conviction. In *The Picnic at Sakkara* (1955) and *A Guest and his Going* (1959) Newby has set his sights lower: the result is superbly executed light comedy.

DENTON WELCH (1917–48) died at thirty-one as a result of a road accident sustained when he was a boy; he lived in extreme discomfort and, in the last stages of his illness, acute pain. His books, *Maiden Voyage* (1943), *In Youth is Pleasure* (1944) and *A Voice Through a Cloud* (1950)—there was also a volume of stories and sketches, *Brave and Cruel* (1948)—are candid, subjective explorations of his self-pity and homosexuality. His was only a minor talent, but a sufficiently exquisite one to have kept his work alive for a quarter of a century. Like Jocelyn Brooke, who edited some of his literary remains, Welch wrote autobiography in the form of fiction; his unbaring of his personality is quite remarkable—and even unnerving. His technique consists of a series of extremely detailed impressions; there is no generalization. Welch's narcissism and hypersensitivity sometimes obtrude into his work (especially in *In Youth is Pleasure*), but when these are under control his writing provides a unique insight into the homosexual mentality.

ANTHONY BURGESS (1917) is the most gifted English novelist of his generation; but he has not yet produced the major novel of which he is so clearly capable. He is a talented musician, learned in linguistics, and with a real grasp of all sorts of knowledge. He is also an active journalist and critic. No writer of our time is more obviously highly intelligent—and aware of the essentially subversive function of the writer. No contemporary novelist more clearly displays genius. And yet no single book has yet contained all this genius and sensibility. This is partly because he is too clever, too aware, too self-conscious, too versatile: swarms of objective correlatives present themselves to him, and become too articulate too soon; he can't help knowing too well what he is doing. But in too many cases this extremely sentimentive (q.v.) type of writer allows himself to be inhibited into complete silence; we are grateful for Burgess' prodigious output, for the fecundity for which he has unfairly been blamed. Notable among his novels is the *Malayan Trilogy* (1956-9), which is essentially a tragedy on the subject of Britain's withdrawal (of interest as well as power) from its empire. Burgess is a Tory (in the old, Johnsonian, sense) unable to recover from the shock of realizing that Toryism died with Ford's Tietjens (a statement with which he would certainly agree). This horror has led him into over-frenzied journalistic activity, into a no-nonsense, professional approach to his craft that tends to obscure his seriousness, dedication and stature—and into excursions into the area where horror merges with comedy. *Nothing Like the Sun* (1964) is a *tour de force* on Shakespeare's life—the only tolerable novel on the subject—which seems to be based on Fripp's rather than Chambers' better known biography. Perhaps his most powerful novel, in which we see more of the author himself than elsewhere, is the devastating *Honey for the Bears* (1963).

It is the habit of literary journalists to compare all women novelists with Jane Austen—which is both an injudicious and a foolish procedure. Two writers who have had too much pseudo-critical attention paid to them are MURIEL SPARK (1918) and IRIS MURDOCH (1919). Neither of these has come near to the writing of a major novel, but both are fluent, skilful and creatively ambitious. Muriel Spark is clever and sometimes amusing (her jokes go less far than her admirers claim, however), but her Roman Catholicism seems to function as something more distinctly personal than universally divine (if one may so put it). She writes well and concisely, and this has tended to obscure the psychological superficiality and sheer petty malice of her content. Like Evelyn Waugh she indulges herself in callousness; but she doesn't have Waugh's intelligence or weight. Her stature is exactly summed up (if unwittingly) by a phrase thrown off by the ladies' columnist Katherine Whitehorn: 'top-notch Spark'. This mock-critical ejaculation exactly echoes her real voice—even if it filters out the uncanny literary adroitness. *Memento Mori* (1959) is the most successful of her novels. She lacks wisdom, emotional substance and all compassion, but the surface of her novels is exceedingly attractive. Her limitations were not fully revealed until she attempted a large-scale novel, *The Mandelbaum Gate* (1964), in which most of the writing is simply dull.

Although considerably less adroit, Iris Murdoch is more serious. She (unlike Muriel Spark) has the potentialities of a good novelist; but she has in effect refused to write a novel, and has instead resorted to desperate tricks: pretentious symbolism and crass sentimentality. At times both her characterization and her dialogue are at a woman's magazine level (as in *The Nice and the Good*, 1968); she leaves us with the impression that she dares not contemplate her true attitude towards life, but instead must hurry on to the next novel. She is a teacher of philosophy by profession, and her own philosophy (it is outlined in the astonishingly entitled pamphlet *The Sovereignty of Good Over Other Concepts*, 1967) gives a useful indication of her fictional intentions. These are not (apparently they dare not be) imaginative —but philosophical. Alas, philosophy has never been a satisfactory *raison d'etre* for the creative writer. And Iris Murdoch's philosophy is not distinguished: a pallid and sentimental Kantian substitute for Christianity. In the later novels some of the characters search for Murdochian virtue; the results are as mediocre as the philosophy, and they are not improved by the author's insertion of clothes- and pet-notes of interest only to an audience for whom the public library is now a (doubtless unsavoury) substitute for the defunct circulating library. The earlier novels are superior—the least organized, *Under the Net* (1954), is in some ways the best of all because it has no pretentious control superimposed on it, and the hero is simply allowed to wander. For in Iris Murdoch control is nearly always pretentious in terms of the creativity—the ability to create autononous character and situation—that has been revealed. She can descend to such depths as this piece of dialogue, supposed to be exchanged between a very young man and woman after their first sexual encounter:

> 'Was that really it?'
> 'Yes.'
> 'Are you sure you did it right?'
> 'My God, I'm sure!'
> 'Well, I don't like it.'
> 'Girls never do the first time.'
> 'Perhaps I'm a Lesbian' . . .
> 'Oh Barb, you were so wonderful, I worship you.'

The novel that demonstrates that Iris Murdoch is above the kind of thing she is now content to perpetrate is *The Bell* (1958), which most critics have agreed is her best. Here the action, which concerns a homosexual founder of a religious community, is convincing in itself—with the result that the author's symbolic intentions do not seem to be contrived. Otherwise, despite excellent passages, the 'mysteriousness' of Iris Murdoch's fiction, even if it is regarded as 'deep' in some quarters, is no more than meretricious trickery. What has happened to this talented writer by now is that she cannot see her people as people, and so in her despair she has become increasingly reckless, using every modish cliché—spying, sex, incest, mythological allusion, the Gothic, whips—to distort her and her reader's attention from her inability to imagine situation.

More gifted than these two novelists are OLIVIA MANNING, BRIGID BROPHY (1929) and MAUREEN DUFFY (1933). Olivia Manning's most considerable achievements are in her *Balkan Trilogy* (1960–5) and *The Rain Forest* (1974). She is an unobtrusively careful and subtle novelist, who uses atmosphere and landscape to reflect mood and inner states of mind. Her novels are widely read but have hardly yet received the critical attention they deserve. Brigid Brophy is a mixture of Shavian rationalist, high-class journalist and imaginative writer. So far she has most fully realized her genius in her remarkable study of Firbank (q.v.), *Prancing Novelist*, which is an account of an exploration of its subject's life and work. Her best novel is *The Snow Ball* (1964). Her journalism is lively and contentious, as it is supposed to be. Maureen Duffy treats of the lonely and subversive in such novels as *The Microcosm* (1966) and *Wounds* (1969), and is one of their most imaginative spokesmen. She has written some delicate and elegant lesbian love-poems in *The Venus Touch* (1971), which gain much of their strength from their total lack of furtiveness.

KINGSLEY AMIS (1922) caught a universal post-war mood in his very funny first novel *Lucky Jim* (1954). In this book the Pooterish Jim Dixon represents honesty; a university lecturer, he rejects culture not so much because of what it is as because of its snobbish and hypocritical associations. He is not likeable: he is not only exasperated, anti-phoney and furious, but also a sly and ambitious go-getter. He resembles Denry of Arnold Bennett's *The Card*, but lacks his mobility and warmth: there is something feral about his snarl: this is a deprived young man who is going to be revenged. The high comedy does not obscure the inner determination. But Jim Dixon is real, and his preoccupations are powerfully conveyed. Nor are we entitled to assume that the author has put Dixon forward simply as a hero: on the contrary, I doubt if Amis objects in the least if we object to his boorishness and pity his accident-proneness. We laugh at him as much as we laugh with him. This was an unusual novel, a necessary variation on the theme initiated in *The Card*. It is all the more unfortunate, then, that Amis' fiction has, over the past twenty years, consistently deteriorated. This seems to be because Amis has identified with the simplistic, materialist side of himself—at the expense of the sensitive side, as is sometimes presented in his earlier poetry. In a word, he is coarse; rather than be driven by his comic imagination and his dislike of sham, he has allowed himself to be taken over by the aggressive, conservative moralizer who features so unpleasantly in the press: the taunter of 'lefties' and advocate of British participation in Viet Nam. He is now no more than a popular novelist who turns his private conflicts to good commercial account. One might put it in another way: that Amis was not intellectually capable of developing the *Lucky Jim* theme any further than he did; that the succeeding novels simply exploit various kinds of smartness and cynicism until the author became tired and settled into a straight novel-a-year man. . . . But one cannot help wondering if Amis did not once possess the capacity to illuminate the reactionary slyness which he portrays so uncannily well.

JOHN WAIN (1925) is less accomplished but more straightforward. *Hurry on Down* (1953) was—as Anthony Burgess seems to have been the only critic to note—an inept performance, ill-written and almost insultingly badly constructed; but its subject matter, the rejection of bourgeois values by an educated anti-hero, was fashionable; and, as far as it went, it was well-meant. Better was Wain's Empsonian (q.v.) early verse, with which he apparently took some trouble. The successors of *Hurry on Down* have been, if anything, less distinguished; the poetry has degenerated through want of direction; but in his short stories Wain exhibits some of the control he so badly lacks in his other work. He seems in this form to be able to master his excitement about himself, and his sensitivity and feeling are given fuller expression.

THOMAS HINDE (ps. THOMAS CHITTY, 1926), who has been somewhat neglected by the critics, is a master-delineator of the British at their nastiest and most small-minded, and is one of the best realist novelists of his generation. *Mr. Nicholas* (1952), his first novel, is also his best—and one of the best to appear in England since the Second World War. He set himself a very high standard with it. It is about the tyranny of nastiness, age and insanity—a memorable and deeply-felt portrait of an impossible-to-love, and yet pathetic human being, together with an account of how the young struggle in the cruel nets laid by their elders and betters. Hinde conveys the sense of decency (this is not, alas, definable in public-school, Christian, or any other moralistic terms), of the decent man's helplessness in the face of bourgeois malice or ill-will, better than any novelist of his time. He shows this in many of his later novels, including *Happy as Larry* (1957), *For the Good of the Company* (1961) and the African novel *The Cage* (1962). It is possibly a matter of regret that he has latterly turned to a self-conscious symbolism, for his social observation is so acute that one misses it—and the symbols do not arise from the action, but are arbitrary. But clearly he is a novelist, still young, of major potential.

The novels of ALAN SILLITOE (1928) are all more or less wrecked by their author's extreme simplicity of mind. Few writers who have managed to acquire his reputation can have been so much at the mercy of crude emotion. The nature of his mental difficulties is probably best illustrated by an equation made in one of his poems— between 'cancer' and 'racism'. His first novel, *Saturday Night and Sunday Morning* (1958), is as atrociously written as Wain's *Hurry on Down*, and is not particularly psychologically plausible, but has the power and freshness of youth. *Key to the Door* (1961) is distorted by wishful thinking and poor construction; the succeeding novels consist mostly of puerile anti-authoritarian fantasy, although there are flashes of good description. Sillitoe is better in his short stories, and has never been more powerful than in *The Loneliness of the Long Distance Runner* (1959): in this narrative of a Borstal boy Sillitoe's hatred of injustice, hypocrisy and exploitation found an effective objective correlative (q.v.). He has written other simple, precise and moving stories; one of the best is *The Ragman's Daughter* (1963), also the title of a collection.

PHILIP TOYNBEE (1916) is, like Heppenstall, Connolly and Jocelyn Brook (qq.v,), an exquisitely clear stylist, as he demonstrates in *Friends Apart* (1955), reminiscences of his early years. He is one of the most interesting of modern English novelists, but has never realized himself. However, he does experiment intelligently (*Tea with Mrs. Goodman*, 1947; *The Garden to the Sea*, 1953), and is thus more deserving of attention than most of his contemporaries. His series of novels in free verse, still in progress, have perhaps been unduly neglected: they begin with *Pantaloon* (1961).

FRANCIS KING (1923) is an uneven novelist, but at his best a deft and sensitive explorer of the ambiguous, unexpressed sexual tensions that can exist between groups of people. He has been much and fruitfully influenced by Japanese fiction, as in two of his best novels: *The Custom House* (1964) and *The Waves Behind the Boat* (1965).

V

The Thirties in Britain were dominated by the four poets whom Roy Campbell (q.v.), in an otherwise poor satire, conflated as 'MacSpaunday'. Actually CECIL DAY LEWIS (1904–72), LOUIS MACNEICE (1907–63), W. H. AUDEN (1907–73) and STEPHEN SPENDER (1909) were never all together in one room until after the Second World War, and the notion of them as a genuine foursome is a wrong one. But all four, like many intellectuals in the Thirties, were Marxist (or at least left-wing), and all four were associated in the public mind. What they had in common was age, an admiration for Hopkins and Eliot's *The Waste Land*, and a feeling that revolutionary changes were needed. They were, however, very different. The Irishman Day Lewis, despite his gestures towards modernism, was not a modern poet at all, and was never able to deal with modern issues. Presumably his odd penchant for writing verses on public occasions got him the laureateship. Day Lewis had energy and strong feeling, and was a brilliant pasticheur (Hardy, Emily Bronte and others); but diligent search through his *Collected Poems* (1954) and its successors yields all too little poetry in Day Lewis' own voice. His best poetry appears in the wartime collection *Word Over All* (1943) and in his translations —from Valéry (q.v.) and Virgil. As early as 1939 Philip Henderson noted that Lewis is 'only a poet . . . when he forgets the Marxist mountain [today one would substitute Her Majesty, the bully-boys in the back rooms working for good old Britain, and so on] . . . and allows his natural, and after all quite Georgian, lyrical talent free play'. Day Lewis is the sort of poet one would like to praise more than one is able to; even in his modest neo-Georgian vein he is too frequently tepid or over-parodic, his rhythms metrical rather than personal (they have been called slick).

Louis MacNeice, also an Irishman, was the most extroverted of the poets of the Thirties: as well as being a student of the classics, he was a keen player of games and (like Norman Cameron, q.v.) a popular boon-companion. He was a minor poet who never really took poetry quite seriously enough. A good deal of his output, particularly *Autumn Journal* (1939) and *Autumn Sequel* (1954), consists of prosy pseudo-philosophical rambling. But he was intelligent and honest: if his poetry gives most pleasure to members of the middle classes who feel doomed, bewildered and sorry, but still continue as they are, he cannot fairly be called a middlebrow—in the sense that Day Lewis is middlebrow, a substitute for 'difficult' poets: poetry was for MacNeice a limited instrument, and he was never pretentious. But his poetry does little more than reflect the fears, hopes and anxieties of his class; it describes much, sometimes felicitously, but illuminates nothing. His work abounds in the tired, sophisticated clichés of the audience at which it is aimed; whenever he becomes serious the atmosphere becomes highbrow-taproom. His best poetry is satirical-funny, as in the famous 'Bagpipe Music'—he exploited the same vein very successfully in one or two of his radio plays. It is often said that in his last poems, published in *The Burning Perch* (1963), he reached a new intensity; and certainly he succeeded here, at last, in purging his language of its unfortunate Chelsea-like glibness ('May come up with a bouncing cheque,/An acid-drop and a bandage') and professionally blasé tone. These poems do, too, expertly describe what it is like to be middle-aged, in love, intelligent, tired, possessed by forebodings of death, and suffering from advanced alcoholism; but the slick, journalistic manner had been with MacNeice too long: none is more than neat and appealing. The elements of surprise, a truly individual voice and technique, the capacity to express the intensity of feeling that was, I think, genuinely there, are missing. MacNeice, whose *Collected Poems* appeared in 1967, could entertain poetically, and he could touch the heart; he could be appealing; but his poetry is not durable.

W. H. Auden's early *Poems* (1930) was the most energetic and promising collection of its time; its excitement still casts a spell— and there are many of Auden's own generation who have never escaped from this spell, and who consequently have never been able to judge his achievement dispassionately. The poems in his first collection are frequently incoherent, and their author is clearly hopelessly confused between a Kiplingesque imperialism and a Marxist-Freudian revolutionary attitude; there are echoes of other poets—Blunden, de la Mare, Graves, Laura Riding (qq.v.), and so on; but excitement and feeling are both present: this is a poet of technical brilliance who has a genuine lyrical gift. *The Orators* (1932), which again mixed Freud, Groddeck and Kipling, was just as con- fused; but in *Look Stranger* (1936) Auden had reached his lyrical apogee, and had purged himself of his more irritating public-school mannerisms. From then on the story of his poetic career is one of steady decline and disappointment: like his friend Isherwood, he never grew up. One is presented with the extraordinary spectacle of a man of very great facility, with fine intuitions about poetry (Auden is one of the best anthologists of our time), who has nothing of intellectual and little of emotional substance to say. For all his energy and versatility and intellectual curiosity, Auden has no more to offer than the following messages: that poetry changes nothing (he agreed, in fact, with Laura Riding, q.v.—but continued to write), that poetry should be entertaining above all else (this is consistent: entertainment is all it is good for); and that life should be led as graciously as possible. Thus, Auden's 'philosophical' poems, the poems in which he tries to make 'major' statements—*New Year Letter* (1941), 'The Sea and the Mirror' (1945: included in *For the Time Being*, 1945), *The Age of Anxiety* (1948)—are essentially superficial. *New Year Letter* contains Auden's ideas (of that time) about all subjects; it is rather like a glossy 'dictionary of thoughts', and when it surprises it does so because Auden is so adept at the expression of truisms. *The Age of Anxiety* is just what it seems: the prelude to a conversion to Christianity that can make sense only to Auden himself. But not many critics claim that the later Auden, the Auden of the later Fifties and Sixties, carries real weight. If he is really the major poet he has for so long been supposed to be then this is for the poetry collected in the earlier *Collected Shorter Poems* (1950) and perhaps for the poems in *The Shield of Achilles* (1955). Now if vigour and the ability to move the reader (Auden lost both these qualities during the Fifties) were enough to make a major poet then Auden would be major. But they are not. Again, if what Alfred Alvarez has called 'catching the tone of the age' ('catching the tone' is just right: it does not imply explaining, exploring or illuminating) were the attribute of a major poet, then certainly Auden would be one. But it is not; and he is not. He is an important phenomenon; he had excellent qualities; but he failed to develop—and became the greatest disappointment of his age. Even in the most celebrated of his poems —the elegies on Yeats and Freud, 'Musée des Beaux Arts'—there is a spurious quality. In the best poems the superbly memorable phrases are isolated, have no context: they are the notes and impressions of a clever and sensitive adolescent, not of a mature man. The immaturity of which the clowning was a symptom in the earlier poetry has persisted: this poet has failed to examine his personal situation: his casual stance towards poetry may be more the result of this than conviction. And yet until about the mid-Fifties—when his poems began to deteriorate into facetious trivia—Auden concealed his emotional rawness and intellectual superficiality with remarkable skill. Sometimes he did this by apeing another poet—he is a superb mimic. A good example of this is 'Their Lonely Betters' (1951), which is, as one would say, 'pure Graves'—but without being pastiche-homage in the manner of Day Lewis. Auden injects his own casual manner. (Graves himself once called Auden 'a synthetic poet who probably never wrote an original line in his life'.) Auden has real feeling for the poets whose procedures he appropriates. Indeed, those of his best poems that are not imitative owe what viability they have to their quality of sincerity. *Spain* (1937 rev. 1940), on the Spanish Civil War, remains moving in spite of its rhetoric; 'In Praise of Limestone' (1951), when one looks carefully at it, has little meaning—but does embody a fascination with England. A great deal of the responsible admiration that Auden attracts is actually admiration of his *performance* rather than of his achievement; future critics who cannot be dazzled by his performance will assuredly wonder why we saw so much in him.

Stephen Spender had markedly fewer technical resources than Day Lewis, MacNeice or Auden; his ear is considerably less sure; but his poetic impulses were deeper and more serious—and have survived longer. He has written much lush, tentative, over-sensuous poetry, but his best has qualities more enduring than that of most of his contemporaries. In recent years he has been able to integrate his sense of humour—often in evidence in his criticism—into his poetry. Spender has written an outstanding novel about life in an unpleasant preparatory school, *The Backward Son* (1940), and a book of stories, *The Burning Cactus* (1936); two later stories, published under the title *Engaged in Writing* (1958), are less successful. He is also an uneven but always stimulating critic.

The poems in Spender's first collection, *Poems* (1933; there were two earlier, privately printed pamphlets), were altogether more emotionally *réussis* than the earlier poems of Auden, MacNeice or Day Lewis. There are obvious faults—lack of humour, obscurity resorted to in order to avoid sentimentality, confusion—but one is drawn into the unmistakable presence of a poet. And although Spender has remained a poet (in a way that Auden and Day Lewis quite certainly did not), has not become corrupt or tired or mechanical, has retained his sensibility, has learned to do certain things better—I doubt if he has ever written a more exciting and appealing book. There is a sweetness and a breathlessness about Spender's early poetry that he has never quite been able to recapture This quality is seen at its most vulnerable but nevertheless most potent in the very early 'Epilogue':

> Time is a thing
> That does not pass through boredom and the wishing,
> But must be fought with, rushed at, over-awed,
> And threatened with a sword:

For that prodigious voyager, the Mind,
Another self doth find
At each hour's stage, and riven, hewn and wrought
Cannot foretell its port.

Let heart be done, shut close the whining eyes,
And work, or drink, or sleep, till life defies
Minute, month, hour and day
Which are harrowed, and beaten, and scared away.

Spender charmingly foresaw the weaknesses of his later poetry: he 'expected always', in a manner genuinely Shelleyan, 'Some brightness to hold in trust,/Some final innocence/To save from dust'. But this was not always apparent: Spender's lyricism and sensitivity were not usually strong enough to shore him up against the shocks of war and of the kind of personal sexual difficulties common to us all. He lacks the less often acknowledged, sceptical, toughly intellectual side of Shelley. *The Still Centre* (1939) and *Ruins and Visions* (1942) showed a falling off after *Poems*, and there was not even quite enough in *Collected Poems* (1955) to state positively that Spender had either fulfilled his promise or developed satisfactorily. But adjudgement of his performance now means less to him, and in more recent poems, now collected in *The Generous Days* (1971), he has notably succeeded in integrating his subtle sensibility and his intellectual intricacy, although everything has been transposed into a minor key. Whereas Spender had previously always been open to the charges of clumsiness, emotional over-indulgence and unnecessary ambiguity, the author of these less grandiose poems is firmly in control. Is this new modesty a gain? One can only repeat what George Barker said of the *Collected Poems* ('. . . if you come across a cripple walking you can be . . . sure that he wants to get somewhere') 'the true presence itself . . . moves and operates'. With Spender this has always been the case, and one has learned to be grateful for it.

However, just as the homogeneity of 'MacSpaunday' was false, so was the concept of their dominance of the Thirties. There were poets as good—or better. Prominent among these was NORMAN CAMERON (1905–53), whose genius is only just now in the process of being recognized—though he has had imitators since the Fifties. Cameron, a Scot with Calvinistic conscience and a penchant for occasional reckless behaviour, wrote a witty and metaphysical poetry— frequently laced with deep feeling—that foreshadowed the style of the so-called Movement (q.v.) of the Fifties. He resembled Graves and was a close friend of his and of Laura Riding's—but he was not substantially influenced by either. He formed his style while still at

Oxford, as the sequence of poems included by Auden in *Oxford Poetry 1927* shows. Perhaps nothing demonstrates the general insensitivity to real quality in poetry of official, academic or fashionable critics, anthologists and literary historians so much as their neglect of Cameron, whose excellence and originality are evident to anyone who truly cares for poetry. Cameron made the best English translations from Villon and Rimbaud; his *Collected Poems*, a slim volume, appeared posthumously in 1957. He did not really develop (he was doubtful and suspicious about the importance of poetry)—in this respect he resembles his compatriot Andrew Young—but his sardonic, tender sensibility was always capable of dealing with problems as they arose. Cameron's was the perfect twentieth-century traditional manner: he had no innovatory ambitions and was (over-) modest about his achievement—but cliché and poeticism are so entirely absent from his poetry as to render it exemplary in style alone. Its emotionally dense texture is the result of stubborn honesty and of intellectual and emotional self-appraisal. Cameron's is a poetry that will appear increasingly strong and original as work more ambitious in scope, but ephemeral, falls away.

When one compares the achievement of RONALD BOTTRALL (1906) (*Collected Poems*, 1961; *Poems*, 1975) to, say, that of MacNeice, one is again struck by the obtuseness of the regular critics. For Bottrall far exceeds MacNeice both in dedication and performance. Possibly his reputation was harmed when both F. R. Leavis (q.v.) and Edith Sitwell—a notoriously hysterical and unreliable critic—praised him. At his best he has real style and feeling; above all, he truly feels the pressure of the modern world (Auden tended to enjoy his own success in it, however he may have protested), and it evokes a complex and lively response from him. Moreover, he has an original lyric gift, as he shows in 'Four Orders':

> I am a trembling leaf
> I am a withered arm
> I am a sunken reef
> I am a trampled worm.
>
> Leaf, be the caterpillar's joy
> Arm, enfold the new-born boy
> Reef, flower into a coral isle
> Worm, fertilize the soil.

A serious critical exploration of Bottrall's poetry would reveal a versatile and immensely well-informed mind, a linguistic turbulence frequently controlled, and an exquisite humour.

JOHN BETJEMAN (1906) could have been a poet, but—in Spender's words—he has never been able to escape being 'the schoolboy who pretends that he is only pretending to be a poet'. Betjeman is bound to irritate serious readers of poetry for this reason: so much wilful silliness, thumping metre, and deliberate pastiche of earlier and now inadequate modes from a writer so clearly capable of sensitivity and rhythmical tact. By silliness one means the sort of impulse that can lead him to say—on one of his too frequent appearances on television—that he prefers 'Tom Moore' to Donne. . . . This refusal to be serious haunts and ultimately vitiates his verse, which is enjoyable but none the less coffee-table. One has to be crass to be a best-selling poet in these days, and Betjeman is crass; but he has qualities that other best-selling poets have not usually possessed. He is capable of real feeling; his nostalgia has style. One is not inclined to praise him for this, however: he has squandered his gift— and, even worse, has used it to slyly persuade those who buy his books that they are reading serious poetry. Most reprehensible is the cunning manner in which he indulges his own sentimentality: some of his lines move his non-literary readers, while his sophisticated audience may take them as satire. The most complete edition of his *Collected Poems* appeared in 1970. He is now Poet Laureate.

GEOFFREY GRIGSON (1905) published his *Collected Poems* in 1963; most unusually, he has written nearly all his best poetry since then. Grigson, a tough, scholarly and always provocative critic, is another of that dying breed, the genuine man of letters. Grigson edited the influential poetry magazine *New Verse*, which he had founded, throughout the Thirties. Since then he has supported himself by a series of critical and other works of a high standard; outstanding among these is the autobiographical *The Crest on the Silver*. His early poems were impressionistic, even imagist (q.v.)—and correspondingly slight. During the Sixties he broadened his scope without sacrificing the precision and luminosity that, at his best, he had always had.

It is through Grigson that the memory of CLERE PARSONS (1908–31) has been kept alive. Parsons did not have time to fulfil his promise, but what he did accomplish shows that he was potentially a major poet. He was mainly influenced by his contemporaries at Oxford (Auden, Spender) and by Laura Riding.

Curiously, since he is famed for his cerebral qualities, the keynote of the poetry of WILLIAM EMPSON (1906) is repressed passion. His output is small. He has published two collections; his *Collected Poems* appeared in 1955. He is best known as a critic—for *Seven Types of Ambiguity* (1930 rev. 1953), *Some Versions of Pastoral* (1935) and *The*

Structure of Complex Words (1951). And he is, too, one of the most suggestive and subtle, although recondite, critics of his time. But he is also a good poet, and one who has been consistently misunderstood. The reason for his extreme intellectuality is his extreme intensity and depth of feeling, both political and personal; this feeling is apparent, but has not been searched for diligently enough by his critics and even his disciples. Thus, Alfred Alvarez, who began as a disciple of Empson and then swung (predictably enough) to D. H. Lawrence—and then to confessionalism and suicido-confessionalism —called his subjects 'impersonal'. Now it is true that from time to time Empson indulges in 'crossword puzzle' poetry—his enthusiasm for this, as a critic, has sometimes led him into an indiscriminating attitude—as in such poems as 'Rolling the Lawn' ('You can't beat English lawns. Our final hope/Is flat despair. Each morning therefore ere/I greet the office, through the weekday air,/Holding the Holy Roller at the slope. . . .'). But the essential Empson has 'learned', as the last line of 'This Last Pain' announces, 'a style from a despair'. This is, however, as Alvarez insists, a limited achievement. Empson was concealing deep feelings—but not a rich lyrical gift. The achievement has been important because it kept 'wit' alive over a period when it counted for little in poetry: Empson's best lines—'Not to have fire is to be a skin that shrills'; 'Twixt devil and deep sea man hacks his caves'—have an Augustan toughness as well as a metaphysical concentration of feeling. Empson had his reasons for turning poetry into a minor project—it is one of the features of his minor poetry—and it is not his fault that the poets of the Fifties imitated his manner and produced no more than a series of drab anti-romantic statements. He himself has disliked his influence, and has pleaded, by implication, for 'honey' and for 'a singing line'— although his own lines seldom 'sing'.

w. R. RODGERS (1909–69), an Ulsterman who had been a protestant priest and who wrote highly praised radio features, was at one time held up as a possible rival to Dylan Thomas and George Barker (qq.v.); but his poetry has now, it seems, been almost forgotten. In his first poems, collected in *Awake* (1941), he was over-intoxicated by words and too heavily influenced by Hopkins ('Now all our hurries that hung up on hooks'); verbal pyrotechnics, assonance and dissonance and rhetoric too often obscured the fact that he had something to say. He was always plainer than Thomas and Barker, though: a strong-thewed Augustanism lay behind even the comparative exuberance of the earlier poems. The American poet and critic Kenneth Rexroth compared him to Marvell; this is not too far-fetched, as the poems in *Europa and the Bull* (1952) demonstrate.

But Rodgers failed to develop: his poetry was too uneven, too unexcitingly 'physical' (it remained difficult to justify most of his verbal effects), too little worked out. The strength and unfashionable openness were there; but so was an unaccountable carelessness. His best poetry is simple, like his description of the airman who must be pitied because 'he'll/Halt, hang hump-backed, and look into his crater'.

BERNARD SPENCER (1909–63) was associated with Lawrence Durrell (q.v.) in Cairo during the Second World War; a few of his poems had appeared in such magazines as Grigson's *New Verse* (q.v.) in the Thirties, but he did not publish a book—*Aegean Islands*—until 1946. He killed himself. His *Collected Poems*, which drew on two later collections and added ten more poems written in Vienna at the end of Spencer's life, appeared in 1965. His poems resemble him: well-bred, restrained, fastidious, acutely sensitive (to the point of breakdown) behind a tight-lipped reserve. His early poetry is elegant, unpretentious, over-civilized, passive; but a note of menace begins to creep in about 1950 (he ends a poem of that year by asking 'what towns born on what darker coast of sleep,/how many histories deep?'). It is a profounder note; but Spencer never gave it a quite full expression. But he did find single images into which he concentrated his feelings of sexual guilt and shame, and his premonitions of death: for example, in 'By a Breakwater' he sees what he takes to be lovers—but the man, 'middle-aged', is emptying a syringe into the woman's arm. . . . Spencer's work was never trite, and it deepened in intensity as he grew older. He is most likely to be remembered for his later poems; but *Collected Poems* is a distinguished volume, a testament to integrity and seriousness and purpose.

KATHLEEN RAINE (1908), who published her *Collected Poems* in 1956—*The Hollow Hill* followed in 1965—has since the Forties been an uncompromising Platonist and symbolist. Her poetry is limpid, musical, deeply serious; frequently it is so removed from life that it hardly touches the ground (after all, even the Platonist is rooted in life); but when Kathleen Raine writes of the real mystery she helps to restore meaning to it:

> We look up and the sky is empty as always; only
> Assembling the scattered for-ever broadcast light
> Here, or there, in his creatures, is seen that Face.

JAMES REEVES (1909) is widely read but has not had the attention of critics. For long it was commonplace to hear him referred to as of the 'school of Graves', on the strength of his friendship with the older poet and because Laura Riding prefaced his first collection, *The Natural Need* (1936). In fact the early poems included in this owe at least as much to Eliot, Pound, Richard Aldington and the imagists (qq.v.) as they do to Graves or Laura Riding. On the other hand, Reeves' later poems owe more to Edmund Blunden, Andrew Young and John Crowe Ransom than to Graves—whose consistency of energy and 'attack' his poetry has never pretended to have.

Reeves' poetry requires selection. There are some metrical wastes, where energy and linguistic inventiveness have been low, and where consequently the effect is commonplace and even Georgian in the worst sense. *Selected Poems* (1967) is a valuable pointer towards what he can achieve at his best.

Reeves, perhaps the only genuinely crepuscular (q.v. 3) poet in the English language—yet he has never heard of the *crepuscolari*—writes in three distinct manners; but, as Edwin Muir (q.v.) wrote in reviewing one of his volumes, 'Perfection does not call attention to itself': the surface of the poems is not striking. Most approachable of Reeves' manners is his quiet pastoralism, which in its way is as authentic as Blunden's, although it is less observant of natural detail and frequently takes a wryly satiric look at human obtrusions. In 'Ghosts and Persons' he writes of 'slow heads drowsing over sums' and the 'mower's distant sound' whining through high windows, but also of 'The forward smile and stupid eyes/Of a youthful village charmer'. Human 'progress' in its urbanizing forms amuses Reeves, but finally, especially in pastoral settings, arouses his resentment.

Reeves' angry, Kafkaesque manner, as beautifully exemplified in 'Greenhallows'—ostensibly an account of a journey to an interview for an important position—is less familiar, more original and harder to interpret. In this vein, Reeves appears violently to reject his normally calm acceptance of—even refuge in—his bourgeois backgrounds and to express attitudes quite alien to his usual self as expressed in poetry. The same kind of uncharacteristic energy is to be found in the sequence 'Letter Before a Journey' and in some of the satirical poems included in *The Questioning Tiger* (1964).

Finally, Reeves is the author of a handful of deeply felt, and powerfully expressed lyrics, such as 'All Days But One', which begins:

> All days but one shall see us wake to make
> Our last confession:
> Bird notes at dawn revive the night's obsession.

Guilt, regret, anger, desire for stability—these are among the staple elements in Reeves' best poetry. Few have more memorably portrayed the pains, pleasures and sinister or unhappy nature of the conventional life than Reeves; few are more startling beneath a tranquil surface. *Subsong* appeared in 1969, *Poems and Paraphrases* in 1972; *Collected Poems* in 1974.

*

'MacSpaunday' and those whom they influenced (Kathleen Raine, who had not discovered her true manner, and Bernard Spencer were among them) were sometimes called the 'New Country' school: this was the name of an anthology, edited by MICHAEL ROBERTS (1902–49), a distinguished intellectual—he wrote a good book on T. E. Hulme (1938)—and a minor poet of some distinction (*Collected Poems*, 1959). Roberts had also edited *New Signatures* (1932); he went on to produce what is arguably the most influential anthology of this century, the original (the revised versions of it are worthless) *Faber Book of Modern Verse* (1935). Roberts included in this excellent collection three poets whose work was recognized at the time as reacting away from the socio-political concerns of the so-called 'New Country' poets. It was not that GEORGE BARKER (1913), DYLAN THOMAS (1914–53) and DAVID GASCOYNE (1916) were anti-left-wing—all three were sympathetic, for example, to the legal government of Spain—but that their main concerns in poetry were non-political.

Of the three Barker is at once the most uneven and the most gifted. It is unfortunate that he has had to write under the shadow of his more immediately striking but also more meretricious contemporary Dylan Thomas. The general verdict is that Thomas is the better poet; but this is not the case. Barker is a prolific, hit-or-miss poet who can write quite indescribably badly—and with great power and authority. Barker was not much influenced by surrealism; his confusions came naturally to him, and harked back to Smart and the Blake of the prophetic books rather than to France. His early poetry was tragic and guilt-laden, consisting of great clusters of words that are flung at the reader with a deliberate lack of tact. In many ways Barker anticipated Berryman (q.v.), who looks somewhat less original when put by his side. Barker, a capable prosodist, distrusts neatness and can inflict hideous cacophonies upon his readers—'Satan is on your tongue, sweet singer, with/Your eye on the income and the encomium'—he has not really developed his procedures since his early days—but he scores a rather higher proportion of successes. However, it is perhaps fair to say, as David Daiches does, that he has never integrated 'his talents into a wholly satisfying poetic complexity'. But he is not that kind of poet: we have to look for his best and most integrated work in single poems. Barker, a most original poet (he is in fact more original than Thomas), is in love with the paradox—sometimes too facilely, but at others with surprising authority. Not afraid to be absurd, he can be more successfully elemental than almost any of his contemporaries:

> Step, Primavera, from your bed,
> Dazzling with existence;
> Put the Sun and the Moon and the Systems right;
> Hang heaven on circumstance:
> Lean from all windows like waterfalls,
> Look, love on us below:—
> And so from their somnolence in sense
> All things shall rise to you.

Barker needs rigorous selection (his *Collected Poems* appeared in 1957). There is no doubt that he is one of the most rewarding and interesting of contemporary poets—and one who deserves a great deal more critical attention than he has had. Although the generally accepted notion of Barker as an uneven poet is correct as far as it goes, there is more to him than this: he has plenty of wit and skill, and quite often his failures are considerably less disastrous than they appear. Finally, Barker has done things in English that only Bottrall (q.v.) has even dared to try.

Dylan Thomas has been overrated and overpraised, largely, no doubt, because of his somewhat spectacular life and death. He was a simpler and less prudent man than Barker; despite the many books —particularly in America—that have been written about his poetry, this is usually not well accomplished, and leans heavily on violent rhetoric. Thomas' early inspiration came from James Joyce (q.v.), translations of Rimbaud (perhaps by Norman Cameron, who became his close friend) and the Bible; the wild and whirling, irrational manner of his early volumes (*Eighteen Poems*, 1934; *Twenty-five Poems*, 1936) was certainly highly original. But, as his leading critics themselves admit, he is never lucid (Barker very often is). If, then, he is the major poet that we are so often invited to celebrate, we should need to discern a method in this lack of lucidity. But there is none. When we have conceded the powerful effect of the rhetoric and the unfamiliarity of his surrealist-like verbal juxtapositions (but he is always closer to a Welsh revivalist spell-binder than to a genuine surrealist), we have to admit that Thomas is frequently irresponsible in his use of words. There is a strong emotional pressure behind his poetry, and a feeling for the sound of words (though his ear was faulty, as in 'There is a saviour/Rarer than radium. . . .'); but Thomas suffered from an insensitivity to the *meanings* of words, a result of his inability to come to terms with reality. Like many alcoholics, he was at bottom an appealing man; but he never grew up, or even tried to. He was no Baudelaire or Rimbaud; his counterparts are to be sought in the nineteenth century, among similarly immature men: Swinburne, Dowson, Francis Thompson. Where Thomas is comparatively lucid, as in the elegy for Ann Jones, he is usually weakly adjectival: strip the poem of its not, on second inspection, so striking adjectives and nothing is left. Thomas is in some respects a dirty little boy, and the imagery of the earlier poems (many of them about masturbation) is simply 'dirty'. The much vaunted complexities and profundities of his work invariably prove to be the projections of critics.

But Thomas does have vitality—and, where he is not too ambitious, some small successes, such as 'The Hand That Signed the Paper'. But it is a pity that this vitality, and his sensuousness, have led even such sensible critics as David Daiches to over-praise him, and to regard him as a profound thinker. Daiches' account of his 'thought', in fact, unwittingly reduces it to the series of commonplaces that it is. Thomas' later poems—'Over Sir John's Hill', 'In Country Sleep'—do attain a greater simplicity than his earlier in that they are less clotted and wilfully sexual in their imagery; but the kind of simplicity they seek is rhetorical, and their individuality is restricted to tone. The most complete edition of Thomas' *Collected Poems* appeared in 1971. He wrote some exquisitely funny prose, printed in *Quite Early One Morning* (1954) and *Adventures in the Skin Trade* (1955); but the success of the radio drama *Under Milk Wood*, skilfully done though it is, is not artistically deserved: Joyce is plundered, T. F. Powys is imitated—the script is ingenious rather than felt, and a lack of real clarity is everywhere apparent.

David Gascoyne was more directly influenced by surrealism than either Barker or Thomas—or, indeed, any other English poet. Gascoyne's first book of poetry, *Roman Balcony*, appeared when he was sixteen; his novel *Opening Day* followed in 1933, when he was seventeen; *A Short Survey of Surrealism* (1936) was published when he was twenty. When he published *Poems 1937–42* (1943) he had reached his maturity, although he was not yet thirty. Influenced by Jouve (q.v.2) and by the philosophy of existentialism, Gascoyne is a most unusual phenomenon in English poetry; yet his 'Europeanness' does not give his poetry an un-English flavour. On the contrary, he remains the most English of poets, a genuine visionary writing in the tradition of Blake and Dante Gabriel Rossetti's 'The Woodspurge'. His early surrealism, where successful, achieves innocence. Unfortunately, however, the latter stage in Gascoyne's development is wanting: his later poetry has the strength of sincerity, but is grey, defeated and lachrymose.

> Not from a monstrance silver-wrought
> But from the tree of human pain
> Redeem our sterile misery,
> Christ of Revolution and of Poetry,
> That man's long journey through the night
> May not have been in vain.

This is too deeply felt and dignified to be platitudinous; but it is disappointed in the light of the earliest poetry. Gascoyne's *Collected Poems* appeared in 1965.

VERNON WATKINS (1907–69) was considerably older than Thomas and Barker, but did not become known until the Forties. His first book, *The Ballad of the Mari Lwyd*, appeared in 1941. Watkins was the best of the British poets to be associated with the so-called romanticism of the Forties, and until the end of his life he continued to write in his own unfashionably lyrical or Platonic styles. He began as a self-consciously Celtic imitator of Yeats; but at his best his manner is seventeenth- rather than nineteenth- or twentieth-century. He is humourless and often takes himself too bardically seriously; much of his poetry is monotonous and dull; but every so often he is pellucid, illuminating and original. It is ironic that so heavyweight an effort as Watkins' should in the end produce only a few lyrics; but it is also an object-lesson. A *Selected Poems* appeared in 1948.

The poetry of JOHN HEATH-STUBBS (1918) suffered for many years from its author's theoretical neoclassical preoccupations; but his *Selected Poems* (1965) reveals a poet of more strength and individuality than is perhaps generally realized. Heath-Stubbs is a genuine literary conservative. As a craftsman in traditional forms he has few peers; and his light verse is perhaps the most readable of his time. Mainly he is a graceful occasional poet, for whom style represents passion; but he has written a handful of personal poems (for example, the beautiful and subtle elegy 'Address Not Known') of great distinction.

HENRY REED (1914) has published only one collection of poems. *A Map of Verona* (1947), but this is widely read—it has remained in print for a quarter of a century. He has earned his living as a translator and writer of radio scripts—including the famous 'Hilda

Tablet' series. Reed has written several distinctly different kinds of poem: the metaphysical, influenced above all by Marvell; a narrative, contemplative poetry influenced by Eliot; parody—as in 'Chard Whitlow', which was Eliot's own favourite parody of himself; a narrative poetry influenced not by Eliot but by Hardy—such as 'The Auction Sale'. Reed's justly famous 'Lessons of the War' sequence is in his metaphysical vein, exploiting *double entendre* to its limit, varying the tone from the wistful to the broadly comic (as in the third poem of the sequence). The less well known 'The Auction Sale' handles narrative as well as it can be handled in this age. Reed is a poet of greater range than is usually recognized; only his Eliotian contemplative poetry really fails to come off, and even this is eloquent and rhythmically interesting.

*

Two Irish successors of Yeats are outstanding: PATRICK KAVANAGH (1905–69) and AUSTIN CLARKE (1896–1974). Yeats had preferred F. R. HIGGINS (1896–1941), but Higgins never really progressed beyond a pleasantly expressive occasional poetry. Kavanagh (*Collected Poems*, 1964) wrote a narrative poem about the poverty of the land and the people in his home county, Monaghan: 'The Great Hunger'. He also wrote a good autobiographical novel, *Tarry Flynn* (1949); he was for some years a newspaper columnist. His best poetry is subtler than his ostensibly careless, conventionally romantic attitude ('. . . this soul needs to be honoured with a new dress woven/From green and blue things and arguments that cannot be proven'), combining self-satire with lyricism in an unusual and moving way. Clarke (*Later Collected Poems*, 1961) is a fastidious minor poet who has over the years performed a number of technical experiments, within the tradition, of interest and importance. He is above all a classical poet, and is an honourable example of one; but although his integrity is beyond question, the usual fault of his work is that there seldom seems to be sufficient emotional impulse to draw it together. However, Ireland has not yet produced—leaving aside the more robust Kavanagh—a worthier successor to Yeats.

*

During the Second World War itself, it was the loss of SIDNEY KEYES (1922–43) that attracted the most attention. Keyes (*Collected Poems*, 1946) was certainly promising, but it is hardly possible to prophesy what he might have done: his poetry is (understandably) a hotch-potch of influences (Rilke, Yeats, Eliot—and others), and there are hardly as yet the glimmerings of an original manner. Two other poets, lucky enough to have a little more time to develop than Keyes was allowed, were more important: the Welshman ALUN LEWIS (1915–44), whose *Collected Poems* finally appeared in 1966, and KEITH DOUGLAS (1900–44): *Collected Poems* (1951 rev. 1966).

Alun Lewis, who seems to have died by his own hand, while serving in Burma, had time to develop, to purge his poetry of trite-ness and over-romantic diction (often apparent in his first collec-tion, *Raider's Dawn*, 1941). His greatest difficulty lay, it seems, in knowing when to stop. But he was a poet of great power, who described the loneliness of military life in the early Forties with unique eloquence and accuracy; he wrote, too, exciting and original love poetry.

Douglas did not actually achieve more (he had less time), but his extrinsic importance would probably have been greater. In him we see romanticism not rejected, but tempered by intellectuality—and a poetic intelligence not equalled by any poet since. His poems often lack finish, but this does not obscure his tough fusion of feeling and 'wit', his generous awareness of the world around him.

ROY FULLER (1912) also made his reputation during the war, in which he served but which he fortunately survived—he had in fact been publishing poetry, criticism and fiction since the mid-Thirties. His *Collected Poems*, which appeared in 1962, established him as a major poet among the younger generation: it was generally felt that here was the best living poet of his generation, one just a few years younger than that of MacSpaunday. But his poetry does not make as clear an impression as it should. He is intelligent and sensi-tive, but lacks power and drive. His early poetry is too evidently influenced by Auden, his later by Yeats (this is particularly impor-tant, because here he apes a manner that rather clearly does not suit him). He began well, but chose a disappointing direction in which to develop. For all his later poetry's interesting and intelligent unravelling of small Freudian knots, its chief function seems to be to keep any real kind of poetic vision at bay. Thus Fuller—in his weakest type of poem—mourns his political impotence and bour-geoisdom (he is a Marxist), but does absolutely nothing about it. His parodies of Yeatsian richness do not complement this apathy, because they entirely fail to convince. And yet there is enough that is good in Fuller to compel us to judge him from high standards: he has always tried to deal honestly with his experience, and even his latter-day posturing is rhetorical in intention, rather than self-deceit. He has written enough to make us regret that his ultimate stance should be to defend so limited a position.

It is difficult to understand why Fuller's near contemporary, c. h. sisson (1914), who did not become known until the publication of his first collection of poems, *The London Zoo*, in 1961, is not better appreciated. The author of an extraordinary novel, *Christopher Homm* (1965), Sisson's voice is unquestionably contemporary. His diction is chaste, sometimes almost puritanical in its clarity and savage directness; but beneath this temperamental severity fires burn—fires which throw up passionate and memorable lines, such as 'If we have reasons, they lie deep'. The 'if' here is characteristic: Sisson appears to be an extreme pessimist—intelligence and gloom have never, of course, been fashionable attributes—part of whose theme is corruption, or, in theological terms, original sin. But the careful reader of his poems (*Numbers*, 1965; *Metamorphoses*, 1968) will discover that they are coloured by an extreme, though subtly ironic, good humour. For another part of his theme is grace: both the grace inherent in the human creature to endure its terrible corruption, and the grace that is therefore inherent in the situation itself. The 'if' in the line quoted above is characteristic, then, because Sisson refuses, with unobtrusive courage and a poetic sharpness of intelligence, to exploit his own certainties, to step beyond the known grounds. Sisson's poetry displays a tough, curious, informed mind under continuous pressure from experience; it ranges from exuberant and deliberately villainous scatology ('The Theology of Fitness' is the prime example of this) to sustained passion.

*

Scotland has not yet produced another poet of the calibre of MacDiarmid; but at least three poets writing in Lallans, and four in English, are worthy of note. robert garioch (ps. r. g. suther-land, 1909) is a good, witty, acerb poet in Scots; many of his best poems are satires. He is well represented in *Selected Poems* (1967). He uses Lallans as though it were his own language, not a literary device, and expresses comic and outrageous emotions in it that could not possibly be expressed in any other language. sydney goodsir smith (1915), who also writes in Scots, is more ambitious and more uneven. Many regard him as the natural successor to MacDiarmid; but MacDiarmid's own lyrical successes very often show up his lyrics as forced and artificial. Nor does his Rabelaisian, comic verse always succeed. But when it does it is revelatory; 'Sydney Slugabed Godless Smith', upon whom 'Auld Oblomov has nocht on' can be genuinely exhilarating. What one finally misses in his work, however, is the ability to modify his romanticism (in which he over-indulges himself under the disguise of linguistic gusto) or his sense of fun, which spills over into facetiousness. TOM SCOTT (1917) is altogether more austere; but his use of Lallans, while not as exuberant as Goodsir Smith's, is ultimately more responsible. He began by writing in English, but in 1953 produced his remarkable *Seeven Poems o Master Francis Villon made owre into Scots.*

NORMAN MACCAIG (1910), originally a member of the extreme romantic group who called themselves the 'New Apocalyptics', writes in English—but has, as has been pointed out, an unmistakably Scottish sensibility. He has, perhaps, written too much; but he has never written badly, and has developed consistently towards a truer self-expression. He has the acute observation of his countryman Andrew Young, and he has combined this (latterly in free verse forms) with metaphysical speculation. His best books include *The Sinai Sort* (1957) and *Measures* (1965). W. S. GRAHAM (1917) had verbal energy, best displayed in *The Nightfishing* (1955), an obscure but exciting sequence; *Malcolm Mooney's Land* (1970), in which he indulges his intellectual confusions rather than purges them, shows that he has failed to develop. G. S. FRASER (1915) wrote, in *Home Town Elegy* (1944) and *The Traveller Has Regrets* (1947), some of the most honest and carefully wrought poetry of the Forties; readers will turn back to it when the time comes to reappraise the period. *Leaves Without a Tree* (1952), published in Japan, is his most substantial collection of poetry, and contains most of his best poems. At his best, when he is not susceptible to the influence of Yeats, he is a gritty, subdued poet—certainly one of the best of his generation. IAN CRICHTON SMITH (1928) is an uneven poet; but no one writes more densely or compassionately than he does at his best. His main collections are: *The Law and the Grace* (1965), *In Bourgeois Land* (1970) and *Selected Poems* (1971). He combines a subtle humanitarianism with a brooding, self-deprecatory Calvinism that gives his poetry great strength and originality.

*

The Fifties saw a reaction to the romanticism of the Forties, although the name of the 'Movement' given by a journalist to such poets as Davie, Gunn, Larkin and Amis (qq.v.) was unhelpful. The Sixties and early Seventies saw a great proliferation of versifiers of all kinds (mostly bad because lazy, careless, ignorant or derivative). It remains here to pick out the more outstanding. ELIZABETH JENNINGS

(1926) has been cruelly used by fashion. Her first collection, *Poems* (1953), was rightly praised for its modest and sober strength, and its unusual way of looking at landscape and experience. The chief influence on these early poems was Edwin Muir (q.v.), whom Elizabeth Jennings also resembled in lacking a personal, 'attacking' rhythm. Throughout many volumes (*Collected Poems*, 1967), she has sustained her sobriety and honesty of tone—but she has run out of experience. It is as if she gave up all to be a poet, and now has nothing to write about except her approach to the writing of poetry and her acute disappointment. But her potential as well as her earlier achievement remain.

DONALD DAVIE (1922), one of the most intelligent and aware critics of his generation, has never quite been able to escape from his didactic inclinations. His poetry is brilliant, but nearly all of it is factitious—verse not as poetry (which is produced under the kind of pressure that cannot be faked) but as various kinds of didactic criticism. He has wit, ingenuity and technique—but his work is controlled by what he prescribes as necessary ('for poetry') at the time of its composition: everything is for 'the good of poetry'. The best poetry does not come into being in this way: experience is primary in it, and its author is first a poet—and then (if he likes) a critic. Davie is first a critic. But there is a wry and bitter feeling which takes over in some earlier poems; and no critic illustrates his prescriptions more cleverly or more interestingly. His wit and the remarkable movement of his intellect are his own; it is a pity that the emotion in his poetry should so often be non-existent or aped. Much of his best work is in *New and Selected Poems* (1962), *Events and Wisdoms* (1964). *Essex Poems* (1969) is less good.

Davie's exact contemporary PHILIP LARKIN (1922) aptly reveals his severe limitations (it is a matter of the difference between actually being moved and simply being in a state of admiration or intellectual fascination); it is ironic that he, in his turn, should exhibit severe critical limitations, the chief of which is his refusal to consider European poetry as being of interest. But the student of true poetry becomes used to such ironies. For Larkin, although a minor poet, is the best since 1945. His first collection, *The North Ship* (1945), is not more than promising (it was Charles Madge, q.v., alone who prophesied his future from this volume); *The Less Deceived* (1955) and *The Whitsun Weddings* (1964) contain his important poetry; it has traces of Hardy and Graves, but there is no doubt of its originality. That this is apodictically as good as it is demonstrates the sceptical quality of the imagination. Larkin faces what seems to be a merely squalid predicament ('truth', for him, is a 'trite truss advertisement'),

and yet he moves us. His best poems remain on the right side of
sentimentality. One may sympathize with Charles Tomlinson (q.v.)
when he complains that 'a movement in which he is the star performer can scarcely be thought of as having the energy to affect the
ultimate destinies of English poetry'. But Tomlinson, like Davie, is a
critic-poet and not a poet-critic: the 'ultimate destinies' of any
poetry exist only retrospectively; meanwhile, poets do what they
can. As Tomlinson points out, Larkin's subject is 'largely his own
inadequacy'; he goes on to deplore 'Larkin's refusal to note what
had been done by the French before 1890 in the ironic self-deprecat-
ing mode'. But if Larkin could 'note' Laforgue and Corbière's
poetry then he would certainly not be capable of the fine ironic self-
deprecating poetry he wrote in English in the Fifties and Sixties. . . .
So much for criticism.

CHARLES TOMLINSON (1927) is, like Davie, an excellent and sensitive
critic. He has a fine sense of landscape, a fascination with decay
(which he seems not to acknowledge), and he is a good craftsman.
An American admirer of his perception and his intelligence, however, has characterized him as 'no poet'. One sees what he means.
Tomlinson has all the equipment of a poet except the capacity to
deal with emotion. This has led him to try to realize himself in other
men's styles: he has thus imported the procedures of Williams,
Vallejo (qq.v.) and other poets into English poetry—but he has not
absorbed them, and he has been unable to compensate for his own
deficiencies. He is a frustrated painter, and his best effects have been
gained from poem-pictures, where landscape acts as a metaphor for
mood; but self-satisfaction or complacency (reflected in the prissy
and exasperated tone of his criticism) seem to preclude the self-
criticism, the self-exploration, the irony and the humour to which
he would need to subject himself if he were to succeed in recording
more than a series of moods. This is a loss to poetry. But as it is his
poetry is far too cool and delighted with itself: one can hear the
taps of the ferule as he sets about instructing his calm little world in
how to organize itself—all ignorant of another, rougher world outside. His books include *The Necklace* (1955), *Seeing is Believing* (1958),
A Peopled Landscape (1963) and *The Way of a World* (1969).

BRIAN HIGGINS (1930–65), by contrast, was a hit-or-miss poet
(somewhat in the manner of his friend George Barker, q.v.), who
had too little time to exercise control over his considerable intelligence. His poems were published in *The Only Need* (1960), *Notes
While Travelling* (1964) and *The Northern Fiddler* (1966). His best
poems were full of urgency (an urgency that now seems poignant),
primitive energy and directness of purpose. They combine passion,

humour and subtlety. 'Genesis' demonstrates something of his quality:

> Language is the first perversion of the senses.
> The alphabet was written on the gates of Eden.
> Reason is an angel in mathematics, a castration
>   in literature, and a devil in life.
> The first and last speech was a curse.
> When the moon was numbered the stars grew pale.
> It was God who conspired with Satan in that garden
> When, lowering the snake, he sent words to prove
>   the Fall.

Of poets of Higgins' generation the two most discussed are TED HUGHES (1930) and THOM GUNN (1929). Hughes began (*The Hawk in the Rain*, 1957; *Lupercal*, 1960) as an elemental poet of power; he was inchoate, but fruitfully aware both of the brute force of creation and of the natural world. Then—a naïve (q.v.) poet—he began to assume a mantic role; he has now turned into (*Crow*, 1970) a pretentious, coffee-table poet, a mindless celebrant of instinct. Gunn's best poems were in his first book, *Fighting Terms* (1954 rev. 1962), of which the original version is preferable. His later poetry (*My Sad Captains*, 1961; *Moly*, 1971) has remained interesting, but the tug between the classicist influence of Yvor Winters (q.v.) on the one hand and the 'tough', male, leather-jacketed world of American pop on the other has proved destructive: it is not, perhaps, a fundamental conflict.

Of poets younger than this DOUGLAS DUNN (1942) is perhaps the best. He (*Terry Street*, 1969) has feeling and a sense of occasion; he is the most substantial poet of his age-group.

Canadian Literature

The pressures on Canadian writers have been more diverse than in some of the other ex-colonies: there have been two 'home cultures', French and British—as well as the presence of the strongly-developing American culture to the immediate south. The fact that the French and the British (one should perhaps say English and Scottish) cultures exist side by side brings up the question of whether there is even now such a thing as a single, indigenous *Canadian* culture. Certainly it is only very recently that young Canadian writers have felt anything like confidence that there is—and this is largely owing to the emergence of an international feeling (among young people) that racial and political differences belong to an older generation. . . . And yet from this supposedly 'boring', archaic and 'square' society emerged the first 'unsquare', new-style prime minister in the history of the modern world: Pierre Elliott Trudeau (Olof Palme of Sweden was the next). It is true that when a Canadian politician was kidnapped and subsequently killed by Canadian separatists Trudeau in mid-crisis looked (and spoke and acted), suddenly, very much like any other conventional politician; but it is still their world—not his.

There is not much in the poetry and fiction of the nineteenth-century Canada that can be offered as interesting except in a historical or local sense. The one exception, Isabella Valancy Crawford, whose poetry contains some magnificent lines and passages, died in 1887, aged thirty-seven. It was not until during and after the war that a Canadian literature began to develop. It is true that STEPHEN LEACOCK (1869–1944) began writing his humorous sketches in 1910 (he also wrote serious works on politics), but he was seldom more than an Englishman commenting on Canadian life. The exception is *Sunshine Sketches of a Little Town* (1912), in which the narrator's ambiguity of attitude betrays the stirrings of a truly Canadian consciousness.

As is usual in colonial literatures, it was the poets who first made themselves heard—in the Twenties. But two early French-Canadian poets should be mentioned. The invalid ALBERT LOZEAU (1878–1924) was not a modernist, but his short lyrics—written from his bed—were, when not sentimental, elegant and moving records of a life necessarily devoted to reverie. The precocious ÉMILE NELLIGAN (1879–1941), born in Montreal, had an Irish father and a French-Canadian mother; before he was twenty he had become hopelessly insane, and spent his last forty years in an asylum. He can justifiably be thought of as Canada's Rimbaud or Campana (q.v. 3). He is really a part of the French rather than the French-Canadian tradition, but this makes him all the more important: he introduced symbolism to Canada, whose English poets, however, made nothing of it. He read his poems aloud, but they were not published until 1903; the *Complete Poems* (*Poésies complètes*) appeared in 1952. The chief influences on his work were Rimbaud and Verlaine, and the theme of his lush but suggestive poetry, which is astonishingly precocious in accomplishment, is the inaccessibility of beauty in the ordinary world. (OBCV)

The English-Canadian poets became active in the mid-Twenties, but their group anthology, *New Provinces*, did not appear until 1936. Canadian publishers were not much interested in issuing poetry until the years of the Second World War. The father-figure of modern Canadian poetry is E. J. PRATT (1883–1964), born in Newfoundland. Pratt, who began as a Methodist priest, is a good, forceful narrative poet who has affinities with Masefield and Roy Campbell (qq.v.); he had little lyrical gift but his language is admirably lucid and his versification masterly within its limitations. He broke with the old, mechanically picturesque procedures to form a poetry that actually observed both natural and urban processes. He is a truly dynamic poet, who will introduce any kind of relevant scientific information into his work. In this (alone) he resembles MacDiarmid (q.v.); but he is never prosy. He takes public themes (*Towards the Last Spike*, 1952, is on the building of the Canadian Pacific Railway) but spices them with irony. If he failed to gain an international reputation then this is because, finally, he never resolved his ambiguous attitudes: his vitalism, sometimes jaunty like Campbell's, but never schoolboyish, veers between grimly ironic naturalism—with much emphasis on 'nature red in tooth and claw'—and a compassionate calm; and faith and a theism simply exist as opposites in his work. He never found a language of resolution, and therefore lacks that ultimate wisdom which characterizes the work of a major poet. He came nearest to it in *Brébeuf and His Brethren* (1940), the narrative of a Jesuit priest who is martyred by Indians. The fullest retrospective edition of his work was published in Canada in 1944: *Collected Poems*.

The poets of the so-called 'Montreal School' of the Twenties learned from Pratt to widen their scope to include all aspects of life;

but they employed shorter forms. A. J. M. SMITH (1902) has been important as an influence and anthologist as well as a poet. He appeared in *New Provinces* with Pratt, Klein and Scott (qq.v.). He is essentially a cautious modernist, and his work remains more or less in the formal tradition, often reminding one of the Sitwells (qq.v.), and drawing on the English metaphysical tradition. His deliberate pastiche of such poets as Yeats (q.v.) and Vaughan is brilliantly educated and displays extraordinary sensitivity and skill; but since his best effects are in this kind of poetry one wonders if his function is not predominantly critical. He has an admirably hard style in his 'own' poems, but seems too often to lapse into rhythmical obviousness and a tone slightly false to his own educated sophistication. F. R. SCOTT (1899) is a satirist, a love poet and a nature poet—in that order. As a young man at McGill University he played a large part in making his contemporaries aware of Pound and Eliot. He has led a public life, as Professor of Law at McGill and as an active socialist (he was chairman of the C.C.F., the Canadian socialist party, 1942–50), and has been a lively figure. He has done much as publicist and translator to promote French-Canadian literature. Canadian literature would not have been what it is without him (OBVC)

The most interesting and gifted of this Montreal group was the Jewish poet A. M. KLEIN (1909–72), who remained poetically silent after 1948, when he published *The Rocking Chair*, his fourth collection. His first volume was called *Hath Not a Jew . . .* (1940). This was followed by the *Hitleriad* (1944) and *Poems* (1944). *The Second Scroll*, an experimental novel, appeared in 1951. Klein, 'a Jewish poet in the sense that Claudel [q.v.] was a Catholic poet' (A. J. M. Smith), is the poet of Quebec, whose French-Canadian conservatism he views from his own Hebraically conservative position. He is very much an odd man out, although his work is held in high regard. He wrote from the point of view of a sophisticated but committed Jew: even when dealing with such themes as an Indian Reservation he considered them—if only obliquely—in the terms of an alienated, tortured Jew who yearns for Jerusalem. But he is unique because of his involuntary (and still very Jewish) irony, and his remarkable use of language. One feels that he did not go to secular Israel (he worked in public relations in Montreal) because, under such circumstances, he preferred to work in a less frustratedly secular Canada. Nevertheless, he was zealously concerned with the establishment of Israel as well as with protest against the Nazi atrocities. His latest poetry achieved an idiosyncrasy of diction which was necessary for the complex feelings it expressed. Was Klein an influence on John

Berryman (q.v.)? He ends his poem 'Montreal', in *The Rocking Horse*:

> City, O city, you are vision'd as
> A parchemin roll of saecular exploit
> Inked with the script of eterne souvenir!
> You are in sound, chanson and instrument!
> Mental, you rest forever edified
> With tower and dome; and in these beating valves,
> Here in these beating valves, you will
> For all my mortal time reside!

Here is the same kind of mixture of heroic poesy, old high manner, archaism and quaintness that characterizes much of Berryman's later work. Certainly Berryman's own manner differs from Klein's; but this approach among others could well have provided him with the confidence to go forward. Despite his long silence, Klein was Canada's most original English-language poet, and perhaps the only one of his generation who, although so rooted in the past of his race, was entirely unsatisfied with the poetic procedures of the nineteenth century (OBCV).

The younger poets whose work began to appear in the Forties had less creative confidence than Klein, and consequently a more eclectic and 'international' approach. They were galvanized into activity by an energetic Englishman, PATRICK ANDERSON (1915), who became a Canadian citizen, but eventually returned to Great Britain. He was only in Canada for ten years. What Anderson really did was to export to Canada the styles and preoccupations of the English poets of the late Thirties; his own poetry was a sensitive instrument for the recording of these (particularly of Auden, MacNeice, Barker, Gascoyne, qq.v.) rather than an *œuvre* in its own right. But his application of this Thirties-style sensibility was intelligent and fluent, and his presence in Canada entirely beneficial. His best published work is contained in autobiographies (*Snake Wine*, 1955) and travel books. Although called, with some justice, 'a kind of tea-drinking Dylan Thomas', on account of some of his over-fluent Canadian poems, Anderson is an exceptionally intelligent man who has an engaging line in criticism of his earlier selves. (OBCV) Anderson established the magazine *Preview*, and it was there that the work of P. K. PAGE (1917) first appeared. P. K. Page was born in Swanage, Dorset, England, but was educated and grew up in Canada. A characteristically rigorous selection of her best work, with new poems, was included in *Cry Ararat!* (1967), her most recent volume. Her start as a poet of social protest under the influence of Scott and Anderson (qq.v.) was in fact a false one; her real concerns emerged in the poems of *The Metal and the Flower* (1954): satire of lonely bourgeois personalities merges into psychological and biographical concern. These were perhaps her most successful poems: her more recent work, for all its purity of line (reminiscent of Kathleen Raine, q.v., and of some other good woman poets), is not entirely convincing. Such thoughts as 'A single leaf can block a mountainside;/all Ararat be conjured in a leaf' are better left where they belong: with William Blake. But if its mysticism fails, this is still an attractive and limpid poetry. (OBCV)

EARLE BIRNEY (1904), a noted scholar and critic, born in Alberta, was in his early years a farm labourer, logger, bank clerk and sailor; later he became an academic, though no conventional one. He has been one of the most independent of Canadian writers, and is now a universally respected veteran. The influences on his verse have been manifold. Much of its strength comes from his scholarly concern with early English poetry and Chaucer. Then there is his non-dogmatic, tough radicalism and feeling of kinship with the working-classes. More recently—for Birney will cheerfully expose himself to any influence that he feels may be of use to him—there have been the Beats and the American Black Mountain poets (qq.v.); such as is silly or brutal about these has been resolutely rejected. Chiefly, however, Birney has written out of himself: out of an innate scepticism and humanitarianism, and a vision rooted in the Canadian Rockies where he spent his childhood. He is in fact at his best when writing in terms of nature, as in 'Slug in Woods',

> For eyes he waves greentipped
> taut horns of slime. They dipped,
> hours back, across a reef,
> a salmonberry leaf.

where his attention is directed onto the minute detail of what he has observed. But he is never unreadable or pretentious. His *Selected Poems* appeared in 1966. He has written two excellent novels: the picaresque *Turvey* (1949) and *Down the Long Table* (1955), on the depression years. (OBCV)

Another Canadian original is IRVING LAYTON (1912), who was born in Rumania. His parents emigrated to Canada when he was only one year old. Layton is a highly gifted poet, a 'natural', who simply has to mix in his sillinesses and rushes of blood to the head with his more straightforward lyrical poems. He can seldom express his opinions about affairs without a childish rage or petulance; his wisdom is deliberately withdrawn. But when he writes of that experience which ought to temper his opinions he is a bright minor poet, and justifies the comparisons—often made—between himself and Blake and Whitman. He has been overrated (he is nowhere near so accomplished a poet as Klein, even though he has been referred to as 'great') because his immense energy tends to obscure his incapacity, even at his best, to organize his emotions. The concluding stanza of 'The Birth of Tragedy' gives a good sense of his achievements and his limitations:

> A quiet madman, never far from tears,
> I lie like a slain thing
> under the green air the trees
> inhabit, or rest upon a chair
> towards which the inflammable air
> tumbles on many robins' wings;
> noting how seasonably
> leaf and blossom uncurl
> and living things arrange their death,
> while someone from afar off
> blows birthday candles for the world.

There is more cliché here than the sincere vitality of the surface suggests there might be, and there are confusions; the last two lines insufferably indulge a penchant for whimsy; but the emotion which the poet is not altogether successfully trying to capture is pure, powerful and moving, and the line 'and living things arrange their death' has been its reward. Layton's *Collected Poems* were published in 1965. (OBCV; CWT)

The Montreal poet LOUIS DUDEK (1918) has been a vital and helpful influence on Canadian poetry without, perhaps, contributing much to its permanent qualities. He originally appeared in the *Preview* anthology, *Unit of Five* (1944), which introduced P. K. Page. Dudek's friend RAYMOND SOUSTER (1921) is a useful, generous and lively influence; his poetry is direct, pleasant and prosy. For many years he was also at the centre of Montreal literary activity. A *Selected Poems* appeared in 1956, and he has published many other collections.

Later English-Canadian poets have divided themselves into academic and U.S.A. schools. JAY MACPHERSON (1931), a university teacher who has stated that she stopped being a poet in 1957, makes poetry out of previous poetries, of which she has extensive knowledge.

She was first taken up by Robert Graves, who printed her *Nineteen Poems* (1952) on his long-defunct Seizin Press (he revived it again for Terence Hards in 1964); but her best-known, and much-acclaimed, book is *The Boatman* (1957). These poems represented one of the cleverest and most attractive literary retreats from sexuality of their decade. Reluctantly influenced by Graves' pagan beastliness (as one might, from the general tone of the poems, put it), they combined elements of fable and learned Biblical reference with great skill and charm. The subtly organized scholastic surface does not conceal a wistfulness for robust experience. (OBCV) JAMES REANEY (1926) founded, and edits, a magazine called *Alphabet*, which follows the theories of the important Canadain critic Northrop Frye (1912), a minister of the United Church of Canada and university teacher who has been described by Mordecai Richler (q.v.) as 'our keeper of true standards'. Frye's most ambitious and influential book is *Anatomy of Criticism* (1957), in which he contentiously attacks value judgements and makes a prophetic bid to reduce literature to its socio-anthropological and mythopoeic components (his project has interesting, though tenuous, affinities with the programme of the Russian Formalists, q.v. 4). Reaney's poetry seeks to order his experience into recognizably Fryean categories, and to subsume them under a general Christianity. The most interesting and original of his four books are *Twelve Letters to a Small Town* (1962), written in a mock-infantile style, and *A Suit of Nettles* (1958), satirical mock allegory. Despite some surrealism, Reaney has yet to burst out of his over-scholastic theorizings and to face himself in his poetry; but it already displays the lineaments of experince. (OBCV; CWT)

BERTRAM WARR (1917–43), killed in the Second World War, should also be mentioned. He did not have time to realize his gifts, but the poems in *Yet a Little Onwards* (1941) display remarkable sophistication and potential—as the final lines of 'The Deviator' illustrate:

And as I sat here this morning, thinking my thoughts amid the
  sounds,
Suddenly, all these, the definables, began telling their meanings to me,
Saying there is no aloneness, there can be no dark cocoon,
With room for one, and an empty place, if love should come.

(OBCV)

Little need be said of LEONARD COHEN (1934), who long ago smothered his gift in whimsical, sickly lushness. (OBVC; CWT) Some point to ALFRED PURDY (1918) as one of the first of the younger Canadian poets to find an expression for 'the emergence of a new nation', but this seems over-confident: his sprawling verse entirely lacks a rhythmical coherence, and suggests that his natural form is antibiographical prose. (CWT)

*

In French-Canadian poetry only ROBERT CHOQUETTE (1905) rivalled E. J. Pratt's (q.v.) gift for creating on an epic scale. His first volume. *Through the Winds* (*A Travers les vents*, 1925), contained passionately lyrical poems about the northern part of Canada. He is a rhetorical and romantic poet, in some ways a French counterpart of Birney (q.v.)—but with smoother rhythms and much less toughness of mind. (OBCV) The first really important poet after Nelligan (q.v.) was HECTOR DE SAINT-DENYS-GARNEAU (1912–43), whose volume *Gazes and Games in Space* (*Regards et jeux dans l'espace*, 1937) initiated the modern movement in Canadian poetry. Saint-Denys-Garneau did almost all his poetic work between 1934 and 1937—he suffered from a heart condition—and, like Nelligan, was more a part of the French than the French-Canadian tradition. He was aware of Rilke (q.v. 2), and his poetry is more individual and more pioneering in its use of free verse than any of his Canadian-English counterparts. 'Birdcage' demonstrates his quality.

> I am a bird-cage
> Bone-cage
> With a bird
>
> The bird in his bone-cage
> It is death who makes his nest
>
> When nothing happens
> You hear his wing-ruffle
>
> And after a burst of laughter
> If you suddenly stop
> You hear his coo
> Deep down
> Like a tiny bell
>
> It's a captive bird
> Death in my bone-cage

> Wouldn't he love to fly away
> Is it you who holds him back
> Or me
> Or what
>
> He can only escape
> When he's eaten me all
> My heart
> My source of blood
> My life
>
> In his beak will be my soul
>   (tr. Miranda Britt. See also OBCV; CWT)

His *Journal* (1954; tr. J. Glassco, 1962), which explores both his own spiritual unease and Canadian problems, is one of the great modern examples of the genre.

Saint-Denys-Garneau's cousin ANNE HÉBERT (1916) has written with similar purity and insight, although she succeeded in transcending her invalidism where Saint-Denys-Garneau ultimately failed. She is highly regarded; and publishes in France. 'Manor Life'. in F. R. Scott's (q.v.) version, is one of her most characteristically sombre and exact poems. It concludes:

> See, these mirrors are deep
> Like cupboards
> There is always someone dead behind the quicksilver
> Who soon covers your reflection
> And clings to you like seaweed
>
> Shapes himself to you, naked and thin,
> And imitates love in a long bitter shiver.
>
>   (CWT)

Anne Hébert has also written a delicately evocative novel, *The Wooden Rooms* (*Les Chambres de bois*, 1958). (OBCV; CWT)

The best known French-Canadian poet of the younger generation is JEAN-GUY PILON (1930), whose poetry is, however, more deliberately cosmopolitan than personal. (OBCV; CWT)

*

Fiction that is not merely provincial has been even slower to establish itself than poetry in Canada. The chief places of honour must go, in English, to MORLEY CALLAGHAN (1903), and in French to GABRIELLE ROY (1909). Callaghan, a Canadian newspaperman, was first encouraged to write fiction by Hemingway (q.v.), who later introduced him to the American expatriates in Paris, about whom he has written understandingly in *That Summer in Paris* (1963). Callaghan is a realistic novelist of very high quality, whose achievement has not been fully recognized except in his native Canada, and then belatedly. His harshness is somewhat modified by his devout Catholicism, but this is never really to the fore (unless compassion be a solely Christian quality). *Strange Fugitive* (1928), his first novel, was about a bootlegger. Much better was *It's Never Over* (1930), a haunting account of the sufferings of the friends and family of a man hanged for murdering a policeman. His first major work is *Such Is My Beloved* (1934), dealing with a Roman Catholic priest's attempt, which leads to his destruction, to redeem two prostitutes. Here Morley dwells upon the dangerous resemblances between Christian love and opportunistic lust. His attitude towards his prostitutes is, for the Thirties, refreshingly unsentimental and unhysterical. *The Loved and the Lost* (1951) examines, with the same poignancy, Negro-white relations in Montreal; this shocked Callaghan's fellow Catholics. *A Passion in Rome* (1961) is a story of a love affair between two Canadians living in Rome, and raises the same issue as the earlier work: to what extent is love sexual opportunism? The short stories are collected in *Morley Callaghan's Stories* (1959). They are among the best of our time. Callaghan is a writer worthy to be classed with Green (q.v. 2), Greene (q.v.) and other explorers of the Catholic view of sin.

Gabrielle Roy was born in Manitoba; she was a teacher and an actress before becoming a writer. Her first novel, *The Tin Flute* (*Bonheur d'occasion*, 1945; tr. H. Josephson, 1947) is a humourless but moving study of slum life in Montreal, with a bitter undertone of social accusation. *The Cashier* (*Alexandre Chenevert, caissier*, 1954; tr. H. Binsse, 1955), her subtlest book, presents a bank-clerk, a character reminiscent of Duhamel's Salavin (q.v.). The well-written *Street of Riches* (*Rue Deschambault*, 1955; tr. H. Binsse, 1957) consists of autobiographical sketches. *The Hidden Mountain* (*La Montagne secrète*, 1961; tr. H. Binsse, 1962) tries to trace the mainsprings of artistic inspiration through the career of a painter who seeks beauty in Canada and then in Paris; this excursion into symbolism is unconvincing. *The Road Past Altamonte* (*La Route d'Altamonte*, 1966; tr. J. Marshall, 1967), short stories many of which have their source in childhood experience, shows a return to form. Gabrielle Roy's strength as a novelist lies in her uncluttered view of ordinary lives, and her refusal to regard commercial 'progress' as a true human benefit.

HUGH MACLENNAN (1907), born in Nova Scotia, is another writer who from the beginning showed an awareness of the real problems facing Canadians; he has continually urged his countrymen to abandon their collective inferiority complex and to face their problem of a divided culture with realism and maturity. After Princeton MacLennan went on to Oxford as a Rhodes Scholar, and while there travelled widely in Europe. He wrote, but did not publish, two novels in the early Thirties, while teaching in Canada; but then became aware that there was 'no known contemporary fiction being written in Canada' (either he had not read, or had misunderstood, Callaghan), and so set himself the task of rectifying the omission. The result was *Barometer Rising* (1941), about the great munitions ship explosion in Halifax Harbour in 1917 (which he witnessed). *Two Solitudes* (1945) was the first Canadian novel to explore in depth and with real understanding the conflict between the descendants of the British and the French. *The Watch that Ends the Night* (1959) is a rather over-solemn novel about communism and Canadian intellectuals; but it is intelligent and humane. Like Gabrielle Roy, MacLennan has little humour; in this respect both writers are overshadowed by the more cosmopolitan Callaghan. *Each Man's Son* (1951), however, is a major novel, in which compassion and insight fully compensate for the author's lack of a comic sense. This is one of the outstanding English-language studies of a too enclosed community.

Although of an older generation, ETHEL WILSON (1890) did not publish her first novel, *Hetty Dorval* (1947), until she had reached almost sixty. The wife of a Vancouver doctor, Ethel Wilson is justly honoured by the younger generation as a shrewd, ironic and intelligent experimental novelist. *Hetty Dorval* is a subtle study in promiscuity. All its successors are about love or emotions and attitudes that pose as love. *Equations of Love* (1952) describes a love affair through the eyes of a number of people, and then examines it in terms of the person who experienced it. *Love and Salt Water* (1956) is more overtly satirical. Ethel Wilson shares at least an acerbity of mind with Ivy Compton-Burnett (q.v.).

The French-Canadian novelist, ROGER LEMELIN (1919), 'the bad boy of present-day Canadian literature', began brilliantly with two realistic novels about the Lower Town of Quebec, where he had worked. Again like Gabrielle Roy, Lemelin compels attention by his refusal to settle for a complacent view of French-Canadian society. *The Town Below* (*Au Pied de la pente douce*, 1944; tr. S. Putnam, 1948), a disrespectful and satirical tale, won a prize in France. *The Plouffe Family* (*Les Plouffe*, 1948; tr. M. Finch, 1950)—taken up as a weekly serial on television—is about an opera-singer who becomes a monk but then leaves his monastery to fight Nazism.

Two minor novelists, exact contemporaries, who share a concern with the Canadian creative predicament, are ERNEST BUCKLER (1908) and SINCLAIR ROSS (1908). Buckler's most outstanding novel is his study of a mute artist in *The Mountain and the Valley* (1952). Ross is less pessimistic; *As for Me and My House* (1941) is about a clergyman's and his wife's struggle to exist physically and spiritually in a prairie town. More interesting and vivid is the analytical *The Well* (1958), which deals shrewdly and sympathetically with a young man of criminal mentality.

Younger prose writers include MORDECAI RICHLER (1931), who has long made his home in London, BRIAN MOORE (1921), who now lives in America, JACK LUDWIG (1922), who works as a university teacher in the state of New York and MARGARET LAURENCE (1926), who lived in Africa before settling in England. The fact that these and other highly self-consciously Canadian writers live abroad must mean something; it is probably, however, an indictment of the social rather than the strictly cultural environment. The French-Canadians tend to stay at home, although most of them publish in France—a few, such as Anne Hébert (q.v.), in France only.

Richler, a lively and intelligent writer much concerned with Jewish problems, has not yet—despite massive and somewhat irrelevant publicity campaigns—written the novel of which he is capable. His novels deal with the same kind of material as the poems of Klein (q.v.): he was brought up in a Jewish family in Montreal. He has not bettered his second novel, *Son of a Smaller Hero* (1955), about Jewish life in Montreal. *The Apprenticeship of Duddy Kravitz* (1959) is less sure in touch, but is written with verve and humour. The satirical *The Incomparable Atuk* (1963), about an Eskimo writer's success with Toronto intellectuals, is slighter but extremely funny. *Cocksure* (1968) is more ambitious and less effective.

Brian Moore is a Belfast Irishman who emigrated to Canada after the Second World War. *The Lonely Passion of Judith Hearne* (1955) is a tender-tough study of an alcoholic spinster. His best known book, *The Luck of Ginger Coffey* (1960) is also his most specifically Canadian. Ginger Coffey is a middle-aged Irish immigrant in Canada: he finds himself bereft of wife, job and a sense of virility, and he can only respond by fantasizing and self-deceit. The processes through which he discovers the truth about himself and his situation are described with acute psychological penetration and feeling, although not without sentimentality. He has not yet bettered this novel; but its successors, which include *The Emperor of Ice-Cream* (1965), have been of a high standard. (CWT)

Jack Ludwig is more experimental, and has learnt from Saul Bellow (q.v.), with whom he has collaborated on a periodical. Of his two novels, the earlier *Confusions* (1963) is by far the better. Especially notable in this study of an American Jew who goes to teach in California is Ludwig's grasp of the speech-habits of North American Jews (one of Bellow's special provinces). (CWT) Margaret Laurence sets the best of her three novels, *Jest of God* (1966), in a small Canadian prairie town, Manawaka. The story of an unhappy and unfulfilled teacher's abortive love affair is told by herself with dignity and insight. The relationship between erotic and religious disturbance is delicately explored, and, as in all Margaret Laurence's fiction, small-town pressures on decency are rendered with fearful exactitude. (CWT)

The leading younger French-Canadian novelists are ANDRÉ LANGEVIN and CLAIRE MARTIN (PS. CLAIRE FAUCHER). The more vigorous talent is that of Langevin, whose best novel remains, however, the early *Dust Over the Town* (*Poussière sur la ville,* 1953). Claire Martin is at her best as a short story writer (*With and Without Love, Avec et sans amour,* 1958) and autobiographer (*In an Iron Glove, Dans un gant de fer,* 1965); but her later novels, including *Doux-Amer* (1960) are shrewd, and lucidly written. (CWT)

*

A good deal of theatrical activity goes on in Canada, but there have so far been few really successful dramatists worthy of consideration. The French branch has had more vitality than the English. The dominant theatrical personality in Canada for the past thirty years has been the versatile actor, producer and playwright GRATIEN GÉLINAS (1909), known as Fridolin because of the series of revue sketches he wrote and played in between 1938 and 1946: these featured himself as the Chaplinesque Fridolin. *Lil' Rooster* (*Tit-Coq,* 1948; tr. 1950), a shrewd comedy about French-Canadians in the overseas Canadian armies during the Second World War, was more substantial, and enjoyed an immense and widespread success (except in New York). *Bousille and the Righteous* (*Bousille et les justes,* 1959) was another success in both English and French. Other French-Canadian playwrights include GUY DUFRESNE, FÉLIX LECLERC (1914)

—both authors of fairly successful plays—and the more serious PAUL TOUPIN, whose *Brutus* and *The Lie* are interesting, but have not attracted the public. However, JACQUES LANGUIRAND, a close disciple of Beckett and Ionesco, has aroused some interest. The leading playwright of the younger generation is the prolific MARCEL DUBÉ (1930) whose *Zone* (1955) and *Florence* (1950) are black farces of some originality.

English-Canadian drama is sparse on the ground, although there are numerous performances in many cities. James Reaney (q.v.) has written interesting verse plays. Canada's most distinguished English-language playwright is ROBERTSON DAVIES (1913), also a novelist (whose work has been overpraised by Bellow, q.v.). Davies, an ex-actor and now an academic, gained success with the one-act *Eros at Breakfast* (1948), which he followed with the full-length *Fortune My Foe* (1949). His novels portray small-town Canadian life satirically but lovingly. He adapted *Leaven of Malice* (1954), a satire on intellectuals, for the stage in 1960. He is an intelligent writer whose work is unfortunately not free from a sentimentality and a heavy mock-profundity that too often masquerades as wisdom.

New Zealand Literature

New Zealand has not only to look at the mother-country, but also, jealously and out of the corner of her eye, at Australia; this has affected her literature, which feels itself to be, and is, smaller than that of its neighbour. New Zealand has as yet produced only one major prose writer, Frank Sargeson (q.v.), but the quality of its run-of-the-mill writing is higher than that of Australia. Geographically New Zealand presents a contrast to Australia: where the interior of the latter is harsh, hostile and mysterious, New Zealand is greener and more—in geography-book terms—'scenic'. Beautiful and mysterious it may be, but it is undoubtedly more welcoming.

The beginnings of literature in New Zealand were English. Writers have never had prestige with the New Zealand middle-class, which does not regard creativity as 'honest work'. This has led to some of the sharpest of contemporary English-language satire. Writers have none the less instinctively felt that one of their functions is to record specifically New Zealand experience, which is neither British nor Australian—nor, as C. K. Stead has well said, 'the product of some strange mutation of spirit induced by Pacific sun'. No one can today be interested in the Victorian verses of WILLIAM PEMBER REEVES (1857–1932), who in any case relinquished his interest in literature for politics. The socialist JESSIE MACKAY (1864–1938) aspired to create a genuinely New Zealand literature, and was more intelligent than Reeves; but she did not understand the distinction between imagination and worthy social causes, and her verse is crude. BLANCHE BAUGHAN (1870–1958), born in Putney, London, went to New Zealand in 1900. She had less skill than Mackay, but looked more closely at what was going on around her, and created a popular form all on her own—unlike Australia, New Zealand has no ballad tradition to fall back upon. She was an active socialist and fighter against injustice and the cruelty of the prison system. She wrote some notable sketches, collected in *Brown Bread from a Colonial Oven* (1912). One might claim her as New Zealand's first innovator, even if a few poeticisms are mixed in with her generally colloquial and unpretentious offering. FRANK S. ANTHONY'S

(1891–1925) *Follow the Call* (1936) and *Me and Gus* (1938) were published posthumously. They portray the life of pioneer farmers in a
prose that draws fully and freely on genuine New Zealand
idiom.

The novelist WILLIAM SATCHELL (1859–1942) made the first
attempt to describe the New Zealand scene. *The Toll of the Bush*
(1905) is about the New Zealand outback; his most famous novel,
The Greenstone Door (1914), is about the troubles with the Maoris in
the Sixties that resulted in their being granted part of the North
Island (1870). This is weak in characterization and sentimental,
but Satchell's intended objectivity is evident.

KATHERINE MANSFIELD (PS. KATHERINE MANSFIELD BEAUCHAMP,
1888–1923), who married the English critic John Middleton Murry
in 1918 (a marriage to George Bowden in 1909 had resulted in an
immediate separation), escaped provincialism—she was educated in
London, and finally came to Europe at the age of twenty. She was a
gifted and delicate author, but has been overrated as a short-story
writer. Her stories are often autobiographical; the best, about her
childhood in New Zealand, were written soon after the death of her
brother Leslie Beauchamp in action in France in 1915, an event
which upset her profoundly, since she had just previously spent some
months in his company recreating their common childhood back
home. Even in these tales—published in the collection *Bliss* (1920)—
Katherine Mansfield sacrificed a certain amount of spontaneity to
'art'. Later stories are more tragic; reflecting her fear of loneliness
and the consequences of arrogance, they distil the essence of lonely
or embittered lives. She died in 1923 of tuberculosis, in Gurdjieff's
community at Fontainebleau, after publishing *The Garden Party*
(1922); two posthumous collections followed: *The Doves' Nest* (1923)
and *Something Childish* (1924). At her very best (in the stories of
innocence, about New Zealand, and in later work such as 'Life of
Ma Parker') Katherine Mansfield does reach a lyrical perfection,
even if her scope is limited in the interests of stylistic effect. But her
most substantial writing is to be found in her *Letters* (1928; 1951)
and her *Journals* (1954): here she records her coming to maturity
in the face of imminent death, and describes her relationship with
the Lawrences—D. H. Lawrence (q.v.) ended their friendship when,
in one of the most terrible letters ever written, he attacked her for
suffering from the very disease that was to kill him. *Collected Stories*
was published in 1945. She is a minor writer of great interest; and
she is particularly relevant to New Zealand literature because she
wrote her best stories about life there. Probably the supreme example
is 'At the Bay', which opens *Something Childish*.

A truly indigenous New Zealand literature began to appear at home in the Twenties. JANE MANDER (1878–1949), in contrast to Katherine Mansfield, was artless and sentimental, but showed a shrewd understanding of the problems of women living in rural conditions. Her best novel is *The Story of a New Zealand River* (1920); *Allen Adair* (1925) was her most popular.

It was R. A. K. MASON (1905–1971), who studied classics at Auckland University, who wrote the first truly native poems. He more or less dried up in his mid-thirties and when (after the war) he became well-known he had stopped writing. Mason was an angry pessimistic radical, a non-Christian concerned wonderingly with Christ. Clearly he was influenced by Housman and Hardy, but his voice had its own rawness and harshness:

> Oh I have grown so shrivelled and sere
> *But the body of John enlarges*
> and I can scarcely summon a tear
> *but the body of John discharges....*
>
> (ANZP)

His example has been important to the poets who followed him. Allen Curnow (q.v.) has called him New Zealand's first 'wholly original, unmistakably gifted poet'. Harold Monro (q.v.) took up the cause of his poetry in the Twenties. His achievement may be small, but his place is secure.

MARY BETHELL (1874–1945) was born in England thirty-one years before Mason, but did not publish her first book, *From a Garden in the Antipodes* (1929), until six years after his. It appeared under the pseudonym of 'Evelyn Hayes'. Mary Bethell who spent her middle years in England but is very much of a New Zealand poet, is at her best when writing about her garden. Clearly Lawrence (q.v.) influenced her first poems; but these are more plainly descriptive of nature than his. Her later work, upon which the influence of Hopkins has been suggested, is more ambitious but not less successful or original. Her *Collected Poems* appeared in 1950. Mary Bethell's genius consists of the capacity to select what to describe, a fine plainness and modesty, and a deep love of nature. Her later poems, which dwell on God and death, are quite remarkably interesting— and invite critical investigation and appreciation. (AZNP)

ROBIN HYDE (ps. IRIS WILKINSON, 1906–39) produced much before her early death. She was born in South Africa, came to New Zealand when young, went to China in 1938 and then on to England, where she died. She was a novelist and poet of high distinction, and her death was a major loss to letters. Her poetry is lucid and tender, and often of considerable subtlety. *The Houses by the Sea* (1952) consists of autobiographical poems, some almost transparent in their intense nostalgia, purity of feeling, and haunted sense of erotic unfulfilment. Her distinction is well shown in these lines from her sequence 'The Beaches'. She has been watching two lovers—a man seducing a girl —and has afterwards gone to lie in their 'bed':

> I never meant
> To tell the rest, or you, what I had seen;
> Though that night, when I came in late for tea,
> I hoped you'd see the sandgrains on my coat.

Much of her best poetry, which developed interestingly and quickly, is in this autobiographical vein. Her fiction was the best written in New Zealand in the Thirties. *Passport to Hell* (1935) and its sequel *Nor the Years Condemn* (1938), in the form of reminiscences told to her by a friend, portray New Zealand before and after the First World War. *Check to Your King* (1936), about the adventurer Baron de Thierry, has been described as New Zealand's best historical novel. She, again, requires serious critical attention. (ANZP)

The four writers who dominated the literary scene of the Thirties, associated either with the magazine *Phoenix* (1932) or with the Caxton Press (founded 1935), were all poets. A. R. D. FAIRBURN (1904–57), a lecturer at Auckland University, was the most limited. A kind of more genial and soft A. D. Hope (q.v.), he had a tendency towards rather obvious satire. This was balanced by a not unsentimental lyricism, as in

> He was such a curious lover of shells
> and the hallucinations of water
> that he could never return out of the sea
> without first having to settle a mermaid's bill. . . .

He is better when sardonic, as in 'I'm Older than You, please Listen', and conversational, but even in this vein he lacks edge. He was most useful as a personality on the literary scene. (ANZP)

CHARLES BRASCH (1909), founder of the important post-war periodical *Landfall* (1947), lived and studied abroad and did not return to New Zealand until after the war. His earlier poetry was less regional in tone than that of his contemporaries, although obviously written by a New Zealander. Like the baby Sebastian in his poem 'Photograph of a Baby' he

> has the air of one looking back, by death set
>   free,
> Who sees the strangeness of life, and what things are
>   trying to be.

The subject of his later, ruggedly honest, poetry is just how much it is possible and proper to establish as true, out of a general scepticism. His answers are often in terms of South Island landscape:

> Ask in one life no more
> Than that first revelation of earth and sky,
> Renewed as now in the place of birth
> Where the sea turns and the first roots go round. . . .
>   (ANZP)

DENIS GLOVER (1912), typographer and founder of the important Caxton Press, is an acerb poet of narrow range but more achievement than he is sometimes given credit for. He has been a significant influence in his capacity as publisher and as printer. He began as a satirist (*Six Easy Ways of Dodging Debt Collectors*, 1936), but in the Fifties broadened out into a sardonic observer of the human scene in New Zealand—with work that is satirical in tone but also often lyrical. His best work in this vein is in *Sings Harry* (1951). Harry is a tough and lonely character through whom Glover seems to be able to express himself effectively and fully.

> Once the days were clear
> Like mountains in water,
> The mountains were always there
> And the mountain water;
>
> And I was a fool leaving
> Good land to moulder
> Leaving the fences sagging
> And the old man older
> To follow my wild thoughts
> Away over the hill,
> Where there is only the world
> And the world's ill,
>   *sings Harry*.
>   (ANZP)

ALLEN CURNOW (1911) has a versatile technique at his command, and his statements about New Zealand poetry are important. He contends—sensibly—that the New Zealand poet must be regional in order to be international; his own poetry fuses his knowledge of New Zealand history with the New Zealand present. His views are now being vigorously challenged by the poets of a younger generation. He, too, began as a satirist—*Enemies* (1937) was published by Denis Glover—but his scope widened soon, and amply. His potentiality had been shown early on in such lines as 'Fear made the superior sea/The colour of his new car'. Poems such as 'Landfall in Unknown Seas', on the 300th anniversary of the discovery of New Zealand by Tasman (1642), are intelligent and display graceful rhetoric, but are not as successful as his more personal poems. Then he has an original manner of investigating the metaphysical aspects of his experience, both plain in language and yet not over-simplified:

> What it would look like if really there were only
> One point of the compass not known illusory,
> All other quarters proving nothing but quaint
> Obsolete expressions of true north (would it be?),
> And seeds, birds, children, loves, and thoughts bore down
> The unwinding abiding beam from birth
> To death! What a plan!

Curnow's language seems to have been slightly influenced by Dylan Thomas (q.v.), but more considerably by the English Elizabethan and Jacobean poets. His poems, of which there is as yet no collected edition, are rather more impressive in bulk than read singly or in groups in anthologies. He is important on his own scene, but has not become the 'major poet' New Zealand thought it saw in him. (ANZP)

The best-known poet of the younger generation was JAMES K. BAXTER (1926–1972), who established an international reputation. He was called the 'focus of highest hopes for the future'. He believed in poetry as 'a cell of good living in a corrupt society' and mixed socialism with what has been called a 'histrionic' Catholicism (he was a convert). Rather a self-consciously wild man, although well endowed intellectually, Baxter wrote in a number of styles, none of which absolutely coheres. His ballads are fairly successful, but superficial; his most convincing mode is that employed in *Pig Island Letters* (1966): the conversational. His 'wild youth' remained a consistent theme in his poetry, which is largely of the hit-or-miss-kind: he rejected his own intellectualism as a distraction. Baxter's energy and intelligence are probably sufficient to justify his high position in New Zealand poetry; but except in a few poems he failed to prove himself a satisfying poet. He remained, disappointingly, over-intoxicated with his own energy, and never manifested convincingly qualities of restraint to balance it. But at the end he was leading, so far as he could, a saintly and simple life, and in the last poems there is a new, sadly promising and sombre note. He published a selection: *The Rock Woman* (1969). (ANZP)

KENDRICK SMITHYMAN (1922), who is an academic, is possibly the more gifted poet, although the obscurity of much of his work has robbed him of an international audience. But this obscurity represents a struggle for self-expression that is at least sometimes less self-indulgent than Baxter's bursts of vitality. Smithyman can certainly indulge himself in windy rhetoric ('. . . the days of the weeping woman/between the terror of love and the tremor/history shakes in a bride bed. . . .'), and one suspects that he has been over-influenced by George Barker and Dylan Thomas (qq.v.); but when he builds a poem around an objective situation rather than a set of only nominally personal and romantic clichés he discovers a language of his own, as in the syllabic 'Waikato Railstop'. (ANZP)

There are other New Zealand poets of promise and achievement: HONE TUWHARE (1922), LOUIS JOHNSON (1924), C. K. STEAD (1932), an excellent critic, FLEUR ADCOCK (1934), who has published two volumes in England, VINCENT O'SULLIVAN (1937).

*

Three writers of fiction are outstanding in contemporary New Zealand literature: Roderick Finlayson, Frank Sargeson and Dan Davin. The work of RODERICK FINLAYSON (1904) is not as well known as it should be. His contribution has been towards the understanding of the Maoris of the country around Auckland, where he was born. He has written a standard work on the Maoris and their culture: *The Maoris of New Zealand* (with J. Smith, 1959). Finlayson portrays the Maoris with humorous sympathy but no patronage, and has reproduced their speech to great effect. *Tidal Creek* (1948) and *The Schooner Came to Atia* (1952) are novels; short stories are collected in *Sweet Beulah Land* (1942). Where Satchell (q.v.), although a pioneer, was forced to oversimplify his Maoris, Finlayson has taught his contemporaries that this is not necessary.

The novelist FRANK SARGESON (1903), born at Hamilton, south of Auckland, is the most important—and influential—writer so far produced by New Zealand. He is an undisputed master of the vernacular, and while never prepared to sacrifice coherence he has not been afraid to experiment—as in the autobiographical *Up Onto the Roof and Down Again* (serialized in *Landfall*, 1950–1). Sargeson belongs to the same hurt, puzzled, liberal-humanist tradition as E. M. Forster (q.v.), who praised him, and James Hanley (q.v.); and the same kind of bruised sensitivity exists below the tougher and more defiant surface-skin of his writing. Like so many New Zealand writers, Sargeson began as a satirist, stung to expression by a bourgeoisie that is apparently, judging by what it has invited in the way of protest, peculiarly complacent. His first pamphlet of stories, *Conversation with My Uncle* (1936), satirized suburban life from an orthodox left-wing point of view. But since then he has gone on to make emancipation and spiritual redemption his main theme. His earlier stories suffer from a somewhat crude distinction that he makes between capitalism and the values of the working classes; eventually Sargeson became more concerned with general human values, although he has remained a radical. He has dealt with homosexual themes more fully and frankly (for example, in *That Summer*, q.v.) than Forster was able to do, but his women—although beautifully observed—are never as subtly presented as Forster's in *A Passage to India*.

It was in *That Summer* (1943–4) that Sargeson's genius first fully emerged: for the first time he revealed both his unfailing ear for local dialogue and his unsentimental compassion. A more leisurely narration replaces the cryptic and laconic style of the earlier stories. *I Saw in My Dream* (1949), a novel set in the early years of the century, traces the revolt of a son from respectable parents to his eventual spiritual victory. Sociologically rich, this is also a skilful presentation of a rather negative figure; critics who said that the hero was 'too negative . . . to excite interest' missed the subtlety that Sargeson had by now developed. *I, For One* (1954), in the form of letters, is a more overt study-in-depth of suburban mentality. *Memoirs of a Peon* (1965) represents a new departure. Its defeated narrator, John Newhouse (i.e. Giovanni Casanova), is intelligent and fully articulate; his account of his rakish progress in the New Zealand Depression is the first picaresque novel in Antipodean fiction. *The Hangover* (1967) deals with the pressures that build up in adolescence; few more convincing picture of the motives behind the behaviour of what is usually known as a 'juvenile delinquent' exists in modern English-language fiction. Sargeson is a major writer, legendarily modest, who continues to go from strength to strength. *Collected Stories* (1969) includes *I, For One*. *Wrestling with the Angel* (1964) contains two plays: *A Time for Sowing*, about the missionary who wrote the first primer of the Maori language, and *The Cradle and the Egg*.

DAN DAVIN (1913), who has for many years worked as a publisher in England, never bettered the short stories in his early collection *The Gorse Blooms Pale* (1947). These are set in an area of South Canterbury settled by Irish Catholics, and in the Middle East during the Second World War. His novels cover much the same ground. In a Scandinavian country they would probably be described as a 'novel-cycle', since thematically they are intimately linked. They make use of autobiographical material: Davin differs markedly from Sargeson in having little—some would say too little—faith in his imagination: he deliberately eschews invention. His first novel, *Cliffs of Fall* (1945) is melodramatic; it seems to consist in part of bitter self-appraisal, and probes expatriate guilt. His next, *For the Rest of Our Lives* (1947), based on his war experiences and set in the Middle East, is his best. There is no better account of the New Zealander at war. *Roads From Home* (1949) is set in New Zealand, *The Sullen Bell* (1956) in London. Davin is a sensitive novelist, meticulous in his social observation, but so far without the imaginative depth of Sargeson. His earliest work in the short story suggests, however, that inventiveness is a quality he restrains rather than lacks. Recent novels have been disappointing.

JAMES COURAGE (1903–63) lived for the latter half of his life in England. He wrote well (*The Young Have Secrets*, 1954; *Desire Without Content*, 1950) of the wealthy landowners in Canterbury, showing how their attempts to be 'English' amounted to self-destruction. In 1959, he published what must have been up to that date the most physically candid (though in no sense 'pornographic') English novel in English about homosexuality: *A Kind of Love*. He also left a handful of exquisite short stories. RUTH PARK, who lives in Australia, wrote an excellent comedy of New Zealand working-class life in *The Harp and the South* (1948), but her later books declined into a more forced robustness. MAURICE SHADBOLT (1932) is the most promising of the younger writers. His novel, *Among the Cinders* (1965), is a kind of New Zealand *Catcher in the Rye* (q.v.). *This Summer's Dolphin* (1969) is a more carefully written symbolic work, but too obviously influenced by Patrick White (q.v.); however, it reveals its author as a novelist of potential.

South African Literature

South African literature comprises literatures written in English, Afrikaans (a form of Dutch that eventually replaced Dutch as the official language of South Africa) and African languages.

I

A true Afrikaans literature began only in this century. On the familiar colonial pattern, the first truly native poetry preceded the prose. It was in EUGÈNE MARAIS (1871–1936), TOTIUS (ps. J. D. DU TOIT, 1877–1953), JAN CELLIERS (1865–1940) and C. LOUIS LEIPOLDT (1880–1947) that Afrikaans poetry first found its authentic voice. Marais, a lawyer, wrote only one volume of verse; it contained 'Winter Night', which is considered to open the Afrikaans epoch. His wife died young, his own health was broken, and he finally killed himself. He wrote well in prose of animals and insects, especially in *The Soul of the White Ant* (1934; tr. W. De Kok, 1937): this had appeared in a periodical some sixteen years earlier and was plagiarised by Maeterlinck (q.v. 2) in his inferior book on the same subject. (PSAV) Totius was a minister in the Dutch Reformed Church and a professor of theology. His verse is stark, simple and sometimes effective; he was influenced by late nineteenth-century Flemish poetry and by protestant hymnology. (PSAV) Celliers was the least interesting of this group, but deserves his place for his technical ability. Leipoldt was one of the most gifted South Africans of his generation: he was a politician, journalist and doctor as well as poet. He was also a novelist, dramatist, botanist and notable personality. 'The Banded Cobra' is a fine poem showing at the same time his deep hatred of war and the love of nature in which his bitterness about humanity took refuge:

> The copper cobra comes out of his slit
> On the ridge and slides around.

'The rain has fallen; the veld is wet,
 And wet the red-gold ground.'
The meercat comes, his eyes two gleams,
 And watches bolt-upright.
The ancient porcupine says: 'It seems
 It will rain again tonight.'
But the lizard squeaks: 'Why, that's not rain,
 It's red and sticky and dark:
Such rain will you ever see again—
 So smooth, so fine, so stark?'
And the wise rock-owl weighs in his words:
 'It's blood, it's human blood!
 It's living blood at the bushes' roots
That feeds them in its flood.'

                                    (PSAV)

The only Twenties writer to make a lasting mark was G. M. VAN
DEN HEEVER (1902–57), born in one of the world's first concentration
camps (the British one at Norvalspont), whose fiction is probably
more important than his poetry. His best novels are *Late Fruit* (1939)
and *The Harvest Home* (1935; tr. 1945); like much Afrikaans fiction,
van den Heever's is weak in psychology; but he gives a poignant
picture of farmers forced by failure to the city and exploitation.
(PSAV)

The dominating personality in Afrikaans letters today, however, is
still N. P. VAN WYK LOUW (1906–70), a university lecturer. He is a
genuine intellectual, and has written criticism and a verse drama—
Germanicus (1956)—of some importance. Some of his dramatic and
yet metaphysical lyrics are distinctly unusual and original, as 'Oh
the Inconstant':

        Oh the inconstant child: young girl
        fantasy-making, fantastic, neurotic—
        bound forever to the hardest:
        wood never could be hard enough for her knife;

        lime was too crumbling
        (granite again beyond her forbearance),
        'form' she had in her, to her—oh the light
        play-haunches that filled a universe—

        but the role of free hetaira was
        concentration-camp wire parting

her from the double-bed and babies
and the too wide sheet plus the pillow;

the cool sheet, and the separated pillows
were two mountains and a finlandic mere
between her and her 'sanctity',
between her bestowal and her desire.

(PSAV)

This plainly shows the influences of German and possibly Dutch expressionism.

Another important Afrikaans writer is UYS KRIGE (1910), who is an anthologist and translator into Afrikaans (from French, Spanish, Italian, Portuguese) of note as well as a poet. He has been influenced by the Latin-language poets from whom he translates, but has acclimatized them to his own Afrikaans voice. His subject-matter is usually war or the suffering inflicted by man upon man; but this he often sees against the natural background of South Africa, which he renders with a hard precision. The last two stanzas of 'Farm Gate' illustrate his lyrical powers:

Now after all the years I'll open
a gate again.
Where have my paths
till now not led
to bring me to this farm-road gate
with all illusions shed
but hope, hope in my heart
and clear dreams in my head?

The gate stands in
a maroola's shade.
A wholeness in me, harmony
and no bitterness, no hate.
I lift the catch . . . and in my heart
opens a gate.

(PSAV; see also SAWT)

Uys Krige is the author of many stories, and of a book about his escape from an Italian prisoner-of-war camp during the Second World War.

D. J. OPPERMAN (1914), like Louw, continued to experiment within traditional forms, and is generally regarded as the leading

Afrikaans poet of his generation. He is a clever and attractive
poet:

> Under a dung-cake
> with the rain in spate
> two earthworms held
> a terse debate
>
> on 'you' and 'me'
> and 'my native land',
> on 'my mud-hut
> was first to stand'.
>
> A casual spade
> by chance sank through,
> the earthworms both
> were chopped in two:
>
> Four earthworms now
> jerk slimily along
> the 'I's' and the 'you's'
> doubt where they belong.
>
> In the next thick mush
> of a meeting place
> politely each
> greets his own face.
>   (PSAV)

ELIZABETH EYBERS (1915), deeply influenced by Emily Dickinson,
was the only outstanding Afrikaans woman poet until the advent of
Ingrid Jonker (q.v.). She now lives in Holland. Her subject-matter
is the same as that of the Australian poet Judith Wright (q.v.):
motherhood, womanhood, loneliness. . . . But she is terser and less
inclined to sentimentality, and there is a note of subdued bitterness
running through her work. *The Quiet Adventure* (tr. 1948) is a selection
of her poems in English translation. (PSAV)

The suicide of INGRID JONKER (1933–65) has had an unquestionable symbolic significance for all South African writers. Her poetry
is disturbed and disturbing. The comparison with Sylvia Plath (q.v.)
is inevitable; but she yielded to the British influence of Dylan Thomas
more than to that of Roethke (qq.v.), the figure most obviously
behind Plath. But the poetry of both anguishedly explores the link

between birth and violence: 'but sewer O sewer/my blood child lies in the water' writes Ingrid Jonker. And just before her suicide she expressed her feelings about the situation in South Africa:

> My black Africa
> follow my lonely fingers
> follow my absent image
> lonely as an owl
> and the forsaken fingers of the world
> alone like my sister
> My people have rotted away from me
> what will become of the rotten nation
> a hand cannot pray alone.
>
> (PSAV)

Selected Poems appeared in English in 1968.

II

With only a few exceptions, those South Africans who write in English and are known internationally are exiles; few of them are even thought of as being South African. ROY CAMPBELL (1901–57) did not stay in South Africa long, although long enough to make his mark as a satirist and to write his best poetry. He and William Plomer (q.v.) founded the magazine *Whiplash* (1926), to 'sting with satire the mental hindquarters . . . of the bovine citizenry.' Then Campbell left, stormed London (challenging his literary enemies to duels), fought for Franco in the Spanish Civil War and then for the Allies in the Second World War, worked for the B.B.C., and finally went to live and farm in Portugal, where he died in a car crash.

Campbell never grew up, and as he grew older became increasingly brash and egocentric, while his satire became thin. He became a Roman Catholic, but an unpleasantly militant one, sharing the hysterically nihilist mood of some of the fascist rebels in Spain, who rationalized their brutality by the slogan, 'Live Christ the King'. He himself was no fascist, simply a naïve (q.v.) who lamented—but without ever bothering to take serious thought—modern technology's erosion of individuality. Much of his work, like his personality, was vitiated by his inability to examine the nature of his ultra-romantic compulsions. But he had real warmth, and his egocentricity—which occasionally involved hitting people he disliked in public—may be

looked upon as an accidental sickness. Without it he might have
remained a fairly good vitalist poet. His early satire, in which he
attacked the pseudo-romantic self-indulgence of bad colonial
poetry, was excellent: the famous epigram 'On Some South African
Novelists'—

> You praise the firm restraint with which they write—
> I'm with you there, of course:
> They use the snaffle and the curb all right,
> But where's the bloody horse?

—gives a hint of his power and wit. Later satire is vigorous and
ingenious in its compression; but its points of view are too often sick:
Jews are funny, force equals Christ equals glory, and so on. There
was however, a lyrical purity in him; and before he came to London
and became too involved with his own megalomania this came out
in a handful of beautiful poems. The best is the comparatively long
'Tristan da Cunha', the real subject of which is that very poetic
loneliness which drove him into egocentricity. It is a magnificent
poem, of major proportions, more complex than its lucid surface
immediately suggests; one prophetic stanza is:

> My pride has sunk, like your grey fissured crags,
> By its own strength o'ertoppled and betrayed:
> I, too, have burned the wind with fiery flags
> Who now am but a roost for empty words,
> An island of the sea whose only trade
> Is in the voyages of its wandering birds.

Campbell's poems and translations were collected in three volumes:
Collected Poems (1949–60). David Wright (q.v.) has written of
Campbell with wisdom and understanding.

The turning point from colonial to South African came with
Campbell and WILLIAM PLOMER (1903–73). The colonial had been
mainly represented by such poets as F. C. SLATER (1876–1954),
KINGSLEY FAIRBRIDGE (1885–1924) and the Rhodesian ARTHUR
SHEARLY CRIPPS (1896–1952), none of whom is more than historically
interesting. Both Campbell and Plomer saw and accepted what the
earlier poets had escaped from by rooting themselves in the Victorian
British tradition: the nature of their new country. Both looked not
to the worn-out home tradition, but to the vigour of the Africans
themselves, and to European modernism. Plomer, a still undervalued
writer, is a distinguished novelist and poet. He combines the

humanism of his close friend E. M. Forster (q.v.) with a colourful sense of the bizarre. His *Collected Poems* appeared in 1973. His poetry may be divided into comic extravaganza on the one hand, and more personal work on the other. There is no one like him in the world in the former genre; as a 'light poet' he is preferable to John Betjeman —as fluent in traditional forms, his work is never vitiated by refuge in the poetical or high sentimental, and his choice of words is subtler, funnier and altogether sharper. In his other vein Plomer is fastidious, reticent, elegant and the author of some memorable and moving lines, such as (in his elegy, 'The Taste of the Fruit', for Ingrid Jonker and Nathaniel Nasaka, who killed himself in the same month): 'Where sour beer and thick smoke/Lewdness and loud/ Laughter half disguise/ Hope dying of wounds;/He is not there'. There is no doubt that Plomer has been underrated as a serious poet. He has had more of his due as a novelist, and it is on the whole well acknowledged that he was the first South African writer of English fiction to try to see the black man as he actually is. His first novel, *Turbott Wolfe* (1925), bears obvious signs of its author's youth; but it remains a passionate demonstration that a human way for South Africa would be through miscegenation. After three relatively minor books, Plomer produced his best novel:*Museum Pieces* (1952), a study of a man who cannot find a place for himself in the modern world. *Museum Pieces* is a sad novel, about a failure; but it affirms and even comes near to defining certain elusive personal values of the past that might be forgotten. Its equivalent at a lower social level is the English novelist Geoffrey Cotterell's *Go Said the Bird*.

Other English-speaking exiles from South Africa may be dealt with here. CHARLES MADGE (1912) left very early, and has never returned. He became associated with the leading English poets of the Thirties, and was for a time married to Kathleen Raine (q.v.). His only two published books of poetry are *The Disappearing Castle* (1937) and *The Father Found* (1941). He was co-founder, with Tom Harrison, of Mass Observation, and later became a publisher, planner in a new town, and, finally, a professor of sociology. He is now retired and lives in the south of France. Madge has since the Second World War been a much neglected poet, most of whose best work has not yet been collected. He began as a reasonably straightforward Marxist; but even his two early volumes contain indications of the direction he would take in his post-war work, of which the most important are the sequence, *Poem by Stages*, and the long poem *The Storming of the Brain*. That no honest publisher has yet taken these up (a publisher did, but left them unpublished) is not short of scandalous, for Madge is the one and only genuinely 'sociological' poet writing in English, and is also extremely original. His Marxism has become tempered by observations of practical communism (and its betrayal), by an increasing understanding of the anthropological bases of religious feeling, and by a personal—and sweetly old-fashioned—romanticism. The resultant poetry is of major interest, and a revelation. It should be made available without delay.

R. N. CURREY (1907), who has been a schoolmaster in Essex since 1946, did his most distinguished work as a war poet; his more recent development as a specifically South African poet (something Charles Madge never attempted) has been of a more academic nature. His war poems are in *This Other Planet* (1945). ANTHONY DELIUS (1916) did not leave South Africa until more recently. He now works for the B.B.C. in London. He has written a celebrated long poem, 'Black South Easter', satires, and a number of shorter poems on exclusively South African themes. F. T. PRINCE (1912), Professor of English at the University of Southampton, is a distinguished scholar whose elegant, fastidious, reticent poetry is collected in *The Doors of Stone* (1963). One of his poems, 'Soldiers Bathing', has become an anthology piece.

DAVID WRIGHT (1920), who is deaf, has not returned to South Africa except on visits. As well as a poet, he is a superb although unobtrusive critic (*Seven Victorian Poets*, 1965), a fine translator (Chaucer, *Beowulf*) and writer of travel books (about Portugal) in collaboration with the painter Patrick Swift. *Deafness* (1969) is the best general book on the subject; one is tempted to say the only good one. As a poet Wright has two styles: one romantic, more or less rhetorical, and the other sardonic, hard. In the first he seldom wholly locates his own voice; but there are exceptions which make the misses worth while. For example, on Wordsworth:

> There is a cragbound solitary quarter
> Hawk's kingdom once, a pass with a tarn
> High on its shoulder. Inscribed on a stone
> With graveyard letters, a verse to his brother
> Says it was here they parted from each other
> Where the long difficult track winding down
> A bald blank bowl of the hills may be seen
> Leading the eye to a distant gleam of water.
> After that last goodbye and shake of the hand
> A bright imagination flashed and ended;
> The one would live on, for forty years becalmed
> Among the presences he had commanded—
> Those energies in which the other foundered
> Devoured by wind and sea in sight of land.

Another aspect of Wright's more lyrical poetry is its fineness of technique: a deaf man's sense of music. In his sardonic manner, which comes to him as and when it can, Wright is both more detached—

> With paper and pen, with a room, and with time to think,
> Everything, in fact, unnecessary to the Muse. . . .

—and, as Anthony Delius has put it, 'dry-eyed'. He is an original poet, much read but little noticed by reviewers, who dislike the manner in which his anthologies studiously and obstinately ignore their own verses and their current preferences.

The Rhodesian novelist DORIS LESSING (1919) has lived in England since 1949. She made her reputation with her first book, *The Grass is Singing* (1950), which remains, technically her best. This is about a white farmer and his wife, and their African servant. Here the author's social and political concerns are implicit in the story; they are not superimposed from without. Succeeding work has not fulfilled the promise of this book: although it has proved popular, and is worthy, it has not, on the whole, succeeded on a purely imaginative level. The most successful was *Five* (1953), short stories. *The Golden Notebook* (1962) impressively and despairingly records Doris Lessing's own creative problems. Essentially she is a writer searching for a new language to describe old truths; she now finds it most nearly in her short stories.

LAURENS VAN DER POST (1906), of the generation of Plomer (q.v.), has also left South Africa. He is partially a humanist like Plomer; but he also has a mystical streak which he has not succeeded in integrating into the scheme of his fiction. His best work is non-fiction about Africa: *The Lost World of the Kalahari* (1958) and *Venture to the Interior* (1951). His novels are unquestionably the products of a distinguished and humane mind, but they fail to reconcile the scientist in him with the seer: rather than resolve his conflicts, they tend to make for more confusion. The best is *The Heart of the Hunter* (1961). Earlier novels include *Flamingo Feather* (1955) and *The Face beside the Fire* (1953). All his fiction contains magnificent descriptive writing; but he cannot decide how to handle or even to see his characters. He is, significantly, a 'Jungian'.

*

South African fiction begins with OLIVE SCHREINER (1855–1920), famous for her *The Story of a South African Farm* (1883), which founded the South African novel proper. This, set on an ostrich farm on the veld, is at the beginning a powerful novel, even if too obviously influenced by *Wuthering Heights*; it later becomes a piece of fine social preaching (reminiscent of Shaw, q.v.), rather than a novel. The description of the veld itself, and of a childhood on it, is magnificent. Jesus Christ comes to Mashonaland in *Trooper Peter Halket of Mashonaland* (1897) and preaches racial justice. But Olive Shreiner's most interesting book is her very early—but posthumously published —*Undine: A Queer Little Child* (1928), which describes both her morbid death-wish as a child, and the manner in which her family's Calvinism drove her to atheism. South Africans are proud of Olive Schreiner, a passionate and complex personality, of whom Roy Campbell (q.v.) wrote in 'Buffel's Kop (Olive Schreiner's Grave)':

> In after times when strength or courage fail,
> May I recall this lonely hour: the gloom
> Moving one way: all heaven in the pale
> Roaring: and high above the insulated tomb
> An eagle anchored on full spread of sail
> That from its wings let fall a silver plume.

SARAH GERTRUDE MILLIN (1889), the wife of a judge, has been a prolific and worthy chronicler who writes lucidly and with great competence—if not more. She has covered most aspects of South Africa's recent history with sympathy, skill and accuracy, though not with any outstanding psychological penetration. She is particularly concerned with the plight of the 'coloureds' (those of mixed descent), who since the Second World War have been denied the right to vote, as in *The Dark River* (1919) and *King of the Bastards* (1950).

Racial conflicts between black and white were the theme of the single novel, *Bayete! Hail to the King* (1923) of the South African politician—previously police commandant—GEORGE HEATON NICHOLLS (1876–1942), who was born in England. This was certain, of course, to become the increasing concern of serious writers of South African fiction—which is why the contemporary novelists look back to Olive Schreiner, Sarah Gertrude Millin, and then to Plomer, rather than to the comfortable colonial writers who simply ignored the problem, or treated the Africans as picturesque furniture. FRANK BROWNLEE (1875–1952), although a minor writer, deserves honour in this respect. He lived among the people of the Transkeian territories and wrote stories about them which show understanding without a trace of patronage: *Ntsukumbini, Cattle Thief* (1929), *Corporal Wanzi* (1937), *Lion and Jackal* (1938).

It is quite possible that posterity will regard H. C. BOSMAN (1905–51) as the most oustanding South African writer of fiction in the first half of the century. An Afrikaner who wrote in English, and poet as well as prose writer, he served four and a half years in prison for shooting his stepbrother ('culpable homicide') in a family brawl. He was originally sentenced to death, but was reprieved. His first stories (some of them written in prison) were collected in *Mafeking Road* (1947); these are told by an old Boer farmer and trekker; the result is a remarkably objective picture of an isolated Afrikaner community. The laconic prose is outstanding. Bosman is the best of all South African story writers because he is the least compromising; yet no malice distorts the picture. If these men of the backveld are sly and mean, they are also courageous and—on occasion—generous. *Cold Stone Jug* (1948) is one of the best of the many books that have been written about life in prison. His novel, *Jacaranda in the Night* (1946), was not a success. He never bettered the sketches in *Mafeking Road*.

One might regard Bosman as an exile: he lived away from South Africa for a long time. But he went back there, and he regarded himself only as a South African writer. He has rightly been compared to Maupassant and (for his cruelty) to Saki (q.v.); but he has his own characteristic flavour.

Contemporary fiction in English from South Africa is somewhat disappointing. Not much written by supporters of the governmental policy of *apartheid* has any relationship with literature (this is a statement of fact, not of opinion); nearly all the fiction by opponents of *apartheid* tends, naturally enough, to be on that subject. Unfortunately few of these writers have major imaginative talent—or energy. Most of the vigour comes from black writers with feelings of oppression. This is not to suggest that the humane, human, high journalistic value of such books as ALAN PATON's (1903) *Cry the Beloved Country* (1948) is not great; but such a book as Plomer's *Turbott Wolfe* quickly shows up their literary pretensions. Perhaps the outstanding contemporary writer of English fiction living in South Africa is NADINE GORDIMER (1923), who is less overtly political and more concerned with the human results of *apartheid*. Thus, she emphasizes feelings rather than makes political arguments. She is at her best in the short story: *Six Feet in the Country* (1956), *Not for Publication* (1965) and two other collections. She has written five novels, all of which, like her stories, sensitively explore the psychological and emotional consequences of *apartheid*.

*

One poet who remains in South Africa deserves mention: GUY
BUTLER (1918), Professor of English at Rhodes University. Butler is
a versatile experimenter within traditional forms; his main concern
is to bring together the strains of South African and European
within himself; he is sensitive to European and English poetry, and
tends to write poems that either record his South African experience
in a European manner or to describe Europe (he is fond of and knows
Italy well) from the point of view of a South African. His two main
collections are *Stranger to Europe* (1952) and *South of the Zambesi* (1966).
His poetry is elegant, subtle, lyrical and yet meditative, as these
lines from 'Common Dawn' indicate:

> Submitting to a sentry's fate
> I concentrate
>   On the day's way of dawning—
>
> Grey clouds brighten, birds awake,
> Wings and singing shake
>   The curtained silence of the morning.
>
> And gentle as a bird, the breeze
> Brushes the grass about my knees
>   So softly that the dew remains
>
> On every blade from here to where
> Alien sentries, watching, share
>   The view of fatal plains. . . .
>   (PSAV; SAWT)

*

PETER ABRAHAMS (1919), son of an Abyssinian father and a
coloured mother, was the first South African of mixed blood to make
an international name for himself as a novelist. He escaped early
from the native township where he was born to come and live in
London. His novel *Mine Boy* (1946) was the first novel by a black
South African to appear in sixteen years. He had previously published a book of short stories: *Dark Testament* (1942). Abrahams
became well known on the publication of his autobiography *Tell
Freedom* (1954). He is by no means a major novelist: characterization
is not above average and plots, especially in recent novels, tend to
creak. But he is an intelligent and valuable one. *Mine Boy* was one
of the first novels to reveal the true effects of white exploitation upon

black South Africans. The best of his other novels are *Wild Conquest* (1966), about the Great Trek of the Boers to the Matabele, *A Wreath for Udomo* (1956), set in West Africa and prophetic of the rise and fall of Nkrumah of Ghana, and *This Island Now*, which deals with the rough and tumble of politics in a Caribbean island (Abrahams now lives in the West Indies).

ALEX LA GUMA (1925), whose work may not be published or quoted in South Africa, was accused in the notorious Treason Trial of 1956, but the charge was dropped. In 1967 he escaped to Britain; the British version of *apartheid* introduced by the Maudling Act of 1971 (on the precedent of Callaghan's action against the Kenyan Asians, which actually introduced the principle of *apartheid* into the British constitution) has hardly yet been developed to a point where it will trouble him. But doubtless he watches with apprehension. *A Walk in the Night*, a long short-story, was published alone in 1962 and then in a story collection of the same title in 1967; it is one of the most vivid of all modern African stories. It is set in Cape Town's District Six, one of the toughest places in the world. Here lives Michael Adonis, sacked for answering his white foreman back. It has been compared to Paton's *Cry the Beloved Country* (q.v.) and to Doris Lessing's *Five* (q.v.); one is bound to say that it is superior to both: it really has, as one critic claimed, 'Dostoevskian overtones'. *The Stone Country* (1967) is a novel about South Africa's prisons. (SAWT; AWT)

In *Road to Ghana* (1960) ALFRED HUTCHINSON (1924) memorably describes his flight from South Africa, where he was prosecuted by the government for his opposition to their policies. It has pace, lucidity and humour; and its record of stupidity and the brutality that this leads to amounts to one of the most powerful denuciations of some supporters of South Africa's Nationalist Party. (SAWT)

EZEKIEL MPHAHLELE (1919), banned from his profession of teacher because of his opposition to the Bantu Education Act, now lives in Nigeria. He has summed up a feeling common to many South African writers, in a remarkable statement: 'I feel very gloomy about the whole situation as far as creative writing is concerned. I think right now we are being sucked into this battle between the ruling whites and the Africans . . . our energies go into this conflict to such an extent that we don't have much left for creative work . . . why could this not be a spur towards creative writing? . . . I think it's a paralysing spur. . . . You won't get a great, white novel, I don't think, and you won't get a great black novel until we get to a point where we . . . [are] integrated'. *Down Second Avenue* (1959) is a vivid evocation of a ghetto area in Pretoria; the long, four-part *The Wanderers* (1970), is in part a semi-autobiographical account of a black journalist forced out of South Africa, in part a shrewd study of a liberal white journalist. It is an intelligent and moving work, as complex and subtle as anything to come out of Africa in the last few difficult and embittering years. (SAWT; AWT)

LEWIS NKOSI (1936), trenchant critic of much mediocre black literature, displays a similarly fine intelligence. He was barred from South Africa in the early Sixties. He is mainly a critic; but *The Rhythm of Violence* (1964) is a powerful play, set in Johannesburg, about racial tensions against a background of stupidity and violence (AWT)

Select Bibliography

by the late F. Seymour-Smith

Reference books and other standard sources of literary information; with a selection of national historical and critical surveys, excluding monographs on individual authors (other than series) and anthologies.

Imprint: the place of publication other than London is stated, followed by the date of the last edition traced up to 1971. *OUP*= Oxford University Press, and includes departmental Oxford imprints such as Clarendon Press and the London OUP. But Oxford books originating outside Britain, e.g. Australia, New York, are so indicated. *CUP* = Cambridge University Press.

GENERAL AND EUROPEAN

Baker, Ernest A.: A Guide to the Best Fiction. *Routledge*, 1932.

Beer, Johannes: Der Romanführer. 14 vols. *Stuttgart, Anton Hiersemann*, 1950–69.

Benét, William Rose: The Reader's Encyclopaedia. *Harrap*, 1955.

Bompiani, Valentino: Dizionario letterario Bompiani delle opere e dei personaggi di tutti i tempi e di tutte le letterature. 9 volumes (including index volume). *Milan, Bompiani*, 1947–50. *Appendice*. 2 vols. 1964–6.

Chambers's Biographical Dictionary. *Chambers*, 1969.

Church, Margaret: Time and Reality: studies in contemporary fiction. *North Carolina*; OUP, 1963.

Contemporary Authors: an international bio-bibliographical guide. *In progress. Detroit, Gale*, 1962.

Courtney, W. F. (Editor): The Reader's Adviser. 2 vols. (Vol. 1: Literature). *New York, Bowker*, 1968–71.

Einsiedel, Wolfgang: Die Literaturen der Welt in ihrer mündlichen und schriftlichen Uberlieferung. *Zurich, Kindler*, 1964.

Ellmann, Richard and Charles Feidelson (Editors): The Modern Tradition: backgrounds of modern literature. *New York, OUP*, 1965.

Esslin, Martin: The Theatre of the Absurd. *Penguin Books*, 1968.

Fleischmann, Wolfgang B. (Editor): Encyclopaedia of World Literature in the Twentieth Century. 3 vols. *New York, Frederick Ungar*, 1967–71. (An enlarged and updated edition of Lexicon der Weltliteratur im 20 Jahrhundert. *Infra.*)

Ford, Ford Madox: The March of Literature. *Allen and Unwin*, 1939.

Frauwallner, E. and others (Editors): Die Welt Literatur. 3 vols. *Vienna,* 1951–4. *Supplement* (A–F), 1968.

Freedman, Ralph: The Lyrical Novel: studies in Hermann Hesse, André Gide and Virginia Woolf. *Princeton; OUP,* 1963.

Grigson, Geoffrey (Editor): The Concise Encyclopaedia of Modern World Literature. *Hutchinson,* 1970.

Hargreaves-Mawdsley, W. N.: Everyman's Dictionary of European Writers. *Dent,* 1968.

Harward, Timothy B. (Editor): European Patterns: contemporary patterns in European writing. *Dublin, Dolmen Press; OUP,* 1963.

Hoppé, A. J.: The Reader's Guide to Everyman's Library. *Dent,* 1971.

Josipovici, Gabriel: The World and the Book: a study of the modern novel. *Macmillan,* 1971.

Kearney, E. I. and L. S. Fitzgerald: The Continental Novel: a checklist of criticism in English, 1900–66. *New Jersey, The Scarecrow Press,* 1968.

Keller, Helen: The Reader's Digest of Books. *New York;* and *Allen and Unwin,* 1947.

Kindermann, Heinz and Margarete Dietrich: Lexikon der Weltliteratur. *Vienna, Humboldt,* 1951.

Kindlers Literatur Lexikon. 5 vols. *Zurich, Kindler,* 1965–9. (A–Ra; in progress.) Based on Bompiani *supra.*

Kronenberger, Louis and Emily Morison Beck (Editors): *Atlantic Brief Lives:* a biographical companion to the arts. *Atlantic Monthly Press Book: Boston, Little Brown,* 1971.

Kunitz, Stanley J. and Howard Haycraft: Twentieth Century Authors. *New York, the H. W. Wilson Co.,* 1942. *Supplement,* 1955.

Laird, Charlton: The World Through Literature. *New York;* and *Peter Owen,* 1959.

Lexikon der Weltliteratur im 20 Jahrhundert. 2 vols. *Freiburg, Herder,* 1960–1.

Magnus, Laurie: A Dictionary of European Literature. *Routledge,* 1926.

Melchinger, Siegfried: Drama: Zwischen Shaw und Brecht. Translated by George Wellwarth as: *The Concise Encyclopaedia of Modern Drama. New York;* and *Vision Press,* 1966.

Mondadori, Alberto: Dizionario universale della Letteratura contemporanea. 4 vols. *Verona,* 1959–62.

Mukerjea, S. V.: Disjecta Membra: studies in literature and life. *Bangalore,* 1959.

Murphy, Rosalie (Editor): Contemporary Poets of the English Language. *St. James Press,* 1970.

The Penguin Companion to Literature. 4 vols. *Penguin Books,* 1969–72.

Poggioli, Renato: The Theory of the Avant Garde. *Belknap Press, Harvard University Press,* 1968.

Priestley J. B.: Literature and Western Man. *Heinemann,* 1960.

Smith, Horatio (Editor): Columbia Dictionary of Modern European Literature. *Columbia University Press,* 1947.

Steinberg, S. H. (Editor): Cassell's Encyclopaedia of Literature. *Cassell,* 1953.

Studies in Modern European Literature and Thought Series. *Bowes and Bowes* (*The Bodley Head*) and *Yale University Press,* 1952.

Van Tieghem, Philippe and Pierre Josserand: Dictionnaire des Littératures. 3 vols. *Paris, Presses Universitaires de France,* 1968.

Ward, A. C.: Longman Companion to Twentieth Century Literature. *Longman*, 1970.

Wellwarth, George E.: The Theatre of Protest and Paradox: developments in the Avant Garde drama. *New York*; and *MacGibbon and Kee*, 1965.

West, Paul: The Modern Novel. *Hutchinson*, 1965.

Writers and Critics Series (British, European and American). *Oliver and Boyd*, 1960.

AMERICAN (*United States of America*)

Beach, J. W.: American Fiction, 1920–40. *New York, Macmillan*, 1942.

Bradbury, Malcolm and David Palmer (Editors): The American Novel in the Nineteen Twenties. (Stratford-upon-Avon Studies, 13). *Edward Arnold*, 1971.

Browning, D. C.: A Dictionary of Literary Biography: English and American. *Dent*, 1960.

Burke, W. J. and W. D. Howe: American Authors and Books, revised by Irving and Anne D. Weiss. *New York, Crown Publishers*, 1971.

Dodsworth, Martin (Editor): The Survival of Poetry: a contemporary survey by Donald Davie and others. *Faber*, 1970.

Freedman, Morris: American Drama in Social Context. *Southern Illinois University Press*, 1971.

Gerstenberger, Donna and George Hendrick: The American Novel, 1789–1959: a check list of twentieth-century criticism. *Chicago, Swallow Press*, 1961.

Gregory, Horace V. and Marya Zaturenskay: A History of American Poetry, 1900–40. *New York, Harcourt Brace*, 1967.

Guttmann, Allen: The Jewish Writer in America: assimilation and the crisis of identity. *New York*; *OUP*, 1971.

Handy, William J.: Modern Fiction: a formalist approach. *Southern Illinois University Press*, 1971.

Hart, James D.: The Oxford Companion to American Literature. *OUP*, 1965.

Herzberg, Max J. and others: The Reader's Encyclopaedia of American Literature. *New York, Crowell*; and *Methuen*, 1963.

Jones, Howard Mumford: Belief and Disbelief in American Literature. *University of Chicago Press*, 1969.

Lutwack, Leonard: Heroic Fiction: the epic tradition and American novels of the twentieth century. *Southern Illinois University Press*, 1971.

McCormick, John: American Literature, 1919–32: a comparative history. *New York*; and *Routledge*, 1971.

Maxwell, D. E. S.: American Fiction: the intellectual background. *Columbia University Press*; and *Routledge*, 1963.

O'Connor, William Van (Editor): Seven Modern American Novelists. *University of Minnesota; OUP*, 1964.

Pamphlets on American Writers: series. *University of Minnesota: OUP* 1959– *in progress*.

Rosenthal, Macha L.: The Modern Poets: a critical introduction. *New York; OUP*, 1960.

Rosenthal, Macha L.: The New Poets: British and American poetry since World War II. *New York; OUP*, 1967.

Spender, Stephen and Donald Hall (Editors): The Concise Encyclo-

paedia of English and American
Poets and Poetry. *Hutchinson*, 1970.

Spiller, Robert E., W. Thorp, T. H.
Johnson, and H. S. Canby
(Editors): Literary History of the
United States. 3 vols.; Vol. 4:
*Bibliography supplement. New York,
Macmillan*, 1948; Vol. 4, 1959.

Tanner, Tony: American Fiction,
1950–1970. *Jonathan Cape*, 1971.

Thorp, Willard: American Writing
in the Twentieth Century. *Harvard;
OUP*, 1960.

Turner, Darwin T.: In a Minor
Chord: three Afro-American writers and their search for identity.
Southern Illinois University Press,
1971.

Unger, Leonard (Editor): Seven
Modern American Poets: an
introduction. *University of Minnesota; OUP*, 1967.

Wager, Willis: American Literature:
a world view. *University of London
Press*, 1961.

AUSTRALIAN

Argyle, Barry: An Introduction to
the Australian Novel, 1830–1930.
OUP, 1971.

Green, H. M.: A History of Australian Literature. 2 vols. *Sydney,
Angus and Robertson*, 1961.

Keirnan, Brian: Images of Society
and Nature; seven essays on
Australian novels. *Melbourne OUP*,
1971.

Miller, E. Morris: Australian Literature from its Beginning: a bibliography, edited by F. T. Macartney.
Angus and Robertson, 1956.

Semmler, Clement: Twentieth Century Australian Literary Criticism. *Melbourne: OUP*, 1967.

Wilkes, G. A. and J. C. Reid:
Australia and New Zealand (*The
Literatures of the British Common-
wealth* series). *Rider College; The
Pennsylvania State University Press*,
1970.

BRITISH

(*English; Irish; Scottish and Welsh*)

Annals of English Literature, 1475–
1950. *OUP*, 1961.

Boyd, Ernest A.: Ireland's Literary
Renaissance; with a bibliography.
Dublin, 1922; *Grant Richards*,
1923.

British Book News: 1940 to date.
Published monthly by the British
Council.

Browning, D. C.: A Dictionary of
Literary Biography: English and
American. *Dent*, 1960.

Burgess, Anthony: The Novel Now:
a student's guide to contemporary
fiction. *Faber*, 1971.

Clarke, Austin: Poetry in Modern
Ireland. *Dublin, Three Candles*,
1951.

Dodsworth, Martin (Editor): The
Survival of Poetry: a contemporary survey by Donald Davie and
others. *Faber*, 1970.

Ellis-Fermor, Una: The Irish
Dramatic Movement. *Methuen*,
1939.

Fletcher, John: New Directions in
Literature: critical approaches.
Calder and Boyars, 1968.

Gord, Boris (Editor): The Pelican
Guide to English Literature:
Vol. 7: The Modern Age. *Penguin
Books*, 1964.

Gwynn, Stephen: Irish Literature
and Drama, *Nelson*, 1936.

Harvey, Sir Paul: The Oxford
Companion to English Literature,
revised by Dorothy Eagle. *OUP*,
1967.

Myers, Robin: A Dictionary of

Literaure in the English Language: from Chaucer to 1940. 2 vols. *Pergamon Press*, 1970.

Press, John: Rule and Energy: trends in British poetry since the Second World War. *OUP*, 1963.

Rosenthal, Macha L.: The Modern Poets: a critical introduction. *New York, OUP*, 1960

Rosenthal, Macha L: The New Poets: British and American poetry since World War II. *New York, OUP*, 1967.

Schorer, Mark (Editor): Modern British Fiction. *New York, OUP*, 1961.

Sisson, C. H.: English Poetry, 1900–50: an assessment, *Hart-Davis*, 1971.

Spender, Stephen and Donald Hall (Editors): The Concise Encyclopaedia of English and American Poets and Poetry. *Hutchinson*, 1970.

Stewart, J. I. M.: Eight Modern Writers: Vol. 12 of *The Oxford History of English Literature, OUP*, 1963.

Watson, George (Editor): The Concise Cambridge Bibliography of English Literature 600–1950. *CUP*, 1958.

Writers and Their Work: a series of monographs in paperback on notable British writers from Chaucer to living authors of the twentieth century published as supplements to *British Book News* (*supra*) by Longman.

CANADIAN

Brown, Edward K.: On Canadian Poetry. *Toronto, The Ryerson Press*, 1944.

Brunet, Berthelot: Histoire de la littérature canadienne-française. *Montreal, Editions de l'abre*, 1946.

Klinck, Carl F. (Editor): Literary History of Canada: Canadian literature in English. *University of Toronto Press. OUP*, 1965.

Pacey, Desmond: Creative Writing in Canada: a short history of English-Canadian Literature. *Toronto, The Ryerson Press*, 1961.

Rhodenizer, Vernon B.: Handbook of Canadian Literature. *Ottawa*, 1930.

Story, Norah: The Oxford Companion to Canadian History and Literature. *OUP*, 1967.

Tougas, Gérard: Histoire de la littérature canadienne-française. *Paris, Presses Universitaires de France*, 1960.

Watters, Reginald E.: A Check List of Canadian Literature and Background Materials, 1628–1950. *University of Toronto Press. OUP.* 1959.

NEW ZEALAND

McCormick, Eric Hall: New Zealand Literature. *OUP*, 1959.

Smith, Elizabeth M.: A History of New Zealand Fiction: from 1862 to the present time. *Wellington, New Zealand, A. H. and A. W. Reed*, 1939.

Wilkes, G. A. and J. C. Reid: Australia and New Zealand (*The Literatures of the British Commonwealth* series). *Rider College. The Pennsylvania State University Press*, 1970.

SOUTH AFRICAN

Nathan, Manfred: South African Literature. *Cape Town*, 1925.

Index

Also available from Teach Yourself Books

GUIDE TO MODERN WORLD LITERATURE
Martin Seymour-Smith

All these books are available at your bookshop or newsagent or can be ordered direct from the publisher: Teach Yourself Books, P.O. Box 11, Falmouth, Cornwall.
Please send cheque or postal order. No currency, and allow the following for postage and packing:
1 book—10p, 2 books—15p, 3 books—20p, 4–5 books—25p, 6–9 books—4p per copy, 10–15 books—2½p per copy, 16–30 books—2p per copy, over 30 books free within the U.K.
Overseas—please allow 10p for the first book and 5p per copy for each additional book.
While every effort is made to keep prices low, it is sometimes necessary to increase prices at short notice. Teach Yourself Books reserve the right to show new retail prices on covers which may differ from those previously advertised in the text or elsewhere.